The Great Betrayal

The Great Betrayal

Christians and Jews in the First Four Centuries

SHELDON W. LIEBMAN

WIPF & STOCK · Eugene, Oregon

THE GREAT BETRAYAL
Christians and Jews in the First Four Centuries

Wipf & Stock
An Imprint of Wipf and Stock Publishers
199 W. 8th Ave., Suite 3
Eugene, OR 97401

www.wipfandstock.com

PAPERBACK ISBN: 978-1-5326-6003-0
HARDCOVER ISBN: 978-1-5326-6004-7
EBOOK ISBN: 978-1-5326-6005-4

Manufactured in the U.S.A.   10/22/18

This book is dedicated to the memory of three old friends:

William A. Cox
John F. Gibbons
David K. Stigberg

Contents

Introduction

"The Evangelists were addressing a primarily non-Jewish public, and the period when they wrote (just after the disastrous Jewish War of AD 66–70) was one during which anti-Jewish feeling was rife throughout the eastern Roman Empire. They are accordingly at pains to emphasize the differences between Jesus' doctrines and those of orthodox Judaism; to show the Jews as hostile to him and responsible for his death, and the Roman authorities as impartial but weak." (David Flusser)

AT THE PRESENT TIME, anyone who comes to the subjects of early Christianity, the New Testament, or the life of Jesus for the first time will be surprised by two things: first, the amount of scholarship in the last half century that has been devoted to examining the Jewish background of Jesus and, second, the broad consensus among scholars in these fields that neither Jesus nor his earliest disciples ever abandoned their origins.[1] Indeed, the sheer quantity of such studies and the extraordinary extent to which they agree should suggest that no one can really understand the New Testament in general and Jesus in particular without coming to terms with the connection between Jesus and Judaism, as well as the immediate product of that connection: Jewish Christianity. As one historian says, "The rediscovery of this Jewish Christianity is one of the achievements of recent scholarship."[2]

1. On this point, see, for example, Pelikan, *Jesus Though the Centuries*, 11–13, 19. Bainton says that "Jesus was a pious Jew who like his people went up to Jerusalem for the great religious festivals." Furthermore, "The cardinal affirmations of Judaism became those of Christianity" (*Early Christianity*, 9). Jesus observed the Jewish law except in extreme circumstances, and his teaching included all the major tenets of Judaism (17–18). Neusner similarly argues that "the bulk of the ethical sayings attributed to him are commonplaces in the Judaism of the age" (*Judaism in the Beginning*, 36). Robinson comments: "We [meaning the contemporary scholarly community] of course realize that Jesus was a Jew" (*Gospel of Jesus*, 55). Indeed, Robinson adds later, "Jesus was immersed in Jewish culture" (64). See also Senior, *Jesus*, 78–80, 94–95, 135. Besides the fact that "Jesus was a Jew" and that "his disciples were Jews," Davies says, Christians remained Jews "for some time" after the Crucifixion (*Invitation*, 26).

2. Danielou, "Christianity as a Jewish Sect," 275. This kind of Christianity "died out completely, so much so that its history and the relevant mentality are only now being painfully pieced together" (262). Danielou adds that "Christianity belonged to the Jewish world because its founder did." Furthermore, Jesus' disciples also "continued to be faithful observers of the Law and of the worship in the Temple" (275). According to Cwiekowski, "One of the unmistakable results of contemporary biblical and historical studies is the realization of the Jewishness of Jesus and of the early church" (*Beginnings of the Church*, 205). Gager says: "Judaism was the dominant force in the world of early Christianity.

At the same time, however, the more one examines the first four centuries of Christianity, the more obvious it becomes that, although Jesus never stopped being a Jew, the religion that evolved out of his words and deeds slowly separated from its Jewish roots and grew increasingly hostile to the Jews.[3] This happened despite the fact that the Jews not only founded this faith, but also sustained it, without much help from gentiles, for at least a generation after the Crucifixion: "For decades the earliest Christianity was kept going solely by Jews."[4] In Acts of the Apostles, Luke says that the Jews (excluding, of course, "rulers and elders and scribes") not only approved of the Christians (Acts 2:47; 4:21; 5:13; 5:26), but also joined the Jesus movement in large numbers (2:41; 2:47; 4:4; 5:14; 6:7; 9:31). According to Eusebius, the fourth-century historian of Christianity, until the Jewish Revolt of AD 132, "the entire church of Jerusalem consisted . . . of practicing Hebrews" (*Ecclesiastical History*, Bk. 4, 5:2–4).

As the years passed, although Christians converted many gentiles—some affiliated with Judaism (i.e., so-called God-fearers like Cornelius and perhaps the Ethiopian eunuch), and Samaritans, who considered themselves to be Jews—proselytizers like Paul continued to visit synagogues (Acts 13:4–5), even after he and Barnabas announced that they were turning to the gentiles (14:1). In fact, while Paul carried his mission to "the uncircumcised," Peter evidently continued his mission to "the circumcised" (Gal 2:7). These Jewish Christians—i.e., Paul, Barnabas, and Peter—used the Jewish network of synagogues, which included congregations in every major city

---

While at one level this is simply a truism, its various implications have not always been fully appreciated" (*Origins of Anti-Semitism*, 113). Clark contends that the Jewish identity of "Jesus and many of his first followers" was "a fact often disregarded *until the mid-twentieth century*" (*Christianity and Roman Society*, 4; my emphasis).

3. Pelikan notes that the Church gradually developed a "de-Judaized" view of Jesus: "To the Christian disciples of the first century the conception of Jesus as a rabbi was self-evident, to the Christian disciples of the second century it was embarrassing, to the Christian disciples of the third century and beyond it was obscure" (*Jesus Through the Centuries*, 17). The de-Judaization of Christianity is partly attributable to the Gospels themselves. According to Robinson, "The Gospels of the New Testament are all documents of the gentile church, and hence do not go into great detail about the many practices of daily life to which Jesus of course conformed" (*Gospel of Jesus*, 77). Thus, by the fourth century, the view of Jesus as rabbi or Jewish prophet was heretical. See also Young, "A Cloud of Witnesses," 14; "Two Roots or a Tangled Mass?" 87; Goulder, "Jesus: The Man of Universal Destiny," 61–62; and "The Two Roots of the Christian Myth," 81.

4. Schillebeeckx, *Jesus*, 485. Danielou notes, "Until AD 70, when its centre at Jerusalem was destroyed, a Jewish form of Christianity was dominant, and the Hellenizing tendencies represented by Paul were followed only by a minority" ("Christianity as a Jewish Sect," 262). Danielou discusses the Jewish-Christian missions—the earliest, he emphasizes—in various parts of the Mediterranean basin and areas east of Palestine (276–77). Indeed, "Judaeo-Christianity continued to be dominant culturally" until the middle of the second century—more specifically, "until after the repression of the last Jewish revolt" (277).

in the Roman empire, to spread Christianity throughout the Diaspora.[5] And, in this early period, the Romans always saw the Christians as members of a Jewish sect, not as members of a new and separate religion (e.g., Acts 16:20). That is, "Roman pagans . . . found it quite difficult to distinguish between Jews and Christians."[6]

For such reasons, many historians argue that Christianity remained an essentially Jewish institution at least until after the Jewish Revolt of AD 66, which resulted in the destruction of the Temple and a sharp decline in the power of the Jerusalem church and its overwhelmingly Jewish-Christian majority—if not *exclusively* Jewish-Christian membership. Indeed, some scholars contend that Judaism remained a *major* influence on Christianity, as well as an important source of converts, for centuries after the Revolt.[7] Yet, perhaps a decade or so after the Crucifixion, some Christians (like Stephen and Peter, at least according to Acts of the Apostles) began to blame Jews generally for killing Jesus. Some Christians (like Paul and John) accused Jews of being unable to understand either Jesus' identity or his moral program. And, eventually, some Christians (like Ambrose and John Chrysostom) argued that Judaism should be destroyed. The irony is, of course, that, if the Jews had actually been incapable of accepting Jesus, there would have been no Christianity at all.

Let me restate these points as clearly as possible. On one hand, according to most scholars today, Jesus and his earliest disciples were not only born Jews, but also lived and died as Jews. That is, the Church, insofar as it was represented by Jesus and his first disciples, did not repudiate Judaism. Jesus' followers are, therefore, best described as either Christian Jews or Jewish Christians. Indeed, they were unquestionably Christian *Jews* (that is, members of a Jewish sect, like the Pharisees and the Essenes) before

---

5. "Diaspora Judaism is of crucial importance for the history of Christianity, for it was one of the main avenues through which the new faith expanded throughout the Roman Empire" (Gonzalez, *Story of Christianity*, I, 12). Stark says that "conversion tends to proceed along social networks formed by interpersonal attachments" (*Rise of Christianity*, 18). That is why "Christianity arose through pre-existing [Jewish] networks" (56).

6. Sandmel, *Jewish Understanding*, 312.

7. Stark, for example, argues, "Perhaps only a sociologist would be foolish enough to suggest that, contrary to the received wisdom, Jewish Christianity played a central role until much later in the rise of Christianity—that not only was it the Jews of the diaspora who provided the initial basis for church growth during the first and early second centuries, but that Jews continued as a significant source of Christian converts until at least as late as the fourth century and that Jewish Christianity was still significant in the fifth century" (*Rise of Christianity*, 49; see also 138, 139, 143). Stark cites, as evidence, the Church's rejection of Marcion's anti-Judaic theology, the ongoing Christian attack on Judaism as a competing religion, and John Chrysostom's battle with members of his Antiochene diocese who evidently found Judaism to be to some degree attractive as well as compatible with Christianity (65–67). Weiss makes a similar point in *Earliest Christianity*, II, 666–71. Senior says that, to some Romans, Christianity remained a Jewish sect until at least AD 120 (*Jesus*, 11). Danielou argues that, at least in the East (Palestine, Arabia, Transjordan, Syria, and Mesopotamia), Jewish Christianity remained strong until the third and fourth centuries ("Christianity as a Jewish Sect," 281–82). Commenting on the composition of the Jerusalem church, Robinson says that it "was made up of the immediate disciples of Jesus, all of whom were Jews" (*Gospel of Jesus*, 8).

they became Jewish *Christians*–that is, members of a cult that saw itself and was seen by others not as a wholly non-Jewish entity, but as neither Jewish nor gentile.

On the other hand, as a consequence of separation, the Church tried, by various means, to deny this fact. Specifically, the synoptic Gospels, especially as the Church has interpreted them, appear to demonstrate that Jesus rejected Jewish dietary laws, Sabbath restrictions, and all Temple practices; Acts of the Apostles plays down the authority of Jesus' brother James, who seems to have been a pious Jew as well as a Christian, and gives center stage to Paul, who actually *did* repudiate Judaism (at least as, by itself, a means of salvation); and the Gospel of John portrays *all* Jews, not just the Jewish aristocracy, as Jesus' enemies.

As the last point suggests, the great divide between Judaism and Christianty was not established in a friendly and conciliatory manner. The sticking point was (and, to a large extent, still is) the accusation that the Jews killed Jesus. Never mind that (as most modern scholars claim) the Jews had no authority to execute anyone (John 18:31); that the Romans regularly, as a matter of course, arrested and crucified all Jews (and others) who even remotely appeared to threaten the status quo; and that the Jews' involvement in the arrest of Jesus occurred because the Jewish establishment had the responsibility of maintaining law and order in Palestine. As I will argue in the following pages, the Church, for complex reasons, found it expedient not only to separate from Judaism, but also to treat the Romans (represented by Pontius Pilate) throughout the New Testament as innocent bystanders and to blame the Jews for whatever bad things happened to Jesus and his followers.

The problem is, this exculpation of the Romans and accusation against the Jews did not fade away over the centuries but was sustained by the Church for nearly two thousand years. Indeed, the idea that the Jews killed Jesus is a commonplace in German and French criticism of the late nineteenth and early twentieth centuries.[8] It is worth remembering, as well, that many of the writers of the last century or so who blamed the Jews, rather than the Romans, for the murder of Jesus also claimed that whatever happened to the Jews after the Crucifixion was self-inflicted. That is, the suffering of the Jews after the establishment of Christianity as the official religion of the Roman empire and the oppression they faced as citizens of Christian countries throughout the Middle Ages were nothing more than God's own punishment of them for the sin of killing Jesus. For some scholars, "there is a logical connection between" Judaism "and all the later disasters and persecution which came upon it, even in the modern European countries." Specifically, "These sufferings can be understood at most as the result of the failure of Judaism to perform its task—or of its denial of this

8. In her book on anti-Judaism, Klein devotes an entire chapter to this subject. Among the Bible scholars who, based on the Gospel accounts, accused the Jews of killing Jesus, Klein mentions Joachim Jeremias, Joseph Blinzler, Georg Fohrer, Gunther Schiwy, Leonhart Goppelt, Max Metzger, Romano Guardini, Michael Schmaus, Heinrich Schlier, Eduard Lohse, Walther Zimmerli, Martin Dibelius, Ethelbert Stauffer, Rudolf Bultmann, Adolph Schlatter, Marie-Joseph Lagrange, and Joseph Bonsirven (*Anti-Judaism*, 92–126).

task—which itself includes the rejection of Jesus." In his death at their hands, "Judaism passed decisive judgment upon itself." And "it was not the war with the Romans that left the Jews permanently homeless." Rather, "it was "the hostility of the Christians"—who, implicitly, were justified in their actions because the Jews were guilty, and, equally implicitly, authorized by God himself because He was justifiably angry.[9]

Of course, it does not require a comprehensive reading of scholarly books on the New Testament to discover that the word *Jews* seldom appears in the synoptic Gospels (four times, besides the references to Jesus as "King of the Jews") and that the word *Romans* never appears. Jews are specifically mentioned once in the Gospel of Matthew only as rumor-mongers, who spread the story that Jesus' body was stolen by his disciples after his Crucifixion (Matt 28:11–15). In the Gospel of Mark, Jews are referred to once as people who unnecessarily followed certain "traditions," which Jesus considered hypocritical (Mark 7:3–16). What is missing in the synoptic Gospels is not merely the negative portrayal of "the Jews" as a named entity, which occurs throughout the Gospel of John and the Acts of the Apostles, but any positive connection between Jesus and Judaism. Indeed, the Synoptics provide their readers with a thoroughly de-historicized account, in which almost no one is given any national or religious identity.

Reading these Gospels, especially considering their flattering treatment of Pilate, no Roman would be put off by the identification of Jesus as a Jew or offended by the accusation that Jesus was executed by Romans. The reason is that Jesus is not so identified, and the Romans are not so accused. According to one Church historian, even in the Gospel of Mark, "Christ is clearly and deliberately dissociated from the Jewish revolt, and his loyalty to Rome is stressed." In this way, the Gospels served as "a highly effective instrument for the propagation of Christianity," but not as an effective instrument for understanding the Christians, Jews, and Romans of the first century.[10] The result of the evangelists' interest in missionizing rather than truth-telling is that the earliest Christianity is "very different from our conventional picture of it." In short, "[t]he conceptual framework of the New Testament writers led them to present" Christianity as an anti-Jewish and pagan-friendly movement—*not* as a troublesome

---

9. *Anti-Judaism*, 17, 95, 112. The idea of Jewish punishment for Jewish guilt *ad infinitum* was defended by, among many others, both Dietrich Bonhoeffer (118) and Pierre Benoit (122–26).

10. Danielou, "Christianity as a Missionary Religion," 294. In his introduction to the same volume, Toynbee says, "The historical Jesus . . . is difficult to discern, because he has been overlaid by the 'image' of him that the Church began to build up immediately after his death" (14). As Robinson argues, "The texts of the New Testament are products of Diaspora Christianity, literacy, Greek hegemony, the cosmopolitanism of of Antioch, Ephesus, Corinth, and the like." However, this was not the world in which Jesus lived. Thus, "the emergence of the Gospels has to do with the transition from the barefooted, pennyless, unlettered, mendicant, transient native to the moderately educated, literate, sedentary, cosmopolitan, hellenized Evangelist." It was "the Evangelists and their Greek Church" who "obscured" the social and cultural differences between themselves and "Jesus, his family and followers" ("The Gospels as Narrative," 106). See also Crossan, *Jesus*, 37.

former Jewish sect that would struggle with Roman opposition until its final acceptance in the fourth century.[11]

Ultimately, then, the story of early Christianity was told in an ethnic and religious vacuum, in which Jesus and his followers live in a kind of cultural limbo, where words and phrases like "commandments," "Son of David," "kingdom of God," "Pharisees," "the law and the prophets," "Son of man," "Messiah," "elders," "gift," "Levite," and "holy spirit" have no contextualized meaning. One can only imagine a gentile from the Middle East, North Africa, or Southern Europe reading these words and simply ignoring or misinterpreting them because they are incomprehensible without some knowledge of Judaism. In fact, the presence of this language—whose meaning would have been perfectly clear to Jews, though mystifying to everyone else—prompted the second-century Christian theologian Marcion, who denied *any* tie between Jesus and Judaism, to revise the Gospel of Luke by eliminating *all* references to Judaism and to promote this Gospel alone, along with Paul's epistles, as the only Christian scriptures.

The real problem is, therefore, not merely what the Gospels include, but also what they leave out. Remarkably, none of the Gospels refer at all to the social, political, and economic circumstances that make the relations between Christians, on one side, and Jews and Romans on the other, understandable. They omit the fact that Rome was a tyrannical dictatorship that crucified hundreds of thousands of Jews, slaves, and other rebels and inspired periodic rebellions in Palestine during the first two centuries of the Roman occupation. Self-proclaimed Jewish messiahs and kings (as well as just plain bandits, terrorists, and assassins) started riots, led revolts, and engaged in random acts of violence as expressions of frustration with and hostility toward the ruling class. Except for the reference to Barabbas as an insurrectionist in the Gospel of Mark (15:7), there is no indication in any of the Gospels that Palestinian Jews were so deeply dissatisfied with Rome and its indigenous representatives (i.e., the High Priest and other Jewish appointees of the Romans) that they—*alone among the residents of the empire*—rebelled at every opportunity.

Also completely ignored in the Gospels is the fact that Jewish peasants, representing as much as ninety-five percent of the Jewish population, hated the Jewish elite as well as the Roman occupiers because they were denied political freedom and economic opportunity. Indeed, they had lost their independence as a nation-state since the Roman conquest in 63 BC; had been systematically deprived of their small, family-run farms through excessive taxation and exploitative lending practices for even longer; and were periodically insulted by Hellenistic rulers (including sometimes their own people) who mocked their religion and disrespected their traditions. And there is no mention in the New Testament of the fact that the vast majority of Jews, being hostile to both the Jewish aristocracy (elders, priests, and scribes) and the Romans, with whom the ruling Jews collaborated, would not have supported the execution of

---

11. Danielou, "Christianity as a Jewish Sect," 262. On the inextricability of Christianity and anti-Semitism, see Ruether, *Faith and Fratricide*, 5, 7, 64, 170–71, 180–181, and 246–49.

Jesus any more than they supported the execution of other Jewish dissidents, of whom there were many during the first century AD.

In *that* context, consider the fate of a charismatic Jewish leader who warned that the Kingdom of God was imminent, gathered together a sympathetic Jewish following in Galilee, entered Jerusalem amid cries of praise and clear demonstrations of popular support, made seemingly hostile statements about the Temple, turned over tables within the Temple walls and dismissed the merchants and money changers who worked there, and was arrested at night because the authorities feared the reaction of his followers, as well as other Jews (Luke 22:53). True, he might not have been as dangerous as Barabbas, who had both participated in an insurrection and committed murder in the process. But he was surely more of a threat than John the Baptist (recently arrested and executed, presumably without a trial). Consider, too, the tendency of the Romans to arrest and execute *all* of the mob-leading rebels (real and perceived) whom Josephus, the Jewish historian, refers to in his history of the period—again, not only without a trial, but also without the help of any Jewish intermediaries.[12]

By the end of the first century, it is evident that Jews were no longer to be merely ignored by the Church, as they were in the earlier Gospels, but disparaged. Most of the more than sixty references to "Jews" in the Gospel of John imply that few of Jesus' followers were Jews, but that all of his enemies were. At this point, the ethnic cleansing of Jews from the sacred scriptures of Christianity gave way to simple, straightforward anti-Judaism and anti-Semitism. In the synoptic Gospels, the Jews are present, if unnamed, but in the Gospel of John the Jews are not only visible, but uniformly and relentlessly portrayed as hostile and vicious—even Satanic (John. 8:44). By this time— that is, a generation after the Revolt of AD 66, in the wake of which Jews were often looked upon as enemies rather than supporters of Rome—many Christians found it expedient to identify themselves as Christians rather than Jews. In addition, they were

---

12. On this point, see the discussion of the beheading and crucifixion of Jewish rebels by Romans, based on Josephus' account, in Levenson, "Messianic Movements," 531–34. Robinson says that one of the achievements of recent scholarship is the recovery of the social, political, and economic background of early Christianity: "Especially over the past generation, during my lifetime, the quest of the historical Jesus has been renewed by valuable new tools that have become available. As a result, we know a lot more about Jesus' world than did previous generations. The actual circumstances of Galilee under Roman rule and the social structures against which Jesus' lifestyle and parables make sense have been brought increasingly into view: the exploitation of the native population, the patronage system used by those who wanted to get ahead, the abysmal economic status of a peasantry taxed into poverty" (*Gospel of Jesus*, 89). Senior says, "[I]t was also a world of ominous and mounting political tension, a world that seemed to be moving toward an inevitable holocaust, a world in which the birthright of God's people had been diminished by oppression and despair" (*Jesus*, 45; see also 26, 39, 44, 64). According to Robinson, it was partly these circumstances that drove poor people to Jesus: "[C]ommon people, who suffered the most from the evils of society, flocked to him hoping for the deliverance he promised" (*Gospel of Jesus*, 112).

evidently finding a more responsive audience among gentiles, to whom they now, in large measure, turned their attention.[13]

At this time, too—that is, in the Gospel of John—Jesus is shown to be in total control of the situation ("I have overcome the world" [John 16:33]), simply fulfilling his God-given destiny, and no longer "distressed and troubled" as well as "forsaken," as he was in the Gospel of Mark (14: 34; 15:34); "sorrowful, even to death," as he was in Matthew (26:38); or in "agony" and perspiring heavily, as he was in Luke (22:44). The Jesus in John, unlike the Jesus in Mark, unquestioningly accepts the cup his Father has given to him and has no need to submit his will to God's: Father and Son are in complete agreement (John 12:27; 18:11). Barabbas is now merely "a robber" (John. 18:40), though he was formerly described as one among many "rebels in prison, who had committed murder in the insurrection" (Mark 15:7). Gone, too, are Aramaic words and phrases, which appear in Mark because they were, presumably, the exact words spoken by the first-century Jews who were part of the Jesus movement.

In fact, in the words of one scholar, "John's Jesus is in every way less *Jewish*" than he was in the synoptic Gospels. He does not argue about ethical and ceremonial issues with the Pharisees, he does not engage in the traditional Jewish practices of exorcism or fasting, he has nothing negative to say about gentiles and nothing good to say about Jews, he is called "rabbi" only by his enemies, and he rejects the authority of Jewish law for Christians: That law is invariably *theirs*, not his (John 8:17; 10:34; 15:25). In the Synoptics, Jesus regularly preaches in synagogues, but does so only once in John. And, when "he goes to a Jewish festival such as the Passover or the Feast of Tabernacles, he goes not as a participant, as in the Synoptics, but as a missionary." At the Last Supper—which, in John, is conspicuously not a Passover meal, as it is in the other Gospels—Jesus encourages his disciples to wash each other's feet rather than partake of the Eucharist, which was based on the Jewish pre-meal blessings on wine and bread.[14]

In addition, the original members of the Jesus movement are now, in John, remembered as the revered founders of the Church, who are privileged to hear, in Jesus' farewell address, a thorough and explicit explanation of both his role as a messenger from God and the responsibilities of his followers henceforth. They are no longer the questioning and uncomprehending disciples who, in Mark, especially, seem never to

13. Sandmel comments on this development: "As the child of its parent, Christianity naturally would hope for the favorable status which Judaism had earlier obtained. Initially it could be argued that the child was entitled to the legacy of its parent. But when Christianity had matured, it went a step further; it ceased to regard Judaism as its parent, but rather as a kind of misbegotten stepbrother. The Judaism of the day was regarded as of illegitimate birth; it was the Judaism of the past as whose legitimate heir Christianity had come" (*Jewish Understanding*, 214–15).

14. The quotations and examples in this paragraph are from Foster, "John Come Lately: The Belated Evangelist," 124–25. In the Gospel of John, Sandmel says, "Jesus is portrayed as though not a Jew, and thus the group from which he is here fully dissociated can bear the brunt of the animosity which has been kept more subdued in the Synoptic Gospels. In its utility for Jew-haters, the Fourth Gospel is pre-eminent among New Testament writings" (*Jewish Understanding*, 269).

understand anything Jesus says to them. In John, after Jesus' powerful discourse, they exclaim: "Ah, now you are speaking plainly, not in any figure! Now we know that you know all things, and need none to question you" (John 16:29). In this Gospel, John the Baptist does not send disciples to Jesus to ask if he is the one "that should come" (Matt 11:3). Rather, he announces in the first chapter that Jesus is, in fact, "the Lamb of God" (John 1:29).

To be sure, the significance of what many scholars call the Church's *de-Judaization* of Christianity lies in its two major consequences. First, *it misrepresented Jesus*, the religion he practiced, and the message he communicated. Although this statement may surprise both Christians and Jews, it is the latest conclusion of a centuries-long quest among Bible scholars to separate the historical Jesus (that is, as he appears in the broadest possible historical context) from the theological Jesus (that is, as he appears in the New Testament). In the last half-century, the ongoing effort in the field of Jesus studies to recover the "real" Jesus, as well as the "real" original community that he founded, has resulted in the widely held view that both were Jewish. In short, there has been a serious attempt to correct the biblical record that remained largely unquestioned for almost two millennia.[15]

Second, *this misrepresentation has had a devastating impact on Jews*, whose religion was portrayed as superannuated, whose character was demeaned, and whose alleged treatment of Jesus became a justification for hatred, exclusion, and violence, including extermination. As one historian explains, when the Roman empire adopted Christianity as its official religion, it "presented Jews with a challenge more severe than the destruction of the Temple." This is because "Christianity claimed to be Judaism, Christians to be Israel." In other words, having assumed, since the second century,

---

15. In this book, my goal is to present that correction, based on the findings of what I take to be a majority of contemporary scholars. Like Sandmel, in his words, although I have not refrained from citing Jewish scholars, "I [have] attempted to reflect the general stream of what Christian scholars [have] thought and written about the New Testament writings." Furthermore, again like Sandmel, "Where I [have] expressed my own opinion this was almost entirely limited to selecting from a range of differing Christian opinions those that appealed to me as right" (*Jewish Understanding*, xxi). Of course, I do not wish to imply that all scholars either support my views or even subscribe to the so-called Jesus Quest—that is, the search for the historical Jesus. Indeed, for some Christians, it has not been a worthwhile effort. In a book published in 1996 and entitled *The Real Jesus: The Misguided Quest for the Historical Jesus and the Truth of the Traditonal Gospels*, Luke Timothy Johnson begins, sarcastically: "Recent years have been very good for the Jesus business in America. I don't mean the Jesus business that goes on in churches, but the profitable trade in Jesus by a variety of publications that by creating a commotion in both the academy and the church also create a media-fed demand for more of the same. Sales in scandal are high, stocks in shock are rising, and futures on the historical Jesus are sound. Commerce in the Christ has rarely been better" (1). As many scholars note, however, what is sometimes dismissively referred to as the Jesus Quest has been going on for decades and, in some respects, for centuries. Even Johnson refers, however briefly, to Luther's influence on the early stages of this scholarly enterprise, which was sustained in the eighteenth and nineteenth centuries by such representatives of the so-called Higher Criticism as Hermann Samuel Reimarus and David Strauss (69–71). In the twentieth century, the tradition of closely reading the New Testament for evidence of "the real Jesus" was maintained by practitioners of Form Criticism and Redaction Criticism.

that it had superseded the Synagogue—that Christianity had supplanted Judaism—the Church now had the power to treat Judaism as a defunct religion and the Jews as a doomed race. Just as the Church, aided by the imperial government, began "the delegitimization of paganism," it also initiated "the systematic degradation of Judaism." At first, Jews were forbidden to proselytize, to circumcise slaves, and to punish Jews who converted to Christianity. Later, they were forbidden to marry Christians and to acquire slaves of non-Jewish origin. By the early fifth century, the patriarchate in Jerusalem was abolished, and Jews were not allowed to hold public office, to become soldiers, or to practice law. Christians often regarded it as an act of piety to attack synagogues, as well as Jewish people and their property. Thus, Jews faced not only "physical insecurity in their own villages and towns," but also a radical reduction of their rights and privileges in the empire.[16]

Ironically, however, as I have suggested, according to a majority of scholars writing in the last fifty years, the Church's persecution of the Jews as the enemies of Jesus is, was, and always will be utterly unwarranted. For, if Jesus did not reject Judaism, and the Jews did not, in any meaningful sense, reject him (let alone execute him), then 2,000 years of Christian hostility toward the Jews and their religion—manifested in occasional attempts of mass murder as well as persistent acts of oppression of various kinds—has been based on what many contemporary scholars consider to be an inaccurate picture of reality.

What made matters worse in this regard is that many prominent Bible scholars in the half century or so leading up to World War Two, the vast majority of them from Germany, not only failed to correct this misrepresentation, but perpetuated it. On the one hand, they argued, God chose the Jews as recipients of His divine law, presumably because He believed they were, insofar as they were represented by the patriarchs and other Jewish leaders (like Joseph, Moses, Joshua, and David), righteous and therefore worthy of his gift. On the other hand, however, post-Exilic Jews proved undeserving of God's love. They were stubborn and disobedient, and, as time passed, their religion—originally pure and divinely inspired—degenerated into something narrow, self-serving, and ungodly. Ethical concerns were replaced by a focus on ceremonial practices, and Judaism became a religion of law rather than love.[17] Jesus arrived in ancient Israel in order to restore the original relationship between man and God. Although the Jews failed to appreciate his effort and change their ways, gentiles

16. Jacob Neusner, *Judaism in the Matrix*, 17–22. Summing up the fate of the Jews in the Middle Ages, Jaher says that the Christians did to the Jews what they accused the Jews of doing to them: "It was Christians who stole and despoiled Jewish property, desecrated Jewish objects and places of worship, compelled conversions, seduced and raped Jewish women, and slaughtered Jews, including children" (*Scapegoat*, 74).

17. According to Sandmel, "Indeed, sober Christian scholarship until rather recent times" consistently emphasized the superiority of Christianity over Judaism: "Contrasts were drawn, uniformly unfavorable to Judaism, and a curious by-product of such scholarly partisanship was the fantastic corollary that every applaudable sentiment in the New Testament had in the Rabbinical literature some parallel of despicable content" (*Jewish Understanding*, 313).

slowly but surely recognized Jesus' authority and accepted his message. In this way, Christianity replaced Judaism.[18]

Furthermore, although acknowledging that the Church was founded by Jews, led by James and Peter after the Crucifixion, and predominantly Jewish until the Jewish Revolt of 66 AD, many scholars also claimed that the early Jewish Christians were unable, merely by virtue of their Judaism (or even Jewishness), to understand the Gospel in the terms in which Jesus actually meant it to be understood. As a result, true Christianity—that is, the Gospel according to *Jesus*, rather than Peter or James or John the son of Zebedee—had to wait until a later, non-Jewish Christianity enabled the Church to establish a solid foundation of beliefs that were not distorted or corrupted by Jewish misinterpretation. According to this large body of highly respected scholars, Jewish exegesis, whether it was directed at the Jewish Bible or at Jesus' message, was undermined by legalism and literalism. Indeed, the contrast was drawn not only between Jews and gentiles, but between Hebrews (i.e., the Jewish members of the Jerusalem church) and Hellenists (the Jewish members of Diaspora churches): "The Hellenists, being universalistic in outlook and liberal in temperament, came after a short time to realize (in a way in which their narrow, conservative Hebrew fellow believers could not) the true ramifications of the gospel of Jesus Christ."[19]

Given the influence of this long-term scholarly assault on the Jews of the first century and their progeny over the next two millennia, it is hardly surprising that one well-known scholar has asked whether there would have been a Holocaust if Jesus had not been de-Judaized: "Would there have been such anti-Semitism, would there have been so many pogroms, would there have been an Auschwitz, if every Christian church and every Christian home had focused its devotion on icons of Mary not only as Mother of God and Queen of Heaven but as the Jewish maiden and the new Miriam, and on icons of Christ not only as Pantocrator but as Rabbi Jeshua bar-Joseph, Rabbi Jesus of Nazareth, the Son of David, in the context of the history of a suffering Israel

18. Klein has thoroughly examined the modern scholarly tradition in which this interpretation of Judaism was presented. In the second and third chapters of *Anti-Judaism*, she mentions, among many others, Martin Noth, M. Schmaus, G. Schiwy, Georg Fohrer, Werner Forster, and Martin Metzger, as well as Rudolf Bultmann, Martin Dibelius, and Joachim Jeremias as scholars who have described Judaism after the Exile as a religion in decline: "They see [the change] as a break with the true Yahweh-faith of ancient Israel. Something new emerged, a kind of ethical world view which can scarcely be called religion any longer." In short, according to these scholars, Judaism "abandoned the true faith proclaimed by the prophets and replaced it after the Exile with ritualistic and legalistic piety" (16). In Klein's words, George Foot Moore, an American specialist on ancient Judaism, accused the Germans in particular of "an *a priori* biased attitude towards [Jewish] sources, and objected to their continual use of a method of comparison which tended to depreciate everything Jewish and to upvalue everything Christian at the expense of the former" (3).

19. Hill, *Hellenists and Hebrews*, 3. Hill continues: "The Hebrews . . . are portrayed most unflatteringly in much of the relevant secondary literature. While Hellenist theology flowered into Christian universalism, Hebrew thinking sank into a retrenched Jewish legalism. In light of the diversity of first-century Judaism, it must be asked whether this depiction of the Hellenists and Hebrews is founded upon anything but stereotype" (3).

and a suffering humanity?"[20] The answer is not necessarily "no," but the fact that many scholars have asked the same question suggests that the negative consequences of the Gospel accounts of Jesus and Judaism are worth re-examining.[21]

This point needs to be emphasized. The evangelists who told the story of Jesus' life and the letter writers who tried to explain their beliefs to their fellow Christians were primarily interested in sustaining the faith of Christians and inspiring it in non-Christians.[22] Furthermore, although gentile Christians were in the minority before the Jewish Revolt of AD 66, the war changed everything: "The Jews were now discredited throughout the Empire, and the Christians tended to draw away from them

20. Pelikan, *Jesus Through the Centuries*, 20. Correcting the Gospel versions of the Passion, because they have been the source of "two thousand years of theological anti-Judaism and even racial anti-Semitism," was Borg and Crossan's stated motive for writing their book on the Passion stories (*Last Week*, xi). For their conclusion on this point, see, 127–28. Maccoby argues, "Because Jesus was raised above politics, the Jews became the victims in a real political as well religious sense, when they became the pariahs of Christendom, deprived of political and economic rights and subject to constant persecution" (*Mythmaker*, 50). Akenson says that Christian anti-Judaism goes back to the Gospels themselves because their "goal was to modify, minimize, or exorcise [Jesus'] Jewishness" (*Saint Saul*, 3). Based on his reading of the Passion stories, Herzog says, "[T]here is nothing to support the mean and abusive uses to which the show trial of Jesus has been put. Crossan is surely right to connect his concern for interpreting the trial of Jesus to the problem of anti-Semitism" (*Jesus, Justice*, 245). Herzog says earlier that to treat the Jews as if they were persecuting a Christian "is anti-Semitic, anti-Judaic, historically anachronistic, and horribly misguided. No one holds twentieth-century Italians responsible for what first-century Romans did" (219). Speaking of the New Testament, Cwiekowski adds, "The polemics of some of these texts had a role in encouraging in later centuries a reprehensible anti-Semitism that at the time seriously compromised the Christian element of the history between the two groups" (*Beginnings*, 205). After stating "that Jesus was executed by the Romans . . . as a political insurgent," Senior argues that the evangelists misrepresented these facts, the result of which was disastrous for Jews: "One of the most tragic and shameful blots on Christian history has been the use of the passion story as an excuse for antisemitism" (*Jesus*, 137–38; see also 40–41).

21. Indeed, a number of historians have answered with a definite "yes." Baum, for example, says that the Holocaust "would not have been possible if hostility to the Jews had not been fostered by Christian preaching which spoke of Jews and Judaism almost from the beginning only in terms of rejection" ("Foreword" to Klein, *Anti-Judaism*, ix). According to Tillich, the earliest "Christian anti-Judaism . . . is one of the permanent sources of modern anti-Semitism" (*Systematic Theology*, II, 152). Jaher says: "[A]nimosity embedded in Christian doctrine, while by no means the only source of anti-Semitism, has exerted a primary influence since the early days of Christianity. Research has uncovered abundant evidence of anti-Jewish sentiment in Catholic and Proestant theology, canon law, church councils, papal and clerical edicts, and abusive action" (*Scapegoat*, 9–10; see also 23).

22. Smith says that "the gospels were written, not merely to record events, but also to produce and confirm faith in Jesus the Messiah," who was "not a historical figure, but a mythological one." Furthermore, the same bias has affected Bible scholarship as well: "Most of the scholars have not been historians, but theologians determined to make the documents [i.e., the Gospels] justify their own theological position" (*Jesus the Magician*, 3). Of course, one need not regard the idea that Jesus is the Son of God as mythological to consider the Gospels more theological than historical. The latter point is widely shared among recent Bible scholars. Morgan, for example, says: "The Early Christians . . . worked backwards *from* the answer *to* the question and said that Jesus died because it was God's will. Then they retold the story complete with this theological explanation in order to illuminate for others the whole meaning of Jesus as they understood it . . . This does not disprove the historical accuracy of what they relate, but it does cast a shadow of doubt over it" ("A Concluding Postscript to Historical Research on the Trial of Jesus," 139).

. . . Christianity disengaged itself socially and politically from Judaism, and became a third force."[23] Thus, the New Testament was written at a time when relations between Christians and Jews were beginning to deteriorate, especially in Palestine, and Christians were inclined to turn away from the Jews and appeal to gentiles for acceptance, in every sense of the word. Their goal was to fend off the harsh criticism of Christianity by prominent Romans (e.g., Tacitus, Porphyry, Lucian, and Celsus), reduce or eliminate the kinds of persecution they received from governors like Pliny and emperors like Nero, and even demonstrate to ordinary people that Christianity was a reasonable and unthreatening faith.

This is why, when the Gospels were written, forty to sixty years after the Crucifixion, the writers not only left out some extremely important background information, but also mischaracterizied the roles played in the Passion by Jews and Romans. These falsehoods were proffered by an institution that was not only increasingly dominated by gentile converts, but also influenced by Greco-Roman ideas at the same time that it abandoned its connection to Judaism—the faith of Jesus and almost everyone else mentioned in the Gospels. In other words, this division between Christianity and Judaism grew in the context of a very gradual, but quite definite transformation of the Church itself. By the second century, its expansion was largely in the hands of men who had very little in common with the Jews who had founded it. The new leaders of Christianity— Justin Martyr, Tertullian, Origen, and Clement of Alexandria—were gentiles who were products of Hellenized culture and addressed themselves almost exclusively to people very much like themselves.

The change began some years after a small number of pious men and women implemented many of Jesus' moral guidelines, according to the Acts of the Apostles, by establishing an egalitarian community and practicing a primitive form of communism: "[A]s many as were possessors of lands or houses sold them, and brought the proceeds of what was sold and laid it at the apostles' feet; and distribution was made to each as any had need" (Acts 4:34–35). In this, they were following Jesus' ethical ideas (for example, in Mark 10:17–25; Luke 6:20–36; and Matthew 25:31–46), many

---

23. Danielou, "Christianity as a Jewish Sect," 277. Danielou continues: "The Hellenistic Christian communities gained the upper hand. Paul triumphed posthumously" (277). "It was gradually," Danielou says elsewhere, "as more converts came in from Hellenism, that the Christian Greeks abandoned their original Semitic affiliations and came directly into contact with Hellenism" ("Christianity as a Missionary Religion," 293). According to Sandmel, the evangelists exculpated Romans and blamed Jews because they wrote "in a time of sharp conflict between Christians and Jews" (*Jewish Understanding*, 10). In this "period of extreme antagonism" (162), "the progressive shift of blame from the Romans to the Jews . . . is a result of the need to appease the Romans." Sandmel adds: "There is quite an extensive literature, written by Christians for Christians, deploring the intrusion of anti-Jewish feeling into the New Testament" (204).

of which derived from the Jewish Covenant Code.[24] These values, presented especially in Deuteronomy and the writings of the Jewish prophets, are based on the principle of lovingkindness, especially for the poor and helpless, as well as the principles of fairness and human decency for all members of the community.

By AD 400, that original Jewish-Christian community (which not only pooled its resources and provided for everyone's needs, but also followed the Sabbath, purity, and dietary laws of traditional Judaism) had been declared heretical by the Church, which had become the governing religious body of the Roman empire and had turned into an organization that, for whatever good it did, sometimes betrayed the ideals on which it had been founded. It carried religious intolerance to an extreme never before seen in the empire.[25] It somehow managed to execute more Christians (as heretics) than the pagans ever did.[26] And it reduced all Jews under its jurisdiction to

24. The heart of this code is expressed most clearly in Deuteronomy 15:1–11. The passage most relevant to the community of early Christians is 15:4–5: "[T]here will be no poor among you . . . if only you will obey the voice of the Lord your God, being careful to do all this commandment which I command you this day." Enslin comments: "It would appear from the early narrative of Acts that for a time the early Christians adopted a kind of communism. This has been heavily denied, but apparently with little reason, for even the most conservative political economists can scarcely fail to be satisfied with its disastrous failure. Two parallel accounts are given [Acts 2:44–47 and 4:32–5:11]. In keeping with their view of a speedy termination of the age and in strict compliance with the teaching of Jesus they pooled all their resources and lived on the resulting capital" (*Christian Beginnings*, 177).

25. The reasons for this exceptional degree of intolerance are discussed by Ehrman. The main problem was that Christians, unlike pagans, "refused to worship other gods." Being "exclusivistic in their views," they regarded every other form of worship as unacceptable: "This exclusivity . . . bred an intolerance toward religious diversity. Since there was only one way of salvation, all other religions were in error. And being in error had eternal consequences"—not only that non-believers would burn in Hell forever, but that the Church had the right to execute them, including pagans, Jews, and heretics (*Lost Christianities*, 255–56). Like several other scholars, Stark claims that the number of Christian martyrs in the period before Constantine's rule has been greatly exaggerated. He estimates that the number was less than one thousand (*Rise of Christianity*, 164). In fact, "although Christians stood in formal, official disrepute for much of the first three centuries, informally they were free to do pretty much as they wished, in most places, most of the time" (192). Typically, Stark adds later, quoting Ramsay MacMullen (*Paganism in the Roman Empire*, 129), on most occasions when the imperial authorities executed Christians, "only the leaders were seized, while crowds of obvious Christians went unpunished" (208). This is not to say, of course, that many thousands of Christians were not tortured. They were.

26. Parkes says that "the internal divisions of Christians themselves . . . produced far more victims than their first conflict with Judaism" (*Conflict*, 149). Parkes adds later that this violence was generated not by ordinary Jews and Christians, who generally maintained "friendly relations" with each other, but by "the ecclesiastical or imperial authorities." Thus, Parkes continues, "The picture of fourth century Christianity given us in the polemic writings of the fathers and in their sermons, in the ecclesiastical historians, and in the canons of the councils is a singularly unattractive one." He mentions the "perpetual wars between their rival partisans, mutual intolerance, and vindictiveness against individuals" as major contributions to this portrait of extensive Church-condoned violence (189–90). Senior says, "[T]oo often, the zeal of some in the church became fanatical and their response to error so tainted with cruelty and ambition that the cure was less compatible with the spirit of Jesus than the ill it sought to remedy" (*Jesus*, 155).

second-class citizens who could never practice their ancient religion—indeed, Jesus' own religion—without fear of disapproval, condemnation, repression, and murder.

I believe, as many scholars do, that the Church's expansion, its move from Palestine to the Diaspora, and its acquisition of power have left the world with a religion that, in some respects, Jesus himself would neither approve of nor even recognize as something for which he bore any responsibility.[27] And much of that development can be understood in relation to the Church's slow, but ultimately complete abandonment of Judaism. Again, Christianity was Hellenized at the same time that it was de-Judaized, and the primary result of that change was the formation of a religion based on ideas that were, in some instances, totally foreign to the Galilee in which Jesus was born and raised. One scholar explains: "Inevitably Christianity became, or rather was deliberately made, absolutist and authoritarian. The Jewishness of Jesus' teaching was lost, and has never since been allowed to influence Christology."[28]

The degree to which scholars acknowledge that the Church ignored the religious background of Jesus and his followers, abandoned its connection to Judaism, and not only held Jews alone responsible for the death of Jesus but also punished them unremittingly for the crime is the degree to which they believe that the Church betrayed its

---

27. In the fourth century, Jesus began to be portrayed in the art of the period not only as the Good Shepherd, but also as the Pantocrator, the almighty King of the Universe, especially in the East: "Christ becomes the heavenly emperor, his throne the replica of the emperor's; the nimbus around the emperor's head is appropriated for Christ and his saints." That is, Christian iconography borrowed from imperial art, and "the Church found little difficulty in endorsing with its blessing the old images of the quasi-divine emperor" (Markus, *Christianity*, 101). Cupitt adds: "Christ became the basis of the Christian Empire and of political and ecclesiastical power in the present age. He was invoked to guarantee the very things Jesus had said were passing away" ("The Christ of Christendom," 141). Cupitt contrasts the view of Jesus as Pantocrator with Jesus' repudiation of gentile kingship in Luke 22:25–27 and Matthew 20:25–28. Jesus' point in these Gospel passages is that he himself is a servant, not a king, and that the dispute between the sons of Zebedee over who is "the greatest" among the disciples is misguided because monarchy, a gentile institution, is inappropriate for the followers of Jesus. Thus, Cupitt says, "Early Christianity had repudiated the Emperor-cult but now [i.e., in the fourth century and later] conciliar Christianity came increasingly to be modelled on the Emperor-cult" (139). Senior says that "the dominating tone of this view of Jesus tended to eclipse the palpable humanity of the gospel Jesus whose most evident characteristics were compassion and love, not condemning judgment" (*Jesus*, 156).

28. Cupitt, "The Christ of Christendom," 141. Over time, says Cupitt, "Christianity was very extensively paganized in its faith, worship, organization and social teaching." The development of "a largely pagan iconography of Christ" was "profoundly influenced" not by either scripture or historical facts, but by "political needs and pressures" (138). Closely examining what he considers the radical Hellenization of Christianity, Hatch concludes that by the fourth century the Church had developed a theology that "would probably have been unintelligible to the first disciples" (*Influence of Greek Ideas*, 1). Carrying the point a bit further, Kung says that "the criterion for being a Christian does not lie in the church's theories of Trinity, incarnation and satisfaction developed centuries later (otherwise the early Christians would not be Christians)" (*Judaism*, 389; see also 379). Indeed, he asks, "What would the Jew Jesus have made of such dogmatic formulations of Greek Hellenistic Christianity as," for example, the Nicene Creed? (311). Enslin answers, "Had Jesus been able to attend a church service in Corinth in the year 54 A.D., he would have been astounded, and might well have asked himself in amazement: Is this the result of my work in Galilee?" (*Christian Beginnings*, 182).

origins, if not its founder. I am uncertain as to whether a majority of scholars would accept the term *betrayal* in reference to the Church's relationship to Jesus, but there is no question that for many of them the transformation of Christianity—especially in terms of its attitude toward Judaism—was extreme. Morally, of course, Christianity underwent the kind of change that often characterizes idealistic movements.[29] Whether Buddhists or Franciscans, such groups are founded by charismatic leaders who insist on the highest possible moral standards, and they are sustained by bureaucrats who are as interested in survival as they are in moral principles. In short, adaptation is inevitable.

For Christianity, too, expansion and compromise went hand in hand. As one scholar puts it: "Originally these itinerant radicals"—that is, Jesus and his disciples—"had renounced home, family, possessions and protection, a life style that ultimately was tolerated in mainline Christianity only as the exceptional status of monasticism, an ideal to be honored but not enforced on the church at large." Indeed, Christians in general embraced an ethical code much more conventional and, importantly, more acceptable to their prospective converts in the Diaspora: "[T]he cosmopolitan church opted for a charitable patriarchalism where middle-class virtues such as the Christian home replaced the intolerable and futureless celibate radicalism of Jesus and his followers."[30]

Theologically, the difference between the Church of AD 50, under the leadership of James the brother of Jesus, and even the Church of AD 100 can be seen in the conversation between Jesus and Nicodemus in chapter three of the Gospel of John, as well as in the conversations Jesus has with all of the Jews, including his own disciples, in the rest of that work (John 16:25). By the time of the composition of this Gospel, the Church had moved out of Jerusalem; its mission had turned from Aramaic-speaking Jews to Greek-speaking gentiles; and its leaders were increasingly non-Jews who were trained in Greek philosophy, Greek religion, and Greek rhetoric.

It is not surprising, then, that, in his dialogues with Nicodemus and other Jews, Jesus was speaking Greek, by which I mean that he was using concepts drawn from

---

29. On this point, see, for example, Victor Turner's discussion of "communitas" and "structure" in *Ritual Process*. Turner defines the former as a vision of society "as an unstructured or rudimentarily structured and relatively undifferentiated *comitatus*, community, or even communion of equal individuals" (96). "Communitas itself soon develops a structure . . . [That is,] under the influence of time, the need to mobilize and organize resources, and the necessity for social control among members of the group in pursuance of these goals, the existential communitas is organized into a perduring social system" (132). The principal elements in "structure" are hierarchy and regulations, which are needed in order to protect and preserve the community.

30. Robinson, "The Gospels as Narrative," 106. On the post-Easter conservatism of the Church, see Theissen, who, in *Early Palestinian Christianity*, discusses the replacement of wandering charismatics by local church officials (9); the perception of Christianity "as one of the conciliatory, moderate groups" (60); the change in the role of Jesus from earthly king to "the crucified and suffering messiah" (64, 65, 116); and the abandonment of the "radical ethics of the synoptic tradition," particularly under Paul's influence (115).

Neoplatonism in particular and Hellenistic culture in general: the conflict between spirit and flesh ("That which is born of the flesh is flesh, and that which is born of the Spirit is spirit" [John 3:6]), the idea of a descending and ascending god ("I came from the Father and have come into the world; again, I am leaving the world and going to the Father" [John 16:28]), and the assumption that divine knowledge is inaccessible to the uninitiated ("[T]he hour is coming when I shall no longer speak to you in figures but tell you plainly of the Father" [John 16:25]). None of these ideas appear in the synoptic Gospels, and, of course, many of Jesus' Jewish followers, as well his Jewish enemies, would have found his new message incomprehensible.[31]

In this book, I am concerned with the process by which the estrangement of Christianity from Judaism took place. Its result, as I said, was not simply a transformation of the Church as an institution and a transformation of the way Jesus himself was understood. It provided a perspective—and, to some degree, a disturbingly false one—from which the Church, the events of the first century AD, Jesus, the disciples, and the Bible itself have far too often been misinterpreted. Unfortunate as this may be, its worst result was the consequences for Jews all over the world. Hence, the passion with which I write and the sense of urgency I feel. The issues are not—and never have been—merely historical or philosophical; they are matters of life and death. As one Jewish scholar has put it, "Since in the past, and even in the present, the epithet of 'Christ-killer' has been directed by some Christians at Jews, and the epithet has often been accompanied by physical onslaught—and *this may continue in the future, too*—the search for the historical facts relating to the crucifixion has long been a Jewish concern."[32]

The point of view that I am questioning can be understood as a series of myths—in the sense of more or less deliberate distortions and misrepresentations—which separate Jesus from everyone. Essentially, in the chapters that follow, I am dealing with six myths: (1) that Judaism was (and still is) a hopelessly backward religion, (2) that Jesus rejected Judaism, (3) that Jesus was killed by the Jews, (4) that the earliest disciples rejected Judaism, (5) that the Jews totally rejected Jesus, and (6) that the gentiles understood Jesus better than the Jews did. All of these assumptions are untrue, and all of them have been challenged by many historians, Bible scholars, and theologians. In fact, one of the problems that concerns me most is the gap between what many scholars say and what many people believe. In 1934, one historian lamented that

31. McKenzie comments, "Jesus lived in patterns of thought and language which he did not invent and could depart from only at the cost of becoming unintelligible" (*Old Testament*, 58). According to Carmichael, this is precisely the problem at "the end of the first century and the beginning of the second," when "Greco-Romans were no doubt by far the bulk of the new recruits to the new faith." Carmichael continues: "This meant that there was an audience for the ideas projected by both Paul and the Gospel of John, representing an attitude that was to sweep the field . . . [The Christians] were now speaking about Jesus in ways that would no doubt have flabbergasted him" (*Birth of Christianity*, 140). On the Hellenistic content of the Gospel of John, see Davies, *Invitation*, 396–408.

32. Sandmel, *Jewish Understanding*, 202–3.

recent studies of the Bible had done little to change people's views, especially of the race that gave Jesus to the world and profoundly shaped his thinking: "To-day it must still be said that the popular view of the Jews has little altered through the influence of modern scholarship."[33]

An incredible amount of interesting work has been done since then by men and women, Christians and Jews, who have put aside ancient prejudices and have carefully studied the Bible; examined the social, economic, and political conditions of the first century AD; and traced the development of Christianity from the last year of Jesus' life to the fourth century, at which time the Church reached a broad agreement on the contents of the Christian Bible, accepted the Nicene Creed as its central article of faith, and welcomed the establishment of Christianity as the official religion of the Roman empire. As a result of this scholarly effort, according to one Bible scholar, "Christians are no longer interested in presenting Judaism as a degenerate religion, describing the Pharisees as legalists and hypocrites, making the Jewish people responsible for the crucifixion, concealing the Jewish origin of Jesus, Mary, the disciples, and the early Church as a whole, nor do they want to represent the Synagogue as forsaken by God, to speak of the Jews as a people cursed by God." In other words, they no longer wish to caricature the Jews, make them appear to be contemptible, and thereby "authorize [their] unjust treatment."[34]

Whether this collective examination of Jesus and Judaism and the resulting re-valuation of Jesus and Christianity will change people's thinking remains to be seen. Writing in 1993 (that is, more than half a century after the scholar I referred to above), another scholar said, "[N]either in the university, nor among knowledgeable people in our society, nor among the Christian churches have the results of biblical scholarship ever made much of a difference."[35] Nevertheless, one hopes for the best.

* * *

In the first chapter, entitled "Judaism," a subject usually unexplored even in studies of Jesus and Judaism, I examine the religion in which Jesus was raised. The subject requires attention if for no other reason than that almost everything Jesus said derived from his religious background. Whether it is the idea that the last (the abased) will be first (the exalted), the assurance that those who seek a response from God will receive it, the claim that revenge is unacceptable, the insistence on the Golden Rule or the expectation that the world will be transformed and its inhabitants will ultimately be

---

33. Parkes, *Conflict*, xx. In 1952, in his foreword to a new edition of Herford, *Pharisees*, which was first published in 1924, and after listing the important works on the subject written after Herford's book, Glatzer says, "Yet, despite these and other efforts at an honest, unbiased, historical clarification of the entire issue, the old prejudices, or at least a onesided view, still prevail in the minds of many" (8). Sandmel makes the same point in *Jewish Understanding*, xxiii.

34. Baum, "Foreword" to Klein, *Anti-Judaism*, x.

35. Mack, *Lost Gospel*, 248.

judged, the concept comes, in one form or another, from Deuteronomy (if not the earlier books of the Pentateuch), the prophets, the psalms, or the non-canonical Jewish writings of the inter-testamental period. In fact, most of Jesus' ideas are repeated throughout the literature of the Jews.

As I said earlier, some Bible scholars have ignored the connection between Jesus and his Jewish sources because they accepted the New Testament picture of a Jesus seriously at odds with his forebears. These scholars were working under the assumption that Jesus totally rejected Sabbath, purity, and food laws, as well as Temple worship, even though his earliest followers conspicuously obeyed those laws and continued to pray in the Temple. This assumption has allowed the so-called experts to proffer one of the worst and most damaging scholarly misrepresentations in history: the idea that Judaism was a legalistic religion, which encouraged attention to the letter of the law rather than the spirit, and promoted the belief that one could make up for sins by performing expiatory rituals.[36] The result was that Jews were perceived to be guilty of self-righteousness, arrogance, and hypocrisy, against which Jesus offered self-abnegation, humility, and sincerity.[37]

36. Crossan says that Christians—including Church Fathers as well as modern scholars—"have both trivialized and brutalized Judaism in descriptions down through the centuries" (*Birth of Christianity*, 340). Witherington comments, "The caricature that all early Judaism was grounded in legalism and works righteousness without any emphasis on grace and God's mercy taking precedence in the way God deals with people is simply false" (*What Have They Done?* 201). As Friedman suggests, one could justify this caricature by reading only passages by the so-called Priestly writer of the Jewish Bible and ignoring passages in the sections identified as J, E, and D. P never uses the words "mercy," "grace," and "repentance." The writer of these sections "rather emphasized the divine aspect of justice . . . J and E are virtually the opposite. They emphasize the divine aspect of mercy" (*Who Wrote the Bible?* 238–39). In short, "[t]he oft-repeated image of the 'Old Testament God of justice and anger' has always been only half of the real picture" (240). The same point is made by Davies: "Was their God aloof and their religion dominated by fear and not by love? Many Christian scholars have often in the past urged that this was so. But the otherness of God in Judaism did not mean remoteness . . . God could and did come to many of his own through his Holy Spirit." Furthermore, "Judaism did know the love of God for his own and emphasized this as much as it did the fear of the Lord" (*Invitation*, 28). For similar sentiments, see Senior, *Jesus*, 94.

37. As I argued earlier, many scholars regard this misrepresentation of Judaism as a consequence of anti-Semitism. Akenson, for example, argues that the Church, using Paul's criticism of his former religion, became increasingly hostile to Jews and Judaism. Subsequently, similar attitudes pushed Bible scholars and church historians to exaggerate the separation between Jesus and the Jews. This is particularly true, he says, of German scholars of the twentieth century (*Saint Saul*, 146–47, 234). Akenson says that the German Higher Criticism came to be called by Jewish scholars "the Higher Anti-Semitism" (52–53). The phrase appears, for example, in a very short address by Solomon Schechter, then president of the Jewish Theological Seminary of America. In response to the German Higher Criticism, Schechter asks, "Can any section among us afford to concede to this professorial and imperial anti-Semitism?" (*Seminary Addresses and Other Papers*, 38). The *bête noir* among German Higher Critics for Schechter was Julius Wellhausen. One wonders what he would have said of Rudolf Bultmann. On the Graf-Wellhausen claim that after the period of the prophets Judaism "hardened into a priestly theocracy," see the brief explanation in McConnell, "Introduction," 5. For a refutation of the Graf-Wellhausen thesis, see Kaufmann, *Religion of Israel*, 1–3, 153–57, 175–79.

Portrayed as a religion of fear and ritual, as opposed to Jesus' religion of love and morality, Judaism is, *in fact*, based on the assumption that because God acts on the principles of mercy and justice, so must ordinary human beings. Mercy and justice, which God offered to the Jews as part of his Covenant with them, are especially important to widows and orphans, who cannot fend for themselves, but also to aliens, strangers, and sojourners. Indeed, God's creatures are not only expected to imitate Him, as numerous Jewish texts insist, they are given to understand—particularly by the prophets, among whom this idea is paramount—that morality is far more important than ceremony.

Most compelling of all, human action must be motivated by the two Great Commandments: love of God and love of humanity. These two distillations of the Ten Commandments, which were important to Jesus, are at the heart of Judaism and can be found not only in the writings of Jesus' contemporary, the Jewish philosopher Philo, but also in the words of the Jewish scribe whose mention of the two commandments earns Jesus' approval in the Gospel of Mark: "Thou art not far from the kingdom of God" (12: 28–34). They underscore the idea that mutual love, rather than the threat of punishment, is the binding element in the relationship between God and His people. And these ideals enable God's worshipers to create and sustain a compassionate society in which cooperation is favored over competition and in which generosity prevails over selfishness. The divine-human Covenant is the foundation for the inter-human Covenant.

Another both essential and influential Jewish idea, which can be found in Deuteronomy and the prophets, is the claim that, because God understands the human proclivity to sin and because He loves humanity, He enables people to regain their relationship to Him even after they have violated it. The means by which Jews are redeemed is called *repentance*, which is always interpreted in the Jewish Bible to mean *coming back* to God. That is, one is alienated from God because one has *turned away* from Him. And one is restored to God's favor by *returning* to Him. This is the Jewish equivalent of "rebirth," as Paul and John's Jesus define it, for it results in the acquisition of a new heart and a new soul, as the Deuteronomist, Jeremiah, and Ezekiel make clear. That is, the idea of spiritual change is central to biblical Judaism. And, ironically, if John's Jesus had explained his theory of rebirth to Nicodemus in traditional Jewish terms, which is no doubt the way both Jesus and John the Baptist first heard it, the conversation might have gone more smoothly.

Repentance, from the Jewish perspective—that is, as it is defined in the Bible—consists of three stages: confession, forgiveness, and reformation. The sinner is expected to acknowledge his error, show remorse, and (if necessary) pay restitution to the person sinned against. In response, assuming that the regret is sincere and the atonement satisfactory, God forgives. Indeed, He blots out the sin from both human and divine memory. Henceforth, the sinner sins no more—not because he can pile up supererogatory acts and *compel* forgiveness, as if good deeds wipe out bad ones or as if God can be fooled by appearances—but because God forgives out of kindness, out of love (that is, out of Grace).

So clearly and passionately did Jesus express these covenantal values that one is forced to wonder what he was reacting to in the first century AD. As it happens, the religious, social, economic, and political situation that his people found themselves in at the time might be said to have incited his revival of those Jewish ideals that were severely under assault by the Romans. The Jews were an oppressed people, living under a tyrannical government that proved to be as ruthless and as insensitive to Jewish sensibilities as any that the Jews had endured for more than half a millennium. Small landowners were suffering under the burden of debt, caused by usurious lending practices; dispossession because of royal decree, fraud, and even drought; as well as tributes and tithes demanded, respectively, by Rome and the Temple, and taxes paid out on all kinds of goods and services. Ordinary Jews were alienated from the Jewish elite, who cooperated fully with their Roman superiors. And the old ties of community, tradition, and religion were challenged from all sides.

Not to minimize Jesus' uniqueness or deny the spiritual dimension of his appeal, but it is important to remember that there were many messianic and otherwise revolutionary figures in the first century who not only opposed the Romans and their Jewish collaborators, but also proposed radical changes in the way people lived together and treated each other. Jesus may have been part of God's plan for mankind, but, like many Jews who felt frustrated by hypocrisy and exploitation, he also spoke to the issues of the day and articulated a moral program that promised (threatened, to the Romans) to restore Palestine to its covenant relationship with God and, if the Acts of the Apostles accurately portrays the earliest Christian community, return the people to a more humane society than was possible under Roman rule.

* * *

In "Jesus the Jew," I discuss the well-established facts that Jesus was born into a Jewish family, who performed all of the rituals required of Law-abiding Jews on the occasion of a male birth; that he studied the Hebrew Bible, especially the Torah and the prophets; and that most, if not all, of what he said about Judaism, including its laws and rituals, had been said by other Jews, including Pharisees, prophets, revolutionaries, and Essenes.[38] Most scholars agree that he called only Jews to discipleship and that these followers continued to pray in the Temple, make sacrifices, and keep many of

---

38. Summing up the scholarly view, Ehrman says: "[M]ost scholars today acknowledge not only that Jesus was a Jew but that he was raised in a Jewish household in the Jewish hamlet of Nazareth in Jewish Palestine. He was brought up in a Jewish culture, accepted Jewish ways, learned the Jewish tradition, and kept the Jewish law. He was circumcised, he kept Sabbath and the periodic feasts, and he probably ate kosher" (*Lost Christianities*, 96). Whether Jesus was formally educated is a subject of debate among scholars. Robinson argues that he received no formal training. Rather, it was the educated Greeks who thought of Jesus as "more like themselves" and therefore portrayed him as an expert in Jewish theology (*Gospel of Jesus*, 66, 74).

the purity and food laws enshrined in the Torah. It is worth noting, in this regard, that Jesus told the leper he cured at the beginning of his mission to see a Jewish priest and make an offering (a sacrifice) in the Temple (Mark 1:44)[39]; that some of the women following Jesus deferred going to his tomb on the Sabbath because they rested on that holy day (Luke 23:56); and that Peter had "never eaten anything that is profane or unclean" until the "Lord" told him in a vision to do otherwise, many years after the Crucifixion (Acts 10:14).

The strongest evidence that his disciples did not believe that Jesus had rejected the Law occurs in Acts of the Apostles, shortly after Paul's arrival in Jerusalem, perhaps thirty years after Jesus' death. James, the brother of Jesus and then head of the Jerusalem church, told Paul (proudly, one assumes, and speaking on behalf of "all the elders") that "many thousands of Jews there are which believe; and they are zealous for the law." That is, thousands of Jews had joined the Jesus movement, and all of them remained obedient to Jewish Law. Since these members of the Church had heard that Paul had been telling Jews "to forsake Moses," James ordered Paul ("Do therefore this what we say to thee") to sponsor four men in a rather elaborate Nazirite ritual at the Temple. Paul—despite his apparent contempt for Jewish ritual—underwent a "rite of purification" and accompanied his fellow Jewish Christians, who were going to the Temple to make a sacrifice (Acts 21:20–24). The point is this. If James and the elders, no doubt some of whom had been original disciples, did not know precisely which aspects of Judaism Jesus approved of, who did? And, if they required Paul to perform this ritual in order to demonstrate his obedience to Jewish laws, which ones did they ignore?

Thus, although Jesus regarded moral purity as more important than ritual purity (as other Jews did), he did not (at least in the synoptic Gospels) entirely reject rituals, food limitations, or Sabbath restrictions. Like other Jews, he modified the rules when he found them either too strict (Matt 12:1–5) or too loose (5:17–30). He proselytized only to Jews (Matt 15:24),[40] most of whom seem to have regarded him as a teacher or a prophet, whose principal objective was either to reform the Judaism into which he was born or to encourage his fellow Jews to follow their traditional laws. In the Gospel of

39. Crossan views this incident differently: "Jesus is enjoining the visit to the Temple not as legal observance but as confrontational witness" (*Jesus*, 83). I would argue, however, that Jesus clearly requires the cleansed leper to obey the Mosaic law: "[S]how thyself to the priest, and offer for thy cleansing those things which Moses commanded" (Mark 1:44). The "things that Moses commanded"—that is, the items the leper must offer for sacrifice at the Temple—are listed in Lev 14:4–31. They are many and legion.

40. Hill argues that the so-called gentile mission was slow in coming: "The Christian message, whatever its content, was in the understanding of these first believers [i.e., Jesus' earliest disciples] a message for Jews. Insofar as gentiles were considered, it was probably thought, along the lines of conventional expectation [e.g., numerous passages in Isaiah], that they would share at some future date in the blessings of a *redeemed* Israel. Therefore, Jewish Christians would naturally share their newfound perspective as Jews with Jews" (*Hellenists and Hebrews*, 138). The relevant New Testament passages are Matt 10:5–6 and Acts 11:19.

Luke, when Jesus heals the servant of a Roman centurion, the evangelist makes it quite clear that Jesus was willing to help a non-Jew only under special conditions (Luke 7:1–7). First, the Roman sent a delegation of Jewish elders to appeal to Jesus. Second, he was described by the elders as "worthy": "[H]e loveth our nation, and he has built us a synagogue." Third, he sent his friends to tell Jesus that there was no need for him to come to his home. As one scholar explains, "Such a centurion stationed in Galilee knew quite well that a Jew would feel defiled by entering a gentile house . . . It was the same Luke who in Acts narrated in considerable detail the steps God took to persuade Peter to to enter the house of another gentile centurion [i.e., Cornelius] who also was generous to Jews."[41] As these Gospel stories suggest, there is little evidence that Jesus rejected Judaism and every reason to believe that he remained throughout his short life a Jew who embraced the teachings of the Jewish prophets and who sought to remind his countrymen of the high standards established by Isaiah, Jeremiah, Hosea, Amos, and Zechariah.

In the synoptic Gospels, Jesus argues constantly with the Pharisees, but the animosity between him and this small group of religious Jews is probably exaggerated. First, although the Pharisees are portrayed as rigid, dogmatic, and hypocritical, many scholars now believe that this negative view derives from a retrojection of conflicts between Christians and Jews that took place in the second half of the first century. As for their hypocrisy, the Pharisees of Jesus' day were among the many Jews who were willing to sacrifice their lives for their beliefs. As for their rigidity, they are now generally understood to have been dedicated to applying the Law to everyday circumstances—that is, trying to adjust the Law to changing realities. And, as for their dogmatism, the Pharisees had no way of forcing their judgments and interpretations on other Jews.[42]

Numbering only in the few thousands and having no official position in the Judean power structure, the Pharisees were influential, but not powerful enough to burden anyone with legalisms.[43] In fact, many scholars consider it likely that Jesus either

41. Robinson, *Gospel of Jesus*, 78–79. Robinson also notes that, according to all the evangelists, Jesus invariably went to synagogues to preach and that, in the Gospel of Matthew, he regularly refers to gentiles in a disparaging manner (80–81).

42. Sandmel says, "No group in history has had a greater injustice done to its fine qualities and positive virtues than have the Pharisees through parts of the Gospel . . . And earlier generations of Christian scholarship, going on from these denunciations, have tended to label all of Judaism as no more than the hollow shell of religious observance, or as pure and simple hypocrisy" (*Jewish Understanding*, 24–25). Cwiekowski emphasizes the Pharisees' "flexibility" and tolerance of others (*Beginnings of the Church*, 31). Neusner argues that "often many Protestants and Catholics, speaking of the Pharisees of long ago, really mean ("perfidious") Judaism of today" (*Judaism in the Beginning*, 45). Later, quoting the definitions of *Pharisaic, Pharisaism,* and *Pharisee* in the *Shorter Oxford English Dictionary* (1955), Neusner says that they "are part of the cultural background of the West, an aspect of the anti-Semitism nurtured by Christian theology of a certain sort" (49).

43. On this point, Hill cites Martin Goodman, E. P. Sanders, Jacob Neusner, Morton Smith, and Robert A. Wild (*Hellenists and Hebrews*, 35 n. 63).

belonged to this group or at least shared many of its values and beliefs.[44] What seems to have influenced the evangelists was the survival of the Pharisees after the unsuccessful Jewish Revolt, when other Jewish groups—including the Zealots, Sadducees, and Essenes, for example—were destroyed, and the Pharisees, as Rabbis, became the leaders of Judaism.[45] It is significant that in Mark and Luke's descriptions of the Passion (the notable exceptions are Matthew 27:62 and John 18:3), the Pharisees, despite their alleged hatred for Jesus, have nothing whatsoever to do with his arrest, trial, or execution.

Scholars in the twentieth century justified the biblical characterization of the Pharisees in particular and the Jews in general by arguing that these people practiced a religion based on the commercial principle of *quid pro quo*—literally, *this for that*. In other words, the Jews made a covenant with God that granted them protection in exchange for obedience. This crude caricature has been rejected by most mainstream scholars today.[46] And, indeed, as it happens, the Christians, from the early martyrdoms to the Crusades of the Middle Ages, implemented this principle in ways unimaginable to people living in the time of Jesus. Martyrs and soldiers went into spiritual and physical battle expecting (as they were often encouraged to believe by Church leaders) that they would be rewarded for their sacrifice. In fact, the concepts of penance, pilgrimage, and purgatory are based on the same principle: not only that good deeds can compensate for bad ones, but that saying prayers, visiting holy

44. On Jesus' connection to the Pharisees, see Gonzalez, *Story of Christianity*, I, 10; and Bainton, *Early Christianity*, 14.

45. Cwiekowski claims that the Pharisees are portrayed in the Gospels from a post-war perspective on the Jewish-Christian conflict, when relations between Jews and Christians were increasingly hostile in some areas, and the Pharisees (as Rabbis) represented for Christians not just a sect, but all of contemporary Judaism. "Today," he continues, "the historical setting of the Gospels makes us recognize the apologetic and even polemic motives in the Gospels; hence our estimate of the Pharisaic movement is much more positive" (*Beginnings of the Church*, 30). Klein says that this retrojection explains why "the picture of the Pharisees and scribes given in other historical sources does not correspond to that of the Gospels." Klein points out that, after the Revolt, the Jews themselves regarded the Pharisees as their "natural religious leaders." So it was logical for Christians, encountering opposition from Jews who had become increasingly intolerant of dissent, not only to vilify the Pharisees, but also "to portray them as the enemies of Jesus himself" (*Anti-Judaism*, 67). Klein says that the hostility between Christians and Jews did not become severe enough to justify this mischaracterization of the Pharisees until "six decades after the death of Jesus, at the time of the definitive redaction of Matthew" (76; see also 90). Klein devotes a chapter to an overview of French-German scholarship in which the New Testament view of the Pharisees is presented as historically accurate (67–91).

46. For a balanced view of Jewish ethics in the ancient world, see Barton, *Ethics*, 82–96. Barton identifies three kinds of motivation for the Jews' obedience to the Law, associated respectively with future, past, and present. The first is the threat of punishment and the promise of rewards, the second is gratitude (e.g., for God's past favors, such as the liberation of the Jews from Egypt), and the third is joy (of the kind expressed in Psalm 19). Barton cites E. P. Sanders as the scholar who corrected "the impression often given in studies of Paul that the Judaism of Paul's day was a religion of bargaining with God . . . Sanders has shown that Paul's Jewish contemporaries would have been just as horrified at such an idea of God's covenant with Israel as any modern Christian" (93).

places, and practicing self-denial can expiate past sins. As the author of 1 Peter says, "[C]harity shall cover the multitude of sins" (4:8). This is legalism with a vengeance.

* * *

In the third chapter, "The Crucifixion," I examine the extent to which crucifixion was commonplace in the Roman empire during the first century and used exclusively to punish insurrectionists and rebellious slaves. My point is not to deny that Jesus suffered a cruel death on the cross, but to underscore the fact that many thousands of Jews (among others) had been crucified by the Romans for a hundred years before Jesus' death and that hundreds of thousands would be massacred over the next hundred years.

On the question of responsibility for the murder of Jesus, it must be noted that in the synoptic Gospels the Jews who were obsessed with arresting, trying, and executing Jesus were the members of the Jewish aristocracy—priests, Herodians, landowners, elders, and scribes. What makes the usual charge against them problematic is that they were not only allied with, but also completely dependent on the Roman authorities. The priests, including the High Priest, served at the mercy of the Roman-appointed ruler, whether he was Herod or Pontius Pilate: "The Temple cult was managed by agents of the monarchy, men who purchased the high priesthood at a price, held it at the king's pleasure, and, enriched by the priestly dues, handed it in the accepted Greek manner to the next appointee."[47] In other words, recognizing their dependency, High Priests as willingly submitted to their deposition as they gladly accepted their appointment. Lacking any ability to resist the hiring and firing power of the Roman governor (or the Jewish tetrarch), these so-called leaders came and went. Thus, in the seventy-plus years of Roman rule in Palestine, between the death of Herod the Great and the Jewish Revolt, twenty-seven High Priests were deposed.[48]

Given the historically inferior position of indigenous artistocracies to Roman authorities throughout the empire, it is impossible to believe, that at any time in Jesus' lifetime the High Priest could intimidate Pilate or any other Roman prefect or procurator, despite the claims to the contrary in the Passion stories of the Gospels and by those members of the scholarly community who have taken these stories at face value.

47. Neusner, *Judaism in the Beginning*, 21.

48. Hill, *Hellenists and Hebrews*, 188 n. 116. Ironically, the High Priest under Pilate, Joseph Caiaphas, served longest, from 18 to 36 AD, during the entirety of Pilate's tenure, from 26 to 36. The overwhelming majority of High Priests served for less than two years, which suggests that Pilate and Caiaphas might have had an unusually cooperative, if not cordial, relationship. The point is important since Pilate is known as the first of several hard-line prefects or procurators and was considered particulary uncompromising in dealing with his Jewish subjects. Summing up a brief overview of Pilate's method of "crowd control," Crossan says: "My point is not that Pilate was a monster. He was an ordinary second-rank Roman governor with no regard for Jewish religious sensitivities and with brute force as his normal solution to even unarmed protesting or resisting crowds. Like any Roman governer he was also careful to distinguish between the rich and the poor, the powerful and the powerless, the important and the unimportant, the aristocrat and the peasant" (*Jesus*, 141).

Nor is it possible to imagine that ordinary Jews could have been persuaded by the Sanhedrin or the High Priest to call for Jesus' death.[49] These members of the Jewish aristocracy were, after all, not just opposed, but despised by ordinary Jews, who saw themselves as much victims of the Jewish elite as victims of the Romans. These Jews, who often supported messianic leaders of any kind, were the ones who followed Jesus in Galilee and Judea and not only cheered his entrance into Jerusalem, but, at least in the Gospel of Luke, lamented his conviction by Pilate as they walked sadly behind him on his way to Golgotha (23:27, 48). There is little reason to dispute Luke's account.

The crowd who demanded that Pilate crucify Jesus could not have been these anti-establishment Jews, but representatives of the rich and powerful—that is, those who had something to lose if the Romans decided to punish them for allowing a potential threat to the regime to run amok, which is exactly the argument of the chief priests and Caiaphas in the Gospel of John (11:48–50; 18:14). The same standard was applied to John the Baptist, as well as the long list of both violent and nonviolent Jewish rebels who were invariably beheaded or crucified because they were perceived to be dangerous. It was sometimes the Jews who arrested them because it was their responsibility to maintain law and order in Judea, but it was the Romans who executed all of them. In fact, the vast majority of Jews—six or seven million, scattered across the empire—never heard of Jesus, although many of them would have supported him against the Jewish elite and Roman authorities if they had had an opportunity to choose sides.

Jews were blamed for the murder of Jesus because (as I said earlier) in the period after the Revolt of 66, when all of the Gospels were written, Christians found it advantageous to dissociate themselves from the rebellious Jews and were reluctant to blame the Romans for killing their savior, since they were then struggling to win at least the tolerance, if not the acceptance, of Jesus' executioners.[50] As the later epistles indicate, Christians increasingly presented themselves to the Romans as otherworldly, peaceful, and morally conventional—that is, politically innocuous. The first letter of Peter,

49. The idea that the High Priest and the Sanhedrin compelled Pilate to execute Jesus can be found in the writings of Josef Blinzler, Heinrich Schlier, and Pierre Benoit (Klein, *Anti-Judaism*, 93, 102, 124). The charge that Jewish leaders changed the minds of Jewish peasants is stated by Michael Schmaus and Ethelbert Stauffer (108, 113).

50. Questioning the authenticity of passages in the Passion stories in which Pilate is shown to be innocent of Jesus' death, the compilers of *Jerome Biblical Commentary* argue that the Gospels "were finally edited in a particular historical situation of conflict between Church and Synagogue, and . . . they reflect this situation" (II, 111). Similarly, Reumann says that "the tendency to magnify Jewish responsibility is a later development that scarcely fits the original fact" (*Jesus*, 67). Senior says, simply: "The central fact is that Jesus was executed by the Romans. About that there is no doubt . . . Jesus was executed as a political insurgent" (*Jesus*, 137). The Church accused the Jews, Senior continues, because of historical circumstances: "Christian concentration on Jewish involvement in the death of Jesus stemmed, in part, from the hurt and perplexity caused by the fact that by and large the Jewish people had not accepted the gospel message . . . And it is also probably true that later Christians surely would not want to overemphasize Roman involvement in the death of Jesus when the young church's relationship to the authorities of the state at best was tenuous" (137). See also Kee et al., *New Testament*, 172; Chilton, *Rabbi Jesus*, 21; and Nineham, *Gospel of St. Mark*, 367–68, 417.

for example, reads like a public promise to the Roman authorities that the Church and its members are and will continue to be totally committed to the status quo: All Christians must submit to "every ordinance of man," especially those of kings and governors (2:13–14); servants must obey their masters (2:18); and wives must yield to the authority of their husbands (3:1). The purpose of these commands, says the letter writer to his fellow Christians, is to silence the critics of Christianity who portray Christians as enemies of the state: "For so is the will of God, that with well doing ye may put to silence the ignorance of foolish men: as free, and not using your liberty for a cloak of maliciousness, but as servants of God" (2:15–16).

The accusation that the Jews murdered Jesus is on exactly the same level of veracity as the charge that the Jews murdered all of their prophets. Indeed, the latter claim was used to bolster the credibility of the former.[51] Jesus himself is said to have accused Jerusalem of "killing the prophets and stoning those who are sent to you" (Luke 13:34; 11:47–51; Matt 23:29–37). After the Crucifixion, Stephen asked his Jewish accusers: "Which of the prophets did not your fathers persecute? And they killed those who announced beforehand the coming of the Righteous One, whom you have now betrayed and murdered" (Acts 7:52). Paul also charged that the Jews "killed both the Lord Jesus and the prophets" (1 Thess 2:14–15).

Two sources of this accusation, both attributed to Ezra, appear in the Hebrew Bible and the Apocrypha. In the first source, the book of Nehemiah, Ezra says to God that the Israelites "were disobedient and rebelled against thee . . . and killed thy prophets" (Neh 9:26). In the second source, 2 Esdras, Ezra quotes God as saying to the Jews: "I sent my servants the prophets to you, but you took them and killed them and mutilated their bodies. For their murder I shall hold you to account" (2 Esd 1:32).

A quite different report appears in 2 Chronicles. Summing up the poor record of the last kings of Judah and explaining the destruction of the Temple and the exile of the Jews to Babylon, the chronicler says, "The Lord, the God of their fathers, sent persistently to them by his messengers, because he had compassion on his people and on his dwelling place; but they kept mocking the messengers of God, despising his words, and scoffing at his prophets, till the wrath of the Lord rose against his people, till there was no remedy" (2 Chr 36:15–16).

While several sources in both the Old and New Testaments say that the prophets were murdered, the passage from 2 Chronicles is probably closer to the truth—that is, the Jews *rejected* the prophets, but did not kill them. In fact, while Jeremiah seems at least to have been threatened with death, *only two prophets are actually known to have been murdered*: (1) Uriah, a contemporary of Jeremiah, who was executed by King Jehoiakim (Jer 26:20–23); and (2) Zechariah, a ninth-century priest, who was stoned

---

51. What Jesus suffered was "the lot of all the prophets of Israel; they are rejected by the people of God" (Schillebeeckx, *Jesus*, 414). Schillebeeckx adds, "That prophets are destined to martyrdom was a commonplace in Jesus' time" (496). According to Lieu, Justin Martyr's contention that the Jews killed their prophets provided a "theological framework" for the claim that in Justin's own time Jews wanted to kill Christians, although they lacked the power to do so (*Image and Reality*, 135).

to death in the Temple courtyard by the order of King Joash (2 Chr 24:20–22).[52] Thus, in the words of one scholar: "[T]his general utterance about prophets being murdered is not borne out by the facts of history. A lot of prophets did indeed suffer persecution, but only a few were put to death." For this reason, many scholars assume that the accusations by Jesus, Stephen, and Paul are either exaggerations or were originally stated figuratively. To put it simply, "a murder of the prophets" meant "a defiance of the prophetic message."[53]

After all, although the prophets were often despised by those whose interests they were defending, their target was usually the ruling class—that is, those who were in a position to do the most damage by acting unjustly and unrighteously: "The prophets consistently singled out the leaders, the kings, the false prophets, and the priests as the ones responsible for the sins of the community."[54] That might be why the two prophets mentioned above were executed by kings, not murdered by mobs. In other words, the Jews—if one means by that term the ordinary people, who made up more than ninety percent of the Jewish population at any given time in their early history—may be said to have killed no prophets at all.

Another scholar has suggested that Christians were inclined to exaggerate the fate of the Jewish prophets because they were, at the time the Gospels were written, regularly being excluded from synagogues whenever they tried to proselytize. The post-Revolt Jews had grown less tolerant of dissent, which (in the view of some Jews) had undermined the Revolt, while Christians were more emboldened by their missionary success and more convinced than ever, after the destruction of the Temple,

52. The more famous Zecharaiah son of Berechiah, referred to by Jesus as a prophet killed in the Temple (Matt 23:35), was probably misidentified, according to the editors of *Oxford Annotated Bible*, 1203. See also Bruce, *Canon of Scripture*, 31. Bruce mentions only Zecharaiah and Uriah as prophets killed by the Jews. Hare explains: "Historical research indicates that the number of prophetic martyrdoms was greatly exaggerated in popular tradition. Of the three major and twelve minor prophets of the canon, none died a violent death." Besides the two prophets mentioned by Bruce, Hare notes that, according to Elijah in 1 Kings 19:10 and 14, the entire nation of Israel was responsible for the "slaughter of unnamed prophets," even though it was Queen Jezebel who killed them (1 Kgs 18:4). "We see here," Hare says, "the beginnings of the belief that Israel as a whole is responsible for the death of her prophets and must bear the guilt corporately" (*Jewish Persecution of Christians*, 137). Kloppenborg says that the repetition of this theme in the Jewish Bible "may seem odd, since [this book] itself records no story of the murder of a prophet, except Elijah's killing of the prophets of Ba'al" (*Q*, 76).

53. Schillebeeckx, *Jesus*, 275. Referring to the flogging of Jeremiah and his overnight arrest, McKenzie says, "We have not too many instances of such personal attacks upon prophets" (*Old Testament*, 112. That is, the Jewish prophets met with "little violence" (124). Mack calls the charge "a summary fiction" (*Lost Gospel*, 144).

54. Heschel, *Prophets*, 203. Heschel earlier comments: "The striking surprise is that prophets were tolerated at all by their people. To the patriots, they seemed pernicious; to the pious multitude, blasphemous; to the men of authority, seditious" (19). Newsome says that Uriah was killed because he offended the rich (*Hebrew Prophets*, 109).

that Jews who remained Jews had been punished by God.[55] Speaking of the exploitation by the Church of the Jews' self-accusations, one scholar comments: "No people has ever paid so high a price for . . . the outspoken courage with which they held up an ideal and denounced whatever seemed to them to come short of it. If they had known the use that was to be made of their writings, then, indeed, many of the prophets might have obeyed literally the sarcasm of Irenaeus [a second-century bishop] when he says that 'the Jews, had they been cognizant of our future existence, and that we should use these proofs from the Scriptures which declare [that they] . . . are disinherited from the grace of God, would never have hesitated themselves to burn their own Scriptures.'"[56]

* * *

Much of what Jesus said and did regarding the Mosaic laws can be determined by looking closely at what his disciples said and did, the subject of Chapter Four, "The Disciples." Their words and actions also allow the student of the Bible to see how Paul challenged the tradition Jesus left behind and the extent to which he transformed it. As I said earlier, the followers of Jesus—at least the members of the Jerusalem church—continued to accept the Temple and its practices as legitimate, still honored Jewish festivals, and remained indistinguishable from other Jews, except for their high regard for Jesus as the Messiah, if not literally the Son of God. Furthermore, it took at least a few years for followers like Peter, James the brother of Jesus, and John the son of Zebedee to convert anyone except Jews, Jewish proselytes, and God-fearers. Clearly, as Acts of the Apostles shows, gentiles were eventually converted, but only, at first, on condition that they undergo circumcision and otherwise follow the Jewish Law.

Paul (and possibly others before him) revolutionized Christianity, or what he called the Way, by allowing new gentile members to forego circumcision and obedience to other laws. The religion of Jesus could be said to have changed because Paul's version of the faith—which included not only non-contingent conversion, but also (in some sense) rejection of the Law—was influenced by his own perception of Jesus'

---

55. Robinson, *Gospel of Jesus*, 18; and Mack, *Who Wrote?* 151. Like some other Bible scholars, Mack assumes that the accusation against the Jews in 1 Thessalonians 2:14–15 is a later insertion reflecting the proselytizers' frustration at being driven out of synagogues and thereby hindered from converting God-fearers in attendance, a subject that is addressed not only in Paul's letter (1 Thess 2:15–16), but also in the corresponding passages in Matthew (23:34) and Luke (11:49).

56. Parkes, *Conflict*, 106. Neusner says on the subject of sinfulness among the Jews of the time of Jesus: "It was not a sinning generation, but one deeply faithful to the covenant and to the Scripture that set forth its terms, perhaps more so than many who have since condemned it." The Jews of the first century fought a war "explicitly for the sake and in the name of God. The struggle called forth prophets and holy men, leaders whom the people did not kill or stone, but courageously followed past all hope of success . . . Since they lost, later generations looked for their sin, for none could believe that the omnipotent God would permit his Temple to be destroyed for no reason. As after 586 B.C.E., so after 70 C.E., the alternative was this: 'Either our fathers greatly sinned, or God is not just'" (*Judaism in the Beginning*, 20). Kaufmann makes exactly the same point in *Religion of Israel*, 135, 402–3.

message and his own upbringing in a Hellenized world. In the long run, James (known as a pious, observant Jew, as well as Jesus' brother) was marginalized, the Jerusalem church lost its stature as the center of Christianity, and Jewish Christianity came to be regarded, by the fourth century, as heretical.[57]

The course of this change can be measured by mutations in the meaning of words like *apostle* and *holy spirit* and of rituals like baptism.[58] The most radical change occurred in the meaning and practice of the ceremony that Jesus initiated at the Last Supper in the synoptic Gospels, the Eucharist. Ironically, at the Supper, Jesus merely distributed bread and wine, said they represent his body and his blood, and claimed he would not drink wine until he drank it in the Kingdom of God. In the Gospel of John, after he washed the feet of all of his disciples, he much more obviously and deliberately commanded his followers to repeat this ceremony in the future: "I have given you an example, that you also should do as I have done to you" (John 13:15). In other words, at least in the synoptic Gospels, he did not counsel his followers to eat his flesh and drink his blood. And, in the Gospel of John, He asked them to remember him by treating each other compassionately and deferentially.

Although the Eucharist, as communion, became one of the most important rituals in the Church, it was not implemented in its present form for perhaps as long as two centuries. Most scholars agree that Christians initially held their communal meals without in any way remembering the death and resurrection of Jesus. They met as if they were members of an association—that is, a kind of organization that was commonplace throughout the Roman empire—honoring the god or holy man to whom the group was dedicated. The supper shared by the *Didache* community, in the early second century, was closer in this respect to that of the Essenes at Qumran, for whom the collective meal was similarly just a messianic banquet.[59] Thus, the earliest Eucharist was, as the word implies, a thanksgiving to God the Father for the gift of Jesus, his son. In this respect, the meal itself was only slightly different from a Jewish meal

57. Robinson says that he entitled his book *Gospel of Jesus* partly to distinguish it from the gospel of Paul, which he feels the Church (evidently mistakenly) treated "as the one and only gospel" (*Gospel of Jesus*, 1). Hill similarly argues that Christianity was transformed by Paul, at the expense of the Jerusalem church and Jewish Christianity (*Hellenists and Hebrews*, 194). Hill associates "the traditionally negative portrayal of non-Pauline Christianity" with "the traditional denigration of Judaism by New Testament scholarship" (196).

58. On changes in the meaning of the word *apostle*, see Weiss, *Earliest Christianity*, II, 674–78, 686–87. On changes in the meaning of the Holy Spirit, see Brown, *Churches*, 121–22; and (far more extensively) Bultmann, *Theology*, I, 153–64. Bultmann also offers a lengthy discussion of changes in the concept of baptism on 133–44. Hatch analyzes the evolution of the practice and meaning of baptism in light of influences from mystery religions in *Influence of Greek Ideas*, 294–300.

59. On this point, see Crossan, *Jesus*, 179–80.

at which the Kiddush (the prayer for wine) was recited, along with a prayer thanking God for bread.[60]

By most accounts, Paul was responsible for making the Eucharist what it is today. To the traditional words used by Jesus, he added the command, "Do this . . . in remembrance of me" (1 Cor 11:24–25; see also Lk 22:19 in the KJV, but not in the RSV). And, eventually, the Eucharist began to resemble a mystery-cult ritual in which the consumption of a god's symbolic flesh and blood resulted in a spiritual union with the god.[61] As one scholar explains, Christians embraced "the sacramental idea" that the body of the deceased god was simultaneously "filled with power." Therefore, whoever ate the flesh and drank the blood of Jesus achieved "Life."[62]

In short, over time, the ritual went through several stages. Finally, the sacramental meal was separated from the communal meal—eventually with priestly administration.[63] By the time the Gospel of John was written, at least the Johannine community understood Jesus' description of his blood as wine and his flesh as bread to mean that he was somehow to be consumed for the spiritual sustenance of his followers: "Truly, truly, I say to you, unless you eat the flesh of the Son of man and drink his blood, you have no life in you; *he who eats my flesh and drinks my blood has eternal life, and I will raise him up at the last day*" (John 6: 53–54). At this point, the Jesus movement, at least insofar as it embraced such ideas, had clearly separated from Judaism.

As a result of Christianity's new self-definition, some second-century Church leaders and later Church historians denied the idea that the earliest Christians were practicing Jews (Sabbath observers, Temple worshipers, ritual performers, and unrepentant circumcisers) by arguing that, since Jesus had rejected the Law, so did his

60. Gonzalez says that the earliest Christian communions celebrated the New Age (*Story of Christianity*, I, 20, 93–94). On the celebration at Qumran, see Vermes, *Dead Sea Scrolls,* 46–47. Cumont says that such banquets began in the ancient world as commemorations of the death of a loved one and took place near the tomb or grave of the departed: "No religious ceremony was more universally performed in the most diverse regions of the Empire than this cult of the grave" (*After Life*, 55). Perhaps the most interesting aspect of these ceremonies was the assumption that, in some sense, the dead returned and shared in the repast (54, 56, 57, 59–61, 100). When they commemorated a god or goddess, the banquets were also a means of "communicating with the godhead." Wine was drunk, and bread was eaten. And, when "a sacred animal was consumed," it symbolized the idea "that the god himself was consumed" (120, 200–204).

61. On this subject, see Tabor, *Jesus Dynasty*, 203; and Hatch, *Influence of Greek Ideas*, 300–309. Tabor specifically mentions a ritual in honor of Isis. On Paul's influence, see Maccoby, *Mythmaker*, 112–13.

62. Bultmann, *Theology*, I, 146–147. Bultmann adds that although common meals were "not actual cultic celebrations" in the early church, they were transformed "in the Pauline or Hellenistic congregations" (57–58): "In Hellenistic Christianity the Lord's Supper, like baptism, is understood as a sacrament in the sense of the mystery religions." The idea of communion is common in ancient cults, but "in the mysteries it plays a special role; in them it is communion with a once dead and risen deity, in whose fate the partaker receives a share through the sacramental meal, as we know from the mysteries of Attis and Mithra" (148).

63. Bultmann, *Theology*, I, 149–52. Crossan discusses five stages in the development of the Eucharist from celebratory meal to mystical experience in *Historical Jesus*, 360–67.

earliest disciples. These first disciples were not James and the "Judaizers," but the Hellenized Jewish Christians who left Jerusalem immediately after the murder of Stephen. Only at that point, so the argument goes, did the Law-observant James, the brother of Jesus, assume the leadership of the Jerusalem church and turn what had been a truly Christ-centered organization into a merely Jewish sect. The process, called *re-Judaization*, was understood to be a betrayal of Jesus' unique and revolutionary faith, and it was fortunately reversed as the Church developed outside of its original Jewish milieu.[64]

Still other Church leaders and historians contended that, although the earliest Church was indeed Jewish, its members were unable to understand Jesus' message, either because Jesus did not reveal everything to them or because they could not transcend their cultural and religious limitations. Jesus' real message (e.g., his redemptive sacrifice, his death and resurrection, his unearthly kingdom, his divine identity) was only fully comprehended by Hellenized thinkers who were unfettered by Jewish ideas and had had the time to sift through all of the evidence—some of which was late in coming, especially the revelations reported by the Apostle Paul. Thus, as one scholar notes, "in its attempts to determine the moment at which God's choice was concretely and effectively accomplished in the man Jesus we see within the New Testament some very subtle and delicate changes, pointing to a persistent process of reflection, all the time *refining, correcting and deepening* the first one."[65] Eventually, however, the process ended—at least to the satisfaction of a majority of Christians—at Nicea.

64. For examples of this view, see Catchpole, "The Historicity of the Sanhedrin Trial," 53; Hengel, *Acts*, passim; and Smith, *Jesus the Magician*, 147–48, 171. Hengel's argument is worth exploring. He first claims, based partly on the Antitheses in the Gospel of Matthew, that Jesus rejected the Jewish Law (*Acts*, 94, 112). Peter, as Jesus' closest associate and most devout disciple, was also a "liberal," who was never law-obedient (92, 94, 97, 98) and turns out to have been Paul's best friend (86, 95, 124). Peter was thus, unlike James, a part of the still-surviving *liberal* wing of the Jerusalem church (76–77, 92, 101), as were the Hellenists, who were chased out of Jerusalem after the death of Stephen. Having thus lost its enlightened members, who had been influenced directly by Jesus, the Jerusalem church turned into an outpost of Jewish-Christian conservatism, especially under James, who took over in AD 43 (73, 80, 94, 96). The result was an unchristian "radical obedience to the law" and a reshaping of "the Jesus tradition" in "a legalistic form" (113). It took some time, of course, considering the unreasonable influence of Judaizers everywhere (121), for the air to clear, Jesus' real ideas to emerge (or re-emerge), and the Church to return to its real non-Jewish roots. With Hengel in mind, Hill exhaustively dismantles the idea that the Jerusalem church was conservative, that Hellenists were liberal, and that either Stephen or Paul represented anyone but themselves (*Hellenists and Hebrews*, 1–4, 41–43, 115, 123–24 n. 85, 146).

65. Schillebeeckx, *Jesus*, 548–550; my emphasis. Hegesippus, a second-century historian of Christianity, argued that Christianity was "virgin, pure and uncorrupted" at first and was ruined not by James and the Jerusalem church, but after "all the Apostles and the generations of those who knew them had passed away"—that is, in the second century, when all kinds of heresies arose (Markus, *Christianity*, 62). Like Hegesippus, Hatch claims that Christianity was at its best and most authentic at its beginning, but was undermined later on, in Hatch's view, by the influence of Hellenism (*Influence of Greek Ideas*, 332–33, 351–53). Correcting this view by emphasizing the "divergent and sometimes conflicting traditions" of the *original* Church, Markus, like Schillebeeckx, offers the idea that Christians only later understood Jesus: "It was a gradual *crystallization* in the consciousness of Christians over generations,

The problem with the first interpretation is that the New Testament itself—especially Luke's Infancy narrative, Jesus' modification (but not rejection) of Jewish laws in all of the synoptic Gospels, and Luke's account in Acts of the early Church's consistent respect for the Law and attendance at the Temple—demonstrates that both Jesus and his followers were obedient Jews. That, in any case, is the belief of the majority of historians and Bible scholars.[66] The second interpretation—that the true picture of Jesus

---

akin to the growth of self-discovery in an individual person" (63; my emphasis). Richardson makes a similar point: "While the disciples of Jesus are never called 'Israel' in an exclusive way, a development is begun in the New Testament that reaches a conclusion at least by AD 160. There is a gradual but *inevitable* takeover by the Church of the attributes and prerogatives of the people Israel, so that at some point it becomes an uncontested assumption of the Church that it is 'true Israel' and 'old' Israel has lost all claim to that title of ancient privilege" ("The Israel-Idea in the Passion Narratives," 1–2; my emphasis). What shows these views to be theological rather than historical—that is, based on faith rather than fact—is the words *crystallization* and *inevitable,* both of which suggest that the "discovery" occurred late because it was God's will. In other words, the idea that the Church moved from ignorance in Jerusalem to wisdom at Nicea is simply asserted, not demonstrated factually or logically. The weakness of this interpretation becomes clear when Richardson argues that *Jesus failed to reveal the whole truth* and that the Holy Spirit later enabled the Church to fill in the gaps: "All questions were not finally disposed of once and for all by [Jesus'] teaching. The Church, in dependence upon the Holy Spirit, had to meditate long and hard upon the direction they were to go *vis-à-vis* Israel and the world." From a Nicean perspective, this means that God-as-Jesus first offered a partial explanation, but as the Holy Spirit He eventually revealed everything. If this view sounds bizarre, suggesting as it does God's initial failure to make Himself clear, Richardson offers an alternative. That is, the fault was not in Jesus, but in his Jewish disciples. Here, Richardson manages to bring together the Theory of Belated Revelation, the Theory of Christian Supersedure, and the Theory of Jewish Inferiority. That is, not only did Christianity supersede Judaism, but later Christianity superseded earlier Christianity. And both occurred because Jews—whether they were Jesus' disciples or his enemies—were unable to understand Jesus. And this happened because they were "trapped in the old ways, old views, old traditions which were so largely responsible for the arrest and trial of Jesus" (10). One may therefore choose between two interpretations: first, that Jesus held back so as to allow the gentiles, but not the Jews, to understand his message; or, second, that Jesus explained everything, but the Jews were incapable of understanding it. Tannehill argues that the first of these two theories is incorporated into Acts of the Apostles as an ongoing theme. That is, Luke repeatedly shows that Jesus' followers, with the aid of the Holy Spirit, slowly discovered the will of God. The process involved people having visions and other new experiences, sharing them with others, having them publicly debated, seeking the approval of the Church, and finally working out the implications of the Church's decisions (*Luke-Acts,* II, 131–32; see also 145). Thus, for example, the conversion of Cornelius contributed to "the transformation of a church that has a universal mission but is caught in ethnocentric isolation" (137). Senior also claims that the Church only gradually understood the full implications of Jesus' message: "The evolution that began with the first moment of the church's life was not a betrayal of the teaching of Jesus but a sure sign of the presence of the Spirit. To change and adapt was a sign that the church was alive, that it was willing to bear the responsibility of deepening its understanding of who Jesus was and to proclaim this faith in fresh language to all generations and cultures" (*Jesus,* 154; see also 110, 112, 146–48, 152).

66. Chilton says that "the primitive church," meaning the earliest Church, existed "prior to any conscious separation from Second Temple Judaism" ("James in Relation to Peter, Paul, and the Remembrance of Jesus," in Chilton and Neusner, eds., *Brother of Jesus,* 138). According to Ehrman, "The earliest Christians kept the Jewish law as interpreted by Jesus and insisted that their converts do so as well" (*After the New Testament,* 134). Bauckham says that "it is extremely doubtful whether anyone in the Jerusalem church would have questioned that Jewish Christians should continue to observe the whole law. Debates concerned the relationship of Gentile converts to the law, a quite distinct issue" ("James and Jesus," 105–6). Thus, as Brown puts it, "Christians in Acts are faithful to the piety of Israel"

did not emerge until Greek ideas enabled Christians to see Jesus in a Greek context—is also a minority opinion. The question is, why should the way Jesus was viewed in the second and third centuries by Greek-speaking Romans be considered more accurate than the way he was viewed in the first century by his own companions and country-men, Aramaic-speaking Jews, based as the older view was on more recent memories and face-to-face relations? In other words, what did the gentiles know about Jesus that the Jews did not? Furthermore, if God had wanted Jesus to be understood from a Greek perspective, why did he not only *start* Jesus' career in Palestine, but *end* it there?

* * *

Not only did the Jews, in any meaningful sense of the term, *not* kill Jesus, it can also be said that the Jews did not even reject him, the argument in Chapter Five, "The Rejec-tion." On one hand, Christians claimed that Jews did not accept Jesus as their leader because God Himself wanted to deny them the privilege of becoming Jesus' disciples. In short, it was His plan to have Jesus preach to the Jews but fail to convert them to his faith—principally as a sign of their depravity and faithlessness. On the other hand, however, the Church was created and supported entirely by Jews for many years. That is, it would not have existed at all but for the devotion of eleven of the twelve Jewish disciples, Jesus' Jewish brothers (especially James), and the thousands of Jews who are said to have joined the Church in Acts of the Apostles (e.g., 21:20). To many scholars, Jesus was ignored in Galilee by the people who knew him best (Mark 6:4) because "he

---

(*Churches*, 65). "Joseph of Arimathea," Brown says elsewhere, "a pious member of the Sanhedrin, . . . presumably wanted to observe the law that the body of one hanged on a tree should not remain over night" (*Introduction*, 147). According to Vermes, the ideas of the Jerusalem church, documented in the Acts of the Apostles, "have every probability of mirroring in substance the earliest thoughts of the first Jewish-Christian communities of Palestine." That is, Acts presents "an ideology that still reflects the freshness and lack of sophistication of the original Jewish followers of Jesus before Paul conquered the intellectual high ground in the Church" (*Resurrection*, 112). Kloppenborg adds: The Q gospel (i.e., the sayings of Jesus common to the Gospels of Matthew and Luke, but not in the Gospel of Mark) "gives us a glimpse of the earliest Jesus movement in the Galilee, a different Gospel with a different view of Jesus' significance. It is not a dying and rising savior that we see in Q, but a sage with uncommon wisdom, wisdom that addressed the daily realities of small-town life in Jewish Galilee" (Q, 121). For Robinson, the Q gospel is "the best source that exists today to get back to what Jesus actually had to say; it is also the best source for understanding what he thought he was doing, what he was up to in what he did" (*Gospel of Jesus*, 9). Robinson provides a brief introduction to Q in 23–26. Scholars have also emphasized the persistent and ongoing influence of Judaism on Christianity. Gager says, "From the very beginning there are strong indications that Christianity from Antioch in the West to Mesopotamia in the East was strongly influenced by Judaism. On this issue there is virtual unanimity." Gager mentions especially rituals and beliefs (*Origins of Anti-Semitism*, 24). Furthermore, the Jewish influence remained strong: "For significant numbers of Christians in late antiquity, Judaism continued to represent a powerful and vigorous religious tradition." Unlike their leaders, "they saw no need to define themselves in opposition to Judaism or to cut themselves off from this obvious source of power" (133). See also Tabor, *Jesus Dynasty*, 121.

did not fulfill the prophetic expectations of a Messiah."[67] In particular, it was his death on the cross that made his messianic claim "scandalous": "The response of a Jew to such a claim could not but be one of shock."[68]

The argument in the Gospels indicates that God made the Jews incapable of accepting Jesus or his message. Explaining why he spoke to the public in parables, Jesus said that God permitted his disciples "to know the secrets of the kingdom of heaven, but to them [i.e., the others] it has not been given . . . This is why I speak to them in parables, because seeing they do not see, and hearing they do not hear, nor do they understand" (Matt 13:11–13). Jesus then, in both Matthew (13:14–15) and John (12:40), quoted Isaiah 6:9–10. The translation is more forceful in John: "He [i.e., God] has blinded their eyes and hardened their heart, lest they should see with their eyes and perceive with their heart, and turn for me to heal them." That is, God himself did not want the others to perceive and understand. Thus, in both Matthew and Luke, Jesus praised his disciples, who, unlike the public he otherwise addressed, knew what he was talking about: "But blessed are your eyes, for they see, and your ears, for they hear" (Matt 13:16; Luke 10:23–24).

Scholars say that this use of Isaiah is what the ancient Jews called a *midrash*, a traditional Jewish method of interpretation that has been variously described as a means (1) of filling gaps in a text, (2) of stringing together biblical passages to establish a theme, and (3) of explaining "one biblical passage in light of another."[69] Examples of the first can be found in both the Infancy narratives in Matthew and Luke and the Passion narratives in all of the Gospels.[70] *Midrashim* of this kind are common in the New Testament in descriptions of either events that occurred so long ago that no one can remember the details or events for which there were no eye witnesses. In the narratives mentioned above, the evangelists used Old Testament passages to provide the missing information about both Jesus' infancy and his arrest, trial, and execution. An example of the second type of *midrash* can be seen in the use of various passages

---

67. Klein is summing up the argument of Nineham in *The Gospel of St. Mark* (*Anti-Judaism*, 151). The Jewish Messiah was expected to initiate "the worship of the one true God by all nations and the cessation of war, disease, and injustice." As for Jesus' miracles, there were miracle workers among his contemporaries, both Jewish and gentile (151). Furthermore, the most spectacular miracles he performed (e.g., feeding many people with a small amount of food and reviving the dead) were anticipated in the Old Testament by Elijah and Elisha. On this subject, see Senior, *Jesus*, 111.

68. Davies, *Invitation*, 415–16.

69. Levine, *Misunderstood Jew*, 200; White, *From Jesus to Christianity*, 320; and Schiffman, *From Text to Tradition*, 47.

70. On the infancy narratives as *midrashim*, see Meier, *Marginal Jew*, I, 208–14; Braun, *Jesus of Nazareth*, 24–25; Bornkamm, *Jesus of Nazareth*, 32; and Spong, *Liberating the Gospels*, 224. On the Passion narratives as *midrashim*, see Wylen, *Jews*, 131; and Conzelmann and Lindemann, *Interpreting the New Testament*, 329–32. "The infancy and resurrection narratives leave room for this type of expansion," says McKenzie, "because there was no first-hand account of either series of episodes" (*Old Testament*, 58).

from the Jewish Bible in the Letter to the Hebrews (Ps 8, 40, 95, and 110; Jer 31:31–34; Gen 14:17–20).

An example of the third kind is what we find in the passages dealing with God's rejection of the Jews. In them, Isaiah is used to substantiate the view that the failure of the Jews to accept Jesus was inevitable (because it was imposed by God). However, that attempt suffers from the problem that midrashes almost always suffer from: They are completely taken out of their original context,[71] which is *never* referred to. One scholar comments: "[T]his conception of scripture leads to an atomistic exegesis, which interprets sentences, clauses, phrases, and even single words, independently of the context of the historical occasion, as divine oracles."[72] The quotation from Isaiah is used to explain an event that took place hundreds of years after the passage was written. The question is, of course, does a statement by Isaiah in the eighth century BC actually predict (and therefore authenticate) the claim that God wanted the Jews to reject Jesus (and suffer the consequences) in the first century AD? And this question applies to hundreds of passages in the New Testament.

Of course, the point is not that "the Jews" rejected Jesus. Only a few thousand of them, out of several million in the Roman empire, were likely to have even heard of him during his lifetime. And, if there were fewer than 10,000 Christians (by one estimate) at the end of the first century,[73] why would the Jews have either paid attention or felt threatened? Furthermore, in the Gospel of Mark, Jesus said the same thing to his disciples that he said to the public: "Do you not yet perceive or understand? Are your hearts hardened? Having eyes do you not see, and having ears do you not hear?" (Mark 8:17–18; 6:52). One has to remember that "the others," whom Jesus said God

71. Brown, *Introduction*, 207. Brown also raises the question of whether passages from the Jewish Bible used throughout the New Testament, especially those showing that Jesus was fulfilling an Old Testament prophecy, were cited to prove that point or were in fact the source of the event. On the same kind of use of Old Testament passages to show that the Jewish Bible predicted the coming of Jesus, see Newsome on Isa 7:10–17; 9:1–7; and 11:1–9, in *Hebrew Prophets*, 65, 74–78. What Newsome says of the first passage applies equally to all of them: "[T]he text as it stands seems to say something quite different from the traditional Christian interpretation of it." That is, in this and the other instances, Isaiah is referring to a contemporary situation: "It seems clear that Isaiah has in mind an immediate application of his words" (74–75). And the same point applies to similar passages in Ezekiel, Haggai, and Zechariah. Although, even with the aforementioned caveats, Newsome is somewhat inclined to see these prophesies as the Church has interpreted them, he adds that (1) the prophets were not primarily predictors of future events, but moralists addressing current problems; (2) they were sometimes wrong, as Haggai and Zechariah were in predicting that Zerubbabel would restore the glories of the Davidic kingdom; and (3) none of the so-called predictions of the Jewish Bible "anticipated the fulfillment of the messianic promises in precisely the way in which they came about" (211–13).

72. George Foot Moore, quoted in Grant, *Historical Introduction*, 260. Suggesting that the Essenes used the same kind of literary analysis, Grant says, "In this way [they] were forerunners of the Christian exegetes of the Old Testament" (266). Crossan gives a detailed explanation of the Essenes' interpretive method and the Christian application of it in *Historical Jesus*, 368–70. See also Wylen, *Jews*, 40–41; and Conzelmann and Lindemann, *Interpreting the New Testament*, 224.

73. Stark, *Rise of Christianity*, 4–13.

had rejected, were not discernibly different from his disciples: Both groups were Jews. And the implication in Mark is that *nobody* understood Jesus.

Nevertheless, it was evidently of interest to Christians to make this charge, just as they accused the Jews of three crimes against the followers of Jesus: (1) including in regular synagogue services, as early as the first century, a curse against all Christians, (2) excluding all Christian Jews from synagogue services before the Revolt, and (3) arresting and killing Christians in Judea under Paul's leadership as an anti-Christian Pharisee. It seems probable, however, that the curse was added much later and was addressed to all heretics and that only Christian proselytizers (especially, if they were inclined, as Stephen was, to insult their audience) were kept out of synagogues.

Most important, it is worth asking—at least, according to some scholars—whether Jews actually sought out and executed Christians under Paul's leadership (or anyone else's, for that matter).[74] Paul's portrait of himself as the High Priest's chief heresy-hunter seems questionable if only because the Jerusalem church appears to have been completely unaffected by his work. On the one hand, the entire contingent of Hellenized Jewish Christians are said to have left Jerusalem after Stephen's death. That is, they were frightened by the murder of *one* of their compatriots. On the other hand, as far as we know, the members of the Jerusalem church—despite *many* (and, according to Paul, official!) executions—were unperturbed by the threat of persecution. Indeed, not only does Luke report in Acts that large numbers of Jews converted to Christianity at this time, evidently without reprisal, he also says that "the people" (i.e., the Jews) so strongly admired the early Christians of Jerusalem (Acts 2:47; 5:13) that they prevented the authorities from prosecuting even Christian proselytizers like Peter (4:21; 5:26).

Furthermore, while (presumably) every arrest and flogging in Paul and Peter's careers are documented in Acts of the Apostles, nothing at all is known of the victims of Paul's alleged persecution. He claims they were *put to death* (Acts 9:1; 22:4; 26:10), but this would mean that they constitute the largest group of unknown martyrs in Christian history. They were, Paul says, arrested in their homes (Acts 8:3) and then murdered merely for professing Christianity, a circumstance that distinguishes them from the Christians, like Paul, who were *only* arrested as disruptive propagandists in synagogues and then flogged. One is forced to wonder why, if Paul had such an easy time killing Christians, the Jews had such a hard time killing him.

* * *

74. Hill says, "I do not believe that the Hellenists were especially subject to systematic persecution, since I do not accept that the severe persecution of Acts 8 and 9 is literal historical fact . . . In summary, it is difficult to believe that scholars would ever have interpreted a verse like 8:1 with such minute literalism, except for the fact that an entire superstructure is built upon it." Hill does not contend that Luke "fabricated" the persecution; rather, he assumes that Luke's account "relects what was a genuine heightening of tensions between the infant church and Judaism" (*Hellenists and Hebrews*, 38–39). Hill cites, in defense of his view, W. M. L. Wette, *Kurze Erklarung der Apostelgeschichte*, 67; Johannes Weiss, *Earliest Christianity*, I, 170; and F. J. Foakes Jackson, *The Acts of the Apostles*, 69.

In "Hellenization," the final chapter, the focus is on the four-century-long process by which Christianity as a Jewish sect evolved into a religion much more like a pagan mystery cult than a Jewish messianic movement. This slow, but ultimately radical change occurred partly because Christianity moved out of the Galilean countryside—an area occupied by Aramaic-speaking, rural Jews—to the Greek-speaking cities of the Diaspora, which had been deeply affected by the influence of Greek art and architecture, language, recreation, philosophy, and (of course) religion. Jewish Christians started their proselytizing missions in Jewish synagogues in Diaspora cities, appealing to pagans who had converted to Judaism and God-fearers, the latter of whom could become, as the Church increasingly insisted, "real" Jews—that is, the truly elect—without the agony of circumcision and without the burden of food, purity, and Sabbath laws.

Both Jews and gentiles in the Diaspora had been influenced by the idea that mere human beings could become gods (Divine Men), a concept totally foreign to Palestinian Jews, who, ironically, used the term "son of God" quite loosely and figuratively, but never implied that mere human beings could be thought of as God's progeny or God's equal. Diaspora residents, influenced by Platonism (through, for Jews especially, the Jewish philosopher Philo), thought of human beings as related to the gods through the spiritual element within them. That is, they understood divinity as something shared by all human beings. Thus, Jesus, as a divine being, could be—as were the Pharaohs, the Roman emperors after death, and men who were divinized because of their heroism—thought of as a kind of god.

It was the mystery religions, however, that provided the Hellenized world with a model for understanding Jesus—that is, the cults that celebrated a god who had descended from heaven; appeared on earth disguised as a man, and performed miracles and disseminated wisdom; and who, after being destroyed by earthly forces, ascended to heaven. The process of change in the Church's understanding of Jesus was complex. It is obviously not that Christians cynically did what they needed to do to "sell" Christianity. It is, rather, that people who were immersed in the world view of the so-called oriental religions understood Christianity in the context of their belief system. Jesus *seemed* like a mystery-cult god.

The concept of Wisdom in the literature of late Judaism illustrates how the transformation of Jesus from prophet to god was influenced by Greek thought.[75] Of course, all kinds of goddesses, wise and otherwise, were familiar to the ancient Jews. On one hand, female deities being anathema to traditional Judaism, Jewish prophets (especially Jeremiah, but also Elijah and others in 1 and 2 Kings) railed for centuries

75. Brown says, "Scholars of many backgrounds would recognize that an adaptation of this figure played an important role in the N[ew] T[estament] understanding of Jesus' divine origins" (*Introduction*, 825). White says that Wisdom literature was an attempt by Jews to make their religious concepts "intelligible" to pagans (*From Jesus to Christianity*, 87–88). But it also turned out to be a means by which Hellenistic philosophy influenced Jewish thinking. On the Hellenistic origins of Wisdom literature, see Martin, *Hellenistic Religions*, 90, 107–9; and Koester, *History, Culture, and Religion*, 272.

against the influence of Baal and his female consort. On the other hand, Wisdom, a more or less secular figure who was popular throughout the ancient Near East, was introduced into patriarchal Judaism by the time the Book of Proverbs was written (see chs. 1–9). She also appears in several inter-testamental works, such as *Ecclesiasticus*, *The Wisdom of Solomon*, *Tobit*, and *Baruch*—all of which were deeply affected by Hellenistic thought.

The attributes of Wisdom include her similarity to the Holy Spirit (Wis 1:5; 7:27; 9:17; Prov 1:23), by which means she inspires prophets (Wis 11:1); her availability to all seekers (Wis 6:12; 7:7; Prov 8:17), but only as God's gift (Wis 8:21; Prov 2:6); her promise of immortality (Wis 6:18; 8:13, 17); and her closeness to God, such that serving her is serving Him (Sir 4:14; Prov 8:35). It is also suggestive that one of the ways to gain the kind of knowledge Wisdom provides is to eat the fruit or drink the potion she proffers (Sir 24:19; 2 Esd 8:4; 14:37–40).

It is clear from these characteristics that Wisdom was thought of as a hypostatized or reified entity, who acted only at God's command, but existed in some sense on her own. In this respect, as God's messenger or emissary, she resembles the logos, as it was defined by the Jewish philosopher Philo and made its way into Christian concepts of Jesus, especially in the Gospel of John, in which Jesus *is* the Logos, or Word. The connections between Wisdom and Jesus, especially as Jesus is described in John (1:1–5), are several. First, Wisdom, like Jesus, existed from the beginning of time or earlier (Wis 9:9; Sir 1:4; 24:9; Prov 8:22–29). Second, she is the means by which God created everything (Wis 7:22; 8:6; 14:5; Prov 3:19–20). Third, like the gods and goddesses of other cultures of the time, she descends into the world, offering wisdom, and later ascends (Bar 3:37).[76] Fourth, Wisdom announces in Ecclesiasticus, "I am the word" (Sir 24:3). And, fifth, Wisdom provides both life (Prov 8:35) and light, as Jesus does: She "shines brightly and never fades" (Wis 6:12). "She is the radiance that streams from everlasting light" (Wis 7:26).[77]

---

76. Mack, *Who Wrote?* 94. Commenting on the origins of the Christ hymn in Philippians 2:6–11, in which this pattern appears, Mack says that "ears accustomed to the stories of the gods (and whose ears would not have been?) would have sensed the common myth"—i.e., common to Jesus and the pagan gods—"lurking in the background" (94). Perrin and Duling identify the same myth in Enoch 42:1–2 (*New Testament*, 27). Crossan specifically identifies this myth as Hellenistic (*Historical Jesus*, 232). Cameron, in *Other Gospels*, says, "Such a myth was widespread in the Greco-Roman world and underlies many of the earliest christological formulations of believers in Jesus" (84). He cites half a dozen examples of the latter.

77. See also Baruch 4:2. Peters says that the Gnostics found in Wisdom "a prototype of a hypostatized emanation of God who descended into the world and was, in a sense, its creator." Furthermore, in some Gnostic systems, the female Wisdom was replaced by the male logos (*Harvest of Hellenism*, 658). Townsend says that "a few passages in the New Testament suggest an equivalence between personified wisdom and Jesus Christ" ("Wisdom," 193–94). Robinson discusses a passage in which Wisdom speaks in the Q Gospel (13:34), is replaced by "the wisdom of God" in Luke (11:49), and is replaced by Jesus in Matthew (23:34), speaking in the first person: "Therefore also Wisdom said: "I will send them prophets and sages, and some of them they will kill and persecute" (*Gospel of Jesus*, 192–93).

I am not suggesting that these attributes were arbitrarily attached to Jesus to make him more attractive and accessible to gentiles. I am merely saying that people who were introduced to Jesus as a messenger of God necessarily understood him in the context of their pre-existing ideas of what that messenger would be like. And, if the concept of Wisdom had been one of those ideas, it would not be surprising if people saw Jesus as a Wisdom-like figure. The same point applies to other such figures in the Diaspora—e.g., the mystery cult gods, the logos, and the Divine Man—that did not exist in Palestine, especially in rural Galilee.

Christianity moved in this way from its Jewish roots to the Greco-Roman world; slowly cut off its connection to Judaism without, however, severing its ties to the Jewish Bible (translated into Greek), the prophets, Abraham, the Exodus, Passover, and the Holy Spirit; and, indeed, not only claimed these aspects of Judaism as its own, but considered itself to have superseded Judaism by asserting that Jesus was prophesied by the entire Old Testament. This new faith proceeded to relegate Jesus' own religion (with its emphasis on universal love, non-violence, and voluntary poverty) to oblivion and condemned the Jews to a life of second-class citizenship and both economic and political punishment for the sin of not acknowledging one of their own as King of the Jews as well as the gentiles.

As if by divine decree, the Church turned into the Synagogue, at least, insofar as Christians not only continued to use the Jewish Bible (translated into Greek and ultimately used secondarily as the Old Testament), but also adopted the Jewish liturgy and held worship services (as the Jews did) once a week on the Sabbath. Otherwise, priests replaced rabbis, synods attended by bishops replaced rabbinical councils, and the doctrines established by the Church Fathers replaced the traditions established by the Pharisees—the same kind of traditions that Jesus repudiated because they were not created by God, but by men. Eventually, the pope replaced the High Priest, and the Vatican—as the political, religious, and economic center of a world-wide religion, with its treasury and treasures, storage rooms, and other extra-religious facilities—turned into the Temple.

Chapter One

Judaism

"It has long been commonplace among Christians that the Old Testament is the rule of law, the New Testament the rule of love. Once the Old Testament is accepted as equally the word of God with the New Testament, it becomes embarrassing to speak of the abolition of the Law by Jesus—or ought to become embarrassing." (John L. McKenzie)

DESPITE THE FACT THAT many scholars in the last twenty or thirty years have expressed the belief that Jesus and his disciples lived and died as Jews, few books on the subject have devoted as much as a separate chapter to Judaism. Indeed, the majority of examinations of Jesus' life and work, including even those that focus on his embrace of Judaism, devote relatively little space to the subject. That is, although it would clearly make sense to examine in some detail the religion that Jesus himself practiced throughout his life, Judaism is usually treated only in passing. Scholars occasionally connect an idea or act of Jesus to a parallel idea or act in ancient Judaism. What the reader gets as a result of this intermittent commentary, however, is a very sketchy picture of Judaism and a flawed concept of Jesus' relationship to his native faith.

An even bigger obstacle to the study of Jesus and Judaism, however, is the distorted picture of Judaism that has been traditional among students of religion, ancient history, and the Bible for almost two thousand years.[1] Following the Gospel accounts

---

1. Herford says that the misrepresentation of Judaism goes back to the New Testament itself. First, it is an unreliable source on the Pharisees (*Pharisees*, 14). Second, as a product of the second-generation of Christianity, which succeeded the first generation (at which time the Church was the exclusive creation of Palestinian Jews), it is equally an unreliable source on the Jews in general and on Judaism in particular: "The New Testament as a whole is the product of a religious movement which, *ex hypothesi*, was not Jewish, and its general attitude towards Judaism, apart from individual Jews, is nowhere friendly, and often hostile" (198–199). The evangelists were not "false witnesses," Herford goes on to say, but they were looking from the outside in, for which reason "nothing can be learned from [the New Testament] which directly throws fresh light upon the essential meaning of Judaism" (214). The subsequent history of the relations between Christians and Jews—or at least between the Church and the Jews—Herford calls "a shameful story," which "belongs to the subject of the presentation of Judaism in the New Testament" (224). Winter says that the Gospel portrait of the Pharisees as "the most bitter opponents of Jesus" is "a biased view." "The disciples of Jesus," Winter continues,

of Jesus' hostility to the Pharisees, scholars have emphasized the difference between Judaism's doctrine of obedience and Jesus' doctrine of love—two contrasting ways of defining humanity's relationship to God.[2] To put it simply, it is argued, Jews followed God's laws because God promised to reward them for compliance or punish them for disobedience: "Behold, I set before you this day a blessing and a curse: the blessing, if you obey the commandments of the Lord your God, which I command you this day,

---

"tried to win a hearing, and looked for likely converts among the same classes as those from which the Pharisees were drawn. From the point of view of the history of religion, Jesus himself was much closer to the Pharisees than to any other sect of the time" ("Sadducees and Pharisees," 51). Enslin implicitly attributes the negative view of Judaism to the Gospels themselves, which were written when the Church was becoming more and more gentile and therefore created, forty years after the fact, an account of Jesus and the Jews that was distorted by both the lapse of time and an unsympathetic perspective (*Christian Beginnings*, 148).

2. Sanders says: "Hundreds, possibly thousands of New Testament scholars have charged Jews with being legalistic, and they have attributed to Jesus the desire to overcome the legalism of his native religion . . . The charge of legalism perfectly fitted the Christian need to accuse Judaism of producing bad humans. Legalistic Jews are either anxious or arrogant; they value trivial external actions; they are hypocrites" ("Jesus, Ancient Judaism, and Modern Christians," 49). For Sanders's full explanation of the charge of Jewish legalism, see 48–54. Tabor attributes this view of Judaism to Christian anti-Semitism (*Jesus Dynasty*, 110). On this point, see also Ruether, *Faith and Fratricide*, 62. Brown notes that Jewish and/or Pharisaic legalism has been a subject of "endless debate" in scholarly circles. For his discussion, see *Introduction*, 578–83. Both Glatzer, in his foreword to *Pharisees*, and Herford, the author of the book, lament the misreading of the Pharisees by Christians. Glatzer accuses Christian scholars of "ignoring in the main [the] piety, loving concern, and humaneness" of Pharisaism (1). Herford calls "inadequate and superficial" the idea that Jesus represented "the free prophetic spirit" and the Pharisees represented "the bondage of the Law." He continues, "Such limitations of view vitiate most of what has been written about the Pharisees by Christian scholars" (11–12). According to Enslin, Christians "have expatiated on the decay of a once noble religion into a barren and formal legalism," but "[t]his appears to be an almost total misapprehension" (*Christian Beginnings*, vii). For an example of the ambivalence of some scholars toward the religious practices of the ancient Jews, see Latourette's *History of Christianity*. On the one hand, Latourette says that Jewish legalism is a caricature; on the other hand, however, he says that, according to Jesus, "the radiant life which God desires for men is not to be had through the meticulous observance of the Law [i.e., Jewish legalism], for no one could fully keep the commands which God had given for men's instruction and guidance" (I, 51, 72). Indeed, Latourette's portrait of the Jews elsewhere is quite negative, to say the least. He says (1) that a majority of Jews "either rejected the prophets outright or devitalized their message by compromise" (8); (2) that Jesus was executed because his "teaching" so contrasted with ancient Judaism (50); and (3) that Jesus challenged the leaders of the Jews because, "while professedly standing as the guardian of the Jewish heritage," they neither understood it nor respected it (52). As we shall see later in this chapter, only the last point is at least partially correct. That is, the Jewish elite owed their primary allegiance to Rome and therefore exposed their fellow Jews to political and economic exploitation. Dihle says that "Jesus [took] issue with the Jews' sense of election and replace[d] pious self-concern with unconditional love of one's neighbor" ("The Graeco-Roman Background," 17). Braun, in the same volume, similarly accuses the Jews, with their "meticulous obedience" to the Law, of wallowing in "self-glory," while Jesus offered "unconditional" love as well as "joyful and free obedience" ("The Qumran Community," 74). As Boyarin notes, considering the omnipresence and persistence of the belief that Christianity offered "love and faith" while Judaism was "a grim realm of religious anxiety," some ideas "die very hard" (*Jewish Gospels*, 103).

and the curse, if you do not obey the commandments of the Lord your God" (Deut 11:26–28).[3]

Some Christians, beginning with Paul, regarded this arrangement as merely self-serving. That is, the Jews were willing to cooperate with God only because they expected to receive something in exchange for their cooperation. In short, they saw their religion as a *quid pro quo*—an exchange of "this" for "that." Indeed, if they failed to cooperate, they would not only lose the benefit, they would be forced to suffer, as Adam and Eve and their progeny suffered for their numerous acts of disobedience. There was no middle ground between rewards and punishments. And there was no motive for obedience other than the desire for pleasure and the fear of pain.

This approach to the divine-human relationship was called literalistic, insofar as it emphasized following the letter of the law rather than the spirit. It did not ask, "What does God *want* me to do?" but "What can I get away with?" This form of worship was also called legalistic, insofar as it encouraged obedience based on fear rather than love. It did not ask, "What is the right thing to do?" but "What is the safe thing to do?" And it was considered to be amoral insofar as it allowed men and women to expiate their sins by doing good deeds. At its worst, therefore, it did not discourage sin, but encouraged supererogatory acts that were undertaken only to compensate for wrong-doing.[4] And it has often been suggested that these acts, making up in some

3. Crossan says of the contrast between Judaism and Christianity: "I reject emphatically and absolutely any hint that the God of Judaism was a God of violent force and the God of Christianity was a God of nonviolent love . . . In strictest truth, those disjunctive options cut across Judaism, across Christianity and, for that matter, across Islam as well" (*Birth of Christianity,* 287). For a review of the scholarship on the relationship between Judaism and Christianity, see Parkes, *Conflict,* xi-xx. Herford makes the point repeatedly that Judaism has been misrepresented as a burdensome, rigid, hypocritical, and formalistic religion (*Pharisees,* 75). The synagogue could not have survived if it had been as sterile and onerous as Christians since Paul have supposed, nor was it "deadened" by Ezra's alleged reduction of the religion "to a barren legalism" (100–101). Herford discusses the flexibility of the Law in the hands of the Pharisees, as well as the joy of obedience which they celebrated, as, for example, in Psalm 119 (110–12). Finally, he adds, the Pharisees were wary of hypocrisy and emphasized the importance of "the inward purpose" as much as "the outward sign" (116–18). Herford revisits these subjects in *Pharisees,* 160–63.

4. Bultmann's portrayal of first-century Judaism is a good example of the kind of interpretation that dominated early twentieth-century scholarship. In Bultmann's view, Judaism was both legalistic and non-ethical: Jesus was "against a form of piety which regards the will of God as expressed in the written Law and in the Tradition which interprets it, a piety which endeavors to win God's favor by the toil of minutely fulfilling the Law's stipulations . . . The real result is that motivation to ethical conduct is vitiated" because it is a response to rewards and punishments and therefore a matter of unquestioning obedience." Indeed, Bultmann continues, Jews developed an ethics of "supererogation"—i.e., doing more than is required, simply for the sake of greater rewards and even atonements for past sins (*Theology,* I, 11–12). This view was evidently the basis for Bultmann's establishment of the so-called discontinuity criterion for determining which of Jesus' sayings are authentic. The theory was that only those words and actions that are discontinuous from Judaism (and also, incidentally, not obviously added by the primitive Church) could be considered genuine. Schillebeeckx says that—besides Bultmann—Hans Conzelmann, Oscar Cullmann, and Ernest Käsemann used this standard of judgment, resulting in a minimalization, by fiat, of Jesus' ties to Judaism (*Jesus,* 92). Crossan makes exactly the same point: "Is that [i.e., the criterion of discontinuity] not a conclusion rather than a criterion?"

instances for serious moral infractions, need not be accompanied by remorse, but need only be penitential gestures, like reciting a prayer or performing a ritual.

That, supposedly, was the Covenant that God had established with pre-Jewish humanity, represented by Noah, and, uniquely, with the Israelites, represented by Abraham and his descendants. Theoretically, it was a means of establishing and maintaining order; however, it was morally shallow because it did not depend on the development of "conscience," a Greek concept that Paul and his followers referred to frequently (in Rom 2:15; 9:1; 13:5, and almost a dozen times in 1 and 2 Colossians), but was absent from Jewish discourse on the subject of righteousness. Under the influence of the Pharisees, Judaism was further degraded as it became "a barren formalism," descending "from prophetic freedom to organized hypocrisy."[5]

The New Covenant, suggested by Jeremiah, represents the Christian alternative, which is driven not by hope and fear, but by love; influenced not by God's word, but by His intention; and preoccupied not with salvation at any price, but with human compassion as an end in itself. Willingness to follow God's will is not, in this regard, an act of obedience that will more or less automatically generate pleasure instead of pain and is therefore based on a calculation of consequences, but a spontaneous act of affection for God and respect for others: "I will put my law within them," God says to Jeremiah, "and I will write it upon their hearts" (Jer 31:33). From a Pauline and Johannine—and even Matthean—perspective, the Christian, unlike the Jew, is reborn. He or she becomes a different person, no longer driven by the baser self (the *flesh*, in Paul and John), but moved by the Holy Spirit.

As I hope my examination of Judaism in the following pages demonstrates, the distinction between these covenants would be valid if Deuteronomy and the Book of Psalms had never been written and the prophets had never spoken. The fact is, these books *were* written, and the prophets *did* speak. Of course, it is not that these works

(*Birth of Christianity*, 144). Sanders says simply, "The test rules out too much" (*Jesus and Judaism*, 16). Lace claims that Jews in Jesus' time depended "almost entirely on professional scribes for their interpretation of their scriptures and for religious and moral guidance." Jesus taught them "to think for themselves . . . instead of just obeying rules blindly" (*Understanding the New Testament*, 152). Cook says, without explaining why, Jesus' ethics were superior to those of Judaism (*Introduction to the Bible*, 109, 123). Sanders examines the claim—in the work of Bousset, Bultmann, Bornkamm, Dibelius, Käsemann, Fuchs, and Kummel—that Jesus rejected Judaism because of its moral inadequacy (*Jesus and Judaism*, 18, 26–37).

5. Herford, *Pharisees*, 238. Herford adds, "A greater misreading of history it is scarcely possible to imagine" (238). Of course, one need not directly impugn Judaism in the process of crediting Christianity with inventing the doctrine of love. Stark, for example, says that Christians were innovative in suggesting that "more than self-interested exchange relations were possible between humans and the supernatural." Furthermore, "because God loves humanity, Christians cannot please God unless they love one another." Both ideas—loving God and loving humanity—were "alien to pagan beliefs." Stark begins this discussion by calling these concepts Judeo-Christian, but by the time he is done, the "Judeo" has disappeared. They were "revolutionary" and "new" with the arrival of Christianity, which invented the idea of "a merciful God [who] requires humans to be merciful" (*Rise of Christianity*, 86–87, 212).

merely *offered* the Jews a radically new understanding of Judaism. Just as Confucianism, Zoroastrianism, and Buddhism represented a new attitude that was actually embraced by millions of Chinese, Persians, and Indians, respectively, so prophetic Judaism and other later Judaic works reflected the way many even ordinary Jews looked at the world. Thus, whenever Jesus criticized his fellow Jews for failing to conduct themselves righteously and honorably, he quoted these sources in an effort to persuade his countrymen and -women to become better Jews—and his auditors would have understood him that way. Likewise, Jeremiah himself was a Jew speaking to Jews.

In other words, even if he opposed legalism—the reduction of religion to a set of rules and the transformation of ethics into a blind submission to the rules—Jesus did so in the spirit of Amos and Hosea and Malachi, those Jewish prophets of the eighth through fifth centuries who articulated a more heartfelt and personal understanding of Judaism and served the same purpose in their day that Jesus did in his: to call the faithless and hopeless back to the faith.[6] Thus, when Jesus suggested to the members of his parents' synagogue in Nazareth, after hurling Deuteronomic quotations at Satan in the wilderness, that he would help the poor, release the prisoners, give sight to the blind, and free the oppressed (Luke 4:18–19), he did so by reading a passage from Isaiah, rather than citing a non-Jewish source, such as the Code of Hammurabi or the Sayings of the Compassionate Buddha or Solon's laws. Jewish problems could be solved by Jewish methods.

In this respect, according to one scholar—making a point that many other modern scholars have made—"neither Jesus nor his proclamation was contradictory to Judaism."[7] This is because Jesus embraced not the Judaism of a much earlier time, with its focus on the ceremonial laws, but, like many of his Jewish contemporaries, the Judaism of the prophets, which emphasized ethics, intimacy with God, and individual

---

6. Bultmann, *Primitive Christianity*, 71–72. Against the idea that Judaism was a *quid pro quo* religion in the time of Jesus, as opposed to what it might have been many centuries earlier, see, on the ancient Jewish understanding of "reward" and "merit," Herford, *Pharisees*, 124–35. Enslin explains: "Keeping the law was synonymous with morality and religion. And he [that is, the Jew] sought to keep it with no ulterior motive: He did it because he loved God and wished to do his will . . . He sought to do what was right because it was right—and because he desired to do it. God's will had become his" (*Christian Beginnings*, 99–100).

7. Brown is speaking here about the presentation of Jesus in the Gospel of Luke, but the point has been made more broadly by many others (*Introduction*, 234). Brown says, "We should note that there are two important matching themes [in Luke 2]: how Jesus' parents were faithful to the Law and how Simeon and Anna, representative of devout Jews waiting for the fulfillment of God's promises to Israel, accepted Jesus" (234). "On Luke's view that Jesus supplements [rather than replaces] the Law which has not been done away with," Brown refers to Joseph A. Fitzmyer, *Luke the Theologian*, 176–87 (234 n. 18). As Schillebeeckx makes clear, Jesus cites Isaiah because, like Jesus, the prophets were anti-establishment. "That is why the social 'upper crust' is the butt of the prophets' criticism: it is corrupt, uses bribery, pursues 'class justice', and the population are subject to the bondage of debts and rental payments. But all this shows a disregard for Yahweh, the patron and protector of the people. It is because every Israelite is a fully-fledged member of the people of God in this country . . . that the prophets utter their protest: their critique is a religious one" (*Jesus*, 175).

responsibility.[8] In other words, the Judaism of the first century AD was not the same as the Judaism of a millennium earlier, and Jesus was in many ways a product of that change, as I intend to demonstrate in Chapter Two.

THE COVENANT

For most students of the subject, the essence of Judaism is its moral code, which is presented briefly in Exodus and Leviticus and more fully in Deuteronomy; matched in the works of the prophets; reiterated in Psalms and Proverbs; repeated in the inter-testamental literature; and taken up again in the Mishnah and the Talmud. To many Christians, this claim may come as a surprise, since they are accustomed to thinking of Judaism as a religion that focuses on ceremony rather than morality, which, after all, appears to be Jesus' complaint in the Gospels.

Indeed, a quick glance at the books of the Pentateuch, which are the source of the 613 laws that make Judaism seem to be a rule-bound faith, shows quite clearly that far more space is given over to detailed descriptions of ritual laws than to ethical laws. The latter are covered—intermixed with discussions of ritual laws—in the equivalent of four chapters in Exodus, ten chapters in Leviticus, and fifteen or so chapters in Deuteronomy, out of more than one hundred chapters in all three books (though many of these chapters, especially in Exodus, contain narratives rather than discussions of ritual). That is, discussion of the moral law represents a small portion of the whole.

On the other hand, many of the ceremonial laws have been out of date since the destruction of the Temple nearly two thousand years ago, including laws on sacrifice and the priesthood, which simply became irrelevant after AD 70, with the termination of Temple worship and the elimination of the functions of the priests.[9] In fact, as one scholar says, "the deeper insight, of which the enlarged conception of the Torah is the witness"—that is, the more profound understanding of the Law that had been growing since the time of the prophets—"was already, in times while the Temple was still in existence, recognizing the spiritual value of repentance and attaching less importance

8. On the prophets' view of God as moral and His requirement that His people imitate His morality, see Newsome, *Hebrew Prophets*, 24. On the Pharisaic emphasis on individual responsibility and the lack of conflict between conscience and authority, see Herford, *Pharisees*, 120–21. He says that Ezra, following in the tradition of the prophets, individualized Judaism (57–58). In this way, Judaism paved the way for the "personal piety, without priest and without ritual," that characterized early Christianity (226). Against the claim that conscience was unknown to Judaism, see *The Wisdom of Solomon* 17:11–12 and *Ecclesiasticus* 14:2. These works belong to the Apocrypha and were composed in the inter-testamental period.

9. "[W]hen sacrifices and expiations ceased with the destruction of the temple," says Moore, "repentance of itself sufficed" (*Judaism*, I, 14). Commenting on the prophetic view of the afterlife—for example, in Ezekiel 36:25, wherein God says that He Himself, instead of priests, will purify His people—Moore adds, "It is evident that in such a world the greater part of the laws of the Pentateuch would have no application or relation to anything actual. This was true, however, of many of the laws in the Rabbis' real world. Not only the laws for the king, but much of the civil and criminal law, necessarily fell into desuetude under foreign rule" (272–73).

to the ancient sacrificial system."[10] In other words, what has endured is the moral code, the ritual code being dependent for its survival on historical circumstances, which have not been favorable.

Furthermore, to judge by the preferences of the prophets, it would seem that the ritual laws were often regarded by the leading voices of ancient Judaism as subordinate to the moral laws. At the very least, many of the prophets considered the laws governing activities associated with the Temple, among other things, to be meaningless if God's ethical imperatives were not obeyed. And this may well be ancient Judaism's most important contribution to Western Civilization.[11] In Amos, for example, God says that he despises feasts, assemblies, sacrifices, and songs as long as His worshipers ignore justice and righteousness (Amos 5:21–24). In Hosea, God says that He wants love and knowledge instead of sacrifice (Hos 6:6). The prophet Micah says that God is not satisfied with mere ritual: "He has showed you, O man, what is good; and what does the Lord require of you but to do justice, and to love kindness, and to walk humbly with your God?" (Mic 6:6–8).

Similarly, the books of Psalms and Proverbs have much more to say about ethical issues than about other matters. The psalmist, for example, goes so far as to say that God actually demands *no* sacrifice: "Sacrifice and offering thou dost not desire . . . Burnt offering and sin offering thou hast not required." Rather, "I delight to do thy will. O my God; thy law is within my heart" (Ps 40:6–8). "The sacrifice acceptable to God is a broken spirit; a broken and contrite heart" (Ps 51:17).[12] The worshiper, in short, must have not only "clean hands," but "a pure heart" (Ps 24:4). In such passages, the emphasis is clearly on the often intensely emotional relationship between the individual and God, as is the case throughout the psalms. Indeed, Christians and Jews

---

10. Herford, *Pharisees*, 166 n. 1. Herford adds, "When they were minutely discussed in the Mishnah, that was because they were part of what was ordained in the Torah, not because they were still of primary importance" (166). Neusner says that, after the destruction of the Temple, under the leadership of such Rabbis as Yohanan ben Zakkai, Judaism understood the word *chesed* (as it is used in Hosea 6:6, for example) to mean not merely "conformity to the covenant between man and God," but also acts of "compassion and lovingkindness": "Yohanan thought that through *hesed* the Jews might make atonement, and that the activities now demanded of them were love and mercy . . . He provided an interim ethic by which the people might live while they awaited the coming redemption. The earlier age had stood on the books of the Torah, the Temple, rites, and acts of piety. The new age would endure on the foundation of studying Torah, doing the commandments, and especially performing acts of compassion" (*Judaism in the Beginning*, 96–97).

11. According to Sanders, since Judaism shared with the other religions of the ancient world many of its ritual practices and its proscriptions against murder, theft, robbery, and adultery, its uniqueness lay in its elevation of ethical laws to the level of ceremonial laws. On these points, see *Historical Figure of Jesus*, 33, 36, 38.

12. Moore says that "the summaries" of God's will in the works of the prophets are "solely moral" (*Judaism*, II-III, 84). See also Psalm 50:8–14; Jeremiah 6:20; and 1 Samuel 15:22.

agreed, in the words of one scholar, "that God . . . wants people to behave in a certain way and takes measures to enable them to do so."[13]

Thus, although Jews ordinarily held both kinds of laws in great esteem and regarded both as equally binding, no Jew (ancient or otherwise) would have considered these laws to be equally important. All such laws derived from divine revelation, but many violations that offended God alone could be expiated by various kinds of ritual sacrifice. Violations that offended human beings required more than symbolic action. Instead, they required repentance and, in many instances, restitution. On one hand, if the Jewish Bible was assumed to be the word of God, "there is no incompatibility between the most minute attention to rites and observances, or to the rules of civil and criminal law, and the cultivation of the worthiest conceptions of God and highest principles of morality." On the other hand, however, "Jewish teachers . . . recognized the distinction between acts which the common conscience of mankind condemns as morally wrong and such as are wrong only because they are made so by statute."[14]

If we turn to the Jewish Bible itself, it is easy to discover the principles that made Judaism in the first century AD an object of intense loyalty and devotion among Jews both in Palestine and in the Diaspora and made it appealing as well to countless numbers of gentiles who became converts or, as God-fearers, merely maintained a connection to the ethical aspect of Judaism rather than the ceremonial.[15] Unspoken,

13. Meeks, *Origins of Christian Morality*, 151. Van Leeuwen says, "Throughout the Book of Deuteronomy the note of personal, inward commitment to the Lord, 'with all your heart and with all your soul,' takes precedence over the purely outward and visible performance of ritual sacrifice" (*Christianity in World History*, 93).

14. Moore, *Judaism*, II-III, 18, 462. Crossan says that the prophets demand both ritual and morality (*Birth of Christianity*, 205). Bultmann argues that, "[e]specially after the fall of Jerusalem, when the sacrificial cultus ceased, remorse or repentance took the place of sacrifice as the means of obtaining the forgiveness of God" (*Primitive Christianity*, 71). If Bultmann's implication is that repentance was not an essential part of ritual before this time, he is, of course, wrong. As the evidence in the prophets and psalms suggests, Jews never thought of sacrifice alone as a means of obtaining forgiveness. Sacrifice succeeded in absolving the sinner from guilt only if it was accompanied by remorse. Furthermore, Bultmann argues that "side by side with this sense of sin and urge to repentance," which might tempt us to see Judaism as respectable and authentic, "we find the 'righteous' proud and self-conscious" (71). Where we find them thus is in Luke 18:11–14, but not in any source that could be regarded as other than tendentious and polemical on this issue. Speaking of the sacrificial rites of the Jews, Moore says that they were "conditions of forgiveness" before the destruction of the Temple, but never a sufficient cause: "Judaism, as we have seen, made repentance the condition *sine qua non* of them all, and eventually the substitute for them all . . . In other words, the legal conception of sin [in ancient Judaism] leads directly to the recognition that the only remedy for sin is God's forgiving grace, having its ground in mercy, or his love, and its indispensable condition in repentance, a moral renovation of man which is compared to a new creation" (*Judaism*, I, 117). Later in his book, Moore cites passage after passage attesting to the fact that Judaism always insisted on the indispensability of repentance: "The important thing is that while the temple was still standing the principle had been established that the efficacy of every species of expiation was morally conditioned—without repentance no rites availed" (505; see also 498, 520).

15. Moore, *Judaism*, 232. Sanders says: "Most people in the ancient world were religious, but even so the piety and dedication of the Jewish people stood out. Moreover they were committed to a noble religion, one that inculcated an upright life, love, prayer and repentance" (*Historical Figure of Jesus*,

but very much present throughout the Bible is, first of all, the idea that people cannot merely do what they want to do, but must abide by community standards and divinely authorized regulations. In Numbers, God tells Moses to remind the Jews to follow "all the commandments of the Lord, to do them, not to follow after your own heart and your own eyes, which you are inclined to go after wantonly" (15:39). Moses delivers that message in Deuteronomy: "You shall not do according to all that we are doing here this day, every man doing whatever is right in his own eyes" (12:8). Judaism is, in this regard, an attempt to spell out exactly what it means to live in a world populated by other people and in a universe governed by an omniscient and omnipotent God.

Getting people to live in the light of one or the other or both of those assumptions is, of course, the objective of every world religion. Essentially, it comes down to encouraging people to stop being egoists and to become altruists. In Judaism, this goal is best expressed by the traditional Judaic distillation of the Ten Commandments into two supreme laws: *Love God*, based on the first five commandments and the Shema ("[Y]ou shall love the Lord your God with all your heart," etc.; Deut 6:4–5); and *Love Mankind*, based on the final five commandments and the divine requirement from the Holiness Code in Leviticus: "[Y]ou shall love your neighbor as yourself" (Lev 19:18).

This reduction of ten laws into two laws achieves three goals. First, it translates negatively stated prohibitions into positively stated commands. The eight "thou-shalt-nots," excluding, of course, the fourth and fifth commandments ("Remember the sabbath day" and "Honor your father and your mother") are turned into "thou-shalts." Second, and more important, they are translated into principles rather than laws. That is, the specific commandments are to be understood not just as legal proscriptions, but as manifestations of large moral imperatives. And, third, they are to be acted upon not in regard to their material consequences (rewards and punishments), but as expressions of their emotional and spiritual origins: Fear is supplanted by love.

As I said earlier, many scholars and theologians, starting with Paul, have failed to see Judaism in this light. That is, they regard the religion of the Jews in the time of Jesus as a hodge-podge of laws that lacked coherence (like Hammurabi's Code) and were thereby impossible to follow; a creation of the fanatical Pharisees, who tried to force everyone to obey them; and, consequently, a narrow, self-serving, rule-bound faith that was far more of a burden than a benefit.[16] According to the psalmist, how-

---

47). Commenting on the essential ideas of ancient Judaism, Enslin says: "These were lofty and noble conceptions. Naturally all did not reach the standard set for them then any more than all do now. None the less these were ideals toward which the pious reached. Such was the heritage of the Church from the Synagogue; such the environs that helped to produce a Jesus and a Paul" (*Christian Beginnings*, 104).

16. Bultmann says that Judaism, with its 613 laws, lacks a "unifying principle" and therefore represents "an intolerable burden." Thus, he continues, "[i]t was almost impossible to know the rules, let alone put them into practice" (*Primitive Christianity*, 66). In addition, he says, "The Pharisees, in their zeal, imposed upon the laity their laws of purity which had originally applied only to the priesthood" (65). Of course, as is often the case with Bultmann, he subsequently so qualifies or even contradicts his initial charge against Judaism that one wonders why he made it in the first place. In this instance,

ever, the laws were in fact a "delight." That is, it was a positive pleasure to follow them (Pss 1:2; 40:8; 112:1; 119:16, 24, 47, 70, 77, 92, 143, 174). Furthermore, these laws were biblical, not merely Pharisaic. That is, God made them. On the absurdity of the notion that Jews were burdened by them, one scholar says: "Paul's definition of righteousness as perfect conformity to the law of God would never have been conceded by a Jewish opponent, to whom it would have been equivalent to admitting that God had mocked man by offering to him salvation on terms they both knew to be impossible . . . God was too good, too reasonable, to demand a perfection of which he had created man incapable."[17]

There can be little doubt that Moses himself (at least as he is represented in Deuteronomy) regarded the first Great Commandment—to love God—as a summary statement of the duties accepted by the Jewish people as a result of their decision to honor their Covenant with God. In other words, the Covenant simply required an exchange of love for love. God "keeps covenant and steadfast love with those who love him and keep his commandments" (Deut 7:9). To drive the point home, Moses repeats it again and again in Deuteronomy (e.g., 7:12–13; 10:12–13; 11:13; 11:22; 13:3–4; 19:9; 30:6; 30:15), and it became, perhaps for that reason, the basis for the most important prayer in Judaism.

Moses emphasizes the second Great Commandment in Deuteronomy by explaining in great detail exactly what God meant by following His rules, especially those governing human relationships, in chapters 14–26. Furthermore, this commandment seemed to most of the prophets and many other canonical interpreters of the Law to be a logical extension of the first. Indeed, love of humanity was often understood to be the most important way of fulfilling the requirement to love God: "You shall therefore love the Lord your God, and keep his charge, his statutes, his ordinances, and his commandments always" (Deut 11:1; see also Josh 22:5; 23:11). In this passage, as in all of the passages alluded to in the preceding paragraph, love and obedience are parallel

he goes on to say that the Sabbath and purity laws "were taken so much as a matter of course by the ordinary Jew . . . that he would not have felt them to be a burden at all" (66). Furthermore, "[n]o one was obliged to observe all the Pharisaic precepts." The reason is, although Bultmann does not supply it here, that the Pharisees had no authority to impose their will on others. In other words, the laws were known to the average Jew, and they were not onerous! Furthermore, according to Bultmann, when Jews went to the synagogue, they "*had* to recite the Shemah" twice daily, and "everyone, including women, children, and slaves, *had* to recite the Shemoneh' esre or Eighteen benedictions" (65; my emphasis). They *had* to recite prayers at a prayer service! While acknowledging that the Pharisees made "fine-spun distinctions," Enslin says that they were part of the process of adapting the Law to changing circumstances. Furthermore, Enslin adds, stricter than normal fasting and tithing and other Pharisaic practices were completely voluntary (*Christian Beginnings*, 116). On the scribal/Pharisaic ongoing attempt to fit the Law to the present situation, see 118–19.

17. Moore, *Judaism*, I, 495; see also II-III, 93, 239 n. 6. Like Moore, Maguire argues that Judaism initiated an "unprecedented revolution" in establishing the principles of justice, compassion, and egalitarianism as the lifeblood of religion. "Christians [like Bultmann]," Maguire adds, "have disparaged the genius of Judaism and their filial debts to it partly to aggrandize Jesus and Christianity" (*Moral Core*, 54–55).

and interchangeable acts. Love is the motive, and obedience to *all* of the commandments, including the ones that express a love of humanity, is the necessary action.

What had occurred in Judaism by the time of the prophets and the composition
of Deuteronomy was basically a change in the human perception of God's nature and
therefore a change in the human perception of His requirements for salvation. As a
god to whom sacrifices were made, Yahweh was said (more than thirty-five times) in
Genesis and Exodus, but especially in Leviticus and Numbers, to enjoy the pleasing
odor (or "sweet savor" in the KJB) of animal sacrifices, or burning flesh. That is, in
such passages, Yahweh was understood to be, like the pagan gods, a meat-eating deity
(either literally or figuratively) who depended on human beings for His sustenance.

In Psalm 50, however, a profound change is enunciated, reflecting the sentiments
of many of the passages cited above. Here, Yahweh acknowledges that he receives sacrifices enough from His people. As if He is renouncing this practice, however, Yahweh
says that He will henceforth accept nothing of this kind (including bulls and he-goats)
because "all that moves in the field" is His anyway: "[T]he world and all that is in it is
mine." Thus, He explains, "If I were hungry, I would not tell you," and then He states
explicitly what he wants: "Do I eat the flesh of bulls, or drink the blood of goats? Offer
to God a sacrifice of thanksgiving and pay your vows to the Most High" (Ps 50:11–15).
This kind of sacrifice "honors" God as (presumably) nothing else does. And how is
this thanksgiving to be expressed? After reciting a litany of sins He finds reprehensible
(theft, adultery, deceit, and slander), God says that humanity shows its gratitude by
following the moral law: "[T]o him who orders his way aright, I will show the salvation of God!" (50:23).

God repeats these sentiments in the prophecy of Isaiah, when, at the beginning,
he calls Israel a "sinful nation, a people laden with iniquity, a seed of evildoers" (1:4).
The question He raises is how the Jews can redeem themselves. Like the God of the
psalmist, He explicitly and exhaustively rejects all ritual, including sacrifices, obla-
tions, incense, festivals, and even the celebration of the Sabbath: "When ye come to
appear before me, who hath required this at your hand?" (1:10–15; see also Jer 6:20).
What God requires instead of ritual purity is *moral* purity. Like Jesus, who quotes the
following passage in his first address to the public, in Luke 4:18, Isaiah translates this
commandment into a general program of care and comfort for all of suffering humanity: "[T]he Lord hath anointed me to preach good tidings unto the meek, he hath sent
me to bind up the broken-hearted, to proclaim liberty to the captives, and the opening
of the prison to them that are bound" (61:1).

The essential principles of the moral law that derives from the commandment to
love humanity are summed up in the words that are used most often to describe the
works of God Himself: *mercy* (manifested in acts of generosity and compassion) and
justice (manifested in acts of fairness and equity). Mercy, of course, involves the possibility of forgiveness, while justice requires judgment and, therefore, the possibility

of punishment. But these concepts were not considered to be contradictory; they derived, after all, from the attributes of God Himself.[18] The prophet Hosea, for example, repeatedly uses the Hebrew word *chesed*, usually translated in the RSV as "steadfast love," as the principal characteristic of God (2:19–20; 4:1; 6:6; 10:12; 12:6), along with *mishpat* ("justice"), *tsedek* ("righteousness"), and *rachamim* ("mercy"), words which reappear throughout the works of the prophets and psalmists (e.g., Isa 5:16; 9:7; 30:18; Ps 97:3; 99:4).

In addition, these basic principles were translated into specific laws that were intended to govern the everyday lives of ordinary people. In effect, these laws reflect a desire to preserve the status quo. That is, at least among the ancient Jews, it was important to enable communities to stay intact, help families remain on their farms or in their villages, and keep individuals free from anxiety by defending them as much as possible from adversities created by nature and human nature: natural disasters such as drought and blight, as well as exploitation by the rich or oppression by the strong. God expected His people to "live in safety" and security (Lev 25:18–19; Deut 12:10; 33:12; Jer 32:37; Ps 4:8; 37:3; Isa 14:30), while they put into practice the ideals that figure so prominently in the Jewish Bible.

The importance of this point should not be missed. The way in which Jews were required by God to maintain life as they knew it was by implementing political, social, and economic rules that would enable them to preserve the classless, mutually supportive, and communitarian character of the agrarian villages in which they lived. Theirs was not the sprawling urban civilization of Egypt or Mesopotamia in the third millennium BC and later—with its powerful monarchy, priestly caste, military force, division of labor, and peasant underclass. In the great urban agricultural societies of the Middle East, the people on the lowest rung of the socio-economic ladder lived at the mercy of the king and were compelled to support the construction of political and religious buildings through conscripted physical labor and to meet the needs of the army for housing, food, and weaponry through tithes and taxes. On the contrary, the Israelites dwelt in a pre-urban agricultural world of independent farmers, who lived in small villages, passed on their farms from generation to generation, and—before the establishment of the monarchy—were ruled directly not by a king, but by God Himself.

---

18. Moore, *Judaism*, I, 393. Herford says that Paul misinterpreted Judaism "by leaving out essential elements . . . , in particular the conscious personal relation of the soul to God through which came strength to do the divine will, and forgiveness for repentance after sin" (*The Pharisees*, 220). Following these principles, the Pharisees tried to teach "the doing of right actions for the service of God and man. They sought to strengthen the factors which make for unity and peace amongst men—the sense of justice, truth, purity, brotherly love, sympathy, mercy, forbearance, and the rest—in a word, to raise the moral standard amongst their people from age to age" (111). Borg says that in ancient Jewish texts *mercy* is an "archaic" synonym for the word *compassion*. What it means in Judaism is not merely "forgiveness," but also feeling what someone else feels "and a way of acting that flows out of that feeling" (*Jesus*, 176).

According to the prophets, the status quo was to be maintained by preserving the existing social and economic relationships among the people. To achieve justice, as one scholar explains, the councils of village elders were responsible for "ensuring that proper relations prevailed among the members of the community," particularly by defending "by means of law those who were too poor or too weak to defend themselves." Correspondingly, to achieve righteousness, every individual in the community was expected not only "to maintain a right relationship with his/her neighbors," but also "to restore relationships that have been broken." Since these relationships, as many of the prophets emphasize, were disrupted by the injustices of powerful people, the prophets stress as well that "even the simplest people of the land had rights which not even the king could abrogate."[19]

THE LAWS

Mercy and justice were thus not mere abstractions in ancient Judaism. Rather, they were concrete objectives, which everyone was required to strive for. In the pursuit of them, God simply wanted a world free of poverty: "[T]here will be no poor among you . . . if only you will obey the voice of the Lord your God, being careful to do this commandment which I command you this day" (Deut 15:4–5). The only question was how this goal could be achieved. And the answer appears in an odd context: "You shall not see your brother's ox or his sheep go astray, and you shall not withhold your help from them; you shall take them back to your brother." In fact, "so shall you do with any lost thing of your brother's, which he loses and you find." In Exodus, this requirement extends even to one's enemies: "If you meet your enemy's ox or his ass going astray, you shall bring it back to him. If you see the ass of one who hates you lying under its burden, you shall refrain from leaving him with it, you shall help him to lift it up" (Exod 23:4–5).

What follows this command in Deuteronomy is a moral precept that pertains to more than just returning lost things: *"[Y]ou may not withhold your help"* (Deut 22:1–3). In other words, the commandment applies both to such occasional losses as these examples suggest and to long-term social conditions, especially destitution and helplessness. Daniel says to Nebuchadnezzar, "[B]reak off your sins by practicing righteousness, and your iniquities by showing mercy to the oppressed" (Dan 4:27). Jeremiah says that those who "judge not with justice the cause of the fatherless . . . [and] do not defend the rights of the needy" will be punished (5:28). Proverbs adds, "He who despises his neighbor is a sinner, but happy is he who is kind to the poor" (14:21).

Another way of helping the indigent is to pay a sort of poor tax, called a tithe, which was also used to sustain the otherwise unpaid Levites, who served as Temple

---

19. Newsome, *Hebrew Prophets*, 28, 14.

officials, below the level of priests.[20] "At the end of every three years," a tithe was given to the traditionally dependent and vulnerable—"the sojourner, the fatherless, and the widow" (Deut 15:28–29; 26:12–13).[21] Furthermore, a less formal tithe was supposed to be given to the poor after every harvest: "When you reap the harvest of your land, you shall not reap your field to its very border, neither shall you gather the gleanings after the harvest" (Lev 19:9; 23:22). Specifically, when you have forgotten "a sheaf in the field," let it go. And the rule applies not only to fields, but to olive orchards and vineyards: "When you beat your olive trees, you shall not go over the boughs again . . . [and] when you gather the grapes in your vineyard, you shall not glean it afterward." The gleanings—forgotten sheaves and fallen grapes—"shall be for the sojourner, the fatherless, and the widow" (Deut 24:19–21) or, more succinctly, "for the poor and for the stranger" (Lev 23:22).

In Exodus, there is even a requirement that fields, vineyards, and olive orchards should be left fallow in the sabbatical, or seventh, year, "so that the poor of your people may eat" (Exod 23:11). That is, what is available for the poor is "[w]hat grows of it-self"—more likely grapes and olives than corn or wheat (Lev 25:5). However, as the actions of Jesus' disciples in Mark 2:23 (Matt 12:1, Luke 6:1) suggest, even hungry passersby who found themselves near a field of corn could pluck an ear or two, as long they did it by hand, not with a sickle. Likewise, if they were near a vineyard, they could "eat [their] fill of grapes," as long as they did not take grapes away in a vessel (Deut 23:24–25). In addition to the tithe, the Jews in Jerusalem conducted a daily distribution of food "among wandering paupers" and "a weekly dole to the poor of the city," consisting of food and clothing. The deserving poor could also receive alms at the Temple, which were deposited in secret—"the devout" made their contribution to the destitute in a "chamber of secrets," anonymously.[22]

Because they are helpless, the indigent can also be aided by being shielded from abuse and oppression.[23] God is especially protective, again, of the stranger, the widow,

---

20. Num 18:21–24; Deut 12:19. On the functions of Levites, see Jeremias, *Jerusalem*, 207–10. In the time of Jesus, the tithe was used to support the entire Temple apparatus, including especially the high priests. Indeed, the upper-level priests lived very well off the sacrifices, gifts, and taxes that Jews contributed to the Temple (Enslin, *Christian Beginnings*, 134). This was doubtless another source of the hostility many Jews felt toward the priestly aristocracy, whose income might well have been perceived to be greatly in excess of their labor, which, Enslin says, was limited to "four or five weeks at most during the year" (135).

21. Crossan, *Birth of Christianity*, 199. The editors of *Oxford Annotated Bible* explain, "Israel's God is the protector of the legally defenseless: the stranger (sojourner), orphan, widow, and poor" (96, 245–46).

22. Jeremias, *Jerusalem*, 131–33. Jeremias adds that this practice influenced the provision of basic necessities to the poor in the earliest Christian community: "There can be no doubt therefore that these arrangements served as a model for the primitive church" (131).

23. Crossan says that, although there are parallels in the moral programs of other societies in the ancient world, they in no way diminish "the far, far more serious way in which righteousness and justice, especially as protective of the widows and the orphans, the poor and the wretched, were taken in the [Jewish] Bible" (*Birth of Christianity*, 186). Crossan adds that the devotion to such principles

and the orphan (Exod 22:21–23). In Amos, God condemns those who "trample upon the poor and take from him exactions of wheat, . . . afflict the righteous . . . and turn aside the needy" (Amos 5:11–12; see also 2:6–8; 8:4–6). In Jeremiah, God commands: "Do justice and righteousness, and deliver from the hand of the oppressor him who has been robbed. And do no wrong or violence to the alien, the fatherless, and the widow, nor shed innocent blood in this place" (Jer 22:3; see also 7:5–6). In Zechariah, God says, simply, "Render true judgments, show kindness and mercy each to his brother, do not oppress the fatherless, the sojourner, or the poor; and let none of you devise evil against his brother in your heart" (Zech 7:9–10; see also Prov 28:27).

The language of some of the prophets is surprisingly violent, suggesting that God's anger toward anyone who victimizes the helpless is strong. For example, Micah accuses predators of tearing and flaying skin, as well as eating flesh and breaking bones (Mic 3:1–3). In Isaiah, God accuses the enemies of His people of "crushing" them and "grinding [their] faces" (Isa 3:15; see also 10:1–2; 32:7). In Psalm 14, "the evildoers," God complains, "eat up my people as they eat bread." These proscribed acts are, in fact, violations of human rights: "Open your mouth for the dumb, for *the rights of all who are left desolate.* Open your mouth, judge righteously, *maintain the rights of the poor and needy*" (Prov 31:8–9; see also 29:7; my emphasis).[24]

Since God also considered slaves to be among the weak and vulnerable, He insisted that they be freed from servitude after six years (Exod 21:2). Deuteronomy even requires that the released man or woman not be allowed to go away "empty-handed." Freed slaves—or, in this case, more properly, indentured servants—should not leave their masters' houses without being amply provided for. They must be furnished "liberally out of your flock, out of your threshing floor, and out of your wine press" (Deut 15:13). Furthermore, relatives and neighbors who fall into destitution should not be employed as slaves or otherwise mistreated: "[I]f your brother becomes poor beside you, . . . he shall be with you as a hired servant and as a sojourner," not as a slave,

---

began with God's demand that Abraham "keep the way of the Lord by doing righteousness and justice" (Gen 18:19) (186–87). On this point, see also de Vaux, *Ancient Israel,* I, 143–52. Borg argues "that justice is the social form of compassion." Specifically, it applies to interpersonal relations "from the family to society as a whole" (*Jesus,* 185–86). Van Leeuwen says: "This basic theme of the Torah is fully brought out by the prophets in their tremendous struggle for justice in the face of social pressures, corruption and the pursuit of riches and power. They sound the deepest note of the Torah when they assert that to do justice and to obey God are 'the whole law'" (*Christianity in World History,* 96).

24. This ideal continued to be promulgated in the inter-testamental period. Sirach, for example, writing in the second century BC, laments that the poor are often victimized by the rich: "As lions prey on the wild asses of the desert, so the rich live off the poor" (Sir 13:19). Therefore, he counsels not only protecting and caring for the poor, but also responding to them politely and quickly: "[D]o not cheat a poor person of his livelihood . . . If someone is desperate, do not add to his troubles or keep him waiting for the charity he asks. Do not reject the appeal of someone in distress or turn your back on the poor; when one begs for alms, do not look the other way . . . When anyone who is poor speaks to you, give him your attention and answer his greeting courteously." In addition, the poor should be rescued from people who take advantage of them: "Rescue the downtrodden from the oppressor . . . Be as a father to the fatherless" (Sir 4:1–5, 8–10; see also 29:8–9).

and "[y]ou shall not rule over him in harshness" (25:39–43). Similarly, if a Jew who becomes poor "sells himself to the stranger or sojourner with you, . . . then after he is sold he may be redeemed" by his relatives (Lev 25:47–49).

In addition, workers of all kinds must be paid promptly. In fact, whether "a hired servant who is poor and needy" is Jewish or not, he or she must be paid in a timely manner: "[Y]ou shall give him his hire on the day he earns it, before the sun goes down (for he is poor, and sets his heart upon it)" (Deut 24:14–15). God says in Jeremiah, "Woe to him who . . . makes his neighbor serve him for nothing, and does not give him his wages." Again, the prophet's (and presumably God's) language is extreme: This pursuit of "dishonest gain" is the equivalent of "shedding innocent blood, and . . . practicing oppression and violence" (Jer 22:13, 17; see also Mal 3:5).

Justice in ancient Judaism is generally served in more official settings, such as courts of law. It goes without saying, of course, that judges should "judge the people with righteous judgment." But the judicial system does not work unless everyone follows suit. Thus, says Moses, speaking for God, in Deuteronomy: "You shall not pervert justice; you shall not show partiality; you shall not take a bribe, for a bribe blinds the eyes of the wise and subverts the cause of the righteous. Justice and only justice shall you follow" (Deut 16:19–20; Exod 23:8). Furthermore, it is unacceptable to "utter a false report" or "to be a malicious witness" in the service of "a wicked man" or to otherwise "pervert justice" by yielding to popular opinion ("turning aside after a multitude") and bearing false witness "in a suit" (Exod 23:1–2). As much as the poor are to be protected, they must not be treated partially in court cases (Exod 23:3).

The principle of justice applies particularly strongly in the punishment phase of trials. Perhaps the most obvious application is the lex talionis, which demands "life for life [and] eye for eye," etc. (Exod 21:24–25; Lev 24:17–21; Deut 19:21). A false witness, for example, should be punished according to this rule: "[Y]ou shall do to him as he had meant to do to his brother" (Deut 19:18–19). The law may sound harsh to modern ears, but it was originally meant to eliminate excessive punishments, such as amputation of hands for robbery as well as execution for crimes less serious than murder. Furthermore, one scholar claims that the lex talionis was never actually enforced. At least "a century before the time of Jesus," injuries to victims were not paid for by identical injuries to perpetrators, but by monetary fines.[25]

The law also requires thieves to give back more than they stole, whether through deception, robbery, "oppression," or false swearing: "[W]hen one has sinned and become guilty . . . he shall restore [the ill-gotten gain] in full, and shall add a fifth to it" (Lev 6:1–5; Num 5:5–7). Because the crime is also "a breach of faith against the Lord," the sinner must make a sacrifice in order to be forgiven. Exodus lists restitutions for

25. Herford, *Pharisees*, 111–12. Herford says that the law "may have ceased long before, and it may never have been operative at all." And if it was enforced by the Sadducees, who read the Bible literally, it was not enforced by the Pharisees. Jesus' reference is therefore "apparently to the text in Exodus, and not to anything being still taught" (112 n. 1).

a wider variety of crimes, including neglect, with double payments for instances in which the stolen or neglected object has been sold or consumed by or stolen from the thief (Exod 22:1–14).

The Jewish law is focused as much on fair lending practices as on any other moral issue. And, once again, this concern falls into the category of protecting the poor, for it is especially such people who are vulnerable to the abuses of unscrupulous lenders. The rule that is most prominent in these ancient texts is a total ban on lending money at any interest at all: "You shall not lend upon interest to your brother, interest on money, interest on victuals, interest on anything" (Deut 23:19).[26] The prophet Ezekiel is particularly critical of violations of this law, equating it with oppression, robbery, bribe taking, and extortion (Ez 18:8–9, 12–13, 16–17; 22:12).

Exodus applies this law only to the poor, but it is quite restrictive on the use the lender may make of collateral: "If you lend money to any of my people with you who is poor, you shall not be to him as a creditor, and you shall not exact interest from him." If the "pledge" is something that the borrower needs—that is, a cloak or a mantle—it must be returned to him before nightfall. "[I]n what else shall he sleep?" God asks because, as He says, He is "compassionate" (Exod 22:25–27; Deut 24:10–13). Thus, "No man shall take a mill or an upper millstone in pledge, for he would be taking a life in pledge" (Deut 24:6). That is, since survival depends on breadmaking, "the mill [with which bread is made] cannot be taken as security for a loan."[27] In Leviticus, the lender of money to a Jew who has become poor must not only refrain from charging interest, but also house him and feed him: "[A]s a stranger and a sojourner he shall live with you . . . You shall not lend him your money at interest, nor give him your food for profit" (Lev 25:35–37).[28]

Two additional rules affect the conduct of these transactions. The first says that all debts are forgiven at the end of the seventh year—the same kind of sabbatical holiday that frees the slave from servitude: "[E]very creditor shall release what he has lent to his neighbor" (Deut 15:1–2). Second, one must not only lend money to the poor, but also lend whatever the borrower needs— and do so without resentment: "If there is among you a poor man . . . lend him sufficient for his need, whatever it may be . . . You shall give to him freely, and your heart shall not be grudging when you give to him" (Deut 15:7–8, 10). This law takes into consideration the reluctance a lender

26. Jews could charge interest to foreigners if they were citizens of countries that permitted the practice. Crossan comments, "Since the latter took interest on Jewish loans, interest could be taken from them alone" (*Birth of Christianity*, 192). Furthermore, says de Vaux, "lending at interest was in fact practiced by all Israel's neighbors" (*Ancient Israel*, I, 170).

27. *Oxford Annotated Bible*, 245. While a poor man's cloak must be returned by nightfall, "a widow's garment" cannot be taken as collateral in the first place (Deut 24:17).

28. For the psalmist, giving and lending are two sides of the same coin: The good man "is ever giving liberally and lending" (Ps 37:26). "It is well with the man who gives generously and lends" (112:5). According to Sirach: "He who is compassionate lends to his neighbor; by giving a helping hand he fulfills the commandments. Lend to your neighbor in his hour of need" (Sir 29:1–2). In fact, Sirach says in the same chapter, "Be ready to lose money for a brother or a friend" (29:10).

might have shortly before the termination of the current seven-year cycle: "Take heart lest there be a base thought in your heart, and you say, 'The seventh year, the year of release is near,' and your eye be hostile to your poor brother, and you give him nothing" (Deut 15:9–10).

The most interesting of these laws is one that is intended to restore the status quo ante completely—that is, to protect people who suffer any kind of setback that deprives them of land, freedom, or personal property. After a fixed period of time, what they have lost is supposed to be restored to them, obviously in the interest of preserving ancestral lands, maintaining the social and economic order, and protecting individuals from losing their place in the community of Israel. Theoretically, at least, Jews were expected to celebrate the Sabbath of Sabbaths—at the end of the seventh seven-year cycle, or in the fiftieth year—by proclaiming on the Day of Atonement of that year "liberty throughout the land to all its inhabitants." By "liberty" is meant that everyone "shall return to his property," and everyone "shall return to his family." That is, land that has been lost through debt because of drought or unpaid taxes or royal appropriation is restored to its original owner, and all Jewish slaves are free to return to their homes (Lev 25:8–13, 25–28, 47–55).

The prophets were particularly concerned about the abuses that led to the widespread loss of ancestral lands, which evidently got progressively worse as time passed. That is, from the age of the Seleucids to the age of the Romans, Jews lost more and more land because of excessive taxes, royal appropriation, land speculation, and unfair lending practices. Micah complains about the evildoers who "covet fields, and seize them; and houses, and take them away; they oppress a man and his house, a man and his inheritance" (Mic 2:2).[29] These people sound like the ones Isaiah attacks for expanding their holdings and squeezing out small property owners: "Woe to those who join house to house, who add field to field, until there is no more room, and you are made to dwell alone in the midst of the land" (Isa 5:8). And they are the rich, who, according to Ezekiel, acquire land through extortion and eviction (Ezek 22:7, 12, 29; 45:9), as well as the princes, who "shall not take any of the inheritance of the people, thrusting them out of their property" because they pass on to their own children the property of which others have been "dispossessed" (46:18).

It is impossible, of course, to determine precisely who these "princes of Israel" were and all of the kinds of crimes they perpetrated. But, as Micah indicates, their misdeeds were diverse and onerous. Merchants cheated their customers with "wicked scales" and "deceitful weights" (Mic 6:11). The "heads of the house of Jacob," as well as judges, asked for bribes (3:11; 7:3; see also Isa 1:23). The "rich men" were violent, and lying was rampant (Mic 6:12; see also Isa 5:7). Not only did "the rulers of the

29. Newsome explains: "This expropriation may have taken place by quite legal means, but its effect upon its poor victims was nonetheless devastating, especially upon women and children (2:9). Those who lost their lands also lost their livelihood and were reduced to poverty, perhaps living the remainder of their lives as indentured servants" (*Hebrew Prophets*, 51–52).

house of Israel abhor justice and pervert all equity" (Mic 3:9), but even priests and prophets sold their wares (3:11). We know from other sources that—whether the most powerful and destructive of them were land speculators, powerful Jewish aristocrats, or, later, Roman officials—they were successful in acquiring large tracts of land that would have stayed in the hands of their original owners if the laws of the Pentateuch had actually been enforced.[30]

The principle therein, announced by God to Moses, is twofold. First, the land actually belongs to God, who says to Moses: "The land shall not be sold in perpetuity, for the land is mine; for you are strangers and sojourners with me. And in all the country you possess, you shall grant a redemption of the land" (Lev 25:23–24). The idea evidently originated in a desire to prevent the kind of land-grabbing that could in the long run ruin any kind of community bond because it created disparities between rich and poor and deprived many people of a decent living. In "a statement of the theological premise of the program," scholars explain: "Israelites are strangers and sojourners on land which does not belong to them by right but which the Lord has given them as an inheritance. Thus, the land is not private property, to be bought and sold speculatively. Although there is no evidence that the Jubilee program was ever carried out, the law opposes foreign conceptions of property which resulted in the swallowing up of ancestral holdings."[31] Second, God twice states the human side of the issue: "You shall not wrong one another" (Lev 25:14, 17), which speaks for itself.[32]

To suggest that these moral precepts were too complicated to understand, too many to accomplish, or too demanding to accept is to forget that they were often simplified (as two Great Commandments, for example) and summarized, as in the following four passages from the Jewish Bible, which may be taken to represent descriptions of the ideal Jew. The first comes from Isaiah: "Wash yourselves; make yourselves clean; remove the evil of your doings from before my eyes; cease to do evil, learn to do good; seek justice, correct oppression; defend the fatherless, plead for the widow" (Isa 1:16–17; see also Isa 33:15). Notably, there is nothing in this passage about performing rituals. Even the cleansing that God asks for, juxtaposed as it is with forswearing evil, is clearly moral rather than ceremonial.

---

30. Newsome states that in Isaiah, Amos, Hosea, and Micah, it is "especially the upper classes" who "have become greedy and . . . have allowed their love of material wealth to lead to the suppression of the rights of the weak and defenseless" (*Hebrew Prophets*, 63). Jeremiah identifies the "wicked men found among [his] people" as those who "have become great and rich" and "have grown fat and sleek" by judging "not with justice the cause of the fatherless" and not defending "the rights of the needy" (5:27–28).

31. *Oxford Annotated Bible*, 154–155.

32. Crossan reminds his readers that the ongoing Jewish moral tradition, "from around 750 to 500 BC, repeats the same themes over and over again. It is not the eccentric vision of an individual here or there but the constant vision of a tradition involving this God, this people, this land, this justice" (*Birth of Christianity*, 202). Crossan provides an overview of this tradition (182–202). Borg says that the rules by which Jews evidently lived at this time and yearned to live by centuries later were stated in the Torah, which "contains some of the most radical social legislation in history" (*Jesus*, 99).

In the second passage, from Ezekiel, God says that the kind of person who is worthy of life is "just," which means that he does what is "lawful and right." On the one hand, this includes the prohibition of certain modes of worship and two kinds of sexual crimes. On the other hand, however, the list of *social and economic* requirements of the kind we have been discussing is long and impressive. The just man is specifically one who refrains from oppressing "the poor and needy," committing violence, charging interest on loans, and failing to return collateral. More positively, he has fed the hungry, clothed the naked, and "executed true judgment between man and man." This kind of person, by way of summary, has "withdrawn his hand from iniquity" and has "walked" in God's laws. He will receive God's blessing, and the person who fails to live up to these standards will die (Ezek 18:5–13).

In the third passage, the psalmist asks who will dwell with God (or, more specifically, "Who shall be admitted to the worshiping congregation?").[33] He answers: "He who walks blamelessly, and does what is right, and speaks truth from his heart; who does not slander with his tongue, and does no evil to his friend, nor takes up a reproach against his neighbor; in whose eyes a reprobate is despised, and who honors those who fear the Lord; who swears to his own hurt and does not change; who does not put out his money to interest, and does not take a bribe against the innocent" (Ps 15:1–5). "He who does these things," the psalmist concludes, "shall never be moved," a phrase meaning that the moral person described in the passage will neither abandon his integrity nor lose confidence in God (Pss 16:8; 21:7; 46:5; 55:22; 62:2; see also Prov 12:3).

In the fourth passage, from the Book of Job, Job asks why he is suffering so much despite his having lived according to the highest moral standards: "I delivered the poor who cried, and the fatherless who had none to help him. The blessing of him who was about to perish came upon me, and I caused the widow's heart to sing for joy. I put on righteousness, and it clothed me; my justice was like a robe and a turban. I was eyes to the blind and feet to the lame. I was a father to the poor, and I searched out the cause of him whom I did not know. I broke the fangs of the unrighteous, and made him drop his prey from his teeth" (Job 29:12–17). Regardless of whether Job is right or wrong to complain to God about his condition, it is clear that he is presenting himself as an exemplary Jew. That is, these were the criteria by which moral excellence was judged in ancient Judaism.

Lest it be assumed, furthermore, that these principles had become irrelevant to Jews by the first century AD, it is important to remember that the Essenes at Qumran (and elsewhere) put many of them into practice and were still living by them during the lifetime of Jesus. In fact, in many respects, the Essenes appear to have been, like the members of the earliest Christian congregation in Jerusalem, guided by a revival of Jewish covenant values, the most obvious of which was the requirement that

---

33. *Oxford Annotated Bible*, 664. The editors of this text call this psalm a "liturgy for admission to the temple" (664).

full-fledged members of the Council had to sell all their earthly goods and give the proceeds to the Qumran community. One of the documents found among the Dead Sea Scrolls, *The Damascus Rule*, lists riches as one of three snares by which Satan captures his victims. Thus, "wealth" itself is "wicked," and people sin "for the sake of riches and gain." The same idea appears in one of the Qumranic hymns, which states that God's servants do not "pride themselves in possessions and wealth," but loathe them.[34]

Most important, every initiate into the community, which was regarded by its members as the sanctified remnant destined to inherit the Kingdom of God, was expected to undergo a moral transformation so complete that he was changed from an ordinary sinful human being into one who was fully prepared to live up to the high demands of a perfect God: "He shall be cleansed from all his sins by the spirit of holiness uniting him to His truth, and his iniquity shall be expiated by the spirit of uprightness and humility . . . [After baptism, his flesh] shall be made clean by the humble submission of his soul to all the precepts of God," after which he will be able "to walk perfectly" with the Lord. Ultimately, the saints, transformed as well into warriors, would fight as God's agents to establish the Kingdom of God in a final war in which all nations would be destroyed, and God would reign in Israel. In the meantime, the members of the community promised to "despise kings," "mock and scorn the mighty," and pray for the end to come quickly.[35]

This transformation was not assumed to be merely ceremonial or ritualistic. Going further than the prophets who condemned ritual without righteousness, the Essenes "taught that, even without the performance of sacrificial rites, a holy life was endowed with expiatory and sanctifying value." Indeed, *The Community Rule* (another document from Qumran) states that "prayer rightly offered" and "perfection of way"—i.e., love of God and love of humanity—were more than adequate substitutes for sacrifice. Of course, it had to be determined, during a two-year period of rigorous examination, whether "the holy life" of the initiate was *genuinely* holy—that is, wholehearted, deeply felt, and inwardly experienced: "The Master shall teach the saints to live [according to] the Book of Community Rule, that they may seek God with a whole heart and soul, and do what is good and right before Him as He commanded by the hand of Moses and all His servants the Prophets."[36]

34. Vermes, *Dead Sea Scrolls*, 101, 105, 184. Also: "No man shall stretch out his hand to shed the blood of a Gentile for the sake of riches and gain" (*The Damascus Rule*, 114). Vermes briefly discusses the details of this transfer of wealth (82).

35. The first quotation comes from *The Community Rule*, in *Dead Sea Scrolls*, 75. The second comes from *The War Rule* (139). The kings who were doomed were particularly whoever occupied Israel at the end-time, first the Assyrians and, later, the Romans: "The dominion of the Kittim shall come to an end and iniquity shall be vanquished" (124).

36. *Dead Sea Scrolls*, 46, 87, 72–78. A glance at *The Hymns* of Qumran shows the importance to this sect of such concepts as man's sinfulness, God's forgiveness, God's concern for the poor and needy, the end-time (when God's kingdom will arrive), the Holy Spirit, and Grace (149–201)

REPENTANCE AND REDEMPTION

As the many biblical passages referred to earlier indicate, there can be little question as to *what* God expected His people to do. *How* God expected Jews (or anyone else) to obey His moral imperatives is much more complicated. No doubt, some Jews followed the Jewish Law for the same reason that most people follow the laws of their society. They learned right from wrong and found it socially compelling—or at least, socially useful—to pursue the former rather than the latter. Some Jews were also motivated by the belief that their choice would be rewarded and punished not only by their peers, but also by God Himself. Certainly, however, if they consulted the Jewish Bible, they would have discovered that God is not satisfied with the kind of half-hearted obedience encouraged by hope and fear. As more than a God who rewards and punishes solely on the basis of obedience—like the gods of all pagan societies—Yahweh required a full-fledged commitment to the covenant laws, as befits a God of both justice and metcy, a God who was understood to be a father rather than a king, and a God who demanded, in Deuteronomy 6:5, nothing less than love: "with all your heart and with all your soul, and with all your might."[37]

What enables and enncourages God's people to act lovingly and altruistically is the reciprocal relationship between God and Israel: God loves His people, and His people love Him in return. That is, they are not merely honoring God in their acts of justice and mercy, important as that may be; they are engaged in a relationship that allows nothing less than the exchange of love for love.[38] God's undying love is thus an ongoing theme in Jewish scripture. God says in Hosea "that not even Israel's sin can snuff it out." He "cannot utterly destroy this people since to do so would be a violation of [His] own being." In deutero-Isaiah, He suggests that Israel's salvation is therefore independent of Israel's conduct: "In the nature of the Deity who saves, and not in the people who are saved, is to be found the true quality of the mighty act."[39] Thus, in Amos, God says that he punishes the Jews because they are His people (3:2)—i.e., to correct their behavior, not to penalize them for it.

37. Speaking of the moral development of the Jews as a historical (and historic) event, Herford explains: "The words alone [of God's Law] could not have conveyed any revelation, unless there had been the awakened mind, the enlightened conscience, to apprehend what was revealed, that which formed the meaning and contents of the written words. There was, at least in the loftier minds, a real perception of God through the inward vision of the soul, and not merely the blind subjection to the letter of the law" (*Pharisees*, 143). The concept works as well for the individual perception of the Law as the Jews understood it.

38. Herford says that the relationship of the individual to God is that of a child to a father. "The Pharisaic doctrine of repentance and forgiveness assumes that relationship as its basis . . . [Thus,] the forgiveness of God meeting the repentance of man was the natural way in which love went out to meet love, and there is no more to be said" (*Pharisees*, 167).

39. Newsome, *Hebrew Prophets*, 42–43, 150. Newsome cites Hos 2:14–15; 11:8; and Isa 43:1–7; 43:22–44:5.

This theme is particularly strong in the Book of Psalms, wherein God is repeatedly portrayed as a bearer of "steadfast love," a phrase that occurs almost seventy-five times in approximately forty different psalms. Psalm 136 may be called the Song of Steadfast Love, since the phrase appears in each of its twenty-six short verses. Within this framework, God does not forget "the cry of the afflicted" or the plight of the needy or allow the poor to "perish for ever" (Ps 9:12, 18). He notes the "trouble and vexation" that disturb "the hapless" and "the fatherless" (10:14). He hears "the desire of the meek," "strengthen[s] their heart," and does "justice to the fatherless and the oppressed" (10:17–18). God places the despoiled poor and the groaning needy "in the safety for which" they long (12:5). And, on a national level, "the Lord restores the fortunes of his people" (14:7).

Elsewhere in the remaining one hundred and thirty-six psalms, God is said to care for the brokenhearted and the crushed in spirit, the defrauded and the oppressed, the desolate and the imprisoned, and the downtrodden and the destitute. And every manifestation of divine love is an expression of the covenant relationship between God and man, to which the psalmist refers frequently (Ps 50:16; 74:20; 103:18; 111:5; 132:12). Psalms 78, 89, and 105 may, in fact, be thought of as extended meditations on this relationship.[40]

God's demand for His people's thoroughgoing devotion to His Law is also based on two additional aspects of His nature. That is, He is not only understood to be fatherly and loving. He is also, first, unlike the gods of the pagans, a moral being, who is perfect in every way. Thus, unlike Zeus or Ba'al, He establishes by His very existence a standard of righteousness, or moral excellence. And it follows, as well, that anyone who believes in Him believes also in this standard as a basis for human behavior. In this regard, the fundamental requirement of Judaism is to *imitate* God: "You shall be holy; for I the Lord your God am holy" (Lev 19:2; 20:26).[41] He "practice[s] steadfast love, justice, and righteousness" and "delights" in the human practice of them (Jer 9:24). He "executes justice for the fatherless, and the widow, and loves the sojourner, giving him food and clothing" (Deut 10:18).

Thus, God asks mankind to both help and protect each other because that is what *He* has done. In Ezekiel, God brings back the lost, binds up the crippled, and strengthens the weak (Ezek 34:16). According to Isaiah, He sets an example by being a "stronghold" to the poor and needy and "a shelter from the storm" (Isa 25:4; see also Ps 9:9). He brings down "the inhabitants of the height" and allows the poor and needy to trample the once mighty who are now fallen (Isa 26:5–6; see also 40:17; Ps 35:10;

40. Sirach says of God, "Charitable giving he treasures like a signet ring, and kindness like the apple of his eye" (Sir 17:22). God Himself "never ignores the appeal of the orphan or the widow as she pours out her complaint" (35:14).

41. Moore discusses the imitation of God as a form of worship in Judaism in *Judaism*, II-III, 103–11. See also Newsome, *Hebrew Prophets*, 85; and Herford, *Pharisees*, 140, 163. Enslin quotes Philo, who says that the "proper object of happiness" is simply "to attain to a likeness of God" (*Christian Beginnings*, 101).

and Jer 20:13). Not to imitate God is, of course, to dishonor Him: "He who oppresses a poor man insults his Maker, but he who is kind to the needy honors him" (Prov 14:31; 19:17).[42] That is why God punishes evildoers: His love is unrequited, and He acts accordingly (Prov 22:16, 22–23). "The Lord preserveth all them that love him: but all the wicked will he destroy" (Ps 145:20).

Second, God is not only an exemplary being, as well as the Comforter, the Protector, and the Savior of mankind. He is especially all of these things for His people, the Jews. His principal act of salvation is His liberation of the Israelites from slavery in Egypt. God therefore asks His people not only to do what He has done, but also to do what He has done *for them*. He says, "Love the sojourner *therefore*; for you were sojourners in the land of Egypt" (Deut 10: 19; 24:17; my emphasis).[43] The last point here is reiterated throughout the Bible: "You shall remember that you were a slave in Egypt; therefore I command you to do this" (e.g., Exod 23:9; Lev 25:28; Deut 24:22). In other words, Jews should be generous because God was generous to them: "[A]s the Lord your God has blessed you, you shall give" (Deut 15:14).

Indeed, the exodus from Egypt, conducted by God as the first step in the liberation of His people—followed by the covenant agreement in the desert and the settlement of the Jews in their homeland—has remained throughout Jewish history the most glowing evidence of God's commitment to love.[44] And it is the most compelling argument for "walk[ing] in his ways" (Deut 8:6; 11:22; 26:17), which becomes associated in Deuteronomy with love (10:12; 19:9) rather than mere obedience, which is the usual meaning of the phrase in Exodus and Leviticus. Joshua asks the Israelites "to love the Lord your God, and to walk in his ways, and to follow the commandment and the law . . . and to serve him with all your heart and with all your soul" (Josh 22:5).[45]

42. This passage looks forward to Matthew 25:46., in which Jesus says that being concerned about the plight of the hungry, the naked, and the imprisoned is the same as being concerned about "the Son of man," who, at the Second Coming, will distinguish the sheep from the goats: "Truly, I say to you, as you did it to one of the least of these my brethren, you did it to me." To aid the suffering, in short, is the same as aiding God. Enslin says that sin in Judaism is not simply error: "It was an unfilial act of defiance to a loving, gracious father: in short, rebellion against God" (*Christian Beginnings*, 103).

43. On the subject of aid given to sojourners in ancient Israel, Jeremias says, "We have evidence that the Essenes had in each city . . . their own agents who provided their travellers with clothing and other necessities" (*Jerusalem*, 130). The provision of this service suggests how difficult it was for travelers of all kinds to journey to places where they might otherwise be entirely on their own and, therefore, at least temporarily in the position of the poor and needy.

44. Crossan says: "It is hardly possible to overemphasize that central tradition . . . That God was, therefore, a divinity that freed the oppressed—unlike foreign gods and goddesses, who were divinities that enslaved them" (*Historical Jesus*, 187–88).

45. Again, the emphasis in such passages is not on abject fear, but on heartfelt commitment. Thus, Solomon says, "Let your heart therefore be wholly true to the Lord our God, walking in his statutes and keeping his commandments" (1 Kgs 8:61). Josiah pledges "to walk after the Lord and keep his commandments . . . with all his heart and all his soul" (2 Kgs 23:3). After citing passages in which God is shown to visit the sick, comfort mourners, and help the needy, Moore comments: "These offices of humanity are evidences not merely of the general goodness of God, but of the highest kind of charity which involves personal sympathy and service. In such deeds of kindness God is a pattern for man's

It is particularly the responsibility of kings (and, implicitly, all government leaders) to carry out God's will, says the psalmist, by protecting "the poor of the people" and "the children of the needy" and destroying "the oppressor." The righteous monarch will protect such people "from deceit and violence: and precious shall their blood be in his sight" (Ps 72:4, 12–14). According to Jeremiah, God told the king of Judah to be just and righteous—that is, to "do no violence to the stranger, the fatherless, nor the widow, neither shed innocent blood in this place" (22:3). Yet, if kings and princes fail, as they will, God says that He Himself can be counted on to punish oppressors, feed the hungry, free the prisoners, give sight to the blind, raise up the downtrodden, help strangers, give relief to orphans and widows, gather in the outcasts, heal the broken-hearted, and lift up the meek (Pss 146:3–10; 147:2–6). Thus, although "the son of man"—i.e., any ordinary person—cannot be counted on to obey God in these ways, His laws are nevertheless the standard by which both rich and poor will be judged.

The only kind of action that God permits to Himself but forbids to men and women is revenge. For example, in the Book of Leviticus, God tells the Jews, "You shall not hate your brother in your heart," nor shall you "take vengeance or bear any grudge against the sons of your own people" (Lev 19:17–18). This means that human beings should "[r]efrain from anger, and forsake wrath!" (Ps 37:8). The reason is that God will impose punishment on evildoers Himself: "For they will soon fade like the grass, and wither like the green herb . . . [T]he wicked shall be cut off . . . [T]heir sword shall enter their own heart, and their bows shall be broken." To put it simply, "the wicked [will] perish" (Ps 37:2, 9, 15, 20).[46]

God's love is manifested not only in his administration of justice, however. It is also revealed in his acts of mercy, which include, in addition to acts of protection and redemption, like the liberation of the Jews from bondage in Egypt, acts of forgiveness and restoration. While God's miraculous interventions are initiated by mankind's pleas for help, God's absolutions are responses to mankind's repentance, which should be understood in terms of its original meaning: *turning to God*.[47] Jews are expected to

---

imitation; this is what is meant when it is said, 'Walk after the Lord thy God,' that is, imitate these traits of God's character and conduct" (*Judaism*, I, 44).

46. This evidently anticipates three statements in the New Testament. First, Jesus says, "[E]very one who is angry with his brother shall be liable to judgment" (Matt 5:22). Second, he adds, "Judge not that you be not judged" (Matt 7:1; Luke 6:37; Rom 2:1–2; 14:10, 13). And, third, Paul argues, "[N]ever avenge yourselves, but leave it to the wrath of God," who says, "Vengeance is mine" (Rom 12:19). In Romans, Paul actually quotes Proverbs 25:21–22, in which kindness to an enemy is given a somewhat sinister purpose: Feed him if he is hungry, "for by so doing you will heap coals of fire on his head" (Rom 12:20).

47. On repentance in Judaism, see Herford, *Pharisees*, 166–67; and Enslin, *Christian Beginnings*, 103. Moore makes two interesting points about this subject. First, he says, repentance has been inadequately (and, presumably, inaccurately) explained by Christian scholars: "[I]n the current Christian representations of Judaism neither the character of this teaching nor the central significance of the doctrine of repentance in the Jewish conception of the religious life and of the way of salvation is adequately recognized." Second, Moore describes repentance, as I did in the preceding paragraph, as something far more personal and profound than, say, an apology or a pro forma act. That is, "the

repent after they violate the law. Inadvertent violations—touching a dead body, menstruating, eating forbidden food accidentally—can be forgiven if the "sinner" makes a sacrifice or undergoes purification (or both). Other offenses against God might also require a charitable act. Violations that hurt other human beings, however, require remorse, restitution, and reformation. The guilty person has to confess, show regret, restore the victim to his or her original condition, and forswear the offending behavior.

The terms of punishment are relatively easy since the repentant person is assured, as long as his or her remorse is genuine, that God will forgive the offense. Unrepentant persons are punished by God, but not necessarily denied redemption.[48] One scholar, commenting on the motives for repentance in ancient Judaism, says: "Men may be moved to repentance by the warnings of God in his word and providence, by experience of the consequences of sin and apprehension of worse consequences in this world and another—[that is, in such cases,] repentance induced by fear. But there is a repentance that springs from a nobler motive—love to God; and this is more highly esteemed by God and brings a larger grace."[49]

Repentance begins with a confession—an admission on the part of the sinner that he or she has in fact committed a sin. Daniel, for example, "fasting and [covered in] sackcloth and ashes," starts by acknowledging that the entire nation of Israel has "done wrong and acted wickedly and rebelled." He admits his people's "treachery," transgression, and refusal to obey. And he confesses his own sin as well (Dan 9:3–11, 20). Nehemiah asks God to hear the prayer of one who is "confessing the sins of the people of Israel, which we have sinned against thee." He admits to having acted "corruptly" and failing to keep the commandments (Neh 1:6–7). Later, the Israelites themselves also "confessed their sins and the iniquities of their fathers" (9:2–3).

Confession is often described in terms of *turning away from* evil, as well as *turning or returning to* God. That is, one returns to God if one has earlier turned away from Him. Daniel's confession involves the acknowledgement that his sin was essentially a *"turning aside* from commandments and ordinances" (Dan 9:5, 11; my emphasis). Thus, in Deuteronomy, Moses calls on the Israelites to "return to the Lord your God . . . and obey his voice" (Deut 30:2), which requires that sinners, as Ezekiel says, "turn away from [their] idols" (Ezek 14:6).

transparent primary sense of repentance in Judaism is always a change in man's attitude toward God and in the conduct of life, a religious and moral reformation of the people or the individual" (*Judaism*, I, 507). Elsewhere, he mentions that the Jewish conception contains all the features of the Roman Catholic idea: "contritio cordis, confessio oris, and satisfactio operis" (514). Enslin says, "By the word 'repent,' Jesus meant, as did every other Jew, change of conduct as well as change of heart" (*Christian Beginnings*, 159).

48. On this subject, see Sanders, *Historical Figure of Jesus*, 34.

49. Moore, *Judaism*, I, 514–15. Moore goes on to compare the Jewish idea of repentance with the concept as it is defined in the Westminster Shorter Catechism.

Turning to God, as I suggested, leads to God's forgiveness.[50] The psalmist, for example, says simply that he confessed to God and was then forgiven (Ps 32:5; see also 86:5). In Proverbs 28, "he who confesses and forsakes [his transgressions] will obtain mercy" (v. 13). And God says in Jeremiah, "I will forgive their iniquity" (Jer 31:34). Solomon says, speaking to God of the people of Israel, "if they turn again to thee, and acknowledge thy name, and pray and make supplication to thee in this house," God will "forgive the sin of [His] people Israel" (1 Kgs 8:33). Sirach says: God "leaves a way open for the penitent to return to him . . . How great is the Lord's mercy and forgiveness for those who turn to him!" (Sir 17:24, 29). And, in Psalm 25, the sinner says to God, "Turn thou to me," while he also asks God to "pardon [his] guilt" and "forgive all [his] sins" (vv. 16, 11, 18). Turning *toward* the sinner is, on God's part, of course, an act of forgiveness, just as turning *toward* God is the first step in the redemptive process.[51]

In the final phase of spiritual transformation, the sinner is expected to change his ways so as to demonstrate the genuineness of his confession and his request for forgiveness. In Jeremiah, God says, "Amend your ways and your doings," which means not engaging in the kinds of oppressive and exploitative actions God elsewhere deplores (Jer 7:3–7). And, if the sinner changes his behavior, "the Lord will repent of the evil which he has pronounced against" the sinner (Jer 26:13). One repentance evokes another. God has always had His prophets say, "Turn now every one of you from his evil way, and amend your doings" (Jer 35:15).

---

50. According to Moore, the idea "that God freely and fully remits the sins of the penitent is a cardinal doctrine of Judaism; it may properly be called the Jewish doctrine of salvation" (*Judaism*, I, 500; see also 502–3). This passage should be read as a corrective to Bultmann's claim that, "in view of Christ[,] Christian confidence in the forgiving grace of God is incomparably more certain than the Old Testament-Jewish trust in the effectiveness of repentance" (*Theology*, I, 120). I assume that Bultmann is making a distinction between theologies rather than between their respective efficacies. Treating the Jewish conception of repentance as a strictly quid-pro-quo arrangement, in which deeds are thought to purchase salvation, Bultman elsewhere claims that Jews were nervous about gaining salvation because they were uncertain how many good deeds they needed to succeed: "The prospect of meeting God as their Judge awakened in the conscientious a scrupulous anxiety and morbid sense of guilt" (*Primitive Christianity*, 70). Needless to say, no one seems to be counting good deeds in the psalms or in the writings of the prophets. One wonders where Bultmann got his empirical data. His attribution of anxiety to the Jews must be understood in the context of Luther's condemnation of the Doctrine of Works in Catholicism. Relying on the Catholic belief in the spiritual efficacy of Good Works, Luther says, many Christians "worried whether they had done enough to be saved." Instead, he argued for reliance on Faith alone: "Luther saw the radical sovereignty of God as offering the only reliable assurance of salvation" (Deason, "Reformation Theology and the Mechanistic Conception of Nature," 186).

51. Moore discusses the question of whether God or man initiates the process in *Judaism*, I, 531. Moore cites Malachi, in which God says to the "sons of Jacob," "Return to me, and I will return to you" (Mal. 3:7), which suggests that the sinner must make the first move. Similarly, the psalmist says in Psalm 90, "Return, O Lord! How long?" (v. 13), as if he has asked for forgiveness, but has waited for a response for some time. Moore concludes, however, "God encourages and assists every movement of man's heart towards him" (531).

What this means, especially in Ezekiel, which presents a new, individualized concept of redemption, against the older view that saw it as a collective and national issue, is very close to what it means in the New Testament. For, instead of every individual bearing the guilt of Israel—inheriting the sins of the fathers and passing them on to the sons—"every one shall die for his own sins" (Jer 31:30; Ezek 18:4,20; Deut 24:16). Thus, on the one hand, when Jeremiah promises a radical change in the circumstances of his people, he is looking forward to their restoration by means of their liberation from their oppressors and the eventual reunion of Judah and Israel. But *individual* redemption—not merely as forgiveness and restoration, but as moral development and psychological change—was also becoming an important feature of ancient Judaism.[52]

The most significant aspect of this process is its culmination not just in change or even development, but in *renewal*. Judging "every one according to his ways," God says: "Repent and turn from all your transgressions, lest iniquity be your ruin. Cast away from you all the transgressions which you have committed against me, and *get yourselves a new heart and a new spirit!*" (Ezek 18:30–31; Jer 32:42; my emphasis). That is, the repentant sinner is the beneficiary of a new understanding and a new disposition, and he is expected to experience henceforth a new and deeper relationship with God. In Psalm 51, the penitent says, "Create in me a clean heart, O God, and put a new and right spirit within me" (v. 10).

So *new*, indeed, are the new heart and spirit one acquires under these circumstances that there is no memory of the old ones. The heart of the psalmist is clean because he has asked God to "blot out [his] transgressions" and wash and cleanse him "thoroughly" (Ps 51:1–2). But God "blots out your transgressions *for [His] own sake*," as well as for the sinner's, "and [He] will not remember your sins" (Isa 43:25; see also Ezek 18:21–22; 33:16). According to the prophet Micah, God "tread[s] our iniquities under foot" and "cast[s] our sins into the depths of the sea" (Mic 7:18–19). In cleansing the sins of mankind, He wipes out all records and all memories of them, human and divine (Jer 33:8; see also Ps 25:7). It is as if, as Paul would later put it, the old self has died and a new self has been born. Indeed, the old self is gone forever—lost to memory as well as history.

The person with a new heart is changed in the sense that his devotion to God is single-minded and whole-hearted: "I will give thanks to the Lord with my whole heart" (Ps 9:1; 111:1; 138:1). The redeemed sinner responds completely because he is no longer divided. He is not a liar or flatterer with "a double heart" (Ps 12:2). Nor is he restrained by a false heart (Hos 10:2). Rather, he is a singer of the "new song" that

52. Moore briefly explains the individualization of repentance in *Judaism*, I, 113–14. "The piety of the Psalmists is testimony to the penetration of this idea." Indeed, Judaism "thus became a personal relation of the individual man to God" (114). For the view that individual repentance was supplanted by collective repentance, see Kaufmann, *Religion of Israel*, 234. Kaufmann explains: "The new moral conception, especially as it was expressed by the prophets, was beyond the scope of the ancient, sapiential morality that had never heard of a claim upon society as a whole" (329). Kaufmann discusses the point in relation to Jeremiah and Ezekiel (417 and 439).

God has put into his mouth (Ps 40:3). And, because his heart is pure (Ps 24:4), clean (Prov 20:9), upright (Ps 36:10), "wholly true" (I Kgs 8:61), blameless (2 Chr 25:2), and circumcised (Jer 4:4), it is a tablet on which the law of God can be written, the result of which is a mouth that "utters wisdom" and a tongue that "speaks justice" (Ps 37:30; Prov 3:3) and a person who acts righteously.

The model for the last stage of this process of individual transformation—the redemption that follows repentance—is the earlier idea of salvation for everyone at the same time: the eschatological promise of a new reality for the nation of Israel ("a new heaven and a new earth" [Isa 65:17; 66:22]), a new understanding between God and His people ("a new covenant" [Jer 31:31; 32:41]), and a new personality for the redeemed: "I will take out of your flesh the heart of stone and give you a heart of flesh" (Ezek 36:26; 11:19). Thus, in Jeremiah's proclamation, God "will put [His] law within them" and "write it upon their hearts." Here, the words remain the same as in the passages cited above, but this passage, like many others, applies to the nation rather than the individual: "[T]hey shall be my people and I will be their God, for they shall return to me with a full heart" (Jer 24:7).

In collective redemption, suffering comes first, however, just as in individual redemption the heart is broken before it is healed. "Behold, the days are coming, says the Lord, when I will make a new covenant with the house of Israel and the house of Judah" (Jer 31:31). This restoration follows a period of breakdown, overthrow, and destruction, the equivalent of the individual's alienation and despair. And the final result is the same, at least in quite general terms. That is, sinners, individually or collectively, return to an earlier, purer state of being because they are cleansed and purged by God as a consequence of either their repentance or their suffering. Thus, in Ezekiel, God says, "This land that was desolate has become like the garden of Eden" (Ezek 36:35; Isa 51:3; Joel 3:2). As Jesus says, "Truly, I say to you, unless you turn and become like children, you will never enter the kingdom of heaven" (Matt 18:3). Or they ascend to a new level of existence as a consequence of their acquisition of a new understanding, a new spirituality, a new moral sensibility, and, in the case of the nation, a new political, social, and economic world.[53]

In Isaiah, for example, the end-time—which will come soon (Isa 13:6, 9)—will be characterized by two major catastrophes. First, "The earth shall be utterly laid waste and utterly despoiled." And "the foundations of the earth [will] tremble." This will occur because *all* people "have transgressed the laws, violated the statutes, *broken the everlasting covenant.*" It is for this reason that "a curse devours the earth, and its inhabitants suffer for their guilt." In this cosmic event, even "the heavens [will] languish together with the earth." "Then the moon will be confounded and the sun ashamed." (Isa 24:1–23; my emphasis). Worse yet, "the stars of the heavens and their constellations will not give their light; the sun will be dark at its rising and the moon will not shed its light" (13:10).

53. On the subject of Jewish apocalypticism, see Segal, *Rececca's Children*, 68–78.

The second catastrophe will be the judgment of mankind, which will take place after the people have been "gathered together as prisoners in a pit." And "[o]n that day the Lord will punish [both] the host of heaven . . . and the kings of the earth," as well as all "the inhabitants of the earth for their iniquity" (Isa 24:21–23; 26:21). Even Isaiah's so-called oracle against Babylon prophesies that God "will punish *the world* for its evil" by killing the men, ravishing the women, and dashing the infants "in[to] pieces before their eyes" (!3:11, 15–16; my emphasis). What this means is that the first ("the kings of the earth") shall be last, and the last (the weak and suffering) shall be first. That is, according to Ezekiel, those who are now in power will be replaced by those who are now powerless: "I the Lord bring low the high tree, and make high the low tree, dry up the green tree, and make the dry tree flourish" (Ezek 17:24). If that point is not clear enough, God later says to the "prince of Israel" that "things shall not remain as they are; exalt that which is low, and abase that which is high" (21:26).

After this devastation—"in the day when the Lord binds up the hurt of his people, and heals the wounds inflicted by his blow" (Isa 30:26; 12:1–2)—He will create a paradise of peace and security (32:16–18). For just as God forgives the individual for his sins, so he forgives His nation. The weapons of war will be turned into ploughshares and pruning forks, and war itself will cease (2:4). Predatory beasts will become harmless (11:6–9). The survivors of God's wrath will live in a land in which the produce is "rich and plenteous," brooks run freely, and the moon and sun shine brighter (30:23–26). The dead will be raised (26:19). "Then justice will dwell in the wilderness, and righteousness abide in the fruitful field" because kings and princes will rule justly and righteously (32:1, 16). At last, of course, the Covenant itself will be restored, with "every man [sitting] under his vine and his fig tree"—restored to his "original" independence, self-sufficiency, and economic security (Mic 4:4; Zech 3:10).

In short, heaven and earth will be made new (Isa 66:22). Peace and prosperity will come partly because they are God's gift to humanity after "the day of the Lord," the day of judgment, but partly because human beings have been transformed. God will not only forgive them but will pour his spirit upon them (32:15; 44:3). In Jeremiah, God says that He "will give them a heart to know that I am the Lord" (Jer 24:7; 31:33). Later, he adds, "I will give them one heart and one way, that they may fear me forever" (32:39). In Ezekiel, God says that He "will give them one heart, and put a new spirit within them . . . that they may walk in my statutes" (Ezek 11:19–20; 36:26–27). Ultimately, the Kingdom of God will be established, and the Jews (and perhaps others) will remain safe and secure forever.[54]

54. Enslin says that although "no one view [was] accepted by all," most Jews agreed that "the coming golden age" would have a few "general features": "It was to be in the future, but in the present age. It would be upon this earth. It would be brought about by or be coincident with the recognition of the sovereignty of God." Although there were varying opinions on the fate of the heathen, "all were agreed that when [the golden age] dawned God would be recognized and worshipped by all" (*Christian Beginnings*, 141). Enslin also notes that the idea of a cataclysmic end of the world, from which the righteous are saved after God's judgment, was derived from Persia (141).

Although the phrase "Kingdom of God" does not appear in the Jewish Bible (except as "kingdom of the Lord" in 1 Chr 28:5), the words are an appropriate designation for the long hoped-for reign of Yahweh at the end-time. For Jews believed that, ultimately, God would destroy all existing governments on earth and replace them with His own rule.[55] Furthermore, according to the prophets, he would reign not *in heaven*, over embodied or disembodied souls, but *on earth*. Here, profoundly changed spiritually, but not physically, humanity would enjoy the implementation of God's will ("on earth as it is in heaven"), both because they have been transformed (the dead as well as the living) and because the natural world would no longer be unpredictable and fraught with danger.[56] God would rule either directly or through benevolent kings who have no need to exploit or oppress. And the human world would no longer be either threatened or dominated by the envious, the selfish, and the predatory.

Indeed, the end-time predictions of the prophets indicate quite clearly that the ancient Jews imagined an ideal world based entirely on the principle of social, economic, and political justice. In the words of one student of this ethical program: "The Israelites' project was to rethink the very meaning of authority, and, indeed, to rethink all the rules of life that other people took as eternally valid. To bring this about, they hoped for the end of political despotism in a new society without oppression, poverty, or violence."[57] The prophets embraced this utopian ideal precisely because the monarchies of ancient Israel had become indistinguishable from the other tyrannical kingdoms of the Middle East. The only corrective, as they saw it, was a complete reversal of the status quo. That is, the poor and helpless could not achieve peace and security unless the rich and powerful were defeated. Thus, as one historian puts it, the prophets "spoke or wrote on behalf of the socially and economically disadvantaged, the victims of the gradual and inexorable undermining by the state of the cohesion and ethos of

---

55. In *Moral Core*, 116–17, Maguire cites three scholars on this point. Pixley says: "Yahweh's kingdom is the seminal idea of the Old Testament . . . Jesus was not preaching something new, but announcing a hope with a long history in Israel" (*God's Kingdom*, 3). Stephen Charles Mott (*Biblical Ethics and Social Change*, 82) and T. W. Manson (*Ethics and the Gospel*, 65) agree.

56. Smith comments, "Most Jews believed that in the end [God] would destroy or remodel the present world, and create a new order in which the Jews, or at least those who had followed his law, would have a better life" (*Jesus the Magician*, 5). Tacitus and Suetonius said that the belief in the ultimate triumph of Judea and the establishment of the Kingdom of God was widely held (166). On the uniquely Jewish belief in a physical resurrection, see Vermes, *Resurrection*, xv-xvii. Vermes cites Ezek 37:5–6; Isa 24–27; Dan 12:1–2; and passages in *The Psalms of Solomon* 3:9–12; 2 *Baruch* 30:1; and *The Testament of Judah* 25:4.

57. Maguire, *Moral Core*, 118. Maguire continues: "The 'great reversal' is not from something to an unspecified otherness, but from one set of moral and political assumptions to others at the antipodes. Beyond any doubt, justice is the primary distinguishing theme and hallmark of the new order envisioned by the reign" (126).

a more or less egalitarian system based on the kinship network."[58] Evidently, extreme change was necessary because the situation could not be endured. Even if we ignore the very specific accusations of the prophets against the Jewish elite of ancient Israel, it is easy to see from their extravagant visions of the future that hope had been engendered by excessive hardship.

In all treatments of the end time, the sequence of events is the same: sin, suffering, and salvation. Between sin and suffering, there may be few or many warnings. And between suffering and salvation, there may be little or much contrition. On the national level, suffering sometimes replaces repentance as a step to salvation because it is expiatory and therefore salutary. It both chastens and purifies. One way or another, however, God is expected to respond to human needs simply because He is not only merciful, but *present*. The psalmist can go on and on about his pain and vulnerability only because he assumes that God is near enough to hear him as well as kind enough to help him.

God is thus not transcendent and abstract, as if He were a *principle* of justice operating automatically, but immanent and personal, listening and hearing and acting: "I cry aloud to the Lord, and he answers me from his holy hill" (Ps 2:4). To the righteous, Isaiah says, "Then you shall call, and the Lord will answer; you shall cry, and he will say, Here I am" (Isa 58:9). And to the suffering, the psalmist says that God can be found by those who look for Him: "And those who know thy name put their trust in thee, for thou, O Lord, hast not forsaken those who seek thee" (Ps 9:10). After all, God has said to His people: "You are my son, today I have begotten you. Ask of me, and I will make the nations your heritage" (1:7). In sum, God is not only fair-minded and merciful, but also responsive: "The Lord is just in all his ways, and kind in all his doings. The Lord is near to all who call upon him, to all who call upon him in truth. He fulfills the desire of all who fear him, he also hears their cry, and saves them"

58. The passage (from Blenkinsopp, *Sage, Priest, Prophet*, 147) is quoted in Herzog, *Jesus, Justice*, 62. Herzog comments, "As the state increasingly encroached on the rights, resources, and eventually the land of its peasant base, it coopted the religion of Yahweh and its prophets to serve its purpose and legitimate the newly emerging state policies" (147). The co-opted prophets were obviously not Isaiah and the other great voices of protest, who in fact took on the establishment and railed against its abuses. Herzog discusses the use of religion by rulers everywhere in the ancient world to legitimate the exploitation of peasants (112–13).

(145:17–19).[59] Therefore, "Ask, and it will be given you; seek, and you will find" (Matt 7:7).[60]

In the apocalyptic writings of the prophets, there are two main variables.[61] First, who will be saved—e.g., a remnant of Jews, all Jews, all Jews and all gentiles, or only repentant Jews and converted gentiles? Second, who will initiate salvation—e.g., Elijah, a Davidic messiah, "one like the son of man," or God Himself? In Isaiah, a Davidic messiah ("a shoot from the stump of Jesse") "shall stand as an ensign to the peoples; him shall the nations [i.e., the gentiles] seek." He will "recover the remnant which is left of his people . . . and "gather the dispersed" Jews from everywhere (Isa 11:1,11; 27:12–13). In Jeremiah and Ezekiel, God Himself "will gather the remnant," and a Davidic king will reign forever (Jer 23:3, 5, Ezek 37:21, 24–25).[62] Jews and their converts will occupy their ancestral lands, gentiles ("the peoples") will be their slaves, and the restored Jews will "rule over those who oppressed them" (Isa 14:1–2). God seems to offer salvation (and freedom) to the gentiles—obviously, however, on condition of their conversion to Judaism—when he says, "Assemble yourselves and come, . . . you

59. In the context of these passages, it is beyond human understanding that Bultmann should utterly misrepresent Judaism once more, this time on the subject of God's accessibility. On the one hand, he is correct to say that "Jesus' teaching of God seems no different from that which he has been taught." Specifically, Bultmann is referring to the idea that God is both transcendent (as creator) and immanent (as provider): "For Jesus, as for the Old Testament and Judaism, God is the Creator who governs the world with his providential care . . . God wants men to have a sense of dependence as well as trust." On the other hand, however, Bultmann creates a difference where none exists: "But the terms used to express this dependence and trust show that Jesus had brought God out of the false transcendence to which he had been relegated by Judaism and made him near at hand again" (*Primitive Christianity*, 77, 79; my emphasis). Enslin says, to the contrary, "The notion that for the Jew at the beginning of the Christian era God had become remote, that as the King of the universe he was likened to an Eastern despot, completely inaccessible, to be feared, not worshipped, while still widely held, *is entirely mistaken*" (*Christian Beginnings*, 101; my emphasis). Moore says simply, "That God hears and answers prayer is taught and exemplified in a thousand ways in the Scripture. In the Psalms this fundamental truth of religion becomes a fact of experience, the faith by which men live" (*Judaism*, II-III, 231; see also 238). Moore devotes an entire chapter to this subject in the first volume of his study, 423-42. See especially 438-42.

60. Enslin contends that "'Seek and ye shall find' was a lesson Jesus had learned in the synagogue" (*Christian Beginnings*, 94).

61. Fredriksen says: "Nothing in this scenario, except for the sequence travail/bliss, is fixed. There is no consensus, for example, on whether all the dead will be resurrected or only the saints; on who will lead the apocalyptic battle; on how many of the Gentiles will perish in their sins or turn in the end to God. Most important of all . . . is the breadth of speculation concerning the apocalyptic redeemer figures, the Son of Man and the messiah" (*From Jesus to Christ*, 85). For a brief overview of apocalyptic end-time theories, see 81–84.

62. The remnant appears to be "the righteous," with whom "it shall be well," and the other is "the wicked," whose "hands have done" what "shall be done to him" (Isa 3:10–11). The remnant is "he who is left in Zion and remains in Jerusalem, when the Lord shall have washed away the filth of the daughters of Zion and cleansed the bloodstains of Jerusalem from its midst by a spirit of judgment and by a spirit of burning" (4:3–4). The victims of this cleansing and burning are no doubt "the men that have rebelled against me"—that is, presumably, those who are unrepentant and who will remain forever dead (66:24).

survivors of the nations! . . . Turn to me and be saved, all the ends of the earth!" (Isa 45:20, 22).

To the Jews, it should be noted, "conversion to Judaism" did not mean acceptance of and submission to a tribal god, who was merely a god among gods. The Jews assumed that, since Yahweh was *the* God—and, indeed, the *only* God, the idols of the gentiles being merely *false* gods—anyone who accepted Him would be saved. In other words, everyone was welcome to worship the Creator of the universe, the Forgiver of sins, and the Dispenser of divine justice. Not to accept the exclusive godhead of Yahweh was suicidal, since He—merciful and just to all—saved only those who accepted His exclusive godhead. Thus, the prophets, from Isaiah 40 on, believed that "God would one day be acknowledged and served by all mankind." In this way, "[t]he Jews were the only people in their world who conceived the idea of a universal religion." And what may have looked like the narrowest kind of particularism and ethnocentrism turns out to be the only universalism in the ancient world.[63] The one universal God was available to anyone who believed in Him.

It is evidence of this universalism that Jewish missionary activity was both extensive and successful.[64] And God's welcome of gentiles, even under the rather strict terms by which acceptance into Judaism could be attained, was often warm and welcoming rather than hostile and threatening: "And the foreigners [that is, gentiles] who join themselves to the Lord . . . these will I bring to my holy mountain, and make them joyful in my house of prayer; their burnt offerings and their sacrifices will be accepted on my altar; for my house shall be called a house of prayer for all peoples" (Isa 56:6–7). "Open the gates, that the righteous nation which keeps faith [i.e., converted gentiles] may enter in" (Isa 26:2). The standard by which this determination was made was established as early as Leviticus, wherein God says to Moses, "You shall therefore keep my statutes and my ordinances; by doing which a man shall live" (Lev 18:5). That is, salvation is gained by obedience, not race or ethnicity. Nothing else could have justified the Jewish mission to the gentiles.[65]

63. Moore, *Judaism*, I, 22. "If there be but one God," Moore argues later, "there can only be one religion; and the idea of unity in religion carries with it the idea of universality." That is, sooner or later, Judaism, the Jews felt, "must one day be the religion of all mankind" (228; see also 323). Bainton says, "Judaism in the time of the prophets was universalized," which meant not that every religion was valid, but that everyone was invited to accept the Jewish law and worship the Jewish God (*Early Christianity*, 11). It should be emphasized that Judaism was not tolerant. Other religions were tolerant, but made no claim to universalism. Christianity followed the path of Judaism—i.e., other religions were unacceptable because only Christianity offered the true faith. On Jewish efforts at conversion, see Moore, *Judaism*, I, 323–24. Moore calls for scholars to avoid using the term "particularism," which is "depreciatory" and inaccurate as it applies to Judaism (219). Speaking of Judaism's claim to universality, Moore says, "This is the logical attitude of a revealed religion, and has always been maintained by the Christian church: repentance avails nothing . . . outside the church" (529).

64. On Jewish missionizing, see Segal, *Paul the Convert*, 86–93.

65. As usual, to Bultmann, the differences between Jesus and Judaism—in this case on the subject of the acceptance of gentiles into the Kingdom of God—start out large and then disappear. "Obviously," says Bultmann, erroneously, "the Jews thought of the deliverance of the Kingdom of God as

CLASS CONFLICT

It is important to understand the longstanding and well-established ideals of Judaism in order to understand both the dilemma of the Jews during the Roman occupation and the missionary career of Jesus himself.[66] The most significant fact about this period is that it represented a continuation of a bitter and brutal history characterized by failed wars of survival that resulted in the domination of the Jews by larger and more powerful nations: the Assyrians, the Babylonians, the Persians, the Ptolemies, the Seleucids, and the Romans. In every case, their ideals were challenged either by the desire of the occupying powers to make them accept a new religion or by the mere presence of a culture that had demonstrated its superiority by means of conquest. In that context, Jesus is best understood as, at the very least, a defender of ideals that were threatened by outside forces—i.e., the principles embodied in the Covenant Code— and as a Jewish hero in the mold of Moses, Joshua (after whom he was named), Elijah, Josiah, Ezra, and Judah Maccabee.

From this perspective, the problem facing the Jews in the first century AD was a consequence of their being a subject people under Herod Antipas in Galilee (from 4 BC to AD 40) and the Romans in Judea: They could not live their lives as they wished to. Politically, they were dominated by foreign powers. Even Antipas, son of the famous (and hated) Herod, an Idumean, was perceived to be, at best, a half-Jew, who had little interest in promoting the values of biblical Judaism. Economically, the Palestinian Jews were surrounded by people who saw the land not as a means of sustenance, to be used in support of the entire community, including the helpless, but as

---

deliverance for the Jews." That is, "the favored position of the Jews is taken for granted." "From Jesus," Bultmann continues, "we hear almost nothing" about a Davidic [i.e., Jewish] messiah, the triumph of the Temple and Jerusalem, and the return of the lost tribes of Israel. (Of course, Bultmann had evidently failed to read [or understand] Acts 1:6 and Luke 22:30.) Yet, Bultmann adds, Jesus did not teach the "universality" of the Kingdom of God: "He took for granted as did his contemporaries that the Kingdom of God was to come for the benefit of the Jewish people." In other words, "the preaching of Jesus had not extended beyond the boundaries of the Jewish people; *he never thought of a mission to the Gentiles*"! (*Jesus and the Word*, 43–44; my emphasis). Ironically, Bultmann neglects to say that, in fact, the Jews welcomed gentiles as converts, while Jesus did not. After referring to the "known success" of "contemporary Jewish missionary activity" at this time, Parkes says that the Jews were expelled from Rome in 139 BC and later by both Tiberius and Claudius because of their "enthusiastic" missionizing. "Even in the middle of the wars at the end of the first century the Flavians had to take measures to make the circumcision of Gentiles a capital offense" (*Conflict*, 2, 24). Jews even welcomed gentile slaves into their faith, most of whom accepted conversion (Jeremias, *Jerusalem*, 111). Jews were in fact required to convert all slaves, although the slaves were not required to accept Jewish ownership and conversion. Male slaves were circumcised; female slaves were baptized (Moore, *Judaism*, II-III, 18, 136).

66. Guignebert says, "The only way to understand Jesus' own career as a Messiah is to restore it to its proper background and surroundings: the historical development that led up to it and in a very real sense conditioned it" (*Jewish World*, 153). Discussing the economic issues that made the peasants of Palestine "less contented with their lot," Kaylor says, "Jesus' teachings and actions are so directly related to those economic stresses that a further exploration of economic conditions is necessary to understanding Jesus" (*Jesus the Prophet*, 27).

a means of profit making. Culturally, the Jews were living in a world dominated by Hellenism, a thoroughly alien world view that had been a powerful force in their lives since the conquest of Alexander in the fourth century BC and the subsequent rule of the Ptolemies and the Seleucids.[67] In terms of religion, they were still exposed to the kinds of temptations that Ezra had tried to shield them from—not, in this case, the allures of Canaanite idolatry, but what they must have thought of as the Roman version of a religion they (or at least their religious leaders) had always repudiated.

The Jewish response to this dilemma was rooted in the fact that things had not always been this way. Most important, the Jews had been to some degree self-governing a millennium earlier under Joshua and the so-called judges and during the monarchy of David and his heirs. Indeed, it is likely that the social and economic principles that they codified in Leviticus and Numbers were developed in the years before the establishment of the Jewish kingdom, when the Israelites lived in villages, raised sheep and cattle, and grew crops on small family-owned farms. Presumably, under their own rule—especially before both the monarchy and the Assyrian and Babylonian conquests of the eighth and sixth centuries BC, which destroyed it—they had also been able to implement the laws that were intended to preserve their way of life and were later so clearly repeated in Deuteronomy and reinforced by the prophets and the psalms. The result of the loss of their independence was twofold: frustration and yearning.

The frustration was manifested in the frequency with which both armed and unarmed Jews resisted the occupation of Palestine by foreign powers, beginning with the Maccabees in the second century BC and sustained after the Roman conquest in the next century by recriminations, riots, and revolts, all documented by the Jewish historian Josephus and more or less totally ignored by the writers of the New Testament. The yearning was reinforced, to some degree, by their success under the leadership of the Maccabees (or Hasmoneans), when they threw out the Seleucids, who had tried to destroy their religion and convert them to idol worship, less than two hundred years before the Crucifixion. After less than a century of self-rule, the Jews of Palestine fought the Romans in 63 BC; the surviving Hasmoneans led four rebellions in the 50s

---

67. "Jewish settlements throughout Palestine," says Kaylor, "were surrounded by a diverse Gentile population whose upper classes were thoroughly hellenized . . . Hellenism was especially attractive to the Jewish upper classes, among whom were the main priestly families," some of whom "were inclined to transform Jewish society so that its distinctiveness was replaced by Hellenistic institutions and values" (*Jesus the Prophet*, 24). The Hellenization process actually began with the Seleucid king Antiochus IV, against whom the Maccabees fought in the second century BC, and was continued by Herod, though less militantly. During Jesus' lifetime, Herod Antipas continued the Hellenization project by building (or rebuilding) two centers of Hellenistic culture, Tiberias and Sepphoris (25–26). Toynbee traces the dilemma of the Jews in the time of Jesus to the birth of "monotheistic Judaism" in the eighth and sixth centuries BC, when there occurred "a domestic economic and social crisis which widened the gulf between rich and poor and raised the question of social justice acutely" ("The Historical Antecedents," 42). These are the issues that the prophets raised at the time—rather insistently, one might say.

BC[68]; the Jews rioted in 4 BC, after the death of Herod the Great; and they initiated a major revolt against the Romans in 66 AD. Exactly sixty-six years later, in 132 AD, they tried it again.

In the meantime, especially between Herod's death and the Revolt of 66—that is, during the lifetime of Jesus and his first disciples—there were innumerable violent conflicts, threats by self-proclaimed messiahs and rebel kings, disruptions of the social order by brigands and bandits, and increasing attacks by Zealots and assassins and kidnappers. Josephus refers to thirty leading insurrectionists of one kind or another during this period. And, of course, the tension and unrest that characterize this half century or more of undeclared war culminated in the seven-year-long battle between Jews and Romans in 66, which resulted in the deaths of hundreds of thousands of Jews.

The yearning of the Jews of the first century was based partly on nostalgia, rooted in the memory of better times, and partly on hope, derived not only from the success of the Maccabean rebels, but also, and perhaps more importantly, from the exodus out of Egypt, which, as I have suggested, figured so largely in the writings of the Jews and deeply affected their expectations and aspirations. The example of the Maccabees indicated that liberation from foreign domination was at least possible. And the example of the exodus indicated, especially in the dire circumstances of the first century, that in the worst of times God would intervene and free His people from oppression.

Thus, when rebels arose in the first century, they sometimes called themselves kings, implying that they would restore the old monarchy, and sometimes assumed the mantle of prophet or even messiah, implying that, like Moses, they would lead their people to the Promised Land. In the thirties, a Samaritan leader took his followers up Mt. Gerizim to restore the Temple on a Sinai-like mountaintop. In the forties, the rebel Theudas promised to part the waters of the Jordan River. And, in the fifties, the rebel called simply the Egyptian told his followers that he would bring down the walls of Jerusalem, just as Joshua had brought down the walls of Jericho. It was

---

68. On this subject, see Enslin, *Christian Beginnings*, 39. Enslin says that Galilee was, before Herod's assumption of power, "a turbulent place, seething with discontent" (41). "As we shall see," he adds, "this district was to remain the hotbed of incipient rebellion." Indeed, "the group in Galilee was certainly no mere group of mountain brigands, but militant nationalists," who "hated Rome" (42). According to Schalit, Judea rose to the same level of discontent under Herod, who replaced the Hasmonean chief priests and Sanhedrin with men whom he could trust to be obedient. For the Judeans, even the illusion of self-rule "was now over" since the priesthood "had been taken by the 'impious regime' of the Gentile world power embodied in the hated figure of the 'Hasmonean slave' and 'half-Jew,' Herod." To put it simply, "his reign was interpreted as the beginning of the messianic woes," which were felt, but not expressed under his regime. At his death, "the messianic and apocalyptic currents" that Herod had suppressed "burst all the more forcefully through the constraints which had been set on them, carrying away the poor and the oppressed who were longing for social justice and the political liberation of the nation" ("Herod and His Successors," 37).

evidently difficult, at the time, for these movements to avoid some kind of biblically based identity for the purpose of authentication and, hence, inspiration.[69]

Much of the violence of this time was not between Jews and Romans, however, but among Jews. And, in this regard, it was almost always a manifestation of class conflict. Herod, ever obedient to Rome, had evidently been willing to go to any lengths to keep his royal house in order, and Rome was an imperial state whose government, it should be remembered, was totalitarian. To be sure, many of the insurgents in the Revolt of 66 were educated and middle-class.[70] By and large, however, the great majority of Jews who were involved in the insurgencies of the first century were peasants fighting for change against both aristocratic Jews and ruling Romans. These included beggars and idlers, to be sure, but also "the respectable poor," many of whom had been displaced or dispossessed by economic circumstances and took their resentment out on the rich and powerful. According to two historians, among the latter were farmers, fishermen, farm laborers, city-dwelling day laborers, "wage earners, indebted servants and slaves, as well as artisans, small traders, and businessmen," in addition to the lowest stratum of "beggars, prostitutes, shepherds, and bandits."[71]

69. Horsley discusses these leaders in *Bandits, Prophets & Messiahs*, 161–72. Horsley concludes, "This very pattern of interpreting and anticipating history had been important in Jewish tradition at least since Second Isaiah," and continued "in later apocalyptic literature" (171).

70. Sanders reminds his readers that "it was the priests serving in the Temple who finally declared war against Rome in 66 CE. They were persuaded by a priestly aristocrat (Eleazar son of Ananias)" to stop making sacrifices in honor of Rome and Caesar (*Historical Figure of Jesus*, 43). Nevertheless, their opponents were also the Jewish aristocracy and Agrippa II. Furthermore, by most accounts, the vast majority of the priests who participated in the Revolt of 66 were "the lesser, local clergy living in the Judean countryside" rather than "the Jerusalem-based high priests" (Freyne, *Galilee, Jesus*, 192). Brandon says, "The revolt actually started . . . when the lower priests refused any longer to offer the daily sacrifices in the Temple for the well-being of the Emperor and the Roman people" (*Trial of Jesus*, 57). Painter explains that the lower priests were allied with the peasants and the Pharisees, while "the Sadducean chief priestly party" was connected to the "aristocratic rich" (*Just James*, 250). That is, the conflict between rich and poor priests simply reflected the general hostility between haves and have-nots (265). See also Winter, "Sadducees and Pharisees," 49–50; and Jeremias, *Jerusalem in the Time of Jesus*, 206. Kaylor says that the country priests [i.e., lower priests] were also involved in the Maccabean revolt (*Jesus the Prophet*, 24).

71. Stegemann and Stegemann, *Jesus Movement*, 133. To the extent that many of these workers were economic victims, "this pauperization of the peasantry created a considerable potential for robbery and revolutionary movements" (113). "The great revolt of 66–70 grew out of the economic and social issues that gave rise to bandits, prophets and messiahs" (Kaylor, *Jesus the Prophet*, 43). Quoting M. Stern ("Aspects of Jewish Society: The Priesthood and Other Classes," 2:564), Kaylor adds, "Landless men, displaced persons and casual labourers who had lost their sources of livelihood, proved an unfailing source for the quarrels and public disturbances that broke out repeatedly" (*Jesus the Prophet*, 43). Speaking of the lowest classes, Jeremias says, "It is amazing how many people of this kind emerged in the last decade before the destruction of Jerusalem; they formed themselves into gangs and terrorized the whole city . . . and later carried on the civil war within its walls . . . The social factor played a large part in the Zealot movement. We can see this very clearly in the activities of these liberators of the people, who in AD 66 burnt the Jerusalem archives in order to destroy the records of their debts which were stored there" (*Jerusalem*, 118–19).

What matters most in this regard is that the Romans worked with members of Jewish society who had much more to lose if the Romans lost power—the rich, some members of the priestly class, Herodians, and their retainers (who included political functionaries and religious officials associated with Herod Antipas, the Roman prefect, or the Temple).[72] Many of these people (except, of course, the tetrarch of Galilee and the prefect of Judea), lived in Jerusalem, which "had [always] attracted the wealth of the nation—merchants, landowners, tax-farmers, bankers, and men of private means," as well as the higher priests.[73] In Palestine in general, this group had no connection whatsoever with the poor and disenfranchised. Hostility between the opponents was strong because they had nothing in common except their religion and ethnicity: "The point is that there was a gulf between the governing and the governed in Judea and Galilee which was not bridged by mutual respect or trust."[74]

The most powerful priests were not, as they had been in earlier days, a hereditary class by birth. They were drawn from the rich; had, after the Maccabean revolt, no traditional claim to this role; and represented, therefore, an unusual concentration

72. Stegemann and Stegemann also put estate managers, financial administrators, and tax collectors in this group (*Jesus Movement*, 127-29).

73. Jeremias, *Jerusalem*, 95. Jeremias later discusses the role of the "elders," particularly as members of the Sanhedrin. Suffice it to say that they were simply the heads of the most prominent families, from among whom priests and government officials were chosen (222-28). Enslin says that the Roman procurators lived in Caesaria (*Christian Beginnings*, 69).

74. Witherington, *Jesus Quest*, 19. For further discussion of the Jewish elite as collaborators with Rome and therefore enemies of the common people, see Borg and Crossan, *Last Week*, 12-13, 16, 57. Maccoby says that the Sadducees were prepared to cooperate with anyone: "Among the priests, it was chiefly a few families of great wealth and political influence with the reigning power who were Sadducees . . . People such as these were the natural allies of whatever authority happened to be in power, whether Ptolemaic Greeks, Seleucid Greeks, Hasmoneans, Herodians or Romans" (*Mythmaker*, 26). Summarizing the cast of characters in *The Psalms of Solomon*, written shortly before the birth of Jesus, Trafton indicates that they represent the class war in ancient Palestine between the haves (the Romans and the Jewish aristocracy) and the have-nots (the other Jews). He notes that "the foreign conqueror from the West" represents Pompey, who conquered Palestine in 63 BC, and his opponent is "a particular group of Jews," whom the psalmist divides into two groups. The psalmist "identifies himself with those whom he calls the righteous, the holy ones, the poor, the innocent, and those who fear the Lord; on the other side are the wicked, the lawless, the sinners, the deceitful, and the hypocrites. But he also describes more specific criticisms: his opponents have defiled the Temple and its sacrifices and have set up a non-Davidic monarchy" ("The Psalms of Solomon," 256). According to Trafton, the Psalms demonstrate that "Jews could—and did—criticize the Temple leadership and brand other Jews as hypocrites" (257). Fredriksen objects to the notion of class conflict as a way of understanding Galilean attitudes toward the Jewish elite in the first century (*Jesus of Nazareth*, 177, 182, 283-86). However, on Galileans, including Jesus, as hostile to Sepphoris (as well as other Galilean cities) as "rich and aristocratic" and loyal to Rome, see Sanders, *Historical Figure of Jesus*, 104-106. Lee comments: "Josephus documents Galilean hatred of both Sepphoris and Tiberias. Jesus of Sepphias, a revolutionary guerrilla leader, and some Galileans kill the small Greek population and burn Herod's palace there" (*Galilean Jewishness of Jesus*, 63). Newsome says that class conflict in Palestine goes back to the time of Elijah, when "Israelite society became increasingly divided between the wealthy classes (who professed or at least tolerated Baalism) and the peasants (many of whom remained loyal to Yahweh)" (*Hebrew Prophets*, 13). Newsome discusses the conflict between King Ahab and Naboth (1 Kings 21) as an illustration of this conflict (14).

of arbitrary power (i.e., both political and economic).[75] The higher priests lived in luxurious houses, decorated with wall frescoes and mosaics and furnished with "ritual baths" and "luxury goods."[76] They were totally opposed by the ordinary priests, who "threw in their lot with the people at the outbreak of the anti-Roman rebellion in AD 66."[77] From what we know of the behavior of the higher priests, it is likely that the lower priests objected to their power politics, nepotism, and control over Temple finances.[78]

Furthermore, the divide between them and the peasants was widened by the Ptolemies, Seleucids, and Romans, who ruled Palestine, successively, from the fourth century BC onward (except for the century-long rule of the Hasmoneans) and supported their regimes by allying themselves with members of the indigenous aristocracy. "Such men," says one scholar, "were primarily concerned with the maintenance of a stable government and ordering of society. They had no love for the Romans, but they were realists in recognizing that their own security depended upon their cooperation with the new masters of Israel."[79] In Palestine, this meant, for one thing, that the High Priest collected taxes and was thereby understood to be no friend of the peasant class, but tied to the foreign rulers: "The priestly aristocracy received their [financial] support from the rural areas, primarily through the tax on agricultural products intended to support the Temple—the tithe originally intended for the poor and the Levites. The Romans backed the arrangement by decreeing that the people should bring their tithes to the Temple. Roman help was necessary because, since Hasmonean days, the sympathy of the people for supporting the Temple establishment had diminished."[80]

75. Bruce, *New Testament History*, 40, 67. The most frequently mentioned actors during Jesus' trial are what Flusser calls the "Jewish troika" of elders, chief priests, and scribes, all of whom were connected with the Temple. The scribes were the Temple lawyers (*Sage from Galilee*, 142).

76. Kaylor, *Jesus the Prophet*, 35. Kaylor is quoting N. Avigad, *The Herodian Quarter in Jerusalem*, 10.

77. Jeremias, *Jerusalem*, 207. "We must remember," says Jeremias, "the remarkable wealth of the priestly aristocracy . . . in contrast with the poor circumstances of the ordinary priests" (98). Part of the problem was, says Kaylor, that "[r]ural priests did not share equally in the income [contributed] to the Temple," by which Temple employees were paid (*Jesus the Prophet*, 28).

78. On these subjects, see Jeremias, *Jerusalem*, 195–98, who adds that these priests also controlled a large number of seats in the Sanhedrin. The general complaint, therefore, was that their power far exceeded their merit and reflected nothing more than their financial status.

79. Brandon, *Trial of Jesus*, 29. Brandon continues, "The Jewish aristocracy, though the official religious leaders of the nation, were concerned to keep their people submissive to their heathen overlord" (30).

80. Kaylor, *Jesus the Prophet*, 35–36. See also Stegemann and Stegemann, *Jesus Movement*, 118. Later, Kaylor suggests that the popularity of the priests declined because they got richer thanks to the prosperity provided by the Romans, while the poor got poorer: "Sadducean priests lived in fine houses at the expense of the peasants and the urban poor . . . The opulence was not at the expense of the Romans but of the Jews, who were required by Torah and by Roman law to bring a tithe for its support" (*Jesus the Prophet*, 61). Kaylor describes the increasing landlessness and indebtedness of peasants under the Hasmoneans, Herod, and the Romans on 29–34.

After Herod arbitrarily appointed a High Priest in 37 BC, "the office ceased to be life-long and hereditary," as it had been, which henceforth made "the high priest wholly dependent on political authority." Until that time, for a period of 115 years, eight Hasmoneans had occupied the office. From then until the destruction of the Temple in AD 70, a period of 106 years, twenty-eight priests served, many of them obviously victims of political whim.[81] After the Romans took control of Judea, the High Priest was the putative leader of the Jews but served at the pleasure of the Roman prefect. Beholden to this appointee, who was in turn beholden to the Roman emperor, the High Priest was hardly an independent decision maker who could be said to represent anyone but his Roman superiors and, if he could get away with it, the Jewish nobility.[82]

Herod Antipas, tetrarch of Galilee, but a ruler in name only, "was under constraint by Rome to maintain order and ensure that the tribute was paid annually." In this endeavor, like his counterpart in Judea—Pontius Pilate—he depended on the support of the local aristocracy, whom he included in his "court retinue."[83] This collaboration occurred everywhere in the empire, with Roman overlords protecting the wealthy classes, who compromised with their protectors and thereby garnered, especially in Judea, the hatred of the masses. Throughout the ancient world, "despite the more democratic outlook created by the diffusion of the Greek *polis*," elites governed in their own interest, "to the exclusion of the vast majority of the population."[84] The division was also exacerbated by the desire of the Romans to Hellenize the Jews and the willingness of the Jewish aristocracy to help them: "[T]here developed a dichotomy in Israelite society between many who resisted Hellenistic influence in social

81. Jeremias, *Jerusalem*, 148, 159, 190.

82. "Since Herod himself could not occupy the High Priest's office, he arranged to have the Hasmonean succession broken off," which he accomplished by dismissals and at least one murder. "Then he installed high priests who suited him, and deposed them when reasons of power politics so dictated" (Stegemann and Stegemann, *Jesus Movement*, 130). "In this policy," adds Enslin, Herod "was followed by the Roman authorities." Thus, in the hundred years between Herod and the Revolt of 66, the High Priests served an average of less than four years. However, all of these priests were drawn from a small group of priestly families, who maintained their power and "formed an elite inner circle" by intermarrying and by understanding that their role could be sustained only by cooperating with the secular rulers. The "chief priests" so often referred to in the Gospels were the priests representing these families, who made up a large part of the Jewish aristocracy (*Christian Beginnings*, 133). To scholars who still insist on blaming the Jews for the death of Jesus, it is important to overestimate the power of the priests and underestimate the power of Pontius Pilate, as Reicke does, in "Galilee and Judea," 32–35. Reicke's picture of Pilate includes nothing about the violence for which he was notorious. He was merely a lower level administrator who yielded to the Jews both at the beginning, middle, and end of his term. The level of Reicke's misrepresentation is suggested by his description of Pilate's construction of an aqueduct: "The Jews demonstrated against this too, but Pilate succeeded in getting the work finished with the help of soldiers dressed as civilians." What Reicke fails to mention about what he calls a "creditable" act is that the Jews objected because Pilate funded the project by stealing money from the Temple treasury. Furthermore, Pilate's soldiers dressed up as civilians in order to infiltrate the crowd of Jewish protestors and put down the protest by killing the participants.

83. Freyne, *Galilee, Jesus*, 142–43.

84. *Galilee, Jesus*, 173.

and religious life and those who supported the modernizing process. In some ways this dichotomy was also between the poor and the rich."[85] Thus, in conflicts between peasants and Romans, the Jewish elite made no attempt to intervene. And, in the Revolt of 66, this group (including Josephus) did everything it could to undermine the revolution. In that war, the rebels, both Zealots and Sicarii (dagger men), attacked the Jewish collaborators. Jewish priests, in turn, killed the rebel leader Menahem, among others.

In short, "nearly all of the separate movements [of liberation in Palestine] were popular groups directed against the Jewish ruling elite as well as against Roman rule."[86] They "were much more likely to respect local elders, Pharisees, sages, prophets or holy men, or even messianic claimants, than they were such official leaders."[87] The mere fact that the rebels of Palestine (later called Zealots) were able to hold out for as long as they did (that is, for more than half a century after the death of King Herod) suggests that they were supported by a majority of the people, either clandestinely or, on occasion, overtly.[88]

85. Kaylor, *Jesus the Prophet*, 29; see also 36, 99, 129, 132. Speaking of Herod, Enslin says: "Though an Idumean by birth, he was in spirit a Hellenist. He did not make the mistake of striving to thrust it down people's throats, as had Antiochus Epiphanes. Nevertheless, he introduced it in no less degree." Enslin mentions not only amphitheatres, chariot races, gladiatorial shows, and Olympic games "celebrated every fourth year," but Greek-style buildings, including especially the Temple in Jerusalem— a gift to the Jews, but equally an expression of Herod's dedication to things both lavish and Greek (*Christian Beginnings*, 47, 55).

86. Horsley, *Bandits, Prophets & Messiahs*, xxvii. "The successive Zealot revolts, culminating in the war of A.D. 66, were directed almost as much against the Jewish 'establishment' as against the occupying power" (Bruce, *New Testament History*, 40). "In such circumstances," says Kaylor, "the peasant population would have made little distinction between the Roman rulers and the high priestly rulers" (*Jesus the Prophet*, 36). Crossan cites two scholars, David Rhoads and Shaye Cohen, who call the Revolt of 66 a class war between two groups of Jews (*Historical Jesus*, 99). Cohen describes it as a war "between the rich and the poor, between the upper classes and the lower, between the city dwellers and the country folk" (cited in *Historical Jesus*). As Maccoby notes, the rebels of AD 66 replaced the High Priest with someone of decidedly non-elite status (*Mythmaker*, 39).

87. Witherington, *Jesus Quest*, 23. See also Robertson, *Origins of Christianity*, 59. Speaking of the Roman empire in general, Peters says: "The classic struggle of the haves and have-nots was complicated by the issues of Republic versus Principate, the Hellenized versus the native, the local versus the central—that is, Roman—authority with, in the large urban centers, the Jews thrown in as pawns. Roman policy, which was directed toward prosperity, favored the already prosperous and so indirectly fostered economic class struggle everywhere in the Empire." In this situation, "the revolutionary class" was "the disenfranchised peasantry and the urban proletariat" (*Harvest of Hellenism*, 526). For a more detailed look at this conflict in Palestine, see Carmichael, *Birth of Christianity*, 113–17.

88. Brandon, *Trial of Jesus*, 34. Of course, the support of the people for the Zealots against the Jewish elite was not continuous. Brandon explains: Between the two groups, "the attitude of the mass of the people wavered, according to circumstances. Fundamentally, they hated the Romans, who gave them good cause both by their oppression and their frequent overt violation of Jewish religious sensibilities." They were fearful of the authorities, however, and therefore usually maintained a posture of submission. Yet again, "secretly they admired the Zealots for their active resistance and supported them as and when they could" (30). In short, they desired both peace and freedom. Over time, of course, the wish for the former gave way to the wish for the latter. There were "increasing clashes between the Roman authorities and Jewish resistance groups," which "were symptomatic of increasing

Of course, many Jews were driven by more than political, cultural, and religious concerns. Not only were they opposed to the Roman occupation, offended by Hellenization, and appalled by Roman insensitivities to Judaism; they were also disturbed by economic conditions, which evidently grew worse, beginning with the Seleucid occupation, continuing under the Hasmoneans, and reaching its lowest point under the Romans. The victims in all of these regimes were both peasants and urban laborers, the latter group having expanded over the decades because of the same forces that made rural life in Palestine progressively more difficult. Jewish farmers slowly but steadily lost their land because of excessive taxation, aggressive land acquisition by wealthy urban investors, usurious lending practices, and other manifestations of exploitation by the haves against the have-nots.

These issues were not important only to the Jews. Throughout the Middle East, rulers took over peasant farms and compelled the formerly independent and self-sufficient owners of the land to become tenant farmers or day laborers. They accomplished this by outright land-grabbing (sometimes for building projects); taking advantage of crop failure because of adverse weather conditions; and lending at high interest rates, which often resulted in a downward spiral of debt and, ultimately, foreclosure. Rulers could get away with expropriation and usury because they were protected by armies and by religious rules concocted to make their victims think they were compelled by the gods to cooperate. Peasants were also susceptible to the depredations of warfare. Their crops could be stolen to feed invading armies, and their land could be confiscated if the enemy proved to be victorious.[89]

In the Book of Genesis, Joseph, working for the Pharaoh, manages to buy up all the land formerly owned by farmers by taking advantage of a devastating famine that destroyed much of the corn in Egypt. First, because the farmers have no food, they trade their cattle for bread. Then, when the famine continues, they trade their land for bread: "[T]he Egyptians sold every man his field, because the famine prevailed over them: so the land became Pharaoh's" (Gen 47:13–20). Henceforth, the now-landless peasants are permitted to work the land they no longer own, but they are required to give one-fifth of their crops to Pharaoh: "And Joseph made it a law over the land of Egypt unto this day, that Pharaoh should have the fifth part; except the land of the priests only, which became not Pharaoh's" (Gen 47:26). Throughout the Middle East, members of the priesthood, the army, and the civil service were typically exempt from

---

popular fanaticism, which was continuously stimulated by Roman ruthlessness and inflamed by Zealot propaganda and action" (48–49).

89. These problems are discussed by Horsley in *Covenant Economics*, 6–12. Meeks adds, "It is generally agreed that the Hellenistic and Roman periods brought increasing social distance between the Haves and the Have-nots" (*Origins of Christian Morality*, 43). Herzog says, "There was no mutually beneficial reciprocity between rulers and ruled" (*Jesus, Justice*, 98). Borg points out that the kind of society established by the Romans and endured by the Jews during Jesus' lifetime has become a topic of discussion among New Testament scholars only recently (*Jesus*, 85). Borg explains what he calls this "preindustrial agricultural domination system" (79–92).

such encroachments. Invariably, the peasants were the worst victims of both famine and tyranny.

It is assumed by many scholars that village life in Palestine had traditionally been guided by the so-called covenant values, which I discussed earlier in this chapter and which were intended to prevent the kind of exploitation that occurred in Egypt and elsewhere. These values were shaped by the Covenant Code in Exodus 20–23, the code stated in Deuteronomy 5 and 12–26, and the Holiness Code in Leviticus 17–26. Formulated in these collections of laws were the standards by which rural Jewish society managed to preserve the status quo of small farms, which, at some point in the remote past, were owned and operated in relative security by a people governed only by God.[90]

Judea may have had approximately two hundred and fifty villages, all of which were constructed in such a way as to suggest that they were, if not egalitarian, then at least relatively classless communities, consisting of extended families grouped by clan and tribe. These "first Israelites" of the twelfth or thirteenth century BC, who lived in the hills west of the Jordan River, had no luxury goods, and their small communities of one hundred or more inhabitants had no large buildings. Threatened only by bad weather and the invasion of foreign armies, they lived modestly and frugally, engaged in no external trade, and evidently devoted much time and energy to preserving their idyllic, but certainly fragile and vulnerable existence.[91]

These subsistence farmers "spread the risks of bad harvests from drought, warfare, or natural disasters over a wide range of agricultural products and crops." More important, however, they were aided by laws, based on the aforementioned biblical codes, which minimized the chances of economic disaster. In short, "The laws . . . enabled the People of Israel to maintain a stable system of social relations, economic welfare, and local autonomy."[92] As long as these codes were accepted by the majority and as long as the majority had the power to enforce them, the covenant laws protected their beneficiaries from, as one Bible scholar says, "indebtedness, enslavement, and dispossession."[93]

---

90. "Not only did the Israelites, under the leadership of Yahweh, . . . establish their independence as a peasantry free of any ruling class, they also formed a covenant with Yahweh and each other to maintain that freedom" (Horsley, *Bandits, Prophets & Messiahs*, 5). "[I]t is apparent," Horsley says later, "that Israel originated as a free and independent people," who, "[i]n their very origins, . . . had escaped from servitude to foreign rulers" (5; see also 136–37).

91. Horsley, *Covenant Economics*, 34–35. "Excavations in Israelite towns bear witness to this equality in standards of living. At Tirsah, the modern Tell el-Farah near Nablus, the houses of the tenth century B.C. are all of the same size and arrangement. Each represents the dwelling of a family which lived in the same way as its neighbours" (de Vaux, *Ancient Israel*, I, 72–73).

92. Horsley and Silberman, *Message*, 13, 27.

93. Crossan, *Birth of Christianity*, 188.

It seems likely that most, if not all, peasant societies of the pre-urban type had similar objectives and established similar guidelines.[94] What is unique about ancient Israel is that, during the first millennium BC, these goals and rules were codified, written down, stated repeatedly, and even read publicly. Furthermore, the Jewish Bible demonstrated in passage after passage that God Himself was concerned with the enforcement of these principles among His people, which thereby enabled them to think of the preservation of their way of life—as it was articulated in the Covenant—as a right, not a privilege.[95] Indeed, the fact that these principles were nothing less than commandments from God encouraged Jews to think of them as the means by which He could be worshiped. In short, to love humanity—i.e., to follow the economic imperatives of the Covenant—was to love God.

Functioning, then, as a kind of constitution, the laws not only helped to prevent (or at least reduce the effects of) economic crises for small landowners, but also aided widows and orphans and other victims of forces beyond their control, who were destitute. Deriving from three biblical sources and therefore having the unquestionable authority of God, the laws represented an effort to maintain a relatively equitable and broadly supportive economic system, which was always susceptible to both internal and external disruption, but also, as long as it lasted, stood as a hallmark of what a compassionate society could be. By means of these laws, the Jews "tried to control if not eliminate the inequality of growing indebtedness in several ways, including the forbidding of interest, the controlling of collateral, and the establishment of remission."[96]

Of course, the extent to which the Covenant Code was put into practice is hard to determine. I am aware of no scholar who believes, for example, that the Jubilee (the celebration that was supposed to occur every fifty years, when properties were to be repossessed by their ancestral owners) ever happened. Yet even if none of these laws had been enforced, they certainly stood as an ideal against which Jewish life in the first century could be measured.[97] And it is likely that merely the written record of these commands would have kept the hope for self-determination alive.

94. Horsley comments: "Peasant societies developed an array of socio-economic mechanisms that assured the requisite minimum to the families of a village community." Horsley warns against romanticizing these arrangements, however, and (particularly) not treating them as "egalitarian social arrangements." Rather, they were practical measures intended to minimize adversity throughout the whole community. No doubt these tribal people were moved by the ties of kinship, but their commitment to mutual aid derived at least partly from necessity. Horsley cites as a source James C. Scott, *The Moral Economy of the Peasant* (*Covenant Economics*, 36).

95. Horsley says that the Covenant "aimed to protect people's inalienable right to their ancestral lands"—that is, "the economic rights of all to an adequate living" (*Covenant Economics*, 44).

96. Crossan, *Birth of Christianity*, 191.

97. "Traditions rooted in the distant past formed the attitudes of common people and provided standards for social justice and economic equity" Kaylor, *Jesus the Prophet*, 31; see also 34. Kaylor raises the question as to whether the Jubilee was "observed regularly or not at all" (33–34). De Vaux concludes, "There is no evidence that the law was ever in fact applied" (*Ancient Israel*, I, 175). Yet,

The evidence suggests, however, that charging interest for loans *was* prohibited, slaves *were* released after seven years, and loans *were* forgiven after the same period.[98] The laws were therefore not merely an abstraction: They expressed a sense of unity in those ancient villages and an ideal of mutuality and gave the Jews "a code of conduct and handbook of instructions by which they could survive on the land . . . and perhaps even prosper."[99] Thus, although memories of the system supported by those laws must have faded gradually during the years of oppression, they seem to have remained strong enough to remind their possessors that village life had been better than it became under Roman domination. In fact, it could be said that the Jews of the first century had "a utopian ideal over against which later subjection to kings and foreign empires was measured and found contrary to the will of God."[100]

The goal of these laws was to prevent the very thing that happened in Palestine, increasingly, under successive occupations. The Romans and their predecessors brought with them a different conception of land ownership than the Jews themselves traditionally embraced. With the idea that the land could produce a surplus and thereby turn a profit, it became desirable to own more land and pay lower wages. The people who capitalized on this situation were not those who had a hard time dealing with both higher taxes and the usual uncertainties that plague subsistence farmers, but the already large landowners who could afford to buy them out. The small farmers, in turn, sometimes borrowed to get through bad times, faced mounting debt, and suffered the consequences: always, anxiety and deprivation; often, foreclosure. Thus, although "Roman rule brought prosperity to Palestine," not everyone benefitted from the change: "The countryside did not share equally with towns and cities, and, except for Jerusalem, Judea did not fare well."[101]

---

though it "was never realized," de Vaux, like Kaylor, considers it to have "set out an ideal of justice and social equality" (176).

98. Herzog says, "[T]here is evidence that some of the sabbatical traditions were observed [among Jews] in Jesus' day, such as letting fields lie fallow during the seventh year, [but] others were not." One example of the latter, according to Herzog, was the forgiveness of debts in the seventh year, which the monied interests rendered irrelevant by refusing to lend money in the year or two before the sabbatical year (*Jesus, Justice*, 107).

99. Horsley and Silberman, *Message*, 13, 27. Signs of this community spirit can be seen in the Gospel of Luke, when a large and presumably sympathetic crowd mourned with a widow at the funeral of her only son, whom Jesus later brought back to life (7:11–12); when Jesus referred to the man who willingly awakened at midnight to lend his friend three loaves in order to feed the friend's visitor (11:5–8); and when, in the Parable of the Lost Sheep, the shepherd who found his lost sheep and the woman who found her lost coin called their friends together in order to celebrate their good fortune (15:6, 9). The point is made by Freyne (in *Galilee, Jesus*, 94), who says that "the dominant pattern of social relationship that is featured [in these scenes] is that of a village society in which people have close ties of kinship with each other, sharing goods as well as familial joys and sorrows."

100. Horsley, *Bandits, Prophets & Messiahs*, 6.

101. Kaylor, *Jesus the Prophet*, 27. Kaylor adds, "Increasing trade and commerce led to an increasingly cosmopolitan society that more and more adopted Hellenistic ways" (67).

Even as early as the fifth century BC, in the time of Nehemiah, Jews complained about being exploited—not in this case, however, by foreigners, but by wealthy Jews, suggesting that the ongoing division was not between gentiles and Jews, but between rich and poor: "We are mortgaging our fields and our houses to get grain because of the famine," said the people. "We have borrowed money for the king's tax [a tribute to Persia] upon our fields and vineyards . . . "[W]e are forcing our sons and daughters to be slaves . . . , but it is not in our power to help it, for other men have our fields and our vineyards" (Neh. 5:3–5). Nehemiah introduced reforms, which included lending money without interest, restoring mortgaged property to its original owners, and even returning the one percent per month interest that these small farmers had paid (Neh. 5:10–12).

Not more than three centuries later, the situation that Nehemiah tried to correct reappeared, but there was no powerful Jewish leader like him to restore the status quo ante.[102] Under the rule of Rome, the problem worsened because wealthy Romans and Herodians needed some outlet for their surplus cash. They could save it in the Temple treasury, spend it on luxury goods, or invest it in land or money lending.[103] Influenced by the profit motive, those who chose land acquisition treated the arable land as an investment rather than an inheritance and emphasized the benefits of ownership rather than the responsibilities of stewardship. Land was seen as a commodity instead of a blessing. Says one scholar, "Acquisitiveness and envy . . . arise persistently in a limited-goods society, a zero-sum game in which if you win, I lose, and that is the way economic historians would characterize the the typical perceptions of people in the Roman Empire."[104]

Of course, the consequences were dire. What this transformation of values meant "was a complete dislocation of peasant life, family support, and village security." In many cases, "[i]t meant a move from subsistence on a small family farm to the life of tenant farmer, landless laborer, beggar, or bandit."[105] Competition replaced cooperation, and the longstanding ideal of mutual aid that characterized traditional village life

---

102. "Indeed," say Horsley and Silberman, "the evidence drawn from rabbinic literature and from legal documents of the period suggests that rural indebtedness dramatically increased during the Herodian period, with desperate farmers seeking loans from the Herodian administration and the priestly aristocracy. Yet this stop-gap measure soon had catastrophic consequences" (*Message*, 29). "In such a limited goods economy," Freyne comments, "in which debts were incurred to meet the pressing needs of land-owner or other tax-collector there was always the danger of exploitation and brigandage" (*Galilee, Jesus*, 95).

103. Horsley, *Bandits, Prophets & Messiahs*, 61.

104. Meeks, *Origins of Christian Morality*, 127.

105. Herzog, *Jesus, Justice,* 105–106. Herzog says that farm families also moved to villages for protection against marauding armies. Another important factor was the monetization of the economy: "As contracts are written in terms of monetary values and not as a portion or percentage of the crop, the social relationship between producer [peasant] and consumer [landlord or aristocrat] is further strained." In other words, the social mobility of peasants was all downward.

gave way to commercialization and exploitation.[106] To put it simply, "More and more people had to earn their living from less and less land . . . Hence one can indeed speak of a regular process of pauperization."[107] Furthermore, extended families living on their own land gave way to nuclear families living in villages, which became, with the loss of tribal and clan organizations, the only viable social unit remaining. Surviving sons, without the prospect of inheriting family farms, submitted to the lure of labor for wages in the cities. As urban workers, they became, in effect, social and economic detritus.

One of the major causes of land loss was taxation. Most taxes were collected by private entrepreneurs who bid for tax leases annually and profited by being forceful and persistent in their collections. The Seleucids introduced this system to make the process more palatable to native populations by having their own people, rather than the occupying government, take their money. One result of this, of course, was to make ordinary people hate the indigenous aristocracy, to which many tax collectors belonged, even more. Although it is difficult to determine exactly how much people paid in taxes in the time of Jesus, estimates run as high as forty percent.[108] After all, residents of Palestine paid taxes to Rome in the form of a tribute; farmers gave the Temple tithes for the priests and tithes for the poor, as well as the half-shekel Temple

106. Crossan, *Birth of Christianity*, 176, 209, 330. According to de Vaux, all of these changes "hastened the break-up of family properties in favour of rich landlords . . . These *latifundia* (large estates) were worked by slaves (2 S 9:10), or by paid workmen." Tenant farming "was apparently never practiced in Israel in early days" (*Ancient Israel*, I, 167). For biblical references to this phenomenon, see 76.

107. Stegemann and Stegemann, *Jesus Movement*, 112. "[S]ince the Ptolemaic and Seleucid hegemonies, the free small farmers and their families—that is, the largest part of Jewish society—had been confronted with a permanent deterioration of their circumstances, including the radical loss of their land and thus their independence, and with an increase in slavery and poverty." The situation improved under the Hasmoneans, "but it clearly deteriorated again under the Roman and Herodian hegemony" (126–27). On this subject, see also Schalit, "Palestine under the Seleucids and Romans," 65–66. According to Schalit, "The antagonism grew more acute; for the rich Judaean Jews and the foreign paramount power alike oppressed the lower classes in Judaea both economically and in the field of law"—i.e., through "exploitation," forced labor, and "perverting justice in favour of the wealthy and powerful" (66). Thus, says Borg, the traditional Jewish "understanding of land and debt stood in sharp contrast to what was happening in the time of Jesus. Under the imperial domination system, the growth of large estates and the commercialization of agriculture meant that that an increasing number of peasants were losing their land, the basis of life" (*Jesus*, 100).

108. Herzog sums up the assessment by saying, "When one adds Roman and Herodian tribute and tax collection on top of the temple's demand, peasants living at a subsistence level would be expected to yield between 28 percent and 40 percent (to take Sanders's low estimate and Horsley's high estimate) of their subsistence stores" (*Jesus, Justice,* 122). Grant suggests that the tax rate may have reached twenty-five percent. However, he emphasizes, even at this rate the burden was great on the poor because the tax was not progressive: "Taxes on sales and produce, along with customs and poll taxes, fell evenly, and thus inequitably, on rich and poor alike." Furthermore, Palestine "was characterized by extreme inequality" (*Historical Introduction*, 278). Herzog agrees (*Jesus, Justice,* 122–23).

tax; and everyone paid tolls, fees, duties, and levies on a wide variety of products grown, bought, and sold (including salt and imports and exports).[109]

The result, in the eyes of some historians, was disastrous: "If we presuppose that ["a poor Palestinian peasant"] had to pay taxes for a large family and that his income was close to the minimum existence, the taxes were an unbearable burden."[110] What was particularly problematic for small farmers was the fact that the taxman showed up whether the harvests were good or not. Even in seasons of blight and drought, the taxes had to be paid.[111]

The people of Palestine were not unique in this regard, since taxation had become the standard way throughout the ancient world of supporting national and local governments as well as religious institutions. According to Luke, "In those days a decree went out from Emperor Augustus that all the world should be taxed" (2:1). Palestine was somewhat unusual for two reasons. First, some political leaders proved to be uncontrollably extravagant. Second, a few of them, partly because of their spending habits, raided the Temple treasury, so that Palestinian Jews could feel doubly taxed. Herod the Great gave away large estates, built Greek-style buildings all over the empire, and created for himself and his large family lavish living quarters. Jerusalem itself "was an example of royal splendor, . . . [and] the newly built Temple exhibited a magnificence scarcely known before."[112] Herod's son Antipas continued to live after the fashion of his father, building extensively, living lavishly, and spending irresponsibly.[113] Looting the Temple treasury occurred periodically from the reign of Antiochus IV in the sec-

109. Horsley discusses the great variety of taxes paid by all residents of the Roman empire in *Bandits, Prophets & Messiahs*, 53–57.

110. Stegemann and Stegemann, *Jesus Movement*, 119. These writers discuss the subject of taxation on 113–25.

111. Horsley and Silberman, *Message*, 28. Horsely refers to famines in the twenties and forties, the latter of which "was almost certainly an important factor contributing to the growing social turmoil of the fifties and sixties" (*Bandits, Prophets & Messiahs*, 61).

112. Jeremias, *Jerusalem*, 87. Jeremias describes Herod's spending in more detail on 124–25. He concludes, "At his death Herod left behind him an impoverished country and a demoralized populace with weakened morality, resigned to misfortune." Horsley explains Herod's tax policies: "The peasants in the village communities of Judea and Galilee . . . constituted the principal economic base from which Herod had to extract more production. He increased demands for royal taxes . . . and increased the efficiency of tax collection. In Galilee, for example, he established fortress towns on hilltop sites such as Sepphoris and stored grain and other goods taken in taxes in the royal fortresses there." Josephus says that "overtaxation" became so burdensome that "Herod had to grant temporary tax relief" (*Covenant Economics*, 84). See also Stegemann and Stegemann, *Jesus Movement*, 132; Yoder, *Politics of Jesus*, 68; and Horsley and Silberman, *Message*, 17. Yoder adds: "The peasant situation in Israel was aggravated by still another plague: the absenteeism of the owners. A hierarchy of intermediate functionaries contracted for the collecting of debts. They extorted from the sharecroppers arbitrary sums which widely exceeded the rent and debt and taxes that were really due" (*Politics of Jesus*, 72).

113. Kaylor says that Antipas built Tiberias and rebuilt Sepphoris as centers of Hellenistic culture and as examples of Roman grandeur {*Jesus the Prophet*, 26–27). On this subject, see also Horsley and Silberman, *Message*, 24–26. "[A]t the time of Jesus," these writers conclude, "a growing bureaucracy closely connected to the court of Antipas played a crucial role in creating a crisis of debt and dispossession that touched and transformed the lives of nearly every peasant family in Galilee" (26).

ond century BC to the time of the Roman prefects and procurators, including Pontius Pilate, in the first century AD.

The other important cause of land loss was borrowing. The first problem was that the size and number of farms owned by ordinary people declined over time. When Herod was king, he confiscated peasant-held lands and either farmed them for his own benefit or gave them away to his rich friends. When Rome acquired Herod's lands, they were leased to the people who could afford them. Also, land was frequently appropriated by powerful rulers for special projects, such as building a gymnasium, temple, or fortress. Finally, the unequal distribution of wealth meant that some people had enormous sums of money available for land purchases. Since "the wealthy needed places to invest surplus income profitably," and "Judea offered too few opportunities to invest in enterprises," wealthy urbanites not only bought up properties, but also lent money to needy farmers. Thus, "[t]he rich of Jerusalem had property in the country."[114] And the result was that fewer farmers worked their own land, and more of them became tenant farmers or day laborers.[115]

The second problem was that farmers living on smaller farms were increasingly vulnerable to adverse weather conditions, market fluctuations, and other factors that might even slightly reduce their harvest or affect the prices at which they could sell their produce. Every farmer "needed enough extra grain for seed for the next year's crops, enough feed for a draft animal (if he had one), enough to sell or barter for whatever necessities he could not raise himself, and enough extra to provide for whatever ceremonies might be celebrated to help explain and regulate life."[116] Living on the edge to begin with and faced with uncertainty, farmers sometimes needed "to borrow against future harvests in order to be able to retain enough of their crops and animals to carry them over to the next year." But, short of producing a bumper crop to pay off the loan, meet the demands of the tax collector, pay the Temple tithe, and meet the needs of their families, many borrowers simply fell into worse debt and ultimately lost their land. Too often, getting a loan led, as I said earlier, to a downward spiral that was irreversible.[117]

---

114. Jeremias, *Jerusalem*, 92.

115. Kaylor, *Jesus the Prophet*, 30. Herod, says Kaylor, "increased his holdings through confiscating the lands of his political opponents. Herod and his sons regarded the whole countryside as at their own disposal and removed peasants at will" (29).

116. Horsley, *Bandits, Prophets & Messiahs*, 52. Families often not only had to borrow to survive, but, in particularly hard times, sent family members "to hire themselves out as wage labor to a larger landholder" (58).

117. Horsley and Silberman, *Message*, 28. The writers comment: Borrowing "soon had catastrophic consequences: once a peasant farmer pledged away an even greater proportion of the next harvest, it was unlikely that he could avoid sinking even deeper into debt in the following year. And since the only collateral that peasants could use to obtain loans was the land that had been farmed by their families for generations, their inability to repay mounting debts eventually resulted in foreclosure" Meier summarizes: "Small farmers in particular led a precarious existence, sometimes at subsistence level, subject as they were to the vagaries of weather, market prices, inflation, grasping rulers,

The disparities between rich and poor are evident in the Gospel of Luke, in which one encounters, at one extreme, landowners with servants and stewards (Luke 7:2; 12:36–38). At the other extreme are ordinary workers (day laborers and share-croppers) and slaves (10:2), as well as the thoroughly destitute (including the physically incapacitated), who are non-participants in the new economy (14:13, 21), and among whom, for example, the dishonest steward would be if he were fired: "I am not strong enough to dig, and I am ashamed to beg" (16:3). In between, in the almost non-existent middle class, were small landowners living in one-room houses, who had little prospect of improving their lot and many opportunities, under the circumstances, to lose everything.

In response to this class conflict, Jesus gathered around himself "not only [people] who are literally poor but also those who are in any way marginal by the measure of that culture." Thus, Luke's Jesus welcomed sinners and women, but rejected "those who are wealthy and powerful." Furthermore, according to Luke, even the public response to Jesus—whether favorable or unfavorable—was determined by social class: "The challenge that Jesus poses to the established righteous and wealthy and powerful by his enacted message of God's favor to the poor and the outcast inevitably leads to conflict"—which, it should be added, arose because Jesus was judged according to pre-existing social conditions.[118] It goes without saying, then, that "[t]here is a stark contrast between the affluence of the rich and the penury of the poor," which is why, throughout this Gospel in particular, everyone is enjoined to help the needy (Luke 3:10–14; 6:29–30; 11:8).[119] Left to the rich, however, if the Parable of Lazarus and the Rich Man (Luke 16:19–26) can be read as a reflection of contemporary economic relations, the gap—like the "great chasm" between the opposing characters in Jesus' parable—was unbridgeable.

There was a stark contrast, too, between the cities of Palestine—at least in the neighborhoods in which the tax collectors, money lenders, and landowners lived—and the rural sections of both Judea and Galilee, where ordinary people of, at best,

---

wars, and heavy taxes" (*Marginal Jew*, I, 282). Says de Vaux: "Alienation of family property and the development of lending at interest led to the growth of pauperism and the enslavement of defaulting debtors or their dependents. This destroyed the social equality which had existed at the time of the tribal federation and which still remained as an ideal" (*Ancient Israel*, I, 173).

118. Johnson, *Living Jesus*, 166. Johnson says, "The suffering of Jesus in Luke's Gospel is very much connected to this division that the prophet creates within the people." I would add only that Jesus *found* this conflict as well as created it. Meeks argues that some of the divisions in Paul's churches were also based on social class (*First Urban Christians*, 67–69, 98).

119. Freyne, *Galilee, Jesus*, 95. Luke's treatment of the Galilean social world gives the most detailed account of the realities of any of the gospel writers" (96). Crossan says: "The clear dividing line was, in agricultural terms, between those who possessed land that others worked for them and those who worked their land for themselves" (*Birth of Christianity*, 179). The old world of extended families "passed away, and in its place there arose a society divided into king and subjects, employers and workmen, rich and poor. This transformation was complete, both in Israel and Judah, by the eighth century B.C." (de Vaux, *Ancient Israel*, I, 23).

modest means resided.[120] In some ways, villagers continued to live according to the covenant rules: "Reciprocal relations within the family or with near neighbours arose from common needs and determined the prevailing value system. The Golden Rule . . . applied particularly in that situation. All could expect to be in need, given the limited resources in great things and small (Lk, 11:5), and the fabric of village life was thus established on a network of interdependent relationships."[121]

In other ways, however, this world, Galilee in particular, had no way of protecting itself from the risks and threats of modern economic life, including not only the burden of debt and the uncertainties of dependency, but also primitive living conditions, crowded housing, and invasions by both robbers and foreign armies. "In a word," says one scholar, "life in a Galilean village was never easy and sometimes brutal, constantly under pressure from above, usually from the city-based people that threatened to deprive the less fortunate of the necessities of life, thus reducing them to penury."[122]

The cities, however, at least for the working and non-working poor, were no better off. Buildings were often so badly constructed that they sometimes collapsed. Their inhabitants, most of whom lived in small cubicles in multi-level housing, were more crowded together than residents of the most populous modern cities. Sewage and garbage were improperly disposed of. And the water supply was both inadequate and likely to be contaminated. Given these conditions, says another scholar, "most people in Greco-Roman cities must have lived in filth beyond our imagining," the worst result of which, of course, was disease. Entire cities were depopulated not only by epidemics, but also by fires and earthquakes. "Little wonder," he concludes, "that healing was such a central aspect of both paganism and early Christianity."[123]

Inevitably, the dissatisfaction of the lowest rung of Jewish society turned into hatred, and hatred turned into violence. One need only understand the combination of suffering and wishful thinking that dominated the lives of peasants and laborers

120. Kaylor makes the point that the conflict was also rural vs. urban: "It is no wonder that peasants identified the ruling group in the towns and cities as the main oppressors, and that the 'powerful revolutionary movement in 66 . . . was very largely the reaction of rural Judaism to social injustice.' The ruling groups were allied with the Romans, but it was the Jewish elite more than the Romans with whom the peasants had their dealings" (*Jesus the Prophet*, 30). (Kaylor's quotation is from S. Applebaum, "Economic Life in Palestine," 2:664.)

121. Freyne, *Galilee, Jesus*, 154–55.

122. *Galilee, Jesus*, 153, 155. Freyne adds later: "Poverty then was a basic fact of life. As far as the gospels are concerned it is in Jerusalem that we meet the clearest examples of the urban poor—the widow's mite in the temple treasury (Mark 12:41–44; the blind, like Bar-Timaeus, begging at Jericho or in Jerusalem itself (John 9:1; Mark 10:46; Acts 3:1–2), or those poor on whom the cost of a jar of ointment could well have been spent (Mark 14:3–9) . . . Yet poverty undoubtedly existed in the rural areas also" (160), which Freyne describes at length a few pages earlier.

123. Stark, *Rise of Christianity*, 149–62. Stark adds: "The Greco-Roman city was a pesthole of infectious disease—because it was always thus in cities . . . The majority of those living in Greco-Roman cities must have suffered from chronic health conditions that caused them pain and some degree of disability, and of which many would soon die" (155). Stark's statistics on Antioch's record of disaster are particularly stunning.

to understand the change: "Whatever was the opinion of the politicians and priests ["who cultivated Roman friendship and the Roman way of life"], neither the Pharisees nor the ordinary people felt anything but hatred for the Roman rule" and, more precisely, for both "heathen Rome and its Jewish collaborators."[124] Quite simply, every aspect of the lives of ordinary Jews living in Palestine in the first century AD was affected by acts of oppression, exploitation, and contempt on the part of the ruling class, which first resulted in "tension and unrest," and then exploded in frequent attempts to resist the enemy, all of which culminated in the Revolt of AD 66.

In the midst of this anger and enmity, Jesus began and ended his mission, and the Church was born. He delivered his message at a time of extreme discontent, engendered by social disintegration, religious conflict, and cultural warfare.[125] Herod's rule, "harsh and unpopular, . . . [had] set the stage for a bit of unrest around the time of Jesus."[126] Indeed, from Herod's death, at around the time of Jesus' birth, "until the first revolt, there were constant signs of lower-class resistance to Roman imperial power in the Jewish homeland."[127] The puritans at Qumran prepared for the final cosmic battle. John the Baptist and insurrectionists like Barabbas were arrested and executed. Rebel factions had begun their progress toward full-blown revolution, which would fail in the face of both overwhelming Roman power and the inability of protest leaders to find common ground. In short, in Jesus' time, "Judea was a veritable volcano waiting to erupt."[128] Galilee, too, swept up in the conflicts between rich and poor, city dwellers and farmers, collaborators with and resisters against all things Roman, provided fertile ground for revolutionary action.[129]

124. Parkes, *Conflict*, 22; and Brandon, *Trial of Jesus*, 30.

125. On this point, see Brandon, *Trial of Jesus,* 41; and Klingaman, *First Century*, 168.

126. Mack, *Lost Gospel*, 60.

127. Crossan, *Birth of Christianity*, 210. According to Herzog: "[T]he popular prophets seemed to have tapped into a deep well of discontent . . . They were acting to increase the possibility of their survival, a factor made increasingly difficult by the multiple layers of ruling classes (Roman, Herodian, and priestly) with which they had to contend. Their movements were symbolic appeals to the God who dwelt beyond the present time horizon of their lives to ensure their survival" (*Jesus, Justice,* 57–58). Danielou says that Jesus must be understood in the context of the rebel movements of his day: "The conflict between official Judaism and the reformist Jewish movements is the framework within which the trial and death of Jesus must be envisaged" ("Christianity as a Jewish Sect," 275). At the beginning, Danielou explains, Jesus' followers "were no more than a minority group, on a par with the other Jewish dissenting sects," from which they eventually had to distinguish themselves (275).

128. Zeitlin, *Who Crucified Jesus?* 39, 53, 59–60. Zeitlin discusses the tension in Judea on 53–59. Horsley and Silberman comment: "Through the first century, in fact, there were apparently so many popular demonstrations and riots that it is almost impossible to say with absolute certainty how the authorities may have reacted in a particular case" (*Message*, 80). Markus simply calls ancient Palestine "a perpetually troubled region" (*Christianity*, 8). Klingaman says that, during the lifetime of Jesus, Judea was a "powder keg" (*First Century*, 49). Herzog uses the same words to describe both Judea and Galilee (*Jesus, Justice,* 105). According to Witherington, "Jewish blood began to boil long before it began to be spilled in large quantities" (*What Have They Done?* 209).

129. "[M]any of the Ame Ha-aretz, the farmers, especially those of Galilee, became the rank and file of the various revolutionary sects which stood for such democratic ideals as 'equality of men

Chapter Two

Jesus the Jew

"Jesus was a Jew, not a Christian. This single historical fact opens the door to understanding Jesus as he really was in his own time and place; it's a door that many have never thought to enter. Jesus was circumcised, observed Passover, read the Bible in Hebrew, and kept Saturday as the Sabbath day." (James D. Tabor)

THIS CHAPTER IS ESPECIALLY addressed to those who have never read the New Testament or whose acquaintance with the book is limited to the parts of it they have encountered only in worship services. If this is the basis for their understanding of Jesus, they are working at a severe disadvantage. They are seeing Jesus through other people's eyes, if they are Christians, or failing to see Jesus at all, if they are Jews. To most Christians, Jesus repudiated Judaism, and, to most Jews, Judaism repudiated Jesus. I believe that Jesus would be appalled to find, first, that he has been completely ignored by the people to whom he addressed his mission and, second, that those who took him most seriously failed to understand him in the context of the religion he inherited and the culture that shaped his ideas.

My goal is to introduce both groups to a Jesus who was born a Jew and died one, engaged in Jewish practices all of his life, preached only to Jews, espoused a Jewish ethic that he derived mainly from the Jewish Bible, inspired the devotion of only Jewish disciples (at least during his lifetime), and left his followers with the commandment to love both God and mankind, a message that had been an important part of ethical Judaism since well before the time of Socrates, Lao-Tsu, and Buddha—specifically, since the sixth, seventh, and eighth centuries BC, when the Hebrew prophets established the basic tenets of Western morality. Remarkably, this is the Jesus recognized by most contemporary scholars: "In the present day Quest for the Historical Jesus," says one of

---

before God'" (Zeitlin, *Who Crucified Jesus?* 66–67). Josephus reports that in the Revolt of 66 the Galileans were particularly ferocious in expressing their hatred for what they considered to be the traitors and friends of Agrippa II who lived in Sepphoris and Tiberias. They succeeded in destroying only Sepphoris, however, although "they had the same detestation for" the residents of both cities (quoted in Crossan, *Birth of Christianity*, 231).

them, "the single most repeated assertion of his substance is that Jesus was Jewish."[1] Indeed, says another scholar, "By now, almost everyone recognizes that the historical Jesus was a Jew who followed ancient Jewish ways."[2]

Of course, this is not the Jesus who has come down to us through history. The Church slowly abandoned its ties to Judaism after Paul initiated his mission to the gentiles, in the middle of the first century, and especially after the Jewish revolt against Rome in AD 66. Church membership changed from one hundred percent Jewish to overwhelmingly gentile a century or so after Paul convinced the leaders of the Jerusalem church—Jesus' brother James, Peter, and John the son of Zebedee—to accept converts without requiring them to be circumcised, keep kosher, or obey some of the other laws in the Pentateuch, including those pertaining to the Sabbath and purity. Christians increasingly blamed the Jews for killing their leader, despite the fact that the vast majority of Jews never even heard of him.

Jesus himself gradually became more and more divinized until (and not before) he was affirmed by the Church under the leadership of Theodosius I in 381 to be equal to God in status and identical with God in substance, at the end of a long debate that had gone on since 313, when Constantine declared, in the Edict of Milan, that Christians would no longer be persecuted, that they were free to worship as they

---

1. Akenson, *Saint Saul*, 3 (see also 185, 190). In the "old" view, says Paula Fredriksen, Jesus rejected Judaism and warned his disciples against it ("The Birth of Christianity and the Origins of Christian Anti-Judaism," 9). As I said, however, the idea that Jesus was a lifelong Jew is a commonplace among contemporary scholars. According to Meier, "Jesus was a Jew living in a Jewish Palestine . . . controlled by Romans." Furthermore, he remained "very much a Palestinian Jew himself" (*Marginal Jew*, I, 8; see also 345). "Whatever else he was," says Ehrman, "Jesus was thoroughly Jewish, in every way" (*Misquoting Jesus*, 187). "On the one hand," say Conzelmann and Lindemann, "the Christian church has fully claimed Jesus. On the other hand, he is a Jew in his life and teaching and there are no historically anchored indications that he essentially departed from the premise of Judaism" (*Interpreting the New Testament*, 334). In the words of Sanders, "Jesus lived, on the whole, as a good Jew" (*Historical Figure of Jesus*, 223; and, by the same author, *Jesus and Judaism*, 19). Brown comments, "[F]rom one end of his life to another," according to Luke, "Jesus has lived his life within the confines of Judaism" (*Introduction*, 260). See also Kaylor, *Jesus the Prophet*, 211; Chilton and Neusner, *Judaism*, xiv, xvii; Tabor, *Jesus Dynasty*, 109, 266; Enslin, *Christian Beginnings*, 154; Peters, *Harvest of Hellenism*, 481; Fredriksen, *Jesus of Nazareth*, 203; Crossan, *Birth of Christianity*, xxxiii, 144, 334; Segundo, *Historical Jesus of the Synoptics*, 63; and Placher, *History of Christian Theology*, 18. For a thorough analysis of the debate over Jesus' connection to Judaism, see Sanders, *Jesus and Judaism*, 1–58.

2. Boyarin, *Jewish Gospels*, 22. As long ago as 1888, Hatch stated that the religion preached by Jesus "was rooted in Judaism . . . It took the Jewish conception of a Father in heaven, and gave it a new meaning. It took existing [Jewish] moral precepts, and gave them a new application. The meaning and the application had already been anticipated in some degree by the Jewish prophets" (*Influence of Greek Ideas*, 4–5). Of course, the idea that Jesus' ideas were new—that is, not *entirely* anticipated by the prophets—has become less evident over the past century or so. Even Hatch suggests that some Jews were ready to accept Jesus' innovations presumably because their Judaism had evolved in the same way that his had: "There were Jewish minds which had been ripening for them [i.e., these ideas]; and so far as they were ripe for them, they received them" (5).

pleased, and that they would be indemnified for their losses as victims of Roman persecution.[3]

With the Jerusalem church marginalized after the Revolt of 66 (and possibly no longer in Jerusalem), many of the Christian Jews who survived, including the Ebionites, still maintained that Jesus had been a prophet, but not divine. In the fourth century, however, Christian Judaism was called heretical, as it had been by some Church leaders as early as the second century. And the now-powerful offspring of Judaism—the Catholic Church—with its unquestioned dominance of the West, began a millennium-and-a-half-long career of isolating, condemning, subordinating, and periodically massacring the brothers and sisters of its Savior, Jesus. Charged with deicide, deprived of a country, and representing a faith that, from the point of view of most Christians, had been superseded by their own, Jews also wrote off Christian Judaism as a heresy and closed the book on Jesus forever. Again, my purpose is to acquaint Jews and Christians with an earlier Jesus, before he was declared to be not only the Son of God, but also, along with the Holy Spirit, God's equal, and before the idea of Jesus and his mission was reshaped by followers who understood him, by necessity, from a gentile and Hellenistic rather than a Jewish and Palestinian perspective.

JESUS AND JUDAISM

The picture of Jesus which most people are familiar with today was also influenced by what many scholars now recognize as a failure among earlier students of the New Testament to acknowledge Jesus' Jewish heritage. They saw Jesus as an enemy of Judaism, who repudiated its basic principles, and they uncritically accepted the Gospel accounts of the increasing enmity between Jesus and the Jews.[4] In the twentieth century, Jesus was first seen as an Aryan (i.e., as a non-Jew) as early as 1910, and the theory

---

3. The equality of Jesus and God was first accepted as official church doctrine in the Nicene Creed in AD 325. Its permanent status was interrupted by a number of Church councils over the next few decades, during which the Arian-Athanasian controversy remained unsettled. For a lengthy discussion of this controversy, see Rubenstein, *When Jesus Became God*, passim.

4. This point is made, for example, in Sanders, *Jesus and Judaism*, 18, 27–30, 34. According to Chilton, "Jesus' biography continues to be shrouded in mystery because the huge body of New Testament scholarship has been largely deaf to Judaism." Nevertheless, Chilton claims, Jesus' basic Jewishness "is now fairly well established within scholarship and popular writing" (*Rabbi Jesus*, xxi, xix). Too many studies, Meier says, have produced an "un-Jewish Jesus" (*Marginal Jew*, I, 10). Yet even Meier at least once indulges in the circular argument that Jesus must have departed from Judaism because he was punished for his beliefs: "He did not wind up crucified for being so agreeable" (335–36). The scholarly consensus today is that Jesus was arrested for sedition, not blasphemy. On the subject of the Jewishness of Galilee (and therefore the impossibility that Jesus was anything but Jewish), see Freyne, *Galilee, Jesus*, 54, 146, 167. Freyne says that although Emil Schurer, the nineteenth-century historian of ancient Judaism, regards the Judaism of Galilee as not more than a century old at the time of Jesus, the claim is untrue (169). Schurer's assumption of a reluctantly or superficially Jewish Galilee, Freyne adds, laid the groundwork for Grundmann's book, *Jesus der Galilaer und das Judentum*, in which the Nazi says that Jesus was Galilean, but not Jewish (2).

was later "occasionally accepted not only in the Germany of the Third Reich but also elsewhere."[5] The Nazi-influenced view of Jesus as a non-Jew was articulated by Walter Grundmann, a New Testament scholar at the University of Jena, who "worked in the Institute for the Study and Eradication of Jewish Influence on German Religious Life," whose literature "proclaimed an Aryan Jesus fully divorced from Judaism not only in terms of practice and ideology but also by ethnicity."[6]

The point is not that everyone who denies Jesus' Jewishness is a Nazi, but that the effort to separate Jesus from his racial and religious heritage, which has been particularly strong in German criticism, has degenerated into this kind of misrepresentation.[7] Furthermore, even without the influence of such blatant racism, the Church itself has somehow managed to bring about the same result: "Two thousand years of relatively hostile separation and alienation between Judaism and Christianity has tended to obscure the fact that Jesus grew up in a religious and cultural world that has been almost wholly lost to the subsequent developments of Christianity."[8] The myth of separation and alienation has also been perpetuated by professional historians and students of the Bible: "Throughout the ages, Christian scholarship and piety stripped Jesus of his Jewish soul."[9]

Regardless of the source of this denial, its result is that many people—both Christians and Jews—think of Jesus as a Christian (or at least a gentile) from the time he was born until the time he died. They are surprised to find out that his parents, like the parents of John the Baptist, were not only Jews, but observant ones. (John's father, Zechariah, was a Jewish priest.) After Jesus' birth, Joseph and Mary strictly followed the Mosaic Law by having Jesus circumcised on the eighth day; presenting the baby to God in the Temple as a first-born male forty days later; and, "for their purification

---

5. Bornkamm, *Jesus of Nazareth*, 199 n. 2.

6. Levine, "Introduction," 8–9. Manschreck suggests that the concept of Jesus as Aryan originated with Alfred Rosenberg, Hitler's theologian (*History of Christianity*, 3). Carroll traces the idea to the nineteenth-century philosopher Johann Fichte (*Constantine's Sword*, 72).

7. Parkes says that ancient Judaism has been misinterpreted by scholars "largely in Germany" and motivated by "the desire to prove that antisemitism was something which inevitably accompanied the Jew wherever he went, and which was due to his own racial and unalterable characteristics" (*Conflict*, 1–2).

8. Tabor, *Jesus Dynasty*, 109. As Parkes puts it: "It is not Christian doctrine which has been the main external influence in the Jewish life of the last fifteen hundred years, but the Christian Church . . . For throughout all those centuries a large portion of the Jewish people have lived under the domination of a Christian majority" (*Conflict*, 33). Lieu agrees: "[T]he constructed 'identity' of Judaism, which has continued to form part of the 'knowledge' of many in both church and academy, is at best a distorted reflection of the reality of both past and present" (*Image and Reality*, 1).

9. Maguire, *Moral Core*, 106. Maguire quotes Frederick C. Grant (in *Ancient Judaism and the New Testament*, 109), whom he identifies as "a Christian scholar," as saying in 1959, "The thorough Jewishness of Jesus is assumed by all present-day scholars competent to judge" (106). Herzog discusses specific examples of this scholarship in *Jesus, Justice*, 13–18, 39–42. Yoder says that even if the scholarship has not been "intentionally anti-Semitic," it has been "sweepingly asemitic," by which he means negligently indifferent to "the Jewish Jesus" (*Politics of Jesus*, 114).

according to the law of Moses," offering a sacrifice of two turtledoves or pigeons at the Temple (Luke 2:21–24). The Jewish laws that Joseph and Mary obeyed can be found in Leviticus 12:2–8 and Exodus 13:2, 12.[10]

In the Temple, Simeon—"righteous and devout" (that is, another pious Jew), waiting "for the consolation of Israel" (that is, the salvation of the Jews) and moved by the Holy Spirit (that is, the same spirit that moved such Jewish heroes as Moses, Elijah, and David)—lifted up the baby and predicted that he would be "the glory of [his] people" (that is, the Jews) and save "many in Israel" (Luke 2:25–34). This announcement occurred, Luke notes, "when the parents brought in the child Jesus, to do for him what was customary under the law" (Luke 2:27)—that is, the *Jewish* law—and immediately before the prophetess Anna, who worshiped in the Jewish Temple with "fasting and prayer night and day," thanked God for satisfying "all who were looking for the redemption of Jerusalem" (Luke 2:37–38).[11]

Indeed, Joseph and Mary "finished everything required by the law of the Lord" (Luke 2:39). Luke adds that they went to Jerusalem every year at Passover, as did many Jews in Palestine, and probably came to the Holy City annually for the other two feasts, Pentecost and Tabernacles (Luke 2:41). Jesus' brothers also went to Jerusalem for Passover, according to John (7:10). Joseph and Mary named their sons after Jewish heroes—Joshua (Jesus), Jacob (James), Judah (Judas), and Simon, the last two being the names of Maccabean warriors as well as the patriarch Jacob's sons (Mark 6:3). Furthermore, Jesus' ability to read Hebrew and his habit of teaching and reading in synagogues (Mark 6:2 and Luke 4:16) had to have been the result of his parents' training or, since they probably spoke Aramaic but not Hebrew, training they encouraged him to receive at the synagogue in Nazareth. It is conceivable, as well, that Jesus' visit to the Temple at the age of twelve was on the occasion of his Bar Mitzvah (Luke 2:42).[12]

10. Placher, *History of Christian Theology*, 18; and Vermes, *Changing Faces of Jesus*, 229. "Since [Mary's] means were inadequate for the purchase of a lamb, she bought two sacrificial birds, as the law allowed . . . The visit of the family to Jerusalem took place so that Jesus could be presented to in the temple, in accordance with Exodus 13.2, 'Sanctify unto me all the first-born'" (Grant, *Historical Introduction*, 308). Flusser states that Numbers 18:15 allowed parents to redeem their first-born "through an offering to a priest anywhere." However, "there were devout people who took this opportunity to make a pilgrimage with their son to the Temple in Jerusalem" (*Sage from Galilee*, 10–11).

11. Flusser notes that the phrase "redemption of Zion" was "imprinted on the coins of the First Revolt against Rome" (*Sage from Galilee*, 127). He adds that Luke's emphasis on Jesus' ties to Israel and Judaism are absent in Mark (128, 131).

12. On these two points, see Enslin, *Christian Beginnings*, 155; and Shanks and Witherington, *Brother of Jesus*, 100–101. Meier discusses Jesus' knowledge of Hebrew in *Marginal Jew*, I, 262–64, 267, 272–76. Regarding Jesus' religious training, see 276–78. Flusser argues: "When Jesus' sayings are examined against the background of contemporaneous Jewish learning . . . , it is easy to observe that Jesus was far from uneducated. He was perfectly at home both in holy scripture and in oral tradition, and he knew how to apply this scholarly heritage. Jesus' Jewish education was incomparably superior to that of St. Paul" (*Sage from Galilee*, 12). Flusser adds later, "I belong to those scholars who believe that Jesus' teaching was in Hebrew and that the Semitic language behind the first three Gospels was Hebrew"—that is, as opposed to Aramaic (111). On the traditional Jewish names of Jesus' brothers, Latourette says, "[W]e gather that the family cherished the Maccabean tradition and were loyal to the

What is most remarkable about these passages and others in the first few chapters of Luke's Gospel is not merely that they demonstrate unequivocally that both Jesus and John the Baptist were born Jews and that all the other people mentioned in them except Herod (including Elijah and David) were Jews. What is even more amazing is that, without the assumption that Jesus *was* Jewish, which is nowhere stated anywhere in Luke's Gospel, the significance of these passages would have been completely lost. After all, no one but a Jew would have understood such words and phrases as *the law of the Lord, the Holy Spirit, Christ, gentiles, salvation, redemption*, and even *Israel* (which did not exist as an actual place after the sixth century BC). In the early centuries, reading these words for the first time, without religious instruction, thousands of non-Jews must have been mystified.[13] Even today, most Christians would be unable to grasp the full meaning of these terms without some familiarity with their Jewish origin and history.

As for Jesus himself, Luke says it was his custom to attend the synagogue in Nazareth every Sabbath (Luke 4:16), and he preached in the synagogues of Judea (Luke 4:44). Mark says he preached in the synagogues of Galilee (Mark 1:39), and Matthew, after repeating this passage (Matt 4:23), adds that "Jesus went about all the cities and villages, teaching in their synagogues" (Matt 9:35; see also 12:9 and 13:54)—which were, of course, *his* synagogues. Luke adds that Jesus preached in the Temple daily during his final days in Jerusalem (Luke 19:47). And, in Matthew, Jesus paid the half-shekel Temple tax required of every Jew, according to Exodus 30:13 and 38:26 (Matt 17:24–27). In the Gospel of John, Jesus said to Annas, when he was confronted at his trial by the father-in-law of the High Priest, "I have always taught in synagogues and in the temple, where all Jews come together" (John 18:20).

Appropriately, Jesus was addressed by Jews as rabbi (or master) on numerous occasions (e.g., Mark 9:5; 10:51; 11:21; and 14:45). And, like other rabbis, he gathered pupils, made up proverbs, and spoke in parables. Even the content of his pronouncements was essentially rabbinical, a subject I will examine in more detail later. In short, he "lived as a Jewish rabbi."[14] For now, it will suffice to note that when Jesus offered

Jewish faith" (*History of Christianity*, I, 35). Tabor makes the same point in *Jesus Dynasty*, 104.

13. On this subject, see Meeks, *First Urban Christians*: "To a significant extent the Christians inherited their jargon from Judaism. A great many of the unusual words and phrases in the early Christian documents are translation Greek [i.e., from the original Aramaic or Hebrew], either taken directly from the Septuagint [the Greek translation of the Hebrew Bible] or influenced by its idiom. The liturgy of the Greek-speaking synagogues also contributed patterns and style" (94). Meeks particularly mentions Aramaic words like *abba* and *marana tha,* but also the Hebrew *mashiah*, which meant *ointment* in its Greek translation, *christ* (94). The point also applies to words like *saints, elect*, and *calling*, and concepts like God's love, redemption, revelation, and baptism, which were also derived from Judaism (85, 92–93, 150–57). Richardson says, "[T]he conception of the Messiah is Hebrew and requires for its understanding a sound knowledge of the Hebrew Scriptures" (*Gospel*, 48).

14. Bultmann, *Jesus and the Word*, 58–60. Pelikan says that "it was as a rabbi that Jesus was known and addressed by his immediate followers" (*Jesus Through the Centuries*, 11). Pelikan also discusses Jesus' rabbinical style (including his question-and-answer technique and his use of parables) (12–13). On Jesus' use of Jewish rubrics, analytical methods, and teaching techniques, see Basser, "Gospel and

what has come to be known as his Golden Rule ("So whatever you wish that men would do to you, do so to them" [Matt 7:12]) he added that the saying was "the law and the prophets"—that is, a Jewish idea. Any Jew would have recognized the words *law* and *prophets* as references to two of the three sections of the Jewish Bible: the laws of Moses (i.e., the Torah) and the writings of the prophets. Jesus might have known that the Rule had been expressed by Rabbi Hillel decades earlier. Even if he did not, however, he knew that it was part of Jewish tradition.[15]

Preaching in synagogues and speaking the language of rabbis, Jesus inevitably preached almost exclusively to Jews, but even those who were not ethnic Jews were in the vast majority of cases proselytes (gentiles who were full converts) or God-fearers (gentiles who were drawn to Judaism, attended synagogue services, and followed Jewish ethical prescriptions, but did not follow the more ritualistic rules of the faith).[16] Matthew's Jesus, in particular, was committed to speaking only to Jews: "I was sent only to the lost sheep of the house of Israel" (Matt 15:24). "Go nowhere among the Gentiles," he says to his disciples; "and enter no town of the Samaritans, but go rather to the lost sheep of Israel" (Matt 10:5–6). In Luke, when he sent his followers to Samaria to prepare the way for him, "the people would not receive him" (Luke 9:51–52).[17] In

---

Talmud," 286–93.

15. Levine, *Misunderstood Jew*, 22–23; and Klingaman, *First Century*, 171. On Jesus' preaching in synagogues, learned disputations on Jewish subjects, and immersion in "the outlook and language of the sacred texts of Israel," see Meier, *Marginal Jew*, I, 276. Flusser traces the Golden Rule to the Essenes, who said, "I will repay no one with evil; I will visit men with good, for God judges all things that live and he will repay" (*Sage from Galilee*, 71; see also 82). Sterling quotes a passage from Philo's *Hypothetica* to show another Jewish expression of the Golden Rule: "What someone hates to experience, he should not do" ("Philo of Alexandria," 305). Sterling comments: "The saying is widely attested in the ancient world (Dihle); Philo and the Gospel accounts simply are illustrations of the ethical principle. It would be a mistake to make too much of the fact that the version in Matthew is positive in its formulation while the version in Philo is negative, since early Christians also knew the negative form, for example, in the Western text of Acts 15:20, 29, and *The Didache* 1.2. The value of the Philonic material is, once again, to illustrate the presence of the saying in Judaism" (300). The negative form ("And whatever you do not want to happen to you, do not do to another" [in Ehrman., *Lost Scriptures*, 212]) also appears in *Ecclesiasticus* 7:1, 27:27; and *Tobit* 4:15. Moore comments: "It is often said that the substitution of the positive form of the rule for the negative makes a very different thing of it. That is a point about which it is not worth while to argue. Jewish teaching about the treatment of others, countrymen or aliens, friends or enemies, was not deduced from an aphorism, but based on the positive general rule in Lev. 19:18 (cf. vss. 33–35) and the many specific injunctions and exhortations, both positive and negative, in which the [Jewish] Scriptures abound in all parts" (*Judaism*, II-III, 87).

16. Boyarin says, "Everybody then—both those who accepted Jesus and those who didn't—was Jewish" (*Jewish Gospels*, 2). "Jesus is rarely shown as interested in saving pagans from damnation or promising them a place in God's coming kingdom," says Lang in "Segregation and Intolerance," 128. Lee adds, Jesus "systematically avoids the Greek cities." The Gospels do not say why, but it is reasonable to assume, Lee continues, "that his own sense of living and teaching as a Jew among and for Jews is a likely reason for Jesus' avoidance of less provincially Jewish places" (*Galilean Jewishness of Jesus*, 67). Lee lists the ways in which Jesus "observes the religious customs of the Jews" (69). See also Klingaman, *First Century*, 170, 173; and Meier, *Marginal Jew*, II, 315, 374–75 n. 98.

17. "Although his fame apparently also aroused curiosity outside Galilee, [Jesus] is not described as a welcome visitor in non-Jewish areas. The inhabitants of Gerasa requested him to leave their country,

Matthew, Jesus' goal is to extend his message to as many of "the towns of Israel" as his disciples can reach before "the Son of man comes" (Matt 10:23).

One scholar argues, in fact, that Jesus' message—with its abundant quotations from the Jewish scriptures; its traditionally Jewish eschatology; and its references to things uniquely Jewish, such as the Temple, the Sabbath, and repentance—was "especially adapted to the Palestine of his day." However, given both its form and content, it was thereby unsuitable for (and therefore, to some extent, as I suggested earlier, incomprehensible to) others. That is, "because of its very nature it was not a gospel for the Mediterranean world. It was the natural outgrowth of the hopes and longings of a distinct and different race." And it would not appeal to a wider audience until it separated from Judaism—both institutionally and theologically—but which it would not do until many years after Jesus' death.[18]

The famous line in the Sermon on the Mount—"Do not give dogs what is holy; and do not throw your pearls before swine"—is usually taken to represent a warning to Jesus' fellow Jews not to pass his messages on to the gentiles, "lest they trample them underfoot and turn to attack you" (Matt 7:6; cf. Matt 15:26).[19] In fact, Jesus did not speak very highly of the gentiles elsewhere in the Gospel of Matthew. When he advised his followers to love their enemies, he said that loving their friends was not enough: "Do not even the tax collectors do the same?" "Do not even the Gentiles do the same?" (Matt 5:46–47). That is, these groups represented an inferior morality; being "perfect" requires much more (5:48). When Jesus told his followers to recite the Lord's Prayer, he condemned not only "the hypocrites" in the synagogues, but also the gentiles, who "heap up empty phrases . . . for they think they will be heard for their many words. Do not be like them" (6:7). And when he assured his followers that it was unnecessary for them to worry about food or clothing, he said—evidently contemptuously—that "the Gentiles seek all these things" (6:31–6:34).

These are examples of the ways in which the gentiles, in Jesus' own words, showed their failure to understand the real meaning of love, prayer, and trust. Nor is this all. When the disciples argued among themselves over who was the greatest, Jesus

and as a Jew travelling to Jerusalem he is represented as a *persona non grata* in Samaria" (Vermes, *Jesus the Jew*, 30).

18. Enslin, *Christian Beginnings*, 182. Among other ideas, Pelikan traces Jesus and his disciples' eschatology to its Jewish sources: "[W]e know that the proclamation of Jesus himself about the kingdom of God, as well as such proclamations of his followers about him, resounded with the accents of Jewish apocalypticism, the fervid expectation that the victory of the God of Israel . . . was now at last to break" (*Jesus Through the Centuries*, 23–24).

19. "It is probable," Hare comments, "that 'dogs' and 'swine' refer to Gentile opponents rather than to Jewish" (*Jewish Persecution of Christians*, 123). Hare notes that W. D. Davies believes that the words refer to "outsiders of any kind" (123 n. 3). "As far as the sources allow us to judge," says Flusser, "Jesus had a poor opinion of the non-Jews, the Gentiles" (*Sage from Galilee*, 50–51). See also Brown, *Introduction*, 83–84. Sanders comments: "All the authors of the gospels favoured the mission to Gentiles, and they would have included all the pro-Gentile material that they could . . . What is striking is that the evangelists had so few passages that pointed towards success in winning Gentiles to faith" (*Historical Figure of Jesus*, 192).

said that since he did not take his socio-political principles from the gentiles, neither should his disciples: "You know that the rulers of the Gentiles lord it over them, and their great men exercise authority over them." That is, they govern through power and require obedience. The real principle of governance, he says, is service to others: "[W]hoever would be great among you must be your servant" (Matt 20:20–28; Mark 10:35–45; Luke 22:24–27).

One might say in defense of the gentiles that Jesus found the Jews inadequate as well. But he preached *only* to them, gathered all of his disciples from among them, and turned away the only gentile who asked to follow him. In Mark, when the exorcised demoniac from "the country of the Gadarenes," an area populated by gentiles, "prayed [Jesus] that he might be with him," Jesus said, "Go home to thy friends" (Mark 5:18–19; Luke 8:38–39). On the other hand, "Jesus never turned down any Jew who wanted to be a follower."[20] In short: "The few Gentiles who do come into contact with Jesus are not objects of Jesus' missionary outreach; they rather come unbidden and humble, realizing they are out of place." That is, "during his public ministry, Jesus does not undertake any formal mission to the Gentiles; the few who come to him do so by way of exception."[21] And, otherwise, his opinion of them was consistently low.

This exclusive appeal to his fellow Jews is contradicted in Mark when Jesus, on at least two occasions—i.e., healing the daughter of a Syrophoenician woman and the servant of a Roman centurion—seems to be initiating a mission to the gentiles. However, even when he cures the daughter of the Syrophoenician, he not only at first demurs; he does so by insulting her as a non-Jew: "Let the children [i.e., of Israel] first be fed, for it is not right to take the children's bread and throw it to the dogs" (Mark 7:26–28).[22] Furthermore, the fact that the Ethiopian eunuch (converted by Philip in Acts 8:27–38) and Cornelius (converted by Peter in Acts 10) are mentioned as the first gentile converts, both evidently God-fearers (that is, gentiles who participated to

20. Lee, *Galilean Jewishness of Jesus*, 68.

21. Meier, *Marginal Jew*, I, 64. Meier adds, Jesus' "Galilean ministry [was] restricted to strongly Jewish towns and villages" (268). Furthermore, there is no evidence that Jesus ever visited any of the Hellenized cities of Galilee, where he would have encountered at least some gentiles (284). "It is significant that from the beginning [Luke] points to the entire Jewish realm, rather than only Galilee, as the sphere of Jesus' ministry ([Luke] 4:44; 7:17). Conversely, any reference to an appearance of Jesus outside this realm is categorically excluded" (Conzelmann and Lindemann, *Interpreting the New Testament*, 234). Gerhard Dautzenberg says (and Gustaf Dalman agrees), "According to the Gospel tradition, he only very seldom, if ever, had any contact with the heathen" (cited in Augstein, *Jesus Son of Man*, 236). Furthermore, although Jesus in Acts 1:8 tells his disciples that they will be his "witnesses . . . to the end of the earth," Brown says that they later "had no awareness of having been informed of such a plan" (*Introduction*, 281 n. 6). See also Grant, *Historical Introduction*, 15; and Kaylor, *Jesus the Prophet*, 185. Thus, Schillebeeckx concludes: "That Jesus restricted himself in his message exclusively to Israel (see also Matt 15:24) is nowadays less and less matter for dispute" (*Jesus*, 296)

22. Brown comments, "The stories of the Syrophoenician woman who asked to have her daughter healed and of the Roman centurion whose faith Jesus praised are of exceptional character and do not really settle the problem" (*Introduction*, 330 n. 112). These episodes, says Bultmann, show that gentiles "were received into the Congregation of salvation . . . only exceptionally and hesitantly" (*Theology*, I, 55).

some degree in Jewish religious practices)[23]—events that presumably took place only slightly before Paul's more aggressive attempt to convert gentiles in the 40s, at least ten years after the Crucifixion—underscores the point even more strongly.[24]

Some passages in the New Testament suggest that Jesus not only limited his mission to Jews, but to Jews whom he identified as *needing* salvation—the implication being that some Jews were not in need of his help. He says in the Gospel of Mark, by way of explaining why he dined with "publicans and sinners," "They that are whole have no need of the physician, but they that are sick; I came not to call the righteous, but sinners to repentance" (2:17; Matt 9:12–13; Luke 5:31–32). The point is that some Jews were evidently not the targets of Jesus' preaching because they were both "whole" and "righteous." In the Parable of the Lost Son, the father of the son who had not squandered his inheritance "with riotous living" (and remained faithful to his father) said to him, "Son, thou art ever with me, and all that I have is thine" (Luke 15:31). This son is similar to the "ninety and nine just persons, *which need no repentance*," whom Jesus refers to in the Parable of the Lost Sheep (15:7; my emphasis). In the Gospel of Matthew, these are the sheep "which went not astray" (18:13).

It might also be inferred that Jesus healed the blind, the lame, and the possessed because they too were sinners. That is, according to first-century beliefs, they were ill because they had sinned. On that assumption, Jesus had no reason to help the "whole" *because* they were "righteous." Thus, when Jesus appointed his twelve disciples, "he gave them power against unclean spirits, to cast them out, and to heal all manner of sickness and all manner of disease." That is, their intended audience was sick people who needed to be healed because they were sinners who needed to be forgiven. They were the kind of Jews whom Jesus healed by saying, "[T]hy sins be forgiven thee" (Matt 9:2; Mark 2:5; Luke 5:20) and to whom he said after healing them, "Behold, thou art made whole: sin no more" (John 5:14).

The disciples' assigned task, after all, was to go "to the lost sheep of the house of Israel" and to "[h]eal the sick, cleanse the lepers, raise the dead, cast out devils." They were not only told to avoid "the way of the Gentiles" and the cities of the Samaritans, but also (at least by implication) *the sheep of the house of Israel who were not lost* (Matt 10:1–8). To the lost sheep, "they preached that men should repent," but, presumably, only the men who *needed* to repent (Mark 6:12). Demanding repentance and offering

---

23. The Ethiopian, who "had come to Jerusalem for to worship," was reading Isaiah in his chariot when Philip met him (Acts 8:27–28), which suggests that he had some connection to Judaism. Despite Deut 23:1, which prohibits eunuchs from being Jews (and is contradicted by Isa 56:4–5). Sanders argues that the Ethiopian was, in fact, a proselyte (*Jews in Luke-Acts*, 152–53, 252–53). Cornelius, though a Roman centurion, is described as "a devout man, and one that feared God with all his house, and which gave alms to the people, and prayed to God always" (Acts 10:1–2).

24. Crossan comments, "Early Christian communities symbolically retrojected their own [missionary] activities back into the life of Jesus" (*Historical Jesus*, 328). According to Brown, the acceptance of non-Jews as Christians "was not detectably an issue solved by Jesus in his lifetime since he showed little interest in Gentiles" (*Introduction*, 330).

forgiveness thus went hand in hand with casting out devils: "And he sent them to preach the kingdom of God, and to heal the sick" (Luke 9:2).

It should be noted that in referring to "lost sheep" Jesus was using a phrase that he very likely found in ancient Jewish texts. In Psalm 119, for example, the writer asks for God's "salvation" and calls himself "a lost sheep" because he has "gone astray" (vv. 173–176). In the writings of the prophets, however, the phrase "the lost sheep" is associated with *all* Jews, meaning that all of "the sheep of Israel" were "lost." In deutero-Isaiah, the prophet says, "All we like sheep have gone astray; we have turned everyone to his own way" (53:6). Ironically, this passage is part of the description of the so-called suffering servant or "man of sorrows," so often associated with Jesus by Christian theologians (53:1–12). Here, as in Jeremiah and Ezekiel, God intends to find and save the lost sheep, who, as Isaiah claims, will be rescued by God's "servant" (52:13).

In Jeremiah God says, "My people hath been lost sheep." Unlike Isaiah's God, however, Jeremiah blames the leaders of the Jews for the apostasy of the sheep: "[T]heir shepherds have caused them to go astray" (50:6). In Ezekiel, God promises that He will "seek out [His] sheep and deliver them out of all places where they have been scattered" (34:12; cf. Jer 50:17). Like Jeremiah, Ezekiel seems to imply that the lost sheep are sinners, but not entirely responsible for their sins and, therefore, not irredeemable. Rather, they were "driven away," perhaps by the sheep that Ezekiel's God calls "fat" and "strong." Regarding the Jews who have gone astray, God says that He "will bind up that which was broken, and will strengthen that which was sick." Indeed, He "will feed them in a good pasture." But the others He will "destroy" and "feed them with judgment" (34:14–16).

Since Jesus spoke almost entirely to Jews and Jewish sympathizers, his movement was recognizably like other Jewish reform movements of the period.[25] And he was like other reform leaders in that he tightened some rules and loosened others. Thus, "Jesus was acting exactly like a Jew of his time when, apparently influenced by John the Baptist, he initiated yet another sectarian movement."[26] Perhaps that is why Jesus was unwelcome in areas of Palestine populated by non-Jews (Mark 5:17; Matt 8:43; Luke 8:37). He was just too Jewish.

In fact, in several instances when Jesus had a chance to distance himself from such Jews and their religion, particularly its rituals, he did not. First, as I noted earlier,

25. Witherington, *Jesus Quest*, 141–43; and Theissen, *Early Palestinian Christianity*, 59–76 and passim.

26. Carroll, *Constantine's Sword*, 78. According to Schillebeeckx, Jews were prepared to accept a "christ" in the sense of "anointed prophet," given the tradition established by Enoch, Moses, Elijah, and Samuel. "To the Jews," Schillebeeckx adds, "they are all known as christus, kyrios, son of God" (*Jesus*, 474). Even after his resurrection, Maccoby says, Jesus was understood to remain committed to re-establishing the Jewish monarchy (the Kingdom of God), as were those other Jewish heroes "who had entered Paradise while alive" and would eventually "return to Earth": Enoch, Eliezer, Methuselah, Hiram of Tyre, Eved-Meleck, Bithia, Serach, the sons of Korah, Elijah, and Rabbi Joshua ben Levi (*Mythmaker*, 125).

after curing a leper, Jesus instructed him to go to the Temple and offer a sacrifice: "[G] o, show yourself to the priest, and offer for your cleansing what Moses commanded" (Mark 1:44; Matt 8:4; Lk 5:14). According to Leviticus, a Jewish priest first had to determine whether the leper was cured: "[T]he priest shall look, and behold, if the plague of leprosy be healed in the leper" (Lev 14:3). The leper then had to undergo a rather elaborate ritual (14:4–32). Although Jesus had both cleansed and cured the leper and therefore obviated the need for a cleansing ceremony, he nevertheless told the leper to offer a "gift" at the Temple as "a proof to the people" and as the passage in Leviticus required (14:4–32).[27] The Gospel text is somewhat ambiguous, but, if nothing else, the leper whom Jesus sent to a priest was clearly, at the very least, expected to make a sacrifice at the Temple: a sin offering, a burnt offering, and a meat offering (14:31). This was, precisely, "what Moses commanded."

Second, Jesus said that, when a person is offering a gift at the altar of the Temple but has unresolved conflicts with a brother or sister, he or she should leave the Temple and "be reconciled" to the offended person first—then return to the Temple and offer the gift (Matt 5:23–24). Finally, Jesus criticized the scribes and Pharisees for claiming that oaths are binding if they are sworn by the gold of the Temple or by the sacrifice, but not if they are sworn by the Temple alone or by the altar on which the sacrifice is placed. Actually, he said, the reverse is true: "For which is greater, the gift or the altar that makes the gift sacred? So he who swears by the altar, swears by it and everything on it; and he who swears by the temple, swears by it and by him who dwells in it" (Matt 23:17–21)—that is, presumably, God.

Surely, if Jesus had been interested in debunking Jewish rites in general, but especially those that involve the purity laws, the Temple sacrifices, or the Temple itself, all of which he is alleged to have disdained, here were several opportunities not to be missed. Yet he passed up all of his chances.[28] In these instances, at any rate, his regard for the Temple as the dwelling-place of God, for the offerings made there, and for the priests who serve the institution seems uncompromising.[29] Indeed, it should be added

---

27. Newsome says that "offerings" (sometimes translated as "gifts") are sacrifices (*Hebrew Prophets*, 28). In other words, when Jesus uses the word *gifts*, he is not referring to donations, but to the kind of activity that some scholars believe he repudiated. For two slightly different views of this incident, see Chilton, *Rabbi Jesus*, 88–89; and Fredriksen, *Jesus of Nazareth*, 203–4. Chilton says that Jesus "told the outbreak-sufferer he did not need to to see the local priest and could proceed directly to the Temple and offer a sacrifice" (89). Fredriksen seems to imply that we cannot determine what portion of the elaborate ritual (i.e., "what Moses commanded") the leper participated in.

28. On this subject, see Sanders, "Jesus, Ancient Judaism, and Modern Christians: The Quest Continues," 39; and Flusser, *Jesus and the Synagogue*, cited in Augstein, *Jesus Son of Man*, 250. Conzelmann and Lindemann identify the Jewish parallel in the Babylonian Talmud for the third example: "Transgressions between a person and his neighbor are not atoned for by the Day of Atonement, unless he appeases his companion" (*Interpreting the New Testament*, 316). Fredriksen discusses the first and third incidents in *Jesus of Nazareth*, 203–5.

29. It is puzzling that Jesus' apparent support for oath-making in Matthew 23 contradicts his repudiation of oaths in Matthew 5:33–37. Yet the Deuteronomist makes a similar point. On one hand, it is sinful to break a vow. On the other hand, however, it is not sinful "to refrain from vowing." The

that every time Jesus went to Jerusalem for the Jewish festivals and entered the Temple to pray or preach, he had to have honored the purity rituals required of all participants in Temple ceremonies—a fact that goes unmentioned in the Gospels.[30]

What else could be expected, however, from a Jew who, at his last meal, established for his followers the tradition of blessing, breaking, and sharing bread and also reciting a prayer of thanksgiving over wine (Grk. *eucharista* and Hebr. *kiddush*; Mark 14:22–23; see also Mark 6:41; 8:6; Luke 24:30), both of which acts derive from ancient Jewish practices that are still in effect today[31]; who wore "fringes" (Hebr. *tzitzit*) on his robe (Matt 9:20; Mark 6:56), that is, tassels used during prayer and required for Jewish men in Numbers 15:37–40,[32] and which, Jesus says, some Jews (pretentiously) wore too long (Matt 23:5)[33]; and who, by his own example, initiated for Jewish Christians the rite of baptism, one of the rituals by which female gentiles could become Jews, known as "proselyte baptism," or *mikvah*.[34]

As described by the evangelist John, even Jesus' burial was a strictly Jewish affair—his body wrapped in linen with a hundred pounds of myrrh and aloe, brought by Nicodemus, "as was the custom of the Jews" (John 19:39–40; Matt 27:59; Luke 23:53). Since he died on "the Jewish day of Preparation" (i.e., the day before the Sabbath), he

writer seems to suggest that a promise is a vow: "You shall be careful to perform what has passed your lips, for you have voluntarily vowed to the Lord your God what you have promised with your mouth" (Deut 23:21–23).

30. Chilton says, "Everyone entering the Temple needed to bathe by immersion" (*Rabbi Jesus*, 27). See also Fredriksen, *Jesus of Nazareth*, 205–6. For a brief overview of opposing views, see 289.

31. Stegemann and Stegemann, *Jesus Movement*, 217. Wilson suggests that Jesus and his disciples sang the Hallel, a Jewish prayer, after the Last Supper (*Jesus*, 199). The Hallel consists of Psalms 113–18. Psalm 112:1 reads, "Blessed is the man who fears the Lord, who greatly delights in his commandments!" Psalm 119 emphasizes, one might say to excess, the need to obey God's "law," "testimonies," "precepts," "statutes," "commandments," "ordinances," and "word"—each term repeated many times throughout this unusually long psalm (176 verses).

32. "As a Jewish male," says Tabor, "Jesus wore the fringed tassels (tzitzit) on his outer garment, which indicates his strict observance of the mitzvoth or commandments of the Torah or Jewish Law" (*Jesus Dynasty*, 116). It is important to remember in this context that the tassels Jesus wore were intended to remind him, as God explained to Moses, of "all the commandments of the Lord, to do them, not to follow after your own heart and your own eyes" (Num 15:37–39). Chilton makes the same point in *Rabbi Jesus*, 179 n. 2. Kloppenborg says that the attempt by some of Jesus' followers "to touch even the fringe of his garment" in order to be "made well" (Mark 6:56) echoes a passage in Zechariah suggesting that anyone pursued in that manner is a Jew and therefore blessed by God: "In those days [God says] ten men from the nations of every tongue shall take hold of the robe of a Jew, saying, 'Let us go with you, for we have heard that God is with you" (Zech 8:23) (*Q*, 37).

33. Levine, *Misunderstood Jew*, 23–24.

34. Kee et al., *Understanding the New Testament*, 99 and n. 16. Baptisms and ritual meals also took place among the Essenes at Qumran. On the Jewish practice of these rituals, see Placher, *History of Christian Theology*, 35; Spong, *Liberating the Gospels*, 75; and Bruce, *New Testament History*, 156. Bultmann notes that for John the Baptist, as for the Essenes, baptism was associated with eschatological expectations (*Jesus and the Word*, 23–24). Horsley and Silberman say that, besides the Essenes and John the Baptist, Josephus' mentor, Bannus, also bathed frequently as an act of both physical and moral purification, based, according to the authors, on Isaiah 1:16–17 (*Message*, 31).

was buried immediately, as most Jews were, in a cave so that his bones could later be placed in an ossuary in preparation for the resurrection of his body—that is, in accordance with Jewish practice (John 19:41–42; Matt 27:60; Mark 15:46; Luke 23:53).[35] Later Christians believed that they would be resurrected as disembodied souls, as the Greeks believed and as Paul seems to suggest when he contrasts the earthly "perishable," "mortal," "physical body" with the resurrected "imperishable," "immortal," "spiritual body" in 1 Corinthians 15:40–54. Other Jews, including the early Christians, for whom "the human person was not divisible into an immortal soul and a mortal body but was a single unified being," would be raised from the dead not as a spirit, but as a whole, though transformed, person.[36]

Still, despite all of these indications that Jesus never stopped being Jewish, it might be argued that he remained a Jew outwardly, but developed a religious view that was, if not anti-Jewish, at least sufficiently different from the Judaism of his day as to suggest that he was actually founding a new religion.[37] However, both the content of his message and the form in which he expressed it were so thoroughly traditional that it is difficult to maintain this position.[38] After all, at the center of Jesus' ethical

35. Shanks and Witherington, *Brother of Jesus*, 67–69. Schillebeeckx says that Jesus' reference to "whitewashed tombs" in Matt 23:27 is, like the phrase "invisible tombs," "intelligible in the light of late Jewish rules for purification." He explains: "Just before the Passover feast polluted graves were whitened with a limewash so that no one would 'unwittingly' continue to walk over them and thus become 'unclean'" (*Jesus*, 691 n. 176).

36. Kloppenborg, Q, 80. Kloppenborg cites Daniel 12:2–3 as a source.

37. Yoder, for example, says of Jesus, "Here we have for the first time to do with a man who is not the slave of any power, of any law of custom, community or institution, value or theory" (*Politics of Jesus*, 148). That is, Jesus was unprecedented in human history. Other scholars, though a distinct minority, make the same claim for Jesus as healer, miracle worker, or moralist. Jesus can be said to be unique (i.e., revolutionary), however, only if Judaism is portrayed as backward. To scholars who know something about ancient Judaism, it is difficult to prove that Jesus was an innovator. In explaining what was different about Christianity, especially compared to Judaism, Meeks says it was morality. Yet Meeks is hard-pressed to say exactly what the difference was: "To be sure, it is curiously difficult to say exactly what was new about Christian morality, or to draw firm boundaries around it. The language of virtue that Christians spoke was adapted from older traditions of moral discourse, rather than being invented from scratch. The daily practice of most church members was doubtless indistinguishable in most respects from that of their unconverted neighbors" (*Origins of Christian Morality*, 2). In fact, when Meeks quotes Aristides' claim that Christianity was superior to all other moralities, including Judaism, it is clear that Aristides' Christianity—that is, as a moral system— was warmed-over Judaism. Aristides says that Christians obey the commandments, follow the Golden Rule, refrain from the sexual habits that were (allegedly) typical of pagans, and generally obey the rules of the Jewish Covenant. That is, they share their resources and take care of widows and orphans (8–9).

38. Wilson says, "The centre of Jesus' teaching was his belief in God, and his belief in Judaism" (*Jesus*, 8). Wilson adds later, "John in the desert, and Jesus after him, did not dream up a new or radically altered Judaism." Their message can be summarized in the words "Be Better Jews"—i.e., follow the Law and the prophets (106). According to Lee: "Most christological interpretation has been 'supersessionist,' that is, it has interpreted Jesus as initiating a new Covenant that supersedes Judaism. Historically, it is quite improbable that Jesus had any such thing in mind" (*Galilean Jewishness of Jesus*, 17; see also 56–57). Schillebeeckx reminds his readers, first, that John the Baptist was a Jew who spoke only to Jews and, second, that John and Jesus shared a common vision and program (*Jesus*,

code is the idea that the Ten Commandments handed down by God to Moses can be reduced to two major precepts: love God and love humanity. Thus, one historian of the Church concludes: "Jesus had about him a freshness and originality which gave [his sayings] such vivid expression and put them in such proportion and perspective that they were seen as both old and new." Nevertheless, "for almost all, and perhaps all of his moral and religious teachings, parallels and precedents can be found in the writings of the Jewish sages."[39]

Anyone who thinks that the idea of two Great Commandments is at odds with the mainstream Judaism of the first century, however, should reread Mark 12:28–34. Here, the evangelist tells the story of a meeting between Jesus and a scribe (i.e., one who was trained in the Jewish Law) in which both agreed that these commandments were indeed quintessential. Asked by the scribe which laws were the most important, Jesus answered by quoting Deuteronomy 6:4–5 and Leviticus 19:18: "[Y]ou shall love the Lord your God with all your heart," and "You shall love your neighbor as yourself." The scribe responded, "You are right, Teacher" and added that "this is much more than all whole burnt offerings and sacrifices." Jesus, in turn, seeing that the scribe "answered wisely"—although a few lines later he condemned all scribes for pride, greed, and hypocrisy—told him, "You are not far from the kingdom of God" (Mark 12:34).

The first-century Jewish philosopher Philo similarly divided the Decalogue into two parts, labeling them laws pertaining to God and laws pertaining to humanity. If he had had the opportunity to discuss the subject with Jesus, he might well have responded as the scribe did in the Gospel of Mark. Indeed, as I suggested in Chapter One, the idea that these two laws constitute the essence of religious faith was a commonplace in ancient Judaism.[40] In *Testaments of the Twelve Patriarchs* (a Jewish text

132–35). Schillebeeckx adds that the Church "may have seen a bigger gap [between John and Jesus] than Jesus personally was aware of" (147). Grant asserts that John might have been an Essene and that Jesus' first disciples probably had been John's followers (*Historical Introduction*, 310–13). Bornkamm says, "The forms and laws of scribal tradition are to be found abundantly in [Jesus'] sayings" (*Jesus of Nazareth*, 57). According to Tabor, "As a Jew, Jesus would have affirmed his belief in the one Creator God Yahweh above all other gods or spiritual entities; the divine revelation of the Torah as a blueprint for social, moral, and religious life; the holiness of the land of Israel as a perpetual birthright to the nation; and the notion that the people of Israel . . . had been chosen by God to enlighten all nations" (*Jesus Dynasty*, 115).

39. Latourette, *History of Christianity*, I, 45–46. As a result of his exposure to non-Greek sources of early Christianity as well as Jewish texts, Chilton says that he "began to understand Jesus on his own terms rather than in the categories of conventional scholarship and theology." As a result, he "was stunned to discover that not only the inspiration behind Jesus' teachings, but also its actual content—point by point—was drawn directly from Jewish sources. A portrait of Jesus as an inspired rabbi with an exclusively Jewish agenda began to emerge . . . It became clear to me that *everything Jesus did was as a Jew, for Jews, and about Jews*" (*Rabbi Jesus*, xviii-xix; my emphasis). Enslin argues that Jesus and his disciples' "emphasis upon purity of life and uprightness of character . . . was their heritage from Judaism" (*Christian Beginnings*, 191). He says the same thing of Jesus' "ethical demands of the greatest severity" and his belief that "morality and true religion were indissoluble" (184).

40. Says Carroll, Jesus "was never more Jewish than in this proclamation" of love (*Constantine's Sword*, 118). See also Flusser, *Sage from Galilee*, 61–62. As Sterling points out, Philo summarized the

from the second century BC), for example, Issachar, one of the sons of Jacob says, "Love the Lord and your neighbor, and have compassion on the poor and feeble" (Issachar 5:2; see also 7:6). Dan, another son of the patriarch, says, "Love the Lord with all your life, and one another with sincere heart" (Dan 5:3).

When Rabbi Hillel was asked to recite the whole Jewish Law in as brief a form as possible, he recited his version of the Golden Rule: "Do not do to your fellow what you hate to have done to you," which one scholar has said "was not original with Hillel," but "seems rather to have been proverbial." Paul said virtually the same thing when he quoted Leviticus 19:18 and called it a summary expression of all of the commandments: "[H]e who loves his neighbor has fulfilled the law" (Rom 13:8–10). In other words, both Hillel and Paul reduced the two Great Commandments to one commandment,[41] as Jesus did when he suggested more than once that loving humanity is the best means of loving God.[42]

In all of the synoptic Gospels, for example, when he was asked by a rich young man how he could "inherit eternal life," Jesus, ever the law-abiding Jew, told him to follow "the commandments." What is particularly striking in this passage is that Jesus did not include all of the commandments listed in Exodus (20:1–17) and Deuteronomy (5:6–21). He specified only the prohibitions against killing, committing adultery, stealing, and bearing false witness—that is, numbers six through nine, in the

Jewish law under two headings, "a summary that is broadly similar to the controversy story about the great commandment in the Gospels" in the passage just cited. Philo says, "There are—one may say—two main headings of the innumerable individual rules and teachings: our obligation to God through piety and holiness and our obligation to humanity through love of humanity and justice; each of these is divided into many subcategories that are all praiseworthy" ("Philo of Alexandria," 299, 304). Sanders says that the two words *piety* ("worshipping God with true devotion") and *righteousness* ("treating other people correctly") "were used very widely by Greek-speaking Jews [including Josephus as well as Philo] to summarize their religion" (*Historical Figure of Jesus*, 92; see also 224). "Both major commandments," says Schillebeeckx, "taken separately, are thoroughly Jewish" (*Jesus*, 49; see also 250–56). Mack argues that the better of the "two ways" identified in *The Didache*, an early Jewish-Christian guidebook, "is based on a common Jewish practice of dividing the ten commandments into the two chief commandments, love of God and love of neighbor" (*Who Wrote?* 241). In short, Jesus' "teaching was strongly imbued with the outlook and language of the sacred texts of Israel" (Meier, *Marginal Jew*, I, 276). Ruether says, "Within the teachings of Jesus himself I would find nothing of what I would call Christian anti-Judaism" (quoted in Gager, *Origins of Anti-Semitism*, 27). Schillebeeckx makes the same point: "[T]he historian and theologian can make out a good case that to a large extent Christianity just took over an internal Jewish critique of Israel and that the early Christian interpretation of Jesus is really a Jewish one. The basic trends in Christianity were touched off by Jews and were firmly established long before non-Jewish, Gentile-Christian influences had started to operate. So an anti-Jewish feeling is quite foreign to the earliest trends in Christianity" (*Jesus*, 32). On Philo's *De decologo*, in which he distinguishes two sets of laws in the Ten Commandments, see Koester, *History, Culture, and Religion*, 276–77. For anyone inclined to dismiss the concurrence of Jesus and Philo on this subject, Koester notes, "Philo became one of the most significant factors in the development of Christian theology and for the Christian world view as a whole" (280).

41. Moore makes this point and provides the examples of Hillel and Paul in *Judaism*, II-III, 86–87.

42. As Yoder notes in *Politics of Jesus*, 122 n. 14, the second of these laws was thus also at the center of Christianity. Paul mentions it in Gal 5:14, as well Rom 13:9; and James refers to it in his epistle (2:8).

exact order, at least in Mark (10:19) and Matthew (19:18), in which they appear in the Torah (see also Lk 19:20) and added number five, the commandment to honor father and mother. Conspicuously missing, besides the prohibition against coveting (that is, commandment number ten), are the commandments pertaining to God, numbers one through four.

Jesus included the tenth commandment, more emphatically, by insisting that in order to be saved the rich young man should (implicitly) not only refrain from coveting his neighbor's possessions, but (explicitly) give away everything he owned: "Sell all that you have and distribute [the proceeds] to the poor" (Luke 19:22; Mark 10:21; Matt 19:21). In Mark, Jesus also prohibited fraud, and in Matthew he added, as if to underscore the importance of the tenth commandment once again, the second of the Great Commandments, "You shall love your neighbor as yourself."

It goes without saying, of course, that Jesus did not neglect the other commandments. Participating in synagogue services on the Sabbath, praying to God whenever he had the opportunity, and attending religious festivals in Jerusalem, Jesus was clearly a pious Jew. Therefore, no doubt more obviously and more memorably than many other Jews, he devoted himself to the service of humanity. Luke says that, when Jesus initiated his career in Nazareth, he announced, by way of reading Isaiah 61:1–2, that God sent him "to preach the good news to the poor" (presumably, news of the coming Kingdom) and to "proclaim" that captives would be released, the blind would be restored to sight, and the oppressed would be freed (Lk 4:18–19).

Jesus later demonstrated that he himself was the agent of these changes when two of John the Baptist's disciples asked him if he was the one "who is to come"—i.e., the Messiah or, less grandly, the prophet whose eventual arrival Moses predicted (Deut 18:15–19). By this point in the Gospels of Luke and Matthew, as Jesus reminded John's emissaries, he had healed not merely the blind, but the lame and the deaf, cleansed lepers, raised the dead, and—to link the message explicitly to Isaiah 61:1—preached "good news" to the poor (Luke 7:22; Matt 11:5). In this way, fulfilling two additional and similar passages in Isaiah (29:18–19 and 35:5–6), Jesus showed that his mission and his message were identical. He had been sent to serve God by serving men and women.

Jesus returned to this subject in Matthew 25, at the end of his fifth long sermon (immediately before his arrest, trial, and execution), when he told his followers that "the Son of man," as King on the Day of Judgment, would separate the sheep from the goats on exactly the same principle.[43] That is, their salvation depended on whether

43. Jesus had referred to this forthcoming event on two occasions. First, he said that "the Son of man is to come with his angels in the glory of his Father, and then he will repay every man for what he has done" (Matt 16:27). Later, he added, "Truly, I say to you, in the new world, when the Son of man shall sit on his glorious throne, you who have followed me will also sit on twelve thrones judging the twelve tribes of Israel" (Matt 19:28). The concept of an assessment of human conduct at the end-time was a commonplace in the Judaism of the first century AD. In Psalm 62, for example, God manifests his "steadfast love" by "requit[ing] a man according to his work" (v. 12).

or not they had served mankind and thereby served God—within, of course, their far more limited powers. To emphasize the logical connection between these two kinds of service, however, Jesus said, speaking in the voice of the imperial judge, that the saved are the ones who fed him when he was hungry, welcomed him when he was a stranger, clothed him when he was naked, and visited him when he was in prison. When even the righteous protested that they had had no opportunity to help him in any of these ways, he brought home the point more eloquently and effectively than he could have by stating the message directly, but undramatically: "Truly, I say to you, as you did it to one of the least of these my brethren, you did it to me" (vv. 31–46).

That is, salvation is gained not by praying or fasting or performing rituals—the implication being that God is not truly served or, at least, served at the highest possible level in these acts of piety and worship, no matter how grand and imposing. Rather, the saved are distinguished from the damned by simple acts of human kindness. Performed by and for ordinary people, they are nevertheless simultaneously performed for God. As one scholar puts it, Jesus announced the coming of the Kingdom of God and commanded his followers to prepare for it by repenting for their sins, doing good deeds, renouncing selfishness, and practicing forgiveness[44]—all of these values, as I suggested in Chapter One, deriving from traditional Judaism.

IMITATION OF GOD

To be sure, Jesus often demanded more than good deeds. In the Sermon on the Mount, for example, he forbade not only sins like murder, adultery, and theft, but also the emotions behind them. The idea that he expected his disciples both to refrain from immoral acts and to avoid feeling anger, lust, and envy evidently struck his followers as humanly impossible. After all, it is one thing to resist temptation by suppressing such emotions. It is quite another thing not to experience the emotions in the first place.

Thus, when Jesus explained his advice to the rich young man by establishing the principle that the rich cannot attain eternal life—"Truly, I say to you, . . . it is easier for a camel to go through the eye of a needle than for a rich man to enter the kingdom of heaven" (Matt 19: 23; Mark 10:25; Luke 18:24)—his disciples must have understood him to mean that even *wanting* to be rich disqualified anyone from a place in the Kingdom of God. Not being rich themselves and without even the prospect of attaining great wealth, they were nevertheless shocked: "The disciples were amazed at his words" and "exceedingly astonished." Indeed, they responded as if their own salvation had been jeopardized by this extraordinary declaration. They asked, "Then who can be saved?"

44. Hengel, *Charismatic Leader*, 61. Hengel prefaces this list with the statement "Indeed, according to the Synoptic Gospels [Jesus] did not first and foremost proclaim himself as the divine revealer but rather proclaimed the Kingdom of God as dawning with his activities" (61).

Jesus' reply to their expression of complete dismay could hardly have been consoling: "What is impossible with men is possible with God." Peter's reaction to this statement in all three Synoptics indicates that at least this spokesperson for the disciples remained utterly befuddled and distraught: "Lo, we have left everything and followed you. What then shall we have?" (Mark 10:23–28; Matt 19:23–27; Luke 18:24–28). That is, the disciples had already done what Jesus required of the rich young man. Was that not enough?[45] Jesus' other demands in the Sermon on the Mount—disdain vengeance, love your enemies, give up your cloak as well as your coat, lend freely, give alms secretly, pray privately, forgive others, reject materialism, refrain from anxiety, and avoid judgment—seem equally extreme and must have been interpreted, at least initially, in the same way that Jesus' persistent attacks on riches were: that is, with bemusement and disappointment.

One way of understanding the reaction of even Jesus' closest disciples is to assume that their astonishment derived partly from the sense that they could not possibly live up to his standards and, more to the point of the present discussion, partly from the sense that these moral requirements were entirely unprecedented in ancient Palestine. That is, Jesus was not offering an ethical program that could be understood in the context of contemporary Judaism, but, rather, a radical departure from his disciples' inherited religion. Thus, so the argument goes, this is precisely the point at which Jesus established a new religion that would eventually be called Christianity and the point at which he left Judaism behind.[46]

This interpretation of Jesus' relationship to Judaism is based on the assumption that Jesus *uniquely* required obedience to the spirit of the law rather than the letter and therefore required that the individual's emotions as well as his actions (the inner self as well the outer) be aligned with the will of God: "Jesus has wholly separated obedience from legalism . . . ; he opposes the view that the fulfillment of the law is the

---

45. Fredriksen calls the "ethical instruction in the Gospels" totally impractical: "No normal society could long run according to the principles of the Sermon on the Mount" (*Jesus of Nazareth*, 110). Yet another reason for the disciples' rejection of Jesus' radical views, offered by Freyne, was the fear that if they accepted a spiritually rich but economically weak value system they would be even more easily abused than they already were by rich and powerful landowners: "To expect Galilean peasant farmers to respond with enthusiasm to a message that, if adhered to, would put them at the total mercy of urban exploitation, in the face of which they were already extremely vulnerable, was expecting the impossible in human terms" (*Galilee, Jesus*, 243). Bainton says that Jesus went beyond "the ethical demands of Judaism." In fact, those demands "were intensified beyond the level of human attainment" (*Early Christianity*, 15).

46. Before discussing the so-called Antitheses (in the Sermon on the Mount), Chilton and Neusner make this point: "Speaking with the authority of Sinai, Jesus revises the received commandments, imposing a higher standard for the Christian way of life. These are what is meant by not abolishing but fulfilling the Torah and the prophets" (*Judaism*, 131–32). In other words, in the Antitheses, Jesus moves beyond Judaism. And the result is an imposition "upon the received Torah [of] an entirely fresh set of meanings, new issues, unanticipated possibilities" (160), but principally the idea that "Jesus is . . . the unique means of access to God" (178, 180, 181).

fulfilling of the will of God. For God demands the whole man, not merely specific acts from the man."[47]

The problem with the idea that Christianity succeeded and Judaism failed because of the backwardness of the latter and the progressiveness of the former is that, as I said in Chapter One, it represents a vicious caricature of Judaism that has been generally discredited by scholars in recent years. That is, to support the belief that Jesus so thoroughly reformed Judaism that it could no longer be considered Judaism, critics have had to assume that traditional Judaism, in the words of one historian, was reactionary (i.e., tied to the past and rigid), "narrow" (i.e., exclusive and ethnocentric), "old" (i.e., out of date and out of touch), and "localized" (i.e., nationalistic and Palestinian). On the other hand, Jesus' version of the faith was "radical" (i.e., modern and flexible), "broad" (i.e., inclusive and non-ethnic), "new" (i.e., unprecedented and forward looking), and "non-localized" (i.e., universal and international).[48]

From this point of view, Christianity began with a clean break from Judaism, if not before the Crucifixion, then immediately after it. Jesus was immediately perceived to be the Son of God, the Cosmic Christ, and Christians embraced a moral code that was fundamentally different from and superior to that of the Jews. The only problem with this interpretation is, as I said earlier, that Christians continued to honor the Sabbath, prayed in the Temple, followed the dietary laws, and seemed (to Jews and Romans) to be members of yet another Jewish sect. Most obviously, according to Acts of the Apostles, James the brother of Jesus appears to have been a pious, Law-abiding Jew, who vigilantly monitored the behavior of Christian missionaries (like Peter and Paul), corrected them when they seemed to have violated Jewish laws, and asked Paul to sponsor a traditional Jewish ritual in the Temple in order to prove that he was not telling new converts to Christianity to reject Judaism.

Alternatively, as I said, in the Introduction, some scholars who accept the idea that a more conservative (i.e., Jewish) Christianity prevailed during the first few decades of the Church argue that James and the other "pillars" of the church (John the son of Zebedee and Peter) misunderstood Jesus and "re-Judaized" the Church while it remained in Jerusalem. In this view, Greek-speaking gentiles understood Jesus better than Aramaic-speaking Jews did. Here, the assumption is that, in the words of one scholar, the Church's experience of Jesus after the Resurrection "led to a more developed sense of who and what Jesus truly is." That is, the Church's comprehension grew over time. The evangelists in particular "profit[ed] from the long period" between the

---

47. Bultmann, *Jesus and the Word*, 92. In the Antitheses, Bultmann says, "Jesus sets the demand of law over against the demand of God" (91). Painter argues, however, that "the antitheses are not against the law. They do not advocate breaking or dispensing with the law but are intensifications of it. The righteousness of the disciples must exceed the righteousness of the scribes and Pharisees" (*Just James*, 91). Righteousness in both instances, it should be added, refers to obedience to the law. See also Painter's discussion of the Antitheses in "Who Was James?" 56–57: "The Jesus of Matthew extends the scope of the law but contradicts no scriptural commandment."

48. Freyne, *Galilee, Jesus*, 270.

Crucifixion and the composition of the Gospels. In short, James, Peter, and John the son of Zebedee were wrong, while Paul and John the evangelist were right.[49]

It turns out, however, that such claims have been rejected by many students of early Christianity.[50] One reason is that *everything* Jesus said has a parallel in either the Judaism of the Bible (including especially the Prophets, Psalms, and Proverbs) or the Judaism of the inter-testamental period (including especially Jewish "wisdom" literature). In the words of one scholar, "A century of study by historians of religions has demonstrated that there is hardly a belief attested in the New Testament for which some parallel cannot be found somewhere in its environment or antecedents."[51] Furthermore, "Rabbinic documents," according to two Bible scholars, "would in time come to the same conclusion [i.e., that Jesus came to], to avoid anger, to avoid temptation, to avoid vowing and swearing."[52] And, since, as yet another scholar points out, the Rabbinical literature cannot be dismissed as merely an irrelevant post-Christian body of ideas—for the simple reason that Judaism did not change significantly from the time of Jesus to the time of the Mishnah—it is safe to assume that such ideas would have been present in earlier Jewish texts, as indeed they were.[53]

Thus, despite the commonly held view that Jesus turned his back on the Jews, the evidence suggests that he never wavered in his fundamental loyalty to what he

49. *Living Jesus*, 35, 127. Johnson adds later: "We are most certain that some account of Jesus' passion circulated early—in sketchy form perhaps already in the first days of the movement, but progressively gaining more richness as the full implications of reading Jesus' death through the words of the prophets were realized" (130).

50. Yoder, for example, criticizes those who embrace Paul's doctrine of Grace at the expense of the doctrine of Works, which appears more prominently in the synoptic Gospels. "We now know, the argument [that Yoder is criticizing] runs, that Jesus could not have been practicing or teaching a relevant social ethic." The Jews, as well as Matthew, "who thought he was doing just that . . . misunderstood Jesus . . . Fortunately before long, the explanation continues, things were put into place by the Apostle Paul. He corrected the tendency to neo-Judaism or to early catholicism," with their emphasis on Works over Grace (*Politics of Jesus*, 20–21). Later, Yoder asks why Jesus would have allowed himself to be misunderstood (58–59).

51. Meeks, *First Urban Christians*, 91.

52. Chilton and Neusner, *Judaism*, 133.

53. Moore says repeatedly and insistently, in the first volume of *Judaism*, that the Rabbis retained the essential features of Judaism that had been in place since as early as the time of Ezra. Speaking of *Ecclesiasticus*, written in the second century B.C., Moore says, "the value of the book as a landmark is very great . . . because it enables us to assure ourselves that the theology and ethics of the Tannaim [the writers of the Mishnah] in the second century of our era were substantially the same as those of the Sopherim [or scribes] at the beginning of the second century before it," i.e., 200 B.C. (I, 45). Even "[t]he branches and methods of study were the same [after the war of A.D. 132] as before the war" (94). Continuity was maintained because the works of the Rabbis in c. 200 A.D. were "all compilations, in which the work of previous generations of scholars is preserved, reviewed, and continued to the date of redaction" (97). See also 107, 134, 147, 172, 173, 177, 345, 358. By way of summary, Moore says, "[N]o significant difference is to be discovered between the religiousness of the first centuries of our era and that of the following periods down to the invasion of mysticism" (178). Parkes makes a similar point in *Conflict*, 34, as do Enslin in *Christian Beginnings*, 102; and Maccoby in *Mythmkaer*, 214 n. 2.

took to be the heart of Judaism. A glance at chapter 13 of Mark, for example, shows how dedicated he was to basing his theology on the Jewish Bible. In this short space, he refers to the Psalms, 2 Chronicles, Isaiah (several times), Exodus, Micah, Genesis, Deuteronomy, Joel, and Zechariah. He also alludes to the Book of Daniel no fewer than a dozen times.

Matthew, who uses the Jewish Bible as a collection of prophecies for Jesus, makes him even more prolific in his references to the Old Testament.[54] And, in both Matthew and Luke, Jesus uses three passages from Deuteronomy as if they were magical incantations against Satan, who is trying to test him, as Jesus makes clear, in the same way that God tested the Israelites in their exodus from Egypt (Matt 4:4; 4:7; 4:10; Luke 4:4; 4:12; 4:8). Jesus derived his eschatological (end-time) ideas from Daniel (2:44; 7:14; 18, 27); named twelve disciples to symbolize the twelve tribes of Israel, who would be reunited at the end time;[55] and, as I suggested earlier, used parables in exactly the same way that the rabbis did.[56]

54. According to Grant, Mark's Jesus directly quotes the Old Testament thirty-seven times; Matthew's Jesus quotes the Old Testament sixty-five times. (*Jesus*, 14). Bruce claims that Jesus "regularly appealed to the Hebrew Scriptures to validate his mission, his words and his actions" (*Canon of Scripture*, 27). "Behind all his utterances," Wilson says, "there are the Hebrew Scriptures in which he implicitly believed, and which he neither wished to supersede nor to alter . . . What interested him most was how to be a good Jew" (*Jesus*, 135). "Jesus worked and taught firmly within the tradition of the Jewish prophets that God could only be pleased by human kindness and goodness. Mysticism, exorcism, the power to heal or to cast out devils were no substitute for justice and virtue" (230). Sanders comments, "Jesus thought that the Jewish scripture contained the revealed word of God, and that Moses had issued commandments that should be followed" (*Historical Figure of Jesus*, 224). See also Flusser, *Sage from Galilee*, 62; Tabor, *Jesus Dynasty*, 312; and Ehrman, *Lost Christianities*, 232.

55. Sanders says that Jesus' selection of twelve disciples represented not only the twelve tribes of Israel, but also the redemption of Israel: Jesus "spoke of the Twelve in order to indicate that his mission was to all Israel as well as his expectation that Israel would be fully restored in the coming kingdom" (*Historical Figure of Jesus*, 122). Sanders later discusses the Jewish (and Jewish-Christian) expectation that at the end-time God would "gather all the tribes of Jacob" together, according to the writers of *Ecclesiasticus* (quoted here), *The Psalms of Solomon*, and the *Dead Sea Scrolls* (184–85). On Jesus' appointment of twelve disciples in Mark 3:14–19, Evans says, "Most commentators rightly recognize that the number twelve was intended to symbolize the twelve tribes of Israel, implying that the goal of the ministry of Jesus was the restoration of the whole nation" ("Josephus on John the Baptist," 57). According to Bruce, "That the Jewish Christians continued for decades to regard themselves as the true remnant of Israel, the 'twelve tribes', is implied by the superscription of the Epistle of James" (*New Testament History*, 210). James' letter is addressed "To the twelve tribes in the Dispersion." Meier also notes that the Essenes used the number twelve symbolically (*Marginal Jew*, I, 234 n. 13).

56. Perrin and Duling, *New Testament*, 423. Schillebeeckx claims that "it is in those parables that we can perceive Jesus' solidarity with what is best in the empirical wisdom of late-sapiential Judaism in ethical and religious matters" (*Jesus*, 161). Porton makes the same point: "While parables appear in Greek, Roman, and Hellenistic documents, the parables attributed to Jesus in the Gospels and those assigned to Rabbis in the Rabbinic texts share some commonalities, such as their form, their images, their themes, and in fact their abundance." Thus, Jesus' parables in the synoptic Gospels are "what we would expect from a teacher/scholar/sage/preacher in Galilee in the first century CE" ("The Parable in the Hebrew Bible," 209). That Jesus employed [the parables] to conceal the meaning of his message is a contorted and tendentious explanation" (Vermes, *Jesus the Jew*, 27). Schillebeeckx likewise treats the parables as invitations to deeper thinking (*Jesus*, 155–58). On Jewish themes in Jesus' parables, see

Thus, although Jesus' disciples reacted negatively to his proscription not only of immoral actions, but also of the emotions behind them, it was not because his demand was unprecedented in Judaism. His opposition to anger as well as murder, for example, has (as I said in Chapter One) several antecedents in the Jewish Bible. Since God reserves the right of vengeance to Himself (Deut 32:35), He also denies to His people even the right to feel hatred or anger (Lev 19:17; Ps 37:8). The reason is that these feelings are self-defeating: "Hatred stirreth up strifes" (Prov 10:12; 29:22), and at the very least it should be deferred (Sir 7:9). Indeed, it is a man's "glory to pass over a transgression" (Prov 19:11) since God is, after all, the final court of appeal and the ultimate avenger.

The idea also occurs in the inter-testamental literature. For example, Sirach says: "Whoever acts vengefully will face the vengeance of the Lord . . . Forgive your neighbor any wrong he has done you; then, when you pray, your sins will be forgiven. If anyone harbors anger against another, can he expect help from the Lord?" (Sir 28:1–3). In *Testaments of the Twelve Patriarchs* (another Jewish work of the second century BC), Gad, one of the sons of Jacob, says, "Put away hatred from your heart, and love one another from the heart; and if a man sin against thee, speak peaceably to him, and do not hold guile in thy soul; and if he repent and confess, forgive him" (Gad 6:1, 3–4).

In fact, many of Jesus' most famous sayings have parallels in Jewish writings.[57] Jesus' reference to "the lilies of the field," representing as it does a whole-hearted faith in the benevolence of God, goes back to the psalms and to Jewish wisdom literature.[58]

Drury, *Parables in the Gospels*, passim. For an opposing view of the Jewishness of Jesus' parables, see Bornkamm, *Jesus of Nazareth*, 69–70.

57. See, for examples, Barclay (using Rudolf Bultmann as a source), *First Three Gospels*, 53–55. One of the strangest arguments against this view appears in Hengel's *Charismatic Leader*. Hengel says: "Jesus stood outside any discoverable uniform teaching tradition of Judaism. It is not possible to assign him a place within the development of contemporary Jewish traditions." Of course, Hengel cannot deny that Jesus' ideas appear to correspond in many ways to the ideas that the Jews passed on from generation to generation. I.e., there are "relatively numerous parallels to Jesus' sayings in the . . . ancient Jewish and rabbinal tradition." However, the extent to which his ideas matched those of his contemporaries is not owing to the fact that Jesus was actually influenced by this tradition. After all, it was an "inexhaustible ocean," implying that Jesus' ideas inevitably resembled Jewish ideas simply because there were so many of them. Thus, Hengel continues, it is owing to the fact that these ideas were part of "the spiritual and mental milieu of his homeland and his age." That is, he could not avoid them, which means that he could espouse them without really being influenced by them. In short, "the direct points of contacts between him and Pharisaism [and, presumably, Judaism in general] need not go beyond what was in general the common property of the Judaism of the first century A.D." (49–50). Hengel is forced into the odd conclusion that Jesus' disciples were mistaken in seeing him in terms of Jewish expectations since he was not influenced by Judaism but represented a point of view that was both revolutionary and unique (79). Of course, if we understand that Hengel's objective is, as he admits, "disentangling Jesus from the Religiongeschichte of Judaism" (71), then we also understand that, even if Jesus *was* connected with Judaism, he must be shown to be disconnected from it, whatever it takes. Otherwise, he could not be regarded as the legitimate founder of a new religion. The contorted argument referred to above suggests that Hengel is solidly in the Bultmannian tradition of persuasion through obfuscation.

58. Bultmann, *Jesus and the Word*, 49, 160–1. "When (or if) Jesus said this to fellow Jews, he

That all things come to those who trust in God is stated in *Ecclesiasticus* (2:6, 8, 10–11; 33:1; and 40:26), and that even Wisdom herself comes to those who ask is stated in *The Wisdom of Solomon* (6:12 and 7:7). Thus, "All the works of the Lord are good, and he will supply every need in its time" (Sir 39:33). The Deuteronomist agrees with Jesus in Matthew 7:7 (Lk 11:9) that, if you ask, "it will be given you": "For what other great nation has a god so near to it as the Lord our God is whenever we call to him?" (Deut 5:7), a thought repeated in Psalm 145:18: "The Lord is nigh unto all them that call upon him . . . He will fulfil the desire of them that fear him; he will also hear their cry, and will save them."[59]

The Lord's Prayer, which Jesus suggested was the only prayer Jewish Christians needed, is entirely Jewish in content.[60] To Jews of the first century, God was a father (see, e.g., Mal. 2:10), His name was revered (the Kaddish, addressed to God, begins, "Magnified and sanctified be Thy great name"), the coming of His reign was passionately wished for (see Isaiah, Jeremiah, and Ezekiel), His forgiveness was expected to be matched by humanity's, and temptation was to be avoided. Thus, Jesus' main themes— "that God is our father, that his name should be hallowed, and that the divine kingdom is something ardently to be desired"—would have sounded acceptable to even those Jews who refused to follow him.[61] As for Jesus' demand that his followers love their

would not have been perceived as anti-Jewish at all" (Levine, *Misunderstood Jew*, 115). Conzelmann and Lindemann cite the Mishnah parallel for Matt 6:34: "Therefore do not worry about tomorrow, for tomorrow will worry about itself" (*Interpreting the New Testament*, 316). The theme is conspicuous in Psalm 91.

59. Schillebeeckx identifies as Jewish, especially *Greco*-Jewish, the idea that conversion requires "giving everything away, forsaking family and home," devoting oneself to relieving the poor, and becoming a child (*Jesus*, 223–26). Flusser similarly traces to Jewish origins Jesus' repudiation of anger and lust and Jesus' claim to have received divine knowledge directly from God (cf. Matt 11:25–27 and the Essene prayer quoted by Flusser on 102) (*Sage from Galilee*, 101–2). Yoder says that the Christian ideal of imitating God "was quite current in the Old Testament" (*Politics of Jesus*, 117 and n. 3). Kaylor discusses the Jewish origins of the Kingdom of God and notes the connections between the Beatitudes and Isaiah (61:1–3, 8–9) and between the Antitheses and Jeremiah (31:33) (*Jesus the Prophet*, 79–81, 99, 106). Evans notes the similarities between the Jewish concept of the King and the Christian concept of the Kingdom of God ("Comparing Judaisms," 180).

60. Printing a "made-up parallel to the Lord's Prayer taken from [disparate] Jewish sources" next to the Lord's Prayer from Luke, Perrin and Duling comment, "In sentiment and meaning the two prayers are exactly parallel, and clearly Jesus was echoing his Jewish heritage." However, these writers suggest that there is an important difference in style (*New Testament*, 424). Bultmann, too, claims that the style of the prayer—particularly its simplicity—makes it non-Jewish (*Theology*, I, 23–24). On the Jewishness of the prayer, both substantively and stylistically, see Millar Burrows, cited in Augstein, *Jesus Son of Man*, 272; Enslin, *Christian Beginnings*, 102–103; Sandmel, *Jewish Understanding*, 150; Kaylor, *Jesus the Prophet*, 194–95; and Maccoby, *Mythmaker*, 111. Chilton traces the prayer to the Jewish Kaddish: "Father, your name will be sanctified, your Kingdom will come" (*Rabbi Jesus*, 22). On this point, see also Meier, *Marginal Jew*, II, 241–45, 297–302.

61. Levine, *Misunderstood Jew*, 21. See also Wylen, *Jews*, 87. Wylen adds: "There is no Christology in this prayer, a matter of historical significance. Jews do not recite the Lord's Prayer because of its Christian associations, but the content alone is very Jewish" (87). Tabor reminds his readers that the prayer calls for the realization of God's kingdom on earth—i.e., as the Hebrew prophets promised, and the Jews would have wished (*Jesus Dynasty*, 311, 313). Kaylor, in *Jesus the Prophet*, 82, also emphasizes

enemies as well as their neighbors (Matt 5:43–44), the idea appears in Proverbs 25:21; by contrast, "hate your enemy," Jesus' suggestion to the contrary notwithstanding, appears nowhere in either the Jewish Bible or the Rabbinical literature.[62]

Jesus' eschatological prediction "The first shall be last" (Mark 9:35; 10:43–44; Matt 20:26–27; 23:11–12; Luke 22:26–27) goes back to Jeremiah. That prophet quotes God as saying, "I the Lord have brought down the high tree [and] have exalted the low tree" (17:24). To a "wicked prince of Israel," God promises to "exalt him that is low, and abase him that is high" (21:26). The passage in the Gospels is also an echo of a statement by Rabbi Hillel: "My abasement is my exaltation, and my exaltation is my abasement,"[63] which is repeated by Jesus in the Gospel of Matthew: "[W]hoever exalts himself will be humbled, and whoever humbles himself will be exalted" (Matt 23:12). Similarly, that the meek, the righteous, the poor, and the pure in heart "shall inherit the earth" (Matt 5:3–8) derives directly from Isaiah: "The meek shall obtain fresh joy in the Lord, and the poor among men shall exult in the Holy One of Israel" (Isa 29:19–20). This is also a recurring theme in the Psalms (e.g., 37:11; 34:15; 107:41).[64] The noble sentiments of the Magnificat (Luke 1:52–53), referring to God's dethronement of the rich and mighty and his exaltation of the poor and low-born, echoes the Song of Hannah, in which the positions of the proud and mighty and well-fed, on one hand, and the poor and needy and hungry, on the other, are reversed (1 Sam 2:1–10).

One Bible scholar notes, in fact, that this theme is at the center of apocalyptic Jewish writing from Daniel onward. In the New Age, "conditions are then reversed: the one who weeps now will laugh then; the poor will be rich, the mighty downcast." In addition, "all earthly empires will then be abolished," and "all the structures of society will be changed."[65] According to Isaiah, "the ruthless shall come to nought and the

the earthliness of the kingdom expected in this prayer. Like Tabor, Kaylor adds that Jews would have understood Jesus this way (83). See also Moore, *Judaism*, II-III, 101, 212–13.

62. Zeitlin, *Who Crucified Jesus?* 220 n. 13, 125; and Maguire, *Moral Core*, 211 n. 7. Maguire adds that Judaism's openness to "the alien, who was often presumed an enemy, is the opposite position" (211 n. 7).

63. Both examples are cited by Jeremias, *Parables of Jesus*, 192. Bultmann says that "the earliest Church seems to have transformed a saying already current among the Jews, which spoke of the presence of God with two men occupied with interpreting the Torah, into the saying: 'Where two or three are gathered in my name, there I am in the midst of them'" (*Theology*, I, 48).

64. Maguire says that in blessing the poor and cursing the rich (Luke 6:20, 24), "Jesus was not original, but was the heir of an ancient Hebrew suspicion." Maguire refers to passages in Deuteronomy (8:11–18), Jeremiah (5:25–28), and *Ecclesiasticus* (8:2), as well as other prophetic writings (*Moral Core*, 136–37).

65. Schillebeeckx, *Jesus*, 123. Schillebeeckx says that the humiliation-exaltation scheme "is classical in Old Testament and Judaistic literature" (536). See, for example, *Ecclesiasticus* 10:14. See also Jesus' eschatological message in the parable of the fig tree (Luke 13:6–9 and 21: 29ff), which Flusser connects with Song of Songs 2:13 and with what he calls "a basic scriptural prophetic scheme" that is illustrated in Genesis 15:13–16 and Tobit 14:4–5 (*Sage from Galilee*, 101–102, 125). The words "bearing fruit" at the heart of this and other parables Schillebeeckx calls "a Semitic expression for good works that can turn aside God's punishments" (*Jesus*, 128). Says Cook: "The solidarity of Israel is a very important and pregnant conception, inasmuch as it paved the way for the later conception of the 'Body of Christ' . . .

scoffer cease, and all who watch to do evil shall be cut off" (Isa 29:20). The principle of reversal in the next world means that princes and nations will be replaced by the meek and humble (Sir 10:14–15). Even the Essenes agreed with Jesus "that, in the very near future, the social outcasts and oppressed would become the preferred"—namely, the humble, the contrite, and the mournful, a sentiment expressed as well in *Testaments of the Twelve Patriarchs*, where the grieving, the penurious, the wanting, and the weak are promised joy, wealth, fullness, and strength, respectively.[66]

In short, Jesus' belief in "love, mercy, and grace" would not have set him apart from other Jews.[67] Nor would it have distinguished him from the Pharisees, who are portrayed in the Gospels as Jesus' enemies. In fact, Jesus' connection to the Rabbinical, or Pharisaic, tradition was strong.[68] Jewish scholars in particular have recently questioned the claim that the Pharisees not only disagreed with Jesus, but also plotted against him. As Luke indicates, the Sadducees had reason to challenge Jesus, which they did in Luke 20:29, because, unlike Jesus and the Pharisees, they did not believe in the resurrection of the body. Thus, the Pharisaic scribes in this passage agree with Jesus ("Teacher, you have spoken well" [Luke 20:39]), and elsewhere in Luke the Jews—except for the Jewish elite—are generally friendly toward him.[69] It was the

There was a feeling of corporateness and unity in space and time" (*Introduction to the Bible*, 88–89). Cook later identifies this solidarity—not only among Jews, but between them and Yahweh—as an expression of God's immanence (132).

66. Flusser, *Sage from Galilee*, 69–70. Meeks adds that the eschatology of the Christians was Jewish in origin: "There can be little question about the source from which they drew such talk; it is the special idiom of those apocalyptic circles of Judaism from which the first followers of Jesus had absorbed so much of their language and their perception of the world . . . The point is how natural thought of 'the end' was to the first Christians, and how strange it was to most of their neighbors"—that is, to pagans. Furthermore, the Christians always associated the idea of the end-time with a final punishment in which everyone would receive his or her just deserts—that is, the world would be turned upside down and everyone's position would be reversed—another Jewish idea (*Origins of Christian Morality*, 175, 177).

67. Sanders, *Jesus and Judaism*, 236. To this list, Segal adds justice and egalitarianism (*Rebecca's Children*, 81, 82).

68. Says Lee: "The tragedy for Christians is that we have steadfastly missed the genetic connection between Jesus and the Pharisees. There is more insight into Jesus in his continuity with them than in his discontinuity" (*Galilean Jewishness of Jesus*, 13). See also Joseph Klausner, *Jesus of Nazareth*, cited in Sanders, *Jesus and Judaism*, 51–53; Carroll, *Constantine's Sword*, 76; Flusser, *Sage from Galilee*, 46–47; and Guignebert, *Jewish World*, 72. Parkes comments: "Jesus attacked the scribes and Pharisees because they seemed to Him to obscure that direct relationship between man and God by falsifying the nature of the Torah . . . This was a fundamental point. But it was not a rejection by Jesus of 'Torah'. It was his Gentile followers a century later who, seeing in 'Torah' only a body of prescriptions, saw in Judaism only the observance of a dead law which Jesus had rejected" (*Conflict*, 37). Sanders says: "I am one of a growing number of scholars who doubt that there were any substantial points of opposition between Jesus and the Pharisees . . . Again, a negative cannot be proved. But all the scenes of debate between Jesus and the Pharisees have more than a slight air of artificiality" (*Jesus and Judaism*, 264–65).

69. Fredriksen, *From Jesus to Christ*, 29; and Mack, *Who Wrote?* 170. Maccoby says, "It should be noted . . . that modern scholarship has shown that, at this time, the Pharisees were held in high repute throughout the Roman and Parthian empires as a dedicated group who upheld religious ideals in the face of tyranny, supported leniency and mercy in the application of laws, and championed the rights

chief priests and elders, groups traditionally affiliated with their Roman superiors, who were involved in Jesus' arrest and execution, not the Pharisees.[70] For these reasons, the chief priests arrested Jesus as inconspicuously as possible, because they were fearful of the reaction of Jesus' Jewish followers (Luke 22:1–2),[71] whose large number made a daytime arrest in the middle of Jerusalem a dangerous venture.

Like the Hasids, a term referring to charismatic holy men who appeared occasionally in the post-Exilic period, Jesus emphasized morality over ritual and was indifferent to some Jewish purity rules. Furthermore, Jesus' way of life as a traveling preacher, without a permanent position, is also matched by the Hasids, who similarly led a life of voluntary poverty. They too were more interested in the well-being of others than their own.[72] The Essenes, like Jesus, expected the end of the world imminently, saw in contemporary events the fulfillment of scriptures, and stressed the importance of religion as an inward experience.[73] The Essenes also preached God's forgiveness. They believed they were partners in a new covenant with God. Their leader, who believed himself to be God's last messenger, was executed. They were led by a council of twelve men. Members who lied about their property were excommunicated. They required repentance from new members, who underwent a baptismal initiation rite. They emphasized love of neighbor and believed that members of the

---

of the poor against the oppression of the rich" (*Mythmaker*, 6). Maccoby's endnote cites, in support of his position, Moore, *Judaism*; Herford, *The Pharisees*; Parkes, *Conflict*; and two more recent texts by Sanders: *Paul and Palestinian Judaism* and *Jesus and Judaism* (212 n. 2). In chapter three of his book, Maccoby (1) criticizes the Gospel misrepresentation of the Pharisees, which, he says, has contributed to an anti-Semitic caricature of Jews in general (*Mythmaker*, 19); (2) explains their democratic method of composing the Mishnah and Talmud (20–22); and (3) mentions their emphasis on the acquisition of knowledge and universal education rather than ceremony and ritual (24). His chapter four is entirely devoted to examining the alleged differences and actual similarities between the Pharisees and Jesus (29–44).

70. Vermes, *Jesus the Jew*, 35. "The Pharisees," says Sanders, "had nothing whatever to do with [Jesus'] death" (*Historical Figure of Jesus*, 218). "[T]he prime movers behind Jesus' execution," Sanders adds elsewhere, were "the priestly aristocracy," acting in their capacity "as intermediaries between the Jewish people and the Romans" (*Jesus and Judaism*, 289–90). Speaking of the Gospel of Matthew, Freyne says that chief priests and elders are referred to in connection with Jesus' death (plotting or arresting) nine times. The chief priests are referred to alone three times. They appear with the scribes three times, with the scribes and elders twice, and with the Pharisees only once (*Galilee, Jesus*, 86 n. 24).

71. Fredriksen, *From Jesus to Christ*, 33.

72. Wilson says that Jesus "is comparable to other hasidim, who also went about healing the sick, casting out devils, controlling the weather, and quarrelling with the religious hierarchy in Jerusalem" (*Jesus*, 8). Chilton makes the same point in *Rabbi Jesus*, 109–10, 175, 179. As spiritual descendants of the Hasids, the Pharisees similarly emphasized ethics over sacrifice. They insisted that membership in the spiritual Israel was gained not by birthright, but by observance. On this point, see Schillebeeckx, *Jesus*, 117; Ruether, *Faith and Fratricide*, 54–55; and Jeremias, *Jerusalem*, 152.

73. Vermes, *Changing Faces of Jesus*, 261, 269, 274. Meier discusses Jesus' role as rabbi and teacher in *Marginal Jew*, I, 276. Maccoby says, "Jesus may well have belonged to the Hasidim, who, indeed, of all the Pharisees show the strongest similarity in type to Jesus" (*Mythmaker*, 46).

sect should aspire to moral perfection.[74] Ironically, says one scholar, because Jesus and his followers were less extreme in their beliefs and practices than the Essenes, the former would have been far less distinguishable from other Jews.[75]

It is possible, of course, that Jesus did, in fact, despise the Pharisees and condemned their ideas and actions, as the Gospels claim. Thus, some scholars have accepted the idea that Jesus found the Pharisees objectionable on several grounds. One charge is based on the assumption that Jesus and the Pharisees merely interpreted the Torah in opposing ways. More specifically, the Galilean Jews were conservative and therefore unlikely to "be attracted to what they considered the novelties of the Pharisees." The rural Galileans were opposed to the innovations of groups they thought of as Hellenized, which the Pharisees, living mostly in urban Judea, seemed to be.[76] The Pharisees were "liberal" in their attempt to adapt the Jewish Law to everyday circumstances, which required them to develop supplementary laws. In the Gospels, Jesus criticized these innovations as "traditions" (a subject I will discuss in more detail later in this chapter).

Other criticisms of the Pharisees have been more extreme. One scholar claims that they were Jesus' enemies during his lifetime because they were, in fact, spies for the Temple. That is, employed by the High Priest, they acted as a kind of police force, infiltrating the towns and villages of Judea and Galilee, looking for lawbreakers. In this respect, they favored the haves over the have-nots, the rich and powerful over the poor and helpless, and collaboration over rebellion. In short, their disagreement with Jesus and his followers was as much a matter of politics and economics as it was of theology and hermeneutics.[77]

On occasion, this criticism has been carried even further by attributing to the Pharisees not merely self-serving loyalty to the powers-that-be, but also the worst kind of venality. As one scholar says, they maintained the purity laws only as a means of social distancing. They dominated Jerusalem and the Temple, and they were interested in "social control," as well as "religious control," which they exercised from "their centre of operation" in Jerusalem. In addition, most tellingly, they were loveless,

74. Augstein, *Jesus Son of Man*, 108–120. On these and other parallels between the Essenes and the Christians, see Flusser, *Sage from Galilee*, 18–21; Burrows, *Dead Sea Scrolls*, chapter 15; and Flint, "Jesus and the Dead Sea Scrolls," 111, 119, 130. On the differences between Jesus and the Essenes, see Robinson, *Gospel of Jesus*, 73–77.

75. Theissen, *Early Palestinian Christianity*, 21–22.

76. Meier, *Marginal Jew*, I, 277. As a Galilean, "Jesus was a staunch defender of the Torah against what he perceived to be threats to it from the Pharisees," who "were a kind of reform movement within the Jewish people that was centered in Jerusalem" (Boyarin, *Jewish Gospel*, 103–4).

77. Herzog, *Jesus, Justice*, 154–55, 171–72, 177. Herzog attributes to Rudolph Bultmann and Martin Dibelius the claim that arguments between Jesus and the Pharisees were made up by the Church in response to the Church's own conflicts with the Jews in the post-Resurrection years (8). He calls the Pharisees "a retainer group deeply involved in court intrigues. According to Josephus, they tried to depose Herod (52).

"parsimonious," "rapacious," elitist, money loving, and "selfish."[78] This fairly well sums up the Gospel picture of these nefarious characters, who were so obsessed with enforcing their rules that they followed Jesus and his disciples around to make sure they obeyed these rules to the letter. After all, using the rabbinical literature as a guide, some Bible scholars and historians argue that the hostility between Jesus and the Pharisees matches the kind of hostility that frequently arose between Jewish groups, which suggests that it was little more than an intra-Jewish conflict.[79]

As I have suggested, however, many scholars reject this portrait of the Pharisees as a retrojection of Christian hostility to the Jews that arose not when Jesus was preaching, but forty or more years later, when the Pharisees (as Rabbis and as the only Jewish sect remaining) assumed a leadership position in the future development of Judaism.[80] In this view, the Pharisees in the time of Jesus had little presence in Galilee (and were therefore unlikely to have encountered Jesus there); certainly had no power to enforce their rules in small towns and villages; and, in fact, "had no institutional base of promulgation" even in Jerusalem. They maintained a high level of loyalty to a "life-style" based on laws handed down by God, but there is little evidence outside the Gospels that they were fanatical or mean-spirited or threatening to people who did not accept their way of life.[81] Thus, the debate did not occur during Jesus' lifetime,

78. Freyne, *Galilee, Jesus*, 100–102, 121.

79. Brown comments: "Matt[hew]'s extremely hostile critique of the scribes and Pharisees as casuistic (especially in ch. 23) is not untypical of the harsh criticism of one Jewish group by another Jewish group in the 1st centuries BC and AD—a criticism that at times crossed the border into slander" (*Introduction*, 222).

80. Paul Winter (*On the Trial of Jesus*) and Flusser (*Sage from Galilee*) argue that "the Gospels did not at all describe the conflict between Jesus and his contemporaries [which did not exist, at least in such an extreme form], but the struggle between the church and (pharisaic) Judaism" (Conzelmann and Lindemann, *Interpreting the New Testament*, 334). For Flusser's comments, see *Sage from Galilee*, 40, 42, 47–49. See also Maccoby, *Mythmaker*, 29, 32, 35–36; Lee, *Galilean Jewishness of Jesus*, 102, 114; Brown, *Introduction*, 79, 198; Gager, *Origins of Anti-Semitism*, 28–31, 140–41; and Wylen, *Jews*, 111. Thus, "the 'hypocrisy' [Jesus] condemned [in, e.g., Mark 7:6, where he quotes Isaiah 29:13] was an externality and superficiality, condemned by the prophets before him, for the consciousness of the intimate personal relation between God and man is characteristic of Israel's writers" (Cook, *Introduction to the Bible*, 124).

81. Mack, *Lost Gospel*, 60, 142. According to Sanders (speaking of Jewish laws governing circumcision, food, and purity), "The Pharisees did not invent these laws, nor were they the public guardians of them. Most are not enforceable, but in any case the official keepers of the law were the priests" (*Jesus and Judaism*, 275). Sanders provides a summary of "recent works [that] have sharply diminished or even eliminated the role of the Pharisees as substantial opponents of Jesus," as well as works that explore the phenomenon of retrojection in the treatment of Jesus' relationship to the Pharisees (291–92). Toynbee says that the Pharisees "prevailed on the strength of virtues that outshone their glaring faults [exclusiveness, pedantry, and obsessiveness]: the noble virtues of sincerity, disinterestedness, wholeheartedness, and readiness to expose themselves to persecution for the sake of abiding by their convictions" ("Introduction," 15). According to Chilton, "Although the Gospels portray the Pharisees as the stock villains in the drama of Jesus' life, they were decent (if somewhat pompous) men, with a considered understanding of religion, grounded within the authority of the Torah and reasoned debate in the community" (*Rabbi Jesus*, 118).

and its placement at that time is merely an example of a ploy common among ancient historians—i.e., moving events forward or backward to support a thesis.[82]

The problem here, however, is that, commonplace as this practice may have been, the consequences were dire. In fact, whether the New Testament picture of the Pharisees is true or false hardly matters. It seems that many readers of the text, throughout the centuries, have taken the Pharisees to represent *all* Jews, an interpretation that helps substantiate the idea that Jesus rejected Judaism—and therefore also rejected the Jews. In short, it is not merely that Judaism was shown to be hypocritical, shallow, and dogmatic.[83] Rather, "When the New Testament was canonized as the direct word of God and the original setting for the quarrel was lost, statements of hostility of this type were completely misunderstood and formed the basis of a virulent strain of anti-Judaism in Christianity." Unfortunately, modern Christian scholarship derives largely from this early Christian anti-Judaism, which is ineluctably—and irremediably—enshrined in the Holy Scriptures.[84]

This is not to say, of course, that Jesus was indistinguishable from the rabbis, the charismatics, the Essenes, and other ancient Jewish groups. The rabbis did not agree with each other, and all of these groups, as well as the more militant Jews who later formed the Zealots and the Sicarii (dagger men) before the Revolt of 66 differed on many points of theology, ethics, and politics. Indeed, according to one Bible scholar, "The general trend of Judaism at that time, in most of its more lively focal points and conscious groupings, was to go for the formation of 'sects,' in conformity with the 'holy remnant' concept of the Daniel literature."[85] On the other hand, however, the

82. Meier, *Marginal Jew*, I, 65. Koester says, "The gospels preserve traditions which originated with the sect of Jesus' followers, whose attitudes over against the Pharisees were by no means friendly"—however, not in Jesus' lifetime, but after his Crucifixion (*History, Culture, and Religion*, 239–240). Brown notes that Matthew and John retroject conflicts between the Church and the Pharisees in "the last third of the first century," which Luke does not include in his Gospel but acknowledges in Acts of the Apostles (*Churches*, 125–26). See also Ruether, *Faith and Fratricide*, 58, 59, 62, 63, 65, 267 n. 1); Chilton and Neusner, *Judaism*, 117; Jeremias, *Jerusalem*, 263; Parkes, *Conflict*, 28, 33, 34; Lieu, *Image and Reality*, 3, 284; Schillebeeckx, *Jesus*, 300; and Bultmann, cited in Augstein, *Jesus Son of Man*, 120. Lee says that this point is "generally acknowledged today" (*Galilean Jewishness of Jesus*, 71–72). Freyne, too, says that this view is widely held: "It would be generally agreed among N.T. scholars today that the debates and tensions between church and synagogue in the post-70 period had a fundamental influence on the formation of our gospels." However, he adds, the "general assumption . . . is open to refutation" (*Galilee, Jesus*, 199–200).

83. As Brown explains: "Tragically, as Christianity began to be looked on as another religion over against Judaism, Matt[hew]'s critique became the vehicle of a claim that Christianity was balanced and honest while Judaism was legalistic and superficial" (*Introduction*, 222).

84. Gager, *Origins of Anti-Semitism*, 7. "It is fair to say," says Gager, "that many of these disputes . . . represent occasions not so much from Jesus' lifetime, as from later times, the times of the gospels themselves, which have been read back into Jesus' career" (136). Segal argues that "[t]he degree of hostility described by John is anachronistic . . . The Gospel writer is projecting the level of hostility that he felt in his own day back to the time of Jesus" (*Rebecca's Children*, 156). See also Peters, *Harvest of Hellenism*, 487, 509 n. 4.

85. Schillebeeckx, *Jesus*, 144.

followers of Jesus shared many beliefs and practices with the other sects in Palestine, and Jesus himself had more in common with their leaders than has traditionally been acknowledged.

Except for the Sadducees and the nationalists, especially, most Jews seem to have expected the arrival of a messiah who would end their suffering (both political and economic), the elimination of the Roman empire and its attendant evils, the creation of a utopian society that was accompanied by the re-establishment of the Davidic monarchy, world peace, a return of the lost tribes, the resurrection of the dead, and eternal prosperity. "When Christianity came to the fore in the first century C.E.," says another scholar, "its adherents saw themselves as living in the period of the fulfillment of these visions. They identified Jesus as the Davidic messiah who would usher in the eventual destruction of all evil."[86] Thus, Jesus' disciples said, in reference to his recent Crucifixion, "We had been hoping that he was the man to liberate Israel" (Luke 24:21). And, at the beginning of Acts of the Apostles, they asked, "Lord, will you at this time restore the kingdom to Israel?" It is important to note that Jesus did not respond to this question by telling his followers that Israel would not be restored. He simply said that it was not for them to know when this event would occur because the time was known only to God (Acts 1:6–7).[87]

To be sure, Jesus was a dissident Jew, but in the first century dissidence was *de rigueur*.[88] Palestine was flooded with mystics, bandits, healers, magicians, rebels, and malcontents. Jews were angry about the Roman occupation, economic decline, the land-grabbing of large landowners, and the cozy relationship between the Jewish aristocracy and the occupiers. Many Galileans resented being ruled by the heir of a Hellenizing half-breed whose family intrigues would have filled our tabloids with reports of murders and other outrages year after year. Judeans hated the Roman procurators, who regularly insulted their religious sensibilities by making some kind of public display of images, forbidden by God, or by merely raiding the Temple treasury. Under these circumstances, many Palestinians who were not well-connected and benefiting from their association with the Romans were ready to follow any credible would-be leader who promised liberation.[89]

---

86. Schiffman, *From Text to Tradition*, 149–50. Jesus' baptism of fire (Matt 3:11) has Old Testament roots, as Schillebeeckx explains, fire and wrath being "fitting images of God's approaching judgement" (*Jesus*, 128–29).

87. For a more thorough discussion of Jesus' adoption of Jewish eschatology, see Sanders, *Jesus and Judaism*, 334–340: "The great symbolic acts of his life show that [Jesus] stayed within the general framework of Jewish restoration eschatology" (340).

88. According to Wilson, many Jews assumed that God was unhappy with their situation in Palestine and that the Messiah would rectify it. Thus, Jesus was revolutionary within Judaism. He was not making new laws; he was asking his fellow Jews to reconnect ritual and righteousness (*Jesus*, 98, 137). Cwiekowski says, "A militant opposition to Rome was a sporadic feature of Palestinian life after Pompey took control in 63 B.C." (*Beginnings of the Church*, 265).

89. "As a rule," says Hengel, "the rural population [often bedeviled by "robbers and rebels"] were grateful when a governor took a hard line against the plague of robbers" and other threats to law

And many such insurrectionists arose, offering freedom—if not in the form of revolution, at least in the form of apocalyptic promise. As one scholar puts it, "In the period before the war, charismatic leaders appeared, gathering crowds and promising to work signs: They claimed, says Josephus, to be prophets." All of them understood their mission in conformity with biblical prophecy—as we have seen—expecting the Jordan to part, the wilderness to lead to the Promised Land, and the walls of Jerusalem to fall; all of them were popular, attracting thousands; and all of them met the same fate: "immediate, definitive repression." In other words, not only did these men of conviction and purpose and commitment appear; they also attracted many followers who were ready to share their dreams and support their efforts.[90] "The movements of John and Jesus were [thus] not isolated ones. They rather represent particular expressions of a larger movement or set of movements that took place over several decades and eventually led to the revolt of 66."[91]

In this context, Jesus was—like his fellow protestors, prophets, and messiahs—a devout Jew and, again like the others, unquestionably a reformer of Judaism, whose preaching in Galilee encouraged Jews to repent and to prepare for the coming Kingdom of God. But he seems to have had no interest in establishing a new religion that departed significantly from Jewish Law and the sentiments of the Jewish prophets.[92] He wanted his fellow Jews to reform themselves and thereby demonstrate to God that they were morally qualified to receive the benefits of the Messianic Age.[93] "He did not intend to be the savior of the world; he intended to be a good Jew, faithfully following the path of conscience inspired by tradition and by the fresh presence of God."[94]

---

and order. Thus, ordinarily, residents of the Roman empire applauded even the use of crucifixion as a means of keeping the peace by punishing troublemakers. However, Hengel continues, "[s]emi-barbarian and more disturbed areas were an exception here, and refractory and unsettled Judaea was a special case" (*Crucifixion*, 49–50). That is, Jews sympathized with (and often both supported and protected) bandits, magicians, and revolutionaries who threatened the status quo. To them, almost uniquely, the crucifix did not represent law and order.

90. Fredriksen, *Jesus of Nazareth*, 150–51. Fredriksen adds later, "Messianic hope in Jesus' time was neither uniform nor universal, but it was certainly well established and articulate" (247).

91. Kaylor, *Jesus the Prophet*, 36.

92. Wilson finds the idea that Jesus intended to establish a new religion "fantastic" (*Jesus*, x, 186). Enslin says that, although the view "still persists in some circles that Jesus' aim was to found a Church, distinct from the Synagogue," it "is quite improbable. The gospels themselves bear little trace of such a view" (*Christian Beginnings*, 166). See also Dautzenberg and Josef Blank, cited in Augstein, *Jesus Son of Man*, 86.

93. Witherington, *Jesus Quest*, 39. According to Grant, "To a considerable extent, Matthew presents Christianity as a reformed and heightened Judaism" (*Historical Introduction*, 130). See also Borg, *Meeting Jesus Again*, 22. Hare, on the other hand, argues that Matthew emphasizes the discontinuity between Church and Synagogue (*Jewish Persecution of Christians*, 157, 170).

94. Kaylor, *Jesus the Prophet*, 211. See also Fredriksen, *From Jesus to Christ*, 98–100. Schillebeeckx mentions Jesus' typically Jewish emphasis on good works as the path to salvation: "Thus he identified with a type of preaching which as we have seen . . . simply had in view the proper relationship of human beings to the living God and with one another, the doing of God's will" (*Jesus*, 137; see also 142–43). "Like any other good Jewish teacher," says Sanders, "Jesus thought that people should

JESUS AND THE LAW

Again, like the prophets, Jesus was most concerned not with the irrelevancy or inadequacy of the Jewish Law as it appears in the Jewish Bible, but with the failure of human beings to follow the essential laws, especially those having to do with justice and compassion. He was appalled by selfishness and greed, and he railed fiercely against those who made a mockery of the Law by obeying some tenets but not others or by pretending to obey the Law while they attended to their own personal needs—the hypocrites whom he excoriated not because they were Jews, as the Gospel of John implies, but because they were as misguided as were the objects of Jeremiah's wrath and (not incidentally) equally worthy of God's forgiveness. Otherwise, why waste his time?

Thus, when Jesus departed from the Law, he either tightened up the ethical standards of Judaism or dismissed religious practices that seemed excessively onerous because they had no ethical purpose. The Pharisees, fearful of disobeying the laws laid down in the Torah, expanded them in order to minimize the possibility of even accidental disobedience, a goal that was later called "making a fence around the Torah."[95] But they were not extremists, as the Essenes at Qumran appear to have been, and there is no reason to believe that they would have disagreed very much with Jesus' actions and attitudes or that he would have strongly disagreed with theirs. At any rate, the most important question here is whether Jesus simply rejected the Law, as Paul seems to imply, or whether he actually modified the Law in the interest of preserving it by making it more authentic, more stringent, and more consistent.[96]

---

examine themselves and their relations with others, doing whatever was necessary to put these relations on a good footing." He "was concerned with how people treated others" (*Historical Figure of Jesus*, 202; see also 203–4). As Cwiekowski argues, the claim that Jesus said he was the Messiah and the Son of God, intended to found a new religion and establish a new church, and "dissociated himself from official Judaism" is "the pre-critical approach to understanding the beginnings of the church," but it is no longer "the dominant view" (*Beginnings of the Church*, 6–7). "The historical-critical picture of Jesus which emerges," the current dominant view, "is that of a Jewish rabbi, a prophet, an itinerant preacher, convinced of his intensely close relationship to God and of the mission which God had given to him" (60). See also 51, 53, 59, 64. Cwiekowski concludes: "Jesus conducted his mission as one who proclaimed the dawning of God's kingdom and who sought to bring Israel to the core, as he saw it, of its religious faith" (205).

95. The separation of milk and meat, including utensils and dishes used for consuming these foods, is a good example of this expansion. Segal explains: "The Bible says not to eat a young goat boiled in its mother's milk; it says nothing about keeping separate utensils for meat and milk or about not eating a fowl, which provides no milk for its young, at the same meal as cheese." Yet combining these two foods also became unacceptable (*Rebecca's Children*, 126).

96. Chilton comments: "All too often, even perennially, Jesus has been portrayed as an antinomian, dedicated to tearing down the law that Judaism revered. The portrayal is simply off base. His attacks on public piety and his emphasis on one's 'secret' relationship with God only enhanced the value of the Torah in his own mind" (*Rabbi Jesus*, 140). Similarly, Bultmann's Jesus is thus not merely the anti-legalist (*Theology*, I, 13, 17), but also the reformer within Judaism, who "distinguishes the important from the unimportant, the essential from the indifferent" (15–16). Bultmann says later that Jesus' "critical interpretation of the Law, in spite of its radicality, likewise stands within the scribal discussion about it, just as his eschatological preaching does within Jewish apocalyptic" (34–35). Indeed,

Some scholars, in the interest of portraying Jesus as a radical innovator, like to quote Matthew 11:30: "For my yoke is easy, and my burden is light," as if in this passage Jesus rejected the burden of the Jewish, especially Pharisaic, Law, which Paul found unbearable. But this pericope appears only in Matthew, and it is contradicted by Matthew 5:19–20, in which Jesus advised his followers not to relax even the least of the commandments and to *exceed* (rather than belittle, disparage, or ignore) the righteousness of the scribes and Pharisees. What is "easy," he said in Matthew 7:13, is the way "that leads to destruction." And, as he emphasized in both Matthew and Luke, "the way . . . that leads to life" is hard, and "the gate is narrow" (Matt 7:14; Luke 23:24). These are the Two Ways Jeremiah refers to as "the way of life and the way of death" (Jer 21:8), a concept that also appeared in both Psalm 1 and Deuteronomy 30:19, as well as in *The Didache* (*The Teaching of the Twelve Apostles*), c. AD 100.[97]

Whether Jesus accepted or rejected the Law is no longer much of a question in New Testament studies.[98] Even scholars who see Jesus through Paul's eyes are usually compelled to accept the evidence of Matthew 5 and 6, Matthew 19 (and its parallels in Luke 18 and Mark 10), and Matthew 25. After all, these three passages are, implicitly in the first instance and explicitly in the second and third, answers to the question, How can I be saved, or, to put it in the context of the Two Ways, How can I

---

in the early first century, as Mack notes, the Pharisees, too, might have been a force for simplifying the laws: "From a large system of legal, ethical, and sacrificial law that had been developed during the second-temple period, Pharisees had succeeded in isolating a small list of ritual practices they could perform at home. These could count, they said, as full observance of the Jewish law and tradition" (*Who Wrote?* 57–58). Enslin says, "Although [Jesus} had the most profound respect for the law, as did every Jew, and never opposed it or hinted that it would ever pass away, he seems always to have sought to get at the spirit of it, to stress what true obedience to it entailed" (*Christian Beginnings*, 163).

97. Meeks says that the idea of the two ways or paths "was common in antiquity." Besides the examples in Jewish texts, which should include the first psalm, Meeks finds examples in pagan texts as well, including, for instance, a fable about Hercules attributed to Prodicus and the *Tablet of Cebes*. Meeks notes that the concept often includes lists of virtues and vices, like the ones in Paul's epistles (*Origins of Christian Morality*, 70).

98. Sanders concludes, for example, after a chapter-long analysis of the subject (245–69), that Jesus urged his followers to violate a Jewish law only once: "We have found one instance in which Jesus, in effect, demanded transgression of the law: the demand to the man whose father had died": i.e., to "leave the dead to bury their own dead" (Matt 8:22) (*Jesus and Judaism*, 267). Hengel makes the point even more emphatically: "The saying . . . could be understood not only as an attack on the respect for parents which is demanded in the fourth commandment but also because at the same time it disregarded something which was at the heart of Jewish piety: works of love" (*Charismatic Leader*, 8; see also 10, 11, 14). However, Hengel is quick to point out that Jesus' attitude even in this exceptional demand was not entirely either un-Jewish or unlawful, since God forbade Ezekiel to lament the dead (24:15–24) and required other prophets to break off all family ties. The Essenes, Hengel adds, made the same demand on their novices (11–13). Sanders comments, "Otherwise the material in the Gospels reveals *no transgression by Jesus* . . . He apparently did not think that [the Law] could be freely transgressed, but rather that it was not final," a view he shared with the Pharisees (*Jesus and Judaism*, 267, 248–49; my emphasis). Speaking of New Testament scholarship in general, Sanders says, "[A] major line of New Testament research has held that Jesus did not take a negative attitude towards the law . . . That is,] he had no attitude towards the law other than that of the normally observant Jew: it represents the will of God" (246).

"inherit eternal life?" The unequivocal answer in all of these cases is *Obey the Law*. Be righteous, meek, and merciful; do not judge, do not seek revenge, forgive others, and follow the Golden Rule; give away your possessions and help the poor, the oppressed, and the suffering. These are the Good Works that Jesus asked his followers to do (at least in the synoptic Gospels)—not perfunctorily, of course, but sincerely and lovingly.

Even if we separate the moral law from the ritual law, the record in the Gospels is clear. When Jesus chastises the scribes and Pharisees for being diligent in tithing, but negligent in "the weightier matters of the law, justice and mercy and faith," he still acknowledges tithing (and presumably other ritual acts) as part of the Law, though he sees it as less important. The "weightier matters" are of course things that the scribes and Pharisees "ought to have done," but *without neglecting the others* (Matt 23:23; Luke 11:42; my emphasis). After all, the Jewish prophets who said that God preferred morality to ritual did not advise their fellow Jews to abandon sacrifice. At least, since the Temple continued to function in its traditional manner for several centuries after the prophets delivered that message, during which time they acquired greater and greater authority, no one interpreted them in that fashion.

Furthermore, the way the followers of Jesus understood his attitude toward the ritual laws, especially anyone who had a chance to hear what he actually said, seems to be reflected in their collective and individual decision to live their lives as observant Jews in every respect.[99] I will discuss this matter in more detail later, in Chapter Four. For now, suffice it to say that the Jewish Christians who made up the entire membership of the Jerusalem church honored the Sabbath, followed the purity laws, and obeyed the traditional restrictions on food. Indeed, James, whom Paul calls the brother of Jesus and whom Eusebius, the church historian, calls the first bishop of the church, was (by all accounts) an orthodox Jew, a regular attendee at the Temple, and possibly a Nazirite, bound by a vow to follow sectarian rules that made him even more observant than ordinary Jews. There is no evidence whatsoever that he eschewed even an iota or a dot of the Law and an abundance of evidence that he took it absolutely seriously.

Jesus' respect for the purity laws is reflected not only in Mark 1:44 (as well as Matt 8:4 and Luke 5:14) and Luke 17:14, but also in his encounter with two non-Jews whom he eventually healed: the daughter of a Syrophoenician woman and the slave of a Roman centurion. In both instances, the healing took place at a distance. That is, Jesus neither touched the sufferers nor even entered their houses, thus (presumably) obeying the laws that forbade Jews, in order to avoid impurity, from having close contact with gentiles. After refusing to heal the daughter, whose mother he insulted by calling her, as a gentile, a dog, Jesus relented and announced, "[T]he demon has left your daughter." Mark concludes the episode, "So she went home, found the child

99. On the disciples' favorable attitude toward the Jewish Law, see Sanders, *Jesus and Judaism*, 248. "We have again and again returned to the fact that nothing which Jesus said or did which bore on the law led his disciples after his death to disregard it" (268).

lying on the bed, and the demon gone" (7:25–30). That is, at the moment Jesus spoke, although the daughter was far away, she "was healed instantly" (Matt 15:28).

In the other account, at the behest of "some Jewish elders," Jesus was willing to come to the centurion's home. In Luke's version, this Roman is described as a God-fearer: "[H]e loves our people, and it is he who built our synagogue for us." As if Jesus had not been informed that the man who sent out the Jewish elders as emissaries was a gentile, the centurion sent out other friends to stop Jesus from proceeding farther. His message is instructive: "Lord, do not trouble yourself, for I am not worthy to have you come under my roof; therefore, I did not presume to come to you." After the centurion's profession of faith in Jesus' ability to cure his slave, Jesus healed him, but without getting any closer: "When those who had been sent returned to the house, they found the slave in good health" (Luke 7:2–10). That is, as Matthew puts it, "[T]he servant was healed in that hour" (Matt 8:13) even though Jesus never even saw him.

As one scholar explains, in reference to the centurion, "This devout Roman wanted to avoid the possibility of Jesus contracting impurity through contact with a non-Jew—the dwelling places of Gentiles were considered impure—so he asked Jesus to heal his servant at a distance."[100] Another scholar adds: "Actually all cures 'at a distance' in the New Testament have to do with 'pagans'; it is a consequence of the fact that Jews will not enter pagan homes, as the pagan Judeophile centurion explains."[101] In these incidents, Jesus appears to be respectful of the purity laws; indeed, he seems to take them as seriously as any Pharisee would.[102]

These two events are particularly striking because, immediately before them, Jesus cured a leper by touching him. After them, Jesus entered Peter's house, went into the bedroom of Peter's mother-in-law, and healed her by touching her. Subsequently, he healed two demoniacs, a paralyzed man, and a woman suffering from hemorrhages—all face-to-face. Finally, he cured a synagogue leader's daughter, two blind men, and another demoniac. He healed the daughter inside her house by holding her hand. He healed the blind men inside someone else's house, but also by touching them. He exorcised the demoniac face-to-face (Matt 8:1–9:33).

---

100. Flusser, *Sage from Galilee*, 52. Chilton says: "In sharp contrast to the way Christian scholarship typically portrays Jesus, the story [of the Centurion] also shows that he was wary of direct contact with Gentiles . . . The episode provided every opportunity for Jesus to transgress the boundary between the circumcised and the uncircumcised—yet that is precisely what he does not do" (*Rabbi Jesus*, 166).

101. Schillebeeckx, *Jesus*, 185–86, 415.

102. On the ancient Jewish distinction between ritual purity (which was not considered sinful) and moral purity (which was), see Klawans, "Moral and Ritual Purity," 266–83. Klawans concludes: "Attention therefore must be paid to Mark 7:21–23, Jesus' list of the things that, by coming out of a person, defile the person . . . What is so striking about the list is the degree of conceptual correspondence between the sins listed here and those that were generally understood to be morally defiling by the Hebrew Bible and the Rabbis—as well as certainly many other early Jews." Thus, Klawans continues, "Nothing contained in Mark 7:21–22 puts Jesus in radical opposition to first-century Jewish attitudes toward impurity" (282). See also Fredriksen, *Jesus of Nazareth*, 200–203.

As for the dietary laws, it is fairly clear that Jesus must have kept kosher—that is, avoided eating certain kinds of meat and seafood proscribed in the Jewish Bible. The main evidence is not in the Gospels and not in direct reference to Jesus' actions, but in reference to the behavior of his disciples as it is described in Acts of the Apostles and Paul's letters.[103] In Mark 7:19, Jesus says, "Hear, all of you, and understand: there is nothing outside a man which by going into him can defile him." Mark comments, parenthetically, "Thus he declared all foods clean."[104] The problem with this statement is that it is contradicted by three passages in Acts and one in Paul's letter to the Galatians. In Acts, Peter fell into a trance in which he was told by God, who showed him "all kinds of animals and reptiles and birds," "Rise, Peter; kill and eat." Peter's response indicates that this pillar of the Jerusalem church had up to this point—at least a decade after the Crucifixion—followed the dietary laws of the Torah: "No, Lord; for *I have never eaten anything that is common* [i.e., profane] or unclean" (10:14; my emphasis). The voice of God continued, "What God has cleansed, you must not call common" (10:9–16).

The mere fact that the voice had to repeat three times the declaration that all foods are acceptable suggests that Peter's resistance to change was strong. And it was so presumably because he had never heard Jesus say anything to indicate that the traditional dietary laws established by God at Mt. Sinai were no longer in force. Thus, Peter said later to Cornelius and his family, "You yourselves know how unlawful it is for a Jew to associate with or to visit any one of another nation" (Acts 10:28). After Peter witnessed the descent of the Holy Spirit onto Cornelius and his gentile companions, he was challenged by some of the members of the Jerusalem church ("the circumcision party"): "Why did you go to uncircumcised men and eat with them?" He responded by retelling the story of his revelation (Acts 11:3–10). But he did not

---

103. My argument in this and the following paragraphs is based on the analysis by Levine, *Misunderstood Jew*, 24–26. Sanders says, "[T]here is no indication that Jesus and his disciples did not eat kosher food" (*Jesus and Judaism*, 266). On the other hand, Crossan argues that Jesus was simply indifferent to the ritual laws (*Historical Jesus*, 263).

104. Wilson says that this comment by Mark is "very different" from what Jesus actually communicated to his disciples. Jesus was "merely telling the Jews to keep a sense of proportion about their dietary laws, and to search their own hearts . . . Mark, of course, is writing for Gentiles, who do not observe the Jewish dietary laws" (*Jesus*, 138–39). Flusser says that Jesus' liberalizing statement regarding the dietary laws "is completely compatible with the Jewish legal position. A person's body does not become ritually impure even when one has eaten animals forbidden by the Law of Moses!" (*Sage from Galilee*, 37). Herzog says that Mark 7:1–23 was, according to form critics, built around the original saying of Jesus, in 7:15. That is, vv. 6–14 and 17–23 are later interpolations: "Most of the intervening material is judged to have come from the early church as a justification for setting aside food laws (7:19b)." However, Herzog goes on to summarize an interpretation by Jerome Neyrey that ties most of these parts of the passage together. Yet, again, his conclusion does not support the traditional understanding of the passage: "All of this means, for Neyrey, that Jesus is not abolishing the purity rules but redefining them." In other words, the passage is not about rejecting the rules, but "contrasting conflicting views of purity" (*Jesus, Justice*, 87–88).

support his decision by referring to anything that Jesus said or did during his life-time.[105] Furthermore, he referred to himself as a Jew, not a Christian.

When Paul and Barnabas visited Jerusalem for the famous conference with the leaders of the Church, at least some members of the congregation believed that gen-tiles should not only be circumcised, but also "keep the law of Moses" (Acts 15:1, 5). That "the law" related at least partly to the food laws is suggested by James' solution, i.e., that gentile converts should not only avoid "unchastity," but also refrain from eating meat sacrificed to idols, meat from strangled animals, and meat still contain-ing blood (15:20). Suggestively, however, what is unspoken here is that this solution applied only to gentiles (15:19). Jewish Christians appear to have been expected to maintain the laws of Moses, including the practice of circumcision and the prohibi-tion against certain foods. And this devotion to the Law among Jesus' Jewish disciples, who constituted at this time the overwhelming majority, *could only have derived from either Jesus' advice or his practice (or both)*.

Here, Jesus is close to the traditional Jewish view of the Covenant, which could never be broken: "God is mindful of his covenant for ever." It is "an everlasting cov-enant to Israel" (Chr 16:15–17).[106] In this context, Jeremiah's "new covenant" could not have been a revision of the old one. His point is not that the Law will be changed, but that it will be understood more deeply and acted on more spontaneously. It will not have to be taught because God "will write it upon their hearts" (Jer 31:33–34)—an idea that Jesus expresses in the Sermon on the Mount.

It is also evident, from Paul's account of his quarrel with Peter about eating with gentiles, that Peter remained equivocal about abandoning his Jewish traditions. He first ate with gentiles, implicitly rejecting the dietary laws, but, when criticized for doing so by "certain men" sent by James, "he drew back and separated himself, fearing the circumcision party," as did "the rest of the Jews," even Paul's partner, Barnabas (Gal 2:11–13). Since these men were not just Jews, but *Christian* Jews, and since they were sent by James, the leader of the Church, it seems that the entire Jerusalem congrega-tion took a stand *against* Paul and *in favor of* the purity laws. Furthermore, from Paul's succeeding argument that Faith had replaced Works and that belief in Jesus had sup-planted obedience to the Law—addressed, by the way, to "foolish Galatians"—it seems

---

105. Wylen says that Jesus seems indifferent to the details of the purity laws and critical of those who overemphasized them. "On the other hand," Wylen continues, "Jesus' public career began with his immersion by John, and baptism early became a central Christian rite. It was only some decades after the crucifixion that Christianity permitted non-kosher food, and then only after heated debate as recorded in the book of Acts. Had Jesus outrightly rejected the ritual purity laws there would not have been so much objection to Paul's innovation . . . Jesus' own practices most likely fell within the broad range of pious Jewish practice" (*Jews*, 90). Brown echoes this sentiment: "The hard-fought struggles over kosher food attested in Acts and Paul would be difficult to explain if Jesus had settled the issue from the beginning" (*Introduction*, 137).

106. These words are repeated in Psalm 105:8–9, and the sentiment is reiterated in Psalm 111: "[A]ll his precepts are trustworthy, they are established for ever and ever" (vv. 7–8).

that the recipients of this epistle were, from Paul's perspective, as remiss as Peter and Barnabas and the rest of the Jerusalem church had been.

The point is, of course, that although the Church unquestionably turned a corner under Paul's influence, Jewish Christians were still following the Mosaic food laws in AD 50, twenty years after the Crucifixion, and many continued to do so for many more years. Either Jesus did not urge his fellow Jews to obey these laws and his disciples misunderstood him, or they understood him completely and obeyed him devotedly, at least until Paul took Christianity in a new direction. Matthew's omission of Mark's claim that Jesus made all food clean suggests that Jesus' position on this subject may have been interpreted differently in different communities. In Matthew, Jesus goes so far as to suggest that his disciples must follow *all* the teachings of the scribes and Pharisees because they "sit on Moses' seat," even though they fail to practice what they preach (23:2–3).[107]

The same thing is true of Jesus' alleged rejection of Sabbath prohibitions. His famous statement on the subject seems to imply that the traditional restrictions were, to him, worthless: "The Sabbath was made for man, not man for the Sabbath" (Mark 2:27). This sounds revolutionary, but it helps to remember that a second-century Rabbi said the same thing: "The sabbath is delivered to you and not you to the sabbath."[108] God's directive states that men and women should rest on the Sabbath: "Six days shall you do your work, but on the seventh day you shall rest" (Exod 23:12; Deut 12–15). The problem is, God did not indicate exactly what He meant by "rest." In Numbers, when the Israelites caught a man gathering sticks on the Sabbath, they had to consult God directly (through Moses) as to whether this act qualified as a crime. In this case, God told His people to stone the man to death (Num 15:32–35). But He was not available to say whether it was lawful to heal the sick on the Sabbath, at least during Jesus' lifetime.

In the synoptic Gospels, the Pharisees, in consultation with the Herodians or the scribes, were so incensed at Jesus when he healed a man with a withered arm on the Sabbath they "held counsel . . . how to destroy him" (Mark 3:1–6; Matt 12:9–14; Luke 6:6–11). But Jesus' justification for his action—that "it is lawful on the sabbath to do good" or "to save life" is exactly the answer that the rabbis would have given. In the words of one scholar, it "is in conformity with the view of the rabbis for whom the saving of life superseded the Sabbath precepts." Even if it is argued that the man

---

107. Brown discusses this issue in *Introduction*, 188–89. He elsewhere states that Matthew's Jesus unquestionably supported the Law although he modified it (179). Brown also notes Jesus' silence on the topic of circumcision (308). See also 470; and Brown, *Churches*, 41 n. 60. Weiss states that Jesus never raised an objection to circumcision (*Earliest Christianity*, II, 671, 696).

108. For comment on this point (and an exact identification of the Jewish source), see Flusser, *Sage from Galilee*, 38–40; and Conzelmann and Lindemann, *Interpreting the New Testament*, 316. Lee says, referring to Jacob Lauterbach, "the teaching of Jesus that the Sabbath is made for human beings and not the reverse is good Pharasaic doctrine (cf. Mekilta Shabbata I). Again, if any of these interactions with the Pharisees do come from the mouth of Jesus, it is a Jesus who is speaking from Pharisaic principles" (*Galilean Jewishness of Jesus*, 111).

with the withered hand was not in need of life-saving, "the form of healing by word of mouth or touch which Jesus had adopted did not really count as 'work' prohibited on the sabbath."[109]

Two similar Sabbath events occur in Luke. First, much to the chagrin of the ruler of the synagogue, Jesus healed a woman who had been crippled for eighteen years (Luke 13:10–14) and later healed a man with dropsy (Luke 14:1–3). Jesus explained in both instances that, if it is lawful to lead an animal to water or to pull it out of a ditch on the Sabbath, it is lawful to heal "a daughter of Abraham" who has been suffering for a long time or a man in the same situation. According to one commentator, "The [earlier] story highlights Jesus's action in contradistinction from what the synagogue leader would have preferred. But the crowd—that is, the Jewish majority—had no problem with Jesus healing the woman, and they would have recognized his argument to be a standard for the discussion of legal matters." The point is that physicians rested on the Sabbath, but miracle workers were permitted to continue their spiritual labors.[110] After Jesus explained his healing of the man with dropsy, the lawyers and Pharisees who witnessed the event were silenced by his justification.

Jesus' alleged Sabbath violations in Matthew and John are equally easy to accept within the limits of the Jewish Law. In Matthew, Jesus' disciples "pluck ears of grain" because they are hungry (Matt 12:1), a situation materially different from the one in Numbers, mentioned above, wherein the man who gathers sticks is stoned to death, with God's blessing (Num 15:32). Here, Jesus explained, it was hunger that excused his disciples' labor, just as hunger justified David's eating of the showbread, which was put aside for the priests in 1 Samuel 21:3–6. In the Gospel of John, Jesus cured an invalid, sick for thirty-eight years, whom he directed to "rise, take up [his] pallet, and walk" (John 5:5–8). When the invalid followed Jesus' orders, he was criticized for carrying on the Sabbath, just as Jesus was charged with healing on the Sabbath. In the latter case, Jesus gave no excuse at all.

It is clear in these examples that Jesus was not suggesting that his followers should ignore the Sabbath, as Paul urged the Galatians to do (Gal 4:10). He was simply honoring it as a sacred day on which reasonable acts could be performed and useful services could be rendered. Understanding Jesus from this perspective, the Galatians were not only eager to respect the Sabbath in the traditional manner, they were also ready to be circumcised. Given their conception of Jesus' position on these matters, which seems to match the position of *all* the disciples, except Paul, one is forced to

109. Vermes, *Changing Faces of Jesus*, 210. This paragraph is based on Vermes's discussion on 209–10.

110. Levine, *Misunderstood Jew*, 32–33.

conclude that Jesus was redefining the laws rather than rejecting them.[111] And just as it is clear that he did not reject the Sabbath, he also never repudiated circumcision.[112]

Although these revisions seem random and arbitrary—and therefore perhaps to be understood not as substantive but as expressive of Jesus' sense of his own authority ("For the Son of man is the lord of the sabbath" [Matt 12:8])—there is a method to his modifications.[113] Many of the key passages are those in which Jesus criticized his auditors, especially the Pharisees, for substituting their own tradition for the will of God. Quoting Isaiah, for example, he said, "[I]n vain do they worship me [that is, God], teaching as doctrines the precepts of men." Then Jesus made his objection clearer: "You leave the commandment of God, and hold fast the tradition of men . . . You have a fine way of rejecting the commandment of God, in order to keep your tradition!" (Mark 7:7–9; Matt 15:3, 9).

What Jesus was suggesting in these verses is precisely what seems to have bothered him most about the Pharisees, despite his affinity with them. The "tradition" he repudiated was nothing less than the oral tradition that the Pharisees and others had

111. Flusser says that in these two instances Jesus committed no offense against the Sabbath: "[T]he Synoptic Gospels, if read through the eyes of their own time, still portray a picture of Jesus as a faithful, law-observant Jew. Few people seem to realize that in the Synoptic Gospels, Jesus is never shown in conflict with current practices of the Law—with the single exception of the plucking of heads of grains on the Sabbath." Flussser goes on to suggest, however, that Jesus' disciples were "behaving in accordance with their Galilean tradition" (*Sage from Galilee*, 35). Flusser argues, furthermore, that "the kernel of Jesus' words in the debate . . . is completely in harmony with the views of the moderate scribes" (38–39). On the second incident, he says: "[I]f there was even a slight suspicion of danger to life, any form of healing was permitted. Moreover [as both Vermes and Levine point out; see the preceding two notes], even when the illness was not dangerous, while mechanical means were not allowed, healing by word was always permitted on the Sabbath" (39). See also Maccoby, *Mythmaker*, 40–42; and Sanders, *Jesus and Judaism*, 266–67.

112. "Here," says Sanders, "the great fact is that Jesus' followers did not know that he had directly opposed the law, and in particular they did not know him to have opposed the laws governing Sabbath, food and purity" (*Jesus and Judaism*, 25; see also 55–56). Elsewhere, Sanders is quite emphatic on the point that Jesus did not reject the Jewish law: "Jesus does not propose that any part of the Mosaic code should be repealed" (*Historical Figure of Jesus*, 210). See also, generally, 113, 225; and, on food and Sabbath laws, 213, 215–16, 220–22. Sanders explains that these issues became important to the Church in the second part of the first century, when the Church was interested in minimizing the differences between Jewish and gentile converts. Thus, the rejection of the three sets of laws that separated the two groups: "circumcision, sabbath and food." Sanders continues, "The stories indicating that Jesus broke the law himself, and authorized his followers to do so, are . . . retrojected from the situation of the early church into the lifetime of Jesus" (222). In short, for a time, the disciples "observed the Jewish law, including its ceremonies, circumcision, and the dietary regulations" (Latourette, *History of Christianity*, I, 67).

113. The discussion that follows rests on the insights of Klinghoffer, *Why the Jews*, 55–56. McKenzie explains that "in the theory of the scribes nothing was lacking in the Law; what was not explicit could be reached by scribal interpretation." He continues: "If the precept to observe the Sabbath was vague, it was no longer vague when the scribes had compiled a list of thirty-nine works which were prohibited on the Sabbath." Furthermore, the scribes' "deduction from the Law . . . had the full authority of the Law" (*Old Testament*, 136). McKenzie notes that Jeremiah (in 8:8) said that "the false pen of the scribes" had made the Law "into a lie" (151).

added to the Law for many centuries.[114] It consisted of the commentaries and explanations that groups like the Pharisees and the Essenes believed were necessary not only to elucidate cryptic passages in the Pentateuch, but also to apply the general laws therein to specific circumstances. The goal, rejected by the Sadducees (and Jesus), was to adapt the written laws, received at Mt. Sinai, to the evolving and changing contemporary situation. It was argued that God himself began the oral tradition by announcing laws that were not originally recorded, and that this tradition was expanded, in the millennium after Moses received the Law from God, to include, among other things, laws pertaining to food, the Sabbath, and purity.[115]

Thus, all of the rules that Jesus criticized—"many other traditions" (Mark 7:1–4), namely, lists of activities forbidden on the Sabbath, praying only when ten or more adult males are present, hand washing before meals, cleaning cups and pots, prohibitions against washing and anointing on Yom Kippur, and perhaps even paying the

---

114. On these points, see Brown, *Churches*, 127. Brown notes that Matthew's Jesus honors the Jewish Sabbath (24:20) and that Matthew himself regards Jerusalem as "the holy city" (27:53) (129). Jesus' auditors are, in Brown's words, "Law-observant Jewish Christians" (131). Although Jesus seems to have abolished the Law in the Gospels, McKenzie says, "the primitive church in Palestine regarded itself as Jewish and lived in observance of the Law. Plainly not everything was always as clear as we would like to think it was" (*Old Testament*, 262). According to Conzelmann and Lindemann, "The ethical teaching of Jesus can only be understood against the backdrop of Judaism. Jesus does not intend to introduce new commandments, neither does he insist on supplementing those already in place. Rather, he wants to establish the uncorrupted intent of the commandments of God and for this reason removes the additions made by the pharisaic interpretation" (*Interpreting the New Testament*, 314–15). "What he did not accept," says Tabor, "were certain oral traditions and interpretations that some rabbinic teachers had added to the biblical commandments" (*Jesus Dynasty*, 116).

115. On the other hand, of course, considering the likelihood, as has been suggested by a number of scholars, that the evangelists retrojected the conflict between Jesus and the Pharisees from the last half of the first century to the first half, the attitude of the Pharisees during Jesus' lifetime might well be indeterminable. On the subject of the retrojection of Jewish-Christian conflicts, see Sanders, *Historical Figure of Jesus*, 217–18, 222–23. For example, Mark's claim that "a series of good deeds by Jesus led the Pharisees to want to kill him" is "intrinsically improbable" (218). Indeed, "[t]he traditional Christian view that other Jews hated him because he was good, and because he favored love, which they opposed, will not do" (5). Theissen states, however, that, at least regarding religious prohibitions, Jews at the time were generally inclined to interpret them loosely, if not, as among Alexandrian Jews like Philo, allegorically: "People had a 'liberal' attitude towards the prohibition against images," for example, as well as toward Sabbath rules, restrictions on relations between Jews and gentiles, and purity laws. "It is therefore no coincidence," Theissen continues, "that we find comparable 'liberal' views in Hellenistic Judaism, where there was daily contact with the problem of communication between Jews and Gentiles" (*Early Palestinian Christianity*, 79). As for the Pharisees, Theissen says that they interpreted the purity laws "in a reasonable way." Thus, he finds the demands attributed to the Pharisees concerning hand washing and cleaning kitchen utensils questionable: "Christian polemic is not very convincing here. The law about the sabbath was given a strict but practicable form: it was permissible to help men and animals in distress" (82). Sanders says that the Pharisaic practice of handwashing was only a "tradition," not a law: "Most Jews did not purify their hands before meals. Among the Pharisees, some regarded handwashing as optional: many of them washed their hands only before the Sabbath meal; they disagreed with one another with regard to whether or not hands should be washed before or after mixing the Sabbath cup. Deadly enmity over handwashing is, I think, historically impossible" (*Historical Figure of Jesus*, 219).

half-shekel tax to the synagogue—were not part of the written law that appeared in the last four books of the Pentateuch, but were part of the body of what would eventually become the Mishnah and the Talmud, those repositories of debates on and discussions of the written law, compiled by the Rabbis, heirs of the Pharisees.[116]

Perhaps this is why Jesus condemned the lawyers in Luke: "Woe to you lawyers also! For you load men with burdens hard to bear" (Luke 11:46). And it may also be why at least once (though uncharacteristically, as I said earlier) he called his yoke easy: "Come to me all who labor and are heavy-laden, and I will give you rest. Take my yoke upon you, and learn from me; for I am gentle and lowly of heart, and you will find rest for your souls. For my yoke is easy, and my burden is light" (Matt 11:28–30). In this regard, Jesus was closer to the Torah than the Pharisees were. Moses says to the Israelites in the Pentateuch, evidently speaking for God, "You shall not add to the word which I command you, nor take from it" (Deut 4:2).[117]

On the other hand, however, the Pharisees seem to have created supplementary laws *only for themselves* and did not impose their demands on others. Indeed, in the words of one Bible scholar, although the Pharisees were respected by other Jews, "they had no actual power." Furthermore, no one, including the priesthood itself—and the scribes as well—could force everyone to accept their interpretation of biblical law. Since the law was written, it could be studied, discussed, and interpreted by anyone, which is why "Judaism was not in the hands of the leading Jerusalem priests; lay people could come to their own views."[118]

In this respect, Jesus was merely doing what Jews were expected to do—i.e., interpreting the Law from his own point of view.[119] One scholar suggests, in fact, that Jesus appeared to speak with authority merely because he carried this practice to its

116. Segal says, "As Pharisaism became rabbinism, the rules proliferated" (*Rebecca's Children*, 127). Boyarin argues that Jesus "saw himself not as abrogating the Torah but as defending it." Seeing the Pharisees as "a reform movement" within Judaism, Boyarin says that their so-called traditions "would have been experienced by many traditional Jews as a radical change." In this respect, "Jesus' Judaism was a conservative reaction against some radical innovations" introduced by the Pharisees (and the Scribes) (*Jewish Gospels*, 103–6; see also 124–26). On the same point, see Herzog, *Jesus, Justice*, 171–74.

117. Jeremias's discussion of the scribes and their "esoteric" teachings may throw some light on this subject. Jeremias emphasizes that the scribes, who replaced the prophets and preceded the Pharisees as interpreters of the law, considered some spiritual knowledge—indeed, the most important part of it—to be dangerous to the uninitiated because they might misinterpret it or misuse it. For this reason, it was not written down; it was simply too sacred to be communicated to the masses (*Jerusalem*, 239–45). Jeremias points out (253–54) that, in Luke, Jesus accuses the scribes and Pharisees of quite different sins. The scribes impose inordinately demanding restrictions on the people, while refusing to share their learning; the Pharisees are faulted for hypocrisy (Luke 11:39–52).

118. Sanders, *Historical Figure of Jesus*, 44–45, 47–49. The Pharisees, says Kaylor, "tended to 'live and let live' as long as they were free to live faithfully to the Torah as they interpreted it" (*Jesus the Prophet*, 36). Moore says that the average Jew in Palestine had little to fear from the Pharisees because the Pharisees had no power to enforce their rules. They were, in fact, interested mostly in "keeping themselves at all times from every kind of uncleanliness" (*Judaism*, II-III, 77).

119. Herzog returns to this point repeatedly in *Jesus, Justice*, 66, 109, 168, 176, 180, 185.

logical conclusion, failing, in many instances, to cite authoritative sources, contrary to the ordinary method of the Pharisees: "[H]e taught them as one who had authority, and not as their scribes" (Matt 7:28–29). In other words, he not only interpreted the Law on his own, but refused to justify his interpretations by quoting "the tradition." When he was challenged for his unorthodox actions, he had the audacity to explain, rather than quote Hillel or Shammai. E.g., he spent time with publicans and sinners because they were the ones who needed to be saved. And although his attitude disturbed some of his auditors, he may well have been confident that he was doing and saying the right thing simply because he was a prophet of God, "inspired by the Holy Spirit," and therefore willing to proceed without relying on legal precedent. He cited his fellow prophets rather than his fellow Pharisees.[120]

All of this is to underscore that Jesus meant what he said in Matthew about his protective attitude toward the Jewish commandments: "Think not that I have come to abolish the law and the prophets; I have come not to abolish them but to fulfill them. For truly, I say to you, *till heaven and earth pass away, not an iota, not a dot, will pass from the law until all is accomplished. Whoever then relaxes one of the least of these commandments and teaches men so, shall be called least in the kingdom of heaven; but he who does them and teaches them all shall be called great in the kingdom of heaven*" (Matt 5:17–19; Luke 16:16–17; my emphasis). Jesus was not concerned in this passage with the oral tradition, which he could obviously do without, but with the written law, which he wanted to strengthen rather than ignore or destroy. "For I tell you," he continues, "*unless your righteousness exceeds that of the scribes and Pharisees, you will never enter the kingdom of heaven*" (Matt 5:20; my emphasis). Similarly, Jesus said in Luke that what separates the saved from the damned is hearing Moses and the prophets. Furthermore, looking forward to his own resurrection, he added, "If they do not hear Moses and the prophets, neither will they be convinced if some one should rise from the dead" (Luke 16:29, 31).

What Jesus meant by this, as he explained elsewhere, was following the Law and the prophets, and therefore having more concern for the inner than the outer self, more interest in the spirit of the law than the letter, and a greater commitment to God's intention—specified by Jesus in his list of so-called Antitheses in the remainder of the Sermon on the Mount, which held his followers to a higher standard regarding the negative emotions of anger, lust, vengeance, hatred, anxiety, and greed, as well as the positive actions of almsgiving, prayer, and fasting (Matt 5:21–6:34). In this respect, Jesus' way of "putting a fence around the Torah" was not to create more laws in order to minimize the possibility of mistakes and misinterpretations, but to encourage his followers to undergo an inward change so powerful that their will matched God's will.[121] Thus, his purpose was not to repudiate Judaism, but to bring it—as Socrates

---

120. Enslin, *Christian Beginnings*, 163–164. Enslin adds that this may be why Jesus was sometimes perceived to be, if not possessed, then at least "beside himself" (Mark 3:21) (164–65).

121. "It should be noted," says Fredriksen, "that his teaching in the Sermon on the Mount is not

did with Greek ethics and Buddha and other Indian reformers did with the Hinduism of the Vedas—to a higher level of self-consciousness, individual responsibility, and moral clarity.[122]

RELIGION AS QUID PRO QUO

Jesus *represented* Judaism, rather than opposed it, because, as I suggested in Chapter One, Judaism did not need to be changed or improved. It simply needed to be followed. The point cannot be stressed enough that—like the religions of China, India, Persia, and Greece—the Judaism of the first century AD had already passed through a profound transformation that left it very different from what it had been at the time of David and Solomon: a faith in which God was understood to be one of many gods. Early in the first millennium BC, He was portrayed as a king of the gods, worshiped ceremonially and collectively, and (ideally) obeyed abjectly and unquestioningly. Furthermore, Yahweh was assumed to have a contractual relationship with the Jews (or Israelites) that rested on the concept of *quid pro quo*: God promised that, if His people worshiped Him, He would reward them; if they rejected Him, He would punish them. It was that simple. And it was, at the time, a universal concept.

In Psalms, a transitional work that contains a combination of old-school and new-school Judaism, Yahweh is praised as unique "among the gods" (86:8) for His strength (89:8) and His greatness (95:3). Indeed, He is "above all gods" (96:4, 135:5), which is why "all [the] gods" are told to "worship him" (97:7). From the Israelite perspective, He is simply "*our* God" (48:14, 95:7; my emphasis) rather than theirs—that is, a tribal divinity: "Blessed is the nation whose God is the Lord" (33:12). In this capacity, His principal function is to cause the enemies of His people to stumble and fall (27:2), to "tread [them] down" (60:12; 44:5), and to smite them (3:7), which is why He is persistently solicited for aid: "Destroy thou them, O God," cries the psalmist (5:10; 6:10; 59:13). Such a god protects His people in exchange for worship (34:9–10; 37:4; 50:15) and rewards them for obedience: "Blessed is the man that feareth the Lord, that

presented as an alternative to Torah . . . Jesus here does what the later rabbis will term 'building a fence around the Torah'; that is, he prescribes rules of behavior that extend the prohibition, thus ensuring that the biblical command cannot be broken" (*Jesus of Nazareth*, 104). I would only amend this comment by saying that, to Jesus, it is not merely the obedience that matters, but the attitude behind it.

122. "Clearly," says Ehrman, "we have come a long way from Jesus, a Palestinian Jew who kept Jewish customs, preached to his Jewish compatriots, and taught his Jewish disciples the true meaning of the Jewish law" (*Misquoting Jesus*, 190). Mack emphasizes that Jesus' followers formed many different groups after his death, which is "evidence for the fact that Jesus did not provide a program for starting a new religion." That is, there was no "clear and common conception of the kingdom." Thus, "[t]he road from Jesus to the Christian religion that finally emerged in the fourth century . . . is a very long and twisted path." Furthermore, "[n]o early Jesus group thought of Jesus as the Christ or of itself as a Christian church" (*Who Wrote?* 45). Mack reminds his readers that the Q community—the followers of Jesus who composed the sayings document used much later by Matthew and Luke—was both closer to Jesus and closer to Judaism than other groups and strong evidence, therefore, that Jesus remained closely tied to Judaism (47, 159).

delighteth greatly in his commandments . . . Wealth and riches shall be in his house" (112:1–3; see also 1:3; 18:20–21; 19:11).

However, influenced by the works of the prophets; such writings as Proverbs, as well as many of the psalms; and inter-testamental works like *Ecclesiasticus* and *The Psalms of Solomon*, Judaism evolved into a truly monotheistic faith, in which Yahweh was understood to be the *only* God and therefore, at least for those who believed in him, the God of all. His people conceived of Him as accessible and even fatherly as well as kingly, were commanded to honor Him by imitating His acts of mercy and justice, and (again, ideally) accepted His demands out of affection, not apprehension. In other ways, too, the Jewish view of God became more nuanced and complex—less formulaic. He rewards kindness, rather than mere worship (Pss 24:4; 37:3), offers security (17:7) and salvation (118:14–15; 119:155), not just wealth. And He saves the contrite and repentant as well as the obedient (51:1–17).

The point is that the writings of the prophets; parts of Deuteronomy, Psalms, and Proverbs; and many apocryphal works represent a new stage in the development of Judaism, emphasizing these ideas.[123] "The great prophets," one scholar explains, "were confronted by what was virtually a nature-religion, one, however, not devoid of ethical ideas, and their achievement was to ethicize it, and to emphasize the fundamental principles of the relationship between God, the universe and man."[124] One need only compare the moral code of the first four books of the Torah with that of the later biblical works to see how profoundly transformed Judaism was by the middle of the first millennium.

In the older writings, Lot offers his two virgin daughters to the Sodomites to prevent the latter from sexually abusing the two angels who are staying at Lot's home (Gen 19:1–8); the matriarch Rebekah counsels her son Jacob to deceive his father in order to get his blessing as the first-born son (Gen 27:1–13); Moses begs God not to destroy all the Israelites because the act will damage His reputation in Egypt (Num 14:13–16); and God tells the Israelites to kill all the men, women, and children, as well as the domestic animals, who inhabit the cities God wants the Israelites to occupy (Deut 20:16–17). In the later writings, neither God nor His followers appear to conduct themselves in such morally questionable ways.[125]

---

123. Cook, *Introduction to the Bible*, 61, 92, 113, 161.

124. *Introduction to the Bible*, 6. Horsley says that the god most prominent in the neighborhood of the Israelites was, like Zeus, the storm-god, who was important to agricultural societies because he controlled the weather. The Jews "transformed Yahweh from the Force that had liberated people from bondage in Egypt into the force that established and maintained the order of the universe forever" (*Covenant Economics*, 54–56). Flusser comments, "It would be a mistake to to think of the Judaism of Jesus' time as being identical with the religion of the Old Testament or as being a mere development of the ancient faith of Israel" ("Jesus in the Context of History," 226). Flusser specifically mentions the issue of morality: "If man knows that recompense from God awaits him for his good deeds, can his actions be dictated by a high morality?" (226). This is the kind of question for which Judaism began to provide new answers.

125. Enslin says that Deuteronomy, composed in the seventh century BC, marks the true beginning

In other psalms, for example, one also finds that Yahweh is not merely tribal, but moral. He protects both the oppressed (Pss 9:9; 12:5; 72:4; 103:6) and the needy (35:10; 40:17; 68:5; 72:12–14; 82:3–4). At the same time, He attacks the rich, the proud, and the powerful (10:2–10; 49:6–7; 73:3–12; 94:3–6). And, finally, he strongly emphasizes the universal need for forgiveness (25:6–7; 32:5; 103:3). Here, it is mankind ("the son of man"), not just Israelites, of whom he is "mindful" (8:4). In short, Yahweh is in these (presumably) later verses perceived to be a deity who acts according to well-defined principles; wants all of humanity to act in conformity with them; loves everyone who loves Him; and punishes all those who betray the innocent, the helpless, and the destitute by putting their own interests first: "The Lord preserveth all them that love him: but all the wicked will he destroy" (145:20).

Indeed, one clear indication of the transformation of Judaism from a religion of fear to a religion of love is the redefinition of God as a father as well as a king. In fact, although Jesus has often been credited with introducing (or at least emphasizing) the concept of God as "abba" (Aramaic for "father"), the idea of God as a loving father has deep roots in Jewish tradition.[126] Like other ancient nations, the Jews thought of their kings as sons of God, especially David (Pss 2:7; 89:26–27) and Solomon (2 Sam 7:14). Eventually, however, God was understood to be the father of all Jews. In the Torah, Israel is God's "first-born son" (Exod 4:22–23), and Israelites are "the sons of the Lord" (Deut 14:1), as well as, more comprehensively, His children (Deut 32:6, 18).

Scholars have recently pointed out that the exclusive association of Jesus with this word was first suggested by the Nazi author of *Die Judenfrage* (1933), Gerhard Kittel. Oddly enough, Jesus used the term only once (Mark 14:36), while the Essenes at Qumran characteristically referred to God as Father, as did Philo, the authors of *3 Maccabees* (6:2–4), *Wisdom* (2:16), and *Ecclesiasticus* (23:1), as well as the authors of many other Jewish sacred texts: e.g., Psalm 68:5; 103:13; Isaiah 1:2; 9:6; 45:11; 63:16; 64:8; Jeremiah 3:19; 31:9; Hosea 11:1; and Malachi 1:6; 2:10. Thus, as one student of first-century Judaism declares, "If they [i.e., Jesus and his followers] used 'father' as an address to God, they must have done so not because it was novel and revelatory but because it spoke to the deepest convictions and aspirations of their (Jewish) audience."[127] Furthermore, because of the image of the father in ancient Jewish culture

---

of modern Judaism (*Christian Beginnings*, 99). However, this is true only of the passages in which God established the rules of the community, chapters 12–27, which echo the earliest covenant codes, and emphasized that the basis for these laws is love rather than fear.

126. According to Meeks, God as father-figure "was a firm element in Israel's covenant traditions, and the relationship occasionally could be expressed by parental images of unsurpassed tenderness . . . By and large, the first Christians (like other sects of Jews) were taught to conduct their moral life under the all-seeing eye of a God who was simultaneously a stern patriarch and a forgiving and caring parent" (*Origins of Christian Morality*, 170, 172). "In those days," says Flusser, "'abba' was another common form of address." Flusser also notes that, like 'Rabbi,' 'abba' was used as both "a title of honor" and "a sign of affection" (*Sage of Galilee*, 14, 99 n. 13). On this subject, see also Chilton, *Rabbi Jesus*, 17–18.

127. D'Angelo, "Abba and Father: Imperial Theology in the Contexts of Jesus and the Gospels," 64–65. D'Angelo briefly discusses Joachim Jeremias's perpetuation and expansion of Kittel's thesis

as both authority and provider (especially of instruction), it is not surprising that Jesus frequently emphasized his total subordination to and dependence on God as a father (Luke 21:42; John 4:34; Heb 10:9).[128] He was the source from which everyone had much to gain and much to learn.

Thinking of God as a father, Jews conceived of worship not as ritualistic and perfunctory, but as personal and emotional. Thus, according to Josephus, whenever the Romans desecrated the Temple, Jews always put their lives on the line. They sent delegations to Rome. They removed Roman emblems from the Temple walls. And, when the situation demanded it, they preferred to be executed rather than allow the Temple to be adorned with imperial images.[129] Perhaps more important, they rebelled four times, in the inter-testamental period, against foreign domination not only on political grounds, but also (inseparable as the motivating factors were) on religious and spiritual grounds.

The decision of the Zealots (or Sicarii, as the case may be), who fended off the Romans for several years at Masada in the Revolt of 66, clearly illustrates the point. They chose to kill themselves (including their wives and children) rather than endure the rule of an alien and offensive power, which suggests a dedication to principle that was anything but shallow and hypocritical.[130] A century or so earlier, in 63 BC, faced with the conquest of Pompey, "Many of the priests, though they saw the enemy ap-

---

and adds that the use of the concept expresses not a new idea of God, "but a characteristic attitude of piety in which Jesus and his immediate disciples were brought up." That is, it was a popular idea in first-century Judaism. Furthermore, "approaches to the historical Jesus that seek to contrast him with 'the Judaism of his time' or that ignore the Roman imperial context of his death and life distort the origins of Christianity" (65–67). Carroll quotes John Pawlikowski: "In particular, Jesus' stress on his intimate link with the Father picks up on a central feature of Pharisaic thought" (*Constantine's Sword*, 74; see also 112). For a different view (a la Jeremias), see Schillebeeckx, who claims that Jesus frequently used the word *abba* in reference to God (as did his disciples) and that the concept was rare in Judaism (*Jesus*, 259–63). Schillebeeckx briefly mentions Jeremias's later retraction of his claim that *abba* was not typically used in Palestine in the time of Jesus (693 n. 210).

128. *Jesus*, 262–63. The most thorough examination of this subject is Moore, *Judaism*, II-III, 201–11. The use of the word *Father*, says Moore, represents "the type of piety in which Jesus and his immediate disciples were brought up, and the Gospel of Matthew is a most instructive illustration of it" (211). For a different perspective, see Bornkamm, *Jesus of Nazareth*, 124–29.

129. Wylen makes the point that the Jews were always ready to lay down their lives for their faith, as they did during several violent and non-violent protests (*The Jews*, 52, 82, 166). Latourette comments, "The loyalty of the Jews to their religion was heightened by persecution" (*History of Christianity*, I, 10). As examples, one might cite the execution by Herod's soldiers of forty martyrs who removed a large Roman symbol from the Temple (described in Borg and Crossan, *Last Week*, 42–43) and the mass suicide at Masada in AD 73 (described briefly in Tabor, *Jesus Dynasty*, 300). Peters refers to several incidents in which the Jews of Judea put their lives on the line for their beliefs (*Harvest of Hellenism*, 510, 514, 516). Peters notes that half a million Jews died in the Revolt of 132 (531).

130. Says Bornkamm, "There is no doubt . . . that this rebellious movement was filled with a theo-cratic ideal and fervent Messianic hopes" (*Jesus of Nazareth*, 33). Sanders says, "During the 150 or so years before Jesus' death, we know of at least four substantial upheavals that began during a festi-val—this despite the fact that both Jewish and Roman rulers were prepared for trouble and had force nearby" (*Historical Figure of Jesus*, 23–24).

proach with sword in hand, quietly went on with the sacred rites and were cut down as they poured libations and offered incense, putting the service of God before their own preservation."[131] They continued to honor the Sabbath even if it cost them their lives.

Paul has often been accused of creating the false dichotomy not only between a backward Judaism and a progressive Christianity, but also between an oppressive, law-ridden, God-forsaken Judaism and a liberating, faith-centered, God-begotten Christianity. That is, Paul was principally responsible for the Church's nineteen-century long "condemnation of Judaism," which is (and will always remain) "a cruel injustice."[132] Paul was wrong about Judaism, as I have suggested, but he was also wrong about Christianity. He did not understand that religions change over time and that Judaism had undergone a rather comprehensive transformation by the time of Jesus, just as the Church would undergo a transformation—sometimes for the better, sometimes for the worse—in the centuries after the Crucifixion.

In the eyes of many historians, Christianity proceeded, in some respects (or many, depending on one's perspective), from an emphasis on individual responsibility, social justice, and moral rigor—all of which Jesus inherited from the prophets—to a preoccupation with acceptability (to the Romans), uniformity (canonical, theological, and institutional), and power. These were demonstrably the issues that concerned Church leaders in the second and third centuries. Even in the post-Pauline letters, the focus of the Church sometimes shifts from the noblest concerns of humanity—the plight of the helpless, the needs of the poor, the suffering of the oppressed—to the pettiest issues and most retrograde attitudes, including the demand that women should submit in all matters to their husbands (1 Tim 2:11–14; 1 Pet 3:1, 7), that they should dress modestly (1 Tim 2:9–10; 1 Pet 3:3), that slaves and servants should be obedient to their masters (Titus 2:9; 1 Pet 2:18), and that Christians should accept the authority of all governments (1 Pet 2:13–15).[133]

By the fourth century, the Church had achieved the goals of acceptability, uniformity, and power. Most important, by way of satisfying all three objectives, it became the official religion of the Roman empire; however, the consequences were not entirely positive. One major result was the frequency with which the Christians committed the theological error for which they blamed the Jews: defining the divine-human relationship as a *quid pro quo*.

What I am suggesting is that the scholars who argued that Christianity superseded Judaism by replacing a religion of fear with a religion of love made two claims, both

131. Quoted from Josephus in Klinghoffer, *Why the Jews*, 27. As Wilson notes, 12,000 Jews were killed at the time by Pompey (*Jesus*, 95).

132. Herford, *Pharisees*, 220–21; see also 75. Mack also identifies Paul as the source of the distinction between rigid Jewish legalism and vital Christian spirituality in his contrast between Law and Faith (for example, in Galatians) (*Who Wrote?* 121).

133. Of course, some of these sentiments were expressed in the Pauline and deutero-Pauline epistles—in the case of Paul's work, in the middle of the first century: subordination of women (1 Cor 11:3, 8–9; Eph 5:22–24; Col 3:18) and obedience of slaves (Eph 6:5; Col 3:22–23).

of them wrong. That is, not only did they mischaracterize Judaism as sterile, vacuous, and even dead; they also misrepresented Christianity as everything that Judaism was not. This is not to say, however, that they were wrong about Jesus. There can be little doubt that Jesus connected with what was best in Judaism and brought it, as none of his contemporaries succeeded in doing, to center stage. To put it in the simplest terms possible, he reminded his fellow Jews of the extraordinary tradition they had inherited and called attention to their obligation to live according to its principles.

Nevertheless, it is hard to miss the passages in the Gospels in which Jesus himself threatens non-believers with eternal damnation—e.g., Matthew 18:7–9; 23:33–36; 24:46–51; and 25:31–46. (See also 2 Thess 1:7–8 and 1 Tim 6:18–19.) He was to be, at his return, a judge as well as a redeemer. Thus, although one scholar acknowledges that "Judaism has no hesitation about recognizing the merit of good works, or exhorting men to acquire it and to accumulate a store of merit laid up for the hereafter," he goes on to say that "[t]he most familiar examples are the words of Jesus in the Gospels." Indeed, the threat of punishment and the promise of reward "are as freely employed by Jesus in the Gospels" as they are in the Jewish Bible.[134]

It must be emphasized, however, that Jesus and other Jews more characteristically promoted the standard affirmed by Rabbi Antigonous of Socho: "Be not like servants who serve their lord on condition of receiving reward; but rather be like servants who serve their lord under no condition of receiving reward."[135] "There is a certain irony," says one student of ancient Judaism, in reference to Antigonous, "in the fact that the first recorded word of a Pharisee should be a repudiation of the supposed 'Pharisaic' wage-theory of righteousness." Furthermore, the idea that obeying every commandment not for gain, but "for its own sake"—meaning, of course, for *God's* sake—was (during, before, and after Jesus' lifetime) "frequently emphasized" in Jewish literature.[136] As I stated in Chapter One, it is the bedrock on which Jewish morality was founded, and Jesus could not have escaped its influence.

---

134. Moore, *Judaism*, II–III, 90–91. Moore adds, "The prejudice of many writers on Judaism against the very idea of good works and their reward, and of merit acquired with God through them, is a Protestant inheritance from Luther's controversy with Catholic doctrine, and further back from Paul's contention that there is no salvation in Judaism" (93).

135. Bultmann, who recorded the Rabbi's words and emphasizes the continuity between Rabbi Antigonus and Jesus (*Theology*, I, 14), has some difficulty rationalizing Jesus' many references to heaven and hell as reward and punishment for good and bad behavior, respectively. (See 15 for an example of Bultmann's incomprehensible prose used in the service of obfuscation.) Cook argues, in this regard, that Jesus was as fiercely demanding as Yahweh: "The God of the Bible is also one of wrath; and those of to-day who speak of the 'angry Jehovah' of the O.T. overlook the stern side of Jesus and the uncompromising discipline of the N.T.: Divine Love and Divine Righteousness are inseparable" (*Introduction to the Bible*, 131). Hatch says that the concept of rewards and punishments is common in early Christianity—for example, "in many passages of the New Testament, and not least of all in the discourses of our Lord"; as well as in the *Letter of Barnabas* (4:12 21:3), the Letter to the Hebrews (11:6), *The Didache* (4:7); and in the writings of Irenaeus, Tertullian, Clement of Alexandria, and Origen (*Influence of Greek Ideas*, 224–25, 228, 229).

136. Moore, *Judaism*, II–III, 96–97. In the first volume of this book, Moore refers to "the often

Thus, on one hand, the Church, implementing the covenant values that Jesus emphasized so strongly in the Sermon on the Mount, attracted converts partly because of its generosity and humanity. Even if it did not at all times and in all places take from the rich and give to the poor, there can be little doubt that the Church established itself as a model of social concern and public philanthropy not only for Christians, but for pagans as well. The poor were aided, the families of martyrs were supported, and victims of natural disasters could often count on Christians to help. On the other hand, however, acts of caring and sharing could (and in many instances did) become not so much expressions of love, but efforts to win God's favor. In the words of one historian, "generosity began to degenerate into a good work for the earning of heavenly credit."[137]

Thus, despite Jesus' fundamental agreement with the Jewish view of morality, some Christians appear to have carried the principle of *quid pro quo* much further than either the Jews or Jesus did. That is, they more blatantly and more consistently did what they accused the Jews of doing. Many Christians, for example, embraced the idea of supererogation. That is, martyrs and saints practiced self-sacrifice quite explicitly because they believed it would not only gain God's favor, but also compensate for past sins. This is not at all to say that even most Christians of these types were driven by the desire for rewards. It is merely to recognize that this standard of ethical behavior has been far more widespread than it should have been and as likely to appear in Christianity as in Judaism.

Some martyrs, for example, courted torture and even death on the assumption that they would immediately be admitted to heaven. They would, in fact, as a consequence of their suffering, stand tall among the saved because they had sacrificed themselves so willingly. Their names would be honored by their peers. And they would have the satisfaction of knowing that their persecutors were being punished: "[T]he martyrs were at times inclined to seek satisfaction in the thought that they would be avenged in the world to come, or even that it would be an element in the felicity of heaven to contemplate the appropriateness of punishments justly meted out to those responsible for acts of gross injustice in this present life."[138]

Other Christians, similarly seeking heavenly rewards, fasted and prayed, remained celibate, and gave away their property not so much as acts of self-denial and self-purification (either as ends in themselves or as a way to get closer to God), but as various means of gaining God's goodwill. Some thought that the most unnatural

---

repeated principle [in Judaism] that duty should be done for God's sake, for its own sake (because it is duty), not for the reward of obedience" (I, 35).

137. Bainton, *Early Christianity*, 56.

138. Chadwick, *Early Church*, 30. Parkes adds, "[I]t is one of the most amazing abortions of the religious mentality that with models before them of such exquisite and poignant beauty as the story of Pionius [which Parkes recites on 137–38], they produced the thousands of morally repulsive Grand Guignol travesties of heroism which deface the whole of this literature" (*Conflict*, 138–39). On this subject, see also de Ste. Croix, "Christianity's Encounter with the Roman Imperial Government," 350.

deprivations were the most efficacious; and, for many, withdrawal from society, which became a mass movement in the fourth century, was motivated by a desire to be richly (though spiritually) recompensed by God. Church leaders like Ignatius encouraged all kinds of self-sacrifice by calling the sufferers "the brides and jewels of Christ."[139] The Benedictines, who did not live extremely ascetic or impoverished lives, were able to perform charitable works that would help them get to heaven: "If we wish to escape the punishment of hell," said Benedict, "and attain to eternal life, we must so walk and so live only as to fit ourselves for eternity . . . that we may be worthy to be partakers in His kingdom" ("Prologue," *The Rule of St. Benedict*).

It was easy for people living in the ancient world to accept this religious principle because it was characteristic of all archaic people, especially before some agricultural societies developed new religious concepts and practices in the first millennium BC. That is, even in China, India, Persia, Israel, and Greece—where new ideas about God and morality blossomed between the eighth and third centuries BC—people at an earlier time saw the gods as potentially hostile forces who had to be placated in the hope that they would refrain from inflicting pain and suffering, provide adequate food and shelter, guarantee good health, and even help win a victory in battle. Surprisingly, the amoral character of this concept appears to have occurred to almost no one. (The most obvious exceptions are the authors of the Book of Job and the Bhagavad Gita.) As one historian comments: There was not "the least uneasiness about the self-interested nature of [such] worship. You only made offerings, or promises of offerings, in order to gain favor from powerful beings." It was also unnecessary to be sincere. People were merely demonstrating their dependency, not their loyalty.[140]

The Romans of the early Christian period worshiped gods of this kind, which is why they insisted that everyone in the empire pray either *to* the gods or at least *for* them. They assumed that the empire thrived only because its residents performed acts of worship that demonstrated their devotion to these deities. Although many Roman aristocrats privately scoffed at this idea, Augustus was infuriated by any sign of disrespect to the gods since, as he and many Romans believed, "the Roman religion was at its heart a reciprocal agreement between gods and humans," according to which success was granted only if the appropriate prayers were recited, vows were sworn, and sacrifices were offered.[141] In fact, the times were ripe for all kinds of superstitions.

139. "The belief was strong that Christ would crown those who suffered in this life" (Manschreck, *History of Christianity*, 31). Manschreck discusses the various acts of supererogation in which Christians engaged, especially in the second century and after, on 66–67. The author of the *Letter of Barnabas* says, "For the one who [does good deeds] will be glorified on the kingdom of God. The one who chooses those other things will be destroyed, along with his works. This is why there is a resurrection; this is why a recompense" (21:1).

140. MacMullen, *Christianizing the Roman Empire*, 13, 116. MacMullen adds, "What counted was payment, *do ut des*: payment for ritual, with hymns, incense, and the like in exchange for divine goodwill that might turn into good fortune" (116).

141. Klingaman, *First Century*, 73–74. In pursuit of the kind of moral probity the gods demanded, Augustus passed laws that prohibited adultery, required couples to have children, and made divorce

Augustus himself believed in "the power of dreams, portents, and oracles."[142] But such beliefs, except among the most sophisticated of Romans, were widespread throughout the Mediterranean basin, where the world was thought to be "populated by gods, angels, demons, [and] spirits of the dead," and magic was the only means by which these creatures could be influenced or manipulated.[143]

It should not be surprising, therefore, that Constantine, even after he became a Christian, held such views. That is, he was religious insofar as he understood that his success depended on the disposition of higher powers. And he was a Christian because he believed that one of those powers was the Christian God. Before a battle in 311, Constantine saw a cross in the sky one night and Christ in the sky the next night, took these visions as messages from God, put a cross on his soldiers' shields, and won the battle. This is the strange event that totally transformed Western civilization. *In hoc signo vinces.* His son Constantius said, in the same spirit, that "to people who are zealous in those [Christian] beliefs, all good things in abundance are accustomed to fall, and whatever they set their hand to will answer to their highest hopes."[144]

As a result of the extraordinary favor he received from God, Constantine legalized Christianity, began to subsidize, in his own words, "the lawful revival of the Church," ordered property that had been appropriated by the Roman government in the past to be restored to the Church, and gave the clergy immunity from "all public burdens." His explanation was simply that "protection of this same worship has caused the greatest good fortune to the Roman name and exceptional prosperity to all the affairs of men." His support of this formerly persecuted religion would in his opinion "bring immeasurable benefit to the commonwealth" in the future. He was quite willing to do anything "in order that *whatever Divinity there be in the heavenly seat* can be appeased and propitious to us and to all who are placed under our rule" (my emphasis). In short, Constantine was driven by purely utilitarian motives.[145]

Without the benefit of extensive religious instruction; not realizing that the Christian God might be offended by his equally fervent worship of the Sun God

---

more difficult to attain. MacMullen says, "For both the Christian and the non-Christian, . . . the only thing believed in was some supernatural power to bestow benefits" (*Christianizing the Roman Empire,* 4).

142. Klingaman, *First Century,* 18.

143. Smith, *Jesus the Magician,* 68–70.

144. Quoted in MacMullen, *Christianizing the Roman Empire,* 14. "In the world we are studying, there was nothing to be ashamed of in needing and asking favors from heaven" (14).

145. This is the view of Jacob Burckhardt, as quoted by Pelikan in *Jesus Through the Centuries,* 50. See also Bainton, *Early Christianity,* 63; and Gonzalez, *Story of Christianity,* I, 120–23. Gonzalez points out that—although Constantine, unlike most other Christians at the time, had no formal religious training, continued to participate in pagan rituals, and delayed his baptism until he was on his deathbed—he was not merely an opportunist. He was not primarily interested in gaining Christian support, but in gaining God's support. Gonzalez discusses Constantine's "love of luxury and pomp," his neglect of public works, and his dependence on circus shows to keep his his constituents happy (114).

(manifested in Constantine's celebration of Sunday in his honor); and embracing a particular religion because it was politically, militarily, and economically useful, Constantine was simply applying the same standard that drove many martyrs and monks to self-sacrifice. In his case, however, as one historian explains, he "knew and cared nothing for the metaphysical and ethical teaching of Christianity when he became a devotee of the Christian God: he simply wished to enlist on his side a powerful deity, Who had, he believed, spontaneously offered him a sign." It was a matter of *quid pro quo*—purely and simply.[146]

Many Christians also treated the Christian sacraments legalistically. Even famous Christians, such as St. Augustine's mother, Monica, regarded baptism as a kind of magical rite rather than a symbol of rebirth. She refused to have Augustine baptized at birth because she believed that, since baptism would wash away the sins her son had committed earlier, he would be better off waiting until his youth had passed and with it the sins of passion that might compromise his salvation. Some Christians who embraced this practice even waited until the last throes of a fatal illness to become baptized: "Some authorities in the Church might discourage such delay, but numbers, even of prominent laymen, including more than one of the Emperors, judged it safe and adopted it."[147] Until about AD 400, the postponement of baptism was common, especially among people whose jobs required them to engage in "un-Christian" acts, such as torture and execution. Constantine—clearly a serious, though not deeply informed, Christian most of his adult life—waited until his final days to undergo his formal, sacramental initiation into the Church.[148]

Finally, like the Jews whom they accused of the same moral failing, some Christians thought of acts of charity, mercy, and kindness not merely as ways of enhancing their chances of going to heaven, but also as means of compensating for acts of selfishness, indifference, and meanness. Some martyrs thought they could erase the sins they

146. This paragraph is based on the discussion of Constantine in Jones, *Constantine*, 73–90. Constantine was thus uninterested in the issues on which the Arian controversy was based and called for a meeting of bishops at Nicea not to get to the truth, which seems never to have been his goal, but to establish a God-pleasing unity in the Church in order to avoid God's wrath (132). Jones concludes: "Constantine seems, to judge by his language, to have conceived of God mainly as a God of power . . . Only rarely does he speak of him as the Saviour, and never as loving or compassionate. Twice only does he refer to God as the Father, and on both occasions he seems to envisage Him as the stern possessor of patria potestas [i.e., the total power of the Roman paterfamilias over his family and servants] rather than as a loving protector of his children" (197). On Constantine's visions, Brown says that the emperor "was the recipient of ten thousand such heartening visitations" (*Making of Late Antiquity*, 63). Payne discusses Constantine's continuing respect for pagan gods and heroes, his emphasis on ritual and propriety, and his interest in power as the principal benefit to be derived from worship in *Ancient Rome*, 292–93.

147. Latourette, *History of Christianity*, I, 96, 195. Clark comments, "Many Christians believed that baptism cleansed sin, but that post-baptismal sin could not be cleansed" (*Christianity and Roman Society*, 101).

148. Chadwick, *Early Church*, 127. Peters says that "the practice of late baptism was still common enough to require little explanation in the case of Constantine" (*Harvest of Hellenism*, 689 n. 8).

had committed through this consummate act of expiation.[149] In the fourth century, to make up for not living up to the standards established by monks—who dwelt apart from others in order to avoid temptation, lead simple lives, engage in religious practices regularly (and often almost incessantly), and avoid sexual contact—lay Christians, accepting "a double ethical standard," followed the ideals of Jesus and hoped "to aspire to higher reward hereafter *if they did more than the minimum that was actually commanded.*" That is, they believed, more good deeds could make up for falling short of the monastic ideal.[150]

Ironically, the more the Church succeeded, the more some groups of Christians lamented the change. Unlike two influential Christians, Eusebius (the Church historian) and Ambrose (the Bishop of Milan), who believed that paganism would be conquered by Christianity and who therefore welcomed the newly acquired power of the Church, others preferred to keep their distance: "Quite large sections of Christianity at one time or other during the fourth century saw themselves faced with a profane world and an apostate church that had succumbed to its temptations." Among these groups were the Donatists, who had gained notoriety for their opposition to allowing priests who had apostatized during the persecutions to return to the Church in their former capacities. They objected, as well, to what they considered to be the apostasy of the entire Church in its illicit dalliance with the forces of evil.[151]

Others who believed that the Church was in danger of losing its soul as it gained the world were the members of the monastic movement. The organization was initiated, to some extent, as an indictment of what many monks saw as the corruption of the Church, which, as a result of both its expansion and its assumption of power, had experienced a diminution in moral passion and a consequent erosion in moral rigor. As one historian of this period claims, "In part undeniably [the monks] were reacting against the secularization and paganization of the church through its too hasty success."[152] This occurred largely because the Church was no longer oppressed and powerless, but, with imperial support, able to do whatever it chose to do. In the words of another historian: "The sudden accession of wealth, respectability, and steadily growing prestige did not inhibit Christians in their readiness to share the culture of their contemporaries. It may be that we should interpret the vogue of monasticism in the later fourth century as, at least in part, a kind of protest movement within

149. Latourette, *History of Christianity*, I, 86. Some martyrs were so eager to make the trade of earthly suffering for heavenly bliss that they engaged in what some observers thought was provocative behavior. For example, although he had no objection to suicide on moral grounds, Marcus Aurelius thought that Christians, making much of their prospective martyrdom, were too theatrical (Chadwick, *Early Church*, 31).

150. Chadwick, *Early Church*, 176; my emphasis.

151. Markus, *Christianity in the Roman World*, 120. Augustine, unlike his friend and fellow churchman Ambrose, came to a similar conclusion, doubting that "any secular society," particularly the pagan Roman empire, could be "transformed and conquered by Christianity" (121–22).

152. Bainton, *Early Christianity*, 71–72.

Christianity against its readiness to identify itself so completely with the culture and values of secular society."[153]

In addition, the Church now welcomed large numbers of pagan converts, whose mere presence moved the Church in the direction of Hellenization: "The narrow gate of which Jesus had spoken had become so wide that countless multitudes were hurrying past it." This happened not as a result of life-changing conversions, as had been the case when Christians were a condemned and sometimes persecuted minority, but simply because, at least in some cases, the Church could now offer "privilege and position."[154] "As converts came in no longer by conviction, but for interested motives or merely by inertia, the spiritual and moral fervor of the Church inevitably waned . . . [T]he old corruption and oppression of the masses by officials and landlords went on unabated, and the last remnants of public spirit faded away."[155]

A conspicuous absence of any kind of mind- and heart-altering experience also characterizes the conversion of many pagans to Christianity who came to the Church not for gain, but because they were deeply impressed by miracles and magic and martyrdoms. Jesus himself complained about superficial reasons for following him, when beneficiaries of his miracle of the loaves and fishes came searching for him. In response to their obviously sincere and earnest desire to see him, he said, "Ye seek me, not because ye saw the miracles, but because ye did eat of the loaves, and were filled" (John 6:26). That is, he seems to imply, they sought him for the food he provided, not for "that meat which endureth unto everlasting life" (6:27). Even if they came for the miracles, however, their conversion was as superficial as Constantine's—that is, if they had had no moral instruction and no real understanding of what, exactly, they were converting to. This was the situation of thousands, if not millions, of Christian converts in the fourth and fifth centuries.[156]

---

153. Markus, *Christianity*, 128. Heer makes the same point regarding "the growing ascetic movement" of the twelfth century: "The features common to all of [these groups], flight from the world, exaltation of poverty and the imitation of Christ, can only be understood in the light of the extreme 'worldliness' of the medieval Church and of Christendom at large" (*Medieval World*, 65).

154. Gonzalez, *Story of Christianity*, I, 136. MacMullen notes that Eusebius criticized the hypocrisy of some Christians who converted for material benefits. "It was, in sum," MacMullen explains, "manifestly profitable in worldly terms to declare yourself Christian; and Christians believed that the motive was widely at work among at least the governing classes, on whose conduct their opinions are occasionally reported" (*Christianizing the Roman Empire*, 56). After AD 380, people of all classes suffered "for not subscribing to the religion of the new Establishment" (57).

155. Jones, *Constantine*, 206. Meeks adds: "If a household became Christian more or less en bloc, not everyone who went along with the new practices would do so with the same understanding or inner participation. Social solidarity might be more important in persuading some members to be baptized than would understanding or convictions about specific beliefs" (*First Urban Christians*, 77).

156. MacMullen discusses these issues, including people who are inspired to convert, but do not really change, in *Christianizing the Roman Empire*, 3–5. He adds that, in the accounts of conversions in the work of Eusebius, the primary motive is to avoid the punishments of Hell and to gain the pleasures of Heaven (29). On the appeal of miracles, especially exorcisms, to potential converts, see 36, 40, 61, 87–88, 112. On the phenomenon of conversion by compulsion, see 65, 88–89.

At the same time, as Christianity became more Hellenized, the Church itself became more Romanized: "[J]ust as post-Origen theological treatises resembled, to an ever greater degree, the contemporary philosophical works, so the organization of the post-Nicene Church came more and more to look like its 'parent' organization, the Roman state."[157] Bishops replaced prophets in authority, and wandering charismatics, instead of being welcome as spiritual leaders, became suspect and therefore unwelcome.[158] Those bishops were sometimes chosen for their social status or social skills, rather than for their virtue or spirituality.[159] Certainly, as Christianity became more universal, it became less revolutionary. Disconnected from Judaism, it lost its hostility to Hellenism; disconnected from Palestine, it lost its opposition to Rome; and disconnected from rural Galilee, it lost its repudiation of wealth and status. In the view of one Church historian, Christianity fell to the three temptations rejected by Jesus. It acquired property, it accumulated wealth, and it gained the ability "to impose [its] will on others."[160]

Indeed, many Christians believed that "riches and pomp" were "signs of divine favor," that large and ornate churches were fitting memorials to their patrons, and that "a clerical aristocracy"—modeled on "the imperial aristocracy" and far removed from "the common people"—was an appropriate form of Church governance. In fact, even Christian worship was strongly influenced by "imperial protocol." Incense, which had been used to show respect for the emperor, began to be widely used in churches by the fourth century. Priests, formerly dressed in ordinary clothes, adorned themselves with the "luxurious garments" of royalty. And church interiors, once simply furnished, were lavishly decorated with polished marble, lamps, tapestries, and mosaics.[161]

157. Peters, *Harvest of Hellenism*, 612, 631.

158. In other words, as Manschreck puts it, some of the innovations of Christianity have "turned out to be less than divine." More precisely, despite the many significant contributions of the Church to the advancement of civilization, some of its achievements have "become so ossified and institutionalized in time that they have become more like idols than fruits of the living Spirit" (*History of Christianity*, 4). Kaylor argues that the "Christian faith has not centered on the historical Jesus," meaning that the years between Jesus' birth and death "were of no real consequence to faith" (*Jesus the Prophet*, 212). That is, the ethical Jesus disappeared.

159. "It was such considerations of a material sort that often appear to have been decisive in the selection of late Roman church leaders—like Synesius, not really a Christian, or like St. Ambrose, not even a priest, both of whom were correctly judged to be of the right circles, eloquence, vigor, and place in the world to provide strength at the summit of the community" (MacMullen, *Christianizing the Roman Empire*, 53).

160. McKenzie, *Old Testament*, 59, 107–8. Manschreck comments: "The story of the Middle Ages, replete with heroic deeds and dedicated men of religion, is finally overshadowed and broken by ecclesiastical drives to put the institutional church at the center of all life, in the process of which the church subtly traded service for domination, prophecy for order, and agape self-giving for the self-fulfillment of eros" (*History of Christianity*, 121).

161. *History of Christianity*, 124–28, 134. Perhaps worse than anything, Gonzalez says, in the fourth century Christians (like Eusebius, for example) were inclined to put aside the idea that the Kingdom of God was on its way because, with the advent of Constantine, "the plan of God ha[d] been fulfilled." In short, there was no reason to wait for the second coming of Christ (*Story of Christianity*, 134).

As for monasticism itself, one scholar says, it too sometimes betrayed its ideals: "Imitation was a powerful force among the monks, and rivalries developed wherein zealot competed against zealot for the palm of athletic asceticism. Contests of fasting and penance became veritable Olympiads of chastisement. The most terrible kind of physical pain must frequently have masked a delicious sense of spiritual self-indulgence."[162]

As the Middle Ages proceeded, things only got worse. In the late sixth century, Gregory the Great, contrary to the assumptions of Augustine's mother and Constantine, believed that, even after baptism, sins could be expiated by good works. In the ninth century, Pope John VIII "promised soldiers fighting the Saracens in Italy as much absolution as the Pope himself could give." And, in the tenth century, the Cluny reformers promoted the idea that pilgrimage to Jerusalem could, beyond confession and absolution, further enable penitents to expiate their sins. "These satisfactions [i.e., acts of expiation] had already taken on a legal aspect," says one Church historian. "They commonly consisted of fasting, recitations of psalms, religious journeys, prayers, alms, scourging, and so forth." And they could be replaced by financial contributions, or the penitent could hire a substitute.[163] That is, over time, the moral system, for *some* Christians, became completely bankrupt.

I mention these many instances of what might be called moral primitivism not because they demonstrate that Christianity was, at any time in its history, defined by them. Certainly, that is not the case. As I said earlier, it was as easy in the ancient world as it is in the present to treat religion as a set of rules, obedience to which garners rewards of one kind or another, whether spiritual or material. I merely intend to

---

Tertullian had suggested this as early as the second century, when he told the Roman emperor that Christians prayed for the end of the world and for Jesus' return to be delayed so that the emperor's reign could continue. Mattingly contends that the Church gave up its early "apocalyptic dreams" for earthly power: "It seems to us that one of the most obvious facts about the Empire was that a large measure of liberty was sacrificed without reserve and for ever for what seemed the sufficient price of peace and security" (*Roman Imperial Civilisation*, 45, 53).

162. Peters, *Harvest of Hellenism*, 642. In this respect, "the monk replaced the martyr" (644). Speaking of practices in Syria and Mesopotamia, Chadwick says: "Their recorded mortifications make alarming reading. A heavy iron chain as a belt was a frequent austerity. A few adopted the life of animals and fed on the grass, living in the open air without shade from the sun and with the minimum of clothing" (*Early Church*, 180). In the fifth century, Symeon the Stylite lived atop a column in a few square feet of space and was imitated by others, one of whom practiced the same austerity for thirty-three years.

163. All of these examples come from Manschreck, *History of Christianity*, 108, 137–39. "Depending on the seriousness of the sin," says Manschreck, "acts of satisfaction might extend over weeks or even years. Many could not afford the time, so substitutions in keeping with German legal practices became common. One could give an equivalent in money or hire another person to perform the necessary works. Outfitting a crusader was one of the best means of making satisfaction" (137). On the legalism that Peter Abelard opposed, see Heer, *Medieval World*, 113. Medieval ethics "saw guilt, sin and expiation as a legal transaction made with God: the sinner had to pay God the King a definite graduated fine for each sin, each breach of faith . . . The inner core of personality was barely touched by such rough and ready ethics" (113).

suggest that the Church has been entirely too quick to accuse Judaism of follies that Christians themselves have, on occasion, been guilty of. Both Judaism and Christianity offer the world an extraordinarily impressive code of conduct, which, if it were followed, would, as the Deuteronomist stated, create conditions for human existence of which even God would be proud. Short of that achievement, *everyone* is a hypocrite and a fool.

Chapter Three

The Crucifixion

"Without Easter, we wouldn't know about Jesus. If his story had ended with his crucifixion, he most likely would have been forgotten—another Jew crucified by the Roman Empire in a bloody century that witnessed thousands of such executions." (Marcus J. Borg and John Dominic Crossan)

JEWS HAVE BEEN THE victims of Christian hatred and violence for nearly 2,000 years. The unofficial second millennial anniversary will arrive in about 2050, commemorating the composition of the epistles of Paul, the first Christian texts that spell out the reasons for this apparently unrelenting and—except for some sympathetic words from the leaders of Western governments and religious institutions after the Nazi Holocaust—remorseless hostility.[1] In 1965, for example, Pope Paul VI led the Vatican II Council to exculpate most Jews (that is, all of the living and many of the dead) from the crime of killing Jesus. In addition, the Council removed an anti-Semitic passage from the Easter liturgy.[2] The

---

1. According to some scholars, Paul, writing in the fifties, composed the first Christian anti-Semitic texts, but the extent of his culpability has been the subject of much debate recently. Carroll says, "[W]hen it comes to the question of the origin of Christian hatred for Jews, Paul is at the story's center" (*Constantine's Sword*, 139). According to Maccoby, Paul was "the creator of the anti-Semitism which . . . produced the medieval diabolization of the Jews," if only because he wrote Romans 11:28, if not 1 Thessalonians 2:15–16 (*Mythmaker*, 203–5). Parkes also points particularly to Paul's letter to the Romans "as the doctrinal basis for the attitude of the Church to the Jew throughout the centuries" (*Conflict*, 52). In defense of Paul, see Gager, *Origins of Anti-Semitism*, 197–212 and passim.

2. In "Declaration on the Relation of the Church to Non-Christian Religions," Pope Paul perpetuates the Gospel fiction (and references John 19:6) that the Jews bear the principal responsibility for executing Jesus: "True, the Jewish authorities and those who followed their lead pressed for the death of Christ." Furthermore, "[a]s Holy Scripture testifies, Jerusalem did not recognize the time of [the Church's] visitation, nor did the Jews in large number accept the Gospel; indeed, not a few opposed its spreading." Nevertheless, he goes on, this crime "cannot be charged against all the Jews, without distinction, then alive, nor against the Jews today." The papal judgment, however, is not that the Jews are innocent (and certainly not that the Romans are guilty). The church forbids anti-Semitism as an act of generosity and principle, as it forbids, "as foreign to the mind of Christ, any discrimination against men or harassment of them because of their race, color, condition of life, or religion." It also acknowledges the kinship between Judaism and Christianity established by the fact that the latter is an offshoot of the former and that "the Apostles, the Church's mainstay and pillars, as well as most of the

first and foremost reason for this ongoing rage against the Jews is the charge that the Jews were responsible for Jesus' death, which, over time, was elevated from a homicide to a deicide. It was not only a holy man who was murdered, but God Himself.

The second reason for both the persistence and virulence of Christian revenge is the assumption that the death of Jesus was not only premeditated, but *unusual*— crucifixion being a form of punishment clearly intended to be so cruel as to dissuade anyone capable of witnessing the pain and hearing the cries of the dying from even thinking of committing a similar crime. Any person living in a predominantly Christian country, who has seen portrayals of the Crucifixion in paintings, sculptures, and films; read about it in books and magazines; or heard descriptions of it in sermons and Sunday School lessons might well be so struck by the sheer agony of death on the cross as to assume that Jesus alone suffered this way, if only to illustrate and underscore the sacrifice he made for the sins of mankind.

Ironically (and, of course, tragically), both of these reasons are highly questionable. As to the murder charge against the Jews, it must be said at the outset that, given the number of Jews in the Diaspora (i.e., Egypt, Syria, Babylonia, Asia Minor, Greece, and Italy), none of whom ever saw or heard of Jesus, and the number of Jews in Palestine, most of whom never saw or heard of him, the suggestion that "the Jews"– meaning, presumably, a sizable portion of the total Jewish population—were involved in Jesus' death is ludicrous. Particularly if Jesus never preached outside of Palestine and spent only one year proselytizing within its borders (the claim of the synoptic Gospels), he is certain to have completely missed the five to seven million Jews in the Diaspora and likely to have seen only a small percentage of the half million Jews in the rural areas of Galilee and Judea, where he spent most of his time preaching.[3] It is true that Diaspora Jews came to Jerusalem (maximum estimated population: 100,000; probable population: 25,000) at Passover and swelled the population to hundreds of thousands. But, without the benefits of mass communication technology, Jesus could hardly have addressed more than a few thousand people.

There are, in addition, many other relevant questions pertaining to the Jewish role in Jesus' arrest, trial, conviction, and execution. First, since the disciples scattered when Jesus was arrested, and none of them even witnessed his death (at least in Mark and Matthew), how is it that we know anything about the events of the Passion?[4] To

---

early disciples who proclaimed Christ's Gospel to the world sprang from the Jewish people."

3. Most historians put the number of Jews in the Roman empire at six or seven million, out of a total population of sixty or seventy million. The highest number I have seen is suggested by Klingaman, who estimates that there were eight million Jews and more than seventy million non-Jews in the empire during the reign of Augustus (*First Century*, 3, 22).

4. On this point, see Conzelmann and Lindemann, *Interpreting the New Testament*, 33: "[W]e are told of several incidents which, in the very nature of things, cannot have been experienced by immediate [Christian] witnesses, such as Jesus' trial before Pilate." Indeed, after Peter's denial, the disciples fled and, except for Judas, were not heard of again until Easter (Borg and Crossan, *Last Week*, 126). The Crucifixion was attended only by Jesus' women followers (Matt 26:56; Mark 14:50), except in Luke, where "the women who had followed him from Galilee" watched Jesus on the cross

what extent were the details of the Passion drawn from the Jewish Bible to support the idea that Jesus' death was prophesied by that book?

Second, did Pontius Pilate need to be encouraged to kill Jesus, given his (and other Romans') attitude toward any sign of resistance or rebellion? Is it not likely that if any Jews supported Pilate's hostility to anti-Roman behavior, they would have been members of the Jewish aristocracy and not the public at large? How many Jews from the lower classes, which constituted the overwhelming majority, would have approved of any action on the part of the Jewish elite and the Roman government, which the elite habitually supported?[5] If Jesus was followed to the cross by "a great company of people [that is, Jews] . . . which also bewailed and lamented him" (Luke 23:27), where were they when priests, rulers, and "people" a few moments earlier told Pilate to crucify Jesus (Luke 23:13–23)? That is, which crowd was Pilate trying to satisfy when he ordered the crucifixion of Jesus?[6]

"at a distance" in the company of "all his acquaintances" (Luke 23:49) (151). "Since the disciples are all recorded to have forsaken Him and fled, there is no certain basis for the narratives which follow the scene in the garden of Gesthemane" (Parkes, *Conflict*, 45). There is nothing at all on Jesus' death in the pre-Markan material, Mack says, and the entire story in Mark is implausible: "The list of improbable features is quite long and includes such things as the trial by night, which would have been illegal; the basis for the charge of blasphemy, which is very unclear if not completely trumped up; the failure of the witnesses to agree, which would have called for a mistrial; the right of the Sanhedrin to charge with death, a sanction that they probably did not have at the time; the insinuation of the crucifixion taking place on Passover, which would have been an outrage," and more (*Who Wrote?* 157–58). Brandon makes a similar point, citing the absence of any reference to the trial and crucifixion of Jesus in the common material (called Q) that Matthew and Luke both used in the writing of their Gospels (*Trial of Jesus*, 108). Sanders says generally of the accounts of the evangelists: "[P]erhaps none of the authors knew what took place when (except of course, the trial and crucifixion). Possibly, they had scattered bits of information, from which they constructed believable narratives that contain a fair amount of guesswork" (*Historical Figure of Jesus*, 69).

5. Crossan estimates the size of the aristocracy in the Roman empire at one percent of the entire population. There was virtually no middle class, so everyone else was a peasant or a laborer (*Birth of Christianity*, 186). Jeremias, however, includes in the middle class of the first century importers, shopkeepers, independent craftsmen, and Temple officials (*Jerusalem*, 100).

6. Fredriksen raises this question. Quite possibly, she says, there were two crowds in Jerusalem— one opposed to Jesus, the other supporting him. Less plausibly, she adds, the same crowd might have changed its mind. But "[t]he priests do not have enough time to swing popular opinion around in the course of this single, highly packed interval between evening (when Jesus is so popular that he must be ambushed to be arrested without incident) and morning (when the crowd demands his death)." More important, Fredriksen continues, "the hostile crowd could not have been 'most of the people.'" That is, either Jesus was followed by a very large number of Jews who supported him (which necessitated his arrest and execution as a dangerous threat), or he was rejected by everyone (in which case, he was harmless). The latter option is, of course, unlikely, especially considering the claim that the authorities had to apprehend Jesus under "the power of darkness" (Luke 22:53)—i.e., at a time and place in which his arrest would not stir up "the people" (*Jesus of Nazareth*, 256). Borg and Crossan agree. "Almost certainly, [the crowd that asks for Jesus' death and Barabbas' release] is not the same crowd that heard Jesus with delight during the week; Mark gives us no reason to think that crowd has turned against Jesus. Moreover, it is highly unlikely that the crowd from earlier in the week would be allowed into Herod's palace, where this scene is set. This crowd, the crowd stirred up by the chief priests, must have been much smaller and is best understood as provided by the authorities (somebody had to let them into the palace)" (*Last Week*, 144).

Third, if the murder of James the bother of Jesus by the high priest Ananus was, according to Josephus, strongly criticized by the Sanhedrin (the Jewish supreme court) as well as the Pharisees, why would these same people have supported the murder of Jesus himself? Would not Jesus have been considered, as James was, to be a pious Jew who departed from mainstream Judaism even less than the Essenes at Qumran did?

Fourth, and most important, to what extent did later anti-Jewish and anti-Judaic attitudes on the part of Christians influence the way they told the story of Jesus' death? And, just as important, to what extent did these attitudes affect the way later Christians, all writing after the Revolt of 66 and the destruction of the Temple, depicted the life of Jesus, including his condemnation of "the Jews" in the Gospel of John and that Jewish cry of perpetual self-condemnation that would seem to have justified centuries of Christian anti-Semitism: "His blood be on us, and on our children" (Matt 27:25)?

It might be questioned, of course, whether at this point in Jewish history, a few Jews (twenty-five, a hundred, a thousand?) could impose their guilt not only on their own children, but on the children of the millions of other Jews in the Roman empire. Corporate guilt—i.e., the punishment of the group for the sins of one member or, presumably, even the punishment of the many for the sins of a few—was a feature of Numbers 16, but not of Deuteronomy 24:16 ("every man shall be put to death for his own sin"), Jeremiah 31:30, and Ezekiel 18:4 and 33:1–20. The question is important because, as one scholar says of the Jews' alleged self-condemnation in Matthew, "The influence of the scene depicted is incalculable, and it has imprinted itself indelibly upon the mind of countless generations of Christians."[7] Other scholars have pointed especially to the writings of Justin Martyr, John Chrysostom, and Hilary of Poitiers, as well as the *Epistle of Barnabas*, as subsequent contributions to the ever-growing anti-Semitism of the Church.

THE CRUCIFIXION OF THE JEWS

I intend to answer some of these questions later in this chapter. For now, I would like to deal with the second assumption I referred to above: the idea that Jesus' Crucifixion was remarkable or exceptional. The fact is, in the post-Exilic period, violence in Palestine occurred under both domestic and foreign rulers, the latter of whom, for the most part, were committed not only to establishing Greek cities (with gymnasiums, Greek temples, and schools), but also, on occasion, to imposing Hellenization on the native Jewish population, often with the active cooperation of the Jewish aristocracy, including landowners and priests. Under the Romans, the clearest symbol of domination

---

7. Brandon, *Trial of Jesus*, 97. Brandon adds later, "For those fierce words came to be enshrined in the sacred scriptures of the Christian Church, where they were seen as the self-confession of the Jews to the murder of Christ. In succeeding centuries, down to this present age, those words have inspired hatred for the Jews and justified the cruelest persecutions" (115). Ironically, as Horsley and Silberman point out, "the ugly . . . scene of the people of Jerusalem eagerly, bloodthirstily taking the responsibility for Jesus' execution upon themselves and their children" is "utterly unrealistic" (*Message,* 222)

was the crucifix, which not only, in great numbers, lined the Appian way after the rebellion of Spartacus and his followers in 71 BC, but particularly filled the Palestinian landscape, especially from the sixties BC to the sixties AD. Thus, though we think of the cross as "a ubiquitous symbol of a certain religion"—adopted in the fourth century AD—it "was to Jesus, as a Jew, an equally ubiquitous symbol of a certain politics." That is, before the Christians adopted the cross as a symbol of love and sacrifice, the Romans had used it as a symbol (and instrument) of pervasive, inexorable, deadly force, particularly against the Jews.[8]

In the late 170s and early 160s BC, under Antiochus IV, whose Ptolemaic predecessors took over Palestine after the death of Alexander the Great, a number of Hellenistic reforms were implemented, including the transformation of Jerusalem into a Greek city. Antiochus also seized Temple treasures, stole Temple funds, and ordered the Jews to abandon the practice of circumcision, Sabbath worship, Temple sacrifices, the celebration of festivals, and obedience to dietary laws; desecrated sacred objects and burned Torah scrolls; and threatened the disobedient with death.[9] When a *gerousia*, a Jewish ruling body, complained to Antiochus about these abuses, he slaughtered

8. Carroll, *Constantine's Sword*, 120. See also Hengel, *Crucifixion*, 86–88, who calls crucifixion "remarkably widespread in antiquity." "All over the Mediterranean world," according to Horsley and Silberman, "north to Gaul and across the Channel to Britain, Roman emperors, governors, prefects, and procurators had the power, and even the responsibility, to inflict unspeakable pain and physical suffering on any person whom their officers grabbed from the fields or the streets and identified— rightly or wrongly—as a threat to private property, public order, or state security" (*Message*, 85). "We know from Josephus," says Crossan, "that thousands of Jewish victims were crucified outside the walls of Jerusalem in the first common era century" (*Historical Jesus*, 391). Horsley and Silberman put the number of Jews either crucified or sold into slavery at "possibly" hundreds of thousands (*Message*, 213). For the horrible details of death by crucifixion, see Tabor, *Jesus Dynasty*, 218–19. Tabor says, "The hapless victims of crucifixion, left on the crosses for days, were a common sight to the Jewish population" (218). Despite the extraordinarily large number of Jews who were crucified, especially by Romans in the time of Jesus—by, for example, procurators Cumanus, Felix, and Florus in Judea, as well as Flaccus in Alexandria—Hengel makes the bizarre claim that "the cross never became the symbol of Jewish suffering" (*Crucifixion*, 85). This statement occurs in a surprisingly brief two-page summary entitled "Crucifixion among the Jews." Hengel's overall account begins with Josephus' description of Titus' execution of Jews during the Revolt of 66: "Titus felt pity for them, but as their number—given as up to five hundred a day—was too great for him to risk either letting them go or putting them under guard, he allowed his soldiers to have their way, especially as he hoped that the gruesome sight of the countless crosses might move the besieged to surrender: So the soldiers, out of the rage and hatred they bore the prisoners, nailed those they caught, in different postures, to the crosses, by way of jest . . . and their number was so great that there was not enough room for the crosses and not enough crosses for the bodies" (26). Hengel concludes his review of the subject by stating that the Talmudic literature offers "a whole series of references to the crucifixion of Jews during the later empire" (85), including, no doubt, the tens (or hundreds) of thousands who were executed during the Revolt of 132. Only a few pages earlier, he distinguishes between the attitude toward this unimaginably cruel form of punishment held by "the majority of the inhabitants of the Greek cities" and the attitude held by "the Palestinian peasant." The former "regarded [crucifixion] as a horrible but nevertheless necessary instrument for the preservation of law and order," while the latter, "his sympathies with the freedom movement, saw in it the feared and hated instrument of repression employed by his Roman overlords" (79)—i.e., as a symbol of the Roman occupation as well as ipso facto a "symbol of Jewish suffering."

9. Kee et al., *Understanding the New Testament*, 16–17.

the entire group. Finally, he killed thousands of Judeans and sold many into slavery. These actions fomented the Maccabean (or Hasmonean) revolution, which ended foreign rule in Palestine for nearly a century. However, even Jewish governance in Palestine did not end the violence. In the first half of the first century BC, during the reign of Alexander Jannaeus, a Hasmonean, this king responded to an assault, in which "rebels" threw citrons at him, by crucifying eight hundred leaders, killing their wives and children in front of them, and exiling 8,000 others.[10]

The Romans, who succeeded the Hasmoneans, crucified thousands upon thousands of Jews and barbarians (as well as slaves) because these groups regularly threatened to overthrow the Roman government, the latter of them especially after the third century, when Visigoths, Ostrogoths, and Germans began to invade the Roman empire with increasing success. Among non-Romans living in the empire, the Jews received special treatment because they "alone refused to acquiesce in imperial rule."[11] The Romans even killed many Christians, usually, however, by means that maximized the possibility that before dying they might repudiate Christianity and return to paganism. A gentile Christian was, after all, a former pagan, while a Jewish Christian was still a Jew.

The Roman general Pompey invaded Palestine in 63 BC, destroying whole towns; slaughtering, crucifying, and enslaving their inhabitants; and desecrating the Temple. He is said to have killed 12,000 Jews. Cassius punished a town in this way for failing to pay an exorbitant tax on time, a common reason for exacting a severe punishment for what might otherwise be considered a minor offense. After a revolt in 53 BC, the Romans sold 30,000 Jews into slavery. Often, except when the victims of attacks were bandits, the Romans killed unarmed or inadequately armed Jews. "At the popular level," says one historian, "we find little or no calculation [on the part of the Jews], but spontaneous action, violent or nonviolent depending on the occasion or the movement."[12] These were the Jews who complained to their oppressors impulsively, naively, and ineffectually and always elicited a response that was intended to shut down public shows of discontent forever.

When he came to power in 34 BC, as an appointee of the Romans, Herod the Great continued to Hellenize Palestine, adding a theater, a royal palace, and an amphitheater to Jerusalem. Little protest is visible under his reign because he ruled

10. Wylen notes that John Hyrcanus, as well as Alexander Jannaeus, crucified many Jews (*Jews*, 64–65).

11. Mattingly, *Roman Imperial Civilisation*, 63. "This [Greco-Roman] culture imposed itself on the Empire at large and seldom met with any direct opposition. The Jews . . . *did* fight, and their fight was cultural as well as national" (67). Besides resisting the Roman invasion in 63 BC, rebelling again a decade later, and rioting against the regime of Herod's sons after his death in 4 BC, the Jews initiated two major revolts in AD 66 and 132.

12. Horsley, *Bandits, Prophets & Messiahs*, 253. Closely examining several protests in Palestine from 4 BC to AD 65, Crossan concludes that "all those demonstrations were nonviolent [and] all had very specific [i.e., well-defined, limited] objectives" (*Historical Jesus*, 136).

ruthlessly, insisting on a loyalty oath and forbidding public meetings.[13] Herod celebrated his acquisition of kingship by killing most of the members of the Sanhedrin. When he was rumored to be dying, two Jewish teachers led a movement to remove the Roman eagle that he had placed on the gate of the Temple. Herod burned alive those who were caught in the act and refrained from slaughtering others only because he was implored to do so by leading citizens. At his death in 4 BC, Roman armies marched through Palestine raping, killing, and destroying.[14] Varus, the Roman governor of Syria, burned Sepphoris to the ground, sold its citizens as slaves, and crucified 2,000 rebels. Under Herod's son Archelaus, 3,000 people were killed in 4 BC when Passover crowds became too vocal and threw stones at Roman soldiers because the latter tried to make a show of force. Archelaus finally lost his job in AD 6 because even the Romans felt that his regime was too brutal.[15]

After the deposition of Archelaus, the Romans ruled Judea directly—first through prefects (AD 6–41) and later through procurators (AD 44–66), who kept 3,000 soldiers at Caesarea, while Herod Antipas, one of Herod's sons, ruled Galilee. Antipas' murder of John the Baptist, motivated by his fear of John and his following, not John's personal insult regarding Antipas' second marriage, provides a clear idea of the paranoia that moved rulers in Palestine to overreaction.[16] Of the procurators,

13. Sanders says: "Herod was fully master of his own house . . . [H]e ruthlessly suppressed all opposition, even minor protests. By the end of his life, he had executed three of his sons because he suspected them of treason" (*Historical Figure of Jesus*, 19). Sanders adds later, "Under Herod, no one else had any power, and those who sought it were promptly executed" (45). See also Zeitlin, *Who Crucified Jesus?* 41–51; and Schiffman, *From Text to Tradition*, 140–46. Zeitlin says that Herod "introduced a spy system like that of the modern Gestapo. He did not permit Jews to gather together, to walk together, to eat together. His spies were stationed everywhere. He himself mingled among the people in disguise, to hear what they thought of him." He put critics to death "in the most inhuman and atrocious manner" (*Who Crucified Jesus?* 43).

14. Carroll, *Constantine's Sword*, 83. For comments on Herod's viciousness, see Jeremias, *Jerusalem*, 190, 243–44.

15. Crossan says that the three annual festivals, especially Passover, always drew large crowds to Jerusalem, in response to which the government brought in extra troops to discourage dissent (*Who Killed Jesus?* 54). This and the preceding paragraphs are drawn primarily from Horsley, *Bandits, Prophets & Messiahs*, 10–34. On travel to Jerusalem for feasts, see also Jeremias, *Jerusalem*, 71, 73.

16. Sanders notes that John made two kinds of statements that could have disturbed Herod Antipas: (1) that Herod had broken the law (Matt 14:4) and (2) that the Kingdom of God was imminent (Matt 3:7–10). However, "if we combine Antipas' fear of insurrection (Josephus) and John's prediction of a dramatic future event that would transform the present order (the gospels), we find a perfectly good reason for the execution" (*Historical Figure of Jesus*, 93). On one hand, despite the fact of John the Baptist's execution by Herod Antipas and the leadership of Galileans in Jewish revolts under both Herod the Great, before Jesus' birth, and in AD 66, after Jesus' crucifixion, some scholars contend that Galilee in the time of Jesus (and under Herod Antipas) was politically quiet. Sanders, for example, says that "Josephus records no instance in which Antipas had to resort to force in order to suppress an uprising," which suggests that he was neither "excessively oppressive" nor overbearing in his tax policies (21). In fact, Sanders goes on to say that "[i]n the late twenties and early thirties Jewish Palestine was not on the brink of revolt," in spite of Josephus' claim that tensions built up steadily before the Jewish Revolt a generation later (28). Fredriksen calls Galilee in particular "politically stable" at this time (*Jesus of Nazareth*, 182), a point that Freyne makes repeatedly in *Galilee, Jesus*, 5, 28, 41, 161–62,

Pilate, Cumanus, Fadus, and Florus were the most violent.[17] Despite Pilate's rather benevolent appearance in the Gospels, he is generally understood to have been an unusually cruel and ruthless head of state: "The early procurators seemed to govern wisely and peacefully. With the appointment of Pontius Pilate (26–36 CE) . . . conflict and bloodshed began."[18] Unlike his predecessors, who respected the sanctity of Jerusalem, Pilate desecrated buildings in the city with Roman shields or standards and raided the Temple fund to pay for an aqueduct, much to the extreme anger of the Jews, who were willing to sacrifice their lives in order to change Pilate's mind.[19]

194–95, 235. Freyne's main justification for this view is similar to Sanders's: Jesus was not arrested in Galilee, and his disciples were not arrested in Jerusalem (196). On the other hand, Fredriksen says, "The decades between Jesus' time and Mark's had seen increasing unrest and friction between Judea and its Roman overseers, often over the issue of introducing unacceptable religious images into Jerusalem" (*Jesus of Nazareth*, 86). Freyne says that social banditry, a sign of social unrest, existed in Judea, but not in Galilee (*Galilee, Jesus*, 164). Furthermore, he acknowledges that Galilee was at least somewhat volatile in the first century (162–66, 244, 265, 266, 270). The point of disagreement among scholars is, therefore, not whether the governors of both Galilee and Judea were apprehensive about the prospect of revolt, but whether their fears were merited. Indeed, the threat of two such rebellions, one potentially fomented by John the Baptist, and the other an "insurrection" in which Barabbas, one of "the rebels," is said to have participated (Mark 15:7)—both in one year—suggests that the atmosphere in which Jesus labored was sufficiently tense to arouse an overreaction to his otherwise innocuous movement. As Sanders says, the Jews were not happy, and the Romans had "to exercise wary vigilance" (*Historical Figure of Jesus*, 29).

17. Wylen says, "They displayed contempt for the native customs, oppressing the Jews beyond the requirements of maintaining public order and collecting taxes." Worse yet, adds Wylen, "[t]he era of the procurators was an era of increasing rebelliousness among the Jews" (*Jews*, 75). According to Grant, Palestine and other occupied territories within the Roman empire—all of them potentially threatening to the regime—"were administered by Roman governors or, in some cases, procurators, whose authority was based on the power of legionary and auxiliary troops. About twenty-four legions were stationed in various trouble spots mostly at the frontiers of the empire" (*Historical Introduction*, 247). The troops available to prefects and procurators in Palestine were stationed in Syria.

18. Schiffman, *From Text to Tradition*, 148. See also Horsley, *Bandits, Prophets & Messiahs*, 38, 164; and Crossan, *Historical Jesus*, 129–30. Conzelmann and Lindemann comment, "The tensions between Rome and the Jewish population intensified during the administration of the procurator Pontius Pilate" (*Interpreting the New Testament*, 121).

19. Three such incidents have been described by Yoder, using Josephus' reports, in *Politics of Jesus*, 90–93. Horsley calls these and similar Jewish acts of resistance expressions of "covenant principles" (*Covenant Economics*, 94–96). Klingaman's description of these events, however, illustrates how easy it is to present Pilate positively and the Jews negatively. Thus, Pilate was a "tough-minded veteran military administrator," who was not "squeamish" and had been chosen as prefect by Tiberius because he had "previously displayed a considerable measure of proven ability and grit." The Jews, on the other hand, were "incorrigibly unruly" and had "failed to grow more mellow" over time. They had "peculiar religious customs," which Pilate's predecessors had respected, but Pilate "was determined to teach [them] to respect" Tiberius. Pilate took money from the Temple treasury to build an aqueduct, but his "expenditures almost certainly fell within the existing limitations on the use" of the money. Nevertheless he had to endure a protest by "Jewish pilgrims" to Jerusalem who were "most likely fundamentalist troublemakers from the bumptious northern realm of Galilee." Having lost face in his first encounter with these protesting Jews, Pilate later "availed himself of every opportunity to irritate the notoriously thin-skinned residents of Judea" (*First Century*, 189–92).

More seriously, Pilate, whose "governorship was marked by a whole series of difficult, violent incidents,"[20] attacked the Jews who protested against these actions. In addition, Luke reports that Pilate killed Galileans who were on a pilgrimage to the Temple and mixed their blood with their sacrifices (Luke 13:1). He also attacked a group of Samaritan pilgrims who were following a self-proclaimed prophet up Mt. Gerizim in 35 or 36, routed and captured many of the participants, and executed the leaders, as well as many of the others.[21] Philo, the Jewish philosopher, says that Pilate was known for "his venality, his violence, his thefts, his assaults, his abusive behavior, his frequent executions of prisoners without trial, and his endless savagery" against the resident population.[22] Both the Jew Josephus and the Roman Tacitus agreed with Philo that Pilate was an extremely unpleasant character.

The procurator Fadus (44–46), among many acts of repression, especially against brigands, is best known for beheading the rebel Theudas—who had persuaded many people to follow him to the Jordan River—and killing many of his followers in 45. Fadus also killed some leaders and exiled others from a group of Perean Jews who were engaged in a boundary dispute with a nearby Hellenistic city. Tiberius Julius

20. Grant, *Jesus*, 162. Grant adds, "But the evangelists, in their desire after the Jewish Revolt to incriminate the Jews and deny any serious dispute between the Christians and the Romans, made Pilate so indecisive because they wanted to show that he had not been really hostile to Jesus, and had even attempted, unsuccessfully, to save him" (163). Zeitlin says: "The early Christians sought to ingratiate themselves with the Roman authorities so that they should not look upon a Roman convert to Christianity as one who would side with the Jews, the rebels . . . Since the policy of the early Christians was not to antagonize the Romans, they tried to put the blame for the crucifixion upon the Jews" (*Who Crucified Jesus?* 174). Kaylor calls this interpretation of the Gospels' treatment of Romans and Jews in this context a "generally acknowledged insight" (*Jesus the Prophet*, 87).

21. Flusser provides a rather full portrait of Pilate in *Sage from Galilee*, 145–55. He describes Pilate's crimes against the Jews on 150–52. On Pilate's record of violence, see also Bruce, *New Testament History*, 35–38. Bruce adds: "Luke [13:4] mentions the death of eighteen men when a tower in Siloam . . . fell and crushed them. This may have been nothing more than a tragic accident, but the context in which it appears suggests that it relates to an attempt at insurrection around this time by a group of militant Jerusalemites, which was speedily and violently put down" (37). Bruce provides the context on 188. Tabor says, summarizing Josephus: Pilate "had immediately established himself as a brutal taskmaster with no concern for Jewish sensibilities. He had brought Roman military standards with their busts of Caesar into the holy city of Jerusalem. Shortly thereafter he had taken money from the sacred Temple treasury to pay for costs of finishing an aqueduct into Jerusalem. The Jewish crowds were in an uproar and both incidents provoked riots to which Pilate responded with force, killing large numbers of Jews" (*Jesus Dynasty*, 153–54). Both the High Priest Caiaphas and Pilate lost their jobs at the same time (in AD 36) as a result of their mishandling of an attempt by Samaritans to climb Mt. Gerizim in order meet the Messiah. "Pilate sent a detachment of troops, which routed the pilgrims before they could ascend the mountain" (Evans, "Josephus on John the Baptist," 57–58). Sanders notes that Pilate was one of only two prefects who were dismissed by the Romans, who also deposed two "native rulers," Archelaus and Antipas, for excessive use of force (*Historical Figure of Jesus*, 24).

22. Quoted in White, *From Jesus to Christianity*, 460 n. 15. The text of Philo's description of Pilate can be found in Sterling, "Philo of Alexandria," 303–4. Sterling comments, "Whether the historical Pilate was as problematic an administrator as Philo presents him to be is questionable; Philo had good rhetorical reasons for presenting Pilate in the worst possible light" (299). On the other hand, we have the testimony of both Josephus and Tacitus.

Alexander (46–48) crucified Jacob and Simon, descendants of Judah the Galilean, who had led the rebellion against Antiochus IV. Under Cumanus (48–52), a soldier in the Roman security forces insulted the Jews outside the Temple at Passover and created a riot. As many as 30,000 Jews (by Josephus' probably inflated estimate) died in the ensuing stampede as they tried to escape from the Roman soldiers. Later, after Samaritans attacked Galilean pilgrims, Cumanus allowed the conflict to escalate and then attacked the Jews.

The violence grew in the decade and a half before the Revolt of 66. Felix (52–60) met an upsurge in movements led by charismatic prophets by slaughtering as many leaders and followers as possible, since he considered all such groups to be nascent revolutionary movements. He attacked the followers of the so-called Egyptian as well, killing thousands, although the leader escaped. He executed the brigand chief Eleazar ben Dinai and sent other brigands to Rome for trial and crucifixion. Festus (59–62) also sent infantry and cavalry against yet another of these groups, slaughtering every-one. In 66, Florus (64–66) provoked a demonstration when he stole money from the Temple treasury, arrested and crucified a few leading citizens who were not part of the protest, and allowed his troops to raid part of Jerusalem. This was one of the first steps in the Jewish Revolt, which led to the indiscriminate killing of tens of thousands of Palestinian Jews over the next few years.[23]

These acts of retribution on the part of the Romans were sometimes justified, at least in terms of the legitimate desire of the Romans to maintain order. After all, any small protest could become threatening, given the readiness of Jewish peasants to express their opposition to the imperial occupation. Even the mere formation of a small group could be considered a potential danger worthy of suppression.[24] How-ever, for the most part, the reactions of the Romans were not only excessive; they often involved the murder of people who had nothing to do with the provocation. Whole towns and villages were punished for not capturing bandits. People were picked up off the streets and crucified for acts that others had committed. And even relatives and friends of the guilty parties were either killed by sword or crucified, if captured.

The principle at work here was simply that all members of a definable group were held accountable for the actions of any single member. Thus, when Varus destroyed Sepphoris in 4 BC, killed 2,000 residents, and sold the rest into slavery, "most of them had no connection with the rebels and did not support them."[25] In pursuit of brigands,

---

23 Much of the information in this paragraph comes from Bruce, *New Testament History*, 337–49. The Roman historian Tacitus blamed the local Roman government for the Revolt of 66: "Tacitus em-phasized exclusively," says Crossan, "the malfeasance of the Roman procurators immediately preced-ing the outbreak of hostilities in the summer of 66 C.E. . . . Tacitus, in other words, is ready to blame the Romans rather than the Jews for the war" (*Historical Jesus*, 101)

24. Klingaman says, "Naturally the specter of mass uprisings scared the hell out of Tiberius—as it did all the Roman emperors before and after him" (*First Century*, 156).

25. Sanders, *Historical Figure of Jesus*, 105. "The Roman authorities punished not only the indi-viduals who incited the people against the Romans, but the leaders of the people as well . . . Many

as Josephus reports, Cumanus had his soldiers arrest ordinary citizens for failing to apprehend and turn in the thieves.[26] In AD 61, the Romans executed four hundred slaves because one of them had killed his master.[27] A few years later, Florus allowed his soldiers "to give vent to their anti-Jewish hatred by killing, raping, and looting Jerusalem's markets and residential neighborhoods." Street battles resulted in the arrest and crucifixion of many "peaceable citizens."[28] As a result of this practice of excessive retribution—quite literally, overkill—and "[b]ecause crucifixion was the Roman way of doing capital punishment, crosses with their dying victims attached were not an uncommon sight in the land of the Jews under this oppressive conqueror."[29]

Furthermore, many of the protests initiated by Jews were provoked by arrogant acts perpetrated by Roman emperors who wanted to assert their power and intimidate their subjects. In AD 19, Tiberius exiled thousands of Jews from Italy for refusing to repudiate a Jewish decree that, among other things, freed runaway slaves and rejected all gods except Yahweh. In 40, Caligula sent an army to Jerusalem to set up statues of himself in the Temple. A conflict was avoided only because Caligula died and the order was rescinded.

In 49, Claudius expelled both Jews and Jewish Christians from Rome. In 132, before the second major Jewish revolt against Rome, Hadrian said he intended to build a Roman temple on the site of the old Jewish Temple. Indeed, he tried to destroy Judaism altogether after the war: "In contrast to the aftermath of the Jewish War of 66–70, the Romans [after the later war] took measures which were directed against the very practice of the Jewish religion. Not only were Jews forbidden to enter Jerusalem or even to approach it, but the prohibition also included the practice of circumcision, the observance of the Sabbath and of the Jewish festivals, as well as instruction in Torah ... The Jewish population of Palestine had been massacred or expelled."[30]

In short, between the insensitivities of the Roman procurators and the superciliousness of the Roman emperors, the Jews of Palestine and the Diaspora, driven by their own delusions of grandeur—their complete ignorance of the imposing power

---

Jewish leaders in such circumstances and political conditions had to act as informers against the dissenters and revolutionaries among their brethren in order to save their own lives." Some of them sold out completely—in many cases, "for personal aggrandizement and power" (Zeitlin, Who Crucified Jesus? 172).

26. Kaylor, *Jesus the Prophet*, 41.

27. Robertson, *Origins of Christianity*, 130. Says Hengel, "[T]he 'old custom' of executing (often by crucifixion) all the slaves in a household if the master was murdered was revived in the time of Nero by a decree of the senate" (*Crucifixion*, 59). Hengel adds, "According to Suetonius, Domitian had Hermogenes, a writer from Tarsus, executed because of some objectionable allusions in one of his books, while the unfortunate slaves who had written it out were crucified out of hand" (80).

28. Horsley and Silberman, *Message*, 207.

29. Spong, *Liberating the Gospels*, 42. See also Robertson, *Origins of Christianity*, 76–77; and Levine, *Misunderstood Jew*, 127.

30. Koester, *History, Culture, and Religion*, 410.

of the empire and their expectation of divine interference—faced a situation that was volatile, dangerous, and futile.

The clearest evidence of that futility, largely owing to the willingness of the Roman authorities to crush all real or imagined threats to their power with extreme and overwhelming force, became visible beyond measure in the Revolt of 66. According to Josephus, the Roman army "ravaged the country, killing a great number of the people, looting their property, and burning down their villages." At one point, 6,000 men, women, and children—who had gathered at the Temple at the urgent behest of a prophet who said he had been advised to take people there by God Himself—were all burned to death. Titus, the general whose father had just become the Roman emperor, crucified five hundred Jews per day during the rebellion. Otherwise, thousands were massacred in the streets, thousands were killed in gladiatorial shows, and thousands more were sent to work themselves to death in Egyptian mines. In short, Vespasian had "launched a brutal scorched-earth campaign of destruction and enslavement, intended to extinguish Judea's tendency for stiff-necked rebellion once and for all."[31] Clearly, his son, Titus, did not relent.

In addition, "all land in Judaea was confiscated and sold by auction; and Jews throughout the Empire were made to pay to the temple of Juppiter Capitolinus at Rome the tax which they had formerly paid to the temple at Jerusalem." Of course, this occurred after the Temple was destroyed in AD 70 and thousands of more Jews were thrown out of Jerusalem—only to return later and undergo exile again after the Revolt of 132, similarly futile, similarly bloody and destructive.[32] In the two wars, as many as one and a half million Jews were killed, and at the end of the second war Jews lost their territory as well their identity.[33]

The worst thing about all this bloodshed—of course, aside from the massive amount of human suffering it caused—is that (except for Gamaliel's reference to Theudas and Judah the Galilean and the misidentification of Paul as the Egyptian, both in Acts of the Apostles) *none of it is mentioned in the New Testament*: not the other protesters, brigands, prophets, and messiahs who, along with their thousands of followers, defied the Romans for well over half a century; not the mass murder of

---

31. Horsley and Silberman, *Message*, 209. The authors continue: "Towns and villages across the region were burned and leveled, and tens of thousands of men, women, and children—even those who played no active part in the rebellion—were hacked, burned, or beaten to death . . . According to Josephus, more than 30,000 Galilean prisoners of war were sold into slavery; twelve hundred elderly and infirm captives (having no market value) were executed; and 'six thousand of the most robust' young people of the region were sent off as imperial slaves to Achaia—where Nero still tarried—to undertake the backbreaking labor of digging his Corinthian Canal" (209–10).

32. Robertson, *Origins of Christianity*, 140.

33. Carroll, *Constantine's Sword*, 90. Borg and Crossan comment: "The whole period was a time of great suffering for Jews, including Jewish Christians. In areas of the Jewish homeland and nearby countries with significant Jewish populations, Gentiles persecuted and sometimes massacred Jews . . . Great numbers of Jews were killed by the Romans as they reconquered the Jewish homeland, perhaps as high a percentage of the Jewish people as perished under Hitler" (*Last Week*, 80; my emphasis).

the Jews by the Romans, which occurred partly because of these rebels; and not the Romans' fear of rebellion, which made them overreact to even the smallest and least political threat to their dominion, including Nero's persecution of Christians in Rome at approximately the very time that Paul arrived there in c. AD 60.

The *only* identified perpetrators of violence in the New Testament are Jews, and none of the aforementioned acts of slaughter and destruction are attributed to the Romans, who are not even held accountable for the deaths of Peter and Paul: "Not mentioned or even hinted at in the Acts account of Paul's arrival in Rome to face an imperial tribunal was the Emperor Nero's growing madness, which no one living at the time could have ignored." More specifically, "the Book of Acts concluded without mentioning Paul's ultimate fate; this was another unpleasant historical reality too painful for its larger theological agenda to include."[34] Similarly, Peter's death went unrecorded in the New Testament even though, like Paul's, it occurred before the first Gospel was written.[35]

In other words, if we consult the evangelists, there were no political conflicts, economic troubles, or social tensions worth mentioning during this period. As one scholar says, "The translators [of the words of Jesus and the reports of his Aramaic-speaking disciples] apparently were more concerned with theology than with history. For they took no cognizance of the backgrounds of the times and the social forces of the Jewish state in which Jesus had his birth and lived."[36] In addition, in the view of many scholars, the Church (1) depoliticized Jesus' own movement, making it non-threatening to the Romans, who (therefore) bore no real responsibility for Jesus' death; and (2) turned the Jews rather than the Romans into the enemies of Jesus by

---

34. Horsley and Silberman, *Message*, 197–202.

35. By contrast, Eusebius says, "Thus Nero, publicly announcing himself as the chief enemy of God, was led on in his fury to slaughter the apostles. Paul is said to have been beheaded at Rome and Peter to have been crucified under him. And this account is confirmed by the fact that the names of Peter and Paul still remain in the cemeteries of that city even to this day" (*Ecclesiastical History,* Bk. 2, 25:5).

36. Zeitlin, *Who Crucified Jesus?* 103. "The hazards of village life do not surface in the gospels" (Freyne, *Galilee, Jesus,* 154). And important events—like Emperor Gaius' threat to install a gigantic statue of himself in the Temple, which failed only because Gaius, otherwise known as Caligula, was assassinated—are also unreported. Concurrent with the activities of the Church depicted in Acts of the Apostles, in AD 40, this colossal insult to the Jews in Jerusalem (and across the empire) is not mentioned in Acts, although it is described by both Josephus and Philo. It might be argued that the incident, though important to Jews, was irrelevant to Christians, but James the brother of Jesus, called by Church historians the first bishop of the Church, seems to have attended the Temple regularly, as did, presumably, his fellow Jewish Christians. Brandon comments: "The fact, moreover, that reference is made by Acts to other contemporary political events, none of which had anything like the significance of this threat to the Temple, consequently causes suspicion about its silence concerning the attempt of Gaius and the effect of it on the Christians living in Jerusalem and worshipping in the Temple" (*Trial of Jesus,* 42). Brandon adds, "[T]hose Christian writings which purport to describe the beginnings of Christianity show a strange unconcern for, or elusiveness about, certain seemingly unavoidable involvements of the Jewish Christians with contemporary Jewish affairs" (43).

making them the perpetrators of his death and making Judaism out to be a backward and outdated religion.[37]

CLASS WARFARE

There are four important points to be made about the official violence in Palestine and the rest of the Roman empire in the first century. First, it was so pervasive and bloody and relentless that it makes any single death, whether by crucifixion or other means, almost invisible. As one scholar explains: "In those harsh times—typical, it might seem, of mankind's whole history—one problematic execution among so many was in no way strange. Such an event—a 'mere incident' in the daily record of the time, which despite Acts 26:26 took place in an obscure corner of the . . . 'whole inhabited world'—would appear to have attracted little or no attention in those days. Such instances were legion."[38]

Of course, I do not mean to suggest that the Crucifixion of Jesus was insignificant. I simply mean that it was a death that cannot be distinguished from countless other deaths. All of the hundreds of thousands of Jews and others who died on the cross suffered unspeakably. Indeed, unlike Jesus, many of them remained on the cross long enough to have their rotting bodies eaten by scavengers, their flesh infested by insects, and their bones picked clean by birds. These were the "criminals" who, unlike Jesus, remained unburied either because they had no friends or family or because people who might otherwise have helped them were too frightened to do so, lest they themselves be subjected to the same treatment. (Victims of Jewish justice were

---

37. Kaylor, *Jesus the Prophet*, 170, 93–94. Sanders agrees with Kaylor's claim that the treatment of Jesus by first- and second-century Christians' was revisionist: "The early Christians did not want Jesus to look like a rebel or even a trouble-maker. Christianity, they wished to maintain, produced good and loyal citizens; the rulers of the cities and provinces of Syria, Asia Minor, Greece, Macedonia and Italy had nothing to fear" (*Historical Figure of Jesus*, 258). Brandon says, for example, that the biblical account of Agrippa's execution of James the son of Zebedee ignores the fact that Agrippa saw James as a subversive and murdered him as a threat to the security of Judea: "[I]t seems likely that he . . . endeavored to root out those elements in Judea which he considered dangerous to the peace and well-being of the state." Brandon continues: "Thus, again, we see that the Acts of the Apostles . . . is in fact a tendentious account, designed to present an idealistic picture of the infant faith, triumphing over Jewish opposition and pursuing its way in serene unconcern for the realities of contemporary Jewish politics" (*Trial of Jesus*, 46–48).

38. Schillebeeckx, *Jesus*, 18. Sanders comments: "Jesus became such an important man in world history that it is sometimes hard to believe how unimportant he was during his lifetime, especially outside Palestine . . . To [Roman writers], Jesus (if they heard of him at all) was merely a troublesome rabble-rouser and magician in a small, backward part of the world . . . When he was executed, Jesus was no more important to the outside world than the two brigands or insurgents executed with him— whose names we do not know" (*Historical Figure of Jesus*, 49). In fact, "Jesus was less important in the eyes of most of his contemporaries than were John the Baptist and the Egyptian [a Jewish rebel leader for whom Paul is mistaken in Acts of the Apostles]" (50–51).

sometimes hung on a tree after their death, but, according to Deuteronomy 21:22–23, were removed for burial on the same day.)[39]

Second, it was not only the New Testament evangelists who failed to acknowledge the turmoil that characterized the century before and the century after the birth of Jesus. It was also many of the Bible critics before the middle of the twentieth century. Even the leading German scholar of the modern era, Rudolf Bultmann, focused almost exclusively on Jesus as an individual, as if he had lived in a historical vacuum, and simply omitted any reference to the connection between Jesus and his sociopolitical milieu.[40] Others merely followed suit. The result was presumably what these guardians of the historical record wanted: a picture of Jesus as utterly anomalous in everything he said and did; a picture of the Jews as irremediably evil and destructive; a picture of the Romans as innocent and worthy of Christianization; and a picture of Christianity as a revolutionary religion that owed everything it became not to human effort and historical accident, but to God's will.

Third, the violence of this time was almost always a manifestation of class warfare, a fact that has immediate bearing on the subject at hand. Specifically, it is imperative to see this ongoing conflict, turning often into mutual hostility and violence, between the haves and the have-nots in order to understand the Crucifixion. For one thing, it demonstrates the absurdity of using the term "the Jews" to describe the people who were responsible for Jesus' death. That is, there was no such group. From the Essenes and Pharisees, who hated the Hellenizers and believed in the imminent transformation of the world, to the Herodians and Sadducees, many of whom adored everything

39. Crossan discusses crucifixions in the Roman empire in *Who Killed Jesus?* 160–68. Tabor provides these details: "It took as long as three days to die, the agony was unbearable, and the naked victims served as a shameful and terrifying example for the populace to behold" (*Jesus Dynasty*, 180). "Death resulted from a combination of shock, exhaustion, muscle cramps, dehydration, loss of blood, and finally suffocation or heart failure" (219). Kaylor points out that both Cicero and Quintillian considered crucifixion to be a deterrent (*Jesus the Prophet*, 49). Borg and Crossan call the use of crucifixion by the Romans "a calculated social deterrent" reserved for "runaway slaves or rebel insurgents": "Its victims were hung up as a public warning. "What made this form of execution particularly frightening was the fact that the bodies could be entirely consumed by "carrion birds" and "scavenging dogs" (*Last Week*, 146). Hengel quotes a Roman poet on crucified bodies as "evil food for birds of prey and grim pickings for dogs" (*Crucifixion*, 9). Hengel adds that the poor, almost exclusively, were subject to this form of punishment (34, 83, 87), that flogging almost always preceded the execution itself (25), and that the crucified person was exposed to "abuse and mockery" (41). According to the editors of *Oxford Annotated Bible*, "Bodies of the executed were normally denied burial" (1211), a point that Borg and Crossan make as well (*Last Week*, 153). Horsley and Silberman report: "The general archeological situation in Jerusalem seems to confirm the rarity of proper burial for those who were crucified . . . And despite the fact that hundreds of family tombs—and the bones of thousands of individuals—from first-century Jerusalem have been excavated from a broad swath of cemeteries . . . , only a single skeleton bearing the signs of crucifixion . . . has ever been identified" (*Message*, 89).

40. Kaylor, *Jesus the Prophet*, 1. Sanders laments that both amateur and professional writers of books on Jesus have "misrepresented" the political as well as religious setting of Jesus' life—a mistake that he does not intend to make in his book on Jesus (*Historical Figure of Jesus*, xiv). Freyne refers to "Bultmann's lack of interest in the historical Jesus and the Jewish roots of early Christianity" in *Galilee, Jesus*, 2. See also Horsley and Silberman, *Message*, 93–94.

Greek or Roman and disbelieved in any kind of eschatology, the Jews were characterized as much by their differences as by their similarities.[41] Furthermore, if any Jews called for Jesus' execution, they were certainly the Roman-sympathizing elites, including the chief priests, rather than the peasants. Many of the latter quite readily and indiscriminately supported any charismatic leader who promised liberation (from both Romans and Hellenized Jews).

Finally—coupled with the fact that the Romans, *without any help or encouragement from the Jews*, were fully capable of arresting and crucifying any perceived troublemaker, and the fact that they had by AD 30 actually crucified many thousands of Jews so identified[42]—it is logical to conclude that, for all intents and purposes, "the Jews" had little or nothing to do with the arrest, trial, and execution of Jesus. In fact, the Romans killed as many messianic rebels as they could find, almost always without any assistance from even the Jews at the top of the socio-economic ladder. One scholar, using Josephus' *Jewish Antiquities*, provides three examples of Roman arrests and executions without Jewish help: Fadus' murder of Theudas and his "masses," Felix's slaughter of the Egyptian's "mob," and Herod Antipas' beheading of John the Baptist.[43] One might add Pilate's murder of Galileans (Luke 13:1) and Samaritans. In the latter case, a messianic Samaritan led his followers up Mt. Gerizim to find relics of Moses and was attacked by Pilate's soldiers, who killed many participants in battle and later turned the leaders over to Pilate for execution.[44]

The last point is almost universally supported by contemporary Bible scholars and historians: Given the frequency with which Jews, in a wide variety of actions over

41. Many scholars have noted that Judaism at the time of Jesus was made up of many different sects. As Tabor says, for example, speaking only of the Jews in Palestine, Judaism at the time "was incredibly diverse" (*Jesus Dynasty*, 120). Brown notes that this diversity often generated surprisingly angry verbal insults, which means that the hostile language used in the Gospel of John against the Jews "is well attested in the inner Jewish disputes of the time" (*Churches*, 119). Says Ruether, the Essenes (like the Christians) "vilified the Judaism outside [their] converted community as apostate, sinful, worse than the Gentiles, and even of the devil" (*Faith and Fratricide*, 74–75). So hostile were these Jewish groups to each other that, according to Fredriksen, the vituperative nature of Paul's criticisms of the Jews and Judaism was in some instances actually exceeded by intra-Jewish attacks. While the Jews were relatively tolerant toward outsiders, she says, they were "rancorously, almost exuberantly, intolerant of variety within the fold" ("The Birth of Christianity and the Origins of Christian Anti-Semitism," 15–16). See also Fredriksen, *Jesus of Nazareth*, 62; and Kaylor, *Jesus the Prophet*, 106. Theissen explains that, under pressure to loosen their standards by Hellenistic attitudes among them, many Jews tried to intensify "the norms of the law," which led to further divisions. "In extreme cases," Theissen continues, "members of the various renewal movements persecuted one another. Among the Pharisees, bloody controversies seem to have arisen between the followers of Hillel and those of Shammai" (*Early Palestinian Christianity*, 86–87). Whatever this persecution amounted to, however, there is no evidence that Jews killed Jews for religious reasons.

42. "Josephus describes many messianic claimants, reputedly endowed with miraculous power, who promised 'signs of deliverance', but whom the Romans promptly suppressed" (Brandon, *Trial of Jesus*, 150).

43. Kaylor, *Jesus the Prophet*, 38–41.

44. For a fuller description of this massacre, based on a passage from Josephus, see Klingaman, *First Century*, 206–7.

the last years of the first century BC and the early years of the first century AD, expressed their dissatisfaction with Roman political and economic oppression, it would have been remarkable if the Romans had not been suspicious of even the slightest hint of a threat. Herod Antipas in particular and the procurators in general distrusted everyone.[45] And "everyone" included bandits, prophets, and healers—any person who might possibly mobilize large numbers of Jews with the overt or covert intention of driving the Romans out of Palestine.[46]

Under these circumstances, it is not at all surprising that John the Baptist, who seems to have had an exclusively ethical, as opposed to political, agenda, was arrested and killed.[47] Josephus explains: "When others joined the crowds about him, because they were aroused to the greatest degree by his sermons, Herod [Antipas] became alarmed. Eloquence that had so great an effect on mankind might lead to some form of sedition, for it looked as if they would be guided by John in everything they did. Herod decided it would be much better to strike first before his work led to an uprising."[48]

Nor is it surprising that even such an obviously harmless character as Jesus ben Hananiah, who had no following at all, was arrested and questioned and scourged by the Romans in the 60s. This Jesus, "seized by the Spirit in the Temple" on the Feast of Tabernacles in AD 62, "suddenly poured forth a prophetic malediction in which he foretold [the Temple's] destruction." He was arrested by the Roman procurator Albinus because he continued to curse the Temple all over Jerusalem. Though Jesus

45. Guignebert, *Jewish World*, 209; see also 253. "To Rome, all crowds were dangerous. All leaders who attracted a following were political revolutionaries" (Wylen, *Jews*, 126). Tabor says that what Herod Antipas "most feared was a native revolt that might gain the popular support of those people who were looking for a legitimate ruler from the house of David" (*Jesus Dynasty*, 98). Carmichael traces the frequency of Jewish resistance and rebellion in *Birth of Christianity*, 8–11, 15, 25–28, 30–32, 43, 207. Carmichael says, "Jesus's movement . . . was characteristic of the Kingdom of God agitation that kept Palestine, and Jewry in general, churned up for well-nigh two centuries" (36). As Gonzalez puts it, from Herod onward, the Jews of Palestine engaged in an "almost continuous rebellion" (*Story of Christianity*, 9).

46. Stegemann and Stegemann, *Jesus Movement*, 166. Theissen discusses the execution of Theudas, an unnamed prophet, Jonathan, a Samaritan prophet, and Jesus: "Each time . . . the Romans quickly intervened, inflicted a blood-bath or arrested the leaders" (*Early Palestinian Christianity*, 60).

47. Flusser says, "John's powerful influence over the people led to his execution by Herod Antipas," as Josephus makes clear (*Sage from Galilee*, 18). Crossan says: "No matter what John's intentions may have been, Antipas had more than enough materials on which to act. Desert and Jordan, prophet and crowds, were always a volatile mix calling for immediate preventive strikes" (*Historical Jesus*, 235). See also Hengel, *Charismatic Leader*, 35. For a fuller discussion of Herod Antipas and John the Baptist, see Tabor, *Jesus Dynasty*, 127–29, 173–74. Antipas was eager to lock up Jesus for the same reasons he executed John (107, 175, 217). See also Horsley and Silberman, *Message*, 33–34. Theissen agrees that John was killed for political reasons but notes that this motive goes unnoticed in the New Testament tradition (*Early Palestinian Christianity*, 60–61).

48. Quoted in Horsley and Silberman, *Message*, 39.

refused to desist, Albinus, "considering him to be out of his mind," released him after scourging him "to the bone."[49]

Thus, as a verbal critic of the Temple (like Jesus ben Hananiah) and a prophet with many disciples in tow (like John the Baptist), Jesus of Nazareth could have been executed anywhere in the empire. Particularly as a religious leader who claimed to be a king as well as a prophet (or was at least perceived to be one or the other), Jesus was especially vulnerable to execution in Palestine.[50] As yet another scholar puts it, "in the unsettling political and religious circumstances of inter-testamental Palestine someone could easily lose his life without actually committing any culpable act against the Jewish law or the Roman state."[51] And it made no difference whether the leader or his followers were political or not. Refusing to make distinctions where they were difficult to make, the Romans suppressed all movements, messianic and otherwise, and either "crucified their instigators or executed them in other ways whenever they could get their hands on them."[52]

The Jewish elite were involved in the arrest of Jesus not because he committed blasphemy, but because he was presumed to be yet another insurgent, like Barabbas, John the Baptist, and Jesus ben Hananiah. In other words, he was seen as a threat to Rome. Like all indigenous aristocracies in the Roman provinces, the Jewish leaders were as vigilant (and as punitive) as the Romans were regarding all suspected rebels.[53] Since they ruled to the limited extent that they did only with the support of the Ro-

49. Flusser, *Sage from Galilee*, 122. Flusser later adds, "[T]hroughout their whole empire, the Romans diligently protected all religious sanctuaries. They also evidently made it their business to protect the high priests from importune agitators" (134).

50. Crossan, *Who Killed Jesus?* 58; and Bruce, *New Testament History*, 163. Sanders comments: "If we use this case [i.e., that of the other Jesus] as a guide, we can understand why Jesus of Nazareth was executed rather than merely flogged. Our Jesus' offence was worse than that of Jesus son of Ananias. Jesus of Nazareth had a following, perhaps not very large, but nevertheless a following. He had taught about the kingdom for some time. He had taken physical action in the Temple. He was not a madman. Thus he was potentially dangerous" (*Historical Figure of Jesus*, 267).

51. Vermes, *Changing Faces of Jesus*, 278. Peters says that "in the first century the social and economic circumstances were far too incendiary for the show of Roman force that normally sufficed. The Palestinian Jews had shown before that there was a point where they would choose to resist the Romans to the end" (*Harvest of Hellenism*, 514).

52. Bultmann, *Jesus and the Word*, 22. Bultmann adds: "Here it must be emphasized that some of these movements had no political character . . . The Romans did not distinguish, and indeed they could not; for them, all these movements were suspected as hostile to the Roman authority" (22). Tabor says, "There was zero tolerance for Messiahs," who "were not considered to be harmless religious fanatics but potentially seditious enemies of Rome" (*Jesus Dynasty*, 189)

53. Meeks says that it was customary for Roman emperors "to build a network of personal dependency between the upper classes of the eastern cities" and themselves. "In return for the loyalty of the local aristocrats . . . the *princeps* not only gave them his protection but also materially advanced their careers and those of their sons" (*First Urban Christians*, 12). Meeks adds: "In those areas where a strong local monarchy made it unnecessary or as yet inexpedient for Rome to organize a province, the native kings themselves became clients of the Roman *princeps*. Herod is a well-known and typical, if not entirely successful, example" (13). These kings helped Rome, and Rome helped them. See also Herzog, *Jesus, Justice*, 90–91, 102–3.

mans, they had as much invested in the status quo as the Romans did. Furthermore, they did not appreciate having Jews accused of subversion, *with the possibility that they themselves might be included in the charge.*[54] Every such act not only threatened to undermine the empire, but, short of that accomplishment, also threatened to alienate the Romans and possibly even lead them to punish the Jews who failed to keep order.[55]

In fact, the Jewish High Priest was Rome's chief security officer, ready to cooperate completely with the local Roman authorities and fully prepared to turn over anyone even remotely resembling a revolutionary: "As an appointee of the Romans, the High Priest was not just a ceremonial official with jurisdiction over the Temple; he was, in effect, a chief of police with his own armed force, his own police tribunal which was concerned with political offences, and his own penal system, including prisons and arrangements for flogging offenders." With serious criminals (i.e., seditionists), however—including not only Jesus of Nazareth, but the ridiculously harmless Jesus ben Hananiah—the High Priest gave the offender to the procurator for trial and punishment.[56]

In this respect, the High Priests always served the Romans, not the Jews.[57] Expected to carry out their orders, they were simply agents of the occupying power. They were "held responsible for the pacification of the country," and, therefore, often "wholeheartedly helped the procurators to destroy any opposition against the Romans." The procurators also appointed the members of the Sanhedrin, whose job was "to hunt out the malcontents, the rebels against the state, and to report them to the Roman officials." They did their job because they were rewarded: "Many of the high priests thought that, by appeasing the Romans and helping them to destroy rebellious Jewish patriots, they would gain at least temporary benefits for the Jews," particularly

54. "The aristocracy were the natural allies of the Romans," says Theissen, "because their members were 'peace-loving men, simply out of concern for their possessions'" (*Early Palestinian Christianity*, 70; Theissen is quoting Josephus). Horsley and Silberman add: "[T]he continued wealth of the high-priestly families and their political fortunes were dependent on the Roman authorities . . . Indeed, the High Priests had been the de facto representatives of the Judean people to the Roman authorities and they were saddled with the responsibility of maintaining order in Jerusalem. Roman officials could—and did—appoint them to office or depose them at will" (*Message*, 79). According to Richardson, the Sanhedrin was "the puppet government which the Romans allowed the Jews to maintain." Because it was made up of "mostly Sadducees, there was little likelihood of its incurring the displeasure of the Romans" (*Gospel*, 64). Brandon gives as an example of cooperation between Jewish elites and Roman authorities across the empire the help given by "Jewish leaders" in Alexandria to the Romans "in rounding up and exterminating the Sicarii [i.e., armed Jewish rebels]" in that city (*Trial of Jesus*, 77). See also Klingaman, *First Century*, 50; and Markus, *Christianity*, 17.

55. Bammel quotes Josephus on this subject. At the beginning of the Revolt of 66, Agrippa warned the rebels that, if they persisted, the Romans would destroy Jerusalem and kill all the Jews. The priests, too, implored the rebels not to evoke Roman reprisals, which would put the entire country at risk (*"Ex illa itaque die consilium fecerunt . . . ,"* 22).

56. Maccoby, *Mythmaker*, 58.

57. Kaylor, *Jesus the Prophet*, 24 and n. 18; see also 55.

themselves. And they would avoid the reprisals that could occur if they failed to fulfill their responsibility.[58]

Thus, as John explains in his Gospel, the chief priests argued that, if Jesus is allowed to continue to preach, "all men will believe on him; and *the Romans shall come and take away both our place and our nation.*" In short, "If things went wrong, the high priest"—and, by extension, the rest of the community—"was accountable."[59] The High Priest Caiaphas agreed completely with this sentiment, concluding, as he explained to "the council," that it was better to have one man executed than to risk the lives of everyone else: "[Y]ou do not understand that *it is expedient for you* that one man should die for the people, and that the whole nation should not perish" (John 11:48–50; my emphasis)—and not only the nation of Palestine but "the children of God that were scattered abroad" (John 11:52), suggesting that a sufficiently rabble-rousing leader might endanger the Jews in the Diaspora as well as in Palestine.

As this discussion suggests, the Sadducean High Priest, unlike the Essenes and the Pharisees, had little or no interest in theology and could therefore not have been concerned about such charges as blasphemy and heresy. He was obsessive about sedition, not religious dissent: Thus, "if Jesus' movement had been a heretical one, espousing theological doctrines that contradicted the traditional tenets of Judaism, the High Priest would have been entirely unconcerned . . . The only circumstances under which the High Priest would employ his police force to arrest and imprison people would be if they had shown themselves to be a political threat to the Roman regime."[60] On the other hand, even if the High Priest cared deeply about theological issues, certainly neither the prefects, including Pilate, nor their subordinates were concerned. Thus, when the Jews of Corinth complained to the Romans that Paul was persuading "men to worship God contrary to the law," the Roman deputy of Achaia, Gallio, responded: "If it were a matter of wrongdoing or vicious crime, I should have reason to bear with you, O Jews. But since it is a matter of questions about words and names and your own law, see to it yourselves. I refuse to be a judge in these things" (Acts 18:14–15).[61]

58. Zeitlin, *Who Crucified Jesus?* 50–51, 81, 156.

59. Sanders, *Historical Figure of Jesus*, 27. Sanders notes, "The high priest, often in concert with the 'chief priests', sometimes with 'the powerful' or 'the elders' (influential laymen), was in charge of ordinary police and judicial procedures, and he—alone and in such combinations as just described—figures large in the gospels, in Acts and in Josephus" (25). Sanders adds later: "If the high priest did not preserve order, the Roman prefect would intervene militarily, and the situation might get out of hand . . . To keep his job, he had to remain in control" (265). In AD 50, for example, as a result of a Samaritan-Galilean dispute, the High Priest Ananias was sent to Rome to be tried, evidently for the actions of the Galileans: "He had nothing to do with the trouble in Samaria, but nevertheless he was responsible for good order. We also see that the high priest was only 'first among equals'. Responsibility to prevent trouble fell, to some degree, on all leading citizens" (266).

60. Maccoby, *Mythmaker*, 59.

61. In other words, the Roman authorities were generally indifferent "to the particular religions of subject peoples" and particularly so regarding what they took to be in-house religious squabbles (Fredriksen, *Jesus of Nazareth*, 8).

In other words, Jesus was a threat to the Jews *only* because he was a threat to the Romans: "His teaching was not at all congenial to the Temple authorities and leaders of the Sanhedrin, who feared that any talk of a new kingdom would excite revolutionary sentiments among the people and bring down reprisals from the Romans."[62] After all, as I mentioned earlier, Mark and Luke refer to a recent "insurrection" in which Barabbas, "among the rebels in prison, . . . had committed murder" (Mark 15:7; Luke 23:19), for which, in fact, he was "notorious" (Matt 27:16). And Jesus was crucified between two *lestai* (Matt 27:38; Luke 23:32), which is usually translated as *thieves*. According to a few scholars, however, the word is more likely to mean, if not *Zealots*, then at least *bandits* of the kind who were as much revolutionaries as they were highwaymen.[63]

All of this suggests that the moment was ripe for overreaction. In other words, under such circumstances, Jesus was opposed not by the populace at large, but by those who had the most to lose if he had been permitted to continue—the chief priests, the Herodians, and the leaders of the Sanhedrin.[64] As one scholar concludes, Jesus "was executed by the Romans, and if the Jews had anything to do with it—that is, if he were not executed simply because he caused public disturbance—the instigators of his death would have been those with access to Pilate. Chief among these were the leaders of the priesthood."[65]

It is worth noting that, after the Jewish authorities in Jerusalem arrested Peter and his friends, Gamaliel, the Pharisee, persuaded the mostly Sadducean "council" members, including the High Priest, to let them go. Clearly, however, neither Gamaliel nor

---

62. Bruce, *New Testament History*, 187. See also 189; and Fredriksen, *From Jesus to Christ*, 204.

63. Bruce, *New Testament History*, 191. In fact, the two so-called thieves crucified with Jesus in Matthew 27:38 may have been insurrectionists as well. As Clark explains, the word *lestai*, usually translated thieves, "often implied the kind of outlaws who are called freedom fighters by their friends and bandits, or terrorists, by their enemies" (*Christianity and Roman Society*, 4). Hengel says that, by law, the Romans called rebels bandits rather than enemies (*Crucifixion*, 47–48). See also Brandon, *The Trial of Jesus*, 40, 103, 150, 189); Borg, *Jesus*, 265; and Kaylor, *Jesus the Prophet*, 88 n. 31.

64. Bultmann, *Jesus and the Word*, 26.

65. Sanders, *Jesus and Judaism*, 293. Sanders's argument leading up to his conclusion is worth reading: 288–93. His substantially more nuanced summary of his position appears on 305. But see also 317, where Sanders says that Jesus was probably "executed for sedition or treason, as would-be king." Vermes names the Herodians and chief priests as Jesus' enemies (*Jesus the Jew*, 36). See also *Changing Faces of Jesus*, 20, 178–79. Maccoby adds to the list of Jesus' enemies the High Priest, who "would indeed have been alarmed and hostile to Jesus because of his claim to Messiahship and his threat to the Temple, for the High Priest was appointed by the Romans to look after their interests." The Pharisees, "the party of resistance against Rome," albeit mostly passive, would have disapproved of Judas' actions, as Gamaliel's speech in the trial of Peter in Acts suggests (*Mythmaker*, 48–49). Flusser says that Judas the disciple of Jesus, "the accounts of [whose] death are contradictory," probably simply disappeared after his betrayal of Jesus, "for there were plenty of people who would have repaid him in blood for handing a Jew over to the Romans" (*Sage from Galilee*, 136). Flusser notes that the Pharisees, who "engineered the deposition of Annas [or Ananus]" after he called a meeting of the Sanhedrin "without their knowledge" and proceeded to execute James the brother of Jesus in AD 62, would have been similarly hostile to the execution of Jesus: "[T]hey could not have acquiesced in the surrender of Jesus to the Romans" (138). Sanders agrees in *Historical Figure of Jesus*, 267.

the others saw Jesus' disciples as anything less than revolutionaries since he compared them not to religious extremists like the Essenes, but to two famous rebels, Theudas and Judah (or Judas) the Galilean. His point was that, if the disciples were really dangerous (i.e., "not of God"), they would be executed by the Romans, as were all Jewish insurrectionists (Acts 5:34–38).

The later arrests of Paul and Jason, insofar as they replicate the pattern of apprehension by Jews and transfer to Romans, which Jesus underwent, probably occurred for the same reason. Paul, arrested by the High Priest Ananias, was presented to the procurator Felix as "a pestilent fellow, and *a mover of sedition* among all the Jews throughout the world, and a ringleader of the sect of the Nazarenes" (Acts 24:5; my emphasis). Jason, among others, was accused before "the rulers of the city" by "the Jews" of Thessalonica of having "turned the world upside down" and declaring that there was another king besides Caesar (Acts 17:6–7).[66] These may well have been false charges in the sense that they were based on exaggerations or misinterpretations, but neither the Romans nor their Jewish representatives were capable of making more precise and accurate characterizations of actions that were apparently always understood to be threatening and therefore worthy of suppression and punishment. There is no reason at all to assume that Jesus, Peter, Paul, and Jason were perceived to be blasphemers,[67] particularly since none of the other messianic figures in first-century Palestine were accused of blasphemy.[68] They were all seditionists in the eyes of a hyper-vigilant, if not paranoid, government.

When we turn to the New Testament for evidence of a split between the Jewish aristocracy and the ordinary people, we find a comprehensive and consistent picture of a vast gulf between them, at least in the synoptic Gospels. Clearly, all of Jesus' followers—quite frequently referred to as "great crowds" (or "multitudes")—were Jews, although they are *never* identified that way. Equally clearly, the only Jews who were interested in arresting Jesus were the chief priests (who appear in all of these Gospels

66. Maccoby says that, "as Jesus himself was falsely represented as a victim of Judaism through the depoliticization of his life work, so the tragedies among his followers in the Nazarene movement were removed from the account of Roman oppression and laid at the door of Judaism, in a myth of Jewish persecution of the Nazarenes, who were in fact not at odds with their co-religionists but were loyal both to the Torah and the Jewish nation" (*Mythmaker*, 138).

67. Hare insists that although certain acts, such as "attacks on Torah or Temple," were considered blasphemous in the ordinary sense, they were not considered to be capital crimes in ancient Judaism. As a legal concept, he adds, blasphemy was narrowly defined, which meant, for example, that the Sadducees never charged the Pharisees with committing blasphemy when they added to the laws in the Torah, and neither Jesus nor his followers were charged with this crime when Jesus claimed to be a divine being and his followers believed him. Indeed, "the law of blasphemy was seldom if ever invoked in the Jewish judiciary" (*Jewish Persecution of Christians*, 24–29). Sanders similarly concludes that Jesus could not have been accused of blasphemy in any of his seeming violations of Jewish law: "Either the circumstances [as described in the Gospel accounts] are improbable or the negative reaction to Jesus is disproportionate to his behavior" (*Historical Figure of Jesus*, 213).

68. At least, Josephus does not indicate that other messiahs were so accused. On this point, see Brandon, *Trial of Jesus*, 89–90.

as the enemies of Jesus), elders, scribes, rulers, and captains of the Temple. Conspicuously absent from the pursuers of Jesus were the Pharisees, who make only two appearances during the arrest of Jesus, but do not show up at either the trial or the execution. (They "replace" the elders in Matthew 27:62 and John 18:3.) In all cases, the High Priest was the prime mover, and the "council" or "assembly" (presumably, the Sanhedrin) over which he ruled appears in each synoptic Gospel (Matt 26:59; Mark 14:55; 15:1; Luke 22:66). The chief priests (and/or their representatives), under the supervision of the High Priest, were the people who arrested Jesus, took him to the house of the High Priest, conducted an inquiry, turned him over to Pilate, and directed the crowd (Mark 15:11; Matt 27:20) to demand Jesus' execution.

Of course, the people who called for Jesus' death should not be confused with the Jews who followed Jesus to Jerusalem, greeted him as a king upon his entrance into the city, and, at least in Luke, followed him to Golgotha, beating their breasts in lamentation (23:48)—i.e., "the multitude" who were transfixed ("astonished") by Jesus' teaching in the Temple (Mark 11:18), "the people" who "held that John [the Baptist] was a real prophet" and whom the Jewish authorities were afraid to offend (Mark 11:32), and "the multitude" whom the authorities "feared" when they "tried to arrest" Jesus after he recited the Parable of the Wicked Tenants (Mark 12:12). Thus, although those who demanded Jesus' crucifixion are referred to as "all the people" (Matt 27:25), they were obviously only those Jews who were obedient to the wishes of "the chief priests and the elders."[69] That is, they were members of the Jewish aristocracy or their retainers. The latter were temple officials, palace bureaucrats, tax and toll collectors, members of the military, and scribes—people who "identified with their patrons, not with the peasants from whom they had come but whom they were now exploiting."[70]

Otherwise, the passage in which Jesus' crucifixion is demanded (Mark 15:13; Matt 25:23; Luke 23:21) is impossible to understand. One problem is that the group most hated—even more than Herodians and elders—by the kind of people who followed Jesus was the chief priests.[71] And, therefore, the chief priests would be the

69. Smith argues that, although the high (or chief) priests supposedly "stirred up the crowd to demand the crucifixion" of Jesus, "a number of passages shift the guilt to 'the crowd,' 'the people,' and in John, to 'the Jews.' The stages of this change reflect the progressive separation of Christianity from the other branches of Judaism, concluding in John with its loss of Jewish identity. Accordingly, these passages are not reliable evidence as to Jesus' actual opponents" (*Jesus the Magician*, 36). After discussing the passages from chapters 11 and 12 in the Gospel of Mark, Borg concludes, "Throughout, the opposition is not between Jesus and the people, the 'crowd,' but between Jesus and the authorities" (*Jesus*, 239–40).

70. Herzog, *Jesus, Justice*, 95–96. Except for palace workers, many of them lived in Jerusalem and acted as a kind of buffer for the aristocracy.

71. The Jews who were drawn to Jesus were likely to be peasants, who constituted well over eighty percent of the population and generally disliked both Romans and Jewish aristocrats, who served as the chief priests (Meeks, *First Urban Christians*, 13). These were the Jews who "considered the empire to be the latest earthly incarnation of the scourge of God" (Klingaman, *First Century*, 6). And it was from their ranks that arose the leaders in various protests against Rome in the decades before the Revolt (Herzog, *Jesus, Justice*, 55).

people least likely to be able to change the minds of Jesus' followers. Indeed, more than one scholar has found "the whole account too preposterous and too ludicrous for belief."[72] In Luke, Pilate "called together the chief priests and the rulers and the people" (23:13). However, the description makes sense only if we assume that "the people" did not include either Jesus' Jewish followers or others like them—because as peasants and laborers they did not support the Jewish aristocracy. *That* was the crowd—the Jewish elite—that would have called for Jesus' crucifixion.

Another problem is that the reader is "asked to believe that that a tough-minded Roman governor bargained with a Jewish mob for the release of a prisoner in his custody, whom he [supposedly] knew to be innocent." The fact is, even Jesus himself had heard "of the Galileans whose blood Pilate had mingled with their sacrifices," an incident that, by the way, despite its evident cruelty, seems to have raised no protest by the evangelists against Pilate [Luke 13:1]. Even harder to accept is the notion that Pilate was to release, instead of Jesus, a notorious insurrectionist who had participated in the murder of Roman soldiers. To many scholars, it simply could not have happened.[73]

The third problem is that the followers of Jesus and other Jewish peasants, who appear to have been the vast majority, were the Jews from whom the chief priests and others had to hide their intention to arrest Jesus. In the Gospels of Matthew and Mark, the chief priests, scribes, and elders understood that they had to "take Jesus by subtilty" (or "by craft") in order to arrest him and kill him. That is, they could not arrest him openly, especially on "the feast day," when many Jews were gathered in Jerusalem, "lest there be an uproar among the people" (Matt 26:4–5; Mark 14:1–2). In short, according to Luke, "[T]hey feared the people" (22:2). Notably, there were no "people" at the Passover feast except Jews—and, indeed, Jews who were far more likely to defend Jesus than to turn him in.

Even in the Gospel of John, the Jews were divided: "[S]o there was a division among the people because of him." On the one hand, "some of them would have taken him in"—obviously the Jewish elite. On the other hand, however, "no man laid hands

---

72. Brandon, *Trial of Jesus*, 98.

73. *Trial of Jesus*, 93–102; see also 189–90, 198. Smith comments: Pilate "was notoriously brutal in putting down political disturbances and insensitive to Jewish opinion. If he found an accused man innocent, it is unlikely that he would have hesitated to release him for fear of offending the Jews; that he should have hesitated to execute a man he thought a messianic pretender, is incredible. Therefore the theatrical scenes set off by his alleged hesitation are Christian polemic against the high priests or, in Matthew and John, the Jews" (*Jesus the Magician*, 176). Pobee says, "The spectacle of Pilate trying to protect Jesus (Mark 15.4) . . . is not in agreement with what is known of Pilate elsewhere, namely that he is a 'man of blood.'" Pobee finds "tendentious" several of the details in this scene, including "the undignified role of the high priests . . . campaigning for the release of Barabbas" ("The Cry of the Centurion—a Cry of Defeat," 100 n. 35). For the view that the Jews *persuaded* Pilate to execute Jesus, see Vogt, "Augustus and Tiberius," and Reicke, "Galilee and Judea," 8, 35. Vogt says that Jesus was neither political nor perceived to be, threatened "the *spiritual* leaders of the Jewish people" when he cleansed the temple (my emphasis), and was sentenced to death by "the Jewish authorities who are responsible for Jesus' arrest"—and execution. The Jews "put pressure on Pilate," who was "undecided"— i.e., innocent ("Augustus and Tiberius," 8).

on him" because some of them would have defended Jesus to the death (7:43–44). Thus, the Jewish *leaders* captured Jesus under the cover of night, in response to which he chastised them for not arresting him in the daytime: "I sat daily with you teaching in the temple, and ye laid no hand on me" (Matt 26:55; Mark 14:49). In Luke, Jesus adds, "[B]ut this is your hour, and the power of darkness" (22:53).

Earlier, on his second day in Jerusalem, the authorities "tried to arrest him, [but] they feared the multitude,"—that is, again, the Jewish majority—"because they took him for a prophet" (Matt 21:46; Mark 11:18; 12:12; Luke 20:19). Luke says, "[T]he chief priests and the scribes and the chief of the people sought to destroy him, and could not find what they might do; for *all the people* were very attentive to hear him" (19:48; my emphasis). What is striking in these passages is the suggestion that *Jesus had no enemies among the ordinary people*—only sympathizers and supporters, many of whom who were willing to defend him (violently, if necessary, in some cases [Mark 14:47; Luke 22:49–50]). It is important to note, as well, that the clear distinction between the Jewish aristocracy and Jewish hoi polloi, which is made so emphatically in the synoptic Gospels, is not made at all in the Gospel of John, in which only Jesus' enemies are identified as "the Jews," while his followers are not.[74]

JESUS AND THE TEMPLE

What exactly did Jesus do to get arrested and executed? The importance of this question is that, if Jesus was blasphemous, then the Jews could be blamed for his death. If he was seditious or subversive, however, then the Romans would have to be held accountable. The traditional, Bible-based view is that Jesus offended the Jews by questioning the Torah to the extent that he challenged the purity laws and Sabbath restrictions and also threatened the Temple: "From the gospel records it is clear that the major reason for the determination of Jesus' enemies to have him executed was their belief that he was undermining the moral standards and institutional structures of their religion."[75]

74. In fact, John implies that the "division" among the Jews was not based on their social class, but on their attitude toward Jesus. "Many of the people" thought he was "the Christ," but "some" doubted his Messiahship because he was from Galilee, not Bethlehem. "And some of *them*"—i.e., the doubters or disbelievers—not just the Jewish elite, "would have taken him" (7:40–44; my emphasis). Smith comments: "In some Johannine passages 'the Jews' and 'the world' are hostile to Jesus, and he to them . . . Moreover, John is full of statements that 'many' or 'crowds' believed in Jesus"—however, without identifying them, except in 12:42, as Jews (*Jesus the Magician*, 171).

75. Kee et al., *Understanding the New Testament*, 199. "From the standpoint of official Judaism, it is no wonder that Jesus was regarded as a subversive who threatened its very foundations by setting aside the Law on no other authority than that which he claimed to have from God" (112). See also Barclay, *Introduction*, 133–35. As Sanders points out, the Gospels themselves hold the Jewish leadership rather than the Romans responsible for Jesus' death (*Jews in Luke-Acts*, 3). And, in the absence of any discussion in the Gospels of the political and economic issues that concerned the Jews of Palestine in the first century, Jesus appears to be a religious rather than political dissident. Indeed, says Sanders, the Gospel of Luke not only shows that the Jews manipulated the Romans into approving of Jesus' execution, but

However, as I noted in Chapter Two and as more than one Bible scholar has recently pointed out, Jesus committed no such violations: "If Jesus had declared all foods clean, why did Paul and Peter disagree over Jews eating with Gentiles (Gal 2:11–16)? . . . [W]hy did it take a thrice-repeated revelation to convince Peter (or, rather, leave him puzzled and on the way to conviction [Acts 10:9–17]). And if Jesus consciously transgressed the Sabbath . . . how could Paul's Christian opponents in Galatia urge that the Sabbath be kept (Gal 4:10)?"[76] Furthermore, why did Jesus' own disciples continue to honor the Sabbath? In Mark 16:1, Mary Magdalene, Mary the mother of James, and Salome waited until the Sabbath was over before they went to Jesus' tomb with the spices necessary to anoint him in the traditional Jewish fashion. Luke explains that these women "rested" on the Sabbath "according to the commandment" (23:56).

Similarly, Jesus' followers honored the Temple as much as they respected the Sabbath. After his return, his disciples "were continually in the temple blessing God," as other Jews were (Lk 24:53). In Acts, Luke says, Jesus' followers went to the temple "day by day," where they praised God and, presumably because they did nothing that distinguished them from other Jews, they "gained favor with all the people," many of whom converted (2:41, 47). In their homes, they broke bread together, after the Jewish custom. To be sure, they spent much of their time in the Temple "teaching and preaching Jesus as the Christ" (5:42). But there can be little doubt that the act of blessing and praising God took place in the context of regular Jewish prayer services. Thus, according to Luke, Peter and John went "to the temple at the hour of prayer" (Acts 3:1). In this context, it is hard to believe that Jesus was hostile to the Temple as a place of worship and as the dwelling-place of God (Matt 21:13; Mark 11:17; Luke 19:46; John 2:16).

It is also relevant to note that, according to contemporary accounts and considering the long-standing doctrinal differences between various Jewish sects, Jews did not kill Jews for religious reasons.[77] Indeed, Jews typically disputed with other Jews over

---

also suggests that the Jews themelves actually committed the murder (7, 14–15). Thus, Freyne, like other scholars who are inclined to read the Gospels as historical instead of theological documents, argues that it was the chief priests, scribes, and elders—centered in Jerusalem, of course, all being associated with the Temple, formally or otherwise—who pursued Jesus and wanted to have him executed (*Galilee, Jesus*, 44, 58, 99, 220). Furthermore, says Freyne, Jesus aroused their hostility because he attacked the religious, rather than the political, social, or economic system: "In the absence of any clearly articulated political moves against Jesus in Galilee, the opposition from those who controlled the religious system in Jerusalem becomes all the more significant, suggesting that it was they, rather than those who were in charge of the social and eco-systems (insofar as these three can be differentiated, of course), who felt the real threat of his challenge" (221). They cannot be differentiated, however, because the priests and elders were also the political, social, and economic leaders of Palestine.

76. Sanders, *Jesus and Judaism*, 250. Sanders adds, "We have again and again returned to the fact that nothing which Jesus said or did which bore on the law led his disciples after his death to disregard it" (268).

77. Vermes says, "The purported antagonism [i.e., between Jesus and Jews in the Gospel of John] receives no support from the Synoptic Gospels; neither the historian Josephus nor rabbinic literature

the meaning and applicability of the Law. But they did not "regard their opponents as following Satan rather than God," and did not believe "they should be executed." In other words, "there was quite a lot of tolerance."[78] At any rate, it is unlikely, though the issue is still debated, that the Jewish authorities had the power to execute anyone without the approval of the Romans.[79]

One reason for assuming that the Jews could neither act independently nor greatly influence the Roman governors is the fact that the most powerful Jewish leader in Palestine (the High Priest) and the most powerful court (the Sanhedrin) had fallen significantly in the eyes of both the Romans and the populace. When Herod first assumed office, he not only murdered members of the Sanhedrin, but also fired all the members of the formerly powerful Hasmonean family, who had dominated the priesthood for more than a century. Henceforth, he made his priestly appointments

reports killing of Jews by other Jews for religious, as opposed to political, reasons. Such behavior is completely without theological foundation in the Jewish thought of the age" (*Changing Faces of Jesus*, 20). Referring to the murders of Stephen and the two Jameses (the son of Zebedee and the brother of Jesus), after a detailed study of the subject (20–43), Hare concludes that "in no instance" were they "clearly a matter of judicial execution by Jewish religious authorities for purely religious reasons" (*Jewish Persecution of Christians*, 34). In fact, Hare says later, there were no such executions in the period AD 35–66 (42–43). A majority of scholars, he states, agree that Stephen was lynched, not found guilty and executed by a judicial body (22 n. 1). For a different view of Stephen's death, see Zeitlin, *Who Crucified Jesus?* 188–92.

78. Sanders, *Historical Figure of Jesus*, 205. Hare argues that the Jews were considerably tolerant of dissent, limiting themselves to little more than verbally insulting and ostracizing Christian believers, and flogging and expelling Christian proselytizers (*Jewish Persecution of Christians*, 1–2, 78–79). He says that "there was greater tolerance for halakic [law-related] nonconformity than has sometimes been supposed" (141). On this point, see also Senior, *Jesus*, 39. However, see n. 41 for an opposing view. Sanders identifies seven different levels of disagreement with Jewish laws, the most serious of which—calling for the repeal of a law—"almost never arose." Jesus' disagreements, Sanders continues, fall into the least extreme categories, calling for some laws to be extended or supplemented. Regarding the Sabbath laws, Jesus seems to have argued for "mitigating circumstance in order to justify transgression." On these laws, however, Sanders adds, "there were various competing interpretations" (*Historical Figure of Jesus*, 206–9).

79. Koester says that the jurisdiction of the Sanhedrin was "limited": "Accusations which involved the death penalty had to be brought before the prefect's court" (*History, Culture, and Religion*, 396). In short, this group "did not have the authority to execute wrongdoers" (400). On Pilate's total power in judicial cases, see Peper and DelCogliano, "The Pliny and Trajan Correspondence," 368. Sanders says: "With one exception [i.e., a gentile's entrance into the Inner Sanctum of the Temple], only the prefect had the right to sentence anyone to death" (*Historical Figure of Jesus*, 24). Zeitlin also notes that the Sanhedrin had power to execute only violators of the holy of holies (*Who Crucified Jesus?* xii, 83). Sanders adds in a note: "Who had the right to execute is a contentious point of long standing, but I think that it should not be. Roman historians whom I have consulted think that [Adrian] Sherwin-White (*Roman Society and Roman Law in the New Testament*) was correct in arguing that in equestrian provinces (like Judaea) only the prefect or procurator had the power of life and death. The argument is supported in [Josephus, *The Jewish] War*, 2.117" (*Historical Figure of Jesus*, 310–11 n. 28). Fredriksen says, "[T]he fact that Jesus was crucified rather than executed or killed in any other way still indicates that no one other than Pilate made the actual decision" (*Jesus of Nazareth*, 295). Deferring to Josephus, Brandon says that the Sanhedrin could execute, "subject to Roman confirmation" (*Trial of Jesus*, 90–91). Enslin says that "the sole limit to [the Sanhedrin's] power was in the matter of the death sentence. This apparently could be pronounced by the governor alone" (*Christian Beginnings*, 131).

from not very powerful families he imported from the Diaspora. Popularly regarded as illegitimate because they were unconnected to any recognized priestly family from the past and widely known to be little more than agents for whoever happened to be the actual ruler of Palestine, these priests certainly had less power than they appear to have in the Gospels: *They were not in charge.*[80]

In fact, the priests continued to have as little independence under the direct rule of the Romans as they had had under Herod. Like the deceased client king, the Roman prefects and procurators also hired and fired the priests and the members of the Sanhedrin at will. They did so frequently, quite likely for the same reason that Herod did—to prevent "any single officeholder from consolidating too much power."[81] Herod himself deposed seven High Priests over a thirty-three-year period and restricted their role to religious matters. Rome did the same, as I noted earlier, with eighteen High Priests ruling for a period of sixty years.[82]

Nevertheless, it is clear that, in some way or other, Jesus opposed either what the Temple was or what it represented. After all, he both drove out the money changers and animal sellers and threatened to destroy it. On this subject, the scholarly interpretation is mixed. It is possible that Jesus rejected the Temple cult—that is, the ritual of animal sacrifice. The most explicit account of the so-called cleansing occurs in the Gospel of John, in which Jesus, using "a whip of cords," drove out of the Temple "people selling cattle, sheep, and doves," along with the money changers. He also poured out the coins of the latter and "overturned their tables." Then he told the sellers of doves to remove their birds and to "stop making [his] Father's house a marketplace" (John 2:14–16; see also Matt 21:12–13; Mark 11:15–17; Luke 19:45–46).

Some of these details are missing in the synoptic Gospels, but it seems possible, if not likely, in the view of some scholars, that Jesus was objecting to the use of the Temple for commercial purposes and, implicitly, for the ritual actions that these marketplace activities supported. Indeed, in the Synoptics, Jesus quoted Isaiah (56:7) and Jeremiah (7:11) when he chastised the sellers and money changers: "It is written, 'My house shall be called a house of prayer'; but you are making it a den of robbers." The latter quotation from Jesus (and, no less, its source in Jeremiah) implies that Jesus was not only offended by the commercialization of the Temple, but also concerned about

---

80. Horsley, *Covenant Economics*, 84–85. In other words, the representatives of the Jewish aristocracy who arrested Jesus and the Romans who executed him simply did their job: "Even the authorities responsible for [Jesus'] arrest and execution," says Borg, "can be seen as doing the best they could, given their difficult responsibility of keeping order and placating Rome" (*Jesus*, 161).

81. Herzog, *Jesus, Justice,* 91. "Over time," Herzog adds, "Herod's policy managed to strip the office of its legitimacy in the eyes of many Judeans and Galileans alike" (91). The Essenes at Qumran were even more outraged at the priesthood established by Herod than by the priesthood created by the Hasmoneans, which initially drove them from Jerusalem to Qumran.

82. Borg and Crossan, *Last Week,* 13, 19–20. See also Tabor, *Jesus Dynasty,* 118–19, 210.

some kind of criminal activity that took place there—that is, perhaps, short-changing or overcharging.[83]

On one hand, these accounts are credible—at least, on the assumption that Jesus repudiated Judaism. They indicate Jesus' opposition to yet another aspect of Jewish worship, reflecting his supposed rejection of Sabbath, purity, and dietary laws. On the other hand, however, this interpretation is contradicted by the fact that *Jesus does not elsewhere appear to oppose sacrifice.*[84] Indeed, as I noted above, his disciples continued to offer sacrifices in the Temple after his death. Later in Acts, as I said in Chapter Two, "the elders" of the Jerusalem church asked Paul to accompany four Christians, who were under a Nazirite vow, to the Temple. Paul was advised to "purify [himself] along with them and pay their expenses." The elders argued that by these means Paul would show that he "live[d] in observation of the law" (Acts 21: 23–24), which, presumably, all Christian did. Otherwise, Paul would have said to the leaders of the Jerusalem church, "Are you kidding?"

The ritual that Paul was asked to sponsor and the other Law-abiding Christians were going to participate in required *making a sacrifice*—an "offering" (Acts 21:26)— as specified in the Book of Numbers: two unblemished one-year-old lambs (one male, one female), as well as bread, cakes, wafers, cereal, and the Nazirites' hair (Num 6:13–18). Thus—unless, of course, it could be argued that James misunderstood Jesus— "[t]here is no reason to think that Jesus' action in the temple was caused by any rejection of blood sacrifice or, indeed, had anything to do with sacrifice as such."[85] It is important to emphasize that, if some misunderstanding of Jesus was involved in this instance, it must have included at least the Nazirites *and Paul himself*, if not everyone

83. Bainton says that one reason for Jesus' arrest was the high priests' opposition to Jesus' "interference with racketeering in the temple courts" (*Early Christianity*, 15). However, Bainton does not specify what that criminal activity might have been.

84. Bultmann says, "Polemic against the temple cult is completely absent from the words of Jesus." Bultmann explains that by this time, although the Temple rituals were obediently performed, Judaism had shifted to the synagogue as the center of Jewish life and away from the Temple, partly because the majority of Jews lived in the Diaspora and not in Judea. Thus, Bultmann continues, Jesus paid the half-shekel Temple tax (Matt 17:24–27), and his disciples "held gatherings within the temple area" (*Theology*, I, 17)—not necessarily because they were all enthusiastic supporters of the Temple, but because they remained good Jews. Fredriksen briefly but thoroughly surveys the biblical evidence that Jesus' followers continued to obey Jewish laws and participate in Jewish practices, particularly regarding the Temple, in *Jesus of Nazareth*, 280.

85. Borg and Crossan, *Last Week*, 38. On Paul's support for and participation in the purification ceremony described in Acts, see Maccoby, who says that Paul's sponsorship "was a not uncommon way of showing piety and charity." However, Paul was not necessarily going to take the Nazirite vow. He was going through "the usual purification for one arriving in the Holy Land from abroad, timing this so that he could enter the Temple simultaneously with the Nazirites and offer a free-will offering while they were making their offerings in completion of their vows" (*Mythmaker*, 219 n. 3 [in chap. 13]). Carmichael argues, however, that Paul was supposed to participate in the entire ritual to prove "that he had in fact been living up to the Torah." Because the rite was expensive to sponsor, Carmichael continues, "it was considered a convincing symbol of piety" (*Birth of Christianity*, 72). The point is, either Paul respected the Law as it pertained to animal sacrifice, or he pretended to respect it.

else in the Jerusalem church. There is no record that *any* Christian protested against Paul's participation in this traditional animal sacrifice at the Temple twenty-five years or so after the Crucifixion.

It should be noted that selling animals for sacrifice and exchanging special tokens for Roman coins were necessary to the proper functioning of the Temple as a place where animal sacrifices were made. And these activities were performed in the "outer precinct of the temple, known as the Court of Gentiles," not in the Inner Court, which was strictly limited to religious activities."[86] "Thus, if Jesus were protesting not the sacrifices themselves but the support services necessary for the sacrifices, his gesture would lack practical significance." That is, it would have made no sense to reject the support services if he did not reject the system they supported. "And if he were protesting the Temple sacrifices per se, he would be all but unique in his time and especially among his people."[87]

Like other Jews, Jesus believed that the Temple was his "Father's house" (Lk 2:49 [RSV]; John 2:16); and, as he showed in Matthew (5:23–24; 23:16–22) and Luke (5:14; 17:14), he did not object *in any way* to the sacrificial system.[88] After all, as God says in Isaiah, the Temple *is* His "house of prayer," and He promises that the sacrifices of anyone who obeys the rules of the Covenant, including "strangers," will be accepted there—"for my house," He concludes, "shall be a house of prayer for all people" (Isa 56:7).

If the heart of Jesus' objection was *not* the profanation of the Temple by the sacrifice of animals or by the presence of sellers and money changers, what was it? Many recent scholars have suggested that Jesus' protest was simply an expression of moral outrage against what the Temple *stood* for, rather than what it was. Specifically, in this view, he took a stand against the Temple as a symbol of the ruling class, the very people (chief priests, elders, and scribes) who wanted to destroy him and who were, from his point of view, capable of committing grossly immoral acts (that is, of greed, selfishness, injustice, and oppression). His enemy, after all, was the not the ordinary people, but the Jewish elite, whom he and his followers explicitly and persistently opposed by

---

86. *New Oxford Annotated Bible*, The New Testament, 31. "The animals for sale were acceptable for sacrifice; the money changers converted Gentile coins into Jewish money that could properly be presented in the temple" (65). The Temple was such a vast structure that the inner courts alone were the size of more than two football fields. If the entire Temple Mount was 144,000 square meters, it would have been possible for Jesus to cause a disruption that remained unnoticed by the vast majority of people in the area. According to Schiffman, the inner courts were 150 feet wide and 750 feet long (*From Text to Tradition*, 45). The other figure comes from Tabor, *Jesus Dynasty*, 101.

87. Fredriksen, *From Jesus to Christ*, 112. Fredriksen comments elsewhere, "Even the Essenes, alienated from the current priesthood and keeping their distance from the Temple, did not repudiate the sacrifices per se" (*Jesus of Nazareth*, 209). What complicates matters even more is the claim that the money changers and animal sellers were not even in the Temple district at the time (Stegemann and Stegemann, *Jesus Movement*, 122). And Fredriksen adds that the larger animals were not on the Temple Mount at all, but "in the market area below the Temple" (*Jesus of Nazareth*, 232).

88. Both points are made by Sanders in *Historical Figure of Jesus*, 259 (and 310 n. 17), 224.

condemning riches (Mark 10:23–25; Luke .21:1–3; Matt 6:19–24), encouraging compassion (Matt 25:31–46), abiding by the humane principles of the Jewish prophets (Luke 4:16–19), predicting the reversal of social roles at the end-time (Matt 5:3–10; 19:30), and creating a classless society (Acts 4:32–34). In short, like the Essenes, he rejected the Temple as a symbol of power. Unlike the Essenes, however, he did not reject it as a place of worship.[89]

Of course, what complicates the question is that the Temple represented different things to different people. No doubt, to the Sadducees, the Temple was the House of God. To many others, however, the building itself was inescapably associated with Herod and Hellenization (and, therefore, Roman hegemony) since Herod had built it and designed it in the popular Greco-Roman style that he used for many other public buildings in Jerusalem, Tiberias, Sepphora, and elsewhere.[90] To the underclass, particularly, the Temple symbolized the unholy alliance between the Romans and the Jewish elite, not only because these groups collaborated, but also because the High Priest, the highest political authority among the Jews, always served at the will of Herod and, later, the Roman procurator. Furthermore, "[t]he high priest and the temple authorities had a difficult task. As with the client-rulers before them, their primary obligation was loyalty and collaboration. They were . . . to maintain domestic peace and order. Rome did not want rebellions. Their role was to be the intermediaries between a local domination system and an imperial domination system."[91]

Since the Temple thus stood for the Roman occupation, the subservience of the Jewish aristocracy, and its willingness to act as a law-enforcement agency on behalf of the Romans, it was hated by the Jews who did not benefit from its extra-ceremonial activities—the overwhelming majority of the population. The Essenes at Qumran regarded the Sadducees' control of the priesthood as illegitimate, and other revolutionaries objected to the whole enterprise as a symbol of foreign control and political suppression. Thus, "Jesus was not the only Jewish anti-temple voice in the first century. Given the temple's role in a tributary domination system [i.e., run by the Jewish elite] collaborating with an imperial domination system [i.e., run by the Romans], this should not be surprising . . . Much of the passion of violent Jewish revolutionary

89. Vermes says that the Essenes' stance was much more extreme than Jesus' since they refused to have anything to do with the Temple: "Sacrificial worship as such was not condemned despite the abuses of the wicked priesthood, but the Community's Priests and Levites must in no circumstances actively participate in Temple services" (*Dead Sea Scrolls*, 45–46).

90. "Herod the Great had been so deeply associated with [the Temple's] conception, building, and maintenance that it was recognized the world over as a Herodian family shrine" (Horsley and Silberman, *Message*, 71).

91. Borg and Crossan, *Last Week*, 19. In Judea, says Horsley, the temple-state also "served as an administrative arm of the Persian and later the Hellenistic and Roman imperial regimes" (*Covenant Economics*, 77).

movements was directed against Jerusalem and the temple because of its collaboration with the domination system."[92]

Perhaps even more obviously, the Temple (described by some contemporary observers as one of the grandest buildings in the world) represented the Sadducees' economic as well as political power,[93] the government's expropriation of land, and the landowners' exploitation of the workers (who suffered from excessive taxation, high interest rates, and low wages). After all, the tithes and taxes that supported the priestly class and therefore enabled them to continue to plunder the poor were stored in the Temple.[94] Furthermore, the extra-religious functions of the Temple were manifestly visible in its physical structure. As one scholar explains: "The Temple was not merely a house of worship; it embraced a complex of all sorts of administrative buildings, houses for attendants, offices, stables, and a number of great courtyards . . . [I]t also had a gigantic staff of attendants, numbering some twenty thousand, who performed a wide variety of functions." The Temple was guarded by a Roman garrison of five to six hundred men and a Temple guard big enough to handle large crowds.[95]

All of this is understandable in the context of ancient urban agricultural societies, most of which sooner or later constructed two massive, mutually supporting buildings: a palace and a temple. The palace protected and defended the temple, and the temple authorized and legitimated the palace. In this respect, religion provided a rationale for political power—the kings were the sons of gods. And the priests, who supposedly served both kings and gods, "were also the managers (CEOs) of the local economy and were the local political heads as well." They enforced the divinely required payment of tithes by the people in order to sustain the regime. Cooperation with the state's taxation, expropriation of land, and conscription of labor (for purposes

92. Borg and Crossan, *Last Week*, 15. Freyne makes the point that opposition to the Temple was "a constant feature of Second Temple Judaism," which reflected "criticisms of the priesthood, because of social oppression or other perceived failures" (*Galilee, Jesus*, 187–89). See also Brandon, *Trial of Jesus*, 147. As Mattingly explains, the Sadducees, who represented the wealthiest families and some of whom served as priests, were "politically minded," "worked in touch with the Roman government," and "cared little for religion in any of its other-worldly aspects" (*Roman Imperial Civilisation*, 226). By most accounts, the chief priests worked for only a few weeks every year in their religious capacities.

93. Mack says, "The Romans kept the temple system alive for another one hundred years, however, for it did provide the basic structure for economic and political control in Palestine" (*Who Wrote?* 23).

94. According to Kloppenborg, "[T]he temple was not just a religious site but the focal point for the collection of taxes or tithes that supported a priestly aristocracy and, hence, an economic center and the focal point of economic redistribution in the forms of loans and capital" (*Q*, 85). In short, according to Borg and Crossan, the Temple had become "the central economic and political institution in the country" (*Last Week*, 20). Herzog emphasizes the fact that the Temple in Jerusalem was a bank, housing "large amounts of coins and currency," which enabled Roman authorities such as Sabinus, Pilate, and Florus to loot the Temple treasury (*Jesus, Justice*, 136–37). See also 109–10, 184, 193; and Guignebert, *Jewish World*, 59–61.

95. Carmichael, *Birth of Christianity*, 41–42. Horsley says that temples in the ancient world were typically "storehouses in which tithes and offerings brought to the gods were kept. They were also the political center of the area that they controlled" (*Covenant Economics*, 3).

of both military service and building construction) was thus a religious duty, the violation of which was an offense to both God and country.[96]

To put it simply, the Temple was, like the Vatican, a symbol of power, both political and economic, and Jesus was opposed to the institutionalization of power: "Ye know that they which are accounted to rule over the Gentiles [that is, "kings," in Luke 22:25] exercise lordship over them; and their great exercise authority over them. But so shall it not be among you" (Mark 10:42–43). (Jesus is reiterating here God's opposition to monarchy, which the prophet Samuel explains to the Israelites in 1 Samuel 8:10–17.) Thus, Jesus' enemies were "those leading Jews of the aristocratic class who saw figures like John the Baptizer and Jesus as a threat to their power and control, both of the economics of the Temple and the regulation of religious affairs."[97] They were *his* enemies because he was *their* enemy.[98]

Under these circumstances—that is, Jesus' opposition to the Temple in the context of the socio-political situation in first-century Palestine, which I discussed in the preceding section of this chapter—Jesus' moral stance had two consequences. First, it made him popular with the people because of their hostility "towards the Temple rulers (who controlled Israel's currency and economy) and the Romans."[99] That is, "[t]he people," including supporters of Jesus, "despised them."[100] That is the reason for the Sicarii's assassination of the High Priest Jonathan during the reign of the procurator Felix many years later, increasingly frequent attacks on the properties (and, even-

96. *Covenant Economics*, 9–11. "This is what made the economy work. The people did not just worship the Forces [both celestial and earthly] but *served* them with their produce and labor" (11). On the same subject, see Herzog, *Jesus, Justice*, 112–24.

97. Tabor, *Jesus Dynasty*, 185.

98. On this point, see Borg and Crossan, *Last Week*, 128. What complicates Jesus' reference to Jeremiah ("a den of robbers") is the fact that "den" is, in Jeremiah's usage, "not where robber's rob"—as if "the changing of money and the selling of animals" were some kind of crime—"but where they flee for safety after having done their robbing elsewhere" (49). Thus, Sanders says that the Temple and its priestly workers were not "corrupt," in and of themselves (*Historical Figure of Jesus*, 42). That is, Jesus rejected the Temple as a symbol of collaboration and oppression, which would be destroyed by God, not as a place where commercial crimes were committed. Brandon comments, "The suggestion is that Jesus' action was not against the petty traders of the Temple but was aimed at the priestly aristocracy who managed the Temple for their own profit and power—men, moreover, who collaborated with the Roman rulers of Israel" (*Trial of Jesus*, 84). See also Parkes, *Conflict*, 46; and Borg, *Jesus*, 234–35. Carmichael says that Jesus attacked "the Temple aristocracy because of its corruption" (*Birth of Christianity*, 42–43), but, again, he is thinking of the larger political issues. Indeed, Carmichael claims that Jesus actually seized the Temple with the intention of throwing out of Palestine both chief priests and Romans (188–90). Freyne argues that Jesus might have "taken over the temple and used it for his own purposes," one of which was to undermine "its centrality to Jewish faith" (*Galilee, Jesus*, 60).

99. Schillebeeckx, *Jesus*, 244–47.

100. Tabor, *Jesus Dynasty*, 210. Herzog says that the peasants rejected the Temple as a unifying symbol particularly because the priests were illegitimate, but also because they "consistently sided with their Roman masters and faithfully carried out Roman colonial policy, even to the disadvantage and damage of the people they were supposed to rule" (*Jesus, Justice*, 104–5). In the struggle between higher and lower priests over the distribution of tithes, ordinary Jews seem to have sided with the lower priests (Klingaman, *First Century*, 296).

tually, on the persons) of wealthy Jews everywhere, and the rebels' destruction of the debt records stored in the Temple at the beginning of the Revolt of 66.[101] To the extent that Jesus defended the covenant values that the prophets also sought to defend, he was supported by people who were adversely affected by challenges to those values.

Second, his opposition to the Temple made Jesus a political threat to those very rulers.[102] "This popularity of a man critical of the Temple must have been the first positive reason for political anxiety among the leaders of Israel, the beginning of the fatal outcome of the life of Jesus . . . The] flame of messianism which flared up in connection with Jesus in Palestine [and which arose out of his popularity] would certainly seem to have been the reason for the fateful disquiet of Israel's rulers, who from then on really did keep a watch on Jesus—as the gospels repeatedly suggest."[103] Subsequently, his words were misinterpreted, his actions were exaggerated, and his presence was perceived to be increasingly dangerous. The reason is that, whatever Jesus did in the Temple, the chief priests, elders, and scribes evidently lumped him together with other pious Jews, including the Essenes, who found reprehensible the appropriation of the Temple by the Romans through their Jewish representatives, the priestly aristocracy.

Of course, Jesus' activities in the Temple—especially the perception of them as expressions of revolutionary zeal—must have contributed strongly to the rather (to modern readers) surprising overreaction to his so-called threat to destroy the Temple, with which he was charged at his trial before Pilate. To be sure, some of Jesus' words were susceptible to wide interpretation. For example, when he pointed to "the buildings of the temple" and said to his disciples, "Truly I tell you, not one stone will be

101. Klingaman discusses the first two incidents on 293–96. Of the third event, he says, the rebels "set fire to the city's records office, destroying the mortgages and other financial contracts stored there, in a calculated bid to obtain the support of thousands of impoverished Judeans who were staggering under a crushing load of debt" (313).

102. For a full discussion of Jesus' attitude toward the Temple, see Sanders, *Jesus and Judaism*, 61–86, 268–70; and *Historical Figure of Jesus*, 254–57. Fredriksen says that Sanders's explanation has been compelling for many scholars: "He concluded that Jesus did indeed overturn tables; that the traditional interpretation of his action as 'cleansing' was historically impossible; and that by this gesture Jesus had intended to symbolically enact the Temple's impending apocalyptic destruction— hence its apocalyptic restoration or rebuilding—with the approaching advent of the Kingdom" (*Jesus of Nazareth*, 291–92). Says Theissen, "Messianic expectations . . . would be a good reason for the intervention of the aristocracy and the Romans" (*Early Palestinian Christianity*, 64). See also Kaylor, *Jesus the Prophet*, 60–63. Freyne argues, to the contrary, that Jesus was a threat to the Temple in only "theological terms": "The pilgrim who subverts the place of pilgrimage and its feasts by fulfilling in his person the symbolism attached to that place and those occasions, is indeed paradoxical" (*Galilee, Jesus*, 131; see also 46, 47, 60–61, 85, 85–86, 89, 93, 225).

103. Schillebeeckx, *Jesus*, 247–48. Schillebeeckx assumes that the cleansing of the Temple took place in the middle of Jesus' missionary effort, not at the beginning, as John suggests, or at the end, as the synoptic Gospels contend. Herzog says that the chief priests were, for various reasons, caught "in a crisis of credibility," which both increased their anxiety and intensified "their sensitivity to any criticism of the temple or efforts to undermine its credibility," which, of course, threatened to further erode their own (*Jesus, Justice*, 104).

left here upon another; all will be thrown down" (Matt 24:2, Mark 13:2, Luke 21:6), it would have been easy to conclude that he himself—that is, with the help of his followers—intended to destroy the Temple.

The context in this instance militates against that interpretation, however. For, as Jesus continued to explain his "threat" to his disciples, he made it quite clear that he was talking about an eschatological event of cosmic proportions. That is, the destruction of the Temple would take place at the end-time, in the general holocaust that would occur before the coming of the Son of man (Matt 24:3–31). As one scholar explains: "Overturned tables symbolize not purification but destruction. Through this disruptive gesture, Jesus symbolically enacted the impending apocalyptic destruction of the Temple."[104]

The same point applies to Jesus' other threatening reference to the Temple: "Destroy this temple and in three days I will raise it up" (John 2:19). In Matthew, Jesus says that he will do both the destroying and the rebuilding: "I am able to destroy the temple of God and to build it in three days" (Matt 26:61). And, when he was on the cross, passersby said, "You who would destroy the temple and build it in three days, save yourself!" (Matt 27: 39–40; Mark 15:29). In John, however, Jesus' auditors did not react to this statement as a threat to destroy the Temple; rather, they were surprised that Jesus claimed to be able to rebuild the Temple so quickly: "This temple has been under construction for forty-six years, and will you raise it up in three days?" (2:20). In other words, Jesus' critics seem to have reacted, not to his threat to destroy the Temple, but to his claim that he was powerful enough to both dismantle the building and reconstruct it.

Furthermore, John explains that Jesus was not even referring to the actual Temple, but to "the temple of his body" (John 2:21). Mark's version of the so-called false witness against Jesus at his trial before the assembly of Jewish leaders also undermines the accuracy of the claim that Jesus made threatening statements against the Temple itself. In this accusation, Jesus was charged with saying that the Temple he would destroy was "made with hands," but the Temple he (or God Himself) would build would *not* be "made with hands" (Mark 14:58). That is, just as the new covenant in Jeremiah 31:33 promised to be inward rather than outward, so the new Temple, "reconstructed" in the New Age, would be spiritual rather than physical.

On the other hand, no matter how Jesus' threat was interpreted, it would have been disturbing only to people who regarded it as politically dangerous, not theologically blasphemous, which it was not: "The people who would have been annoyed . . . at Jesus' declaration were the reigning Temple hierarchy, who were collaborators with Rome, owed their appointments to the Roman occupying forces, and had undertaken

---

104. Fredriksen, *From Jesus to Christ*, 112–13. Theissen says: "The radical theocratic movements arose out of the crisis over theocracy. The Jesus movement, too, was connected with the socio-political tensions in Palestine. Its proclamation of the imminence of the kingdom of God could only find a ready echo in a country in which no satisfactory solution had been found to the problem of government" (*Palestinian Christianity*, 65).

to help stamp out Messianic movements which might threaten the Roman occupation of Judaea."[105] It should also be noted that none of the criticisms of the Temple mentioned above were in any respect repudiations of Judaism, but criticisms *by Jews* of abuses of their faith. That is, Jesus was in good *Jewish* company when he railed against the Temple.[106]

More important, Jesus' curse on the Temple would have been understood by educated Jews to have been an echo of Jeremiah, in whose prophecy God himself calls the Temple "a den of robbers" and threatens to destroy it as He did the tabernacle at Shiloh (Jer 7:11–15; 26:2–4)—that is, *God* would wipe out the Temple, not Jesus and his minions. In short, "Jesus' gesture (overturning tables in the Temple court) . . . would have been readily understood *by any Jew watching* as a statement that the Temple was about to be destroyed (by God, not human armies, and certainly not literally or personally by Jesus himself), and, accordingly, that the present order was about to cede to the Kingdom of God."[107] In other words, if "Jesus *did* predict the destruction of the temple," he was preceded by the prophets, including Micah, who "denounced the priests and the false prophets who claimed that since Yahweh was in their midst no evil would come upon them" and predicted that Zion would be destroyed (Mic 3:11–12).[108]

105. Maccoby, *Mythmaker*, 76. "Only the High Priest and his entourage would have been threatened by it," Maccoby continues. "So this charge against Jesus was not a religious but a political charge—one which would stir the High Priest into action, but would not concern the Pharisees or any religious Jews who were not committed to collaborate with Rome" (76).

106. Guignebert, *Jewish World*, 61. Had Jesus actually been disturbed by the presence of merchants in the Court of Gentiles, he would not have been alone. Some very strict Jews would have agreed with Jesus insofar as they too objected to the mixture of spiritual and material activities in the Temple district—"this mingling of the sacred and the profane." On this point, see Flusser, *Sage from Galilee*, 131–32.

107. Fredriksen, *From Jesus to Christ*, 113. In his "temple sermon," in which Jeremiah calls the Temple a den of thieves (or robbers), he is, like Jesus, preaching God's "word" at God's behest, which demands that the people follow God's moral code, specifically by obeying the laws of the Covenant: "For if you truly amend your ways and your doings, if you truly execute justice one with another, if you do not oppress the alien, the fatherless or the widow, or shed innocent blood in this place, and if you do not go after other gods to your own hurt, then I will let you dwell in this place, in the land that I gave of old to your fathers for ever" (7:5–7). Like Jesus, Jeremiah puts morality above ritual (7:21–23); reminds his countrymen that they have rejected God's prophets in the past (7:25–26); and condemns the wealthy and powerful: "[L]et not the mighty man glory in his might, let not the rich man glory in his riches; but let him who glories glory in this, that he understands and knows me, that I am the Lord who practices steadfast love, justice, and righteousness in the earth; for in these things I delight" (9:23–24). See also Jer 26:1–15.

108. Grant, *Historical Introduction*, 352; my emphasis. See also 360. Fredriksen says the same thing: "Mark and Matthew . . . suggest that the High Priest regarded his threat concerning the Temple's destruction as a religious threat (Mark 14:57–60; Matt 26:60–62). Prima facie this was not so. The classical prophets had uttered similar warnings about the first Temple" (*From Jesus to Christ*, 113). See, for example, Amos 9:1. Horsley and Silberman also discuss the prophetic criticism of the Temple in *Message*, 76–77. Borg says that Jesus' actions during Passover week resemble those of the Jewish prophets, "especially those who challenged the monarchies of ancient Israel in the decades before their destruction." They protested the collaboration of the Jewish elite with their Roman overlords, their

Indeed, "It is not the Temple that is under attack" in Jesus' criticism, "but the Temple praxis, as it was with the great prophets, for whom the spiritual quality of the Temple worship lay in the requirement of total obedience to God 'in deed' (Amos 5:21–25; Jer 7:3)."[109] However, the Sadducean priesthood, devoted (unlike the Pharisees) only to the Pentateuch and notoriously indifferent to the writings of the Jewish prophets, would not have been impressed by Jesus' biblical allusions or comforted by the similarities between his ideas and those of some of his contemporaries. As the later case of Jesus ben Hananiah suggests, all threats against the institutions for which the Jewish authorities were responsible, most notably the Temple, were threats against the empire.[110]

THE KINGDOM OF GOD

Jesus was, of course, also accused of claiming to be God (John 10:33), the Son of God (Matt 26:63; Mark 14:61; Luke 22:70; John 19:7), the King of the Jews (Matt 27:11; Mark 15:2; Luke 23:3; John 18:33), and the Messiah (Matt 27:11; Mark 14:61; Luke 22:67). However, according to John, Jesus offered all men the "power to become children of God" (John 1:12), and Jesus defended his claim to be the son of God by quoting Psalm 82:6: "Is it not written in your law, 'I [that is, God] said, you are gods'?" (John 10:34). (Indeed, his auditors might have remembered that the passage continues, "and sons of the Most High, all of you.") In Deuteronomy, God says to the Israelites, "Ye are the children of the Lord your God," by which He means "a holy people," "chosen" by

---

abandonment of the Covenant, and their pusuit of "power and wealth" (*Jesus*, 240).

109. Schillebeeckx, *Jesus*, 244–45. Flusser adds to the prophetic mix—besides Jeremiah— Micah, Amos, and Zechariah. "There was a biblical verse," he says, "that was understood by all to speak about the Messiah, who would build the Temple. 'The man whose name is Branch . . . he shall build the Temple of God' (Zech 6:12)" (*Sage from Galilee*, 133). For a Qumran source for the idea of God as the builder of the new Temple, see 132–33 n. 45. Mack comments: "In the prewar materials from the Jesus movements . . . there is not the slightest hint of interest in or concern about the temple-state in Jerusalem. It was simply there, taken for granted" (*Who Wrote?* 150).

110. Maccoby says that the High Priest's interests were, first, political and, second, ceremonial. That is, this figure was, unlike the pope in Christianity, without theological authority (*Mythmaker*, 27). According to Witherington, since "the Jewish Temple hierarchy was very concerned about maintaining the Temple and their roles in it, . . . they would certainly be opposed to any sort of messianic movements, including the Jesus movement, that might arouse the suspicions of Rome and might lead to their own loss of political power" (*What Have They Done?* 210). Stephen, another anti-Temple Christian, seems to have been stoned to death for threatening the Temple, although the account of his arrest and defense in Acts of the Apostles leaves the reason for his punishment somewhat ambiguous. After all, in his defense before the Sanhedrin, Stephen said that Solomon was wrong to build God a physical Temple, that the Jews had always killed their prophets, and that they had never obeyed the laws handed down to them by God (Acts 7:47–53). It might simply be that Stephen's auditors felt personally insulted by his frontal assault on their integrity. Theissen calls Stephen's killing "a piece of lynch-law" (*Early Palestinian Christianity*, 59). Maccoby agrees: "The death of Stephen . . . was not a judicial sentence, but an assassination carried out by the henchmen of the High Priest" (*Mythmaker*, 81). See also Ruether, *Faith and Fratricide*, 269 n. 20.

God, and esteemed by Him "above all the nations" (14:1). In other words, given the traditionally wide application of the phrase "son (or children) of God" (to kings and prophets and *all* Jews), it would be difficult to argue that Jesus offended anyone with that self-description.[111]

Similarly, given the frequency with which various rebels and bandits called themselves kings and the proclivity with which other leaders assumed the title "messiah," it could hardly be expected that Jesus would be singled out as particularly offensive—except to the Romans.[112] Furthermore, in John, Luke, and Matthew, when asked if he is the Son of God, the King of the Jews, or the Messiah, he generally refuses to answer yes or no (e.g., Luke 22:67, 70). Accused of these supposedly blasphemous claims, including his threat to destroy the Temple, Jesus admits his guilt only once (in Mark) in about ten opportunities before various judges, including the High Priest, Herod, and Pilate.[113] As for forgiving sins, Jesus was matched by the Essenes, who

111. Sanders explains: "In a Jewish context 'Son of God' does not mean 'more than human'. All Jews were 'Sons of God' or even the (collective) Son of God, as in Hosea 11.1 or Exodus 4.22 ('Israel is my first-born son'). Psalm 2.7 refers to the king of Israel as Son of God . . . In the Greek world there was less of a distinction between human and divine than there was in the Jewish world. Greek mythology depicted gods as consorting with humans and producing joint offspring. The Greeks [and eventually the Romans] occasionally declared that a human was divine" (*Historical Figure of Jesus*, 161). Thus, "[i]f Jesus' followers . . . ever said that he was Son of God, they would have meant what Matthew probably meant: he could rely on his heavenly Father to answer his prayers," as he said his followers could do as well in Matthew 7:11 (162). Sanders contends, in addition, that neither Paul nor many of Jesus' other followers saw Jesus as God's son in any literal sense: "They regarded 'Son of God' as a high designation, but we cannot go much beyond that." Indeed, "Jesus was the Son of God, but others could become Sons (children) of God" (244). Sanders's full discussion is on 243–46. Lee says simply, of the Jewish vs. Greek understandings of "Son of God," "A Hellenized Christian meaning replaced a more Hebraic Christian meaning" (*Galilean Jewishness of Jesus*, 18).

112. According to Parkes, the peace that prevailed before the Revolt of 66 was fragile: "It depended on a great deal of tact on both sides, and tact was not a conspicuous characteristic either of the Jews or of the Roman governors. The New Testament records several 'incidents', and it is probable that a multiplication of these would in the end have led to war. But it was precipitated by the flood of Messiahs who sprang up in the first half of the first century A.D." (*Conflict*, 22). Speaking of the first manifestation of this phenomenon in Palestine, after the death of Herod in 4 BC, Horsley and Silberman comment, "When news of the uprising in Jerusalem spread throughout the Land of Israel, messianic pretenders arose in every region, each one surrounded by a gang of tough young followers, and each aspiring to be proclaimed as the long-awaited redeemer-king of Israel" (*Message*, 19).

113. On this point, see Sanders, *Jesus and Judaism*, 297; and Smith, *Jesus the Magician*, 39. Smith explains that, although claiming to be God or the Son of God was not a punishable offense according to the Romans, the claim was often made by magicians, whose practices were assumed to be part of the evidence that they were guilty of "political subversion" (41). Wylen comments: "The gospels say that the Sanhedrin found Jesus guilty of blasphemy. Yet none of Jesus' words or deeds are blasphemous according to Jewish law. It was not blasphemy to claim to be the Messiah, or to claim that one could knock down and rebuild the Temple by God's hand. If anything, these were claims of Jewish piety!" (*Jews*, 125). As Maccoby says: "To claim to be the Messiah was simply to claim the throne of David, and involved no claim to be God. The title 'Son of God' also involved no blasphemy, as every Jew claimed to be a son of God when he prayed daily to God as 'Father'" (*Mythmaker*, 77–78). According to Chilton, "The term 'son' is used frequently in the Old Testament for the special relationship between God and others"—for example, in Genesis 6:2 and Hosea 11:1. Thus, "[w]hen Jesus speaks of himself as divine son, he is not talking in the extravagant, metaphysical language of a later time, which

went unpunished for making the same claim.[114] Many of the charismatic leaders who appeared in Palestine in the first century worked wonders, tried to allay the anxieties of their followers, and probably, in the view of one historian of the period, argued that faith in themselves was the same as faith in God.[115]

The consensus among contemporary scholars is that Jesus was mistakenly arrested as a rebel—that is, someone who was either suspected of plotting to overthrow the Roman government or perceived to be capable of at least trying to do so. As one historian explains: "The procurator of Judaea had already experienced many difficulties with seemingly seditious Jews, as we have seen. Since it was his duty to maintain law and order in this troublesome frontier province, he was bound to suppress any activity even potentially revolutionary."[116] The crime Jesus was accused of was thus not blasphemy, a religious charge, but sedition. The charge may seem absurd to people living in the twenty-first century, but, as I mentioned earlier, it was common practice

---

claimed that he had no human father. Rather he claims that he is of the spiritual lineage of Israel's seers." Chilton gives as an example of Old Testament usage God's presumably traditional blessing of Israelite kings—"You are my son, this day have I begotten you!" (Ps 2:7)—which Luke (in an alternative version) adds to the enthronement formula that also appears in the Gospels of Matthew and Mark (Luke 3:22). The implication is that if David's sonship is figurative in Psalm 2:7, then Jesus' sonship must also be figurative in Luke 3:22 (*Rabbi Jesus*, 58 n. 3). For two opposing views, see the collection of essays by several Cambridge scholars: Richardson, "The Israel Idea in the Passion Narratives," 2–3; and Catchpole, "The Problem of the Historicity of the Sanhedrin Trial," 54, 58, 62, 65.

114. Sanders, *Jesus and Judaism*, 240, 272–73. Sanders explains elsewhere that Jesus' statement "My son, your sins are forgiven" (Mark 2:5) did not suggest that Jesus was doing the forgiving. "In Jesus' culture the passive voice was used as a circumlocution for God: 'your sins are forgiven' means 'they are forgiven by God'. Jesus only announces the fact, he does not take the place of God" (*Historical Figure of Jesus*, 213). See also Hare, *Jewish Persecution of Christians*, 135.

115.Hengel, *Charismatic Leader*, 20–22.

116. Grant, *Historical Introduction*, 366. Koester says of Pilate's tenure in office: "Difficulties mounted and incidents of unrest increased under his administration . . . He did not hesitate to order on-the-spot executions by his soldiers, as is evident from the incident alluded to in Luke 13:1" (*History, Culture, and Religion*, 396). Horsley and Silberman explain Pilate's behavior in terms of the typical career plans of prefects and procurators, whose futures would have been compromised by political disorder: "Pilate therefore had to be ever vigilant to guard against civil unrest anywhere in Judea, lest unfavorable news or unpleasant gossip about his own performance be spread by Herodian supporters among the ruling circles in Rome" (*Message*, 66–69). To ignore even a minor threat was to risk encouraging other dissidents to follow suit (84). Thus, as Tabor explains, it would have been unlikely for Pilate to find Jesus innocent: "Even if Pilate had thought Jesus to have been a harmless and deluded fool, he would have happily condemned him without the slightest hesitation. The portrait the New Testament gospels present of Pilate is simply historically inaccurate" (*Jesus Dynasty*, 216). Tabor reconstructs the trial, "based on the more probable historical facts," on 216–18. Borg and Crossan say that it is also hard to believe that Pilate would have offered to release an insurrectionist like Barabbas (*Last Week*, 143–44). Flusser disagrees, although he acknowledges that the release was rare and had to be strongly pressed for (*Sage from Galilee*, 154). Grant reminds his readers that Barabbas appears in some manuscripts as "Jesus" and that "Bar Abbas" means "Son of the Father." For these and other reasons, he concludes that the whole incident "was probably an invention of the early Church, devised in order to exhibit a simple rhetorical antithesis between the good Jesus and this fictitious bad one, so that the Jews could be shown for evermore to have rejected his authentic, good counterpart" (*Jesus*, 165). On this point, see also Brandon, *Trial of Jesus*, 190–91 n. 113.

for the Romans to execute almost all suspects, no matter how harmless they were in reality.[117]

The Romans were particularly vigilant because a riot or protest in one place could inspire a disturbance elsewhere. Thus, although a rebellion in Palestine could be put down by the Roman procurator (if necessary, with the aid of the governor of Syria), any local revolt could spark an insurgency throughout the empire. There were synagogues in every city already preaching revolutionary doctrines, such as the liberation of escaped slaves, the ending of usury, and a day of rest for all, as well as nurturing a hope for a day, sooner rather than later, on which all existing kingdoms would be destroyed and then replaced by the kingdom of the Jews.[118] Jesus' participation in this popular expectation is clear. The coming event that he announced was "a visible sociopolitical, economic restructuring of relations among the people of God."[119]

117. "It must have been a political accusation that was leveled against Jesus," say Conzelmann and Lindemann, "for the Romans did not concern themselves with purely religious questions." And, as these authors make clear, Jesus' execution was an entirely Roman affair: "The type of execution shows unequivocally that Jesus died as a result of a Roman death sentence, for the execution is not a Jewish, but a Roman method of execution . . . Jesus was not only executed in keeping with Roman instruction, but he was also sentenced by the Romans" (*Interpreting the New Testament*, 332–33). "It was of course by the Romans that he was executed, as the nature of his death—by crucifixion—demonstrates," says Schillebeeckx, "and so on grounds of possible or alleged Zealotic reactions among the people . . . There was one particular—that is to say, political—interpretation of messianism, which admirers certainly attributed to him, within the range of possible situations." The "evidence" of Jesus' guilt in this regard included the presence of some Zealots among his followers (Luke 6:15; Acts 1:3); possibly a Sicarius (dagger man) in Judas Iscariot; and John and James (sons of Zebedee), whom Jesus surnamed "Boanerges"—that is, "sons of thunder" (Mark 3:17); as well as Jesus' cleansing of the Temple, his own apparent threat to destroy it (Mark 14:58), and his promise of a coming kingdom. Schillebeeckx concludes that all of this "may appear . . . as provocation and would in any case make the always rebellion-conscious occupying power antagonistic towards anyone who aroused the feelings of the people." Furthermore, crucifixion was, after all, "the Roman penalty for serious criminal acts or rebellion" (*Jesus*, 300–301; see also 312–17). See also Parkes, *Conflict*, 45; Herzog, *Jesus, Justice*, 59–61, 240–45; Tabor, *Jesus Dynasty*, 120, 154, 198, 217; Smith, *Jesus the Magician*, 16: Horsley and Silberman, *Message*, 57, 80–81; Borg and Crossan, *Last Week*, 88–89, 147; Ehrman, *Lost Christianities*, 169; Brandon, *Trial of Jesus*, 141, 143; Markus, *Christianity*, 19; and Ruether, *Faith and Fratricide*, 67–68. Freyne says that Jesus might have been misunderstood as a seditionist, by both his followers and the Jewish aristocracy (*Galilee, Jesus*, 246–47). Bainton says that none of the Jewish accusations against Jesus "would condemn Him with the Romans[,] who alone had the power to inflict His execution." Rather, Jesus "was crucified through the fear that He was the focus of a rebellion" (*Early Christianity*, 15–16). Yoder calls Jesus "a model of radical political action" and claims that this idea "is now generally visible throughout New Testament studies" (*Politics of Jesus*, 12).

118. Fredriksen, *From Jesus to Christ*, 109; and Roberston, *Origins of Christianity*, 60. Lace says that Jesus "stands as the very coping-stone of the building which God had designed from eternity." Lace continues: "In other words, the figure of Jesus and his teaching, as they are presented in the Gospels, concern the kingdom of God, that is, God's reign over his world. The reign of God is the theme of the Gospels" (*Understanding the New Testament*, 72).

119. Yoder, *Politics of Jesus*, 39. See also 50 n. 36, 60–63. Yoder explains: Jesus never corrects "his disciples for expecting him to establish some new social order, as he would have had to do if the thesis of the only-spiritual kingdom were to prevail. He rather reprimands them for having misunderstood the character of that new social order which he does intend to set up. The novelty of its character is not that it is not social, or not visible, but that it is marked by an alternative to accepted patterns of

Indeed, Jesus very likely became a subject of imperial investigation because, more than anything else, he promised his followers that they would soon enter this kingdom, which he refers to in the Gospels of Mark and Luke as the Kingdom of God and in the Gospel of Matthew as the Kingdom of Heaven. Jesus began his missionary career by announcing the imminence of the kingdom and the need to prepare for it.[120] Repeating the command of John the Baptist, he said, "Repent, for the kingdom of heaven has come near" (Matt 3:2, 4:17; 4:14, 15; Luke 4:43). Furthermore, as the evidence suggests, he preached that message continuously (Matt 4:23; 9:35; 25:34; 26:29; Mark 14:25; Luke 8:1; 16:16; 19:29; 30; 22:16, 18) and, in Luke, sent out his disciples to do the same (9:2, 60). In Matthew, Jesus made the point again when he said, "This gospel of the kingdom will be preached throughout the whole world" (24:14). He continued to insist that the kingdom was near (Matt 10:7; Mark 10:1; Luke 10:9, 11) and even that it had, in some sense, already arrived (Matt 12:28; Luke 11:20; 17:20).[121]

---

leadership": not kingship, but stewardship (46). Kaylor also states that the Kingdom of God, with its attendant implications of social and political change, was the centerpiece of Jesus' preaching (*Jesus the Prophet*, 70–75, 129). It was, for Kaylor, an explicitly political message, which is attested to by Gospel passages and recent scholarly studies (17, 75–78). As Meeks puts it, "The specifically apocalyptic conception of a world made right again [i.e., "a just world"] by the Creator was . . . the view that was or became dominant, and it defined the final chapter of the great Christian moral drama that eventually was to shape so profoundly the sensibilities of Western culture" (*Origins of Christian Morality*, 85–86). See also Robinson, *Gospel of Jesus*, 170.

120. In this respect, the Jesus movement was indistinguishable from other, perhaps more openly revolutionary movements. As Theissen says, "All the opposition movements wanted to realize the rule of God consistently or hoped that it would be realized in a miraculous fashion. All put forward an explicitly imminent eschatology. Here the imminent end of the old world always implied the end of Roman rule" (*Early Palestinian Christianity*, 62). Theissen continues: "Miraculous healings occupied the same place as terrorist actions in the resistance movement. Thus we may not imagine the proclamation of the kingdom of God simply as a theological programme. Its purport was that in the very near future there would be a fundamental change in Palestine, in which a small group of outsiders would become rulers in Israel . . . This would mean the ending of Roman rule and of all earthly governments" (63). On this subject, see also Carmichael, who says that the "concept of the kingdom of God is the key to the agitation that, until about A.D. 135, had churned up Jewry for two centuries" (*Birth of Christianity*, 1). To Carmichael, the Kingdom-of-God movement required action on the part of the Jews, not just patience (5, 7), and it grew steadily from Pilate's time till the Revolt of 66 (28).

121. Enslin says that, although the Church had difficulty with Jesus' prediction that the world was about to be transformed, there is no doubt that Jesus made the prediction: "It is useless to try to smooth this difficulty away. To attempt to explain this as a misunderstanding of his meaning by his hearers or as a view later developed and attributed to him is most unfortunate." Such a view, Enslin concludes, would require the assumption that either Jesus' disciples were stupid or Jesus could not express himself clearly (*Christian Beginnings*, 165). "He is the only Jew of ancient times known to us who preached not only that people were on the threshold of the end of time, but that the new age of salvation had already begun" (Flusser, *Sage from Galilee*, 80). See also 87, 89. Hengel adds that neither the Romans nor the masses "could understand anyone proclaiming charismatically the nearness of the Rule of God without at least hidden political goals" (*Charismatic Leader*, 59). Hengel also suggests that Jesus was misunderstood, a point on which many scholars agree, says Kaylor. "The thesis of [Kaylor's] book is that as a matter of historical truth, the Romans, in conjunction with Jewish political leaders, had good reason to execute Jesus" (*Jesus the Prophet*, 19–20).

Furthermore, most of Jesus' preaching was given over to explaining who could enter the kingdom: the poor, the persecuted, the obedient, the righteous, the humble, and the celibate (Matt 19:12), as well as those who feed the hungry, take in strangers, clothe the naked, and visit both the sick and the imprisoned—each of which of these acts of compassion could be understood to be an expression of repentance. In his parables, Jesus presented the requirements for entry into the kingdom in more subtle ways. Occasionally, his advice was somewhat surprising. Toward the end of the Sermon on the Mount, he said, "Not everyone who says to me 'Lord, Lord,' will enter the kingdom of heaven, but only the one who does the will of my Father in heaven" (Matt 7:21). In short, not Faith, but Works. Indeed, in at least two parables, Jesus says, as he does in Matthew 19:21, it is imperative to give up *everything* for the Kingdom (Matt 13:44–46).

If this kingdom would have been understood by both the Romans and Jesus' fellow Jews in the way the Church later understood it—i.e., as a spiritual kingdom that will be populated by resurrected *souls*, as Jesus implies throughout the Gospel of John—the concept would have frightened no one. Interpreted as it necessarily was, however, in the context of traditional Jewish notions of salvation—i.e., as a physical kingdom populated by resurrected *bodies*, ruled by God himself, and dominating the world because all other kingdoms have been defeated[122]—the idea of the Kingdom of God could only have been understood as a direct threat to the Roman empire, as well as all other earthly kingdoms. As one scholar puts it: "The Jesus movement . . . proclaimed the imminence of the rule of God. And, however one twisted it, the rule of God meant the end of all other rule."[123] It was the restored kingdom of Israel that

122. "Indeed," says Flusser, "the concept that held central importance for Jesus was the kingdom of heaven, and it was exclusively rabbinical" (*Sage from Galilee*, 86). Maccoby adds that the phrase "kingdom of God" was "not coined by Jesus, but [was] part of Pharisaic phraseology" (*Mythmaker*, 31). Thus, Sanders concludes, "If we calmly survey all of the kingdom sayings, we shall see that most of them place the kingdom up there, in heaven, where people will enter after death, and in the future, when God brings the kingdom to earth and separates the sheep from the goats" (*Historical Figure of Jesus*, 176; see also 177–78). Sanders splits the difference between those who argue that Jesus' mere presence represents the arrival of the Kingdom and those who argue that Jesus wished to bring about radical change through revolutionary action. For a survey of opinions across the spectrum, see Kaylor, *Jesus the Prophet*, 70–91.

123. Theissen, *Early Palestinian Christianity*, 59. Flusser discusses the Kingdom of God in *Sage from Galilee*, 76–96. He says that "people in general [meaning "the Jews"] believed that when the kingdom of God came, Israel would be freed from the yoke of Rome. At that time, most Jews hated the occupying power" (77). "This concept was not worked out with any clarity," Mack argues, "but the ways it was used show that something of a social vision appeared in the teachings of Jesus. The kingdom of God referred to an ideal society imagined as an alternative to the way in which the world was working under the Romans" (*Who Wrote?* 40). The Kingdom of God, according to Horsley and Silberman, represented "a social transformation here and now" (*Message*, 56). Brandon says that Jesus' Kingdom of God "denoted the establishment of Yahweh's sovereignty" and "signified in turn the overthrow of the existing political and social order" (*Trial of Jesus*, 143). Kloppenborg interprets the Lord's Prayer, which calls for the immediate arrival of the Kingdom of God, as a request for the protection of the poor from exploitation by the rich (Q, 89–90). Sanders devotes a chapter to this very complicated subject in *Jesus and Judaism*, 222–241. See also Moltmann, *Church*, 90.

Jesus was thought to be promising, especially in the Gospel of Luke (1:32; 2:30–32, 38), which is why Peter and Cleopas referred to Jesus on the road to Emmaus as the one "which should have redeemed Israel" (Luke 24:21) and why he was mocked at his execution as King of the Jews.

In Matthew, Jesus said, "Truly, I say to you, in the new world, when the Son of man shall sit on his glorious throne, you who have followed me will also sit on twelve thrones, judging the twelve tribes of Israel" (19:28). After all, the prayer that Jesus taught his disciples in the Gospel of Matthew was a request for the kingdom *to come*—that is, it was not present, in the fullest sense. And, when it arrived (or so one could have interpreted it), God's "will [would] be done, *on earth as it is in heaven*" (Matt 6:10). That is, the prayer asked God to rule *on earth*, which would occur when His kingdom was established there.[124]

The first basis for suspicion in this case was Jesus' identity as a Galilean, which allied him ideologically with rebels like Judah the Galilean and his progeny, who menaced the countryside and the last of whom eventually fought in the Revolt of 66[125]—that is, rebels who, as I said earlier, proclaimed themselves or were perceived to be either kings or messiahs (or both). As one historian explains: The Galileans who heard Jesus' message "were not placid country-folk, of quiet-going ways, content to

124. Flusser comments: "According to both Jesus and the Rabbis, the kingdom of heaven emerges, indeed, out of God's might, but is realized upon earth, by men" (*Sage from Galilee*, 79). Levine says that "Your kingdom come" means "the divine kingdom, not the one of Caesar or his lackeys [etc.]." And "Your will be done" is a demand for action: doing God's will (*Misunderstood Jew*, 48). Schillebeeckx makes a similar point: "That this kingdom comes means that God looks to us men and women to make his 'ruling' operational in our world" (*Jesus*, 142; my emphasis). Borg says that "the kingdom of heaven" in the Gospel of Matthew is "*for the earth*" since the word *heaven* in this context is a synonym for God, not for an unearthly spiritual place (*Jesus*, 144). He argues later that the Kingdom of God, as it is used in all of the synoptic Gospels, was *political* as well as *religious*": "As a political-religious metaphor, the kingdom of God referred to what life would be like on earth if God were king and the kingdoms of this world, the domination systems of this world, were not." That is, it "involved a *transformed world*," a kind of "utopia" (186–87). Borg returns to this point on 252 and 330 n. 22. Robinson makes the same point about "kingdom of heaven" in *Gospel of Jesus*, 162. Meier argues that Jesus followed John the Baptist in his view of the Kingdom, by which both meant "the triumphant coming of God as king to rule Israel in the last days, a coming promised in the Book of Isaiah and celebrated in the Psalms" (*Marginal Jew*, II, 1042). However, says Grant, the expectations of Jews in the first century AD varied considerably. On one hand, the vision of Zechariah—that God "will become king over all the earth" (14:9)—"became the principal theme of the apocalyptic Jewish writings which proliferated in the times when Israel was once again ground down by foreign imperialism between 200 BC and 200 AD." On the other hand, toward the end of this period, a very different idea developed—namely, that "only some tremendous, superhuman intervention would suffice to introduce the kingdom." Because of the likelihood that Israel itself would be unable to bring this change about, "there was a growing conviction among a minority that in some sense [the change] would be cosmic and extra-terrestrial" (*Jesus*, 16–17).

125. White, *From Jesus to Christianity*, 12–13. "It is most likely," says White, "that a Roman procurator would have viewed any political subversion as an immediate threat. This seems to be the grounds for Jesus' arrest and execution" (32). See also Flusser, *Sage from Galilee*, 143–44. Anyone from Galilee was suspect because it was, according to Reicke, the birthplace of the Zealot movement, "which opposed Hellenism and the Roman presence with violence" ("Galilee and Judea," 29).

wait patiently on God for better times . . . They were people who had been nourished on the Maccabean tradition of holy war against the oppressors of Israel."[126] The second reason for Jesus' arrest was the mere fact that he had gathered around himself a large number of disciples: "It appears that in the eyes of the authorities, whether Herodian or Roman, any person with a popular following in the Galilean tetrarchy was at least a potential rebel."[127]

The third reason was Jesus' assumption of kingship—that is, his claim to be the head of the aforementioned kingdom—reflected by, among other things, his greeting on his entrance into Jerusalem as a king by "a very great multitude": "Hosanna to the Son of David!" (Matt 21:8–9); "Blessed is the kingdom of our father David that is coming!" (Mark 11:10); "Blessed is the King who comes in the name of the Lord" (Luke 19:37–38); and "Hosanna, blessed is he who comes in the name of the Lord, even the King of Israel" (John 12:12–13). After all, Jesus had been called "the king of the Jews" by the wise men from the East who sought him out in Bethlehem (Matt 2:2). And the biblical source for Jesus riding an ass into Jerusalem, quoted by both Matthew (21:5) and John (12:15), says—not to the world, but "to the daughter of Zion": "Lo, your king comes to you" (Zech 9:9).[128]

It is not surprising, therefore, that Jesus' disciples asked him at his Ascension, "Lord, wilt thou at this time restore again the kingdom to Israel?" (Acts 1:6)—implying that Jesus had made this promise before his death. That is also why Pilate asked Jesus in every Gospel whether he claimed to be King of the Jews—an epithet that was not merely a religious (i.e., eschatological) title in the eyes of the Romans, but political, suggesting as it did that the reigning Caesar was *not* the King of the Jews. In short, "[any] man who spoke of a kingdom, spoke against the temple, and had a following was one marked for execution."[129] Furthermore, in every Gospel, as I men-

---

126. Brandon, *Trial of Jesus*, 144. "Zealotism," adds Brandon, "with its gospel of violent resistance and readiness for martyrdom, was their natural response" (144.). "Among the Galilean crowds Jesus was a great success. Large groups formed and accompanied him when the rumour went round that he was on his way to heal the sick, or simply when he travelled" (Vermes, *Jesus the Jew*, 30).

127. *Jesus the Jew*, 50. Mack says that during and after the Jewish Revolt, "leaders assumed the role of the king of the Jews and were killed" (*Who Wrote?* 148). See also Smith, *Jesus the Magician*, 24.

128. For a lengthy discussion of Jesus' entrance into Jerusalem see Borg, *Jesus*, 230–32. Borg argues that the entrance was "a prophetic act" intended to contrast the deliberately humble entrance of Jesus with the deliberately grand entrance into the city made annually at Passover by Pontius Pilate and his regal entourage: "The juxtaposition of these two processions embodies the central conflict of Jesus's last week." The people could choose either "the kingdom of God or the kingdom of imperial domination" (232).

129. Sanders, *Jesus and Judaism*, 295. However, Sanders continues, "no one need have regarded him as a military leader." Again: "Jesus taught about the kingdom; he was executed as a would-be king; and his disciples, after his death, expected him to return to establish the kingdom. These points are indisputable" (307). See also Crossan, *Who Killed Jesus?* 83, 212; Yoder, *Politics of Jesus*, 34–39 (and 46–47); Carmichael, *Birth of Christianity*, 210; Kaylor, *Jesus the Prophet*, 4; Theissen, *Early Palestinian Christianity*, 64; and Bultmann, *Jesus and the Word*, 26. Pagan writers, such as the second-century Lucian and Celsus and the third-century Hierocles—albeit writing many years after the Crucifixion— also regarded Jesus as a justly executed rebel. Indeed, Tacitus seems to have thought that Christians

tioned above, Jesus is mocked as "King of the Jews" or "King of the Israel" during or after his trial (Matt 27:29, 41; Mark 15:12, 32; Luke 23:37; John 19:2–3, 14), and his cross is decorated with the words "King of the Jews" (Matt 27:37; Mark 15:26; Luke 23:38; 19:19).[130]

Thus, when Pilate supposedly offered to release Jesus instead of Barabbas, "the Jews cried out, 'If you release this man, you are not Caesar's friend; every one who makes himself a king sets himself against Caesar'" (John 19:12). This sounds like a cynical and insincere response on the part of "the Jews," who, if they are assumed to have been ordinary Jews, hated both the Romans and their collaborators and had no affection for the Roman emperor. However, if the Jews in this passage were actually "the chief priests and the officers" (or their retainers)—as they are identified in John 19:6—then their argument must be taken seriously (that is, as neither cynical nor insincere), since these "Jews," as members of the Jewish elite, were, in fact, Roman patriots, at least insofar as their power derived from their Roman imperial masters. Fittingly, at the end of this passage, it was "the chief priests" again, responding to Pilate's third or fourth offer to release Jesus, who said, "We have no king but Caesar," and who objected to Pilate's *titulus* on the cross, identifying Jesus as King of the Jews (John 19:15, 21).

Since Jesus was so clearly perceived to be a threat to the Romans and only because of that a threat to the Jewish aristocracy in Palestine, as even these passages in the Gospel of John suggest, why were the Jews accused of crucifying Jesus and not the Romans? After all, the Romans had crucified thousands of Jews in the century before Jesus' death; relatively few Jews in Palestine and no Jews in the Diaspora actually heard Jesus speak; the Romans would probably have arrested Jesus without Jewish help; Pilate was a notoriously cruel ruler who typically suppressed anyone whom he thought to be dangerous; and the charge against Jesus was not blasphemy (an offense against Judaism), but sedition (a threat to Rome). The answer, according to many contemporary historians, is threefold.

---

deserved to die not because of their endangerment of the empire, but because of their immoral behavior (Robertson, *Origins of Christianity*, 90–92). Robertson argues that the Jesus movement in fact "aimed at the overthrow of Roman and Herodian rule in Palestine and the establishment of an 'earthly kingdom of God' in which the first would be last and the last first" (93–96).

130. Stegemann and Stegemann, *Jesus Movement*, 178. For parallels between Jesus and the social bandits, see 212. Sanders says, "Jesus was executed by the Romans as would-be king, that is, as a messianic pretender . . . Not only the Romans, but probably also the 'crowds' and the disciples so saw him" (*Jesus and Judaism*, 223). On the subject of class conflict, Guignebert says, "Those in office [in Palestine], who found it more profitable to maintain an attitude of compromise towards foreigners and unbelievers, had good reason to fear the unrest and disturbance that Messianism might kindle among those who were less contented with their lot and more spiritually minded than themselves" (*Jewish World*, 150). On parallels between Jesus and three self-proclaimed kings who rebelled against Roman rule, see Herzog, *Jesus, Justice,* 238–39. "Like the judges of old, the popular kings were charismatic figures, able to command a following and conduct a limited military campaign. They were of humble origin, not from royal lineage. Their followers were primarily peasants or the disaffected urban poor" (238).

First, the Christians of the post-war generation (i.e., after the Revolt of 66), when all of the Gospels were written, did not want to be identified with the disgraced and rebellious Jews, who, despite the special privileges they had been granted by Caesar himself, were now easy to blame because they had fallen out of favor with the Romans.[131] The Christians, who were perceived by the Romans to be members of a Jewish sect, were easily identifiable as insurrectionists, not only because of their ties to the Jewish rebels, but also because their founder was commonly considered a Jewish rebel himself. Thus, the Gospels reflect "an apologetical interest in warding off the criminalization of Christians in the Roman empire." Luke (in Acts) indicates several times that Christians were apprehended or attacked at least partly because they were taken for Jews. When Paul and Silas were brought before "the magistrates" in Philippi, for example, their accusers said, "These men are Jews and they are disturbing our city" (Acts 16:20), as if their religion or ethnicity made the disturbance understandable, if not inevitable.[132]

Second, besides not wanting to be identified as Jews for reasons of self-protection, Christians were also motivated by the growing hostility between Church and Synagogue after, but not directly because of, the war. Simply put, the relationship between Christians and Jews grew progressively worse after the destruction of the Temple and the demise of or diminution in the influence of all Jewish sects except the Pharisees. Jews became impatient with sectarianism, which they saw as a partial reason for their defeat in the war. Consequently, when Christian Jews came to preach in the synagogues, they were less and less welcome to spread their unavoidably divisive message. And, when the evangelists came to draw their portraits of Jews in the Gospels, the picture got darker as, presumably, Christians felt less welcome with the passage of time. As a result of this growing "alienation," Jewish guilt for Christian suffering, as the Gospel writers saw it, was extended from the Jewish aristocracy—chief priests, elders, and scribes—to all Jews, not only in Palestine, but in the empire, and not only in the present, but forever.[133]

131. Horsley and Silberman, *Message*, 84. Tabor explains: "Anti-Jewish sentiments were prevalent in the reign of Tiberius (A.D. 14–37), spurred on by the notorious prefect Sejanus, the most influential Roman citizen of his day. After the costly and bloody Jewish Revolt, such anti-Jewish feelings were fanned to a flame by the Romans and any association of Jesus with Jewish sedition and disloyalty to Rome had to be avoided" (*Jesus Dynasty*, 216).

132. Stegemann and Stegemann, *Jesus Movement*, 211, 326–27. "In the present context, it is of decisive importance that in the epoch after the Jewish-Roman war, even unarmed fanatical messianic groups were easily in danger of being charged with the crime of anti-Roman rebellion. This opened wide the gate of a corresponding identification of Jesus' followers, the Christianoi, as one of the groups of Jewish insurrectionists against Rome that existed in the Diaspora. This suspicion was also based on the execution of the Christ they worshiped" (329; see also 332); and Carroll, *Constantine's Sword*, 87. If Jesus' crucifixion "could be blamed on the obstinacy of the Jews," says Tabor, "then perhaps the Christian movement could explain its Jewish origins and the shameful death of its leader in a more favorable—that is, less Jewish—light" (*Jesus Dynasty*, 216).

133. Crossan says, "As Christian Jewish communities are steadily more alienated from their fellow Jews, so the 'enemies' of Jesus expand to fit those new situations. By the time of John in the 90s, those

The Gospels record this antagonism, according to many modern scholars, by retrofitting it to the time of Jesus. Thus, according to the evangelists, Jesus argued incessantly with the Pharisees, not with the Romans or their Sadducean representatives. Jesus was accused of a religious crime, important only to Jews, rather than a political offense, important to Romans. And, most consequentially, Jesus was executed by Jews, not Romans—in "an account," says one scholar, "which defies all records of the actual power relations between" the Jewish High Priest and the Roman prefect.[134] That is, as I have said repeatedly, the priest was not only subordinate to the prefect, he served totally at the mercy of his superior. And the idea that Pilate, in this case, was in any way beholden to, afraid of, or even influenced by Caiaphas is difficult to believe because it is contradicted by everything we know about this era that comes from sources other than the New Testament.

Third, by the latter half of the first century, the missionary goals of the Church had changed. Instead of seeking out only Jews as converts, post-war Christians evidently turned their attention, even more aggressively than they had under Paul's direction, to the gentiles. And the gentiles, it should be remembered, *were* the Romans, who had executed Jesus, Peter, and Paul and later persecuted *all* Christians. By the second century, among the Christians who were writing defenses of Christianity, for both protective and promotional purposes, few of them appear to have been interested in converting Jews. Their audience, rather, was the pagan majority, who might be dissuaded from hostility and persecution and attracted by a rational, philosophical, and decidedly non-Jewish religion.

As a result, the Church had to rewrite history: "In the decades after the crucifixion, as the young church shifted its missionary activities from the Jews to the Gentiles, the church shifted the blame [for the death of Jesus] away from potential Christians, the Romans, and toward the Jews, who had rejected Christianity. In shifting the blame, the gospels represent this missionary concern of their own period rather than the historical realities of Jesus' time."[135] Especially after the destruction of Jerusalem

---

enemies are 'the Jews'" (*Birth of Christianity*, 525). According to Cook, "Anti-Jewish feeling cannot be ignored, least of all Matt. xxvii. 24 f., which whitewashes the Roman Procurator Pilate and harshly intensifies the guilt of the Jews . . . This condemnation of the Jews is carried on in Acts, which culminates in Paul's speech at Rome: the Jews had rejected Jesus, God's salvation is now sent unto the Gentiles, it is they who will hear. This is the motive of the book" (*Introduction to the Bible*, 146). On this subject, see also Sanders, who discusses what he calls "the general tendency in early Christianity to blame 'the Jews' for all Christianity's difficulties" (*Schismatics*, 182–83. Sanders argues that much of the alleged hostility between Jews and Christians, especially in Acts of the Apostles, is attributable to the hostility between Jewish Christians and non-Jewish Christians (184–86).

134. Ruether, *Faith and Fratricide*, 88. Ruether continues: "We find an extraordinary need in the Gospels to shift the blame for the deaths of Jesus and his disciples from Roman political authority to Jewish religious authority." Thus, culpability is not only visited on the Jews rather than the Romans but attributed to Judaism itself (88–89).

135. Wylen, *Jews*, 126. For the view that the Jews were, in fact, responsible for the death of Jesus, see (for example) Klingaman, *First Century*, 199, 212; Richardson, "The Israel Idea in the Passion Narratives," 10; Bammel, "Ex illa itaque die consilium fecerunt . . .," 25, 35 n. 136; Catchpole, "The Problem

and the earlier death of James the brother of Jesus, who had run the Church as a distinctly *Jewish*-Christian institution, "the new movement had to find its place in a world run by Rome."[136] Christians were thus "desirous of cultivating the friendship of Rome," which is why Acts of the Apostles (like the earlier Gospels) leaves out anything negative about the Romans, such as the executions of Peter and Paul, and exaggerates the evils of the Jews.[137]

In other words, the misrepresentation of Jesus' apprehension and execution is nothing more than an extension of the earlier misrepresentation of Jesus' relations with the Pharisees, which I discussed in Chapter Two. In fact, the entire Passion, except for the fact that Jesus was arrested, tried, and executed, is viewed by many students of the Bible as a fabrication based on passages from the Old Testament. As two New Testament scholars explain: "The passion story interprets the Christian confession and has been shaped exclusively with this interest in mind. The Christological meaning is further underscored by the adoption of [Old Testament] motifs and quotations"—for example, Jesus' triumphal entry into Jerusalem, the entire story of Judas, Jesus' statements on the cross, and the behavior of Roman soldiers and Jewish spectators.[138] The main problem, especially with the trial, is that there were no Christian witnesses: "Since the disciples are all recorded to have forsaken [Jesus] and fled, there is no certain basis for the narratives which follow the scene in the garden of Gesthemane."[139]

Indeed, some scholars suggest that, considering Jesus' lowly status, there might not have been a trial at all.[140] In the provinces, after all, the Roman prefect's "right to

---

of the Historicity of the Sanhedrin Trial," 54; O'Neill, "The Charge of Blasphemy," 77; and Hoehner, "Why did Pilate hand Jesus over to Antipas?" 90.

136. Fredriksen, *Jesus of Nazareth*, 185.

137. The quotation is from Parkes, *Conflict*, 46. De Ste. Croix comments, "Acts has the propagandist purpose of depicting the Christians as the victims of Jewish vindictiveness, while the Roman officials either maintain a benevolent neutrality or intervene in favor of the Christians" ("Christianity's Encounter with the Roman Imperial Government," 345). Painter says, "The deaths of neither Peter nor Paul give cause for comment in the NT because they were executed by the Romans. On the other hand, Acts records all executions by Jews, including those of Stephen and James the son of Zebedee (*Just James*, 56 n. 21). The final point is made by Ruether (*Faith and Fratricide*, 89–90) and Stegemann and Stegemann (*Jesus Movement*, 323}.

138. Conzelmann and Lindemann, *Interpreting the New Testament*, 328. The Old Testament passages used in the Gospel of Mark are cited on 329–32, after which the authors conclude, "The historical basis of the entire tradition of the passion proves to be relatively thin."

139. Parkes, *Conflict*, 45.

140. Horsley and Silberman offer this possibility, quoting Crossan (*Message*, 81). Crossan says elsewhere: "I am very unsure what level of Roman bureaucratic authority was empowered to eradicate a peasant nuisance like Jesus. I doubt that 'trial' is even a good description of that process even when taken at its most minimal connotation" (*Historical Jesus*, 390). Smith contends, "The accounts of interrogations and trials . . . are unscrupulous dramatizations of uncertain events" (*Jesus the Magician*, 38). Borg says that "there is great historical uncertainty about this scene" (i.e., the trial before the Sanhedrin) because "[t]rials were forbidden at night and on such days" as "the most important Jewish festival of the year." Furthermore, "if it did happen, how did the followers of Jesus know *what*

execute was not only exclusive but also absolute; he could execute even a Roman citizen, and he did not have to formulate a charge that would stand up in a court in Rome . . . If he had the right to execute a Roman military officer without a full Roman trial [which he did], he could treat members of the subject nation more or less any way he wished." In short, the Romans did not need the Jews when they found it necessary to arrest anyone they perceived to be seditious or dangerous. Under such circumstances, "the Romans sent troops—who did not have to wait for a formal Jewish trial before using their swords."[141]

Certainly, from Pompey's execution of 12,000 Jews in 63 BC to Varus' execution of 2,000 in 4 BC and Titus' execution of 6,000 in AD 70 (counting only those who died in Titus' torching of the Temple), the Romans seldom bothered with trials. If one argues that these were acts of war, which required no official proceedings to justify military action, one might say that the Romans did not carefully distinguish between these large-scale reactions to rebellion and the many smaller attempts to quash Jewish resistance (perceived and real) that occurred in the intervening years. There was evidently no need to bother.

It is also instructive to remember that, although the Romans are justly famous for establishing a coherent system of laws that were applicable throughout the empire, these were brutal times, in which such legal principles as equity and justice were not always applied with the fervor that might be expected in a modern civilized society. The Romans were, as I have suggested, fully capable of punishing innocent people—through exile, enslavement, torture, or execution—for the crimes of others. Roman emperors (notably Tiberius, Caligula, Nero, and Domitian) routinely killed their real and imagined enemies, and the emperors themselves were frequently assassinated, sometimes by their wives. Herod the Great executed one of his wives, her brother, mother, and grandfather, and three of his sons, and punished rebels by burning them alive, in the same way that Nero used Christians as human candles after the fire in Rome. Nero also murdered his half brother, his mother, and his wife Octavia. These deaths were not preceded by trials in which evidence was presented and judicial opinions were delivered on the basis of the evidence. Romans not only created the laws of the empire; they also violated them whenever necessity and opportunity converged.

If there was no trial (either Jewish or Roman)—because the Romans had no need to conduct trials to justify *any* execution—and if none of the disciples were present to witness anything that occurred immediately before and shortly after Jesus' death (Matt 26:56; Mark 14:50), it may be that Jesus was simply turned over to the Romans

---

had happened at it. They had all fled" (*Jesus*, 263). Sandmel doubts that any trial took place: "Our knowledge of Jewish practices is in total conflict with the judicial processes [described in the synoptic Gospels]; it would be as reasonable to suppose that an American lower court held an all-night session on New Year's Eve and transferred the proceedings to a higher court on New Year's morning, and that the sentence was carried out on the same day." In other words, "The entire trial business is legendary and tendentious" (*Jewish Understanding*, 128).

141. Sanders, *Historical Figure of Jesus*, 24, 69. See also Horsley and Silberman, *Message*, 86.

by the Temple guard and the Roman soldiers (John 18:3) and then crucified.[142] From this perspective, the account of events between his arrest and burial may well be taken as a *midrash*, a traditional form of Jewish storytelling that involves the use of one or more biblical passages to explain a historical event, whose details are derived from these passages and woven into a coherent (and plausible) narrative.[143] For example, the soldiers casting lots for Jesus' cloak and Jesus' famous seven final words of despair come from Psalm 22; other details may have been borrowed from, among other sources, Isaiah, Jeremiah, and Zechariah, as well as Psalms 26:6; 69:21; and 109:25.

Of course, regardless of whether or not there was a trial, the "facts" in the case are highly suspect because of what we know about the political ferment in Palestine in the first century, the willingness of the Romans throughout their history and across the empire to crush all opposition, the likelihood that Jesus was perceived (correctly or not) to be a revolutionary,[144] and the irrelevance or insignificance of the Jews' role in his crucifixion. In this context, the Passion stories appear to have had one purpose: In the words of one scholar, "They have been completely shaped by a later Christian theological tradition that sought to put the blame for Jesus' death wholly upon the Jewish people while exonerating the Romans as sympathetic to Jesus, with Pilate doing all he could to save Jesus' life."[145]

Even if the Passion narratives were not *entirely* invented, however, there can be little doubt that, as many scholars have stated, the evangelists simply misrepresented the essential aspects of first-century AD Jewish-Christian-Roman relations. And the important point is not merely that the Gospel writers lied, but that their fabrications

142. Conzelmann and Lindemann comment, "The whole scene of the trial is not based on an eyewitness account but has been shaped from the perspective of the believing post-Easter community" (*Interpreting the New Testament*, 331). Tabor comments, "Scholars are agreed that little in these accounts of Jesus' trial is historically credible" (*Jesus Dynasty*, 215). Mack too regards the Passion story as myth (*Who Wrote?* 87).

143. Not only was the trial not witnessed by any of Jesus' followers; everything that happened thereafter, says Fredriksen, is a *midrash*: "The rest of the Gospels' Passion accounts, once Jesus goes from Pilate to the cross, is thickly overlaid with theological themes and obviously shaped by biblical testimonies." Fredriksen then lists the specific sources in Isaiah, Psalms, and Zechariah (*Jesus of Nazareth*, 256). Wylen also uses the word *midrash* to describe the composition of the Passion (*Jews*, 131–32). Smith says, "Luke's story of a trial before Herod was probably invented to fulfill Ps 2.1f.; cp. Acts 4.27. Another such invention was the nocturnal trial before the Sanhedrin (on Passover night, when leaving one's house was prohibited! Exod 12.22)" (*Jesus the Magician*, 38). For a contrary view, see Catchpole, "The Problem of the Historicity of the Sanhedrin Trial," 47–65.

144. Even Freyne, on occasion, acknowledges that Jesus was perceived to be both "religiously radical and socially subversive": "The norms and values of those who control the limited goods society, which the author has graphically depicted through typical characters and situations, are under attack . . . Here lies the reason for the charge of subversion which came to its final expression in Jerusalem" (*Galilee, Jesus*, 106–7).

145. Tabor, *Jesus Dynasty*, 215–16. Tabor says earlier, "There was a tendency in later Christian tradition to put responsibility for Jesus' death on the Jews as a whole[,] and the idea that Jesus was condemned to die at an official convocation of the entire Sanhedrin was one way to support such a claim" (212). According to Parkes, the early Christians, assuming that Jesus died according to God's plan for the salvation of mankind, did not blame the Jews for this event (*Conflict*, 69).

had devastating consequences for Jews. Speaking of the Passion alone, one scholar says, "It is a magnificent theological fiction, to be sure, but entailing a dreadful price for Judaism."[146] And, if there was a "start-to-finish pattern in the Gospels of deflecting blame away from the Romans and onto Jews"—that is, a *comprehensive* effort to shift the responsibility for Jesus' execution in this manner—then the impact on Christian-Jewish relations was even worse.[147]

There were compelling reasons for this Christian revisionism, and it could well have remained a manifestation of a minor intra-Jewish conflict, as it no doubt was perceived to be in the early years of Christianity. Unfortunately, for the victims, the Church gained enormous power, and its self-serving stories of Christian-Jewish enmity have provided a reason for Christians to like Romans and hate Jews. This enmity deepened as time passed not only because the Church grew in size and influence, but also because the portrayal of Jews by Christians became increasingly negative. In the course of the four Gospels, plus the later *Gospel of Peter*, the charge against the non-Christian Jews became broader and broader, extending from sub-groups who were seldom identified as Jews in the synoptic Gospels (Pharisees, scribes, and chief priests) to "the Jews" in general in the Gospel of John, where they are explicitly identified as Jesus' enemies. Indeed, by the time the *Gospel of Peter* was written, the Jews were all alone in their guilt: *The Romans had had nothing at all to do with Jesus' death.*[148]

This total absence of responsibility is underscored by the fact, as I said earlier, that *nowhere in the Gospels is any Roman actually identified as a Roman* (except, prospectively, in John 11:48). And not only are the Romans absent from the story, including its sequel in the Acts of the Apostles (except twice in chapter 16 and once in chapter 25), so is the bitter conflict between the Jews and the Romans and between the Jewish haves and have-nots. The only people identified by their ethnicity in the Gospel of John, Acts (with the aforementioned exceptions), and Paul's letters are the Jews, who were, at least until the Revolt of 66, indistinguishable, in many respects, from the Christians. Yet the Christians in the Passion stories would appear to have come from a different planet (at least morally and theologically) than the Jews. In this

146. Crossan, *Historical Jesus*, 390.

147. Carroll, *Constantine's Sword*, 85.

148. Carroll says that the biblical misrepresentation of the role of Jews and Romans in the development of Christianity "is commonly taken now as evidence of a primordial Christian anti-Semitism, or worse: an anti-Judaism at the service of a craven attempt to placate Roman authorities." He goes on to suggest that the "Christian anti-Semitism" charge is out place in what was basically a conflict between Jews. "If the Gospels, just then [by which he means, after Nero's "scapegoating of the Christian Jews"] starting to jell in their final forms, emphasized a relative friendliness to Rome, there was a reason for it. The followers of Jesus had been slandered, defined not merely as Rome's mortal enemy but as violent insurrectionists. It was not true, and the Gospels were slanted, in effect, to emphasize that followers of Jesus fully intended to render unto Caesar what was Caesar's" (*Constantine's Sword*, 85–86). As Carroll points out, however, the appropriate response to Nero's exile of the Christians was written by a victim of a similar injustice, John of Patmos, who was exiled to that island by Domitian and there finished writing the anti-Roman Book of Revelation (*Oxford Annotated Bible*, 1491). As I suggested earlier, the Gospels' anti-Judaism was more likely influenced by Christian-Jewish relations after AD 66.

way, a Jewish-Roman conflict was transformed, in the course of time, into a Jewish-Christian conflict.

Then came John Chrysostom, Ambrose, Hilary, and the other Church Fathers who, in one way or another, perpetuated this antagonism. In the twentieth century, it was retained and even expanded by scholars who—despite the historical record, the evidence of the Gospels themselves, and the attempt by many contemporary writers to correct the falsehoods that had been repeated for nearly two thousand years—continued to portray the Jews as evil. Thus, the Jews were still said to have embraced a legalistic religion: "Their error was their belief that they could earn God's favor by their deeds . . . [or] by obedience to His law." Jesus was still said to have died because he loved too much: "To love as he loved was bound to evoke the hostility of the authorities." Worse yet, "To live a life of love . . . *entailed* the likelihood of the cross." And, of course, it was still said that the Jews did not understand Jesus as well as the gentiles did: "[I]t was only as [his followers'] reflection on him deepened that they came to recognize what it fully meant" that he was both human and divine.[149] This rumination did not reach its final form, as I said earlier, until late in the fourth century.

In the end, Jesus was crucified by the Romans, with some fellow-traveling Jews playing a subordinate role.[150] However, "the conflict of the story as set in the year 30 took shape to reflect the conflict of the storytellers between, say, 35 and 90—an intensifying conflict ever more with fellow Jews than with Rome."[151] The evidence overwhelmingly supports this point, but some Christian (as well as some Jewish) scholars have been too unwilling to call a spade a spade. If the Gospel writers did indeed retroject Jewish-

149. The quotations in this paragraph are from Latourette, *History of Christianity,* I, 50; Goulder, "Jesus: The Man of Universal Destiny," 57–58; and Pelikan, *Jesus Through the Centuries,* 71.

150. As Conzelmann and Lindemann put it, "A political suspect was executed by the Romans, with the cooperation of Jewish circles" (*Interpreting the New Testament,* 333). Ruether says, "Recent historical studies have shown that the Jewish authorities could have had, at best, a subsidiary relation to the death of Jesus" (*Faith and Fratricide,* 87). Ruether cites Winter, *On the Trial of Jesus;* Bammel, ed., *Trial of Jesus;* and Brandon, *The Trial of Jesus of Nazareth* (269 n. 19). According to Moltmann: "Jesus did not suffer the penalty for blasphemy, which was stoning. He was crucified for political reasons by the Roman occupying power, for inciting unrest and rebellion . . . "[S]ince Pilate had to see to it that there was peace and order in the occupied country, he was bound to misinterpret the trouble-maker from Nazareth as a political trouble-maker" (*Church,* 89). Nevertheless, the Jews were blamed (92). See also Zeitlin, *Who Crucified Jesus?* xii, xix, 3, 210, 211; Tabor, *Jesus Dynasty,* 209; Grant, *Historical Introduction,* 366; Koester, *History, Culture, and Religion,* 396, 400; and Wylen, *Jews,* 126–27. For a more orthodox Christian view, see Latourette, *History of Christianity,* I, 8, 50, 52, 56, 57.

151. Carroll, *Constantine's Sword,* 132. See also, on the subject of retrojection, Stegemann and Stegemann, *Jesus Movement,* 210. I find Carroll's attitude too forgiving toward the Gospel writers' fictions. While it is unnecessary to attribute venal motives to the Christians, I fail to see why they cannot be accused of lying—albeit for understandable, though not forgivable, reasons. I think Carroll is too constrained by his statements early on in his otherwise thorough and fair-minded book to the effect that either the Jews were guilty or "the Gospel writers were guilty of a vicious slander" (40). How about calling the Jews innocent and the Gospel writers guilty of just plain slander? Brandon simply labels the Gospel treatments of Jesus' trial "misrepresentations" (*Trial of Jesus,* 141). Crossan struggles with this issue in *Birth of Christianity,* 523–25.

Christian conflicts of the last half of the first century onto the relations between Jesus and his Jewish contemporaries, then these writers have inflicted a terrible injustice on the Jews, which (though without the motivation of anti-Semitism) is the primary reason for Christian violence against the Jews for nearly two millennia. Two other historians have it right: "The stories of Pilate washing his hands of the matter and the bloodthirsty screams of the rabble who chose Barabbas over Jesus are all the work of later Christian writers who—unlike Jesus—were desperately intimidated by the Romans and turned the blame on the Jews to divert accusations of disloyalty or rebellion away from themselves."[152]

152. Horsley and Silberman, *Message*, 84. Speaking of the Middle Ages, Heer says that the extensive violence against the Jews is wholly attributable to the identification of the Jews as "the murderers of Christ" (*Medieval World*, 10). Heer adds later, "Measured in terms of duration, magnitude and conscious suffering there is nothing in the history of Europe, or even of the world, to compare with the martyrdom of the Jews of medieval Europe" (312). Well before the Middle Ages began, of course, this kind of anti-Semitism "forced [Jewish Christianity] underground and largely exterminated it" (Witherington, *What Have They Done?* 223).

Chapter Four

The Disciples

"No one who favors admitting the Gentiles without circumcision mentions the example of Jesus, saying, 'Jesus told us to do so.' And, of course, the reason is that he never did tell them to do so. Indeed, one may suspect that the only ones likely to have mentioned Jesus would have been those of the circumcision party, arguing that there was no authorization from him for such a radical departure from the Law." (Raymond E. Brown)

LIKE JESUS, THE DISCIPLES whom he personally chose were born Jewish and, for all we know, remained Jewish for the rest of their lives.[1] In fact, they were not called Christians for many years after the Crucifixion (Acts 11:26) and did not apply that name to themselves for decades after that.[2] Thus, in the words of one Bible scholar, "If we call the

---

1. Bruce says that "the first members of the church were without exception Jews" (*Canon of Scripture*, 27). Furthermore, "[e]arly Jewish Christians thought of themselves, not as a specific sect distinguished from other Jews, but as the nucleus of the Messianic renewal of the people of Israel" (Bauckham, *James*, 16). In other words, "the earliest Jewish followers of Jesus . . . did not see themselves as starting a new religion" (Shanks and Witherington, *Brother of Jesus*, 145). On this point, see also Herford, *Pharisees*, 212, 214; Tabor, *Jesus Dynasty*, 266; van Leeuwen, *Christianity in World History*, 222; Gonzalez, *Story of Christianity*, I, 7, 20; Manschreck, *History of Christianity*, 22–23; Ehrman, *Lost Christianities*, 96; Chilton and Neusner, *Judaism*, xiv; Crossan, *Birth of Christianity*, xxxiii; Davies, *Invitation*, 26; and Maccoby, *Mythmaker*, 104. Wilson adds, "These early followers of Jesus were Jews and never stopped being Jews" (*Jesus*, 6). "Presumably," Wilson says later, in spite of Paul's attempt to de-Judaize the faith, "the Jewish Christians went on doing things in their own way, and Paul stubbornly took no notice of their desire to remain within the fold of Judaism" (26). "Naturally," says Bultmann, "the eschatological Congregation does not regard itself as a new religion—i.e. a new historical phenomenon—and does not draw a boundary between itself, as a new religion, and Judaism. It remains loyal to the temple and the temple cult" (*Theology*, I, 53; see also 57). Maccoby summarizes the battle between those who insist on Jesus' Jewishness and those who have denied it in *Mythmaker*, 206–10. The strangest and most reprehensible aspect of this dialogue—both morally and intellectually—is the claim on the part of the latter that the Church of the early years was at some point "re-Judaized," a subject I discussed in the Introduction. In this view, the Church betrayed Jesus' desire to create a new religion and reversed his "clearly" anti-Jewish ideas. This occurred specifically after the departure from Jerusalem of the Hellenist wing of the Church and under the leadership of Jesus' brother James.

2. According to White, the term "Christians" was applied to Jesus' followers "forty to fifty years or

early disciples 'Christians,' we may use this as a term of convenience, but such use at this stage is an anachronism . . . The disciples called their movement 'The Way'; to their fellow-Jews they were known as Nazarenes or, more properly, Nazoraeans."[3] Paul was called a member of "the sect of the Nazarenes" by a Jew in Acts of the Apostles 24:5 and a member of an otherwise unidentified "sect" by some Jews in Rome in Acts 28:22. Earlier, Paul and Silas were identified as Jews by gentiles in Philippi (Acts 16:20). In his defense before Felix, Paul referred to his movement as "the way which they call heresy" (24:14) and elsewhere called its members "the saints" (26:10), as did Ananias (9:14). Luke calls them "brethren" in Acts 9:30, as well as "believers" in Acts 9:42.[4]

In short, the Christians in Jerusalem thought of themselves as Jews, as did the members of other Jewish sects, all of whom—especially the Essenes—considered themselves to be the true people of God who would be saved at the Last Judgment: "The very earliest groups of those who confessed Jesus as the Christ (Messiah) are now generally seen and studied as religious movements within Judaism."[5] For that reason, "[i]t would be more accurate . . . to call them Christian Jews rather than Jewish Christians."[6]

THE DISCIPLES AS JEWS

The reason that Jesus' followers were indistinguishable from other Jews is that they continued to live as Jews.[7] This was especially true of the members of the Jerusalem

---

more" after his death and even then only derogatorily (*From Jesus to Christianity*, 121–22).

3. Bruce, *New Testament History*, 213. "Eventually," says Tabor, "under the thirty-three-year dynastic reign of Jesus' brother James, large numbers of Pharisees identified with the movement that John the Baptizer and Jesus had inaugurated. As surprising as it sounds to modern ears there were in fact Nazarene or 'Christian Pharisees'—and lots of them" (*Jesus Dynasty*, 121).

4. References to "the way" also occur in Acts 9:2; 19:9, 23; 22:4; 24:14, 22; to "the saints" in 1 Cor 16:1; 2 Cor 8:4; 9:1, 12; Rom 15:25, 31; and to "the brethren" in Acts 10:23; 16:2; 17:10; 18:18; 21:17). Hengel contends that in Paul's time Jesus' followers were "still a completely unknown Jewish sect" (*Crucifixion*, 18).

5. Gager, *Origins of Anti-Semitism*, 113. Mattingly says: "Christianity grew up in the world as a kind of sect of the Jews . . . Many of the first Christians were Jews themselves" (*Roman Imperial Civilisation*, 225).

6. Shanks and Witherington, *Brother of Jesus*, 70. See also 26. In fact, says Klinghoffer, "Another misconception about the early Christians is that they were Christians." What Klinghoffer means is that they were not Christians "in most of the ways that in our time would make somebody recognizably Christian." They obeyed the Mosaic Law, waited for the Messiah, as other Jews did, and lived apart from the gentiles (*Why the Jews*, 91). See also Theissen, *Early Palestinian Christianity*, 1; and Maccoby, *Mythmaker*, 119–20. Theissen discusses the wandering charismatics appointed by Jesus, all of whom "remained within the framework of Judaism" (*Early Palestinian Christianity*, 8).

7. "At first," says Chadwick, "Christianity must certainly have appeared only as one more sect or group within a Judaism that was already accustomed to considerable variety in religious expression" (*Early Church*, 13). "It [was] a long time before people clearly distinguished Christianity from its Jewish parent body," and "the tendency persisted to treat the Christians as an extremist branch of Judaism" (Grant, *Climax of Rome*, 224). Manschreck adds: Rome "probably did not clearly distinguish Christians from Jews until about the end of the first century." Thus, the Christians were not persecuted

church, led by Peter, John, and, most prominently, James the brother of Jesus, who assumed the mantle of leadership either immediately after the Crucifixion or, at least, when Peter left Jerusalem on his first missionary journey. "From the very first, the religion of James and his colleagues was basically common Judaism, which they continued to observe and to which they stayed firmly attached, and in which the Temple of Jerusalem still occupied the center point."[8] After witnessing Jesus' Ascension in Bethany, the disciples returned to Jerusalem, where "they were continually in the temple, praising and blessing God" (Luke 24:52–53); "they spent much time together in the temple, . . . praising God and having the goodwill of the people" (Acts 2:46)—"the people" being, of course, other Jews. One might assume that these "people held them in high honor" (Acts 5:13) not only because the disciples of Jesus were, in some sense, honorable, but also because they were observant Jews.

Thus, whatever Jesus might have said about the Temple, his words did not dissuade his disciples from continuing to use it as their place of worship. Indeed, "Jesus' symbolic destruction of the temple would seem to have been forgotten by the early church, which centered its life in Jerusalem under the leadership of James, who was pious and devout in his temple obligations."[9] Nor did the first Christians do much else that separated them from other Jews. Immediately after his death and before they launched their first new mission, Jesus' followers chose a new disciple to bring the

---

"on the basis of the name [i.e., Christians] itself" until the second century. "Not until then were they seen as a new internal threat distinguishable from the Jews in Palestine" (*History of Christianity*, 24–25; see also 65). Markus says that neither pagans nor Jews would have been able to distinguish Christians from Jews at the end of the first century. There were many Jewish sects, and Jesus' followers looked and acted like members of these organizations. "It was sometimes difficult, even for his own disciples, to distinguish the liberation he offered from the sort of liberation others offered" (*Christianity*, 18–20).

8. Vermes, *Changing Faces of Jesus*, 139–40. "The first disciples of Jesus in Jerusalem frequented the synagogues and participated in the temple ritual" (Peters, *Harvest of Hellenism*, 492). "[T]hey worshipped in the Jerusalem temple; and they saw in Jesus the long-anticipated prophet, teacher, and messiah who would usher in the final days of history" (Gager, *Origins of Anti-Semitism*, 113; see also Herzog, *Jesus, Justice*, 123). Specifically, adds Weiss, they made sacrifices, recited Jewish prayers, honored the Sabbath, and performed good works (*Earliest Christianity*, I, 54–56, 81 n. 57, and 82). See also Brandon, *Trial of Jesus*, 21. Enslin says: "In Jerusalem they appear to have settled down as a separate synagogue with no thought of cutting themselves off from Judaism or of going to the gentile world as crusaders for a world mission. According to the fragmentary evidence given in Acts they visited the temple as did their fellow Jews. That the opposition to them which eventually came was due to any laxity regarding the Sabbath or to any attempt of theirs to disregard the prized interpretation of the Pharisees and Scribes is not hinted" (*Christian Beginnings*, 171). Carmichael, quoting Hans Lietzmann, says (suggesting, incidentally, that it was not just the Jerusalem church that maintained a strong connection to Judaism): "In many places it was quite usual for Christians to attend the synagogue, keep the Jewish fasts, and even make gifts of oil on taking part in the festivals celebrated in the synagogue. In Spain there were people who persuaded the rabbi to pronounce a blessing over their fields; so, too, Africa seethed with the observance of Jewish customs and festivals'" (*Birth of Christianity*, 141).

9. Herzog, *Jesus, Justice*, 254. However, Herzog goes on to say, the situation eventually went in another direction, influenced—as the experiences of Peter, John, and Stephen suggest—by "an anti-temple strain of thought in the early church" (254).

symbolic number back to twelve, representing the twelve tribes of Israel. They spoke in tongues at the Pentecost, one of the three main Jewish festivals, which Peter explained by quoting the prophet Joel, suggesting that the "the last days" had arrived (Acts 2:16–21). They heard Peter also quote Psalms 16, 89, and 110 as proof-texts for Jesus' fulfillment of the prophecy of a Davidic messiah (Acts 2:25–35).

Furthermore, although Paul began to convert gentiles, presumably in large numbers, some time before AD 50, the Jerusalem church—touched by the Holy Spirit (i.e., the same spirit that had moved Samuel, Joshua, and Samson)—began its mission with the conversion of 3,000 more Jews to their faith (Acts 2:41). They raised the total of *men* to 5,000 shortly thereafter (4:4), including, eventually, "a great many of the priests" in Jerusalem (6:7), as well as Pharisees (15:5)—in short, there were "many thousands of believers . . . among the Jews" (21:20).[10] Eusebius reports that "innumerable Jews" joined the Church until the reign of Trajan—that is, c. AD 100 or shortly thereafter.[11] Indeed, one scholar notes that Christians' respect for the synagogue as well as their conversion of Jews continued, at least in some places, into the fourth century.[12]

The message Peter and other members of the Jerusalem church preached went back to the message of Jesus' Jewish forerunner, John the Baptist: repentance and forgiveness (Acts 2:38; 3:19; 5:31; and 8:22), two ideas that had special meaning for Jews, as I suggested in Chapter One. And the same message went forward into the post-Crucifixion community, where it reappears, for example, in speeches by Paul (13:38; 17:30–31; 19:4; 20:21; 26:18–20), Justin Martyr's *First Apology* (61), the *Didascalia* (10), *1 Clement* 7:5, *The Shepherd of Hermas*, and especially *2 Clement* (8, 9, 13, 16, 17, 19).[13] In fact, one self-styled Jewish follower of Jesus, Apollos, taught only the message

10. As Brown reminds his readers, in Acts 21 it is James reporting the number of Jewish conversions to Paul, and the year is c. 58 (*Introduction*, 727).

11. Weiss, *Earliest Christianity*, II, 668. Segal says, "Given the number of voices objecting to Paul's solution [i.e., to questions arising from the gentile mission], Jewish Christians cannot have disappeared as quickly as most scholars assume" (*Paul the Convert*, 146). Segal adds later, "Jewish Christianity probably continued to be the dominant form of Christianity for at least two generations and maybe several generations after Paul" (275). Boyarin comments: "For centuries after Jesus' death, there were people who believed in Jesus' divinity as the incarnate Messiah but who also insisted that in order to be saved they must eat only kosher, keep the Sabbath as other Jews do, and circumcise their sons" (*Jewish Gospels*, 10). Markus says that in some places Jewish Christianity survived into the fourth century (*Christianity*, 22). Schillebeeckx discusses opposing views of the Mosaic law in Palestine and in the Diaspora in *Jesus*, 230–33. He examines the Hellenistic influence in more detail on 560–68.

12. Parkes cites, in the first instance, the evidence of John Chrysostom's sermons in Antioch and, in the second, laws preventing Jews from insulting or molesting Jewish converts to Christianity (*Conflict*, 79, 171). The ongoing connection between even gentile Christians and the synagogue is not entirely surprising, since, Parkes says, "[t]he foundations of the Gentile Church were laid almost exclusively among the proselytes or people already interested in Judaism" (24–25). Painter argues, on the other hand, that the mission to the Jews by the Jerusalem church, supposedly headed by Peter, ended at the destruction of Jerusalem in AD 70 (*Just James*, 86).

13. Meeks says of the *Sheperd* that "[r]epentance is its central concern." He continues, "Although

of John the Baptist (Acts 18:25–26), as a result of which his twelve disciples in Ephesus knew nothing about the Holy Spirit when Paul arrived in that city and proceeded to baptize them in Jesus' name (19:1–6).

The early Church also preached the Kingdom of God, an idea common to both Jesus and the Jewish prophets. In Acts, Luke suggests that Jesus emphasized this subject more than any other during the forty days of his post-Resurrection ministry (1:3), which is partly why the disciples asked him whether he would now "restore the kingdom to Israel" (1:6). Philip spread the "good news about the kingdom of God" throughout Samaria (8:12), and Paul promised his followers in Lystra, Iconium, and Antioch that they would soon "enter the kingdom of God" (14:21–22). He reminded his disciples in Ephesus that he had preached "the kingdom" to them for three years (20:25, 31; 19:8), and he spoke to his audiences in Rome for two years about both Jesus and the coming kingdom (28:23, 31). To Jewish hearers, as in Rome, Paul emphasized that the kingdom was "the hope of Israel" (28:20). On other occasions, other Jewish-Christian proselytizers said that the throne on which Jesus would sit would be the throne of David (2:30; 4:25).

If the so-called Q gospel, the common source of both Matthew and Luke (exclusive of Mark), can be used as a guide, mid-first-century Christians from the community that either wrote it down or passed it on orally did not preach Jesus' death and resurrection, as Paul (and Paul's churches) did.[14] These Jewish Christians, who may have been typical of most Christians at the time, preached what could be called the gospel of Jesus: that is, the ethical program summarized in the Sermon on the Mount, repeated in the epistle of James, and originating in the Jewish Covenant Code. Looking ahead to the second century, we find some Christian apologists offering the same gospel. Thus, Aristides' *Apology* is a "predominantly ethical presentation of Christianity," little of which "would not be at home in a Jewish Apology."[15] And even in the fourth century, although by that time both Jesus' divinity and his atonement for the sins of mankind had become doctrinal in all churches, except perhaps among a few surviving Jewish-Christian groups, "the morality which the church was attempting to teach was Jewish morality, as often supported by Old Testament quotations as by quotations from the Gospels."[16]

---

everything else we know of Christianity at Rome in the first two centuries suggests disparate groups, various small house-meetings, and several competing 'schools' attached to individual teachers, Hermas's images imply a remarkably unified and institutional conception of the church" (*Origins of Christian Morality*, 124–25).

14. Horsley and Silberman, who locate the Q communities north of Jerusalem, refer to "their conspicuous silence on the matter of [Jesus'] death and resurrection" (*Message*, 99). See also Kloppenborg, *Q*, 73–84.

15. Lieu, *Image and Reality*, 174. "For the reader," Lieu adds, "Christianity as presented by Aristides is marked by a distinctly Jewish ethos" (175). Lieu refers earlier to Aristides' "explicit and in some ways positive representation of Judaism" (15).

16. Parkes, *Conflict*, 156. As an example, Parkes cites "the battle which the church waged against 'usury' among Christian laity and clergy, and which was based entirely on Mosaic Law" (156 n. 1).

The Didache, another expression of Jewish Christianity, this time from half a century later than the Q gospel (c. 100), took into account that, while Jewish converts could be assumed to understand the ethical requirements of the Church, pagan converts had to be trained.[17] They had to be reminded of "the two ways"—i.e., the way of good and the way of evil, derived from Jeremiah 21:8, Psalm 1, and Deuteronomy 30:19, by way of Matthew 7:13 and John 10:7—the first of which is based on the two Great Commandments: "[Y]ou must love God who made you, and second, your neighbor as yourself" (*Didache* 1:1–2), derived, of course, from Deuteronomy and Leviticus. Many of the instructions that follow "reflect the teachings of Jesus from the Sermon on the Mount in Matthew 5–7," including the Golden Rule, forswearing revenge, and helping the needy.[18]

The earliest church was, therefore, "a quintessentially Jewish sect," whose members not only attended Temple services daily, but also used their homes for communal dining, teaching, and prayers, as other Jews did; preached in synagogues at Sabbath services; and honored Jewish holy days. They especially resembled the Pharisees, who held home fellowships and study groups.[19] Sometimes the objects of intimidation and browbeating, the disciples were nevertheless "pious and practicing Jews,"[20] who started their mission in the synagogues of cities in the Jewish Diaspora.[21] As far as they were concerned, they were orthodox Jews who had found the Messiah, and, although much of their time and energy was given over to that revelation, they still continued to live and worship as Jews.

Most important, these Jewish Christians kept the Law.[22] All properly circumcised, they had no reason to question or doubt the religious efficacy of that ritual or

17. Crossan, *Birth of Christianity*, 367. "The Didache," Crossan adds later, "while admitting pagans into its Christian community, is profoundly Jewish" (372).

18. Ehrman, *After the New Testament*, 385–86.

19. White, *From Jesus to Christianity*, 127. For a discussion of the terms "sect" and "cult," see 129.

20. Bruce, *New Testament History*, 216.

21. Fredriksen, *From Jesus to Christ*, 33; and Vermes, *Changing Faces of Jesus*, 139. See also Armstrong, *History of God*, 90.

22. Sheehan, *First Coming*, 183; Fredriksen, *From Jesus to Christ*, 170; Gager, *Origins of Anti-Semitism*, 113; and Shanks and Witherington, *Brother of Jesus*, 70, 114–15. Bultmann adds, "That Jesus did not polemically contest the authority of the Old Testament is proven by the course later taken by his Church; it clung faithfully to the Old Testament Law and thereby came into conflict with Paul." Thus, although Bultmann attributes Jesus' defense of the Law in Matthew (Matt 5:17–19) to the Church's later influence (i.e., re-Judaization), he says, "this conservative attitude of the Church would not have been possible if Jesus had called into question the validity of the Old Testament" (*Theology*, I, 16). See also 54–55; and Schillebeeckx, *Jesus*, 230, 411–12, 527. "The Palestinian local churches continued to observe the sabbath and keep the Law (Matt 24:20; see Acts 13:3; 14:23); they considered themselves to be a fraternity inside Judaism" (234; see also 235; and Chadwick, *Early Church*, 22). Theissen takes the Gospel of Matthew as the voice of at least some "local communities," which means that "[s]ome communities wanted to see the law fulfilled down to the smallest detail," "felt that scribes and Pharisees were legitimate authorities," and "recognized the temple and its priesthood through sacrifice" (*Early Palestinian Christianity*, 18). Theissen emphasizes the latitude that was tolerated by Christians in the late first century and early second century, which is suggested by this passage in *The Didache*

of any other aspect of traditional Judaism. Indeed, the Palestinian Christians went on believing that circumcision was indispensable, at least for Jewish followers of Jesus, even after that notion was challenged by Paul twenty years after the Crucifixion.[23] The idea that Christians had to follow the laws, including circumcision, was argued in *The Letter of Peter to James* (2:4–5) and the reply from James (1:1), two documents from the early 200s. In *The Homilies of Clement*, the author says that salvation can be attained through good works and by following either Jesus or Moses (Bk. 8, 6:1–2; 7:1–2). The so-called Judaizers, it should be noted, were not Jews trying to change the Church from the outside, but followers of Jesus who not only practiced circumcision, but continued to keep the Sabbath and maintain the purity and dietary laws.

Indeed, the members of the Jerusalem church remained faithful to the religious practices of the original church, endured until about AD 400, and then faded out slowly for another century.[24] As James and the elders explained to Paul in Acts 21:20, the Jerusalem church was made up of "many thousands of Jews" who "believe[d]" in Jesus, but were also "zealous of the law." This means that, besides worshiping in the Temple (Lk 24:53), they rested on the Sabbath (23:56) and, in Peter's case, obeyed the food laws in general (Acts 10:17), including the laws that prohibited Jews from dining in the homes of Christians (Acts 10:28; Gal 2:12)—and that evidently had prevented Jesus from entering the homes of gentiles whom he healed. Particularly in the churches founded by members of the Jerusalem church, gentile as well as Jewish converts continued to be "bound" by such restrictions.[25] And, surely, Peter was not

---

(6:2): "If you can bear the whole yoke of the Lord, you will be perfect, but if you cannot, do what you can" (19). On the fidelity to the Law in Matthew's communities, see also Meeks, *Origins of Christian Morality*, 203–4.

23. Perrin and Duling, *New Testament*, 77. Brown adds, "The N[ew] T[estament] (including Paul) does not debate whether Jewish-Christian parents should have their sons circumcised." Rather, the debate concerned only gentile converts (*Introduction*, 300 n. 55; see also 301, 305). Furthermore, Brown says that not all gentiles objected to circumcision, as the example of the Galatians shows (469, 573 n. 33). See also, on the Galatians' positive attitude toward circumcision, Bultmann, *Theology*, I, 55. According to van Leeuwen, "[C]ircumcision is taken completely for granted" in the Gospels (*Christianity in World History*, 224).

24. Cornfeld, *Archeology of the Bible*, 308–9. Grant says that some Christians, namely the Ebionites and Quartodecimans (who connected the date of Easter to the date of Passover), were still celebrating Passover in the second century and beyond (*Historical Introduction*, 358). For a fuller discussion of the ongoing Judaism of the Jerusalem church, even after its (assumed) move to Pella around the time of the Revolt of 66, see Latourette, *History of Christianity*, I, 120–22. Latourette says that these early Christians maintained a strong tie to Judaism, especially under the leadership of Jesus' brother James. Gager reviews the persistent influence of Judaism on Christianity in *Origins of Anti-Semitism*, 122–43.

25. Brown, *Introduction*, 309. See also, on James and Peter's defense of Jewish practices, Grant, *Historical Introduction*, 393; and, on the disciples' acceptance of Jesus' strict moral principles, Weiss, *Earliest Christianity*, I, 77–82. "Since they regarded the purity codes as compatible with Jesus' teaching, a position with which Matthew, writing much later, would agree, they may have appeared to many merely as a Pharisaic sect" (Mack, *Who Wrote?* 70). However, Mack contends that the Jerusalem church was the only early Christian community to abide by the Mosaic Law (67–68). On the other hand, if the Gospel of Matthew was not written for the Jerusalem church, but for another Jewish-Christian congregation, there was at least one more such group. Schillebeeckx notes, in this regard,

alone in his adherence to laws that evidently stayed in place among many Christians for decades, if not centuries, after the Crucifixion.

It is important to remember that there were, even well into the second century, counterweights to the influence of Paul, including not only the Ebionites, but also three Jewish-Christian gospels, addressed to the Ebionites, the Nazarenes, and the Hebrews.[26] According to the Christian historian Eusebius, the Church itself was ruled by Jewish Christians for a century.[27] He writes of the Jerusalem church, which he treats as the main church in Christendom, that there were fifteen consecutive bishops, all of whom "were Hebrews from the first." Eusebius then proceeds to name these "bishops from the circumcision," from James to Judas. Indeed, he adds, "At that time *the whole church* under them consisted of faithful Hebrews who continued from the time of the apostles until the siege that then took place"—that is, the Revolt of 132 (*Eccl. Hist.*, Bk. 4, 5:2–4).

Not surprisingly, therefore, many members of Christian churches retained Jewish practices. The best known examples are from Paul's churches in Galatia and Corinth, which were visited in 53–54 by "Torah-observant missionaries"—against whom Paul defended his gospel by asserting that he too was a Hebrew and an Israelite and a descendant of Abraham (2 Cor 11:22–23).[28] Like Paul, Ignatius, the bishop of Antioch, faced gentile Judaizers in the Philadelphia and Magnesia churches, who believed that Christians had to adopt Jewish practices and based that judgment on their use of the Jewish Bible for guidance.[29] Antioch was the scene of the strongest reaction to this kind of situation in the fourth century, when John Chrysostom gave eight virulently anti-Semitic sermons because he found his parishioners somewhat more deeply involved in Judaism than he thought proper for true Christians. It seems "that at least some ordinary members of the church saw nothing out of order in attending the synagogue services, joining in other Jewish festivities, regarding the synagogue as a sacred place appropriate for taking oaths, and respecting the supernatural powers of the teachers."[30]

---

that the Q community, against the Pauline churches, retained the idea that both Works and Faith are necessary for salvation (*Jesus*, 235).

26. Meier says that what we know about these gospels is based on "a few scattered fragments" and, more significantly, "statements and quotations of the Church fathers." Worse yet, we have no idea how many Jewish-Christian gospels existed, where any given fragment belongs, and whether our major sources—Eusebius, Jerome, and Epiphanius—were quoting accurately (*The Marginal Jew*, I, 115–16). Nevertheless, says Painter, the existence of these gospels "is now widely accepted" (*Just James*, 184).

27. Weiss, *Earliest Christianity*, II, 721.

28. Horsley and Silberman, *Message*, 177–78. "Apparently," say the editors of *Oxford Annotated Bible*, "the authenticity of Paul's Judaism was called into question" by these Jewish Christians (1405).

29. Ehrman, *Lost Christianities*, 144. See also Lieu, *Image and Reality*, 39–40. There may also have been "trouble" of this kind in Smyrna (49).

30. Lieu, 24. Wylen says, "When he came to the city, he was shocked to find his flock regularly attending the synagogue, enjoying the sermons there and socializing with Jews" (*Jews*, 195). For a lengthy (and depressing) account of John Chrysostom's assault on Judaism, as well as on the Christians

It is also worth mentioning that, although gentile converts generally had less interest than Jewish converts in maintaining Jewish practices, many gentiles who had been converted by Jewish Christians remained adamant supporters of Jewish Christianity. The issue of backsliding into Judaism is addressed not only in Paul's letters, but also in the Epistle to the Hebrews. "Specifically, the author [of Hebrews] thinks that some [Christians] put too much value on the Israelite cultic heritage . . . Apparently those affected by this outlook had already ceased meeting together in prayer with other [i.e., non-Jewish] Christians (Heb 10:23–25)."[31] In fact, many Judaizers were not Jews, but gentiles. (At the same time, Hellenists who wanted to abandon Judaism entirely could as easily have been Diaspora Jews as gentiles.)

The point is, as the example of John Chrysostom's Antiochene Christians makes clear, just as there were Jews who as Christians retained their Jewish ways, there were also gentiles who as Christians were drawn to Judaism: "The Judaizing Christian," says one scholar, "was a Christian, not necessarily of Jewish background, who was attracted to Jewish rites and traditions, while remaining within the mainstream Church." Strange to say, this was a phenomenon of the fourth century, after Christianity had become the official religion of the Roman empire. It arose particularly in communities with a large Jewish population or among Eastern Christians whose culture was similar to that of the Jews. They "practiced circumcision as well as baptism, followed dietary laws and rites of purification, observed the Sabbath as well as Sunday, and participated in fasts and feasts . . . They also associated with the synagogue in other ways."[32]

It is one important sign of the early Church's commitment to Judaism in general and to the Covenant Code in particular that the Jerusalem church (and perhaps others) created what one Bible scholar has called "a sharing community."[33] That is, insofar as the Acts of the Apostles accurately represents this church in the decades between the Crucifixion and the destruction of the Temple, this group of Christians "sold their

---

of Antioch, see Ruether, *Faith and Fratricide*, 170–81.

31. Brown, *Introduction*, 697–98. "The recipients of the letter [to the Hebrews] were on the point of giving up their Christian faith and returning to the Jewish beliefs and practices of their ancestors" (*Oxford Annotated Bible*, 1453). Brown discusses the possible influence of James on the Roman Christian community in *Introduction*, 743.

32. Ruether, *Faith and Fratricide*, 170–71. On gentile Christians loyal to Judaism, see Brown, *Introduction*, 742–43. Mack notes that the Christians in Galatia who were apparently eager to be circumcised and follow the Law were gentiles (Gal 3:2; 5; 4:10, 21), perhaps acting at the behest of "Judaizers" (Gal 2:4, 12; Phil 3:2), although he finds no evidence that such a movement actually existed: "It is the first indication we have that gentile Christians, not Jews, questioned the credibility of Paul's gospel of freedom from the law" (*Who Wrote?* 114, 145).

33. Crossan, *Birth of Christianity*, 472. Meeks says that "Christians [who] established the practice of giving to those of the community who were needy" were "doubtless following Jewish models" (*Origins of Christian Morality*, 106). MacMullen makes the same point in *Christianizing the Roman Empire*, 54. Maguire traces the attitude of the Jesus movement toward the poor to a large number of Jewish texts in *Moral Core*, 131–42. Maguire says: "The distinctive feature of Jewish justice is *the stress on redistributive sharing and remedial systemic changes that favor the poor*" (133). He adds that the Good Samaritan is, in fact, the model Jew, guided by passages like Deuteronomy 15:11 (134–35).

possessions and goods and distributed them to all, as any had need." Thus, they "had all things in common" (Acts 2:44–45). They had "one heart and soul," rejected "private ownership" of anything, had "not a needy person among them" because "as many as were possessors of lands or houses sold them," and gave "to each as any had need" (Acts 4:32–34). This was a community, one might say—not incidentally, like the Essenes at Qumran—that put the economic ideals of Deuteronomy and the prophets into practice.[34]

Many Christian scholars are uneasy with Luke's description, pointing out that giving was entirely voluntary, that some wealthy Christians did not give up *everything*, and that other Christian enclaves operated on less communistic principles.[35] However, when Ananias and his wife "keep back part of the proceeds" of the sale of their land, they are killed, evidently by an angry God. Furthermore, there is nothing either vague or ambiguous about the statement "[A]s many as were possessors of lands or houses sold them" (Acts 4:34).[36] Thus, the same scholar who calls the early Church a sharing community concludes: "What I see in both cases, with the Essene Jews and the Christian Jews, is a thrust toward establishing sharing community in reaction against

34. Horsley and Silberman see the community values embraced by the Jerusalem church as similar to those at Qumran: "At precisely the same time and in the same small province of Judea, another group who condemned the evils of Roman society and opposed the present priestly leadership of the Temple had organized themselves into a community in which admission to full membership entailed handing over all individual earnings and private property" (*Message*, 102). This was an effort, furthermore, "to maintain sacred, ancestral traditions of Covenant and community without abandoning the unique social vision they contained" (104). Capper uses the similarities between the Jerusalem church and the Qumran community to argue against "[t]he critical consensus" that refuses to see any "actual, organized property-sharing behind Luke's account" ("The Palestinian Cultural Context of Earliest Christian Community of Goods," 323–56). Capper concludes, after presenting his argument at some length, "Thus a cumulative case, building from a wide variety of evidence, suggests that the earliest Christian community of goods in Acts 2–6 is a historically verifiable aspect of the life of the earliest Jerusalem community."

35. Bainton says, for example: "With regard to property the Church never espoused a thoroughgoing communism of production and consumption. There was a sharing of goods and a drastic philanthropy for the benefit not only of fellow Christians but also of the heathen, especially in times of calamity" (*Early Christianity*, 56). See also Conzelmann and Lindemann: "[N]othing is said of a general and compulsory, mandated commonality of property" (*Interpreting the New Testament*, 345). Meeks grants that Luke's description of the early Christians in Acts might be an idealization, but it also expresses an ideal that guided the behavior of Christians throughout the early centuries: "To vulnerable people [Christianity] offered the support of small, intensely connected groups, mutual care, mutual admonition, mutual assistance" (*Origins of Christian Morality*, 129). Maguire says that the picture in Acts may be "more symbol than fact," but it was "pressed relentlessly" in both Judaism and Christianity (*Moral Core*, 135).

36. Enslin says, "Attempts have been made to tone down this clear word [in Mark 10:17–31] and to make it a special diagnosis for this particular man, but the evangelists give no support to this attempt to side-step an unpleasant teaching." As evidence, Enslin points to "the more primitive form of the beatitudes in Luke" (6:20–23), the story of both Lazarus and Dives (Luke 16:19–31), and the near impossibility of a rich man getting into heaven (Matt 19:24) (*Christian Beginnings*, 160). Enslin calls the economic system put into place by the earliest Christians "a kind of communism," which was "in strict compliance with the teaching of Jesus" (177).

commercializing community—an effort made, of course, *to live in covenant with God.*"
And, in this respect, it was intended to be a model, a paradigm, an "eschatological
ideal" for all of Christendom.[37]

This point cannot be made strongly enough. The earliest Christians were not
just a sharing community in covenant with God, but *a covenant community*—that is,
a group of men and women who revived the Jewish covenant values that were clearly
stated in the Jewish Bible and had, at one time or another, actually been implemented.
Following Jesus and the prophets, these early Christians believed that the meek and
humble and weak would finally triumph. Following Jesus and the prophets, they retained an explicit trust in God's willingness to respond to their prayers and satisfy
their needs. And, following Jesus and the prophets, they assumed that the conditions
of human life would soon be utterly transformed. Most important, in the meantime,
they created a community that, in most respects, was identical to the ideal community—part real, part imagined—that evidently remained in the minds and memories
of Palestinian Jews in the first century AD. Specifically, they eliminated poverty and
thereby satisfied the demand that God expresses in Deuteronomy 15:4–5.

As I said earlier, many scholars have said that Jesus' expectations were far too
idealistic (and therefore impractical) if life was to go on as it had during the centuries-
long occupation. Thus, considering Jesus' promise that the end was near, these scholars
have suggested that the ideals of the Sermon on the Mount must have been presented
by Jesus and perceived by his disciples as an "interim ethic"—that is, a set of rules
intended to be in force for only a short time, until the imminent end of the world. In
this respect, the earliest Christians were not expected to live as they did forever. Life
would begin on new terms, sooner or later. So, for now, changes in marital status were
unnecessary, and the highest possible moral standards could be endured.[38]

On the other hand, however, the world to come—that is, the Kingdom of God—
was morally indistinguishable from the Jerusalem community as it is described in
Acts. This is because there was, in general terms (at least among Jews), only one ideal
world imaginable. It was a world of justice and mercy. It was a world in which the

37. Crossan, *Birth of Christianity*, 472; my emphasis. Crossan adduces as additional evidence of
this point that Christians in the Diaspora were expected to contribute to "the poor" of Jerusalem—not
to the traditionally poor and needy, but to the church itself, which was poor as an act of faith and
needed support from all Christians (474). Quoting from the Essenes' *Damascus Document*, Crossan
connects the ideals expressed therein with the Covenant Code, which he discusses on 188–208. Bauer
says that the Roman church (perhaps in imitation of Jerusalem's example) "assessed her members according to each individual's resources and ability to give" (*Orthodoxy and Heresy*, 124). That is, Bauer
seems to imply, the church made the decision, not the member, voluntarily. Horsley and Silberman
add, "It is reasonable to assume that at least some of the diaspora assemblies of the Jesus Movement,
founded by apostles from Jerusalem, were based on a similar principle of sharing" (*Message*, 142).

38. The concept originated with Albert Schweitzer, according to Conzelmann and Lindemann,
Interpreting the New Testament, 317–19. See also Pelikan, *Jesus Through the Centuries*, 24; Nineham,
"Epilogue," 194; and Fredriksen, *From Jesus to Christ*, 100–101.

good were rewarded and the evil punished. Indeed, it was a world in which only the good remained—a world without envy, without anxiety, and without mammon. In this respect, the Jerusalem community was not an interim arrangement, but a preparation for and rehearsal of the life to come, when traditional Jewish values, which Jesus' disciples put into place in Jerusalem, would prevail everywhere and forever. Thus, what the followers of Jesus embraced might be better described as a "kingdom ethic" rather than an "interim ethic." As one scholar has said, in reference to the promised Kingdom of God, "To achieve entrance men must begin to live as though the change had actually taken place."[39]

Although many scholars believe that Luke's description of the earliest Christian community—the church of James and Peter and John the son of Zebedee—is an idealized and fundamentally false version of what the community actually was, it is important to remember how strongly Jesus himself emphasized the values on which such a community might have been founded. We are told quite clearly and unequivocally in the gospels that Jesus asked his disciples to give up *everything* in order to become members of what St. Paul later called the "body of Christ." They gave up jobs, traditional responsibilities (such as burying the dead), and even familial relationships in order to "follow" Jesus—that is, to join his inner circle of disciples, whose role would eventually be to exorcise demons and preach the faith at the Temple in Jerusalem and in synagogues throughout the Diaspora. Peter says to Jesus, "[W]e have left [or "forsaken"] all, and have followed thee" (Mark 10:28; Matt 19:27; Luke 18:28).

Indeed, the values in place in the Jerusalem community, as it is described by Luke, appear to be based on Jesus' explanation of what it meant to "follow" him in his command to the rich young man who, in his wish to achieve "eternal life," told Jesus that he obeyed all of the commandments. Jesus replied that this was not enough. He said to the young man, "[S]ell whatever thou hast, and give to the poor . . . and come, take up the cross, and follow me" (Mark 10:21; Matt 19:21; Luke 18:22). That is, if the young man wished to "be perfect" and "have treasure in heaven," he had to go beyond the commandments that all Jews were required to obey. Specifically, he had to strip himself of his wealth and donate everything he had to the welfare of his fellow Christians. In the gospels of Luke and Matthew, selling everything was the first step in securing "a treasure in the heavens that faileth not, where no thief approacheth, neither moth corrupteth" (Luke 12:33–4; Matt 6:19–21). It was the step that demonstrated where one's treasure was and, therefore, in Jesus' moral scheme, where one's heart was. It was the good work that expressed righteousness and merited the ultimate reward, which the young man sought, immortality.

---

39. Enslin, *Christian Beginnings*, 165–166. Enslin says a few pages earlier that the values of the Jerusalem community were "a means of gaining entrance into the fast-approaching kingdom" because the Kingdom would also be based on the standards of justice and mercy—i.e., anti-materialist values (160–61).

Inevitably, of course, the decision to give up one's wealth meant to embrace a lifestyle characterized by poverty. Self-denial was imperative: "If any man will come after me, let him deny himself, and take up his cross daily, and follow me" (Luke. 9:23; 14:25–27; Matt 16:24; Mark 8:34). That is, unless someone "forsaketh . . . all that he hath, he cannot be [Jesus'] disciple" (Luke 14:33). He had to be willing to lose himself in order to find himself, and he had to avoid accumulating money and property since the cost of doing so was the loss of his soul and the loss of any chance at salvation: "For what is a man advantaged, if he gain the whole world, and lose himself, or be cast away?" Indeed, the preoccupation with mammon was the equivalent of rejecting Jesus and being rejected by the Son of man (Luke 9:25–26; Matt 16:25–26; Mark 8:35–37): "The Son of man shall come in the glory of his Father with his angels; and then he shall reward every man according to his works" (Matt 16:27), the most important of which, evidently, was the repudiation of selfishness and materialism.

Part of Jesus' justification for a life of austerity was the idea that God would make sure that his followers got what they needed. In response to Peter's cry of concern— "Lo, we have left all, and have followed thee"—Jesus said, "There is no man that hath left house, or brethren, or sisters, or father, or mother, or wife, or children, or lands . . . but he shall receive a hundredfold now in this time, houses, and brethren, and sisters, and mothers, and children, and lands," as well as "eternal life" (Mark 10:29–30; Matt 19:29). In Matthew, Jesus put this recompense off till "the regeneration" (that is, the Parousia), but in Luke, as in Mark, Jesus said that it would occur "in this present time" (Luke 18:29–30). Besides houses, lands, and family, Jesus added that the disciples would also be provided with food and clothing: "Take no thought for your life, what ye shall eat; neither for the body, what ye shall put on." God "knoweth that ye have need of these things. But rather seek ye the kingdom of God; and all these things shall be added to you" (Luke 12:22, 30–31; Matt 6:25, 32–33).

Significantly, however, Jesus did not merely ask his followers to live simply and unostentatiously. On the contrary, the poverty his disciples were required to embrace was absolute—assuming that the aforementioned passages in the gospels can be trusted—and its consequence was dependency on the generosity of others. Nor did Jesus suggest that food and clothing would fall, like manna, from the sky. Rather, it would be provided by those who accepted the whole of Jesus' moral program: sell *and* give. In other words, the answer to our asking, seeking, and knocking was to come not directly from God, but from those who were doing God's will: "Therefore" (Jesus said immediately after he claimed that God "give[s] good things to them that ask him"), "all things whatsoever ye would that men should do to you, do you even so to them: for this is the law and the prophets." That is, if everyone followed the Golden Rule, which was drawn from the Torah and the words of the Hebrew prophets, no one would need the direct intervention of God. His will would be done—by others (Matt 7:7–12; Luke 11:9–13; 6:31).

The act of giving might be called the second step not only in joining the Christian community in Jerusalem, but also in attaining eternal life. The idea is that, if men and women imitate God, particularly by following his commandments, they will accomplish God's will. As Jesus said in the Gospel of Matthew, "Be ye therefore perfect, even as your Father which is in heaven is perfect" (5:48). "Be ye therefore merciful," he said in the Gospel of Luke, "as your Father also is merciful" (6:36). Thus, Jesus required his followers to do what God Himself would do: "And if any man will sue thee at the law, and take away thy coat, let him have thy cloak also" (Matt 5:40). "Give to him who asketh thee, and from him that would borrow of thee turn not thou away" (5:42). "Love your enemies, bless them that curse you, do good to them that hate you, and pray for them that despitefully use you" (Matt 5:44). "Judge not, and ye shall not be judged," said Jesus in the Gospel of Luke. "[C]ondemn not, and ye shall not be condemned: forgive, and ye shall be forgiven: give, and it shall be given unto you; good measure, pressed down, and shaken together, and running over, *shall men give into your bosom*" (6:37–38; my emphasis).

Here, notably, it is not just God Who gives, but *everyone*. Thus, when Jesus sent his disciples out to the villages of Galilee and Judea, he did not tell them that God would provide. Rather, his proselytizing followers were to be fed and housed by Christian converts or sympathizers. Both the disciples in the inner circle and the seventy who were later appointed were to devote themselves to healing and spreading the gospel and to carry with them nothing of value: "neither staves, nor scrip, neither bread, nor money; neither have two coats apiece" (Luke 9:3; 10:4; Matt 10:9; Mark 6:8–9). Clearly, they were to rely on their hosts for food and shelter as they traveled from place to place. And these providers would, ideally, recognize the hard work and personal sacrifice of their guests: "[T]he workman," said Jesus, "is worthy of his meat." That is, practicing Christians would help their Christian brethren as they would like to be helped under similar circumstances.

Of course, none of this proves that Jesus not only demanded obedience to his moral rules, but also made sharing—selling everything and giving it all to the community—the basis of membership in the Church. What makes it likely that the latter was the case, however, is that Jesus required from his followers not only obedience, but also the severance of all family relationships: "If any man come to me, and hate not his father, and mother, and wife, and children, and brethren, and sisters, yea, and his own life also, he cannot be my disciple" (Luke 14:26). In the Gospel of Matthew, he said, famously, "I came not to send peace, but a sword." What he meant was that his goal was to divide families—or, more specifically, to separate his disciples from their families: "For I am come to set a man at variance against his father, and the daughter against her mother . . . And a man's foes shall be they of his own household. He that loveth father or mother more than than me is not worthy of me" (10:34–37; Luke 12:51–53). That is, it was not just a matter of leaving one's family, but, as these passages suggest, a matter of cutting off all ties with them.

What Jesus offered in return was a new family—or new community—to replace the old, the new one bound by spiritual rather than physical kinship. When his mother, brothers, and sisters came to visit him in chapter 3 of the Gospel of Mark, Jesus rejected them completely: "Who is my mother? And who are my brethren?" Refusing to see them, he announced that he had acquired a new family: "And he looked round about on them which sat about him, and said, Behold my mother and my brethren! For whosoever shall do the will of God, the same is my brother, and my sister, and mother" (Mark 3:33–35; Matt 12:48–50; Luke 8:21). As I noted earlier, even before the establishment of the Jerusalem church, "Jesus and his disciples shared a common purse administered by Judas, who bought provisions and gave to the poor at Jesus' direction (John 12:6; 19:29)." And after the church had been in existence for a quarter of a century, Paul— always reminding his followers that they were members of "the body of Christ" (1 Cor 10:16; 12:27)—insisted that they generously support the Christians in Jerusalem, whom he evidently regarded as not only worthy of help, but also dependent on it (Rom 15:25; 2 Cor 8 and 9).[40]

It is worth emphasizing, as well, that these Christian Jews represented one of a number of movements that, as different as some of their everyday practices and ultimate objectives might have been, shared a set of ideals of human behavior—based on cooperation, generosity, and compassion—that, in retrospect, appear to join together Jewish Christians in Jerusalem, Pharisees in Judea, Essenes at Qumran and elsewhere, Theraputae in Egypt, and revolutionaries throughout Palestine. The Kingdom of God was their common goal. The love of humanity was their common standard. In other words, it is not simply that these movements existed at the same time, but that they were driven by a collective sense of dissatisfaction and frustration and a pervasive set of ideals. Many Jews in the first century AD—except, of course, for the wealthy and powerful Jews who benefitted from the economic system then in place—were committed to restoring the Covenant and creating a community that reflected its values.[41]

It is also evident that the sharing community described in Acts was, to some degree, replicated by other Christians living outside of Jerusalem.[42] Justin Martyr, for example, describes his conversion as a moral transformation that resulted in a complete change in his value system (*1 Apol.* 61:1–3), one manifestation of which was his

40. Ronald J. Sider, "Sharing the Wealth: The Church as Biblical Model for Public Policy," *Christian Century*, June 8–15, 1977. At www.ChristianCentury.org. The quotation is from Richard K. Taylor, *Economics and the Gospel* (United Church Press, 1973), 21. On Paul's commitment to the idea of a sharing community, Sider mentions his reproach to the Corinthians for failing to contribute adequately to his collection for the "saints" in Jerusalem: "I do not mean that others should be eased and you burdened, but that *as a matter of equality* your abundance at the present time should supply their want, so that their abundance may supply your want, *that there may be equality*" (2 Cor 8:13–14; Sider's emphasis).

41. Speaking of the Essenes, in terms that apply to all of these groups, Enslin says that "the movement was a consequence of an attempt to push back the years and to regain those days when the law was workable without interpretation" (*Christian Beginnings*, 123; see 120–25).

42. On this subject, see Horsley and Silberman, *Message*, 142.

participation in a similar community: "[W]e who once took pleasure in the means of increasing our wealth and property now bring what we have into a common fund and share with everyone in need" (1 *Apol.* 14:2–3).[43] The writings of both Clement and Hippolytus, at the end of the first century, suggest that similar practices were in place in the church of Rome.[44] Christians in these communities were simply following these words from the first letter of John: "[W]hoso hath this world's goods, and seeth his brother have need, and shutteth up his bowels of compassion from him, how dwelleth the love of God in him? My little children, let us not love in word, neither in tongue: but in deed and in truth" (3:17–18).

The community for which *The Didache* was written might have been based on the principles that Luke describes in Acts. Much of this early second-century document, the first Christian manual on ritual practices, seems to have been directly influenced by Jesus' ethical commands in the Sermon on the Mount (*Did.* 1:1–4; 2:3–4:10), and the community may have implemented the socio-economic restrictions enforced by the Jerusalem church: "Do not shun a person in need, but *share all things with your brother and do not say that anything is your own*" (4:8; my emphasis). As in Acts, the distribution of goods was based entirely on need: "For if anyone receives because he is in need, he is without fault. But the one who receives without a need will have to testify why he received what he did, and for what purpose" (1:5).[45] Not surprisingly, in AD 165, Lucian, a pagan who was unsympathetic to Christianity, noted that Christians in Palestine "have equally little regard for all things and think them all common [property], taking them over [from the common fund] without [giving] any accurate guarantee."[46]

Even in the fourth century, some Church Fathers promoted the covenant values of the Pentateuch, whether or not they wished to formalize them in a sharing community. St. John Chrysostom, concerned with both his congregants' preoccupation with possessions and the problem of poverty among them, wondered whether "all giving all that they have into a common fund" might solve the problem.[47] Although he did not call for economic reform among his Christian congregants in Antioch, he emphasized the ideas of the Covenant again and again in his work (e.g., Homily XV, on the Gospel of Matthew 5:1–2). Similarly unwilling to impose these values on

43. Justin elsewhere indicates that giving in his community was entirely voluntary: "Those who prosper, and who so wish, contribute, each one as much as he chooses to." Nevertheless, everyone in need was evidently cared for, including orphans, widows, and sojourners, as well as the sick and the imprisoned (1 *Apol.* 67:5–6).

44. The examples of Christian sharing communities in this paragraph come from Meeks, *Origins of Christian Morality*, 35, 107–10. He also refers to Paul's charitable efforts on behalf of the Jerusalem church, the ideals expressed in the Johannine letters, and the rise of the monastic movement as other examples of covenantal values among Christians and Christian communities (60–65).

45. Quotations are from *The Didache*, in Ehrman, ed., *Lost Scriptures*, 212–13.

46. Smith, *Jesus the Magician*, 56. Smith comments, "Lucian is more amused by their credulous communism than angry at their impiety"—i.e., toward Roman gods.

47. 68 Maguire, *Moral Core*, 154, 156.

Christians, St. Basil of Caesarea nevertheless supported their formal implementation in the monastic movement he so strongly endorsed. And, like John Chrysostom, he consistently preached against the selfishness of the wealthy and the dire consequences of their moral failure: the plight of the poor (e.g., Basil's *Sermon to the Rich*).

It was, however, St. Ambrose who promoted not merely the ideal of charitable giving, but also a return to what one historian has called "the primitivistic communism" of Acts. Believing that God wanted "all things to be held in common by all," Ambrose argued not only that Adam's sin was avarice, rather than disobedience or concupiscence, but that every rich man, merely by virtue of his great wealth, was guilty of the same sin. Furthermore, this sin was the source of social injustice: "[A]varice brought about a division of the rights of ownership," which in turn resulted in universal poverty and widespread human suffering. Yet, although Ambrose insisted, in his words, that "sharing is the way of nature," he "apparently found no other way of bringing about a return to what he considered the ideal order . . . than by the voluntary action of individuals in 'sharing' their unrightfully acquired wealth with their fellows, and by the extirpation, through moral suasion, of the acquisitive motive . . . from men's bosoms."[48]

Following Jesus' advice not to cast pearls before swine, the disciples also, for many years, preached only to Jewish audiences.[49] Invariably, they followed Greek-speaking Jewish networks, depending, as they were instructed by Jesus, on the kindness of strangers, the most likely candidates being their religious compatriots in far-flung towns and cities as distant as Greece and North Africa.[50] This way, they could familiarly address their auditors as Jews, as they did not only in Judea, but throughout the Diaspora, calling them "Men of Israel" (e.g., Acts 2:22; 3:12; 13:16), as Gamaliel did (Acts 5:35).[51] Even the Hellenists "who were scattered because of the persecution

48. All quotations in this paragraph are from Lovejoy, "The Communism of St. Ambrose," in *Essays*, 296–307. Lovejoy comments, Ambrose "was zealous to bring about a better distribution of this world's goods; and his invectives against the rich were based less upon the ground that they lacked Christian charity than upon the ground that a social order marked by so great inequalities of economic condition was contrary to 'natural' justice and an aberration from the normal order established at the beginning of human history" (303).

49. "The self-understanding of the new Christian community expresses itself, among other things, by establishing itself in Jerusalem . . . and immediately begins with the mission among the Jews" (Conzelmann and Lindemann, *Interpreting the New Testament*, 342). "There is no record of their going into gentile territory or of conducting any mission to the gentiles" (Grant, *Historical Introduction*, 320). On this point, see Sanders, *Historical Figure of Jesus*, 12, 192. Moore says, "The disciples in Jerusalem had so little notion of exempting themselves from the ceremonial law that they were slow to admit that Gentile believers could be saved without assuming by circumcision the obligation to keep every article of it" (*Judaism*, II-III, 9–10).

50. Perrin and Duling, *New Testament*, 86; Stark, *Rise of Christianity*, 137; and White, *From Jesus to Christianity*, 389.

51. Weiss discusses the continuing mission to the Jews in *Earliest Christianity*, II, 666–72. Summing up, he says, "It must be insisted that the Gentile Christian Church, despite its missionary program for 'all the Gentiles,' did not give up Judaism completely, and that in the diaspora, and not only in Palestine and the east, there were Jewish communities, just as in the Gentile Christian churches Jewish

that arose over Stephen"—and traveled to Samaria, Cyprus, Phoenicia, and Antioch—preached "to none except Jews," at least until some of them "spoke to the Greeks also" in Antioch (Acts 11:19–20).[52] Peter and Paul continued to speak only to Jews until their revelations in Acts 10:9–29 and 9:3–5, 15, respectively.

It was also inevitable that Christian churches, their organization especially, would be modeled on the synagogues they replaced.[53] Thus, even though, by the time Ephesians was written (see 2:19–22), Christians had begun to think of the church as an institution that had supplanted the Temple and the synagogue—its foundation being not the entire Jewish Bible, but the apostles and the co-opted prophets, and its cornerstone not Moses and the Law, but Jesus—they used their churches as the Jews had used their houses of worship. Christians "continued the Jewish practice of meeting regularly once a week for group worship," and these churches became, as pagan temples were not, community centers.[54]

Christians established charitable programs and offered other kinds of services that were typically Jewish, but not pagan. Church leaders were called elders (Acts 11:30; 14:23; 15:2; and 20:17) as synagogue leaders were, and church offices (especially in Paul's churches) were functional rather than hierarchical, as synagogue offices were.[55] Nevertheless, these leaders went through a formal ordination process, simple though it may have been. Just as Joshua was commissioned by Moses (Num 27:21–23), rabbis were ordained as Torah students by the laying on of hands. Among Christians, this was the method by which the Holy Spirit was passed on from disciple

---

Christian minorities were never lacking" (II, 671). Hare says that the mission to the Jews ended in the eighties (*Jewish Persecution of Christians*, 155). Hare also briefly discusses the two opposing forces that influenced the post-Revolt Christian mission to the Jews: Christian interest in appealing to Jews demoralized by the devastation caused by the Revolt and Rabbinical hostility to Christian proselytizing, especially in the synagogues (128).

52. Grant says that these Hellenists did not convert any gentiles in Samaria, Acts 8:1–25 to the contrary notwithstanding (*Historical Introduction*, 393). Brown disagrees in *Churches*, 103. The Samaritans claimed to be Jews but were not accepted as such by the Jews of Palestine. Stark argues that the Jews of the Diaspora were particularly ripe for conversion to Christianity in *Rise of Christianity*, 57–63.

53. "The earliest Christians had followed the Jewish custom by which each synagogue not only possessed scribes and priests but also a body of ruling elders" (Grant, *Climax of Rome*, 228). Bishops acquired special powers in the second and third centuries and finally ruled the churches in the fourth century (228). Brown makes a similar point in *Churches*, 33–34; and *Introduction*, 81, 645, 646 n. 12. See also Weiss, *Earliest Christianity*, I, 48. Weiss adds that Diaspora Judaism—with its scattered yet unified synagogues, whose members were joined by religion rather than ethnicity—served as a model for the church even in terms of its international organization (II, 618–19). It might also be said that Christians treated the Mother Church in Jerusalem in the same way that the Jews treated the Temple. They not only contributed to its treasury, but may well have deferred to its authority, as Luke suggests in Acts. Grant says that Paul's establishment of Christian judges and courts (1 Cor 6:1–6) similarly followed Jewish models (*Historical Introduction*, 404).

54. Perrin and Duling, *New Testament*, 225–26.

55. Fredriksen, *From Jesus to Christ*, 17; Stegemann and Stegemann, *Jesus Movement*, 279, 281; and Ehrman, *After the New Testament*, 317.

to disciple (Acts 6:6) and the means by which, as 1 and 2 Timothy indicate (e.g., 1 Tim 4:14), the Spirit was given by the elders to new members of the ministry.[56]

With Christian Jews still praying in synagogues, except in Rome and Antioch as early as the forties (when separate churches were established in these cities), it was only natural that they considered the Jewish Bible to be their only scripture—but, for Greek-speaking Jews in the Diaspora, only in its Greek translation, called the Septuagint. This remained true in some cases well into the second century, when other texts, especially the Gospels and Paul's letters, began to acquire the same status.[57] As Jews as well as followers of Jesus, Christians "thought that what one could know and needed to know of God and his will was peculiarly mediated by the scriptures of Israel." Later, even gentiles shared that assumption: "Even as the majority of Christians came to be converted gentiles, they were instructed in those same scriptures."[58]

The liturgy in the churches also followed the pattern established in the synagogues: prayer (perhaps including supplications, thanksgivings, doxologies, and the Lord's Prayer); reading from the Septuagint; preaching, teaching, and exhorting (perhaps all in the form of a sermon); and singing psalms and hymns (both largely drawn from Jewish sources, but supplemented by Christian works, such as the Magnificat).[59] Gradually, other Christian texts were introduced—Paul's letters, Revelation, and some apocryphal works. Later, the Gospels themselves were read in church services, a project greatly facilitated by the possibility that one or more of the Gospels were originally composed as liturgical works.[60] We know, thanks to Justin Martyr, that the gospels of Matthew and Luke were read in some churches by AD 155. Matthew is said to be laid out in the form of five sermons, deliberately imitating—and in some sense replacing—the Five Books of Moses.

At least in Rome (and probably elsewhere), the liturgy of the church was still dominated by the liturgy of the synagogue as late as AD 100. And, although Diaspora churches used Greek scriptures by necessity, Hebrew continued to be used in

56. Kee et al., *Understanding the New Testament*, 411.

57. Placher, *History of Christian Theology*, 51. "In general, in the first half of the second century, before Justin, sayings of Jesus were still not quoted too frequently . . . They were not yet untouchable 'sacred text' in the strict sense" (Hengel, *Four Gospels*, 27). A similar point is made in White, *From Jesus to Christianity*, 448.

58. Meeks, *Origins of Christian Morality*, 89. Meeks discusses the different ways in which the Jewish Bible affected Christian moral discourse on 89–90.

59. "The synaxis, or service of the word, was a continuation of a synagogue practice that consisted of reading and expositing Scripture, singing psalms, and reciting prayers. The Gospels record that Jesus participated in these services on the Jewish Sabbath (see Matthew 13:53–58; Mark 6:1–6; Luke 4:16–30)" (Peper and DelCogliano, "The Pliny and Trajan Correspondence," 367). See also Metzger and Ehrman, *Text*, 46; Perrin and Duling, *New Testament*, 377, 415; Conzelmann and Lindemann, *Interpreting the New Testament*, 347; and Ehrman, *After the New Testament*, 343, 361. Bultmann says that the public readings were "probably" at first exclusively from the Old Testament, which, he says, is attested in 1 Tim 4:13; *2 Clement* 19:1; Mark 13:14. Evidence that non-Jewish writings were used does not appear until Paul's letters (1 Thess 5:27) and the Book of Revelation (1:3) (*Theology*, I, 122).

60. Barclay, *Introduction*, 25; and Spong, *Liberating the Gospels*, 63–64.

Palestinian churches throughout the early years of Christianity.[61] Furthermore, when the members of the primitive church prayed, they sent their songs and hymns not to Jesus, but to God, quoting Exodus and Psalms (Acts 4:24), as even Paul and Silas did while they were imprisoned in Philippi (16:25), many years after the Crucifixion.[62]

The consequence of this continuation of Jewish practices among Christian Jews is that they were often mistaken for Jews: "As different as Judaism and Christianity might appear to us today, they appeared similar [to each other] to first-century gentiles; indeed they were often indistinguishable."[63] The first and only time in the New Testament that any member of this Jewish sect called himself or herself a Christian was in 1 Peter (4:16). Since the word *christos* is Greek for the Hebrew word *mashiah*, *Christian* means *follower of the Messiah. Jesus Christ* in Palestine therefore meant *Jesus the Messiah*. To gentiles who spoke Greek, however, the word meant nothing, since they had no concept of a messiah. Thus, they used the word *christos* as if it were Jesus' last name. Otherwise, spoken in conjunction with the Greek word *Kyrios* (*Lord*), it could also mean *master*, whose servants would be known as *christianoi*. Yet another variation was the Greek word *chrestos*, meaning *useful* and as such commonly used as a slave name.

Clearly, given such confusions, it took some time to get the proper meaning of the word *Christian* worked out, which may be why it was not in use until the second century, when it was adopted by Arsitides, Justin Martyr, and Ignatius.[64] Called

61. Hengel, *Four Gospels*, 129; and Cornfeld, *Archeology of the Bible*, 333.

62. Bultmann says that "'calling upon the Lord' probably did not consist in liturgical prayers addressed directly to Christ. So far as we can see, such prayers were preponderantly addressed to God alone" (*Theology*, I, 126). Schillebeeckx argues that "in the period before Nicea the liturgy had addressed prayers only to the Father, albeit 'through Christ our Lord'" (*Jesus*, 566). Crossan quotes Aaron Milavec: "[T]he Didache [*The Teaching of the Twelve Apostles*, c. AD 100] provides structures of prayer which parallel, in both ritual and rhetoric, the oldest Jewish prayers" (*Historical Jesus*, 363). Brown notes that the great Jewish prayer, the Shema, enshrined as it is in Mark 12:29–30, along with a line from Leviticus—as are, one might add, many other quotations from the Old Testament—was taught to gentiles for "decades after Christian beginnings" (*Introduction*, 143–44). In general, says Brown, the early Christians "continued to say prayers that they had known previously, and new prayers would have been formulated according to Jewish models." Furthermore, the Jewish Bible was authoritative for both Jews and Christians. "Thus, early Christian teaching would for the most part have been Jewish teaching." As for the references to the so-called Old Testament in the New Testament, Brown says that they represent, as an indication of Christianity's dependency on this text, "the tip of the iceberg, the bulk of which is the unmentioned, presupposed teaching of Israel" (288, 289, and 289 n. 25).

63. Segal, *Paul the Convert*, 210. Segal adds: "Gentile motivations for converting to either Judaism or Christianity would also have been similar. The same people tempted to convert to Judaism would have been tempted to convert to Christianity as well" (210). For a brief overview of Jewish influences on Christianity, see Grant, "Foreword," in Hatch, *Influence of Greek Ideas*, ix-x. Grant says that Tannaite Judaism was the primary influence on "Christian organization, worship, and religious thought." In fact, "[t]he vocabulary of the very earliest Christian theology was borrowed from the Greek-speaking Jews of the Diaspora." Hatch himself says that earliest Christianity was untouched by Greek ideas, which did not begin to supplant Jewish ideas for well over a century (124–25).

64. Bruce, *New Testament History*, 267–68; and White, *From Jesus to Christianity*, 117–22. King Agrippa II uses the term "Christian" in a conversation with Paul in Acts 26:28.

(besides Nazoraeans) the Elect and the Faithful, as well as the Saints, the Brethren, and the Way,[65] but not called anything that would suggest radicalism of any kind or even dissent from Judaism, the Christians were, in some places well into the second century, seen as just another Jewish sect, especially to outsiders.

Even as late as c. 120, the Latin writer Suetonius says that *Jews* were expelled from Rome (in about 49) by the emperor Claudius because they were "indulging in constant riots at the instigation of Chrestos." We also know, from Acts 1:3, that Christian Jews, like Aquila and Priscilla, were exiled at that time along with non-Christian Jews. It is clear, however, that neither Suetonius in 120 nor Claudius seventy years earlier made any distinction between Christians and Jews.[66] A few years after the Crucifixion, in counseling the Jews in Jerusalem to be tolerant of the Christian Jews, Gamaliel referred to the latter simply as "these men" (Acts 5:38). After this incident, whenever Christian Jews were confronted by Romans, they were identified as Jews, albeit as Jewish associates of Jesus, the executed rebel (e.g., Acts 16:20; 18:14–15). In Acts 17:6–7, they are referred to simply as "these."[67]

The emperor Nerva, in c. 98, seems to have identified Christians as a group separate from Jews when he freed them from paying the *fiscus Judaicus*, a tax imposed on Jews as a punishment for their rebellion in 66.[68] Christian texts with a strongly anti-Roman slant, however, like the Book of Revelation, did not help separate Christians from the rebellious Jews, balanced though these works were by some of the later epistles, which were written in part to suggest that, unlike the Jews, Christians were good citizens who were loyal subjects of the emperor and committed to the social, political, and economic status quo.

JAMES VS. PAUL

The most obvious indication of the connection between Judaism and Christianity is the strongly Jewish identity of the head of the Jerusalem church, Jesus' brother James. At least by the time of the Jerusalem Conference, but almost certainly earlier, James had assumed the sole leadership of the mother church.[69] Despite the prominence of

65. Guignebert, *Jewish World*, 2.

66. Bruce, *New Testament History*, 295–300. Lieu says of Suetonius' reference to Jews removed from Rome, "[T]he confusion among scholars as to whether there is [here] a reference to Christ(ians) reflects not only the middle of the first century when Christians were little more than (a) group(s) within Jewish communities, but perhaps equally Suetonius's own confusion" (*Image and Reality*, 162).

67. Stegemann and Stegemann, *Jesus Movement*, 326–27, 349–51.

68. Schiffman, *From Text to Tradition*, 154.

69. On James' early assumption of the leadership of the Jerusalem church, see Akenson, *Saint Saul*, 8; Tabor, *Jesus Dynasty*, 121, 165, 244; and Brandon, *Trial of Jesus*, 50–51. Painter says repeatedly that James was not merely an early leader, but the first (*Just James*, 42, 44, 84, 179, 233, 271–72, 274). Meier discusses the question of whether Jesus actually had brothers (and sisters) in *Marginal Jew*, I, 324–32. Painter insists that there is no question about the brotherly relationship of James and Jesus (*Just James*, 96, 199–200, 214–15, 271). Brown says that "if one had only the N[ew] T[estament] one

Peter in the early chapters of Acts, James is always either mentioned first among the leaders in Jerusalem (Gal 2:9) or referred to as the leader among "the elders" (Acts 21:18; Gal 1:19). At the Jerusalem Conference, James alone delivered the final decision on the issues raised by Peter, Paul, and Barnabas (Acts 15:13). When James' agents told Peter to refrain from dining with gentiles, he complied (Gal 2:11–12). And when Peter was freed from prison by an angel, he asked his friends to "[t]ell this to James and to the brethren" (Acts 12:17). In the *Pseudo-Clementine Recognitions*, the reader is warned, "Wherefore observe the greatest caution, that you believe no teacher, unless he bring from Jerusalem the testimonial of James the Lord's brother" or his successor (4:35). Thus, despite his relative obscurity, compared to Peter and Paul, "James of Jerusalem was one of the most important people in N[ew] T[estament] Christianity." Indeed, says another scholar, "James the brother of Jesus held central stage for some time."[70]

Furthermore, there is every reason to believe that James became the head of the church immediately after the death of Jesus. The claim that he was Jesus' first successor comes from Clement of Alexandria, the early third-century Church Father, and Hegesippus, the second-century Church historian, by way of Eusebius. Clement claims that James was elected by the other leaders of the Jerusalem church (*Ecclesiastical History*, Bk. 2, 1:3–4). Hegesippus is quoted as saying that James "received the government of the church with the apostles" (*Eccl. Hist.*, Bk. 2, 23:4). And, as I suggested earlier, Eusebius himself identifies James several times as the first bishop of Jerusalem (*Eccl. Hist.*, Bk. 2, 1:3; 23:1, 4; Bk. 7, 19:1). One scholar has therefore concluded, "[The] tradition is unanimous that James was the first leader of the Jerusalem church."[71]

In fact, a number of ancient texts state that James was actually chosen for the position of Church leader by Jesus himself. *The Gospel of Thomas* reports that Jesus told his disciples, after they asked him who their leader would be after his death, "No

---

would assume that they [i.e., the brothers of Jesus] were the children of Mary and Joseph, born after Jesus—a view held by Tertullian and by most Protestants today" (*Introduction*, 724 n. 2).

70. The first of the last two quotations is from Brown, *Introduction*, 741; the second is from Painter, *Just James*, 3. Brown adds that James was celebrated as "a hero" in the *Pseudo-Clementines*, a collection of works from the late second century, "which is strongly attached to Judaism and is antiPauline" (*Introduction*, 727 n. 6). "It was [James] who took the initiative in demanding that Gentile Christians respect certain aspects of Jewish regulations" (Kee et al., *Understanding the New Testament*, 241).

71. Painter, "Who Was James?" 35. Painter makes the same claim repeatedly on 24, 31–32, 56. Chilton, in the epilogue of the same volume, sums up the scholarly "consensus" of the contributors to his and Neusner's collection of essays in this way: "James the Just was, in the time between Jesus' resurrection and his own death, the most prominent and widely respected leader in Christendom" (185). Chilton's argument is more fully presented in his own essay in the same book, "James in Relation to Peter, Paul, and the Remembrance of Jesus," 157–58. Akenson says that because Acts of the Apostles demonstrates that his emissaries, such as Peter and Barnabas, were always obedient to him, James must be considered "the most powerful figure" in the Church (*Saint Saul*, 160). Indeed, Peter was little more than James' "errand boy" (169). Brown says, "[T]here is no evidence that Peter was ever local administrator of the Jerusalem church . . . Probably as soon as there was an administrative role created for the Hebrew element of the Jerusalem church, James held it, not illogically because he was related to Jesus by family ties" (*Introduction*, 302).

matter where you go you are to go to James the Just, for whose sake heaven and earth came into being." According to the *Ascents of James*, "The church in Jerusalem . . . [was] ruled by James who was made Overseer over it by our Lord." In the *Second Apocalypse of James*, found at Nag Hammadi, the author says that Jesus told his brother James, "Behold I shall reveal to you everything[,] my beloved."[72] Eusebius states that James was made first bishop of Jerusalem by "our Savior" (*Eccl. Hist.*, Bk. 7, 19:1).

James' significance in this context is that, like many Christians of the mid-first century, he was known as "a strictly observant Jew."[73] This means that he was committed to "the continuing law observance of Jewish believers."[74] According to Christian sources (e.g., Galatians 2 and Acts 15), as well as Josephus, the Jewish historian of the first century, James was in fact "someone with a reputation [i.e., among the Jews] for deep piety and righteous character," which is why he was known even by Jews as James the Just or James the Righteous. Eusebius refers to James' "elevated virtue and piety." Hegesippus says that James "was consecrated [a Nazirite] from his mother's womb." And Josephus calls him preeminently just (*Eccl. Hist.*, Bk. 2, 23:2, 4, 20). Eusebius adds that James was "so admirable" and "so celebrated . . . for his justice" that "even the wiser part of the Jews" believed that the High Priest's execution of James caused the "siege of Jerusalem" in the Revolt of 66 (*Eccl. Hist.*, Bk. 2, 23:19). That is, the city was destroyed because God Himself was angry about the murder of James.

72. The relevant passages are quoted in Tabor, *Jesus Dynasty*, 255–58. Tabor comments, "What is impressive about these sources is the way in which they speak with a single voice, yet come from various authors and time periods" (258). Painter says, referring to two passages in Eusebius' *Ecclesiastical History* (Bk. 3, 5:2; Bk. 4, 22:4), "The first quotation from Clement names James as bishop of Jerusalem in a context which implies that he was the first to hold that office but which does not name him as the first. There is also a quotation from Hegesippus that names Simeon, the successor of James, as the second bishop, thus implying that James was the first" (*Just James*, 112). Painter also quotes a passage from the Gospel of the Hebrews (quoted by Jerome), in which Jesus is said to have appeared first after his resurrection to James (184). Painter identifies this passage as coming from "fragment 7," although Ehrman identifies it as "fragment 5" in *Lost Scriptures*, 16. This passage is also the source of the claim that James was at the Last Supper. Acts puts James at the Pentecost, among the "brothers" of Jesus, who were with Mary in Jerusalem when the other disciples returned from Mt. Olivet, where they witnessed Jesus' Ascension (Acts 1:12–14).

73. Bruce, *New Testament History*, 261. Akenson says that James was, in fact, an "ascetic," whose devotion to Judaism was "rigorous." (*Saint Saul*, 161). According to Klingaman, James was "a rigidly orthodox Jew" who "adamantly insisted that membership in the Way required strict adherence to the Law—which, for reasons of ritual cleanliness, precluded close association with Gentiles—and particularly to the ancient ritual of circumcision" (*First Century*, 56). Brown says that James was a "faithful adherent of the Jewish cult" (*Introduction*, 699) and "a conservative Hebrew Christian" (307). Hill rejects the idea that James, though Law-abiding, was either "rigidly orthodox," as Hegesippus insisted, or even conservative, as most scholars believe: "That he was more conservative than Paul seems assured; that this made him a conservative does not." Rather, he had "a moderating influence" on the Jerusalem church (*Hellenists and Hebrews*, 183–85).

74. Painter, "Who Was James?" 54. In his own book on James, Painter says, "The historical James 'the Just' epitomized conservative Jewish Christian values" (*Just James*, 173). Brown calls James "a conservative Jewish Christian very loyal to observing the law" (*Introduction*, 727). Witherington calls James "a Torah-true Jew." He insisted on "the inclusion of Jews [in the Church] who would remain observant of the Mosaic Law" (*What Have They Done?* 204; see also 176–77).

What Hegesippus claimed is that James was probably a Jewish ascetic, as his request in Acts 21 that Paul either participate in or sponsor a Naziritic ritual suggests.[75] Hegesippus added that, as a Nazirite himself—in addition to refraining from wine and meat and neither shaving nor bathing—James was uniquely allowed to enter the Temple sanctuary, habitually worshiped at the Temple alone, and prayed on his knees for "the forgiveness of the people" (*Eccl. Hist.*, Bk. 2, 23:5, 6). At his death at the hands of a High Priest, Josephus says, those members of the Jewish community who "seemed most accurate in observing the [Jewish] law were greatly offended," appealed to the king, and successfully persuaded him to dismiss the murderer of James (*Eccl. Hist.*, Bk. 2, 23:22–24).

It should be emphasized that, although Luke seems to imply that "the circumcision party" was composed of Christian Pharisees (Acts 15:5), as distinguished from the supposedly centrist party of James, there is no reason to assume that Paul was spied upon, challenged, and ordered to come to Jerusalem by anyone except James himself. In other words, Paul's enemies were not just a small group of conservative Jewish Christians within the Jerusalem church, but the entire church, led by James.[76] Thus, unlike Paul—who was regularly beaten and run out of one city after another—James reigned as bishop (or, at least, head of the Jerusalem church) from AD 30 (or shortly thereafter) until his death in AD 62, and, under his leadership, "[t]he Jerusalem Christians were . . . zealous to demonstrate their loyalty to Judaism."[77] As a result, during those years, "the church *throughout all Judea and Galilee and Samaria* had peace and was built up; and walking in the fear of the Lord and in the comfort of the Holy Spirit it was multiplied" (Acts 9:31; my emphasis). James was simply a Christian Jew "who believed that Jesus was the Messiah but also followed the full Jewish Law." And, unlike Stephen and James the son of Zebedee, "James was not attacked, persecuted, or

---

75. Shanks and Witherington, *Brother of Jesus*, 113–14; and Chilton, "James in Relation to Peter, Paul, and the Remembrance of Jesus," 146–47.

76. Paul "was isolated from every other Christian Jew by his own account in Galatians 2:11–13: James, Peter, Barnabas, and 'the rest of the Jews'" (Chilton and Neusner, *Judaism*, 100). The point is that, while Paul questioned the relevance of certain aspects of the Jewish Law, as well as the salvific efficacy of the Law in general, "it is extremely doubtful," as Bauckham says, "whether anyone in the Jerusalem church would have questioned that Jewish Christians should continue to observe the whole law" ("James and Jesus," 105–6). To the contrary, van Leeuwen argues that both "James and Peter continued to waver in their attitude over various matters, for fear of the circumcision party," who were "extremist Judaizers" (*Christianity in World History*, 222).

77. Kee et al., *Understanding the New Testament*, 241. Weiss says that the Jerusalem church "had enough to do to maintain itself in the good will of public opinion through adherence to the Law . . . It was apparent, therefore, that it was actually held in good esteem among influential classes of people and that the ruling party in the Sanhedrin could find nothing against it" (*Earliest Christianity*, II, 707).

executed until the early 60s"[78]—and even then not by Jews in general, but by the High Priest, acting alone, possibly for either personal or political reasons.[79]

On the basis of the elders' statements in Acts 21, it is evident that the Jerusalem church under James required all Jewish Christians to obey the Jewish Law, including circumcision.[80] It also seems fair to say that—at least, until the Jerusalem Conference—James agreed with other members of the Jerusalem church, including the Pharisees, that gentile initiates into "the Way" were similarly required to follow all of the other requirements specified in the Pentateuch. Otherwise, there was no reason to summon Paul and Barnabas, who were converting gentiles without demanding that they undergo circumcision, to appear before the elders of the Jerusalem church.

However, James and his church got along with the Jewish community in Jerusalem not because they were willing to compromise their principles, but because, except for their faith in Jesus as the Messiah, their religion was virtually indistinguishable from the religion of other Jerusalem Jews. As one scholar says, James "was eager to maintain good relations with the Jewish leaders, especially since his own convictions and practices were strongly legalistic."[81] Even James' compromise at the conference still required the pagans who had been visited by the Holy Spirit to obey the Jewish laws prohibiting Jews from eating "pollutions of idols" (animals killed in pagan sacrifices), "fornication," eating "things strangled" (not killed according to Kashrut, the Jewish food laws), and drinking blood (Acts 15:20). James explained this decision not by suggesting that Jewish laws be suspended, but by referring to laws in Leviticus

78. Crossan, *Birth of Christianity*, 467. As Enslin says: "Although the authorities are pictured as being suspicious of these Galileans and to have attempted from time to time to restrain them—or at least their leaders—the community as a whole regarded them with no unfriendly air. They were pious Jews and showed no trace of breaking away from the Judaism that had mothered them" (*Christian Beginnings*, 177). See also Horsley and Silberman, *Message*, 193–94.

79. According to Kee et al., "Probably Annas [Ananus] wanted to destroy James out of resentment for his popularity with the people, who seem to have admired James for his piety. Since James was famous for his fidelity to the Law, the charge brought against him by Annas was almost certainly false" (*Understanding the New Testament*, 241). Painter says that the priests who joined the Jerusalem church in Acts 6:7 were not the wealthy members of the Jewish aristocracy, but the poorer priests, who "harbored dissidents and even gave support to revolutionary groups." Painter speculates that James was associated with the latter priests and might have shared (or was alleged to have shared) their "anti-Roman sentiments," thus incurring the wrath of the High Priest Ananus (*Just James*, 250, 288). See also Maccoby, *Mythmaker*, 138, 218 n. 12 and 13. Hill examines the accounts of James' death thoroughly in *Hellenists and Hebrews*, 184–191. He speculates that James' failure "to repudiate the criminal Paul" might have led to to his execution by the High Priest (181).

80. Meier says that James "was associated with Christian Jews of a conservative bent who were intent on preserving the observance of circumcision and food laws, at least by Christian *Jews*" (*Marginal Jew*, I, 277; Meier's emphasis). Meier cites Sean Freyne, *Galilee from Alexander the Great to Hadrian*, 259–343, on the subject of "the conservative, non-Pharisaic Judaism of Galilean peasants" (308 n. 138). Witherington asks, "Should we take seriously the suggestion that there were many observant Jews among the early Jewish Christians in Jerusalem?" "Yes," he answers: "I think we must, and it must be noted that they apparently were quite content with having James as their leader, which speaks volumes about James" (*What Have They Done?* 193; see also 190–91, 200).

81. Kee et al., *Understanding the New Testament*, 240–41.

17–18. After all, "[t]he prophets foretold that the Gentiles would come, and the Law of Moses allowed uncircumcised Gentiles to live among the people of God provided they abstained from certain listed pollutions."[82] The point here is not that James wished to change Judaism in order to attract and accommodate gentiles. He required gentiles to separate themselves from paganism by following the so-called Noahide laws in exactly the same way that gentiles did who became God-fearers—that is, former pagans who accepted the Jewish God and were affiliated with the synagogue, but not formally converted to Judaism.[83] Quoting a passage from Amos, which states that gentiles will have an opportunity at the end time to become Jews, James was simply following Jewish precedent, except that, unlike pagan God-fearers, who did not become full-fledged Jews until they underwent full conversion, these pagan God-fearers evidently became full-fledged Christians.[84] In fulfillment of Amos' prophecy, God had "visited the Gentiles" and had thereby taken "out of them a people for his name" (Acts 15:14).

This compromise represents the outer limit of James' willingness to depart even a little from Jewish Law. His insistence that Peter not dine with gentile converts, his reverence for the Temple, and his demand that gentile converts obey the Noahide laws—all of which policies implicitly or explicitly reflect the traditional Jewish concern for purity—suggest that he was conservative, not necessarily compared to other Jewish Christians in the Jerusalem church, but compared to Paul. In fact, whether or not he was himself a Nazirite,[85] his request that Paul prove his loyalty to Judaism by paying for the participation of four other Christian Jews in a Nazirite ritual suggests that he was thoroughly orthodox in his Judaism. James and the elders justified their request by telling Paul that the Law-abiding Jews who made up the majority of the Jerusalem church had heard that he was teaching Jews "not to circumcise their children or observe the customs." Paul's support of the Nazirite vow would thus prove that he

82. Brown, *Introduction*, 307. James' decree was thus "in keeping with the general practice of Jewish groups throughout the Roman world." That is, God-fearers were not required to be circumcised and abide by all of the laws in the Torah but were expected to follow the so-called Laws of Noah, which are similar to "a list of ethical requirements for non-Jews" in the second-century BC Book of Jubilees, 7:20–33. These are "the universal ethical requirements that the Torah prescribed for all humankind" (Tabor, *Jesus Dynasty*, 254, 267, 341 n. 4).

83. On this point, see Chilton and Neusner, *Judaism*, 104–8. These authors argue that James quotes Amos to justify his actions because he regards Jewish scripture as still binding on his actions. That is, James accepted gentiles because they are welcomed by Amos (9:11–12). And he could just as relevantly have quoted Micah 4:2; Jeremiah 12:14–17; Zechariah 14:16–19; and Isaiah 42:6–7; 45:22–23; 49:6.

84. Parkes says, "The Apostles took the basis on which the Jews accepted 'the proselytes of the gate' [i.e., God-fearers], the 'Noachian commandments', and made them the basis of Gentile participation in the Church." However, Parkes adds "that the observance of these regulations admitted the Gentiles to full membership and not only to partial adherence to the fellowship" (*Conflict*, 50).

85. Chilton argues—based on passages from Hegesippus, Josephus, and Acts—that James was indeed a Nazirite. He explains Hegesippus' seemingly "exaggerated" claim that James was permitted to enter the Holy of Holies in the Temple, otherwise closed to all but the High Priest, by citing a passage in Numbers 6:18–20 showing that "Nazirites were to be presented in the vicinity of the sanctuary" ("James in Relation to Peter, Paul, and the Remembrance of Jesus," 146–47).

was obedient to the Jewish Law (Acts 21:20–25)—a set of laws, by the way, that were obviously inviolable to James and the members of the Jerusalem congregation.

In the long run, however, James' version of "the Way" disappeared: "Jewish Christianity simply died out."[86] The problem was that, after the Revolt of 66 (and especially after the Revolt of 132), it became more difficult to be Jewish in the Roman empire. That is partially why the Gospels are totally silent about James and why Luke is obviously unwilling to acknowledge James' stature in Acts of the Apostles. Thus, as one scholar puts it, "after the catastrophe of AD 70, the Mother Church of Christianity, the original centre of faith and authority, completely disappeared." After the second war, Jews were exiled from Jerusalem, which Emperor Hadrian turned into a Roman city, renamed it Aelia Capitolina, and built a temple dedicated to Jupiter on the ruins of the Jewish Temple.[87]

Of course, the change in the Romans' attitude toward the Jews resulted in a radical change in the status of Christians vis-a-vis Judaism, since, before these revolts, many Christians felt they were better off as Jews because they were able to claim to be part of an old and therefore respectable religion and less likely to be persecuted by the Romans.[88] After the revolts, Christians were vulnerable to Roman contempt as either Jews or non-Jews: "As soon as Christianity became recognizably distinct from Judaism, the Christians' refusal to acknowledge state, civic, and family cults would have made them appear a gang of undesirables, deserving punishment because they utterly rejected an essential element in the 'Roman way of life' and thereby imperilled the very foundations of the community and showed themselves to be enemies of the state."[89]

86. Kee et al., *Understanding the New Testament*, 247. Kee adds that "the Jerusalem wing of Christianity had already lapsed into such complete obscurity by the end of the second century that there were no precise recollections of what had happened to it after the city of Jerusalem fell to the Romans" (245). "It has long been recognized," says Mack, "that the Gospel of Matthew is a document of Jewish Christianity, a form of the Jewish legacy that may have been more prevalent during the first centuries than the histories of early Christianity recorded in the New Testament let us see." Mack continues, "Since this form of the Jesus movement did not survive the emergence of 'orthodox' Christianity in the fourth century C.E., there is a touch of irony in the fact that Matthew's gospel became the preferred 'gospel of the church,' and that it was given the privilege of first place in the canon of the New Testament" (*Who Wrote?* 162).

87. Brandon, *Trial of Jesus*, 59. Brandon discusses this issue on the preceding pages, 48–59.

88. Ehrman says, "By embracing 'true' Judaism, that is, by taking over the Jewish Scriptures and claiming them as their own, Christians overcame the single biggest objection that pagans had with regard to the appearance of this 'new' religion" (*Lost Christianities*, 112; see also 144–45). As de Ste. Croix explains, "The Jews were equally 'atheists'; but they could be excused, as the Christians could not [at least, outside the umbrella of Judaism], because they were practising, as all men should, their ancestral religion, admittedly older than Rome itself" ("Christianity's Encounter with the Roman Imperial Government," 347).

89. Parkes comments: "As long as Christianity was a Jewish sect it enjoyed the protection extended to Judaism . . . When they were recognized as separate, the Christians were exposed to the possibility of suppression" (*Conflict*, 85). See also Enslin, *Christian Beginnings*, 183–84. As Segal explains, however, after the Revolt of 66, "Jews and Judaism went through a period of disfavor." Domitian disallowed

In addition, changes occurred in Christian theology that made it difficult to see James as the head of the Church. At first, most prominently in Paul's letters, for example, James was simply called "the brother of the Lord." In that capacity, it was easy to believe that Jesus had passed the leadership of the Church to him. However, "in the second century, the view developed that Mary had not only conceived as a virgin but had remained a virgin," and "the status of James and the brothers was significantly downgraded."[90] Thus, Luke, with his account of Jesus' virgin birth, never identifies James as his brother. And James is completely absent from the later epistles, except, of course, the letter he allegedly wrote himself. Furthermore, Luke minimized James' importance because he was uncomfortable with James' "hard–line position on the place of circumcision and the keeping of the law, a position that Luke himself did not wish to maintain."[91]

Although James had clearly led the Jerusalem church in the middle of the first century—for as long as three decades— neither the Church nor students of its history have paid much attention to him since. Peter is honored as Jesus' most prominent disciple, possessor of the keys to the kingdom and prototype of the pope; Paul, author of a major portion of the New Testament, has come down to us as the principal interpreter of Jesus' message and the virtual founder of the Christian—as opposed to the Christian-Jewish—Church; and even John the son of Zebedee is remembered as Jesus' "beloved disciple." The irony is that Jesus and James (that is, insofar as the Letter of James reflects the latter's theology) were closer in doctrine than Jesus and Paul, whom, of course, Jesus never met.[92] The letter thus brings Jesus and Judaism together,

conversion to Judaism, and Hadrian made circumcision illegal. Under these circumstances (and in some places more than others), it was more attractive to become a Christian than to become a Jew. Choosing the latter option was always surgically dangerous and often "politically inexpedient" (*Paul the Convert*, 105–6). According to Wright, Christians nevertheless claimed to be the real Jews in order to retain the protection of that identity under Roman law: "Christians, in pressing their claim for exemption, had to undermine the Jewish claim for legitimacy. They argued that Jews had forsaken their own god by killing his son" (*Evolution of God*, 294).

90. Painter, *Just James*, 61. Painter cites the *Protoevangelium of James* as an early source for the idea that James was Joseph's son by a prior marriage, a view that was perpetuated by Jerome and Augustine. However, Painter says, "[m]odern Western scholarship has tended to regard this approach to the 'brothers' of Jesus as indefensible legend" (2).

91. *Just James*, 56. Painter later says, by way of summary, that James was marginalized because of "Pauline opposition to the authority of James, the disappearance of the Jerusalem church, and the emergence of Peter as a more ecumenical transformation of the James tradition" (178). See also 181, 269–76.

92. Wilson, *Jesus*, 249. For a similar view of James, Jesus, and Paul, see Conzelmann and Lindemann, *Interpreting the New Testament*, 267–71; Enslin, *Christian Beginnings*, 182; Tabor, *Jesus Dynasty*, 272–77, 282–84); Grant, *Historical Introduction*, 221; Painter, *Just James*, 98; Levine, *Misunderstood Jew*, 74–78; and Brown, *Introduction*, 739. Brown states, however, that F. C. Baur, in arguing that the Jewish-Christian church under James was the "antithesis" of the gentile-Christian church under Paul, "goes considerably beyond the N[ew] T[estament] evidence" (727 n. 6). Hill similarly disagrees with Baur's thesis in *Hellenists and Hebrews*, 5–17. Meier suggests that James had two reasons for opposing Paul: (1) Paul was an ex-Pharisee, and (2) he was "a literate tradesman" rather than "an illiterate peasant" (*Marginal Jew*, I, 308–9 n. 139).

once again, since it has been described as both a Jewish document and a restatement of Jesus' Sermon on the Mount.[93]

Furthermore, lest it be thought that, despite heading the Church for many years, James was not recognized by early Christians as, in some sense, Jesus' successor, it should be remembered that many contemporary scholars regard him not only as Jesus' chosen replacement, but the first in what has come to be seen as a royal dynasty in Christendom: "Whatever may be the situation with regard to the bishops outside Jerusalem, there is sufficient testimony for a monarchical episcopate in Jerusalem, on the 'throne' of James, which was regarded by the early Jewish Christian Church as *the continuation and the provisional equivalent of the throne of David, which was to be occupied by Jesus.*"[94] As we have seen, Hegesippus calls James a bishop (as do two other Christian historians, Eusebius and Epiphanius, as well as Clement of Alexandria), and he was succeeded, for a time, only by family members (his half-brothers or cousins Simeon (Simon) and Justus (Judas).[95]

The remnants of the original Christian-Jewish church eventually moved east and had little impact on the subsequent development of Christianity. Among them were

93. Brown compares the Epistle of James and the Sermon on the Mount to establish James' connection to Jesus (*Introduction*, 734–36). Furthermore, he says, the letter "echoes in many ways traditional Jewish belief and piety," specifically, the Old Testament Wisdom books. (728). See also Kee et al., *Understanding the New Testament*, 384; and Conzelmann and Lindemann, *Interpreting the New Testament*, 267. The editors of *Oxford Annotated Bible* contend that James' letter "is a remarkably pure specimen of the ethical teaching found in the Sermon on the Mount" (1416). Tabor compares the letter and Jesus' sayings in the Q source in *Jesus Dynasty*, 274–76.

94. Weiss, *Earliest Christianity*, II, 721–22; my emphasis. Weiss later refers to "the nearly dynastic reverence which was paid the family of Jesus after the death of James" (732). Tabor argues that Jesus, as the inheritor of the throne of David, began a dynasty that continued "for over a century after his death" (*Jesus Dynasty*, 247). On the succession of Jesus' half-brother (or cousin) Simon (or Simeon), see 289–92. On what he calls the Christian caliphate of Jesus, see Danielou, "Christianity as a Jewish Sect," 276. Danielou says: "The undisputed head of the 'Hebrew' Christian Community [which, after the departure of the Hellenists, was the *only* Christian community in Jerusalem] was James, the brother of the Lord. Side by side with the Apostles, James was the most important personality in the Christian community at Jerusalem." As evidence of James' role as "the founder of Judaeo-Christianity," Danielou cites Eusebius, the *Gospel of the Hebrews*, Clement of Alexandria, the *Clementine Recognitions*, the *Second Apocalypse of James*, and the Edessan *Gospel of Thomas*. Danielou concludes: "[T]hese authorities all agree in making James the outstanding figure in the Judaeo-Christian Church. Moreover, James was a typical Judaeo-Christian in his assiduous attendance at the Temple and in his taking of the vow of a Nazerite [*sic*]" (276).

95. Eusebius says that Simeon (whom he identifies as Jesus' "cousin german") and Justus succeeded James as the second and third bishops of Jerusalem, respectively (*Ecclesiastical History*, Bk. 3, 11:1; 35:1). Simon and Judas are given by Matthew as the names of Jesus' brothers (Matt 13:55; Mark 6:3). Brandon also discusses the succession of Jesus' blood-relatives as evidence of a "dynastic principle" at work in the Jerusalem church (*Trial of Jesus*, 51–52). Sanders adds: "According to I Cor 9:5, Jesus' brothers (plural) were missionaries. Later Christian tradition named Judas ... as a leading member of the Christian movement. It attributed to him the epistle of Jude in the New Testament." Hegesippus, according to Eusebius (*Eccles. Hist.*, Bk. 3, 32:5–6), says that Judas' grandsons were investigated by Domitian in the first century (*Historical Figure of Jesus*, 303 n. 4). See also Brown, *Introduction*, 742.

the Ebionites, whose name derived from the Hebrew word *evyonim*, or "the poor."[96] They "may have been the survivors of Jewish Christianity" and, at least to a number of scholars, appear "to have been directly related to the Jerusalem community."[97] The Ebionites were a diverse Christian-Jewish sect that believed in Jesus as the Messiah, but also followed Jewish laws. They embraced a view of salvation based on good works, used a Hebrew version of the Gospel of Matthew, and rejected Paul as an apostate.[98] As Irenaeus describes them, in *Against Heresies* (c. 177), "As to the prophetic writings, they endeavor to expound them in a somewhat peculiar manner; they practice circumcision, persevere in the observance of customs that are enjoined by the law, and in their Judaic manner of life they also venerate Jerusalem as if it were the house of God" (I, 26:2).

The Ebionites' most important departure from Christian orthodoxy, however, might not have been their retention of Jewish practices, but their "low" christology: "According to this, the begetting of Jesus to be the Son of God took place not at the birth but at the baptism, and it is thus connected, not with a wonderful birth, but with election." That is, Jesus was a man, raised to divine status by God because of his righteousness: "They considered him a plain and common man and justified only by his advances in virtue."[99] Although the Ebionites traced their origin to the primitive

96. "It is very likely that the name 'Ebionites' . . . was but one way of referring to a broad stream of Jewish Christianity that resisted the general abandonment of Jewish observance and tradition by other, typically gentile, forms of the Christian movement" (White, *From Jesus to Christianity*, 406). The relationship between this group and the Nazarenes, who also survived under that name for many decades, if not centuries, is uncertain. Both, while remaining Christian, are associated with Jewish practices. The Nazarenes either took the name of the original followers of Jesus or never gave it up (Acts 24:5). Weiss locates the Ebionites in the Transjordan and the Nazarenes in Coele-Syrian Beroea (*Earliest Christianity*, II, 736). Fitzmyer discusses the Ebionites in *Essays*, 437–41, 447–53; and the relationship between this group and the Nazarenes in *Essays*, 441–47.

97. Kee et al., *Understanding the New Testament*, 246. Kee says that the name "the poor" may be another link with the Jerusalem church, which might have used the word as a self-designation (Gal 2:10; Rom 15:26; Luke 6:20: "Blessed are you poor.") (156). Weiss also connects these Jewish-Christian groups to the early church (*Earliest Christianity*, II, 730–34). Painter says, "A connection between early Jerusalem Christianity (the Hebrews) and the later Ebionites is probable" (*Just James*, 229). See also Strecker, "On the Problem of Jewish Christianity," 272–73. Bauckham rejects the tie between the Ebionites and the Jerusalem church because their christologies did not match: "We may now assert quite confidently that the self-consciously low Christology of the later Jewish Christian sect known as the Ebionites does not, as has sometimes been asserted, go back to James and his circle in the early Jerusalem church" ("James and Jesus," 135). On this point, see also Witherington, *What Have They Done?* 224–25.

98. Tabor, *Jesus Dynasty*, 303.

99. As reported by both Eusebius and Hippolytus, according to Weiss, *Earliest Christianity*, II, 734. The passage quoted is in *Ecclesiastical History*, Bk. 3, 27:2. Caird says that "in the original Judean tradition," most notably in the Gospels of Mark and John, "Joseph was regarded as the father of Jesus" (*Gospel of St. Luke*, 31). In the Gospel of Luke, according to Caird, aside from 1:34 and 3:23, "the story reads like an account of a normal human birth, miraculous only because through it God has chosen to act for the deliverance of his people. Joseph is consistently referred to as Jesus' father, and it is through Joseph that Jesus is descended from David." Caird adds that both Luke and Matthew make use of the prophecy of Isaiah 7:14, but, as Jews understood it, the prediction of Immanuel's birth claimed only

Church and thereby to Jesus himself, they were increasingly ostracized by both Jews and Christians.[100] In the words of one scholar, "The very practices that preserved the Jewish identity of Jesus' earliest followers, those practices that Peter and James had cherished, would become eccentricities; eventually they would become heresies." In c. 400, Augustine wrote to Jerome, of groups like the Ebionites, "Desiring to be both Jews and Christians, they are neither one nor the other."[101]

Whether the Ebionites were actually an offshoot of the original Jerusalem church is impossible to determine.[102] There are so many parallels, however, among the many Jewish-Christian communities in the early days of the Church that it is impossible to deny not only the prominence of this form of Christianity even in the second century, but also its persistence, despite the growth in the number of gentile Christians and the increasing influence of Hellenism on Christianity, both theologically and christologically: James' church in Jerusalem, the Ebionites and the Nazoreans, the earliest so-called Q community (from which the Q source of Matthew and Luke came),[103] the

---

that his mother would be a young woman, not a virgin—*almah* (in Hebrew), not *parthenos* (in Greek). "As long as the story circulated in its original Judean setting, the Immanuel prophecy could have carried only its Hebrew connotation. But when the gospel was disseminated throughout the Greek world, and the Immanuel prophecy was cited in its Greek form as the authoritative word of scripture about the birth of Jesus, it would naturally give the impression that Jesus was born of a virgin" (30–31).

100. Consequently, Tabor adds, the role of John the Baptist was minimized, James was almost entirely forgotten, Christianity severed its ties to Judaism, and Paul's followers created a new religion: "The message that Jesus preached was transformed into the person of Jesus as the message—the proclamation that Christ had come and died for the world. By the middle of the 3rd century AD a new religion had been born, shaped by these theological perceptions, and completely separated from all forms of Judaism." What disappeared, Tabor continues, "was the original story, which was Jesus' own story, what he in fact was in his own time and place, as a 1st century Jewish Messiah who [laid] claim to the throne of David and inaugurated a Messianic Movement with the potential to change the world" (*Jesus Dynasty*, 306–7). Flusser says that Jewish Christianity began to be marginalized by the second century (*Sage from Galilee*, 49). According to Kee et al., "Jewish Christianity of the Torah-abiding type became isolated from the mainstream of the developing church" (*Understanding the New Testament*, 163).

101. Levine, *Misunderstood Jew*, 84. Maccoby says that, unlike gentile Christians, who were regarded as too disconnected from Judaism to be considered unacceptable, the Ebionites were declared heretical by the Rabbis as early as 135. "The pressure to join one or [the] other of these two religions was enormous, and by the fourth century the Ebionites had ceased to be a discernible separate community." Thus, this group has been ignored by modern scholars, despite its roots in primitive Jewish Christianity (*Mythmaker*, 179–80).

102. "Possibly," says Ehrman, "the name goes back to the earliest days of the community. It may be that members of this group gave away their possessions and committed themselves to lives of voluntary poverty for the sake of others, like the earliest communities mentioned in Acts" (*Lost Christianities*, 100). They "continued to reverence Jerusalem," believed they were "authorized" by James and Peter, thought of Jesus as a man raised to divinity by God at his baptism, and treated Paul as their arch enemy (100–101).

103. As Bainton explains, "The common view, though sometimes challenged, is that Mark was a source for Matthew and for Luke and that in addition they had another source called Q from which is derived that which they have in common" (*Early Christianity*, 14). The speculation that such a source exists is based on the fact that the Gospels of Matthew and Luke have common material—all of them sayings of Jesus—whose similarity cannot be explained otherwise. Thus, there appears to be

Jewish Christians wrote *The Didache*, the so-called Judaizers everywhere (most notably in some of the churches of Paul, Ignatius, and John Chrysostom), "the twelve tribes in the Dispersion" who were the intended recipients of the Epistle of James,[104] and (later) those who produced some of the documents collected in the *Pseudo-Clementines*.[105]

In this context, there can be little doubt that some of the earliest Christian communities were *Jewish* Christian and embraced the Jewish Law as firmly as they embraced the messiahship of Jesus. And, most important, the Jerusalem church, guided by Jesus' first disciples and headed by his brother James, was clearly not merely Jewish, but *conservatively* Jewish, and represented what can only be called the true heritage of the church's founder.[106] It was, after all, in every respect, the creation of Jesus himself, and *no other church could make that claim*. Thus, Hegesippus himself, based on his familiarity with some of these Jewish-Christian congregations, regarded the Jerusalem church as what one scholar calls "the authentic prototype of orthodoxy."[107]

---

little debate over whether the Q source existed. The primary question pertains to its exact contents. The secondary question is whether it was written down or passed on orally. The tertiary question is whether Luke's or Matthew's use of Q is closer to the original. The most orderly and succinct examination of these issues is by Stein in *Synoptic Problem*, 89–112. Stein rejects the possibility that Luke borrowed from Matthew or vice versa. And he calls attention to Luke's claim that "many [including "eyewitnesses"] have undertaken to compile a narrative of the things which have been accomplished among us" and that he has "followed all [such] things closely" (Luke 1:1–4). Stein's only caveat—and this distinguishes him from some other students of the Q material—is that the original document cannot be satisfactorily reconstructed and that, therefore, we cannot determine what the Q community (i.e., the source of the document) was like (112).

104. According to Mack, "the Letter of James represents a Jewish-Christian movement that must have been strong and vigorous for at least the first three centuries" (*Who Wrote?* 214).

105 Horsley and Silberman comment: "Just as the traditions of the Q Community remembered Jesus' sayings about the difficulty of rich people entering the Kingdom of God and the virtue of selling all one's possessions as the key to separating from the injustices of the Roman economy and returning to the ideals of the clan-based Israelite villages, so too can the shared treasury of the Jerusalem community be seen as a conscious attempt to create a 'village' in the streets and slums of the city" (*Message*, 103). On the connection between the Epistle of James and the Q community, see Kloppenborg, *Q*, 111–21. Says Kloppenborg, "While Matthew and Luke give us the closest to verbatim copies of Q, it is the letter of James which perhaps gives us the best idea of how Q was intended to be used" (120). On the ties between James' letter, the Q gospel, and *The Didache*, see Painter, *Just James*, 260–65. On parallels among James, Qumran, and Rabbinical Judaism, see Evans, "Comparing Judaisms: Qumranic, Rabbinic, and Jacobean Judaisms Compared," 161–83. Evans concludes: "Although not wishing to minimize the differences of the Judaisms of Qumran, the Rabbis, and the Jacobean community, one cannot help but be struck by the extent of systemic agreement. Piety, practice, authority, heritage, sense of the rule of God—in all of these things we find significant overlap" (182).

106. "Jerusalem tended more and more as the years went by to become the stronghold of the distinctly conservative and Jewish wing of Christianity" (Enslin, *Christian Beginnings*, 179).

107. Strecker attributes these sentiments to Hegesippus in "On the Problem of Jewish Christianity," 276. Bauer had quoted Hegesippus as finding in Palestine churches in which "'the basis of faith' had been 'the Law and the Prophets and the Lord'" (196–97). Strecker says, "Jewish Christianity, according to the witness of the New Testament, stands at the beginning of the development of church history, so that it is not the gentile Christian 'ecclesiastical doctrine' that represents what is primary, but rather a Jewish Christian theology" (241). Thus, Strecker adds in a footnote (n. 1), quoting H. Koch, "the heresiarchs [by which is meant Pauline Christians] accused the 'Ebionites' of apostasy or of relapse into

What appears in Acts of the Apostles to be the orthodox, mainstream Church, represented by the Hellenized view of salvation and redemption enunciated by Paul, would have been regarded as a strange and heterodox interpretation of Christianity, at least to James and Peter and Barnabas.[108] Disparaged among many Jewish Christians, "with their bitter hatred of [him] and the resulting blunt rejection of everything influenced by him,"[109] Paul was no doubt in the minority, at least in Palestine, particularly given his penchant for crude insults, the tendency of some of his followers to embrace Gnosticism, his apparent hypersensitivity, his urban background, and his exposure to Hellenistic culture. Fighting what he considered to be backsliding in his churches into Jewish literalism and legalism, when, in fact, many of the early churches had no objection to expressions of Judaism, with which they failed to find the same faults, Paul may be said to have been "the only heresiarch known to the apostolic age—the only one who was so considered in that period, at least from one particular [i.e., Jewish-Christian] perspective."[110]

Always self-conscious about his belatedness as an apostle in the Christian Church, Paul begins his Letter to the Galatians with the claim that his apostleship is "not from men nor through men, but through Jesus Christ and God the Father" (Gal 1:1). Since he makes this point repeatedly throughout his letters, it seems reasonable to assume that he was deeply disturbed about his position in the Church hierarchy. The reasons are obvious.[111] First, he was not among either the twelve disciples chosen by Jesus or the one hundred and twenty disciples at the Pentecostal visitation of the Holy Spirit after Jesus' Ascension. Second, he was clearly subordinate to the elders of the Jerusalem church—especially James, Peter, and John—two of whom were original disciples and all of whom were present at the Pentecost. According to Luke, James, along with Jesus' other brothers, was with the twelve, as well as Mary, in Jerusalem after Jesus' Ascension (Acts 1:14).

Paul's persistent description of himself as chosen by Jesus was evidently intended to remind his friends as well as his enemies that he was as much an apostle as James and Peter were and as much an authority as they were on "the Gospel of Christ." The effort, however, seems to have been an uphill battle. To put it simply, "[i]f one considers that the Jerusalem church encompassed some of the original disciples, a

Judaism while in reality they were merely the conservatives who did not go along with the Pauline-hellenistic developments."

108. McKenzie says that Luke's portrait of the Jerusalem church as Hellenized—at least, in terms of its theology, which appears to be expressed more or less identically by Peter, Stephen, and Paul—can be justified only because it was the view "which had permanent value and meaning in the life of the church." After all, the theology of the "Judaizers" who actually led the church "had [by Luke's time] simply ceased to exist" (New Testament, 166).

109. Bauer, Heresy and Orthodoxy, 213.

110. Bauer, Heresy and Orthodoxy, 236. Bauer adds: "I am limiting myself to what is attested. Whether the Judaists also came into contact with others who preached Christ apart from the law, and how they dealt with such, is not reported to us" (236 n. 12).

111. On Paul's lack of qualifications for discipleship, see Tabor, Jesus Dynasty, 203.

goodly number of believers who had known Yeshua when he was on earth, and also the members of Yeshua's own family, the heads of the church must have found it very tempting to tell Saul to go away, that he was not of the real Yeshua-faith." Rather, they tolerated this somewhat presumptuous outsider, "who had the vexing habit of telling them how to interpret not only Torah in general but Yeshua in particular."[112]

It is important to understand Paul's dissatisfaction with his status in the Church in order to understand his attitude toward the leaders of the Jerusalem church, whom he refers to with extreme bitterness in Galatians. "James and Cephas [Peter] and John," he says, are "those who were of repute," "those who were reputed to be something," and those "who were reputed to be pillars" (Gal 2:2, 6, 9). Although to the Christian Jews in Jerusalem, these men were, in fact, the leaders of the church, Paul says that they "added nothing to him," no doubt suggesting that he had no need for their advice or guidance—and certainly no reason to accept their authority on theological matters. After all, Paul had been set apart by God before his birth and "called . . . through His grace." More important, God "was pleased to reveal his Son" to Paul and by that means gave him his divine assignment to preach his gospel to the gentiles (1:15–16; see also Rom 1:1).

All of this was clearly intended by Paul to establish his claim that *his* gospel of Faith over Law, which he explains in Galatians 2:15–5:15, was the *true* gospel. For Jesus not only appeared to him personally, but also gave him his gospel directly. The implication was, of course, that others received their gospel in a different—and inferior—manner. Thus, Paul argued that he was "seeking the favor of . . . God" rather than man. His gospel was "not man's gospel" since he "did not receive it from man." Instead, "it came through a revelation of Jesus Christ." Furthermore, Paul "did not confer with flesh and blood, nor did [he] go up to Jerusalem to those who were apostles before [him]" (Gal 1:10–112).[113] True, after three years, he briefly visited Peter and "James the brother of Jesus" (1:18). However, even the Jerusalem Conference, which Paul attended fourteen years later and which Luke describes in Acts as a mandatory and public meeting with the elders, Paul refers to, again resentfully, as a private conversation with "those who were of repute" and which, according to Paul, was prompted not by the command of James, but by "revelation" (2:1–2). Paul went at God's, not James', behest.

Paul's hostility toward James, Peter, and John is underscored by his warning to the Galatians that a "different" gospel, obviously a gospel of Law over Faith, which had

112. Akenson, *Saint Saul*, 163. Akenson adds that it was, after all, the esteemed members of the Jerusalem church who assumed the right to exercise their authority. On one hand, it was "the most powerful group in the development of Christianity between the death of Yeshua and the destruction of Jerusalem." Yet, it was also "the one group whose influence the shapers of the canonical New Testament did everything they could to minimize in the historical record: the Family Firm" (165; see also 168, 169).

113. "We are left wondering why on his conversion [Paul] did not at once contact [Peter and the Palestinian apostles] and learn what they could tell him. Why this insistence that he owes them nothing? Why these angry anathemas? A former prosecutor lecturing his new comrades on their imperfections is unconvincing" (Robertson, *Origins of Christianity*, 106).

been preached to them by Judaizers and which prompted him to write his letter, is a *perversion* of "the gospel of Christ." For this reason, anyone who preached this gospel should be "accursed" (Gal 1:6–9). On his final return voyage to Jerusalem, perhaps a decade or so later, Paul left the elders of the church in Ephesus with a similar warning: "I know that after my departure fierce wolves will come in among you, not sparing the flock; and from among your own selves will arise men speaking perverse things, to draw away the disciples after them" (Acts 20:29–30). Paul similarly counseled the Corinthians not to "accept a different gospel" from the one he gave them. It was from "false apostles, deceitful workmen, disguising themselves as apostles of Christ" (2 Cor 11:4, 13). Like the gospel offered to the Galatians, this one also came from Judaizers, as Paul's later comments suggest: "Are they Hebrews? So am I. Are they Israelites? So am I" (11:22). His claim not to be "in the least inferior to these superlative apostles" suggests his usual lament that he was not taken as seriously as those who presented themselves as his superiors (11:6; 12:11).

Of course, what raises questions about Paul's contention that he was God's special envoy, the apostle singled out for a unique assignment, and uninfluenced by the gospel of man rather than the gospel of God is the fact that his claim is unverifiable. The original disciples could argue that they all received the same message from Jesus. By contrast, Paul was the only source (except, perhaps, for the otherwise obscure figure of Ananias) for the validity of his claim. That he encountered strong opposition to his self-portrait is suggested by his exclamation in the middle of his extraordinary self-defense to the Galatians: "In what I am writing to you, before God, I do not lie!" (Gal 1:20). In his Letter to the Romans, Paul felt compelled to make the same statement: "I am not lying" (Rom 9:1). And to the Corinthians, he said, "The God and Father of the Lord Jesus, he who is blessed forever, knows that I do not not lie" (2 Cor 11:31).

What raises questions about Paul's description of the Jerusalem Conference is not only Luke's quite different account of it in Acts, where it appears to be investigative in purpose, but also Paul's rueful admission that he "laid before them" (i.e., James, Peter, and John) his gospel to the gentiles, "lest somehow I should be running or had run in vain" (Gal 2:2; see also Phil 2:16)—that is, wasting his time, from the point of view of the leaders of the Jerusalem church. He seems to be fully aware here that he was called upon to defend his mission.[114]

Paul also makes it clear that he was under surveillance by "false brethren secretly brought in, who slipped in to spy out our freedom, which we have in Christ Jesus, that they might bring us into bondage" (Gal 2:4). The possibility that the "false brethren"

114. Brown says that Paul's mention of "the possibility that he had run in vain" may mean that he was "admitting the power of the 'pillars': Should they deny his Gentile churches koinonia with the mother church in Jerusalem, there would be a division that negated the very nature of the church" (*Introduction*, 306). That is, he was in danger of having his gospel rejected. According to Witherington, there was no question that James and the pillars were in charge. Rather, Paul's expression of hostility toward the leaders of the Jerusalem church "reflects [his] concerns about his own status and whether his mission to Gentiles would be recognized as legitimate" (*What Have They Done?* 179; see also 180).

were sent by James and the elders is suggested by the fact that precisely at this point Paul launches into his attack on them (2:6–9). Thus, his claim that "we did not yield submission [to them] even for a moment" (2:5) could as easily apply to James, Peter, and John as to a minority of Judaizers who did not represent the leaders of the Jerusalem church. In fact, Paul would more likely be proud of not submitting to the leaders of the church than of not submitting to a group of extremists unsupported by either James or the elders.

Furthermore, the people who persuaded Peter to stop eating with the gentiles, the subject Paul turns to next, were not radicals in the church, as they have been called: i.e., "Judaizers" with "narrow prejudices."[115] On the contrary, they "came from James" himself. Peter "acted insincerely," in Paul's view, because he feared "the circumcision party" (Gal 2:12), which, again, was not a small minority, but very likely the whole Jerusalem church (i.e., "the rest of the Jews" [2:13]), including even Barnabas, but not Paul. In this instance, as in many others, Paul was clearly on the outside looking in. Why Peter would fear anyone but James and the elders of the Jerusalem church is one salient question. And why Paul would resent anyone except James and the elders is another.[116]

Considering the evidence, although it is customary to consider "the circumcision party" in Acts and Paul's epistles as the *conservative* wing of the Jerusalem church, the claim is untenable. First, Paul, the opponent of the circumcision party, did not level his contempt at any *minor* figures in the church—i.e., a conservative minority like the "the party of the Pharisees" in Acts 15:1–5—but at James and his fellow apostles, the leaders of the church. They were, according to Paul, the ones who "might bring [the Church] into bondage," who had reputations exceeding their worth, and to whom Paul refused to submit (Gal 2:4–9). Paul says that his followers in Corinth were unduly influenced by Peter (whom he calls Cephas in 1 Cor 1:12; 3:22), along with Apollos, both of whom proffered a gospel different from his. In Galatia, he criticized Peter "to his face," for "fearing the circumcision party," acting "insincerely," and evading "the truth of the gospel" by refusing to eat with gentile Christians there.[117] In other words, despite the differences between James and Peter, "Paul saw the two as part of the common circumcision mission." In fact, after Barnabas sided with James and Peter, Paul henceforth traveled with Silas instead.[118]

115. *Oxford Annotated Bible*, 1409–10.

116. "Given the status and standing of Peter, some great authority must have been behind the circumcision party and been the source of his fear. This can only be James" (Painter, *Just James*, 69). "In this particular case," says Klingaman, "Peter was probably acting on orders from James, because his own views on the subject appear to have been far more liberal" (*First Century*, 259).

117. Horsley and Silberman contend that the leaders of the Jerusalem church were as unhappy with Paul as he was with them: "*They* knew exactly what Paul had been preaching and, having little patience for his radical universal critique of patronage, saw it as a direct threat to Israel's national struggle against Rome" (*Message*, 194).

118. Painter, *Just James*, 82, 71. The opposition between the two groups seems to have pitted Paul

Second, what Paul objected to—circumcision and obedience to Jewish Law—were the very practices that were defended by the entire Jerusalem church, at least as they applied to *Jewish* Christians. It is logical to conclude, then, that no one except Paul and other Hellenized Christians could have embraced the idea that "all who rely on works of the law are under a curse" (Gal 3:10) or that those who preached the need for circumcision should "mutilate themselves" (5:12). The elders of the Jerusalem church, including James, later explained to Paul at his last visit to Jerusalem that the church was made up of Jewish Christians who were "all zealous for the law" and thus opposed to Paul's alleged demand that Jewish, as well as gentile, Christians should "forsake Moses, telling them not to circumcise their children or observe the customs." For this reason, James and the elders told Paul to show his fellow Christians that he "live[d] in observation of the law" (Acts 21:21–24).

As these differences between Paul and the members of the Jerusalem church suggest (and as Paul spells out in more detail in the later chapters of his Letter to the Galatians), there were two opposing groups in the ancient Church.[119] One, in Jerusalem (and probably all of Judea, if not Palestine), was led by James, and the other, in the Diaspora, was led by Hellenists like Paul. As Paul says in Galatians, there were two missionary parties because there were two groups of potential converts. One, organized by him, was "entrusted with the gospel to the uncircumcised," and the other, headed by Peter, was "entrusted with the gospel to the circumcised." While Paul therefore went "to the Gentiles," "they"—*meaning not only Peter, but also James and John and the whole church*—went "to the circumcised" (Gal 2:7–9). Of course, it must be acknowledged that Peter proselytized to gentiles as well as Jews and that Paul appealed to Jews as well as Gentiles. However, while James accepted both missions, though he actively participated in neither, he was "committed to the mission of and to the circumcision."[120]

More important, each party had its own message. To the Jews (the circumcised), James, Peter, and John obviously preached obedience to the Law. To the gentiles (the uncircumcised), Paul preached the irrelevance of circumcision and the inability of the Law to provide salvation.[121] In this context, "the circumcised who came with Peter"

against apostles who "may have had a greater right than [he] to declare what the faith was all about. It is entirely plausible that they may have had a more accurate knowledge of the historical Yeshua than did Saul" (Akenson, *Saint Saul*, 151–52). This is a tentative judgment of the "false apostles" whom Paul refers to in 2 Cor 11:13, but a far more certain one regarding Peter and John the son of Zebedee.

119. "The story is intelligible only if Pauline and Palestinian Christianity represented two separate and opposed tendencies . . . Paul found the Palestinian apostles in his way. His gospel was not their gospel, nor his Christ their Christ" (Robertson, *Origins of Christianity*, 106).

120. Painter, *Just James*, 74; see also 70–71, 75. Although "[t]here is a widespread tendency to distance James from the circumcision party," Painter says, "[t]he circumcision party is to be identified with James" (68 n. 31, 69). On this subject, see also Meeks, *First Urban Christians*, 112–13. Notably, at this time the membership of the Jerusalem church was either entirely or almost entirely Jewish.

121. Painter says: "According to Acts, the Jerusalem church maintained a mission to the Jews based on circumcision and the keeping of the Mosaic law, including Sabbath, food, and purity laws. Paul's

(Acts 10:45) to Caesarea and witnessed the conversion of Cornelius and his household were simply Jewish Christians who represented James and the entire Jerusalem church. Certainly, although they accepted the conversion of gentiles, they shared the sentiments that Peter himself expressed to Cornelius: "how unlawful it is for a Jew to associate with or to visit any one of another nation" (10:28). And "the circumcision party" who, when Peter returned to Jerusalem, criticized him for violating this law ("Why did you go to uncircumcised men and eat with them?" [Acts 11:2–3]), was the same "circumcision party" that persuaded Peter to stop eating with gentiles in Antioch—and whose members, in that case, are specifically identified as coming "from James" (Gal 2:12).

In each case, "the circumcision party" had no objection to the conversion of gentiles. Hearing Cornelius and his household "speaking in tongues and praising God," Peter's Jewish Christian companions were "amazed," but unopposed. That is, when Peter asked, "Can any one forbid water for baptizing these people who have received the Holy Spirit just as we have?" nobody said no (Acts 10:45–48). And, after Peter explained to the Jewish Christians in Jerusalem what had happened in Caesarea— i.e., that God had allowed the conversion of gentiles—every one of them appears to have accepted the news joyfully: "And they glorified God, saying, 'Then to the gentiles also God has granted re-entrance into life'" (Acts 11:18). What is confusing in these incidents is that, while Jewish Christians were willing to accept the conversion of Christians—at least after they witnessed God's approval by giving gentiles the Holy Spirit—they did not resolve two issues. First, they did not, until the Jerusalem Conference, decide whether gentiles could join the Church without being circumcised. And, second, they seem never to have settled, at least formally and explicitly, whether Jews could (to use Peter's phrase) "associate with" gentiles.[122]

Cloudy as these issues remained, however, James insisted that *Jewish* converts to Christianity *always* had to obey Jewish laws.[123] He was, on the one hand, like the other

---

circumcision-free mission in the diaspora was restricted to Gentiles" (*Just James*, 55). This is why many of the churches in the Diaspora were virtually split down the middle. To put it simply, they had been exposed to two different missions and two different messages. Bauer describes two different groups of Jewish Christians in Corinth: "(1) those who identify themselves with Cephas and, like their hero, hold fast to Jewish practice for themselves but do not demand the same from their uncircumcised brethren; and (2) the 'Christ' group, who had the same requirements even for gentile Christians" (*Orthodoxy and Heresy*, 99). Ehrman describes the same situation in Galatia in *Lost Christianities*, 160–61.

122. Segal comments: "Waiving circumcision for gentile salvation was not in itself a startling conclusion, for not all Jews insisted that conversion was necessary for gentile salvation. There were a variety of opinions within the Jewish community," as well as among Jewish Christians. What "was more innovative" was Paul's "claim that the saved Jews and Gentiles could form a single new community and freely interact." What concerned both Jews and Jewish Christians "was not how the gentiles could be saved but how to eat with them and marry them" (*Paul the Convert*, 194).

123. According to Conzelmann and Lindemann, "Even after the Apostolic Council [the Jerusalem Conference] the Jerusalem community remains a strictly Jewish-Christian community which seeks to maintain the association with Judaism, especially by observing the legal code" (*Interpreting the New*

elders in the Jerusalem church, less extreme than the Pharisaic party, which insisted on the circumcision of gentiles (Acts 15:1–5), but more conservative than Peter, who ate with gentiles in Antioch until a delegation from James objected. Thus, as at least one scholar has claimed, "[t]he evidence justifies the description of his position as Judaizing." James was, after all, not only a pious Jew, always either defending the Law or finding biblical justification for amending it, but also, as the head of the Jerusalem church, "the leading authority in Christian Judaism." And, although he "was not actively involved in a Judaizing mission to the nations, he exerted a Judaizing pressure upon those who were, such as Peter and Barnabas at Antioch."[124] It seems likely, in fact, that many of the members of the Jerusalem church (if not all of them) were Judaizers, a probability that Luke ignores in Acts of the Apostles because his hero is Paul, not James.[125]

Notably, fighting Judaizers in Corinth, Philippi, and Galatia, as Titus did in Crete (Titus 1:10), Paul seems to have disagreed on doctrinal matters with *everyone* in the Jerusalem church, as well as Judaizers in the Diaspora, who may well have been influenced by Jewish Christians from Judea.[126] Thus, he opposed, argued with, and vilified those "who were reputed to be pillars" in Jerusalem—James, Peter, and John—whom Paul thought of as pretentious (Gal 2:9); Peter and Barnabas, whom Paul called insincere and who had evidently been influenced by "certain men [who] came from James" to Galatia (Gal 2:11–13); the men who "came down from Judea" to Antioch, insisting that converts be circumcised and obey the Mosaic Law, with whom "Paul and Barnabas had no small dissension and debate," after which Paul and the others were "appointed" to report "to the elders and the apostles about this question" (Acts 15:1–2); the agents who preached justification by works and circumcision to the Galatians and whom Paul hoped would castrate themselves (Gal 5:12); the "superlative" and "false apostles" who had preached "a different gospel" to Paul's converts in Corinth and who seem to have questioned Paul's Judaism (2 Cor 11:4–5; 13, 22–23); "the dogs" and "the evil-workers" in Philippi, whom Paul accused of "mutilat[ing] the flesh" (Phil 3:2); and James "and all the elders," who directly confronted Paul in Jerusalem with the

---

Testament, 348). By c. 150, however, Justin Martyr was saying that Jewish Christians who insisted that their practices be accepted by gentiles were heretics (348–49).

124. Painter, *Just James*, 96, 274. Conzelmann and Lindemann, however, argue that some Judaizing groups were not *sent* by James, but merely *appealed* to him for support (*Interpreting the New Testament*), 172). Brown similarly argues that "those of the circumcision party" in Antioch merely "claim[ed] to represent James" (*Introduction*, 472; my emphasis).

125. Sanders credits F. C. Baur with correctly observing "that Jewish Christians must have generally opposed the move to let Gentiles be absolved from the requirements of the Law" (*Jews in Luke-Acts*, 119). In other words, "[p]ushing the Torah on the Gentiles is not the work of the Pharisees or of some other minority [in the Jerusalem church] alone; it is the work of the Jewish Christians" (123–24)—i.e., of the *whole* Jerusalem church.

126. McKenzie says that the evidence in Paul's letters shows "that those with whom Paul disputed included nearly all of the most respected figures in the apostolic church, meaning those who had been personal disciples of Jesus" (*New Testament*, 59).

charge that he was teaching Jewish Christians "to forsake Moses" by ignoring the law of circumcision and other Jewish customs (Acts 21:18–21).

On the other hand, however, by AD 60, thirty years after the Crucifixion, James and the Jerusalem church had come a long way. By then, they had accepted not only the conversion of gentiles, but also the conversion of gentiles without circumcision. What remained problematic, at least insofar as they seemed to make gentiles second-class members of the Church, were two restrictions: (1) as I said, the prohibition against Jews and gentiles dining together and (2) the demand that newly converted gentile Christians follow the Noahide laws specified by James at the Jerusalem conference (Acts 15:20, 29).

According to the first demand, gentiles could not join Law-observant Jews for important sacramental meals, such as Eucharistic dinners or once-yearly Passover celebrations. Since the dinners were modeled on the Last Supper, which was a Passover meal, and attendance at the latter was limited to the circumcised, uncircumcised gentile Christians could participate in neither. According to the second demand, although Jews could become Christians merely by declaring their acceptance of Jesus as the Messiah, gentile converts also had to separate themselves from their pagan compatriots because they were forbidden to eat the kinds of meat that were commonly consumed by unconverted pagans. Jews could remain Jews, but gentiles had to change.

Under these circumstances, it is hard to imagine that the Jerusalem church could have expanded outward to the Diaspora, where Jews and gentiles were already socializing more freely than they were in Judea and, especially, in rural Galilee. Proselytizing far from these predominantly Jewish areas, Paul argued that God does not recognize *any* distinctions between Jews and gentiles, circumcised and uncircumcised. Therefore, he criticized Peter for being equivocal about dining with gentiles. And he claimed that real Judaism had nothing to do with obeying ritual laws, but had everything to do with spiritual change, which was equally available to Jews and gentiles (Rom 2–4). Eventually, the two missions proved to be irreconcilable, which Paul seems to be aware of in Galatians.[127] There, he defines what appears to be a kind of cosmic dichotomy, in which circumcision and uncircumcision, Works and Faith, Law and Jesus, Bondage and Freedom, and Flesh and Spirit define two discontinuous realms of being. Furthermore, to use a formula that Paul uses elsewhere, the former is the world of Death, and the latter is the world of Life. That is, he not only challenges

127. Brown says that, as a result of the Jerusalem Conference, "the following of Jesus would soon move beyond Judaism and become a separate religion reaching to the ends of the earth" (*Introduction*, 306). Brown later explains: "In fact that road would lead away from Judaism. Even though the savior for Gentiles was a Jew born under the Law, Christianity would soon be looked on as a Gentile religion quite alien to Judaism, especially to a Judaism for which the Law would become ever more important once the Temple was destroyed" (308). Van Leeuwen refers to the divide between the two missions as an "unbridgeable gulf" and goes on to describe the separation of Christianity and Judaism in the same way that Brown does (*Christianity in World History*, 222–25).

the validity of the other gospel, he positively dismisses it as a rejection of God and as an insurmountable obstacle to salvation.[128]

In the meantime, the Jerusalem church, under James, monitored its missionaries—like Philip in Samaria (Acts 8:14), Peter in Caesarea (11:1–2), and Paul in Antioch (15:1–3)—by sending observers to watch out for innovations; calling proselytizers to Jerusalem for interrogation; and, perhaps, even appointing observers afterwards to make sure that the church's instructions, like the decree announced at the Jerusalem Conference, were being followed (15:22).[129] After the Temple was destroyed (in AD 70) and the Jews were exiled from Jerusalem (in AD 135)—before which time, according to Eusebius, the Jerusalem church was almost entirely populated by Jews as well as led by so-called bishops who were circumcised—this church lost its influence and eventually, in its remaining manifestations, was regarded as not only irrelevant, but heretical.[130] By the second century, James, the brother of Jesus and quite possibly appointed by him to head the Church, was beginning to be marginalized. And Paul, the former heretic, was beginning to be recognized as the major contributor to the Church's new definition of orthodoxy.

During his lifetime, however, perhaps recognizing his position as a minor player in the Christian enterprise—impugning the integrity of the Church's leaders, brooding over his lack of recognition, and always feeling the need to defend his legitimacy—Paul was, at least when the occasion demanded it, a Jew as well as a Christian. Despite his refusal to require gentile converts to Christianity to practice Judaism, Paul, like other Jewish Christians of his generation, often referred to himself as a Jew and seems to have engaged in many Jewish religious activities—even sponsoring and to some extent participating in a Nazirite ritual, for example. First, he was "a Jew by birth" (Gal 2:15), after which he was "circumcised on the eighth day." Thus, he was unquestionably "of the people of Israel, of the tribe of Benjamin, a Hebrew born of Hebrews." Furthermore, he was (or at least had been) pious and law-abiding: "as to the law a Pharisee, as to zeal a persecutor of the church, as to righteousness under the law blameless" (Phil 3:5–6). He emphasized this point in his Letter to the Galatians: "I advanced in Judaism beyond many of my own age among my people, so extremely zealous was I for the traditions of my fathers" (Gal 1:14).

---

128. On these points, see Painter, *Just James*, 65 n. 23, 70. "Conflicting understandings of the accord"—i.e., between the two parties—"made actual conflict inevitable" (67).

129. This precaution might have been necessary in Paul's case, since, according to the editors of *Oxford Annotated Bible*, "He did not absolutely forbid food offered to idols (1 Cor. 10.27–29) and he rejected other restrictions on food (Gal. 2.11–12; Col. 2.21)" (1339). Senior argues that the Jerusalem church "kept a close watch over the orthodoxy of new groups coming into the church" (*Jesus*, 151).

130. Segal says, "Time was on the side of the gentile community." The Jerusalem church survived, "but their political and economic situation seems to have deteriorated as the gentile community increased and flourished" (*Paul the Convert*, 272–73). Nevertheless, "Jewish Christianity probably continued to be the dominant form of Christianity for at least two generations and maybe for several generations after Paul" (275).

Paul emphasizes his Judaism even more strongly in Acts of the Apostles. After Roman soldiers saved him from death at the hands of a Jewish (or Jewish-Christian) mob in Jerusalem, he said to the tribune, in Greek, "I am a Jew, from Tarsus" (Acts 21:39). To the crowd of Jews assembled, he repeated his claim in Hebrew and went on to say that, in addition to studying with Gamaliel, he had been "educated according to the strict manner of the law of our fathers, being zealous for God as you all are this day" (22:3). He reiterated these claims before the Sanhedrin (23:6), the procurators Felix (24:14) and Festus (25:8), and Herod Agrippa (26:4–8). And they reappear in Paul's second letter to the Corinthians (11:22) and his letters to the Galatians (1:14) and Philippians (3:4–6).[131]

In all of these instances, Paul argued that he had been unfairly arrested because he was an obedient Jew who was simply promoting the idea of the resurrection of the dead (24:15). In the cities of the Diaspora, Paul always began his preaching either in synagogues (his usual venue) or in other places where Jews were known to gather (Acts 16:11–15).[132] In addition, he and his Jewish-Christian companions may have delayed their departure from Philippi because of the Festival of Unleavened Bread (Acts 20:6). He said he wanted to be in Jerusalem at Pentecost (Acts 20:16), and he had recently come to Jerusalem "to worship" in the Temple (Acts 25:11), just as he had prayed in the Temple the first time he returned to Jerusalem after his conversion (22:17).

Before his arrest in Jerusalem and subsequent departure for Rome, Paul, albeit at the behest of James and the elders of the Jerusalem church, agreed to sponsor four men who, having taken a Nazirite vow, were to participate in a Jewish ritual requiring them to remain in a state of "separation" for an unspecified period of time (Acts 21:23–24; see Num 6:1–21). The purpose, as we have seen, was to prove to other Jews that Paul was a Law-abiding Jew (Acts 21:21–24). He first "purified himself and went into the temple, to give notice when the days of purification would be fulfilled and the offering presented for every one of them" (Acts 21:26). The rite that the Nazirites performed involved consuming no food or drink made from grapes, avoiding the use of a razor, and staying away from dead bodies. The Nazirite shaves his head at the end of the period of separation and offers, as I said earlier, two lambs and a ram, as well as bread, cakes, and wafers mixed with oil—adding up to burnt, sin, peace, cereal, and drink offerings, or sacrifices (Num 6:1–21). Paul had to undergo purification rites,

131. Meeks says, in defense of Paul's Judaism, "It is now generally acknowledged that no one can understand the peculiar form of early Christianity we call Pauline without first gaining some understanding of contemporaneous Judaism" (*First Urban Christians*, 32). Meeks points out that Paul worshiped the Jewish God (190) and never departed from Jewish morality (*Origins of Christian Morality*, 19–20; see also 152, 156).

132. Bruce, *New Testament History*, 145, 146, 270. Rome had eleven synagogues, and many of the large cities on the eastern Mediterranean, as well as in Mesopotamia and Asia Minor, had one or more (146). Antioch, Thessalonica, and Corinth, for example, figured largely in the Christian mission because they were the capital cities of Syria, Macedonia, and Greece, respectively.

but whether he himself participated in the Nazirite ritual is unclear because it was interrupted prematurely (Acts 21:23–27).

What is intriguing about this event is the question it raises about Paul's motives. Was he simply trying to cooperate with James in the interest of Church unity? Was he compromising his principles in order to extricate himself from a difficult situation? Or was he, despite his apparent opposition to Jewish Law elsewhere, demonstrating a sincere commitment to it? The last alternative is made at least plausible by the statement in Acts 18:18 that Paul had years earlier "cut his hair" because "he had a vow," in Cenchreae, near Corinth.[133] Was Paul, then, a Nazirite, preparing to undergo the ritual because he chose to do so? Was James' request not that Paul should perform the ritual in the Temple, since that was what he already intended to do, but to sponsor four other Jewish Christians as well?[134] On the other hand, people were not above performing this ritual (and, no doubt, other religious acts) cynically, as was the case with Herod Agrippa's wife, Bernice, who participated in a Nazirite ceremony to display her fidelity to Judaism, which, like her husband's, "was more than counterbalanced by the thoroughly profligate lives they lived."[135]

After his arrest in the synagogue, Paul apologized for insulting the chief priest by quoting Exodus 22:28: "Thou shalt not speak evil of the ruler of thy people" (Acts 23:5). That is, he acknowledged that *his* people were the Jews. To Felix, he said that he "came to bring alms to [his] nation, and offerings" (Acts 24:17).[136] That is, he was not only giving a donation to the Jerusalem church, which he had collected from fellow Christians during his missionary travels; he was also prepared to make sacrifices at

133. Kee et al. briefly explain the Nazirite ceremony and summarize the possible reasons for Paul's cooperation in *Understanding the New Testament*, 217–18. They suggest that Paul's earlier hair cutting was "a step in the direction of conformity to ritual requirements . . . in preparation for his pilgrimage to the Temple" (217). As I said, Paul traveled throughout Greece and "Asia," spending two years in the latter, between Cenchreae and Jerusalem (Acts 19:10). What seems likely is that he actually *participated* in the ritual in Cenchrea. The only step that remained, since head shaving came at the end of the rite, was "a temple offering, which would mark the completion of the vow." Horsley and Silberman continue, "Acts implies that this is what happened" (*Message*, 238).

134. This incident is somewhat complicated by the fact that at least three years intervened between Paul's haircut in Cenchreae and his sponsorship of the ritual in Jerusalem. What must be astonishing to most modern Christians, of course, is that all of these Christians—James, Paul, and four other members of the Jerusalem church—had, as late as the late fifties, any interest whatsoever in this elaborate Jewish ritual that required adherence to purity laws as well as making eight different sacrifices in the Temple.

135. Kee et al., *Understanding the New Testament*, 222. Paul was always ready to compromise, Segal says, as long as the action had no bearing on his or anyone else's salvation. Since performing the ritual had nothing to do with that issue, Paul agreed to it in the interest of Church unity (*Paul the Convert*, 239).

136. Of course, Paul's self-identification as a Jew was sometimes, if not always, self-serving, as was the case when he was saved from the mob in Jerusalem and when, seeing that the Sanhedrin was composed of Pharisees and Sadducees, he got the Pharisees to exculpate him by calling himself a Pharisee. He simply lied to Felix when he said he had been arrested only for his belief in "the resurrection of the dead" (Acts 24:21), a claim he also made to Herod Agrippa (Acts 26:8). On these points, see Tabor, *Jesus Dynasty*, 269. On Paul's exaggerations elsewhere, see Hill, *Hellenists and Hebrews*, 167.

the Temple. Thus, given his self-presentation as not merely a Jew, but an extremely religious one; not just a Pharisee, but one who had studied with Gamaliel; and not just a worshiper in the Temple, but either a participant in a demanding ritual there or, at least, a sponsor, making a contribution to the Temple large enough to pay for the participation of four other Jewish Christians, it seems logical to conclude that "Paul died thinking of himself as a Jew," as at least one scholar has argued.[137]

THE GENTILE MISSION

This is, however, as much as one can say about Paul's Judaism, especially compared to that of James or even Peter. For Paul's idea of following Jesus meant not only that salvation came through the recognition of Jesus' leadership and moral authority. It also meant that his acceptance of Jesus as divine made obedience to the Mosaic Law—at least its ceremonial aspects— unnecessary. Furthermore, obeying the Law was not, to Paul, a means of salvation. As one historian explains: "Jesus had observed the law except in extreme situations where it conflicted with the obligation of man to man. The Apostle Paul went further and contended that through Christ the law was at an end, because man cannot be saved by the keeping of the commands of the law but only through faith in Christ."[138]

In addition, although Paul regarded the Jewish Bible as morally valuable, it was especially authoritative insofar as it could be mined for evidence of Jesus' messiahship.[139] Otherwise, it could be, as Paul claims it had been for him (Rom 7), more of a hindrance than a help: "[F]or the written code kills, but the Spirit gives life" (2 Cor 3:6; see also Gal 3:19–29). To Paul, the Church replaced the Synagogue, Jesus replaced Moses (2 Cor 3:3, 12–16), Faith replaced the Law, and Grace replaced Good Works (Rom 11:5–6; Gal 2 and 3). Thus, on the one hand, Jewish Christians like James and Peter seem to have regarded Christianity as an outgrowth of Judaism and very likely thought of the two bodies of ideas and beliefs as irreversibly connected spiritually, logically, and historically. Paul, on the other hand, as the first supersessionist, thought of them as fundamentally contradictory and related as Truth and Falsehood, Freedom and Slavery, Salvation and Damnation, not merely as Present and Past.[140]

137. Carroll, *Constantine's Sword*, 138. According to White, "[T]here was no sense that [Paul] had left Judaism behind either by becoming a follower of the Jesus movement or in his reaching out to non-Jews . . . Paul had not converted away from Judaism. Rather, he had merely 'converted' from one sect of Judaism, the Pharisees, to another, while staying within the same worldview and set of values" (*From Jesus to Christianity*, 157). Says Parkes, "Paul never ceased to regard himself as a Jew" (*Conflict*, 55).

138. Bainton, *Early Christianity*, 18.

139. On this point, see Segal, *Paul the Convert*, 262.

140. Chadwick comments: "The first Christians were Jews differentiated from their fellow-countrymen by their faith that in Jesus of Nazareth the Messiah of the nation's expectations had now come. They took it for granted that his coming, being a fulfillment, must be continuous with the past revelation of God to his people and could not mean a break either with the old covenant made with

Of course, considering the irreconcilability of the sum total of things Paul is alleged to have said and done, it is difficult to separate truth from fiction. Indeed, the real problem with this and anyone's assessment of Paul is the ultimate impossibility of determining with any certainty who he really was and what he really thought. Luke's account of him is flawed because Luke, in Acts, is interested in minimizing Paul's outright opposition to the church in Jerusalem. As his letters reveal, Paul obviously rejected the authority of its leaders and disagreed with them on doctrinal issues, particularly those raised by the elders in Acts 21. Luke also shows little interest in or awareness of the theology that Paul articulated in his letters.[141] In Acts, both Peter and Paul preached the ancient Jewish doctrines of repentance, forgiveness, and the Kingdom of God, as well as salvation through faith in Jesus the Messiah.[142] The only offensive statement both were guilty of (as Stephen was, as well) is the charge that the Jews killed Jesus (Acts 2:23, 36; 3:13–15; 4:10, 27; 5:30; 10:39; 13:28). The Jews that Peter and Paul addressed, throughout the Diaspora, were evidently provoked by this charge and particularly by Stephen's more sweeping accusation that Jews have *always* "resist[ed] the Holy Spirit," "persecute[d]" the prophets, and disobeyed God's laws. The fact that they "betrayed and murdered" Jesus was, to Stephen, only the last in a long series of outrages against God.

In Acts, Paul claimed to the procurators Felix and Festus (disingenuously, if measured against his sentiments in his letters) that he remained obedient to Jewish Law (Acts 24:14; 25:8) and that he was in trouble with his Jewish accusers merely because he believed in the resurrection of the dead (24:21), a belief he shared with the Pharisees (23:6–8).[143] Paul's idea of Atonement (Rom 3:25; 6:6–9; 1 Cor 15:3; 2 Cor 5:14–15), his objection to circumcision for everyone (Rom 2:28–29; 3:30; Gal 5:2–3; 6:15; Phil 3:2–3), his rejection of Jewish Law as a means of salvation (Rom 3:21; 1 Cor 8:8; 10:25; Gal 3:10–12; Eph 2:15), and his insistence on the priority of faith over good works—all of these are unmentioned in Acts (except, quite vaguely, in 13:37–39), although they are at the heart of Paul's Christianity. At least three of these doctrines are

Abraham, symbolized by circumcision, or with the Law given to Moses on Mt. Sinai" (*Early Church*, 9; see also 12). On Paul's supersessionism, see Cullman, *Early Church*, 70–74. Sometimes, Paul says that Jesus replaces the Law and that Paul himself replaces Moses (70).

141. Conzelmann and Lindemann note that the author of Acts shows no "familiarity with the peculiarities of Pauline theology." For that reason, "[t]he Paul of Acts is considerably different from the historical Paul as we know him from his letters" (*Interpreting the New Testament*, 237). Brown agrees, but mentions some similarities (*Introduction*, 324).

142. The evidence that Acts offers inauthentic speeches and "does not address the theology of the respective speakers" is that Peter's several speeches in the early pages of Acts and Paul's speech in ch. 13 are standardized "missionary addresses to Jews," which follow "the same pattern" and offer essentially the same content (Conzelmann and Lindemann, *Interpreting the New Testament*, 242).

143. Tannehill comments: "Paul's claim that he is on trial 'concerning hope and resurrection of the dead' seems strange in context. No charge of this kind has been leveled against Paul. Furthermore, Paul's statement seems to ignore the real theological issue between Paul and his Jewish opponents, namely, Paul's claim that Jesus is the Messiah . . . Paul speaks as if he were simply defending a Pharisaic doctrine" (*Luke-Acts*, II, 287). In other words, Paul is not telling the truth.

the very ideas that James, certainly, and Peter, probably, would have found strange, as did the angry Jews in city after city who accused Paul of being anti-Jewish. At the very least, he was sufficiently guilty of the charge to have frightened many of the Jews who heard him speak: "The cry of the accusers in the temple is the cry of a people trying to maintain itself against a perceived threat to its identity."[144]

In this context, one is forced to question (though certainly not reject outright) Luke's claim in Acts that Paul was interested in celebrating Jewish holidays, that he prayed in the Temple, that he honored the decree James issued at the Jerusalem Conference, that he had any reason other than expediency to sponsor a Nazirite ritual, or even that he was harassed and beaten by Jews for merely being a Christian and espousing the innocuous doctrines that he seems to have proffered in Acts. Indeed, although (according to Luke) Paul's only public accusation that the Jews killed Jesus occurred in Pisidian Antioch (Acts 13:28), he may well have said this wherever he went. That is, it is likely to have been part of his stump speech.

Paul might also have repeated two doctrines that he states in this speech (though, as I said, not very clearly): the idea that Jesus died for the sins of mankind ("through this man forgiveness of sins is proclaimed to you") and the idea that the law of Moses is henceforth inefficacious for salvation ("everyone that believes is freed from everything from which you could not be freed by the law of Moses") (13:37–39). Had he expressed these points more explicitly—they are almost unintelligible in their present form—the fact that he usually incurred the wrath of many of the Jews in the synagogues he visited for the purpose of converting his auditors to Christianity would be more understandable. As it is, according to one historian of the early Church, if the speeches in Acts reflect the style and content of the actual speeches of Paul and his Christian contemporaries, "one wonders not at the clashes when they did come, but at the long-temperedness of those who from their high seats heard reports of what must have seemed to them dangerous millennial nonsense."[145]

---

144. *Luke-Acts*, II, 272. As Tannehill acknowledges, the charge that Paul's movement was anti-Jewish was thus not unreasonable. The accusation against him in Acts 21:28—that he teaches "men everywhere against the people and the law and this place [i.e., the Temple]"—is based on Paul's anti-Temple views in 17:24–25 and his promotion of non-Law conversions for gentiles in 15:10–11, as well as in the passages in Paul's letters referred to in the text (271–272). Tannehill says elsewhere, "Although Paul does not *teach* apostasy from Moses, Jewish Christians will find it difficult to maintain Jewish identity and the Jewish way of life while mixing with Gentiles and isolated from the synagogue" (236). Sanders, citing Gal 2:11–14, claims that the charge against Paul "may, in fact, accurately describe the behaviour of the real Paul" (*Jews in Luke-Acts*, 283). Witherington points out that, although "Paul continues to view himself ethnically as a Jew," he indicates "very clearly that he has made a break with that community." Furthermore, "he no longer sees himself as obliged to observe the Mosaic Law." Thus, "it is not inappropriate to call [his views] a radical critique of Judaism" (*What Have They Done?* 232–33). On this point, Witherington cites J. Becker, *Paul: Apostle to the Gentiles*, 2. On Paul's radicalism (in relation to James'—as well as the Jerusalem church's—moderation), see Hill, *Hellenists and Hebrews*, 151–52.

145. Enslin, *Christian Beginnings*, 196.

Furthermore, as I suggested earlier, Paul's theology also alienated many Christians. In fact, he was considered an enemy of the Church throughout much of the Jewish-Christian community. In the *Letter of Peter to James*, Paul is the source of "a lawless and absurd doctrine" (2:3); in the *Homilies of Clement*, Peter is the true prophet, and Paul, in the guise of Simon Magus, is the false one.[146] Jewish Christians, like non-Christian Jews, evidently because they found his rejection of Law and Good Works highly objectionable—these being the bedrock of traditional Judaism—not only repudiated him, but attacked him, at least verbally. In the words of one scholar, Paul "does not give Judaism much of a continuing positive place in God's plan."[147] Speaking to Jewish audiences, he was opposed, reviled, whipped, beaten, and stoned (Acts 13:45; 18:6; 14:19; 2 Cor 11, 24–25). After all, if he plainly stated and explained the ideas he expressed in his letters, he was offering what appeared to many Jews, at least, a new religion and attacking—often quite bitterly—an "old" one.[148]

146. Ehrman, *After the New Testament*, 137, 140. According to Irenaeus, the Ebionites saw Paul as a heretic (Wilson, *Jesus*, 7). Bruce says that many Christians saw Paul and James as opposites and chose one or the other as their spiritual leader (*Canon of Scripture*, 152). Fredriksen adds: "Also, though Paul presumably knew many of Jesus' original followers, including and especially Peter, he had differences with them on important matters of principle. Thus, at some points, in other words, what he says represents something other than what Jesus' earliest followers were saying." Of course, Paul justified his interpretation of Jesus based on direct revelation, which, evidently, some Jewish Christians disputed. The question was (and is): "How much of what Paul says can actually be consonant with what Jesus might have taught, especially if he disagrees so pointedly with those who had known Jesus 'according to the flesh'?" (*Jesus of Nazareth*, 78). Enslin says, "It is today perfectly obvious that there is a vast difference between the nature of the messages of Jesus and Paul" (*Christian Beginnings*, 182).

147. Segal, *Rebecca's Children*, 111. Citing Romans 10:14–21, Brown says: "Paul offers Israel little excuse [for rejecting Jesus]: The gospel was preached already by the prophets, but Israelites did not believe. They cannot even have the alibi of not understanding; for they are a disobedient and defiant people, while the foolish nation of the Gentiles has responded" (*Introduction*, 570). For a fuller discussion of this subject, see Ruether, *Faith and Fratricide*, 96–107.

148. For a Jewish view of Paul's ideas, see Klinghoffer, *Why the Jews*, 106–12. See also Wylen, *Jews*, 188. Wilson says repeatedly that Paul is the founder of Christianity (*Jesus*, e.g., 22, 23), as does Maccoby (*Paul and Hellenism*, passim). Tabor calls the New Testament Paul's book and considers Paul to have been, if not the inventor of Christianity, at least the founder of Christian theology (*Jesus Dynasty*, 311). Bury makes exactly the same point in *Later Roman Empire*, 4. Mack says that Paul "looms so large in the pages of the New Testament that what he called his gospel has served for the Christian church as the definition of the new religion" (*Who Wrote?* 99). Brown states the claim more gently: "Next to Jesus Paul has been the most influential figure in the history of Christianity" (*Introduction*, 422). Fredriksen sums up the scholarly situation this way: "Often scholars who work on the historical Jesus see Paul as a sharp contrast rather than a corroborating witness to the early Jesus traditions: The more Jesus of Nazareth is fit into a first-century Jewish culture, the more Paul is seen in some sense as the actual inventor of Christianity, contributing to the 'de-Judaization of the pristine gospel of the Graeco-Roman world' (so Vermes, *The Religion of Jesus the Jew*, 213, characterizing the joint effect of Paul and John the Evangelist on developing Christian tradition)" (*Jesus of Nazareth*, 278). Segal denies "that Paul was the second founder of Christianity." However, he "defined Christianity's gentile future by radically revaluing its Jewish past" (*Paul the Convert*, 267). Segal refers to the view of Francis Watson (*Paul, Judaism, and the Gentiles*, 38–48), "who feels that Paul's actions and thought changed Christianity from a reform movement [within Judaism] into a sect [outside it]" (348 n. 13); and quotes Sanders at length, on the same point. To Sanders—because he replaced Law with Faith, circumcision with baptism, and the synagogue with the church—Paul created "a third entity," which was "neither

This new religion prevailed because gentiles, who often had little interest in circumcision and Jewish laws in general, replaced Jews in the new Christian Church.[149] The Church that grew up after Paul's fundamental transformation of Christian theology, ethics, and christology (and that therefore attracted an entirely different clientele) would have had little in common with the Jews who became Christians upon hearing the appeal of Jesus and his first disciples.[150] And the Gospels, written under similar influences, would very likely have seemed equally alien and strange—not the least because they blamed the Jews for the death of Jesus, as Paul had done years earlier, and implied that Judaism had been superseded by Christianity.[151]

Thus, when Paul preached in synagogues, he often wound up afterwards in private homes, usually addressing audiences made up of God-fearers, as well as Jews.[152] Utterly opposed to the circumcision of gentiles, as is evident in his refusal to circumcise his disciple Titus (Gal 2:3), Paul nevertheless circumcised Timothy "because of the Jews that were in those quarters"—that is, for appearance' sake. In other words, at the risk of having his critics charge him with disloyalty, he "considered it expedient to regularize Timothy's position in the existing state of society by circumcising him— thereby legitimizing him in Jewish eyes."[153] And when he identified himself as a Jew (a Pharisee, a student of Rabbi Gamaliel, and a speaker of Hebrew [Acts 22:2–3]), he may have merely been employing a rhetorical strategy that he explains in 1 Corinthians: "For though I be free from all men, yet I have made myself servant unto all, that I might gain the more. *And unto the Jews I became as a Jew, that I might gain the Jews*" (1 Cor 9:19–20; my emphasis). Similarly, he continues, he became whatever he needed to be to those under the Law or without it. In short, he says, "I am made all things to all men, that I might by all means save some" (1 Cor 9:22).[154]

Jewish nor Greek" (264).

149. Segal, *Rebecca's Children*, 113. Moltmann explains, "Historically, the church moved from being a community of Jewish Christians to being a community made up of Jews and Gentiles; and from there to being a community of Gentiles" (*Church*, 141).

150. Brown resists the idea that Paul is solely responsible for the high christology that many scholars associate with him, but asks (citing the so-called Christological Hymn in Col 1:15–20), "How within fifty years (at the latest) did Christians come to believe that about a Galilean preacher who was crucified as a criminal?" (*Introduction*, 604, 617).

151. Wilson, *Jesus*, 7. For Peter and James, says Wilson, Jesus had been a Jewish prophet (38). Enslin says that "the apotheosis" of Jesus into the Son of God "was far from the thoughts of the early disciples as they began their lives in Jerusalem" (*Christian Beginnings*, 174).

152. In Acts 13:16, 26, Paul addressed both "Men of Israel" and those "that fear God," the latter of whom were "particularly receptive" to his message (Lieu, *Image and Reality*, 108), although in this instance he was followed after "the meeting of the synagogue broke up" by "many Jews and devout converts to Judaism" (13:43). Commenting on Paul's conversion of gentiles in Chapter 13, Sanders says that they were "[s]urely those who had already been hearing him in the synagogue, i.e., the God-fearers and worshipping proselytes in the congregation" (*Jews in Luke-Acts*, 139). Sanders notes that Paul met with the same kind of gentiles in Acts 16 and 17 (140).

153. Bruce, *New Testament History*, 306.

154. It is not surprising, then, that Paul referred to the Jewish Bible when his audience was made up

One student of ancient Judaism has, on the basis of Paul's rejection of some aspects of his Jewish past and his willingness to do almost anything to promote Christianity (as he understood it),[155] offered the daring suggestion that Paul might not have been Jewish after all.[156] At the very least, Paul was, after his conversion to Christianity—and unlike his fellow Christians in the Jerusalem church—no longer a *practicing* Jew: "Presumably, among Gentiles he was willing to 'live as a Gentile,' which certainly no Jew observant of the Law could ever do."[157] The problem, as Paul saw it, was that the Jews themselves were no longer Jews, spiritually speaking: "For not all who are descended from Israel belong to Israel" (Rom 9:6). In short, whatever they were, he was not one of them. They were self-condemned, but Paul was part of "a remnant, chosen by grace" (Rom 11:5).[158] In passages like these, it would seem, the breach could not be mended.

Of course, it must be emphasized that Paul did not reject the Torah as an expression of *moral* law. After all, in at least the external sense, such laws would not have divided Jews and gentiles. It was not their content that was exceptional in the Roman empire, but their justification.[159] As I stated in Chapter One, the motive for obedience—according to Deuteronomy, the prophets, and the psalms—was not fear, but love. What Paul objected to, as I said before, was the Jewish *ceremonial* law, which did, in fact, not only distinguish Jews from others, but also physically separated them:

---

of Jews but quoted the Greek poets when he addressed pagans (313). For his references to Epimenides and Aratus, see Acts 17:28 and the accompanying footnote in *Oxford Annotated Bible*, 1342.

155. Segal says, "From the perspective of Jewish Christians, Paul was indeed recommending that Jews give up Torah" (*Paul the Convert*, 263). Segal quotes Sanders as saying that "Jewish Christians would have to give up aspects of the law if they were to associate with Gentile Christians" (264). McKenzie says, more bluntly, "Paul's thinking led to a conclusion which he never uttered in so many words (Galatians 3:28 comes close to it) that one must cease to be a Jew in order to become a Christian" (*New Testament*, 61; see also 62, 65).

156. Klinghoffer, *Why the Jews*, 112–13. Maccoby says, "According to the Ebionites, Saul was not a Pharisee and not even a Jew by birth. His parents in Tarsus were Gentiles, and he himself had become a convert [to Judaism]" (*Mythmaker*, 60; see also 172).

157. Tabor, *Jesus Dynasty*, 269. Was Paul telling Jews that they need not observe God's commandments? This was the charge that James and the elders raised, not on behalf of Jews (it might be noted), but Jewish Christians, "all zealous for the law," who had been told about Paul and would "certainly hear" that he had arrived in Jerusalem. These were not Jews, but "Jews . . . who have believed," said James, and they were very likely the ones who were stirred up by "the Jews from Asia" (also, presumably, Jewish Christians), who later attacked Paul in the Temple (Acts 21:20–22, 27). Tabor answers the question that Paul never answered by quoting Paul's letter to the Philippians: "Look out for the dogs, look out for the evil-workers, look out for those who mutilate the flesh" (3:2).

158. The editors of *Oxford Annotated Bible* note that in passages in which Paul claimed to be Jewish (e.g., 2 Cor 11:22), he was responding to charges to the contrary: "Apparently the authenticity of Paul's Judaism was called into question" (1405).

159. Some scholars claim that Jewish morality was actually an attraction to pagans who found their own moral code wanting. Bruce, for example, says, "'God-fearing' Gentiles who frequented the synagogue and conformed in some measure to the Jewish way of life did so largely because they appreciated its superiority to current pagan morals" (*New Testament History*, 281).

"dietary laws, holiday observances, purity, and circumcision."[160] His only objection to the moral law (aside from his somewhat unintelligible struggle with it) was that it was, though inviolable and indispensable, not salvific. That is, salvation was attainable not through obedience to this law, but only through faith in Jesus Christ.

However one estimates the degree to which Paul helped to transform Christian Judaism into gentile Christianity and regardless of his actual origin, training, and former commitment to Judaism, he marks a clear turning point in the evolution of Christianity. As I suggested above, the change was based on two developments that took place mainly because of Paul's influence: first, the idea that Christians should aggressively convert gentiles and, second, that these converts did not have to become Jews in order to become Christians—or, again, at this point, followers of Jesus.[161]

Paul introduced these ideas to the leadership of the Jerusalem church in the late forties at what has come to be known as the Jerusalem Conference (or Apostolic Council) and which may be considered the watershed event in the relationship between Christians and Jews, at least until Theodosius I's establishment of Christianity as the official religion of the Roman empire in 381.[162] As a result of this meeting between the leaders of the Jesus movement, the Church began to loosen its ties to Judaism and established a policy that would henceforth make it easier for gentiles to become Christians, but more difficult for Jews to become Christians. Exactly what happened at this religious summit that truly may be said to have changed the world?

Since it is generally assumed that his first missionary journey lasted from 46 to 49, Paul must have begun to proselytize among gentiles, as well as Jews, more than a decade after his conversion and only shortly before the Jerusalem Conference.[163] It would seem, in other words, that he was called to account for his Law-free preaching

160. Segal, *Paul the Convert*, 124. Segal says: "Paul is not theologizing [in his anti-Law statements]. He is talking about the proper role of Jewish observances in the Christian community. Works of the law are the material effects of the special laws on the unity of Christian community . . . Paul says nothing about the value of law-abiding or moral behavior. If asked, he would certainly be in favor of Torah as a standard for moral behavior" (124). He simply rejects "the whole body of commandments that distinguish Jews from gentiles" (161; see also 210–11).

161. Placher, *History of Christian Theology*, 36. It is possible, however, that the Hellenized Jewish Christians who left Jerusalem after Stephen's execution preceded Paul in actively pursuing gentiles as potential converts. Brown says that "seemingly the aggressive effort to convert Gentiles began with the Hellenists" (*Introduction*, 301). Paul claims late in Acts (22:18–21) that Jesus told him in a vision when he first visited Jerusalem after his conversion, "Make haste and get quickly out of Jerusalem, because they will not accept your testimony about me . . . Depart; for I will send you far away to the Gentiles."

162. According to Brown, the Conference "may be judged the most important meeting in the history of Christianity, "for implicitly [it] decided that the following of Jesus would soon move beyond Judaism and become a separate religion reaching to the ends of the earth" (*Introduction*, 306). Furthermore, says Lee, "the decision, when generalized beyond its local circumstances, has driven a wedge between Christian faith and the Jewish faith that was, and could still be in many ways, its nurturing matrix" (*Galilean Jewishness of Jesus*, 8).

163. Brown says that during Paul's first mission, which he dates AD 46–49, Paul may have preached *only* to Jews (*Introduction*, 303–4, with n. 65). Schillebeeckx says that Paul preached only to Jews for fourteen years (*Jesus*, 370–71; see also 374).

to gentiles a few years after it began.[164] In the meantime, Peter had had his own vision, sometime in the forties,[165] in which a celestial voice said, apparently talking about food, "What God hath cleansed, that call not thou common" (Acts 10:14). Interpreting this statement to mean that "God hath shown [him] that [he] should not call any man common or unclean," Peter gave a brief sermon, after which Cornelius, a Roman officer (as well as "an upright and God-fearing man, who [was] well spoken of by the whole Jewish nation" [10:22]), and other gentiles spoke in tongues. Astonished that the Holy Spirit had come upon these God-fearing gentiles, Peter proceeded to baptize Cornelius and his household, to the amazement, as I said earlier, of those "of the circumcision" who accompanied Peter (Acts 10:34–48). When he reported this strange turn of events to the church in Jerusalem, some Jewish Christians strongly objected—not to the conversion of the gentiles, but to Peter's violation of the purity laws by eating with Cornelius and his family (11:3). After Peter explained the result of his visit, however, they "glorified God" and concluded, "Then to the Gentiles also God has granted repentance unto life" (Acts 11:1–18).

It is important to understand that Jewish Christians, generally, were not opposed to the conversion of gentiles. When some of the Hellenists who left Jerusalem after Stephen's murder converted gentiles in Antioch, Barnabas, possibly sent from Jerusalem to investigate, was gladdened by the event, sought out Paul, and returned with this companion to Antioch for a year (Acts 11:19–26). Later, on their way to Jerusalem, Paul and Barnabas, visiting Christian churches in Phoenicia and Samaria, reported the conversion of gentiles and thereby "gave great joy *to all the brethren*" (Acts 15:3; my emphasis). Still later, when Paul returned to Jerusalem and "related one by one the things that God had done among the Gentiles through his ministry," James and the elders "glorified the Lord" (Acts 21:19–20).

The issue that the Jerusalem Conference was obligated to resolve was, therefore, not whether Peter and Paul should continue to preach to gentiles. By that time, the issue of gentile conversion had been settled.[166] Furthermore, it need not have come up in the first place since Jews had been proselytizing among gentiles for a long time. This is why Paul preached to gentiles initially: They were already, as Jewish proselytes and God-fearers, attending synagogue services and therefore fraternizing with the

164. These dates are referred to as "traditional" by Brown in his Pauline Chronology (*Introduction*, 428). Early dates are called "revisionist."

165. Fox, *Unauthorized Version*, 305–6. Dates for such events as Paul's conversion, Stephen's martyrdom, and Peter's revelation and conversion of Cornelius are difficult to determine. Most scholars put Paul's revelation in the early to mid-30s and then, fourteen (or seventeen) years later, the Jerusalem Conference in c. 48–50. What happened and when, in the intervening years, is indeterminable. Conzelmann and Lindemann comment, however, "It was undoubtedly the hellenists who, on the basis of their attitude to the law, were prepared to accept Gentiles into the community; that began not only with Antioch" (*Interpreting the New Testament*, 352). That is, Peter and Paul were not the first Christian missionaries to convert gentiles.

166. "As far as we can see from Galatians . . . no [Jewish-]Christian group objected to the Gentile mission; they objected only to its terms and conditions" (Sanders, *Jesus and Judaism*, 220).

Jews. They were, as I said earlier, part of his audience.[167] Even the gentile slaves of Jews were encouraged to undergo circumcision and thereby gain full status in Judaism.[168] According to one Bible scholar, Jews in the time of Jesus, at least in the Diaspora, interacted relatively freely with their gentile neighbors. They could share a common courtyard, engage in a business partnership, and have a meal with them. Indeed, the aggressive proselytizing associated with Paul was anticipated by his Jewish compatriots: "The missionary zeal displayed by the Christian Church toward the Gentiles ought therefore to be viewed not as a departure from Judaism but as a continuation of a strong tendency within the parent religion."[169]

Paul and Barnabas were dealing simply with the question of whether the new converts had to be circumcised, a concern raised by "certain men from Judea" (that is, Jewish Christians) who told the gentile Christians in Antioch, "Except ye be circumcised after the manner of Moses, ye cannot be saved"—the same reaction Paul and Barnabas got from the conservatives in Jerusalem, who also insisted that the new converts "keep the law of Moses" (Acts 15:1, 5). At this moment, Peter supported Paul and Barnabas by saying that salvation comes through "grace," not Law, and suggesting that the Law was something that neither Jews nor their fathers "were able to bear" (Acts 15:10–11), a point Paul makes frequently in his epistles. Of course, the "fact" that Peter supported the suspension of the Law in this instance is contradicted by Peter's refusal to dine with gentiles, at James' behest (Gal 2:11–12), and by his claim to some celestial figure that he had "never eaten anything that is common or unclean" (Acts 10:14).

At the end of the conference, after justifying the mission to the gentiles by quoting Amos 11:9–12, James offered his compromise and thereby pleased "the whole church" (Acts 15:22).[170] In the full passage from Amos, which concludes this prophet's message, God promises to "raise up the booth of David"—that is, "restore the fortunes of [His] people Israel"—which includes their possession of "the remnant of Edom and all the nations [i.e., gentiles] who are called by [His] name" (i.e., convert to Judaism; vv. 11–14). The implication seems to be, as I suggested earlier, that, since the gentiles would ultimately be included in the Kingdom of God, James asked the rhetorical question: Why not welcome them now? And here the key word is *now*. There is no

---

167. Fredriksen, *From Jesus to Christ*, xxiv-xxv, 16–17, 149–50, 166.

168. Jeremias makes these points in *Jerusalem*, 111, 267. By these means, he adds, Judaism was on its way to becoming a universal—i.e., trans-ethnic—religion (267).

169. Hare, *Jewish Persecution of Christians*, 8–10. Hare adds, however: "The importance of circumcision in Judaism should not be ignored. It was not unusual for Gentiles to retain a lifelong relationship to the synagogue without undergoing the ritual operation" (11). Bruce says that the Hillel school accepted gentile converts to Judaism without circumcision (*New Testament History*, 283).

170. However, the whole church might have been pleased only with the idea that two members of the congregation were appointed to accompany Paul and Barnabas to Antioch, perhaps to make sure that they at least implemented the strictures laid down by James.

reason to assume that the Jerusalem church (or any other) had theretofore admitted gentiles into the movement without circumcision.

What made James' decision dramatic was his willingness to re-envision Christianity and welcome gentiles under new, but biblically justifiable, guidelines. Having heard testimony from Peter and Paul, James concluded, "Therefore my judgment is that we should not trouble those of the Gentiles who turn to God" (15:19). Notably, he added that this apparently unprecedented pronouncement was made under divine influence: "For it has seemed good to the Holy Spirit and to us" to require only the Noahide restrictions as a precondition for full-fledged Church membership (15:28–29). Perhaps because the decision was revolutionary, the elders also decided to send two seasoned representatives of the church, Judas and Silas, to carry a letter with the new instructions to Cilicia, Antioch, and other towns in Syria (15:22–34).

Paul's version of the Jerusalem Conference, which he notes occurred at least fourteen years after his revelation (Gal 2:1), suggests that it was a far less important event in his life than it appears to be in the Acts of the Apostles. As I said earlier, he claims to have met the leaders of the Jerusalem church "privately," not publicly, as is the case in Acts. Also, instead of saying that he and Barnabas had been "appointed . . . by the [Antioch] church" to go to Jerusalem (Acts 15:2–3), he says that he "went up by revelation"—i.e., at the urging of Jesus—and simply told James, Peter, and John what he was saying to the gentiles. The leaders of the church, says Paul, "perceived" that Jesus had given him "the gospel of the uncircumcision," just as Jesus had given Peter "the gospel of the circumcision." Then, they warmly shook his hand and told him that he "should go unto the heathen." Significantly missing from Paul's report is any mention of the conversion requirements that James is said in Acts to have demanded. Paul merely says that he was asked to "remember the poor"—that is, make collections for the Jerusalem church (Gal 2:1–10). The net effect of this version of the story is that Paul appears to be in complete control of the situation. It is likely, however, that, given his inferior position in the Church, he was not.

As I have said, in the Gospels, Jesus showed no interest in preaching to the gentiles (vs. the parables in Mark 12:9–11; 13:27).[171] Half a dozen or so passages in the synoptic Gospels hint at a gentile mission, but Jesus' repudiation of non-Jews in Matthew is explicit rather than implicit. Furthermore, if Jesus had been even mildly

171. Witherington, *Jesus Quest*, 143; Bultmann, *Jesus and the Word*, 43; and Hengel, *Four Gospels*, 184. Weiss is quite emphatic on this point. In *Earliest Christianity*, he says repeatedly that the earliest mission was limited not only to Jews, but to Jews in Palestine (I, 5, 7, 53, 136–37, and 171–72). Eventually, of course, the Church insisted that the gentile mission had been the only mission from the very beginning (II, 661). And Latourette agrees. Universalism, he says, "was of the essence of the Gospel" (*History of Christianity*, I, 68). That is, "[i]t is clearly implied in the commission to make disciples of all the nations, teaching them to observe all that Jesus commanded the inner group of his disciples" (119). Lee argues, however: "There is no evidence in the synoptics that Jesus has a sense of mission to the Gentiles. The mandate to go to all nations, at the end of Matthew's Gospel, is generally accepted as a development in the church's sense of mission and is not an original saying of Jesus" (*Galilean Jewishness of Jesus*, 67).

concerned about converting gentiles, he could have visited them in the largely gentile cities of Galilee, including one only a few miles from Nazareth, or in Decapolis, a generally gentile section of Palestine, through which travelers from Galilee to Judea could pass. As one scholar explains, "The Jesus movement originally had close ties with the country." Jesus and his fellow Galileans avoided "the more important towns," and Jesus himself refers to the lives of country people—"farmers, fishermen, vintners and shepherds"—but not artisans, shopkeepers, or traders.[172]

In Acts, however, Jesus initiated the gentile mission immediately after his Crucifixion, when he told his disciples that they would be his witnesses not only in Judea and Samaria, but also "to the end of the earth" (Acts 1:8). In Paul's "vision," according to Luke's earliest report of it in Acts, Paul was told by Jesus to stop persecuting his followers (Acts 9:6).[173] In a simultaneous vision, the disciple Ananias was told by Jesus that Paul was his "chosen instrument . . . to carry [his] name before Gentiles and kings and the sons of Israel" (Acts 9:15). When Ananias met Paul in Damascus, however, he blessed and baptized him, but did not tell him exactly what his mission was. In Luke's second report of Jesus' communication to Paul, Jesus again neglected to tell him that he was supposed to save the gentiles, but this time said nothing about it to Ananias. However, Luke says, Jesus caught up with Paul three years later, when he was praying in the Temple. Appearing to Paul in a trance, Jesus told him to leave Jerusalem because Jesus would "send [him] far away to the Gentiles" (22:10; 17, 21). In Luke's third report of Paul's conversion, Jesus repeated his first message: Paul was appointed to "bear witness" of Jesus to both "the people" (i.e., the Jews) and "the Gentiles"—"to open their eyes, that they may turn from darkness to light" (Acts 26:16–18). In the frequent accounts of this communication in his own words, Paul simply says that Jesus asked him to "preach him among the Gentiles" (Rom 1:14; 11:13; 15:16; Gal 1:16; 2:2; Eph 3:1). He more than implies, however, that this mission was his special assignment from God (Gal 2:7–8; Eph 3:7–9).

What is surprising about these accounts is that Paul, like the Christians who actually heard Jesus' announcement of the gentile mission, did not immediately preach to gentiles.[174] In almost every city in which he proselytized—beginning with Damascus, Salamis, and Pisidian Antioch—he went to synagogues first, as the Hellenists did (Acts 11:19). And, presumably, he converted Jews in all of these cities,

172. Theissen, *Early Palestinian Christianity*, 47–48. Mack notes that there were thirty-five Hellenistic cities in pre-Revolt Palestine, twelve of which were within twenty-five miles of Nazareth (*Who Wrote?* 24, 39). Jerusalem, on the other hand, was "inland and insular, provincial and partisan, and often hostile"—that is, to the Roman occupiers (Borg and Crossan, *Last Week*, 3).

173. Schillebeeckx sees Paul's conversion as consistent with the Jewish conversion model, found in stories of gentile conversions to Judaism, which always involved "a brilliant light" and a disembodied voice. This experience was seen as a kind of enlightenment by Hellenistic Jews (*Jesus*, 383–85).

174. According to Brown, Acts "goes on to show that the disciples had no awareness of having been informed of such a plan" (*Introduction*, 281 n. 6). In having Jesus announce the gentile mission, Luke was merely saying that it was something that "Christ willed for his church" (281).

despite opposition in Damascus and Antioch. According to Luke, many Jews objected to Paul's ministry because they were jealous (e.g., Acts 17:5). That is, Christians were stealing both Jews and gentiles from the synagogue. Since, for Paul, gentiles could become full-fledged Christians without undergoing circumcision, many were drawn away from Judaism, under the rules of which they remained, in a sense, second-class citizens. Opposition could also have come from Jews who objected to the presence in the synagogue of unaffiliated gentiles; from Jewish Christians who promoted a gospel different from Paul's; and from Jewish leaders who were concerned less about Paul's message than about the reaction of local Roman officials, who could blame the Jewish community for allowing the propagation of subversive ideas or for not preventing the civil disorder that often ensued in the course of Paul's visits.[175]

It is worth remembering that, during the period of Paul's ministry, Jewish–Roman relations became increasingly strained by the growing hostility of the Jews of Palestine to both their Jewish rulers and the imperial government. Paul himself was mistaken for one of the rebels, the Egyptian, when he was arrested by a Roman tribune in Jerusalem (Acts 21:28). Nor was the Diaspora immune to the problem. For example, after Claudius' expulsion of the Jews from Rome, the same kind of "disturbances" that precipitated Claudius' action occurred in Thessalonica. Thus, when the Jewish leaders of the city claimed that Paul and his companions were "turn[ing] the world upside down," they meant exactly that: "The wording of the charge fits well into the picture of unruly movements within Jewish communities throughout the empire more or less 'messianic' in character . . . which constituted a threat to public order in places where Jews were resident, and which were deplored and denounced by responsible Jewish leaders who knew the importance of maintaining acceptable relations with the Roman power."[176] It would have done Paul, Silas, and Jason little good to say that they were merely promoting the acceptance of Jesus as the Messiah. The charge against the Christians in Thessalonica was that "they [were] all acting against the decrees of Caesar, saying that there [was] another king, Jesus" (17:7).

In Pisidian Antioch, however, Paul seems to have regarded the Jewish opposition to his proselytizing as unacceptable, whatever the cause. He said he was turning away from the Jews, many of whom, but by no means all, rejected his message: "[S]eeing ye put it from you, and judge yourselves unworthy of everlasting life, lo, we turn to the Gentiles" (Acts 13:46). Threatened with death in Damascus (9:23), chased out of town

---

175. Horsley and Silberman argue that the doctrine Paul preached—among other things, the coming of the Kingdom of God—could have drawn the wrath of local officials: "For those pragmatic Jewish leaders who were primarily concerned with communal survival, the outspoken anti-imperial gospel of Jesus posed a clear political danger" (*Message*, 120).

176. Bruce, *New Testament History*, 300, 308. Bruce discusses the presence of more conservative Jewish Christians in Corinth (331–35), whose influence Paul disparages in his letter to the Corinthian church. Tannehill comments: "Both Jews and Gentiles view the mission as a threat to the customs that provide social cohesion, to the religious basis of their cultures, and to political stability through Caesar's rule" (*Luke-Acts*, II, 203).

in Antioch (13:50), and stoned at Lystra (14:19), Paul announced to his followers in Syrian Antioch that God "had opened a door of faith unto the Gentiles" (14:27). And, after similar experiences elsewhere, Paul said to the Corinthian Jews: "Your blood be upon your heads! I am innocent. From now on I will go to the Gentiles" (18:6).

What remains surprising, however, is that, despite his angry threat in Pisidian Antioch to give up on Jews, Paul continued to preach in synagogues—in Iconium, Philippi, Thessalonica, Beroea, Athens, Corinth, Cenchrae, and Ephesus—sometimes addressing both Jews and Greeks (Acts 14:1; 17:4; and 18:4), but sometimes addressing Jews alone. In almost *every* city Paul visited, he went to the synagogue first. In Athens, for example, he addressed pagans at the Aereopagus, but only after he argued with Jews in the synagogue. In fact, Paul's record of speaking to gentiles alone is shockingly paltry. Even when he "withdrew from" the synagogue in Ephesus (after preaching there to some stubborn and disbelieving Jews) and moved to the hall of Tyrannus, he was still addressing a mixed audience. Ironically, although he condemned the Jews of Pisidian Antioch, announced that he was turning to gentiles, converted many on the spot, and helped spread "the word of God . . . throughout the region" (13:42–49), this may have been Paul's most successful moment in his gentile mission—and, based on the evidence in Acts, virtually his only one.[177]

Thus, as I said above, although Paul started his preaching in Corinth to the Jews of that city and then said to the Corinthians that he would preach to the gentiles "from now on" (Acts 18:6), his next convert was the ruler of the local synagogue, "together with all his household" (18:8). Then he "argued with the Jews in the synagogue in Cenchrae (18:19), where "he cut his hair, for he had a [Nazirite] vow" (18:18). After visiting the churches in Caesarea, Antioch, Galatia, and Phrygia, Paul argued and pleaded in the synagogue in Ephesus. No doubt, he preached to gentiles after he moved his base of operations to the hall of Tyrannus. Nevertheless, in the end, as a result of his extensive travels, "all the residents of Asia heard the word of the Lord, both Jews and Greeks" (19:10).

Paul actually preached to gentiles outside of synagogues only in Philippi, Lystra, Athens, and Ephesus. He exorcised "a slave girl" in Philippi, but the only result was that a "crowd [of pagans] joined in attacking" him and Silas, both of whom were arrested, beaten, and jailed (Acts 16:20–24).[178] The accusation against them—"These men are Jews and they are disturbing our city" (16:21)—matches the charges made by Jews

177. It is entirely possible, however, that Paul gave his Antioch speech (Acts 13:15–41) over and over and achieved the same results in city after city. Perrin and Duling say that "Paul's sermon in Acts 13 is not a report of a speech delivered on a specific occasion, but a sample of what Paul must have said many times to Jews and 'God-fearers'" (*New Testament*, 295).

178. The girl, who "had the power of divination," recognized that Paul and his companions were "servants of the Most High God, who proclaim to you the power of salvation." Paul exorcised her not because he was particularly interested in *her* salvation, however, but because, when she followed the missionaries "crying" the aforementioned words, "Paul was annoyed." His attackers, "her owners," were angry because the girl had brought them "much gain by soothsaying" (Acts 16:16–18).

against Paul and his companions in the synagogues (e.g., 17:6). Furthermore, suggesting that the mission to the gentiles had more serious obstacles than Paul may have been aware of, one of the residents of Philippi complained, "They [that is, Paul and the other apostles] advocate customs which it is not lawful for us Romans to accept or practice." The implication here is that *the conversion of Romans to Christianity was forbidden* (16:21).[179] Because of a presumably supernatural earthquake, which opened the doors of the jail and loosened the missionaries' fetters, the magistrates, evidently fearful of Paul's powers and, later, his claim to be a Roman citizen, asked their former prisoners to leave the city (16:35–39). In the meantime, Paul had converted the jailer and his household, but no one else (16:30–34).

Earlier, in Lystra, after Paul and Silas healed "a cripple from birth," the pagans offered them sacrifices, as if they had been gods, but no one in the gentile audience seems to have been brought to the faith (Acts 14:8–9, 18). Later, in Athens, speaking in the Areopagus (having been dragged there by curious Stoics and Epicureans), Paul described God as a spiritual being who was inappropriately worshiped in the Athenian manner. Then, he briefly explained judgment, repentance, and "the resurrection of the dead" (17:22–31). To all this, Paul and Silas received a mixed reaction, converting "some" men and women, but others "mocked" them, while still others wanted to hear more (17:32–34).[180]

In Ephesus, a maker of "silver shrines of Artemis" publicly accused Paul of interfering with the business of the silver workers and possibly damaging the reputation of Artemis by "saying that gods made with hands are not gods" (Acts 19:23–27). A crowd gathered in the theater, "dragging with them" two of Paul's "companions in travel" (19:29). Paul was advised not to interfere (19:30), and the potentially violent meeting was quieted and finally terminated by "the town clerk," who assured everyone that the missionaries were "neither sacrilegious nor blasphemous of our goddess" (19:35–41). When Paul finally returned to Jerusalem, he told James and the elders "one by one the things that God had done among the Gentiles through his ministry. And when they heard it, they glorified God" (21: 19–20). Given the evidence in Acts, however, one wonders what they were really celebrating.

Not only did Paul fail to convert many gentiles other than God-fearers—at least as far the evidence in Acts demonstrates—many of the gentiles he encountered in his extensive travels were already professing Christians. There is little doubt, of course, that he exerted a strong and important influence on "the brethren" everywhere he went. There is also little doubt that, as his letters show, he taught, exhorted, and comforted them, and quite likely, by such means, helped sustain them and enlarge the membership of their churches. The point is, however, that many of the Christians

179. See, on this point, *Oxford Annotated Bible*, 1340–41.

180. Kee et al. describe Paul's treatment by the philosophers in Athens as a citizens' arrest and his speech before the Areopagus as a defense before "the council of city officials who were charged with maintaining order in the agora" (*Understanding the New Testament*, 179).

he met had been converted from at least the mid-thirties onward by both Hebraists like Peter and Hellenists like Philip. Ironically, in contrast to Paul, some of these missionaries were very successful: "And the hand of the Lord was with them, and a great number that believed turned to the Lord" (Acts 11:19–21). Subsequently, Luke reports, "the word of the Lord grew and multiplied" (12:24).

Furthermore, Paul often found these Christians, whom Luke refers to as "disciples" or "brethren," already organized—not only in Antioch, but also in Damascus (Acts 9:19), Lydda (9:32), Joppa (9:36), Lystra (14:20), Thessalonica (17:10), Caesarea (18:22), Galatia and Phrygia (18:23), Ephesus (19:1), and Tyre (21:4). In Corinth, Paul was preceded by Aquila and Prisca (18:1–2). Thus, while he might have founded some churches, like the church in Philippi (16:15), thanks to his conversion of Lydia and her household, he was evidently only one of many proselytizing visitors to all of these churches (including monitors and observers sent by the Jerusalem church) and, except for his extraordinarily hard work, especially his willingness to stay in some places for months and sometimes years, just another competing voice in the gospel competition. Again, some of the members of these churches might have been gentiles, but many of them had been Jewish proselytes or God-fearers, some with lingering ties to Judaism, and many members were Jews: "The Jews and their sympathizers (proselytes and 'God fearers') likely were the initial converts to Christianity outside of Palestine as well."[181]

Of course, the main question raised by Luke's account of the gentile mission—whether conducted by Paul or by the Church in general—is whether it ever happened at all, at least on the grand scale implied by Paul's statements and extensive travels.[182] First, as I said earlier, no one seems to have responded very quickly to Jesus' initiation of the mission in the first chapter of Acts. At least a few years had passed after Jesus' Ascension even before Philip converted "multitudes" of Samaritans, who considered themselves, as residents of the former Northern Kingdom of Israel, to be Jews anyway.[183] The Jerusalem church leaders must have thought of them as Jews—that is,

181. Conzelmann and Lindemann, *Interpreting the New Testament*, 364. Bruce notes, for example, that "in its earliest stages Roman Christianity was thoroughly Jewish, and long after the apostolic age it continued to exhibit certain features of its Jewish provenance" (*New Testament History*, 299). Regarding Paul's recruitment of God-fearers, Bruce says: "Paul recognized in the 'God-fearers' on the fringe of synagogue congregations a providentially prepared bridgehead into the Gentile world." These worshipers of the Jewish God "were familiar with the messianic hope in some form." However, their participation in its "blessings," was, from the perspective of the Jews, dependent on their full conversion to Judaism. Told that, as Christians, salvation was available to them without surgery, "such people could not but welcome the good news" (276–77).

182. Meeks warns against taking Luke too seriously on the success and scope of Paul's mission: "From the letters, although they by no means contradict all aspects of the Acts picture, we receive on the whole the impression of a less grand and public mission" (*First Urban Christians*, 28). Meeks also questions whether Paul actually preached in the public spaces he is said to have visited in Athens, for example: "We must also ask whether the more public settings in Acts may not often reflect some of the author's subtle literary allusions, such as the several hints of Socrates in the encounters in the agora and Areopagus in Athens" (26).

183. According to the editors of *Oxford Annotated Bible*, "Samaria was inhabited by mixed remnants

circumcised, though heretical—since "the apostles," upon hearing "that Samaria had received the word of God," sent Peter and John to give them "the Holy Spirit" after their baptism by Philip (Acts 8:5–6, 14–17).

Nor did Paul react very quickly to the assignment of proselytizing among the gentiles, which Jesus gave him at the moment of his conversion in the mid- or early thirties.[184] His first visits were, as we have seen, to the synagogues in Salamis and Pisidian Antioch, and they were initiated by the leaders of "the church at Antioch," who "sent" Paul and Barnabas off to missionize at the urging of "the Holy Spirit." Their assignment was, in the words of the Holy Spirit, to do "the work to which I have called them," which was not to preach to the gentiles, but simply to continue the mission to the Jews (Acts 13:1–3).

Second, it is eminently notable that neither Peter nor Paul ever *deliberately* set out on anything that could be called a gentile mission.[185] After he healed Aeneas and Tabitha, the immediate result of which was the conversion "of all the residents of Lydda and Sharon," as well as "many" in Joppa, Peter converted Cornelius only at the behest of "the Spirit" who spoke to him in the midst of his rooftop prayer. Indeed, it was Cornelius, prompted by direct instructions from an "angel," who sought out Peter by sending three of his men from Caesarea to Joppa, a journey of thirty miles. Peter's objections—that he had "never eaten anything that is common or unclean" and had refused "to associate with or to visit any one of another nation" (Acts 10:14, 28)— are evidently intended to reveal that this was an event of great consequence for the Church precisely because *gentiles had not yet been converted*. That is, Peter's converts in Lydda and Joppa were Jews or Jewish proselytes, not gentiles.

At this historic moment (and this moment only), Luke says, "the apostles and the brethren" in the Jerusalem church, who had challenged Peter on the same grounds that he questioned himself (Acts 11:2), declared, "Then to the Gentiles also God has granted repentance unto life" (11:18). Surely, they were persuaded not only by Peter's detailed report of the event—which included his reception of a divine message,

---

of the northern tribes who worshiped the Lord and used the Pentateuch. The Jews despised them as mongrels. In one tradition the disciples are forbidden to visit their towns (Matt 10.5), but, according to others Jesus was friendly to Samaritans (Luke 10.30–37; 17.11–19; John 4.4–42). Philip also baptized the Ethiopian eunuch, whom the editors of *Oxford Annotated Bible* say "was probably a Jew" (1327–28), although he is more often understood to be a God-fearer.

184. Thus, Brown suggests, assuming that Paul ever actually turned to the gentiles, that the decision does not appear to have derived from either Jesus' statement in Acts 1 in AD 30 or Jesus' commission of Paul in a vision a few years later. Rather, it "may have stemmed from experiment": i.e., the fact that Paul "found (as Acts indicates) more success" with gentiles than with Jews (*Introduction*, 304). That is, McKenzie points out, "Paul declares that he turns to the Gentiles only in response to the hostility and incredulity of the Jews." In other words, "Paul is described as responding to a practical situation rather than to a commission from the risen Lord" (*New Testament*, 170).

185. Conzelmann and Lindemann say that, although Luke is generally right about the expansion of the Church, including its growing effort to convert gentiles, "one may have to imagine the development as less systematic and less structured" than Luke describes it (*Interpreting the New Testament*, 351).

as well as his observation of the descent of the Holy Spirit onto Cornelius and his household—but also by the eye-witness verification of "the believers from among the circumcised who came with Peter" and were equally "amazed" when the gentiles spoke in tongues and praised God (10:45–46). True, Cornelius was a special case, as "a devout man who feared God with all his household, gave alms liberally to the people, and prayed constantly to God" (10:1–2). That is, he followed Jewish laws (except circumcision, among others), contributed to the welfare of the Jews of Caesarea, and attended a synagogue for Sabbath services. For all that, he was not a Jew—not being circumcised—and yet he had been visited by "an angel of God" and "the Holy Spirit."

In Luke's account, this announcement appears to have authorized the gentile mission of the Hellenists who had left Jerusalem after Stephen's death. Even at this point, however, Luke says that in Phoenicia, Cyprus, and Syrian Antioch they initially spoke "the word to none except Jews."[186] Nevertheless, "some of them . . . spoke to the Greeks also" in Antioch, "and a great number that believed turned to the Lord" (Acts 11:19–21). Apparently concerned about every development in the Diaspora churches, the leaders of the Jerusalem church then "sent Barnabas to Antioch." Since "he was glad" to see this first manifestation of the Church's new direction, he encouraged the believers "to remain faithful," the result of which was an expansion of the Antioch church, under his guidance: That is, "a large company was added to the Lord." And the church—including, no doubt its gentile membership—grew even more with the help of both Barnabas and Paul, whom Barnabas eventually asked to join him in Antioch (11:22–26).[187]

Yet, despite these successes, not only had the gentile mission been inordinately and unexplainably delayed as well as initiated more or less unintentionally by its participants—that is, only at the very strong urging of the Holy Spirit, who, as I said, brought Peter and Cornelius together—it was also so seldom sustained that it could hardly be called a mission. Luke says that Paul went to the Jews first and then to the gentiles, but, after his first major announcement that he would stop preaching to Jews and start preaching exclusively to gentiles (Acts 13:46–47), Paul, as we have seen, embarked on a tour of the Jewish Diaspora, with a few stops at places where gentiles might be seen, but without any systematic plan to address his intended audience.

In this regard, it is worth remembering that Judaism, by the first century AD, had attracted a large number of gentiles, not all of them to full proselytism, of course, which required circumcision, but to the strong affiliation with Judaism indicated by the terms "God-fearer" and "God-worshiper." In the words of one historian of the

186. "After Cornelius' conversion demonstrates to the Jewish Christians that God has cleansed the Gentiles, the apostles do not directly participate in the gentile mission" (Tannehill, *Luke-Acts*, II, 281).

187. Of course, it is impossible to be certain of the chronology in these passages. Luke's order of events suggests that the acceptance of gentiles into the Church was approved by the leaders in Jerusalem after Cornelius' conversion and before the Hellenists' conversion of gentiles in Antioch. The editors of *Oxford Annotated Bible* comment, "This mission to the Greeks may have occurred before Peter's conversion of Cornelius" (1333).

Church, "The monotheism and ethics of the Jews had a magnetic attraction for the Hellenistic world, which turned thousands into 'worshippers of God.'"[188] That is why, as a result of Paul's mission to the synagogues, his churches consisted of "(a few) Jews and (a considerable number of) Greeks," many of whom were "Hellenistic frequenters of the synagogue."[189] According to another historian, "As everyone knows, a tradition of advocacy of faith and of drawing other people to the veneration of God was recognized in Judaism and taken over by and fortified in Christianity."[190] However, it was not merely the case that Christians followed the example of Jews in attracting gentiles. It was, rather—perhaps far more often than many historians have realized—that Christians actually converted the gentiles who had first been drawn to Judaism. Indeed, since Paul never stopped speaking in synagogues, some of his churches may well have been made up *mostly* of Jews and God-fearers, as were Peter's, even after Paul gave up on converting Palestinian Jews.[191]

It seems fair to conclude, as well, that Paul may have met and converted few gentiles other than those he encountered in the synagogues he visited. Even if he spoke frequently in marketplaces, where he could find gentiles, as he did in Athens, he was unlikely to encounter very many potential converts. In such venues, presumably, he was not addressing large, more or less captive audiences, of the kind he found in the synagogues, but shoppers and passersby. Even when he preached in the hall of Tyrannus in Ephesus, he was evidently compelled to wait for curious visitors who heard of him only by word of mouth. In short, whatever the actual case may have been, Luke gives no indication that Paul found a means of addressing gentiles in situations that would have allowed for anything more than one-on-one meetings. Furthermore, aside from spending weeks and months preaching in synagogues, Paul also spent a great deal of time revisiting churches that he had established himself or congregations with whom he had developed good relations. Thus, it might reasonably be supposed that there was no large-scale gentile mission to speak of.

188. Van Leeuwen, *Christianity in World History*, 223. Meeks says that Jews attracted gentile followers not only because of their monotheism, but also because of their worship without idolatry and their communitarianism (*First Urban Christians*, 36). Meeks adds that the Jews were so successful at proselytizing that the Romans frequently tried to suppress their efforts (207 n. 175). On this point, see Segal, who mentions the expulsion of Jews from Rome on two occasions, for trying to convert Romans to Judaism. Segal says that it is impossible to determine how aggressive this missionizing was among Romans. "But the undeniable truth was that they did convert in sufficient numbers to cause anxiety in the pagan world" (*Paul the Convert*, 86). On Judaism as "a missionary religion," see Sandmel, *Jewish Understanding*, 41–42.

189. Van Leeuwen, *Christianity in World History*, 121.

190. MacMullen, *Christianizing the Roman Empire*, 105.

191. Hengel, *Four Gospels*, 154. Segal says that many early Christians were God-fearers and that Paul's audiences consisted almost entirely of Jews, proselytes, and God-fearers (*Rebecca's Children*, 43, 98). Hare argues that "the nucleus of many of the Pauline churches was drawn from the synagogue and included both Jews and 'God-fearers'" and that that even as late as Matthew's Gospel (at least as far as Matthew was concerned) "Jews compose[d] the nucleus of the Church" (*Jewish Persecution of Christians*, 112 n. 4, 153–54).

However, by the time Luke wrote his history of the early Church, it had grown sufficiently to justify an idealized portrait of Paul and an exaggerated account of his accomplishments. That is, the mission itself, as it appears in Acts, may have been more theological in purpose than historical.[192] Specifically, it represented or symbolized an effort that, by the end of the first century, had successfully converted thousands of gentiles, but only as a result of the work of many Christian proselytizers over a period of more than fifty years.[193] Short of this hypothesis, we are left with the conclusion that Luke simply neglected to show where, when, and how Paul successfully converted Gentiles other than those who were in one way or another associated with Judaism; or that Paul was either inept or self-deceived—that is, he was either unable to find the gentiles he so desired to speak to or merely thought he wanted to speak to them, but actually did not.[194]

Thus, when Paul finally got to Rome at the end of Acts, he did what he had always done. On one hand, he says in his letter to the Roman church that he yearned to see its members, that he looked forward to their mutual support and encouragement, and, particularly—especially in relation to this discussion—that he would be fulfilling his special mission by "reap[ing] some harvest among [them] as well as among the rest of the gentiles." He was, he adds, "under obligation to both Greeks and barbarians." For that reason, he was "eager to preach the gospel" in Rome (Rom 1:11–15). On the other hand, however, at least according to Luke's account in Acts, neither objective was fulfilled.

192. Like many scholars, McKenzie regards Acts as "more theological than historical" (*New Testament*, 161). As for Paul's attempt to convert non-Jews, McKenzie says that "the tactics described [by Luke] can be called a mission to the Gentiles only by straining language" (170; see also 168–169). Segal notes that "Paul's fragmentary accounts of the import of his mission differ significantly from and even contradict the Lukan description" (*Paul the Convert*, 12). This is partly owing to Luke's "biased and ahistorical . . . reporting." That is, although "there was no reason for [Luke] deliberately to fabricate the details of the mission," he may be describing "the social situation" of his own time: "Luke clearly has actual experience of this kind of proselytism, whether or not it corresponds to Paul's experience" (270; see also 272). Sanders quotes Arland J. Hultgren as saying that Luke portrayed Paul as both the "ideal persecutor" and the "ideal missionary" (*Schismatics,* 7). In the view of both Sanders and Hultgren, he may have been neither.

193. Horsley and Silberman regard Paul and Barnabas' first missionary journey "as both a commemoration of the efforts of two of [Antioch's] most extraordinary leaders and the distilled recollection of the efforts of many unrecorded individuals from the Antioch community as they fanned out to preach and organize in the surrounding regions over the course of several years" (*Message*, 130).

194. Tannehill calls the gentile mission "not as successful as early Christians hoped." More specifically, in relation to this mission, "Paul's life is not a simple success story" (*Luke-Acts*, II, 239–40). Considering Luke's report that Paul nearly always went to synagogues first (and seldom to any other venue), Brown says that "scholars have wondered whether Acts is accurate here" (*Introduction*, 304). Brown argues that Paul's letters are addressed "to churches evangelized in later missionary journeys at a time when Paul turned to converting Gentiles" (304). The problem with this claim, however, is twofold. First, Paul *continually* visited synagogues and, as far as Luke is concerned, *never* "turned" away from that practice. Second, most of the churches Paul wrote to were in cities in which he initially visited the synagogue: Corinth, Thessalonica, Philippi, and Ephesus.

When Paul arrived in the capital of the empire, he seems to have spent very little time with "the brethren," who met him thirty or forty miles outside of the city (Acts 28:15), and little time preaching to gentiles. Surely, the self-proclaimed apostle to the gentiles would have been expected to seek out some of the objects of his missionary intentions. And the writer of that long, thoughtful, even passionate letter to the Christians of Rome would have wanted to see how they responded to it. But neither of these logical expectations was borne out in Paul's case, at least as Luke, who knew nothing of Paul's letter, describes it. Paul simply "called together the local leaders of the Jews" and told them about his struggles with the Jews of Jerusalem.[195] When they returned to him later and Paul tried "to convince them about Jesus both from the law of Moses and the prophets," he was, as usual, dissatisfied with their response and consequently announced that he was turning to the gentiles (28:17–28). Acts of the Apostles ends with that persistent, but somewhat pointless condemnation.

THE SPLINTERING OF THE FAITH

In his avoidance of gentiles, Jesus was following the traditional Jewish belief that in the Messianic Age gentiles would be, if not destroyed (Joel 3:17–21), then either included subordinately (Zech 8:20–23) or (the most common view) included without any limitations, both contingent on their repentance.[196] On the other hand, Paul might have been preaching to (and converting) gentiles (albeit mostly Jewish proselytes and God-fearers) without opposition for some time (Gal 1:15, 2:1). At some point, however, Paul's success among these groups might have angered both Christian and non-Christian Jews, the latter because the Jesus movement was drawing converts away from the synagogues.[197] The members of the Jerusalem church might have objected because gentiles were beginning to outnumber Jews in the churches outside of Palestine, and the balance of power was slipping away from Palestine to Paul's churches in the Diaspora.

The divide between the two wings of the Church is important, particularly considering that Pauline Christianity eventually triumphed, and Jamesian Christianity completely disappeared.[198] While either Peter or Philip might have been the first apos-

---

195. Brown comments: "That in fact Paul was involved with synagogues is strongly suggested by his statement in II Cor 11:24: 'Five times I received from Jews thirty-nine lashes'—a synagogue punishment. Even at the end, Acts will continue to show Paul, when he arrives at Rome *ca.* 61, speaking first to Jews" (*Introduction*, 304 n. 65).

196. Sanders, *Jesus and Judaism*, 214; Guignebert, *Jewish World*, 155; and Levine, *Misunderstood Jew*, 68–69.

197. Bruce, *New Testament History*, 147, 266, 276–77; and Spong, *Liberating the Gospels*, 48.

198. "It would seem that for as long as Law-observing Jewish-Christianity endured, there was friction between the Palestinian and the Gentile church which ended in a split, and the progressive eclipse of the original form of the Jesus movement coincided with the triumphant rise of Gentile Christianity" (Vermes, *Changing Faces of Jesus*, 154).

tle to convert a gentile, Paul was the one who continued to either establish or expand churches in Greece, Macedonia, Asia Minor, and Syria. Whether he maintained James' requirements among gentile converts is doubtful.[199] What is certain is that, while the Jerusalem church converted "many thousands of Jews" (Acts 21:20), Paul (and other Christian missionaries in the Diaspora) brought into the church many more gentiles. And the more gentiles he (and others) converted, the more the Church moved away from Moses and the Law and towards Paul and his doctrine of Faith. Indeed, "[o]nly the growing number of gentile believers, as well as the destruction of the temple and its consequences, would permit Pauline Christianity to become representative of the movement as a whole."[200]

Some contemporary scholars have argued that Paul did not reject Judaism and the Law *for Jewish Christians*, but it is likely that "all ancient readers" assumed that he did.[201] And, in fact, the hostility of the Jews toward Paul—giving him thirty-nine lashes on five occasions, stoning him and leaving him for dead, and having him arrested whenever possible—suggests that either his message or his method (or both) offended Jews more than the preaching of other Christian proselytizers did. Of course, assuming that his public declamations mirrored his attacks in his letters, his reference to Jews as Christ-killers and enemies of God (1 Thess. 2:13–16) probably made few friends for him among the recipients of these allegations. As one Bible scholar puts it, "He had expressed himself intemperately."[202]

The shift from James to Paul was momentous in the history of the Church because, by most accounts, Paul was a cosmopolitan Diaspora Jew, who had been exposed to and was therefore influenced by Greek philosophy and culture, as Jesus, James, Peter, and John were not. These Palestinians were not even from Jerusalem, the somewhat Hellenized spiritual and intellectual center of Palestine, but from Galilee, which was notorious as a hotbed of radicalism and a cultural outpost characterized,

199. Weiss says that Paul ignored the decree (*Earliest Christianity*, I, 260). See Conzelmann and Lindemann, *Interpreting the New Testament*, 362–363, for a discussion of the contradictions between the accounts in Galatians and Acts. Grant presents a good case for concluding that, although Paul does not mention the decree, he seems to follow it in, for example, 1 Thess 4:3–7 and 1 Cor 5:1–5; 10:32 (*Historical Interpretation*, 395).

200. Chilton and Neusner, *Judaism*, 111.

201. Gager, "Paul, the Apostle of Judaism," 58; see also 73–75. Conzelmann and Lindemann ask: "Is it in keeping with Pauline theology when the validity of the law was nevertheless recognized for Jewish Christians? Based on the doctrine of justification, would Paul not have had to demand freedom from the law for Jewish Christians as well?" (*Interpreting the New Testament*, 363). Weiss says that Paul was then, as he is now, difficult to read (*Earliest Christianity*, I, 154). And Paul himself complained that his followers misunderstood him (1 Cor 5:9–13; 6:12–20; Gal 1:6–17; 5:11–12). According to Mack, "Paul's gospel was not comprehensible and persuasive for most people of his time, including many other Christians" (*Who Wrote?* 99).

202. Brown cites, in support of this charge, among other examples of Paul's indulgences in "gutter crudity," his wish that his Jewish-Christian enemies who were promoting universal circumcision would "castrate [or mutilate] themselves" (Gal 5:12) (*Introduction*, 473–74).

at least according to Judeans, by illiteracy and ignorance.[203] Paul was from Tarsus, "a flourishing commercial city [that] contained many of the religions prevalent throughout the Greco-Roman world. It had a well-known Stoic philosophical school. In fact, Tarsus rivaled Athens and Rome as an educational center." The letters of Paul suggest that he had a formal Greek education, enabling him to speak and write Greek well and use some of the literary devices taught by Greek philosophers of the period.[204]

It is hardly surprising, therefore, that Paul's ideas, particularly on God and ethics, were different not only from those of James and Peter, but also from those of Jesus.[205] Besides rejecting the Mosaic Law in favor of Grace, Paul shifted the attention of the Church from the Kingdom of God to Jesus' Resurrection and Atonement,[206]

203. Conzelmann and Lindemann note that "Judaism in Palestine intermixed less with hellenistic elements than in other areas of the empire" (*Interpreting the New Testament*, 118). Grant says that Jews were less willing than other ethnic groups in the Roman empire "to amalgamate cults and gods"—that is, to practice the syncretism that was "characteristic of the period" (*Historical Introduction*, 249). Indeed, according to Mattingly, "The Jews alone [that is, among all the residents of the Roman empire] refused to acquiesce in imperial rule" (*Roman Imperial Civilisation*, 63). Davies says, "The only province that broke the peace [i.e., the Pax Romana], which began with the accession of Augustus and continued to the death of Marcus Aurelius (A.D. 180), was Judaea" (*Invitation*, 15).

204. On Paul's use of Greek literary methods, see Koester, *History, Culture, and Religion*, 109. Meeks says that Paul uses "the conventions and topics of Greco-Roman moral advice" in 1 Thessalonians and that the Corinthian letters use "paraenetic language," which demonstrates both "how flexible were the strategies offered by ancient rhetoric" and how skillful Paul was in using all the traditions he inherited (*Origins of Christian Morality*, 80, 132). Brown mentions Paul's ability to write good Greek, his "basic Hellenistic rhetorical skills," his knowledge of scriptures and other writings in Greek, his familiarity with Greek religion, and his probable familiarity with Greek philosophy (*Introduction*, 425). Maccoby identifies the exact sources of Paul's quotations of Menander (1 Cor 15:3), the Stoic poet Aratus (Acts 17:28), and Epimenides (Titus 1:12) (*Mythmaker*, 215). See also Perrin and Duling, *New Testament*, 135; Grant, *Historical Introduction*, 65, 176, 251; and Wylen, *Jews*, 48. Bruce, however, states that there is no evidence that Paul either studied in a Greek school or under the tutelage of a Greek teacher: "[T]he knowledge of Greek literature and culture that his letters reflect was part of the common stock of educated people in the Hellenistic world at that time, whether they were Jews or Gentiles" (*New Testament History*, 238). Paul also came into closer contact with Hellenistic culture when he was preaching in Syria-Cilicia in the years before the Jerusalem Conference (245).

205. Thus, Herford concludes that Paul "cut the Church loose from Judaism" and thereby became "the founder of the Christian Church, no longer Jewish but universal." Paul questioned the right of Judaism to exist and consequently called for its termination. Its preoccupation with law made it legalistic, and Jesus was a divine agent sent by God to replace it (*Pharisees*, 215–19). Herford accuses Paul of misreading Judaism, however, and of unjustly and unnecessarily proclaiming it to be not only invalid, but obstructive and dangerous. In all this, Paul simply went too far because he understood too little (220–21).

206. Grant, *Jesus*, 178. Additional comments on the differences between Jesus and Paul can be found in Meeks, *First Urban Christians*, 9, 34; Maccoby, *Mythmaker*, 3; Nickelsburg, "First and Second Enoch," 89; Weiss, *Earliest Christianity*, I, 78–79, 163; Flusser, *Sage from Galilee*, 162–65; and Meier, *Marginal Jew*, I, 54 n. 24. Kung says, "Today even conservative Christian theologians concede that [unlike Paul] Jesus himself put the kingdom of God at the centre of his preaching and not his own role, person, dignity." Furthermore, both "Christian and Jewish interpreters largely agree" that "Jesus himself never used the designation messiah or any other honorific title of himself, except, perhaps, the ambiguous title 'Son of Man'" (*Judaism*, 330–31; see also 333, 376–77). Thus, when Paul "arbitrarily" used "some concepts and notions from his Hellenistic environment"—son of God, Divine Man,

identified the essential human conflict as a battle between soul and body or spirit and flesh,[207] and replaced Jesus' emphasis on Good Works as a means of salvation with his own idea of Faith.[208] That is why it can be said that, along with the evangelist John, although he may not have *invented* Christianity, Paul certainly brought it closer to the Hellenistic views not only of his contemporaries Stephen and Philip, but, more im-

---

mystery god—"those Jews and Christians who came to the letters of Paul from the Jesus tradition" heard "the message of Jesus in a somewhat alien light: fused to quite different perspectives, categories and conceptions, translated into quite a different entire constellation" (365). "Nevertheless," Kung strongly rejects the idea that "Paul misunderstood Jesus" and thereby became "the real founder of Christianity" (363). In order to make this argument, however, Kung must speculate that Paul had to have heard more about Jesus from the disciples in Jerusalem than he suggests in his letters. That is, he must have relied on "eye-witnesses," even though the witnesses themselves remained Law-abiding! In this way, Paul supposedly discovered that Jesus had not been executed as a subversive by the Romans, but as a "critic of the Law," regarding which "conservative Jewish Christian moralists," such as those in Galatia (but also presumably those, like Peter and James, in Jerusalem), were "confused." In other words, it was *they* who misunderstood Jesus. What Paul said, therefore, was a continuation and completion of what Jesus had said "only implicitly": "So Paul did no more and no less than draw out those lines which had already been charted in the preaching, conduct and death of Jesus. In so doing he attempted to make the message understood beyond Israel, for the whole of the then known world." That is, when Paul Hellenized Jesus (i.e., by presenting him in the context of new perspectives, categories, concepts, and constellations), he took him exactly where he wanted to go, although Kung acknowledges that, if it was a "continuation," it was "a *radical* continuation" (364–68; my emphasis). The question is, of course, when does "a radical continuation" become a discontinuation?

207. Bultmann says that Paul "does not think of man in terms of the anthropological dualism of Hellenistic mysticism; that is, he does not speak of the tragedy of man, of the entangling of the divine soul in the earthly body" (*Jesus and the Word*, 48). See also Fredriksen, *From Jesus to Christ*, 63; and Segal, *Paul the Convert*, 160. However, it is hard to interpret Romans 7:22–24 otherwise: "For I delight in the law of God, in my inmost self, but I see in my members another law at war with the law of my mind and making me captive to the law of sin which dwells in my members. Wretched man that I am! Who will deliver me from this body of death?" (my emphasis; see also Gal 5:16). Meeks suggests a middle ground on this subject in *Origins of Christian Morality*. That is, in contrasting flesh and spirit, Paul is not associating the flesh with the body. Nevertheless, Meeks continues, Paul's warnings against "the body" are akin to those of Seneca and the Stoics. And the body/soul conflict in Christianity took a much more Neoplatonic turn in the Thomas and Valentinian traditions (133–38). According to Perrin and Duling, Paul's lists of virtues and vices are drawn from conventional Hellenistic morality (*New Testament*, 199). On Paul's Hellenism, see Sandmel, *Jewish Understanding*, 44–45. On Paul's idea of the conflict between the physical and the spiritual, see 51, 59–60, 69–73. Russell argues that the early Church embraced the Jewish idea "that life in the other world is life in the body": "The early Christians, like the rabbis, understood that union with God was union of the whole human, both soul and body, with him." In the third century, however, "Platonic ideas of the soul's great superiority to the body promoted the idea of the survival of souls apart from bodies" (*History of Heaven*, 15; see also 19, 39).

208. Vermes, *Changing Faces of Jesus*, 104–5. In contrast to Jesus, Paul shows "no special interest in socio-economic problems and especially none in the topic of poverty and wealth" (Stegemann and Stegemann, *Jesus Movement*, 295). In fact, Paul pays little attention to (and actually seems to be totally unaware of) Jesus' ethical concerns. Klingaman says that Paul "evinced no interest at all in Jesus' ethical teaching" (*First Century*, 265). Maguire says that, while older scholars claimed to have found hundreds of parallels between Paul's letters and Jesus' sayings in the synoptic Gospels, "[m]ore objective scholars today" have found very few. Maguire concludes, therefore, that "it is not at all clear how Jesus and Paul would have meshed in a theological conversation" (*Moral Core*, 94). Yoder, on the other hand, blames F. C. Baur for exaggerating the "polarity of Jesus and Paul" (*Politics of Jesus*, 170).

portant, of the later reconcilers of Christianity and Platonism who led the Church out of Palestine and into the heart of the Roman empire—Clement of Alexandria, Justin Martyr, Tertullian, Origen, St. Jerome, John Chrysostom, and St. Augustine.[209] After Jerusalem was destroyed and Palestinian Christianity declined, the Church continued to march toward Hellenization without impediment and away from the Judaism that was its origin.[210]

The exportation of Christianity to the Diaspora was not, at first, a unifying process. Serious divisions in the Church arose between Jewish and non-Jewish Christians, Palestinian and Diaspora Christians, and rural and urban Christians. Furthermore, as different apostles went to different towns and cities, they spread their own ideas of what Jesus said and did. And, when these ideas were received by people who were sufficiently impressed by them to become Christians, they understood them in the context of their own cultural and experiential situation. That is, they interpreted the gospel that was presented to them in terms of their backgrounds as Greeks, Mesopotamians, or Egyptians; in terms of their past religious affiliations (e.g., with a mystery religion, like the cult of Isis, or a philosophy, like Epicureanism); and in terms of their personal experience as family members, tradesmen, peasants, slaves, or scholars.

The result was—perhaps not hundreds of sects in the strictest sense of the word—but a variety of religious attitudes, from asceticism to libertinism, from Pharisaic Judaism to Gnosticism, and from mysticism to dogmatism. All of these many different interpretations of Christianity were manifested in an equally rich variety of religious practices. Jewish Christians were likely to adapt their traditional liturgy to their new Christian faith, former Stoics were inclined to understand Christianity as a rational religion, and ex-members of mystery cults no doubt interpreted baptism,

---

209. Segal says that Paul moved Christianity closer to paganism and the mystery cults: "Paul's writing, by stressing his experience of conversion, helped bridge the gap between the apocalyptic Jewish seer and the dominant Hellenistic Christian community of piety and mystery" (*Rebecca's Children*, 116). Schillebeeckx makes exactly the same point in *Jesus*, 383. "Because of his pagan background," says Maccoby, "Saul would have read into the story of the death and resurrection of Jesus meanings which were in fact absent from the minds of the Nazarenes themselves," for these people were "utterly opposed to pagan schemes of salvation based on dying and resurrected deities" (*Mythmaker*, 101). Carmichael discusses Paul's familiarity with mystery cults in Tarsus in *Birth of Christianity*, 92–94, 96–104, 133. Bultmann claims that Paul saved Christianity from remaining a Jewish sect (*Theology*, I, 37). He later calls Paul "the founder of Christian theology" (187). On this point, see Vermes, *Resurrection*, xv; and Pixley, *God's Kingdom*, 90, cited in Maguire, *Moral Core*, 94–95.

210. Like many scholars, Bornkamm says that the Jerusalem church moved out of Jerusalem before the Revolt of 66. And many Jews moved to Babylonia after the war (*Jesus of Nazareth*, 195–196 n. 2). Maccoby offers a different view of the fate of the Jerusalem church, however. He says that the departure of the church from Jerusalem before the Revolt of 66 is a "legend" made up by Church historians Eusebius and Epiphanius. Maccoby cites S. G. F. Brandon, who claims that the Jewish Christians stayed in Jerusalem throughout the war, fought on the side of their ethnic compatriots, and only after their defeat abandoned the city (*The Fall of Jerusalem and the Christian Church*, 168–73; cited in *Mythmaker*, 174). Maccoby adds that, at this point, the Pauline church filled the vacuum. Weiss questions whether all Christians left Jerusalem in *Earliest Christianity*, II, 723–24.

communal meals, and prayer based on their experience in the worship of Serapis, Cybele, or Aphrodite.[211]

In Paul's churches, for example, there were differences not only between one church and another, but sometimes among the members of a single church. Not only were Corinthians unlike Galatians and Philippians, but members of these churches disagreed among themselves. After all, many congregations attracted a wide variety of members—not only Jews and gentiles, but slaves and masters, as well as natives and foreigners. In his first letter to the church in Corinth, Paul pleaded with the members of this congregation to end their "dissensions" and strive for unity.[212] Apparently, disagreements arose partly because different members had been baptized by different apostles (1 Cor 1:10–12). As a result, the church was plagued by "jealousy and strife," perhaps suggesting that different converts had gotten different messages from Apollos, Paul, and Peter or that the name of the baptizer was being used to justify this or that interpretation of the gospel these missionaries had delivered (3:3–4).

Other factions seem to have been based on differences in social class, resulting in the more well-to-do eating and drinking at the church love-feast, while the less well-to-do looked on enviously: "When you meet together," Paul wrote, "it is not the Lord's Supper that you eat. For in eating, each one goes ahead with his own meal, and one is hungry and another is drunk. What! Do you not have houses to eat or drink in? Or do you despise the church of God and humiliate those who have nothing?" (1 Cor 11:20). The love-feast, Paul concluded, should be a sacred meal: Thus, "if any one is hungry, let him eat at home—lest you come together to be condemned" (11:33–34).[213]

The largely gentile church in Corinth, influenced by Greek ideas and established in a city notorious for its libertinism, clearly had a difficult time understanding Paul's gospel as Paul wished it to be understood.[214] Thus, Paul also faulted the Corinthians for being proud of their newly acquired "wisdom" and displaying their superiority by the so-called loftiness of their ideas and the so-called eloquence of their speech. "Jews

211. On the subject of diversity among early Christian sects, Brown mentions Bauer, *Orthodoxy and Heresy in Earliest Christianity*. See also, on the variety of Christian communities in the far-flung corners of the empire—Mesopotamia, England, Egypt, and Spain—Chadwick, *Early Church*, 62–65. Carroll says that Constantine was primarily responsible for the ultimate unification of the Church, a need for which "was first defined not by the Lord, a Jew who identified with dissenters; nor by his apostles, who did not hesitate to differ from one another; nor by their successor bishops who defended regional interests; nor by evangelists who produced not one version of the Jesus story but four; nor by theologians who introduced innovative Hellenistic categories into Scripture study; nor by preachers who readily put their eccentric personal stamps on the kerygma" (*Constantine's Sword*, 189).

212. As the editors of *Oxford Annotated Bible* put it, "One gathers from the two letters to the Corinthians that Paul's subsequent relations with this church were disturbed from time to time by doubts and suspicions on both sides" (1378).

213. On the issue of social class conflict, especially among Paul's Corinthian followers, see Meeks, *First Urban Christians*, 67–70.

214. "Paul was not the only teacher to which these Christians were listening, and it is clear that his views on the meaning of the 'cross of Christ' and the 'law of Christ' were difficult for the Corinthians to accept and understand" (Mack, *Who Wrote?* 124).

demand signs," he said, "and Greeks seek wisdom." The wisdom they sought, however, was worldly, and those who acquired it were boastful, whereas the wisdom Paul passed on was "secret and hidden"—so much so that it looked like foolishness to the worldly (1 Cor 1:17–2:8; 3:18–21). According to one Church historian, this spiritual error was committed not by every Corinthian, but by members of "a spiritual aristocracy," who believed they had achieved perfection and therefore "regarded their fellow Christians as inferior beings." They had also been influenced by Gnosticism since they were "dualists" who believed that "the spirit is everything, the body nothing."[215]

Other offenses of the Corinthians included spiritual immaturity (1 Cor 3:1–2; 13:11–12), taking legal complaints to public courts rather than settling disputes within the community (6:1–8), idolatry (10:14–22), failure to realize that speaking in tongues is not as useful a spiritual gift as prophecy (ch. 12–14), denying the resurrection of the dead (15:12–58), and licentiousness. Not only were the Corinthians tolerating "a man living with his father's wife"—a sin forbidden by pagans as well as Jews—they were also "arrogant" about it (5:1–2). Paul thus instructed them "to deliver this man to Satan for the destruction of the flesh" and to stop associating "with immoral men" (5:5, 9).

More seriously, in the sense that the problem was evidently more common among church members (and possibly a consequence of Paul's suspension of the Law in favor of Faith), Paul accused the Corinthians collectively of a variety of sexual crimes. They had argued that satisfying their sexual desires was no worse than satisfying their hunger and that the sacraments relieved them of all moral responsibility because they promised spiritual fulfillment. Paul reminded them, however, that because their bodies are "a temple of the Holy Spirit" their bodies as well as their souls are God's possessions (1 Cor 6:9–20).[216]

Obviously, despite his occasional eloquence, Paul often had difficulty making himself clear, since these interpretational problems seem to have surfaced at most of the churches he felt responsible for. He also had trouble with both Christian and non-Christian missionaries whose messages were different from his. In 2 Corinthians, he complained about "peddlers" of the gospel (2 Cor 2:17), who "practice cunning" and "tamper with God's word" (4:2). Arguing that he had "betrothed [the Corinthians] to Christ," Paul felt "a divine jealousy" because they were flirting with other ideas: "For if

215. Chadwick, *Early Church*, 33–34. They "adopted extreme ascetic opinions, so that husbands and wives withheld conjugal rights from one another and betrothed couples abstained from consummating their marriage. Consistent with this dualism, they rejected as crude the Hebraic doctrine of the resurrection of the body, preferring the Platonic doctrine of the immortality of the soul" (34).

216. See also 2 Peter on the subject of "false prophets" who teach "licentiousness" and encourage people to "indulge in the lust of defiling passion and [to] despise authority" (2 Pet 2:1–3, 10). "The teaching maintained in Corinth," say Conzelmann and Lindemann, "apparently sounded something like this: The knowledge we have as Christians makes us free in every respect (e.g., in the realm of sexuality), including religious matters (i.e., with regards to idols)" (*Interpreting the New Testament*, 186). The Letter of Jude also addresses the problems of divisiveness and licentiousness (Jude 1:4, 10–16, 19). On this point, see Chadwick, *Early Church*, 36.

some one comes along and preaches another Jesus than the one we preached, or if you receive a different spirit from the one you received, or if you accept a different gospel from the one you expected, you submit to it readily enough." These interlopers were, however, "superlative" or "false apostles, deceitful workmen, disguising themselves as apostles of Christ." And just as Satan pretends to be "an angel of light," so his "servants . . . disguise themselves as servants of righteousness" (11:1–6, 13–15).

In this instance, the false apostles were Judaizers—notably, not Jews, but Jewish Christians—who inspired Paul, as we have seen, to claim to be just as Jewish as they were ("Are they Hebrews? So am I"), but also, as an indication of his superior credentials, a victim of Jews, non-Jews, and nature itself: "in danger from rivers, danger from robbers, danger from my own people, danger from Gentiles, danger in the city, danger in the wilderness, danger at sea, [and, of course,] danger from false brethren" (2 Cor 11:22–29). Being easy prey, these Corinthians were also in danger of being seduced into idolatry—not simply by a tendency to backslide, but by idol-worshiping pagans, with whom the Christians in Corinth were "mismated": "What accord has Christ with Belial? Or what has a believer in common with an unbeliever?" (6:14–16).

Judaizers also appear in Paul's letter to the Galatians, among whom the other Corinthian problem—internal conflict—seems to have been a serious matter: "But if you bite and devour one another take heed that you are not consumed by one another" (Gal 5:13–14; see also 5:26).[217] He told the Galatians that they had been "bewitched" (3:1), they had been made "much of" (i.e., flattered; 4:17), and they had been lied to. The Judaizers had told the Galatians that circumcision was necessary because it distinguished Jews, who were accepted as members of a legitimate religion by the Romans, from uncircumcised Christians, who were not similarly protected. Furthermore, said Paul, "they desire to have you circumcised that they may glory in your flesh" (6:12–13)—an accusation that might have been understandable to the Galatians, but remains somewhat incomprehensible today. (One scholar interprets *glorying in the flesh* to mean something like "counting scalps."[218])

The First Letter to Timothy, attributed to Paul, but written by an unknown author, deals with the influence of Gnosticism on the church and provides at least a hint of what was to become, from the point of view of middle-of-the-road Christians (i.e., between Judaism and Gnosticism), a serious threat to "genuine" Christianity. The writer accuses his enemies of trying to impose an extreme asceticism on the church: "Now the Spirit expressly says that in later times some will depart from the faith by giving heed to deceitful spirits and doctrines of demons, through the pretensions of

217. "Certain Judaizing teachers had infiltrated the churches of Galatia in central Asia Minor, which Paul had previously founded (Acts 16:6), declaring that in addition to having faith in Jesus Christ a Christian was obligated to keep the Mosaic law . . . So serious was the crisis in Galatia that Paul dispenses with his customary expression of thanksgiving and commendation, and plunges directly into a vigorous defense of his apostolic authority and the validity of his teaching" (*Oxford Annotated Bible*, 1408).

218. Akenson, *Saint Saul*, 159.

liars whose consciences are seared, who forbid marriage and enjoin abstinence from foods which God created to be received with thanksgiving by those who believe and know the truth" (4:1–3). Also condemned are "myths and endless genealogies which promote speculations," "godless and silly myths" (4:7), and "godless chatter and contradictions of what is falsely called knowledge" (6:20; see also 2 Tim 2:14–17).

Like Paul, the author of 1 and 2 Timothy calls his opponents names—in this case, "godless," ignorant (1 Tim 1:6–7), and gangrenous (2 Tim 2:17). But the acme (or nadir) of name-calling (that is, short of Paul's suggestion that his enemies castrate themselves) occurs in 1 Timothy: "If anyone teaches otherwise and does not agree with the sound words of our Lord Jesus Christ and the teaching which accords with godliness, he is puffed up with conceit, he knows nothing; he has a morbid craving for controversy and for disputes about words." What is worse, this antinomianism has a destructive effect on the Christian churches that accept it: It "produces envy, dissension, slander, base suspicions, and wrangling among men who are depraved in mind and bereft of the truth, imagining that godliness is a means of gain" (6:3–5).[219]

With all kinds of competing missionaries trying to influence virtually every new Christian congregation, it is no wonder that, despite the attempt by church leaders like Paul to impose uniformity and agreement, diversity grew. And this occurred even in Paul's churches despite the fact that he vigorously fought off intruders, visited some churches repeatedly, and often stayed for months—sometimes years. The problem was that the marketplace of religious ideas in the Roman empire was relatively free. Furthermore, nobody—from Paul to James to Matthew—really knew what orthodoxy was, other than whatever brand of Christianity any single representative of one of the many different defenders of the faith happened to be promoting. Thus, before the first century ended, Christianity had exploded into an uncountable variety of sects.

Different faith communities, developing their ideas and practices in relative isolation, chose from among many christologies, ethical standards, liturgies, and gospels (including many that were later lost). More than a dozen non-canonical gospels have survived in some form or other, in addition to numerous acts, letters, and apocalypses, all attributed to the original apostles and prominent Church leaders of the following generation. The result was a diversity of faiths whose differences are to some extent reflected in the very distinguishable texts that now make up the New Testament. Before the canon was established, some churches read only the Gospel of Matthew; others

219. It may be that the church in Colossae was also infected by Gnostic ideas. See, on this subject, *Oxford Annotated Bible*, 1426 and 1428. Mack says: The practices described in this letter "would not have been strange behavior for Asia Minor. The list outlines a set of standard practices designed to launch a person into the cosmos by means of ecstatic and visionary experiences" (*Who Wrote?* 186–87). Chadwick says that Paul found at Colossae "a syncretistic amalgam of Christianity with theosophical elements drawn partly from the mystery cults and partly from heterodox Judaism" (*Early Church*, 34). The author of the Letters of John also confronted the problem of Gnosticism in the churches he addressed, several times referring to Gnostics as "the antichrist" (1 John 2:18; 4:3; 2 John 1:7). John's first letter was intended "to correct the heretical views of certain Gnostic teachers who denied that God had really become man in Jesus" (*Oxford Annotated Bible*, 1482; see 1 John 2:22; 4:1–5).

read only the Gospel of John. Still others read Marcion's collection of Paul's letters and a de-Judaized version of the Gospel of Luke. And Syrians, for a few centuries, read only Tatian's *Diatesseron*, a harmonization of the four Gospels.

To get a better sense of this diversity, consider that, in the same way that many texts eventually disappeared, many communities were either written off as heretical or conformed to what, in the fourth century, became known as orthodoxy. That is, in many instances, we have no idea which texts were lost and who these communities were. Even after the fourth century, however, heresies were not completely eliminated. As time passed, new issues arose, which spawned new isms. The Council of Nicea tried to resolve conflicts between supporters of Arius and his enemies, and both earlier and later the Church dealt with Acacians, Albigensians, Bardesanites, Cainites, Carpocracians, Circumcellions, Dissimilarians, Docetists, Donatists, Ebionites, Encratites, Eutychians, Gnostics, Marcionites, Marcosians, Melitians, Messalians, Monarchians, Monophysites, Montanists, Nazarenes, Nestorians, Nicolaitans, Novatians, Ophites, Patripassianists, Paulianists, Pelagians, Phibionites, Quartodecimans, Seballians, and Valentinians. Not surprisingly, well before the Church was divided into Orthodoxy, Catholicism, and Protestantism, it was divided into East and West. Sometimes, the differences have been impossible to reconcile.

Ironically, despite the eventual dominance of his ideas in the development of Christianity, Paul at first all but disappeared as an influence on the early Church. After all, "in his own time he had been an isolated figure"—"both radical and unacceptable to many (if not most) other Christians."[220] One historian claims that Paul's eclipse lasted only a decade, from the mid-fifties to the Revolt of 66, at which time communication between the mother church and Diaspora Christians evaporated, and Paul's ideas gained credibility, especially after the destruction of the Temple.[221] However, another scholar argues that Paul was unimportant throughout much of the first century.[222] In fact, in the second century, Church leaders like Hegesippus, Justin Martyr, and Papias, either reviled him or ignored him (or, as in the case of Ignatius, cited him infrequently).[223] It may be that Paul was too much associated with heretics like Marcion and all kinds of Gnostics. Whatever the case, "The period after Paul's death

220. Chilton and Neusner, *Judaism*, 98–99. Since the influence of both James and Paul declined, the Church exploded in many different directions: "Acts itself, together with the earliest letters of Paul, permit us to see clearly that there were competing views of God's Israel within primitive Christianity" (99).

221. Brandon, *Trial of Jesus*, 62–63. Brandon explains: "The final and catastrophic defeat of Israel, with the destruction of Jerusalem and its famous Temple, would have done little to lessen the danger of the Gentile Christians; but it probably did cause them to recall Paul's teaching about the inadequacy of the Jewish ritual Law . . . Freed from the domination of the Jerusalem Christians, and with their faith in Paul's 'gospel' renewed, the Gentile Christians were doubtless eager to dissociate their religion from its Jewish origins" (63).

222. Crossan, *Birth of Christianity*, xxi.

223. Bauer, *Orthodoxy and Heresy*, 214–18. Paul's letters are singularly missing from the citations of Justin Martyr in the second century (Ehrman, *Lost Christianities*, 239).

would seem to us to have been much more a time of diminution of the Pauline sphere of influence rather than expansion."[224] And yet Paul's star rose. By the time Acts of the Apostles was composed, in c. 90, he had evidently become a hero in some circles, and there he has remained for nearly two thousand years.

224. Bauer, *Orthodoxy and Heresy*, 219.

Chapter Five

The Rejection

"In the early decades of the Roman Empire, a new sect of Judaism appeared and spread rapidly, though not in great numbers, through the cities of the East. It did not stand out among the many 'Oriental' cults being carried from place to place by immigrants and traders . . . Yet it was to become a new religion, separate from, even hostile to, the Jewish communities that gave it birth." (Wayne A. Meeks)

IF GOD HAD WANTED to make it easy for Jesus' followers to create a new religion and to spread it around the world, he would have put Jesus anywhere but Palestine. In the first century, this divided country was an island in the Roman empire.[1] Most of its occupants were monotheistic Jews who, unlike their neighbors, inherited a written scripture, which included what they considered to be their national history, their methods of worship (in extravagant detail), and their ethical system. They also had very definite, though quite varied, ideas of what the future might hold. They were unique in believing that ultimately (sooner or later) the world would be transformed, everyone would be judged on the basis of his or her obedience to God's laws, and all earthly kingdoms would be replaced by God's own kingdom. Other societies had written laws—e.g., the Code of Hammurabi—which contained specific prohibitions and requirements, but the Jewish Bible also emphasized broad ethical principles. And other nation states—most notably, Persia, Egypt, and Greece—had not been subjected to foreign domination for most of the past eight hundred years.

1. Enslin says: "The revolutionary call of Jesus had been especially adapted to the Palestine of his day. But it was not a message, in the form in which he gave it, to exert any considerable influence on the outside world . . . Thus the challenge of Jesus with its insistence on repentance, with its content the impending change, pitched in terms intelligible to Judaism, would have fallen on deaf ears in any portion of the Mediterranean basin except Palestine" (*Christian Beginnings*, 182). And rural Galilee, where Jesus spent almost all of his life, was an island within that island: "The villages of Galilee were far more independent of the local aristocracy than their counterparts in other areas of the empire" (Herzog, *Jesus, Justice*, 93). They particularly resisted the "temple state, client kingship, and Roman rule" (99)—in short, the religious, political, and cultural control that Rome exerted through its local representatives. Thus, "Galilee was not like other areas of the Roman Empire," especially in defense of its peasant lifestyle, its kinship ties, and its covenant values (149–55).

Most important, the inhabitants of Palestine periodically demonstrated—four times in a major way between approximately 165 BC and AD 135, all such protests resulting in massive loss of life and property—their willingness to sacrifice *everything* to reclaim what they considered to be their ancestral land, to protect the integrity of their religion, and to preserve the continuity of their national identity. Most of these Jews lived in rural areas, most of them spoke only Aramaic, and, except for the ruling class—landowners, Herodians, and priests—most of them had no interest whatsoever in Greek culture, pagan religion, or Roman law. In fact, because these things influenced them only negatively, if at all, many of the inhabitants of Palestine were openly hostile to them. Thus, while some Jews in Hellenized cities (including Jerusalem) actually embraced the syncretism that dominated the Roman empire—the assumption that gods with different names (i.e., those given them by different ethnic groups) might be the same—many Jews, especially those in the Galilean countryside, rejected the concept.[2]

Outside of Palestine, thanks partly to the conquests of Alexander the Great, residents of the empire spoke Greek and worshiped many gods. Alexander had brought Greek culture in general to the eastern Mediterranean; and, by establishing a unified empire that was later folded into the one created by the Romans, he also made possible (or *more* possible) the syncretistic polytheism that later characterized the vast Roman state. As a result, the gods worshiped throughout the empire—at least officially—were the gods of the Greek pantheon (renamed, of course), who were thought to be responsible for the success of the Roman empire and therefore eminently deserving of ceremonial acts of gratitude. Residents of the empire worshiped other gods, who, besides Dionysus and Demeter, were not native to either Greece or Italy. They were imported from other places, brought by traders, travelers, slaves and soldiers, who were slowly making the empire a truly multicultural world.

---

2. Armstrong, *History of God*, 66. Meier adds that, although there were Greek-style buildings in Jerusalem (e.g., a theater, a hippodrome, a palace, and Herod's Citadel) and ten to twenty percent of Jerusalemites spoke Greek, many Jews (especially among the devout) resisted Hellenization (*Marginal Jew*, I, 258–59). Theissen agrees (*Early Palestinian Christianity*, 68). See also Bainton, *Early Christianity*, 13; Segal, *Rebecca's Children*, 22–27; Wylen, *Jews* 37, 47; and Wilson, *Jesus*, 24. According to Stegemann and Stegemann, "the followers of Jesus were part of the predominantly Jewish society of Palestine, whereas the Christ-confessing communities in urban residential areas outside of Israel lived in the context of a predominantly Gentile society." The latter "are no longer a phenomenon of Judaism, above all for sociological reasons" (*Jesus Movement*, 3–4). Grant makes a similar point in *Historical Introduction*, 15. Latourette says that Christians were particularly numerous in "the great cities of the eastern part of the Mediterranean Basin, major centers of Hellenistic culture." Furthermore, areas in the East that were less affected by Hellenism were slow to accept Christianity. Non-Greek-speaking Egyptians, for example, were latecomers to the faith (*History of Christianity*, I, 77). The same point obviously applies to rural Palestinians. Boyarin, however, states that the difference in this regard between Palestine and the Diaspora was not so sharp (*Border Lines*, 92). And Meier notes that Martin Hengel would have agreed with Boyarin (*Marginal Jew*, I, 294 n. 39). Crossan says that the difference between Palestine and the Diaspora was not ideological (*Historical Jesus*, 417–18), which may be true of the Hellenized cities in both areas.

Yet, unified insofar as they were by their official worship of Greek and Roman gods and their often unofficial worship of Persian, Syrian, Mesopotamian, Phoenician, Phrygian, and Egyptian gods, the Romans and their subjects had nothing that could be called scripture—a sacred text. Furthermore, the people to whom Paul preached in Asia Minor and Greece were city dwellers who were, to some degree, immersed in Greek culture. And when Christians traveled farther west to Rome or farther south to Alexandria, they encountered a similar linguistic, religious, and cultural milieu. Thus, when Paul and the other Christian missionaries took their faith outside of Palestine, they crossed a cultural boundary.[3] And their departure from one world and their entry into another would eventually have serious consequences for the Christianity they brought with them and for the Jews they would, in many ways, leave behind.[4]

Paul's and other Christians' departure from Palestine had four significant results: (1) the splintering of Christianity into many different sects, already discussed in Chapter Four; (2) the decline and ultimate demise of Jewish Christianity; (3) the demonization of the Jews; and (4) the Hellenization of Christianity, the last of which will be discussed in Chapter Six. The second result occurred simply because most of the gentiles who became Christians had little interest in maintaining Jewish practices.

3. The boundary, other scholars argue, was primarily between rural and urban Jews and only secondarily between Palestinians and Diasporans and, eventually, Jews and gentiles. On the rural/urban difference, see Sean Freyne, "Jesus and the Urban Culture of Galilee," cited by Brown in *Introduction*: Freyne "contends that the Hellenistic cities and the Galilean rural hinterland had very different value systems" (69 n. 32). Brown adds later, "Very Greco-Roman cities in Galilee, for instance, could be surrounded by villages whose inhabitants had very little enthusiasm for Gentile thought and practice and other villages whose commerce brought them into closer contact with Hellenism" (74). Koester says that rural areas in the former Seleucid empire were less affected by Greek influences and that people in the rural areas of the Roman empire continued to worship local gods. In Palestine, the Maccabean revolt represented the Jewish resistance to Seleucid Hellenization (*History, Culture, and Religion,* 55, 97–98). Carroll argues that "many Palestinian Jews would probably have rejected Hellenization, and that is especially true of the rural people, whose experience of the wider world would have been limited" (*Constantine's Sword,* 77). Meier, quoting Shimon Applebaum, says that Palestinian Jews were "less urbanized than the population of other equally developed Roman provinces" (*Marginal Jew,* I, 315 n. 176). Applebaum's essay is in S. Safrai and M. Stern, eds., *Jewish People in the First Century.* See also Lee, *Galilean Jewishness of Jesus,* 63. On the influence of the rural/urban conflict on Judaism in particular and the ancient world in general, Theissen cites L. Finkelstein, *The Pharisees: The Sociological Backgrounds of Their Faith*; and M. Rostovtzeff, *The Social and Economic History of the Roman Empire.* Sanders says that Jesus' indifference to Palestinian cities reflected a Jewish Galilean hostility to Hellenized urban centers (*Historical Figure of Jesus,* 12, 101–7). Hard-working peasants in Nazareth, who could not walk very far on the Sabbath, were disinclined to visit nearby Sepphoris for commercial or recreational purposes (104).

4. "In time, . . . certain Christian groups began to define themselves in opposition to Judaism . . . Some of these groups emerge in Palestine, but many more appear in conjunction with Christianity's gradual expansion into the larger Greco-Roman world. Along with this geographical shift there appears another factor which will have even more significance in the long run. The movement begins to attract increasing numbers of Gentile converts" (Gager, *Origins of Anti-Semitism,* 114). Gager adds, of course, that since Christians met large numbers of Jews wherever they went in the empire, they did not entirely escape from Judaism (114).

Thus, as their numbers increased, the Jewish influence on Christianity declined.[5] Eventually, Jewish Christianity was represented by only a few isolated groups, and finally even these groups disappeared altogether.[6] The third result derived, in part, from the mission failure that Paul blamed for his turn away from the Jews of his adopted homeland to the Jews of the Diaspora and, eventually, to the gentiles of the Roman empire. The bearers of the Christian message found that they increasingly had to deal with the question of Jesus' relationship with his own brethren. Why, they were asked, did Jesus' own people fail to follow him?[7]

Of course, this question has to be understood in the context, as I have tried to emphasize, of Jesus' own continuing embrace of Judaism. It must also be understood in relation to the fact that *all but a few* of his followers—at least until the 40s—were Jews. For this reason, the question of *why* the Jews rejected Jesus has to be preceded by the question of *whether* the Jews, in fact, stopped following him. One answer is that, despite Jesus' initial popularity among his fellow Jews, they eventually lost interest in him. According to the synoptic Gospels, not many of his few remaining followers showed up at the Crucifixion. Furthermore, as one historian puts it, even after Peter's confession, "the report of the people's flocking to Jesus tails off and even ceases altogether."[8]

The precipitate decline in Jesus' public support may owe more, however, to the theological intentions of the evangelists than to the historical facts. The idea that Jesus attracted "multitudes" who first adored him, both during his Galilean ministry and when he entered Jerusalem, and then suddenly turned against him during his trial is, to some commentators, hardly plausible. According to two Bible scholars, "This portrait is predicated upon a synthesis between [the Gospel of John] and the Synoptics. In John 6:66 there is indeed a crisis in the public ministry of Jesus; it is wrong however, to import this presentation into the synoptic Gospels"[9]

5. Brown says, "Acts and Gal[atians] indicate that Christianity coming from Jerusalem was likely to have been more conservative about the Jewish heritage and Law than were the Gentiles converted by Paul" (*Introduction*, 562).

6. Ruether, *Faith and Fratricide*, 83. Brown says that other cities began to surpass Jerusalem in importance during the reign of the three Flavians. "This would probably also have been the time," he continues, "when the number of Gentile Christians surpassed the number of Jewish Christians"—that is, in the two or three decades after the fall of Jerusalem (*Introduction*, 62). Theissen explains why the Hellenized world outside of Palestine was more accepting of Christianity than Palestine itself in *Early Palestinian Christianity*, 118.

7. According to Brown, "All four evangelists, whether or not they were in active contact with Jews, condemn hostilely the Jewish failure to acknowledge Jesus as the Messiah" (*Introduction*, 154).

8. Schillebeeckx, *Jesus*, 193. Schillebeeckx later adds, more specifically: "The Markan gospel clearly says that Jesus' preaching in Galilee met with initial success. But from Mark 7 on, the allusions to 'a great crowd of people' diminish, as do the positive reactions" (295). Schillebeeckx acknowledges that the negative reaction in Mark is associated with the Jewish aristocracy, but he believes that "the rejection of Jesus' message extended beyond these schematic categories" of priests and scribes. After all, he says, Jesus cursed whole towns (Luke 10:13–15; Matt 11:20–24).

9. Conzelmann and Lindemann make this point against what they call the "popular portrait" of

It is possible, to be sure, that the Jews actually supported Jesus at first, but gradually became disillusioned with him. However, since Jesus' *only* followers were Jews for a generation after the Crucifixion, it is also conceivable that the disaffection was invented by the Church when it became convenient for Christians to disavow their connection to Judaism after the Revolt of 66. It is notable, in support of this view, that the Gospels, from Mark to John, grow progressively hostile toward the Jews, particularly insofar as they are increasingly likely to hold the Jews rather than the Romans responsible for Jesus' death, and expand the culpability for the Crucifixion from the leaders of the Jewish community to the entire Jewish population, including their descendants.

GOD REJECTED THE JEWS

The traditional Christian answer to the question of why the Jews rejected Jesus is that it was God's will. As a faithless people, who had always disobeyed God—so the argument goes—the Jews were not only unable to accept Jesus, they were eventually forced to suffer the consequences of their stubbornness and hard-heartedness. Of course, since the evidence of their acceptance of Jesus—to the extent that they were his only followers for many years—is made abundantly clear in both the synoptic Gospels and the Acts of the Apostles, the evangelists must have had some difficulty even demonstrating that the Jews' enthusiasm for Jesus faded and ultimately disappeared.

The Bible reports that, before his trial, Jesus was followed by *multitudes*. His initial success in Galilee was preceded by that of John the Baptist, who drew huge crowds from Judea: "Then went out to him Jerusalem, and all Judea, and all the region round about Jordan" (Matt 3:5; Mark 1:4–5). After Jesus started to preach, he similarly attracted followers—"great multitudes"—from all over, including not only Galilee, but also Decapolis, Jerusalem, Judea, and "beyond Jordan" (Matt 4:25; Luke 6:17–19). In the Gospels of Mark and Luke, one of the disciples says to Jesus, "All men seek for thee" (Mark 1:37; Luke 4:42). His fame thus spread from "the region around Galilee" (Mark 1:28) to Syria (Matt 4:24; Luke 4:14–15, 37). He preached the Sermon on the

---

Jesus' loss of support (*Interpreting the New Testament*, 303–04). Brown says, "The claim that many of his disciples would not follow him anymore ([John] 6:66) is found only in John among the Gospels and may reflect a period toward the end of the century when the koinonia [spiritual community] was being broken" (*Introduction*, 346 n. 33). See also 351. N. T. Wright comments: "People sometimes try to read the early days of Jesus's public career as successful, popular, carrying all before him, but then posit a change, a decline in popularity, and the embracing of a Plan B that included suffering. The texts show nothing of a mid-course change" (*Simply Jesus*, 172). Fredriksen suggests that Jesus' following was quite small to begin with since, if the movement had been as large as the Gospels indicate, Herod Antipas would have acted sooner not only against Jesus, but also against his followers: "Gatherings of four or five thousand people, assembled at one time in one place, would certainly have come to the attention of the tetrarch," who seems to have executed John the Baptist without much provocation. Fredriksen adds that the picture of large numbers of "agricultural workers, villagers, and farmers" following Jesus everywhere "also seems dubious" (*Jesus of Nazareth*, 215–16).

Mount to "multitudes" (Matt 5:1), and afterwards "great multitudes followed him" (8:1).

In Capernaum, Jesus' audience was so large that most people could not get to him (Mark 2:1–2), and he had to cross the sea to escape from the crowd (Matt 8:18). In Nazareth, "the multitudes marveled" at his healing power (Matt 9:8; Mark 2:13–15; Luke 5:17); he gained fame in Nain by restoring a dead youth to life (Luke 7:11–17); and, when he brought back from death the daughter of a synagogue ruler, "the fame hereof went abroad unto all that land" (Matt 9:23–26; Luke 8:40–48). Subsequently, "the multitudes" figured quite prominently among Jesus' followers (Matt 9:35–38; 13:1–2; Mark 3:7–10; and Luke 5: 15). Besides feeding 5,000 and 4,000, respectively, Jesus healed everyone (Matt 13:34–36; Mark 6:53–56) and continued to greet "multitudes," including the crowd that welcomed him to Jerusalem: "All the city was moved" (Matt 21:1–11; Mark 11:1–10; Luke 19:37–38). This assertion, quite late in *all* of the synoptic Gospels, gives the lie to the claim that Jesus' support diminished.

Although Jesus was rejected by some group of Jews at his trial and either ignored or insulted by them at his Crucifixion, the vast majority of passages in the synoptic Gospels that deal with their attitudes toward Jesus show the Jews to be supportive. In these Gospels, as we have seen, it was usually the scribes, elders, and chief priests who wanted to "destroy" Jesus. They refrained from capturing him, as I said earlier, "for they feared him, because *all the people* was astonished at his doctrine" (Mark 11:15–19; Luke 19:47–48; my emphasis). When the priests afterwards "sought to lay hands on him" (Matt 21:46) or challenged Jesus' authority (Mark 11:28; Luke 20:1–2) or wanted to kill him (Mark 14:1–2), "they feared the multitude" and held back from doing anything peremptory or provocative Matt 21:46; Mark 11:32; 12:12; 14:1–2; Luke 20:6, 19; 22:2). In short, as these passages show, Jesus was so popular *among Jews* that his enemies could not arrest him, let alone execute him.

Indeed, in Luke, after the trial, rather than eagerly accept responsibility for Jesus' execution—as the Jews do in Matthew—a *"great number of the people"* followed behind Simon of Cyrene and Jesus on their way to Golgotha, the women among them "beating their breasts and wailing for him" (Luke 23:26–27; my emphasis). After his death, "*all the people* that came together to that sight, beholding the things that were done, smote their breasts," presumably, again, in deep sympathy (Luke 23:48; my emphasis). Furthermore, when Cleopas and Peter met someone who later turned out to be the resurrected Jesus on the road to Emmaus, they were surprised that he knew nothing about what had just occurred in Jerusalem—since, implicitly, *everyone* knew. In other words, Jesus was that famous. Thus, the synoptic Gospels' description of the response of Jesus' Jewish audience is favorable, particularly Luke's. As I said, these accounts seem to put the blame for hostility toward Jesus on the Jewish elite (scribes, chief priests, and elders) and emphasize the widespread popularity of Jesus among ordinary Jews at every moment of his career.[10]

10. As Horsley shows in *Bandits, Prophets & Messiahs*, Jewish peasants, especially in Galilee,

Again, the only exception to this formula occurs during the public phase of Jesus' trial and his subsequent execution. On one hand, it was "the chief priests and elders" who "persuaded the multitude" to "destroy Jesus" (Matt 27:20; Mark 15:11). On the other hand, however, it is clear that the crowd addressed by Pontius Pilate *was* hostile to Jesus, regardless of the influence of the Jewish elite. When Pilate asked "the multitude" whether to release Jesus or Barabbas, they called for Jesus' death (Matt 27:22–23; Mark 15:13–14; Luke 23:18–23). Unlike these people, especially in Matthew, Pilate absolved himself of responsibility (Matt 27:24; Mark 15:6–15; Luke 23:24–25) but yielded to public sentiment because he was "willing to content the people" (Mark 15:15) and feared the "tumult" they created (Matt 27:24).

Later, after the Roman soldiers mocked Jesus, the crowd of Jews did too (Matt 27:39–40; Mark 15:29). Indeed, Luke and John imply that Pilate released Jesus *to the Jews* for execution: "he handed Jesus over as they wished," and "they led him away" (Luke 23:25–26 and John 19:15–16 vs. Mark 15:16). In Luke's Gospel, unlike Matthew's and Mark's, the soldiers remain unmentioned until after Jesus has been placed on the Cross. In Matthew, the "people as a whole" said in response to Pilate's claim of innocence, "His blood be on us and on our children!" (Matt 27:25).

As I suggested earlier, however, the rather sudden disaffection of the Jews immediately before Jesus' Crucifixion makes little sense. (Indeed, as I noted above, it is completely contradicted in Luke.) Three points are worth making here. First, as the evidence in the synoptic Gospels demonstrates (cited in Chapter Two), Jesus was feared and hated only by the Jewish elite. Again and again, the evangelists indicate that the only Jews who wanted Jesus eliminated were those who had reason to suppress any threat to the Roman empire—that is, those Jews whom the Romans held responsible for maintaining peace in Judea. They were beholden to the Romans because the Romans supported their claims to power and eagerly defended them when they were threatened by rebels and angry mobs.

Second, despising the Jewish elite as much as they hated the Romans, members of the Jewish underclass always supported the messianic leaders (from Judah the Galilean in the first century BC to Rabbi Kochba in the second century AD) who rejected the Roman occupation and promised liberation from the pagans and Jews who opposed them. In other words, it is hard to imagine that the kinds of Jews (that is, non-elites) who supported rebels like Theudas and the Egyptian would not have supported Jesus.

---

generally supported bandits, magicians, and messianic figures, while the Jewish aristocracy opposed them. Jeremias notes that successive generations of the first-century BC rebel Ezekiel, all of whom claimed messianic identity and Davidic descent, were lauded by all Jews except those in power (*Jerusalem*, 277 and n. 9). Crossan and Borg discuss the implausibility of any mass Jewish rejection of Jesus at his trial in *Last Week*, 87–91. The passages from Mark cited in the preceding two paragraphs (11:1–10; 15–19; 12:12; 14:1–2) also appear to contradict Schillebeeckx's claim that Jewish support declines in Mark after ch. 7.

Third, as the evidence in the synoptic Gospels shows, Jesus was followed by multitudes, who are often identified not merely as large groups, but as *everyone* in this or that area. Considering the hostility between the Jewish elite and the kinds of Jews whom Jesus would have attracted, it is unlikely that the latter would have been either surprised or disillusioned by the arrest and execution of their leader. That was the fate of most Jewish dissidents whom the authorities were suspicious of. And it is equally unlikely that this crowd would have been swayed by their enemies to turn on one of their own. It is possible, of course, that *some* group could have been influenced by priests and elders, but it could not have been either large or in any way identifiable with ordinary Jews, including Jesus' followers. Thus, while all of the Gospels portray the Pharisees as well as the priests and elders as Jesus' opponents, many of the other Jews in Mark, Matthew, and Luke were supportive of Jesus until the end of his life. Consistent with their ongoing loyalty, as I said in Chapter Four, these Jews remained Jesus' *only* followers for nearly two decades.

What many Christians seem to remember is the scenes in which the Jews are shown in the worst possible light—the accounts of Jesus' Passion and Luke's portrait of the Jews as the murderers of Jesus in Acts of the Apostles (2:26; 3:14–15; 4:10; 5:30; 7:52; and 10:39). Even more incriminating, however—and, it appears, more indelibly imprinted on the Christian historical consciousness—is the entire record of Jesus' relation to his fellow Jews in the Gospel of John. Here, the evangelist, from the very beginning, impugns the motives and condemns the actions not just of Pharisees and priests, but of *all the Jews*, who seem never to have responded favorably to Jesus' message at any time or to any appreciable degree: "He came unto his own, and his own received him not" (John 1:11).

Thus, according to John, "the Jews," collectively, did everything wrong from the very beginning of Jesus' mission. They asked for a sign from him (2:18), wanted to "slay" him because he healed on the Sabbath and made "himself equal with God" (5:16–18), and "murmured at him" because he claimed to be the bread from heaven (6:41–52). At the end of his travels in and out of Jerusalem, as well as Samaria, Jesus returned to Galilee and decided he could not go back to Judea (or "Jewry," in the KJV) "because the Jews sought to kill him" (7:1). Jesus had to travel to Jerusalem for Tabernacles secretly because "the Jews sought him at the feast . . . and no man spake openly of him for fear of the Jews" (7:10–13). Subsequently, Jesus' disciples were put out of the synagogues (9:22), and Jesus himself continued to be in mortal danger because "the Jews" tried to stone him (8:59; 10:31).

To put it simply, "the Jews did not believe concerning him" (9:18). Of course, "the Jews" in the Gospel of John reappear during the trial of Jesus in their familiar role as Jesus' enemies (18:31, 38; 19:7, 12, 14). But it is hardly surprising in this Gospel because John has been at great pains to prove to his readers sixty or seventy years after the Crucifixion that Jesus was *from the beginning* a victim of all the Jews. "You are from your father, the devil," Jesus tells them, "and you choose to do your father's desires" (John 8:44). With this pervasive, unequivocal, and eminently quotable indictment, one is forced to wonder—with "the Jews" hunting, plotting against, and trying to stone Jesus whenever the opportunity arose—first, who admired him and, second, what took the others (i.e., the overwhelmimg majority) so long to execute him?

Ironically, the evidence in John, as in the synoptic Gospels, is that the Jews constituted one hundred percent of Jesus' followers, although these followers are not referred to as Jews in the Gospel of John, but as "many" (John 2:23), "men" (3:26), "disciples" (4:1), "a great multitude" (6:2), "they" (6:15), "the people" (6:22, 24; 12:18), "some" (7:12), "many of the people" (7:31, 40), "all the people" (8:2), "many" (8:30; 10:42), and "much people" (12:12). John refers to Jews in a favorable way only at the death and redemption of Lazarus in chapters 11 and 12. For example: "[M]any of the Jews" comforted Mary and Martha on the death of their brother (11:19); after Jesus brought Lazarus back to life, "many of the Jews . . . believed on [Jesus]" (11:45); "[m]uch people of the Jews came to see Lazarus (12:9); and "many of the Jews . . . believed on Jesus" (12:11). Furthermore, starting in Chapter 7 (v. 32), it is increasingly the Pharisees and the chief priests, rather than "the Jews," who pursue Jesus with the intention of killing him (see especially 11:47–53, 57; 12:10).

Aside from these exceptions, however, John's treatment of the Jews is fairly clear and consistent.[11] Almost invariably, when the Jews support Jesus, they are not identified as Jews. But, when (evidently) *some* of the Jews are hostile to Jesus, they are simply and comprehensively "the Jews." Thus, on the one hand, the Pharisees, supporting the notion that Jesus was an amazingly popular figure, say, "[t]he world is gone after him" (John 12:19), implying that *all* of the Jews—there being no one else around—joined the Jesus movement. On the other hand, however, John, who wants to show that the Jews—and not just the Jewish elite—rejected Jesus, says, "Although he had performed so many signs in their presence, they did not believe in him" (12:37).

Indeed, Jesus himself condemns the Jews in this Gospel as incapable of accepting him because God wanted them to fail to appreciate the Messiah and Son of God. And this became the Church's explanation of why the Jews rejected Jesus: *They had to.* Jesus first made this point when he was speaking to "those Jews which believed on him" (John 8:31). One might assume that these were true believers, but the fact that John's Jesus called them Jews ought to suggest that they were less than genuine disciples. Indeed, when Jesus began a dialogue with "those Jews," it is quite obvious that they had no idea what he was talking about. He said that the truth would make them free; they said they were not in bondage. He said that they were slaves to sin because they followed the teachings of their father. They said that their father was Abraham. Then Jesus pointed out that the Jews did what they did because God was not their father;

---

11. Ruether points out that in both Acts and John all non-Christian Jews are shown to be worthless (*Faith and Fratricide*, 88–90, 111–13, and 116). On John's treatment of Jews, see Reinhartz, "The Gospel of John: How 'the Jews' Became Part of the Plot," 105–6, 112–14. Reinhartz says that John's anti-Judaism was influenced by hostilities between Christians and Jews in the late first century (111, 115–16).

the devil was (8:44). Since the devil is the father of lies, the Jews were simply unable to hear the truth: "He that is of God heareth God's words: ye therefore hear them not, because ye are not of God" (8:31–47). *Quod erat demonstrandum.*

This high-level intellectual debate went on, with the Jews accusing Jesus of *having* a devil (instead of actually *being* one), Jesus defending himself with the obscurest of statements so far ("Before Abraham was, I am"), and Jesus escaping when the Jews picked up stones to kill him (John 8:52–59). Stoning Jesus, however, proved to be as difficult as understanding him. As Jesus later explained, "For judgment I am come into this world, that they which see not might see; and that they which see might be made blind" (John 9:39). Clearly. And after this illuminating comment, he concluded, immediately before retiring permanently from public life, by quoting Isaiah to the effect that God himself did not want the Jews to understand: "Therefore, *they could not believe*, because that Isaiah said again, He hath blinded their eyes, and hardened their heart" (12:39–40; my emphasis).

John's method of discrediting Jews by identifying them as Jews when their behavior was reprehensible and merely calling them "the people" (or some other neutral term) when they supported either Jesus or his followers is matched by Luke in Acts of the Apostles, particularly in the early pages of the work.[12] Thus, the apostles had "favor with all the people" (2:47); the Jewish elders let their Christian captives go because they were afraid of "the people" (4:21); "the people held [the Christians] in high honor" (5:13), and Gamaliel, who argued for the release of the apostles, was "held in honor by all the people" (5:34). It was not the Jews who responded favorably to Philip's signs and wonders, but "the multitude" (8:6); nor was it the Jews who were "added to the Lord," but "a large company" (11:24). Of course, in all of these instances, "the people" *were* Jews, since the scene was Jerusalem in the first century, where almost all of the population was Jewish. What is further confusing is that Luke also uses the term "the people" to refer to gentiles in Lystra (14:13–14) and Ephesus (19:26). To be sure, although Luke is by no means entirely consistent in hiding the identity of Jews when they respond to Jesus and the apostles favorably, the obfuscation works to a large extent. One can only assume that by the time Acts was read in the Diaspora, especially by non-Jews, they would not understand that "the people" in many of these passages were actually Jews.

Of course, when "the people" in Acts are identified as "of Israel" or "of the Jews," they are accused of killing Jesus (4:10) or of unjustly arresting Peter (12:11). Indeed, when "the Jews" are explicitly identified as such, they are often trying to either arrest or murder the apostles. Thus, "the Jews plotted to kill [Paul] in Damascus" (9:23). Herod "pleased the Jews" by killing James and arresting Peter (12:3). "[T]he Jews . . .

12. Sanders makes the same point in *Jews in Luke-Acts*, 48–49. Sanders also discusses Luke's habit of substituting often-unidentifiable pronouns for "Jews" in general or the members of the Jewish aristocracy: Luke "so often omits subjects for his verbs when he wants to imply that 'the Jews' are guilty of something but does not quite want to say it" (79; see also 249).

stirred up persecution against Paul and Barnabas" in Pisidian Antioch (13:50) and "stirred up the Gentiles and poisoned their minds against the brethren" in Iconium (14:2). The "Jews" in Lystra "stoned Paul and dragged him out of the city, supposing that he was dead" (14:19). In Thessalonica, "the Jews . . . stir[red] up and incite[d] the crowds" against Paul (17:13). In Greece, "a plot was made against [Paul] by the Jews" (20:3); and, in Jerusalem, "the Jews made a plot . . . neither to eat nor drink till they had killed Paul" (23:12). There are more than forty examples of Jews behaving badly in Acts, but very few examples of Jews behaving well or honorably.

This portrayal of the Jews as opponents rather than supporters of Jesus and his disciples first appeared long before the Gospel of John and the Acts of the Apostles, however. Indeed, since Paul must have been among the first Christians to be confronted by the question of Jewish indifference or hostility to Jesus, he was among the first to deal with it. He did so by reviling the Jews as Christ-killers who lost God's favor (1 Thess 2:14–15).[13] And he said in 2 Corinthians, "In their [i.e., the Jews'] case the god of this world has blinded the eyes of the unbelievers, to keep them from seeing the light of the gospel of the glory of Christ" (2 Cor 4:4; see also Rom 11:7). In his Gospel, Matthew carries this accusation a step further by suggesting that the Jews had always rejected God's representatives. Thus, the Jews as a people possess "that specific kind of wickedness which is peculiar to God's Chosen People." As the special beneficiary of God's goodwill, they alone have murdered His messengers, a theme that Luke reiterates (through Stephen) in Acts of the Apostles: "You stiff-necked people, uncircumcised in heart and ears, you always resist the Holy Spirit. As your fathers did, so do you" (7:51).[14]

Eventually, the idea that the Jews were innately unable to worship Jesus became a major theme in Christianity. Later, the writer of *The Epistle of Barnabas* claimed that the Jews misinterpreted Moses by understanding him literally rather than figuratively (10:9). They had from the beginning, therefore, "propagated a false religion" and were

---

13. Jesus makes the same point in Mark 4:11–12 by way of explaining his secretiveness about his true identity. On this subject, see Weiss, *Earliest Christianity*, II, 663–64. Weiss says that, in Mark, Jesus did not want to be recognized and therefore deliberately tried not to be understood (691, 695). Schillebeeckx, however, argues that Jesus' communications were not intended to be incomprehensible. His parables were originally meant to open up minds and challenge preconceptions (*Jesus*, 156–57, 169–70). See also Chilton, "Targum, Jesus, and the Gospels," 246. Brown calls the passage in Mark "an offensive text if one does not understand the biblical approach to divine foresight where what has in fact resulted is often presented as God's purpose" (*Introduction*, 133). This explanation can provide little comfort to Jews, however, considering that few Christian readers seem to have understood Jesus' words in this fashion.

14. Hare, *Jewish Persecution of Christians*, 140–41; see also 170–71. Hare contrasts Matthew's indictment of all Jews with Mark's and Paul's much less comprehensive and less insistent charge on 149–156. Thus: "Matthew's pessimism concerning Israel is unrelieved. There is no doctrine of the remnant. There is no prophecy of a future restoration. In Matthew's gospel the rejection of Israel is permanent and complete" (153). Hare offers as evidence his analysis of Matthew 21:43, 22:7f., and 23:37–39.

equally incapable of accepting Jesus.[15] Justin Martyr was one of many Christians to accuse the Jews of a "hardness of heart" so severe as to disable them from ever embracing Jesus (*Dialogue with Trypho*, ch. 17). In his *Homilies on Luke*, Origen says that the Jews not only failed to appreciate Jesus' miracles, they were in fact unable to understand his divinity: "To this very day the people of Israel are mute and dumb" (Homily 5:2). And in this they had no choice: "Only those whom Jesus judged worthy of beholding him really saw him" (Homily 3:4).

The point is, having been asked by gentiles, especially in the new Pauline churches, why the Jews did not, by and large, follow Jesus, the members of the movement said that the Jews rejected him because it was part of God's plan.[16] This, at least, became the indictment in the second century, when the percentage of Jews in the Church declined, the percentage of gentiles steadily grew, and (the Jews being anathema in the empire after their rebellion in 66,[17] the Jerusalem church long gone or marginalized, and Christians in an explanatory bind), the divide between Jews and Christians expanded. As the century wore on, especially after the Revolt of 132, Christians increasingly vilified their former brethren, and, by the fourth century, Christians were trying to decide whether to kill the Jews (St. Ambrose) or simply use them as an example of what happens to people who deny the divinity of Jesus (St. Augustine).

They have come to different conclusions in different times and places.[18] Of course, that Jesus was born and lived a Jew, that he grew up in the largest Jewish enclave in the ancient world, that his Jewish followers spread his message for several decades, and that almost all of the texts sacred to Christianity were written by Jews or Jewish converts are ironies that seem to have eluded the gentiles who have struggled with the Jewish question for many centuries.

OTHER OPTIONS

There are, of course, several easier answers to the question of why the Jews rejected Jesus. The most obvious answer is that *they did not reject him*. If the synoptic Gospels are correct, Jesus failed to state *publicly* that he was either the Messiah or the Son of God. And, therefore, the Jews who did not acknowledge Jesus' role in either category were not denying anything. In Mark, for example, there is absolutely no attempt on Jesus' part to tell his audience who he is. The message that Jesus was even special was granted only to his disciples and, at his trial, to the chief priests and the Sanhedrin.

15. Ehrman, ed., *After the New Testament*, 96.

16. On this point, see Weiss, *Earliest Christianity*, II, 663–666; Bultmann, *Theology*, I, 44–46; and Ruether, *Faith and Fratricide*, 113.

17. According to Wylen, "The unsuccessful Jewish rebellion against Rome in 66–70 CE increased anti-Jewish feeling, as Jews now seemed seditious" (*Jews*, 39). Ruether says that, after their exile from Jerusalem, the Jews were regarded as rebels, but not otherwise punished (*Faith and Fratricide*, 27).

18. Bultmann explains the paradoxical relationship between Christianity and Judaism in *Theology*, I, 95–97.

After Peter said that he believed "Jesus was the Christ"—i.e., the Messiah, not necessarily a divine figure—Jesus "charged [his disciples] that they should tell no man of him" (Mark 8:29–30). It is also suggestive that, in his letters (contrary to the claim attributed to him in Acts), Paul does not justify turning to the gentiles by accusing the Jews of rejecting Jesus. The only reason he gives is that Jesus told him to proselytize "among the heathen," a point he makes in Galatians 1:16 and 2:8.[19]

Thus, if the Jews did not join his movement, the cause may be laid at Jesus' feet: He made no claim that could have been rejected. Jesus healed sick people and performed miracles, but he could have been taken as no more than a prophet, on the order of Elijah, to be sure, but merely a God-inspired prophet nonetheless. As one historian explains: "The Jews had for many centuries accepted the idea that many sorts of miracles, in addition to healings, took place. They were presented as credentials of religious leadership," not of divine status.[20] John the Baptist, when asked if he himself was "the Christ," announced that one "who is mightier than" he—presumably, the *real* Christ—was coming (Luke 3:15). But even John, after his arrest, despite his having heard that Jesus raised a young man from the dead, sent a delegation to Jesus asking if he was "the one who is to come" (7:18–19), a reference either to a messianic figure or, more specifically, to the prophet whom Moses predicted would arrive some time in the future: "God will raise up for you a prophet like me from among you" (Deut 18:15). In short, John, who knew Jesus personally and had at least heard of his miraculous acts, remained uncertain about Jesus' identity.

If you neglect to tell people who you are—one might have said to both Jesus and the angry, vengeful Christians of the second century and after—you certainly cannot hold them responsible for not knowing. As Paul said, "[H]ow shall they believe in him of whom they have not heard?" (Rom 10:14). Paul himself knew that it was easy to mistake a man for a god since he was once the beneficiary of that error (Acts 14:11–12), and Jesus had warned against "false prophets" (Matt 7:15, 24:11; Mark 13:22; Luke 6:22), as well as "false Christs" (Matt 24:24; Mark 13:22), as did both Jeremiah (5:31; 14:14; 29:9) and Yahweh Himself (Deut 18:20–22). Credentials were not easy to establish, and all claims were suspect. Although Gideon, doubting the authenticity of both God and His angel, asked for and received three signs (Judg 6:11–22, 36–40), Jesus refused to offer "a sign from heaven" that would verify his divine connection:

---

19. "The author of Acts . . . sought to account for the separation [between Paul and his prospective Jewish converts] by imagining Paul trying in every place first to win the Jewish community whole and withdrawing to the gentiles only when forced to by Jewish hostility. Perhaps that happened, but Paul says nothing of it" (Meeks, *First Urban Christians*, 168). "The radical change in the course of his own life is therefore explicable only by this revelation from God" (176).

20. Grant, *Saint Peter*, 6. Grant continues: "Elijah and Elisha were seen to have been powerful enough to arrest and change the course of nature itself, and there were specific Old Testament precedents as well as rabbinical analogies for some of the miraculous acts attributed to Jesus, such as the Stilling of the Storm" (6).

"Truly, I say to you, no sign shall be given to this generation" (Mark 8:11–12; Matt 16:1–4; Luke 11:29).

Second, although Jesus is sometimes referred to as a savior (e.g., Matt 18:11; Mark 16:16; Luke 2:11; John 4:42), this identity was forgotten by his family and hidden from others who knew him in Nazareth. That is, despite the claim that both Mary (in Luke) and Joseph (in Matthew) were told by an angel of God that Mary would give birth to a son who would receive "the throne of his father David" and "save his people from their sins" (Luke 1:26–32; Matt 1:20–21), neither Mary nor Joseph remembered this event when they returned to Jerusalem after Passover to retrieve Jesus, whom they had inadvertently left behind when they began their journey back to Nazareth. They "were amazed" to find their twelve-year-old son in the Temple carrying on a dialogue with "the doctors" of the Law, who "were astonished at his understanding." When Mary accused Jesus of being delinquent ("[W]hy hast thou thus dealt with us?"), he answered: "How is it that ye sought me? Wist ye not that I must be about my Father's business?" In response to this explanation, which rested explicitly on the assumption that Jesus was indeed the Son of God and implicitly on the assumption that he was an exceptionally gifted child, Luke indicates clearly that they had no idea what he meant: "And they understood not the saying which he spake unto them" (Luke 2:42–50).

Later, three additional events underscore the fact that Jesus was not even regarded as a prophet, let alone a savior, by the people who were closest to him. First, when he began his missionary career by addressing the members of his home synagogue in Nazareth, they were shocked by his eloquence (i.e., "the gracious words which proceeded out of his mouth") presumably because they had no reason to expect that he was not only a competent reader of the Torah scroll but also a confident interpreter of the text. Jesus' audience had no idea that he was anything but the son of a local carpenter: "Is this not Joseph's son?" (Luke 4:18–22; Mark 6:3; Matt 13:55). In the Gospel of Mark, they ask: "From whence hath this man these things? And what wisdom is this which is given unto him, that even such mighty works are wrought by his hands?" (Mark 6:2; Matt 13:54). In response to what they must have interpreted as his arrogance or pretentiousness, "they were filled with wrath, and rose up, and thrust him out of the city." After all, Jesus had not only claimed that "the Spirit of the Lord" was upon him, but also that he was a "man of God," capable of reviving the dead, like Elijah, and of curing leprosy, like Elisha (Luke 4:25–29). He had presented himself as a prophet, but he was not accepted as such by his friends and neighbors. He explained, "No prophet is accepted in his own country" (4:24), but the irony is that this was where his claims to moral and spiritual superiority should have been most obvious.

Elsewhere in the Gospel of Mark, Jesus' "friends," similarly shocked by his unexpected words and deeds, tried "to lay hold on him" because they thought he had lost his mind: "He is beside himself" (Mark 3:21). And when his family came to see him, quite possibly to bring him home and give him the care they thought he needed, Jesus ignored them, claiming that his mother and brothers were not those who denied him, but "whosoever shall do the will of God" (3:35; Luke 8:19–21). Thus, in Mark, he added to those who failed to honor him as a prophet "his own kin" as well as "his own house" (6:4). In the Gospel of John, Jesus' brothers did not "believe in him" and seem to have encouraged Jesus to go to Jerusalem to meet his death: "[S]how thyself to the world," they said, as if to urge him to risk everything (John 7:3–5). In short, those who knew Jesus best—that is, his parents, despite having received a divine message; his brothers and sisters, who heard his words and observed his deeds throughout his childhood and young manhood; and his neighbors, though witnessing his works and wisdom—continued to see him as an ordinary human being who was, if not delusional, at least behaving strangely.

Third, given the extensive descriptions of the Messianic Age in the writings of the prophets and in the apocalyptic writings of the inter-testamental period—as well as the many rather full-blown descriptions of the Messiah himself in both sources—it must have been well-nigh impossible for Jews to see in Jesus the initiator of the New Era. As one Bible scholar puts it, "To call Jesus the messiah was for most Jews completely ludicrous."[21] Thus, when the High Priest asked him if he was "the Christ, the Son of the Blessed" and Jesus answered, "I am" (Mark 14:61–62), there was no reason to take him seriously. There were, in the first century, many prophets and many messiahs. Without a sign, how was anyone to distinguish the authentic savior from the pretenders?

The first problem for most Jews was that Jesus died—a fate that had characterized almost no previously described Jewish messiah.[22] Originally, messiahs were the anointed ones—the kings who obeyed God's will, rose to power, and ruled over a glorious and blessed kingdom; or the priests who ruled after the kingdom was destroyed. Later, the idea of the Messiah was expanded to mean a savior of the Jews, particularly one who would redeem his people and introduce a New Age. Thus, it might have been acceptable if Jesus had died, as long as by his death (i.e., as a warrior-king defeating the forces of evil, but dying in battle) he initiated a transformation of the universe so thorough that Israel was restored to its original glory (under someone in the mold of King David); the Jews in the Diaspora returned to Israel; the "nations" recognized the superiority of Judaism and embraced the faith; and—under the rule of God—peace reigned, swords turned into ploughshares, and lions lay down with lambs. But what is

21. Ehrman, *Misquoting Jesus*, 188; and Nickelsburg, "First and Second Enoch," 92. Maccoby says: "Jesus failed by being crucified, and the assurance by the Nazarenes that he would return had not been fulfilled. The conclusion reached by most Jews, therefore, was that Jesus was just another failed Messiah. As for his alleged prophetic powers, these must have been delusions" (*Mythmaker*, 179).

22. As Brown notes, it was not just that Jesus had died, but that he had been "hanged as a criminal" that stood in the way of Jewish acceptance (*Churches*, 57). "The salvation for which most of the Jews had been hoping," says Lace, "was salvation from the Romans." Thus, "the claim that Jesus was the Messiah must have seemed ludicrous to people who were expecting the Messiah to save Israel by restoring her political freedom" (*Understanding the New Testament*, 149). McKenzie makes a similar point in *Old Testament*, 104–5. For a different view of Jesus' qualifications for messiahship, see Carmichael, *Birth of Christianity*, 63–64.

a messiah who fails to bring with him the Messianic Age?[23] In 4 Ezra 7:49, the Messiah dies at the end of his 400-year reign, but not until the Messianic Age has not only been established but has also flourished for four centuries.[24]

Christians evidently worked very hard to find passages in the Jewish Bible that could be held to prove that Jesus' existence as the Messiah was prophesied therein. Many scholars have suggested, however, that this process was excessive in its zeal and, consequently, erroneous in its claims. The so-called Servant Song in Isaiah (chs. 41–53), for example, in which God's Servant is explicitly identified as the Jewish nation, is claimed to apply to Jesus. The passage repeatedly addresses "Israel, my servant, Jacob" or "my chosen" (41:8–9; 42:1; 43:10; 44:1–2, 21; 45:4; 48:1, 12, 20; 49:3, 5–7), just as elsewhere in the Bible God addresses Abraham, Jacob, Moses, Joshua, David, Elijah, and Job in the same manner. In fact, the word "Israel" occurs forty times throughout the Song. Halfway through chapter 50, however, the Servant is no longer, except once, addressed as Israel, but as "Zion" or "Jerusalem" (50:14; 51:3, 16–17; 52:1, 7). It is clear, nevertheless, that God is still speaking exclusively to His people, whom he assures again and again throughout these chapters that he will save them from oppression and injustice.

Beginning with Isaiah 52:13 ("my servant shall prosper, he shall be exalted and lifted up") and ending with 53:12 ("he bore the sin of many"), fifteen lines have traditionally been quoted out of context to refer to Jesus as the Servant who suffers, who in suffering atones for the sins of others, and who yet will be exalted. A Jew would protest that the lines refer to the suffering of Israel, as deutero-Isaiah witnessed it in the sixth century. As the editors of *Oxford Annotated Bible* conclude, "The poem describes the purpose of God's people, the covenant community"—that is, the Jews.[25] For Christians, however, the exegetical extremism that led to identifying Jesus as the Servant probably resulted in a net gain in the sense that, while they failed to convince Jews (and, in fact, no doubt offended them), they very likely succeeded in impressing gentiles with Jesus' Jewish credentials.[26]

23. On this subject, see Klinghoffer, *Why the Jews*, 160–61. Klinghoffer makes another interesting point: "Neither in the Bible nor in the later Jewish sources was there any notion that a person would have to wonder whether or not the Messiah had appeared" (159; see also 210). Klingaman says: "Surely the inglorious circumstances of Jesus death did not represent the triumphal climax Israel had awaited for so many centuries. The Romans still ruled Judea, and the Jewish people were still dispersed throughout the Mediterranean world" (*First Century*, 213).

24. Weiss says, "But that the Messiah should die at the beginning of his work, and that his death was to be one means—or the chief means—of fulfilling this mission, is nowhere suggested" (*Earliest Christianity*, I, 111). Schillebeeckx, however, suggests that, although the connection between Jesus and Isaiah's Suffering Servant was developed long after the Crucifixion, Christians could understand Jesus to be the righteous one who suffers, based on other Jewish traditions. The idea was not explicitly associated with atonement, although it was understood among Jews that martyrs died for others, i.e., sacrificially (*Jesus*, 282–92).

25. For extended analyses of the Suffering Servant passages, see Heschel, *Prophets*, I, 148–58; and Newsome, *Hebrew Prophets*, 145–56.

26. In Psalm 2, for another example, God says, "You are my son, today I have begotten you." The

Fourth, if Jesus spoke to the Jews the way the evangelists indicate, it is no wonder that the Jews rejected him. On one hand, he had little difficulty explaining his moral code. This, I believe, without minimizing the ambiguities, comes through quite eloquently and accessibly. On the other hand, however, no one can read the Gospels and come away with the feeling that Jesus even *tried* to make anything else clear—not only his identity, but his expectations, as well. He spoke in parables to the public, which the public usually misunderstood. And, when he explained his ideas to his disciples, especially in the synoptic Gospels, he was often surprised that they were equally unable to comprehend. Indeed, as time passed and the Christian view of Jesus became more Hellenized, it must have become increasingly incomprehensible to many Palestinian Jews.

The point is best illustrated by the frustrating experience of Nicodemus in the Gospel of John, which I discussed briefly in the Introduction. This Pharisee was evidently well educated, so much so that Jesus was apparently very disappointed when he failed to get the message: "Art thou a master of Israel, and knowest not these things?" (John 3:10). It is important to notice that Nicodemus saw Jesus as "a teacher [who had] come from God" (3:2).[27] That is, Nicodemus was not an enemy, but a believer, who later defended Jesus against other Pharisees (7:50–51), helped Joseph of Arimathea carry Jesus to his tomb, and prepared his body for burial (19:39–40). Yet Jesus talked to him in a Platonic language that a Palestinian Jew—including Jesus himself—could hardly have been expected to understand. The point is that this entire passage represents a dialogue in which the audience of one (Nicodemus) was evidently trying to get the message, but the speaker (Jesus) was either unwilling to compromise or simply unable to communicate clearly and effectively. Of course, this was not the historical Jesus' failure. John created this dialogue to underscore his favorite point: The Jews (even the best of them) were incapable of understanding Jesus.

<hr/>

words appear at Jesus' baptism in some old manuscripts of the New Testament, as if the psalm prophesied this event. However, the words are addressed not to Jesus, but to a Jewish king. In fact, the proclamation is "a formula of adoption"—presumably used during the monarchy—"whereby the king became God's son" (*Oxford Annotated Bible*, 657). Klinghoffer says that the Old Testament sources used by Christians in the ancient world to "prove" that Jesus was the Messiah (Mic 5:1; Gen 5:10; Isa 53, Isa 7:14; Jer 31:31; and Ps 32:16) were badly misinterpreted. He adds, "[O]n point after point, Christian exegesis was found to be dubious to anyone who could read the Bible for himself in its original language" (*Why the Jews*, 168–69). Segal discusses the problem of Christian exegesis in *Rebecca's Children*, 88–95. He comments: "This [pattern of novel interpretation] explains why Christianity had so much trouble persuading Jews that the messiah had come. Nothing that the Christians maintained seemed self-evident to the majority of the Jewish community, and the Jews were the only ones who expected the messiah." That is precisely why, Segal notes, Paul said, "We preach Christ crucified, a stumbling block to Jews and folly to gentiles" (1 Cor 1:23) (94).

27. Thus, Freyne calls Nicodemus "an honest inquirer" (*Galilee, Jesus*, 121). Chilton and Neusner explain that "[t]he Jewish resistance to Jesus is within John not a historical happenstance, but a theological necessity." Thus, "Nicodemus . . . tries to appreciate Jesus as a teacher come from God," but "Jesus replies with riddles that befuddle Nicodemus, and Jesus taunts him." The point is that Nicodemus no longer belongs to "Israel" and therefore cannot be expected to understand either God or His emissary (*Judaism*, 122).

Thus, to the fictional Nicodemus, everything the fictional Jesus said must have sounded like gibberish, but the latter was unyielding.[28] Jesus told him that one must be born anew and that one must be born of the Spirit. By way of explaining, Jesus added, "The wind blows where it wills, and you hear the sound of it, but you do not know whence it comes or whither it goes; so it is with every one who is born of the Spirit." When Nicodemus asked, "How can this be?"—in other words, "I have no idea what you are talking about"—Jesus responded, "Truly truly, I say to you, we speak of what we know, and bear witness to what we have seen" (John 3:3–11). From this point on, neither knowing what Jesus knew nor seeing what Jesus saw, Nicodemus was either silent or absent because he was completely dumbfounded.

The same kind of "dialogue" occurs in chapter 6, where members of Jesus' synagogue audience asked, "Rabbi, . . . [w]hat shall we do, that we might work the works of God?" (John 6:28). To this evidently sincere query, Jesus said he was "the bread of life," among other cryptic statements—including the suggestion that his auditors should eat his flesh and drink his blood, to which his disciples responded, "This is a hard saying; who can hear it?" (6:48–60). After all, Jews were forbidden to eat the flesh of any animal that did not chew its cud and were also ordered by God never to drink the blood of any creature.[29] Surely for those reasons, "many of his disciples drew back and no longer went about with him" (6:66). Jesus also stated more directly than he did in his conversation with Nicodemus (3:13–16) his claim to have descended from heaven and his promise that he would return to heaven and thereby give his followers eternal life (6:38–44), another concept totally foreign to the consciousness of rural Galilean Jews.

All of these ideas would have been meaningful to participants in one of the mystery cults that were popular in the Roman empire at this time. However, there is no

28. Brown says that John's metaphors are generally as misunderstood by Jesus' auditors as some of the parables in the synoptic Gospels (*Introduction*, 335). Yet, when he discusses Jesus' metaphorical language in his conversation with Nicodemus, Brown says that the latter's failure to understand was a reflection of his "inadequate faith" (341). However, considering, also, that (as Brown indicates) the passage is characterized by "many plays on Greek words," which make "it very difficult to translate," one can see why Nicodemus did not understand it. Furthermore, the fact that these puns would have been impossible in Aramaic—though other puns would have been possible—makes the exchange even more bizarre. One of the stranger explanations for Jesus' failure to explain his identity clearly and unequivocally to his prospective followers is that he could not find the right words: "So unique did Jesus believe his relationship to God to be that he seems to have found no designation in the scriptures of his people or in common usage which exactly described it. This may account for the reluctance which some of our accounts appear to reflect in him to allow himself to be called the Messiah" (Latourette, *History of Christianity*, I, 49).

29. Vermes comments on Jesus' invitation: "This cannibalistic allegory is hardly attributable to Jesus speaking to his Galilean listeners. Most first-century AD Palestinian Jews, hearing these words, would have been overcome by nausea. The eating of blood was a deeply ingrained biblical taboo," as the leaders of the Jewish Christians at the Jerusalem Conference indicated (Acts 15:20) (*Resurrection*, 68). Smith says that the idea of the Eucharist derives from magic rites: "In them as in it a magician-god gives his own body and blood to a recipient who, by eating it, will be united with him in love" (*Jesus the Magician*, 123; see also 138, 146–47).

way that Jewish peasants attending the synagogue in Capernaum, where Jesus delivered these statements (John 6:59), had any chance of understanding his message. They were simply unaware of the conflict between flesh and spirit, the Platonic theory of the immortality of the soul, the idea of a descending and ascending god, and the concept of eating the flesh and drinking the blood of a divine being. To attribute their response to either Jewish intransigence or God's desire to exclude the Jews from salvation ("No one can come to me unless the Father who sent me draws him," said Jesus [6:44, 65]) is to assume that Jesus' ideas would have been as clear to Galilean Jews as they were to anyone else and that anyone deserving of Jesus' love and God's grace could have have understood them. Paul's theology, similarly influenced by ideas not indigenous to Galilee, must have been equally mystifying.

Fifth, even if he had identified himself unequivocally and explained himself without the obfuscations that people like Nicodemus and the Capernaum Jews encountered, Jesus was, despite the biblical claim that he was followed by multitudes, not particularly well known. The fact is, as the biblical record indicates, there were only 120 disciples at the Pentecost (all of them Jews), and, although many Jews might have fallen away from the Jesus movement, millions more were not a part of it in the first place. With perhaps half a million Jews in Palestine and as many as 7,000,000 Jews in the Roman empire, it is fairly obvious that the overwhelming majority of Jews never heard of Jesus. And even in Palestine, since Jesus limited his preaching to a few small towns near Capernaum, on the northern coast of the Sea of Galilee, he is likely to have been within shouting distance of only a few thousand potential converts.

In short, before his Crucifixion, Jesus might have been popular in rural Galilee, but he was probably obscure in the rest of Palestine and certainly unknown in the Diaspora. Unlike many of the messiah-figures of the first century (and the Gospels to the contrary), he did not inspire a following of vast proportions. He was, as one scholar puts it, "at most a 'blip' on the radar screen" of contemporary Jewish and pagan writers and "simply insignificant" to Jewish and pagan historians.[30] Although many people followed Jesus—mainly because of his spectacular healings—it may well have been the case that few of them actually accepted him as their spiritual leader. Perhaps that is the reason John's Jesus refuses to perform miracles for the purpose of impressing his audience (John 6:26–33). Even in the synoptic Gospels, Jesus calls those who

---

30. Meier, *Marginal Jew*, I, 7–8. Jesus is unmentioned, for example, by the Jewish philosopher Philo of Alexandria and the Jewish historian Justus of Tiberias (Augstein, *Jesus Son of Man*, 351 n. 6). Bornkamm makes the same point in *Jesus of Nazareth*, 27. According to Weiss, "In the dispersion, . . . nothing was known of Jesus except perhaps vague rumors" (*Earliest Christianity*, I, 225). The famous reference to Jesus in Josephus' *Jewish Antiquities*, called the *Testimonium Flavianum*, is a much-disputed passage, the authenticity of which many scholars reject in whole or in part. See, for example, Grant, *Historical Introduction*, 291–92; and Conzelmann and Lindemann, *Interpreting the New Testament*, 290. Brown similarly refers to "later Christian additions" (*Introduction*, 835). "The problem is that Josephus's account is too good to be true, too confessional to be impartial, too Christian to be Jewish. It is either a total or a partial interpolation by the Christian editors who preserved Josephus' works" (Crossan, *Historical Jesus*, 373).

ask for a sign members of "an evil and adulterous generation" (Matt 12:38–39; 16:4; Mark 8:12; Luke 11:29).[31]

Sixth, despite the incredible expansion of Christianity in the fourth century, *Jesus was not accepted by the vast majority of gentiles before this*—that is, for the first two and a half centuries after his death.[32] And, throughout the years during which Christianity grew steadily but slowly, the reason that gentile Christians far outnumbered Jewish Christians is simply that Jews represented, at most, only ten percent of the population of the Roman empire. In other words, if Christianity had appealed equally to both groups between AD 30 and 300, it would have, at the end of that period, consisted of ten times as many pagans as Jews. Ironically, as a result of their Hellenization, the Jews in the Diaspora were probably more ready for the Jesus described in the letters of Paul and the Gospel of John than were the Jews in Palestine.[33] And it is certain that, despite the hostility of the Church toward Jews in the second and third centuries, Jews continued to be aggressively courted by Christians and remained strong in many of the churches throughout the Diaspora, especially in churches—such as those in Rome, Antioch, and Damascus—which had been Jewish before the Pauline gentile mission.[34] Nevertheless, they could not, in the long run, escape being a small minority of Christians.

Finally, the Jews may have rejected Jesus because his standards were too high. If the values of the Christian-Jewish community that Luke describes in the Acts of the Apostles can be taken as a reflection of Jesus' teachings, it is not surprising that even the Church itself eventually turned its back on them. Members of this Christian-Jewish group were expected to sell all of their property and contribute the proceeds to the common fund. Although not all of them practiced sexual abstinence—following Jesus' idealization of the eunuch (Matt 19:10–12) and Paul's opposition to marriage unless it was absolutely necessary (in order to allay an otherwise uncontrollable lust [1 Cor 7:9])—evidently many of them refrained from sex. And, of course, following Jesus' requirement that the disciples travel without any worldly goods, the community adopted a policy of voluntary poverty.

What many Jews (and pagans) very likely found even more onerous was the expectation that the followers of Jesus—influenced as they must have been by the Sermon on the Mount—would undergo a transformation so life-changing that it would be impossible for them to act under the influence of *any* negative emotion, including

---

31. Tabor says, "[W]e don't know how many disciples were following at this time, but one could imagine a cadre of adherents, perhaps several dozen" (*Jesus Dynasty*, 161). See also 184 and 337 n. 8.

32. Ehrman reminds us that the Jews were not alone: "Most non-Christians, of course, completely rejected the Christian message" (*After the New Testament*, 3). Elsewhere, Ehrman estimates the percentage of Christians in the Roman empire in c. 300 at five to seven percent of the total population, which grew to fifty percent a century later (*Lost Christianities*, 250).

33. Stark makes this point in *Rise of Christianity*, 57–62.

34. On these two points, see Weiss, *Earliest Christianity*, I, 166; and II, 666, 671. Weiss says that every church had at least a Jewish-Christian minority (671).

anger.[35] It is useful to remember that the Essenes supported a similarly strict code of behavior—including chastity, at least for the Qumran residents—and attracted only a few thousand Jews to their sect. Indeed, as I said earlier, many scholars regard Jesus' high moral standard not as a long-term requirement, but as an *interim* ethical program, that was expected to end at Christ's second coming.[36] What scholars are suggesting by this explanation of Jesus' ethical regimen is that it could not have been sustained for long.

Furthermore, Christians eventually expected Jews to relinquish their covenant claims—that is, their belief that God established a permanent relationship with them *as Jews*. No doubt, for many pious Jews, this requirement proved unacceptable.[37] There is no reason to think that James the brother of Jesus—or, in fact, any member of the Jerusalem church during the first century—would have submitted to that demand. Nor would any of them have accepted the Christian challenge to "the central symbols of Jewish solidarity," such as the Torah, circumcision, and the Sabbath.[38] In other words, what Jews rejected was not Jesus, but the entire array of attacks on things that Jews held sacred and the appropriation of aspects of Judaism that Jews regarded as their own.[39]

To be sure, Christians could argue, as they did increasingly in the second century, that the New Age had begun with Jesus' mere presence in the world. But a not-so-wise Jew might argue that the world had not improved in any ostensible way—i.e., that nations were still embroiled in conflict; that individuals—even Christians—remained not only critical of each other, but sometimes belligerent; and that not one of the transformations delineated in the futuristic program of the prophets had come to

35. Theissen comments: "The intensification of the commandments against killing and against adultery makes impossible demands on every man: aggressive dispositions and erotic fascination cannot be made subject to human wills. Anyone who is asking that is asking for the impossible" (*Early Palestinian Christianity*, 106). Flusser says, referring to Jesus' demand that his followers love their enemies, "In those days it was obviously very difficult for people to rise up to the heights of Jesus' commandment" (*Sage from Galilee*, 61). Flusser traces Jesus' view of anger and lust to what he calls the Jewish concept of 'Two Ways,' which can be found in *The Didache*: "Be not prone to anger, for anger leadeth to murder . . . [And] be not lustful, for lust leadeth to fornication" (64–65). The idea also appears in the Essenes' *Community Rule* and *Damascus Rule* (see Vermes, *Dead Sea Scrolls*, 75–78, 98–99).

36. Fredriksen, for example, says, "The perfectionist ethical teachings and the miracles, then, are all of a piece . . . Both together attest to the nearness—now but not yet—of the Kingdom" (*Jesus of Nazareth*, 117).

37. Herford explains: "The Jew could not accept Christ without disowning the Torah. But why should the Jew abandon the Torah? He could not do so until he had felt that it was insufficient, and this he did not feel, nor ever has felt down to the present day" (*Pharisees*, 218).

38. Hare, *Jewish Persecution of Christians*, 3–4. "Christians subordinated all [such] symbols to the central symbol of their faith, the Christ" (5). They also challenged Jewish nationalism and religious leadership (7–8).

39. On this subject, see Ruether, *Faith and Fratricide*, 80. Thus, says Tabor, "What Jews have rejected is not so much Jesus as the systems of Christian theology that equated Jesus with God, that nullified the Torah, and that displaced the Jewish people and their covenant" (*Jesus Dynasty*, 314).

pass. Jesus himself had claimed nothing, he had died on the cross like thousands of Jews in the preceding century, and—although, at his death, "the temple was rent in twain from the top to the bottom; and the earth did quake, and the rocks rent; and the graves were opened" (Matt 27:51–52)—nothing had really changed. The wonder is, therefore, not that the Jews rejected Jesus, but that large numbers of Jews actually took him seriously enough to make of the movement he started, the promises he made, and the ethical program he articulated something that lasted, without much of their help after the first century, for two thousand years.

At first, only Jews supported Jesus, and, if they had not responded to his call, Christianity would never have flourished. Nevertheless, since many Jews (as well as many pagans) failed to rally to his cause, later Christians, cut off from their Jewish roots, accused the Jews of all kinds of sins. These "sins," ironically, were merely those that the Jews accused themselves of when they struggled to understand, especially in the first century AD, why God had not intervened on their behalf for more than half a millennium and restored them to their former glory. Indeed, the self-criticism of the Jews—expressed so eloquently and pervasively in the writings of Isaiah, Jeremiah, and Ezekiel, as well as in other Jewish canonical and non-canonical works—became the principal basis for these charges.

The Jews, like other ancient peoples, believed that suffering was caused by sin. Therefore, conquered and subsequently dominated, often ruthlessly, by other nations after the Assyrian invasion in the eighth century—namely, Babylonians, Persians, Ptolemies, Seleucids, and Romans—the Jews assumed that they had been abandoned by God because of their own wrongdoing. The self-accusations may be said to have begun with Amos and Hosea as a way of explaining the Assyrian invasion and by Isaiah as a way of explaining the Babylonian exile.[40] However, it is unlikely that the sins of which the Jews accused themselves were ever actually committed. They "confessed" because they had no other way to explain what had happened to them. Assuming that God is just, they suffered; therefore, they must have sinned.

Specifically, since the Jewish Holy Land had been invaded, many Jews had been forcibly removed from their homeland, and the Temple had been destroyed, the only possible explanation was that they had disobeyed God. Amos called for justice; Hosea called for love. Like them, Isaiah blamed the Jews themselves, whom he called the "people of Gomorrah" (1:10), who accepted bribes, ignored the poor (1:21, 23), and rejected their God-given ethical code (5:20). Jeremiah agreed.[41] And the indictment

---

40. On the main themes of Amos and Hosea, see Heschel, *Prophets*, 27–60. McKenzie says that Jews "did not question the justice of God. God punished in measure, and if the punishment was total it was proportionate to the offense." In short, "if God did it, it must be morally irreproachable" (*Old Testament*, 49). "Man could not," McKenzie says later, "as he could in Mesopotamia, be the victim of demons or of a dispute between gods. Elementary justice demanded that God treat each man according to his own deserts. There could be no failure or pain in the life of a good man" (150). McKenzie applies this point to specific biblical stories on 82, 170, 171.

41. The prophets castigated the Jews, says Carmichael, because "[t]here had to be some explanation

continued throughout the inter-testamental period, particularly in the Apocrypha. Here, the criticisms of the Jews remained as angry and their punishment as horrible as they were in the words of the prophets.

Even before this series of foreign conquests, Solomon had said to God, "[H]eaven is shut up and there is no rain because they have sinned against thee" (1 Kgs 8:35).[42] Moral impurity, the Jews believed, is caused by sin, and it can corrupt both the individual sinner and an entire people. Unlike ritual impurity, which is curable by rites of purification, moral impurity can be reversed only by punishment or atonement.[43] Therefore, the Jews insisted, in the face of what they considered to be oppression, injustice, and exploitation, they had to return to obedience and righteousness in order to win back God's support.

However, what the Christians used as evidence of Jewish culpability in such passages never included the other side of the traditional prophetic vision—i.e., the promise of God's ultimately saving act, his commitment to the Covenant, and his restoration of the status quo ante. From the Christian perspective, the Jews lost that hope because they had sinned too egregiously. Now, they were beyond forgiveness, and the Christians inherited both the Covenant and its promise.

In the inter-testamental literature, especially in the Jewish Apocrypha, the connection between sin and suffering is stated repeatedly. The writer of the Letter of Jeremiah, for example, says to the Jews that they were "being led away captive to Babylon" solely "because of the sins [they] have committed in the sight of God" (Baruch 6:2). The author of Tobit says to God, referring to the Assyrian conquest, "I acknowledge the justice of your many judgements, the due penalty for our sins, for we have not carried out your commandments or lived in true obedience before you" (3:5). In the Book of Judith, Holofernes hears a report from "the commander of the Ammonites" to the effect that the career of the Israelites has wholly depended on their god's attitude toward them, which depended, in turn, on their obedience to his laws. They can be beaten in battle only if they have "violated their law" (5:17–21). Judith herself later acknowledges the truth of this assumption: "[N]o punishment ever befalls our race nor does the sword subdue them, except when they sin against their God . . . for whenever they do wrong they arouse their God's anger" (11:10–11; see also 8:18–20).

---

of Jewish suffering, and since the Creator could hardly be blamed, the Jews had to be" (*Birth of Christianity*, 2–3).

42. Crossan comments: "It was clear from [this] prayer . . . that sin and drought were a continuum, the former begetting the latter and the latter certifying the former. So also was there . . . a continuum between sin and sickness or death" (*Historical Jesus*, 141). According to Koester, the Deuteronomist assumed that "God is justified by historical events; it was always the guilt of Israel which led to repeated setbacks and subsequently to the final catastrophe of the nation" (*History, Culture, and Religion*, 231). See also Wylen, *Jews*, 147; Brown, *Introduction*, 738; and Ruether, *Faith and Fratricide*, 160.

43. Klawans, "Moral and Ritual Purity," 269. See also Flusser, *Sage from Galilee*, 78. This otherwise unexplainable suffering also leads to apocalyptic visions in which the world will be transformed, and human misery will be ended (Schillebeeckx, *Jesus*, 124).

In the non-Apochryphal *Psalms of Solomon,* the poet says, speaking of the Jews, "And according to her sins he did to them, because he abandoned them into the hand of one who was stronger" (2:7).[44]

The claim that Israel had suffered because of its sins would have been bad enough, but some texts went so far as to charge that Israel's punishment was extreme only because Israel's sins were unprecedented. That is, they exceeded the sins of any nation at any time. The author of *Psalms of Solomon,* for example, says, "[N]o one did upon [the earth] as they did" (2:9), "[a]nd there was no sin greater even than those of the nations that they did not commit" (8:13).[45] Baruch, similarly, says that the Jews had been disobedient since the departure from Egypt, they had broken all the commandments, and they had even eaten their children. Thus, "Under the whole of heaven no such things have been done as were done in Jerusalem" (1:17–19; 2:2–3, 12). The author of 1 Esdras asserts that, during the reign of Josiah, the sins of Judah were "graver than anything perpetrated by any other nation or kingdom" (1:23). During subsequent reigns, "both people and priests . . . outdid even the heathen in their abominable practices" (1:45). And they were all punished requisitely (8:75–76, 86–87). In 2 Esdras, the Jews evidently being incorrigible, God threatens to turn to other nations (1:24–25, 35).

Christians of the second, third, fourth, and fifth centuries remembered the self-incrimination of these passages, but, as I said, forgot God's repeated promise that, in spite of their disobedience, the Jews would not only survive, but triumph. It was, after all, not "punishment" that God had imposed on the Jews, but "chastisement," for the purpose of correction and purification.[46] Thus, Tobit ends with a promise of God's mercy, the conversion of the gentiles, and the gathering of the righteous in Jerusalem (13:11–18; 14:6–7), a typical Jewish apocalyptic vision. In 2 Esdras, Ezra argues against the angel Uriel's accusations by claiming that Babylon sinned worse than Zion

---

44. Similar passages appear in Nehemiah, Ezra and 2 Kings: "Here we are, slaves to this day—slaves in the land that you gave to our ancestors to enjoy its fruit and its good gifts. Its rich yield goes to *the kings whom you have set over us because of our sins*" (Neh. 9:36–37). "[W]e have forsaken your commandments" (Ezra 9:10). "After all that has come upon us for our evil deeds and for our great guilt, seeing that you, our God, have *punished us less than our iniquities deserved*, shall we break your commandments again? (Ezra 9:13). "This occurred because the people of Israel sinned against the Lord their God" (2 Kings 17:7; all with my emphasis). The tradition of self-incrimination continued after the destruction of the second Temple in A.D. 70, as Mack notes: "The apocalypses of 2 Baruch and 4 Ezra from the time after the war are full of laments over Jerusalem as a desolate city, expressions of despair in the face of God's incomprehensible failure to protect it, struggles with guilt for the sins that surely must have been the cause of the disaster, and prayers that cry out for some way to imagine a future for Israel despite the destruction of the city" (*Who Wrote?* 149).

45. The passages from *The Psalms of Solomon* can be found in Joseph F. Trafton, "The Psalms of Solomon," 258, 260.

46. Ironically, says Moore, God's punishment of the Jews was "not vindictive," except against those who were irremediably bad. Rather, "God's end in punishment was not to make the sinner suffer what he deserved, but through suffering to bring him to penitence and amendment. So the prophets had taught both for the nation and the individual, and so Judaism understood" (*Judaism,* II-III, 252).

and that, at any rate, all "the inhabitants of the earth" have sinned against God, while Israel alone has (presumably at some points in its history) kept God's commandments (4:28–35). There is no evidence that the angel agrees, but it is clear that at the end of 2 Esdras, as in the final pages of all of these works, God (or his angel) promises that some Jews will be saved.

Furthermore, in the absence of *any* evidence that the Jews were in fact morally inferior to other first-century ethnic or religious groups, it is, of course, tragic that the Christians used the Jews' self-condemnation to justify not only their repudiation of the Jews, but also the violence that accompanied it. Ironically, as one scholar puts it, "It would have been better if the church had also taken over from Judaism rather more of that inexorable self-criticism which distinguished Jewish ethnocentrism from all others."[47] That is, no other people beat themselves up as much as the Jews did. The excessive and unrelenting self-criticism was obviously intended to be both an explanation and a wake-up call, but it turned into a justification for even more abuse, both verbal and physical.

It also remained a theme among Christians who felt the need to justify the idea that Christianity superseded Judaism,[48] as it was for St. Augustine, whose *Tract Against the Jews* portrays the Jews as reprobates undeserving of God's concern.[49] Indeed, as the Church grew larger and more gentile than Jewish, the mere existence of Jews seems to have exacerbated Christian hostility. Jews and Christians competed for converts, and the survival of the Jews appeared to undermine the Christian argument that they had murdered Jesus and therefore deserved to suffer, if not die and endure eternal punishment: "To understand the force of this criticism [by Christians]," one historian explains, "one must recall that Judaism was a thriving religious movement within the Roman Empire in the second century C.E. The Christian movement had

47. Theissen, *Early Palestinian Christianity*, 94. Theissen mentions (1) the identity crisis Israel went though as a result of the clash between its sense of specialness and its position of political, social, and economic inferiority under the Roman occupation; (2) Israel's consequent self-criticism; and (3) the schism this crisis fomented in the multiplication of sects, including Christianity, that offered divergent programs for reform and renewal (93).

48. Lace, for example, persistently refers to the Jews' failure to keep the Law. Indeed, they knew they had violated the covenant by this failure ("Why We Study the New Testament," 7–8; and "What the New Testament Is About," 147). Moule concurs: "The agreement or covenant between God and his People, made at Mount Sinai through Moses, had been broken. God had stood by his people, but they had deserted him" ("How the New Testament Came into Being," 100–101). "We have seen that the Jews were nevertheless conscious of their failure, their sin, their weakness as an instrument for the purposes of God" (Lace, 150). That "we have seen" this means that Lace asserted it earlier.

49. Ruether says that the prophetic pattern of judgment and promise, by which the Jews accused themselves of sinning and yet held out the hope of salvation, was split in two by Christian interpreters, the judgment applied to the Jews and the hope offered to the Christians: "Every negative judgment, threat, or description can then be taken out of context and read monolithically as descriptive of 'the Jews,'" while the "positive side of the prophetic message" was applied to "the future church" (*Faith and Fratricide*, 131–32).

to make its way alongside of, and sometimes in opposition to, well-established Jewish communities."[50]

Of course, the Church did not wait until the time of Augustine, Ambrose, and John Chrysostom to criticize Jews and Judaism. The Gospels themselves do so not only in their claim that the Jews alone were responsible for the death of Jesus, but also in their prediction that Jews would persecute Christians after the Crucifixion (Matt 10:17–23; Mark 13:9–13; Luke 21:12–17). Since the evangelists began to write their Gospels just when Jews began to expel Christian proselytizers from synagogues and punish repeat offenders, as Acts reports, they attributed to the year AD 30 conflicts that arose only much later. The clearest evidence of this revisionist treatment of the relationship between Jews and Christians is the fact that, as time passed, the hostility increased, such that John's anti-Judaism (as I said earlier) is far more extreme than the anti-Judaism in Mark, Matthew, and Luke.[51] For example, John claims (1) that *all* Christians, not just propagandists, were expelled from synagogues; and (2) that this occurred during Jesus' lifetime, not just after the Revolt of 66 (John 9:22; 12:42; and 16:2), although there is no evidence supporting these accusations.[52] Most scholars assert that, sometime in the latter half of the first century, Christians who *preached in the synagogue* on Jesus' behalf were excommunicated, but other Christian Jews were not.

50. Wilken, *Christians*, 113. "From the perspective of pagan critics of Christianity, the existence of authentic Jewish communities was a powerful argument against the claims of the Christians" (188). See also Gager, *Origins of Anti-Semitism*, 16, 31, 112, 114. Most important is the fact "that hostility toward Jews appeared wherever and whenever pagans encountered Jews in the Greco-Roman world" (17). Langmuir explains: "From motives common to most sects, the adherents of the new Christian religions were necessarily anti-Judaic in the sense that they had to demonstrate the superiority of their Christian religions to any Judaic religions." In other words, "Their struggles to establish their own identity were fraught with tensions, including the tension with Judaism" (*History, Religion, and Antisemitism*, 282–83). Langmuir suggests that the Christians' need to explain why Jews rejected Jesus must be understood in this context (283–84). On the consequences of this need, see 284–95.

51. See Reinhartz, "The Gospel of John: How the Jews Became Part of the Plot," 111, 115–16. Citing as an example 1 Peter 2:8, Weiss says, "Anti-judaism . . . becomes sharper and sharper in the later literature." He continues: "The height of this development is to be found in the Gospel of John: its judgment upon the 'Jews' is as severe and devoid of hope as possible: they are sons of the devil (8:44), they are in every respect the typical representatives of the unbelieving and God-opposing world. Indeed, they are incapable of hearing the word and believing its truth (*Earliest Christianity*, II, 666). Ironically, Jesus himself rejected the idea that suffering comes from sin in Luke 13:1–5.

52. "The notion that Jews expelled Johannine believers from the synagogue is problematic theologically, because it blames the Jews themselves for the invective to which they are subjected within the Gospel narrative and discourse materials. It is also problematic historically because no external evidence suggests that any Jewish leader had the authority, the means, or even the incentive to expel Christ-confessors from the synagogue, certainly not in the decade or two after the destruction of the Temple" (Reinhartz, "The Gospel of John: How the Jews Became Part of the Plot," 114–15).

DID JEWS PERSECUTE CHRISTIANS?

One charge that clearly increased the hostility of Christians toward Jews was the claim by Paul that he had been a leading participant in the Jewish persecution of Christians. After he was arrested in the Temple, Paul repeated to the citizens of Jerusalem his statement to Jesus implying that his career as a persecutor started even before Stephen's death: "Lord, they themselves [i.e., the Christians] know that in every synagogue I imprisoned and beat those who believed in thee. And when the blood of Stephen was shed, I also was standing by and approving" (Acts 22:19–20). What is a little confusing about the sequence of events is that Paul had said earlier, "And on that day [that is, when Stephen was killed] a great persecution arose against the church in Jerusalem" (Acts 8: 1)—implying that the persecution *began* with Stephen's death.

Paul and Luke are our main sources for evidence of this persecution. First, Paul refers to his actions in three different letters—Galatians 1:13, 1 Corinthians 15:9, and Philippians 3:6. However, his descriptions here are very brief (e.g., Paul "persecuted the church of God"), and we are forced to rely almost entirely on Luke for details. In Acts of the Apostles, Paul is quoted as saying that he arrested Christians, bound them, and dragged them to prison or turned them over to the chief priests (Acts 8:3; 22:4; 26:10). Neither Paul nor Luke ever specifies the reason for these arrests, but Paul's contention that he arrested Christians in synagogues (Acts 22:19; 26:11) suggests that they were captured when they were proselytizing, as Christians probably were after the Revolt of AD 66 and as Stephen might have been when the members of "the synagogue of the Freedmen" seized him and brought him before "the council"—i.e., the Sanhedrin (Acts 6:12).

Paul makes it very clear that the highest authorities, "the chief priests," authorized his pursuit of Christians (Acts 9:14, 21; 26:12). And in two passages he indicates that he was supported in his efforts by the High Priest himself. When Paul wanted to pursue Christians in Damascus, he asked the High Priest for letters "to the synagogues" of that city (Acts 9:1–2; another hint that these Christians were apprehended for proselytizing). And he adds that both the High Priest and the Sanhedrin ("the whole council of elders") could bear witness to his zealousness (Acts 22:5).

If this was the extent of Paul's activities—i.e., arresting Christian propagandists—then his claims are at least credible. After all, there is no reason to question the accuracy of Luke's account, in Acts, of the repeated arrests of Peter, among other Christian proselytizers. People were invited to address Jewish congregations during or after worship services, and the followers of Jesus evidently took advantage of the opportunity. Assuming, of course, that the speeches of the disciples are accurately reported in Acts, they raised the ire of the Jews not merely because they claimed that Jesus was the Messiah, but because they also accused the Jews of crucifying him and of therefore being in a state of sin so severe that only repentance and baptism could save them from damnation (Acts 2:36–40; 3:13–23; 4:10–12). Peter's public appearance at first only "annoyed" Temple officials (4:1–2), but when he preached again, against the stated command of the council, "they were enraged" (5:33). It was, therefore, not merely the content of his speech, but his defiance of their order that led to his arrest.

Even then, however, despite strong feelings, the authorities in Jerusalem, where Paul is said to have conducted his campaign against Christians, were compelled to proceed cautiously in their treatment of Peter and others because "the people" (i.e., the ordinary Jews) were inclined to protect the Christians. When the High Priest and Sadducees arrested Peter and other apostles because they were—in violation of the Sanhedrin's "strict orders not to teach in [Jesus'] name"—"standing in the temple and teaching the people," the Jewish leaders handled them "without violence, for *they were afraid of being stoned by the people*" (i.e., the other Jews [Acts 5:25–28; my emphasis]). Indeed, at the time of Peter and John's first arrest, the same leaders—"the priests, the captain of the temple, and the Sadducees" (4:1), but later described as "rulers, elders, and scribes," as well as four members of "the high-priestly family" (4:5)—threatened the Christians, but "let them go, finding no way to punish them *because of the people*" (Acts 4:21; my emphasis). Nor does there appear to have been any persecution of Christians in the Diaspora at this time, given the absence of any reference to it in connection with the missionary work of Philip (in Samaria and Gaza, as well as in other coastal towns from north of Gaza to Caesarea) and Peter (in Lydda, Joppa, and Caesarea).

The difference between the response to Peter and the response to Stephen depends on two factors. First, unlike Peter, Stephen was accused of speaking against the Temple as well as against the Law: "for we have heard him say that this Jesus of Nazareth will destroy this place, and will change the customs which Moses delivered to us" (6:13–14). Second, Stephen's final speech before the High Priest and the Sanhedrin was far more insulting than either of Peter's earlier speeches, including as it did the charges that the Jews had *always* resisted the Holy Spirit, *always* killed the prophets, and *always* violated the God-given laws (7:51–53). Stephen not only suggested that the Temple was not the house of God (7:48–50), but also called the members of the council, including the High Priest, "stiff-necked" and "uncircumcised in heart and ears" (7:51). Thus, although no doubt everyone was "enraged" (and their anger was not dampened by Gamaliel's moderating influence, which had led to Peter's earlier release), even before the council could reach a verdict Stephen's accusers acted immediately and stoned him outside the city walls (7:54–58).

Against this background—in which only proselytizers were arrested, treatment of them was usually restrained, and acts of mob violence were rare—Luke's descriptions of Paul's persecution of Christians seem excessive, if only because Paul's actions were both official and violent. He not only "imprisoned," but "beat" Christians he found "in every synagogue" (Acts 22:19). Indeed, in other passages, Luke portrays Paul's activities as both much less discriminating and far more extreme than we have seen so far. He says that many Christians were actually arrested *in their homes*. In Acts,

Luke reports that, "entering house after house," Paul (as Saul) "dragged off men and women and committed them to prison" (Acts 8:3). When Paul says that he "tried to make them blaspheme" (26:11), he seems to be suggesting that he wanted his imprisoned Christians to reject Christ, which implies that they were ordinary people who had committed no act that could be interpreted as disruptive or divisive, as Paul's preaching, especially in Thessalonica, was said to have been: "These men," the Jews said of Paul and Silas, "have turned the world upside down" (17:6). By contrast, Paul's victims were mere believers. Even in the synagogues, he arrested and punished not proselytizers, but "those who believed in" Jesus (22:19).

Furthermore, Paul elsewhere states explicitly that at least some of the Christians he arrested were actually executed. When he went to the High Priest in Jerusalem to get letters to the synagogues in Damascus authorizing his actions, he is described as "breathing *threats and murder* against the disciples of the Lord" (Acts 9:1; my emphasis). "I persecuted the church of God violently," Paul reminds the Galatians, "and *tried to destroy it*" (Gal 1:13; my emphasis). In Acts, Luke says that Paul (as Saul) "*laid waste the church*" as he took both men and women off to prison (Acts 8:3; my emphasis). To the crowd, after his arrest in Jerusalem, Paul claimed that he "persecuted this Way *to the death*" (Acts 22:4; my emphasis). In his defense before Herod Agrippa, Paul presented himself as the unofficial leader of the High Priest's anti-Christian brigade and execution squad, as well as witness: "[A]nd when *they were put to death*, I gave my voice against them" (Acts 26:10). In short, ordinary Christians (as well as proselytizers) were arrested, bound, and beaten and then delivered to the High Priest, tried, and (in some cases) murdered.

If, indeed, Paul played such a large role in the official execution of so many Christians, it is no wonder (1) that Ananias was shocked when Jesus told him to meet Paul in Damascus ("Lord, I have heard from many about this man, how much evil he has done to thy saints at Jerusalem" [Acts 9:13]); (2) that, when Paul began his preaching in that city, his fellow Christians were "amazed" because he was obviously there to arrest Christians and take them "bound before the high priests" (9:20–21); (3) that, when he came to Jerusalem to join the church, "they were all afraid of him" (9:26), and (4) that, after Paul started to preach in Judea, church members said, "He who once persecuted us is now preaching the faith he once tried to destroy" (Gal 1:23). In Damascus, Paul's enemies said, "Is this not the man who made havoc in Jerusalem of those who called on [Jesus'] name?" (Acts 9:21).

The problem with these accounts by Luke and Paul of the latter's massive and sometimes deadly assault on Christians is their implausibility. At the very least, it is hard to accept either the extent or the fatal result of Paul's persecution.[53] First, as to

53. Hare insists, against the clear assertions to the contrary in Acts, that Paul not only did not participate in the execution of Christians (*Jewish Persecution of Christians*, 60), but also did not claim to have participated: "It is noteworthy that although Paul on several occasions mentions that he had been a persecutor of the Church, he never suggests that he had been responsible for the death of any Christian" (35). Hare later says that, in the New Testament, the phrase "persecution to the death"

Paul's claims to have arrested Christians in their homes for being mere confessors of Jesus, there is little evidence that Jews *ever* pursued Christians so earnestly and indiscriminately. At least according to the one scholar who has thoroughly studied the Jewish persecution of Christians, the Jews never arrested or executed Christians based merely on their faith. After the Crucifixion—and perhaps not even then, but after the Revolt of 66—Christians who abused the privilege of speaking in synagogues by accusing Jews of killing Jesus and telling Jews they were damned unless they accepted him were sometimes given thirty-nine lashes—as Paul often was. A Christian who visited a synagogue could be excluded, detained, or flogged "not for a religious offense per se but for a breach of the peace." The punishment, if there was any, depended on the hostility the visitor expressed and the divisiveness he created.[54] Thus, despite Luke's claim that Paul engaged in a comprehensive assault on Christians both in Jerusalem and abroad ("I persecuted them even to foreign cities" [Acts 26:11]), it might never have happened.

Second, Paul's actions seem to have had no effect on the Jerusalem church, then headed by James the brother of Jesus, Peter, and the two sons of Zebedee, John and James. One reason is that, according to many scholars, the persecution was directed solely against Hellenized Jewish Christians, who were likely to visit Greek-speaking synagogues and also to "propagandize against the Temple."[55] Stephen, for example, was "seized" at the synagogue of the Freedmen, Cyrenians, Alexandrians, Cilicians, and Asians (Acts 6:9)—in short, a synagogue established by and for Hellenized Jews. As Diaspora Jews who were influenced by Greek culture, so this argument goes, the Hellenized Christians who preached in this synagogue were less inclined than Palestinian Christians to regard the Temple as the house of God and the Mosaic Law as inviolable. That is, "[i]t is understandable that when such men joined the Christian Congregation, criticism of the Law and the temple cult made itself heard from their midst."[56] Thus, on one hand, since Jewish authorities were prepared to arrest and punish proselytizers who expressed these sentiments in the synagogues of Jerusalem, it is

does not mean "murdered" or "executed." It simply "conveys the thought that the will-to-kill had been present although not actualized" (40–41). The problem with this interpretation is that it suggests that every expression of rage and every stated intent to kill in Acts (9:23; 21:31; 25:3), if not in the entire New Testament, is questionable. Furthermore, Paul claims in Galatians that he "persecuted the church violently and tried to destroy it" (1:13), which suggests some kind of extreme physical action, if not murder.

54. *Jewish Persecution of Christians*, 43–56. For an overall summary of Jewish persecutions, see 78–79. "That it is the missionaries who are the primary target of Jewish persecution is clearly and consistently presented by the First Gospel. Nowhere does this gospel intimate that rank-and-file Christians are liable to Jewish persecution" (125).

55. Brown, *Introduction*, 293–94, 296 n. 43. Klingaman suggests that, although Paul did not persecute Jerusalemites, he attacked Greek-speaking Christians (*First Century*, 255). However, if Stephen was the first such Christian to be murdered and all of his compatriots fled Jerusalem immediately, then there were no Greek-speaking Christians left in the city.

56. Bultmann, *Theology*, I, 56.

logical to assume that Jewish leaders were likely to be more suspicious of Hellenized Christians, generally, than of more orthodox Jewish Christians.

On the other hand, however, there is no reason to suppose that the chief priests and their minions set out to hunt down every Hellenized Christian or to persecute them so fiercely as to drive them all out of Jerusalem. Since it was *Hellenized* Jews who murdered Stephen, one could hardly argue that they were less committed to the Temple or generally less Law-abiding than the Hebraized Jews. And the same hostility to Christian proselytizing of the kind that Stephen indulged in is evident among the Hellenized Jews in the Diaspora cities that Paul later visited. Furthermore, when some Christians left Jerusalem after Stephen's murder, whether they were Hellenists or Hebrews, they refrained at first from preaching to gentiles (they preached "to none except Jews" [Acts 11:19]) even though Peter had already converted Cornelius, and Philip had converted the Ethiopian eunuch. In other words, they do no appear to have stood out as particularly unorthodox or threatening.

If the Greek-speaking Jewish Christians were doctrinally indistinguishable from the Hebrew-speaking Jewish Christians, it is difficult to conclude that they were singled out and attacked by the Jewish authorities. Whether this is the case or not, neither Paul nor Luke specifies that Paul's target was only the Hellenized Christians. Every time he mentions his goal or intention, Paul indicates that he sought to destroy "the church" (Gal 1:13; Acts 8:3), "the disciples" (Acts 9:1), "the Way" (9:2; 22:4), and "the saints" (26:10), not a particular group within the larger movement. Luke says, the "great persecution arose *against the church in Jerusalem*," not specifically against the Hellenists (my emphasis). In response, "they"—presumably members of *this* church (i.e., Hebrews rather than Hellenists)—were all scattered throughout the region of Judea and Samaria, except the apostles" (that is, one assumes, the *leaders* of the Jerusalem church; Acts 8:1). However, if Paul went after the members of the Jerusalem church itself, why was the church virtually unfazed by the attack? That is, there appears to have been neither protest nor even the smallest expression of concern on the part of other Christians in Jerusalem.[57] Even if we assume that it was only "the Hellenists [who] were driven out [of Jerusalem] by persecution,"[58] why were the Palestinian Jews in no way disturbed by Paul's violence against Christians?

Indeed, while the Jews supposedly pursued their bloody course against some Christians, the church in Jerusalem was not only unconcerned, but quite successful in

57. Conzelmann and Lindemann comment: "Acts' portrayal of Christians in the public life is oddly conflicting. On one hand, it speaks of persecution drives against Christians while, on the other hand, the progress in the community's expansion seems to be relatively undisturbed . . . According to Acts 8:1–3 the persecution encompasses the whole community, while only the apostles are allowed to remain in the city; the public protest apparently is directed exclusively against the hellenists" (*Interpreting the New Testament*, 352–53). Sanders raises similar questions about Paul's persecution of Christians in *Schismatics*, 2–4. He concludes, after citing several passages in Galatians: "Paul provides no further direct information. He does not say for what reason he persecuted Christianity, of what the persecution consisted, where it was carried out, or even who the victims were" (5).

58. Brown, *Introduction*, 693 n. 28.

both its pursuit of Jewish converts and its relations with the Jewish community in general. The church gained thousands of converts in Judea (Acts 2:41; 4:4; 5:14; 6:7)—*all of them Jews*. As one Church historian puts it, Acts' author "cannot conceal the fact that the [Christian] community continued its propaganda almost unhindered; even after the persecution at the time of Stephen's martyrdom, . . . it continued undisturbed."[59] Thus, the main problem with Paul's contention that he himself led the Jewish attack on Christians is, as we have seen, the fairly well-established fact that James' church in Jerusalem was not only regarded as inoffensive by the Jewish establishment, but also considered by many Jews to be admirable and even exemplary. According to Acts, the Christians in Jerusalem had "favor" with the Jews (2:47), who "held them [i.e., the Christians] in high honor" (5:13). Eventually, "the church throughout all Judea and Galilee and Samaria had peace and was built up" (9:31). In other words, it is much easier to believe that Jews *protected* Christians when they were arrested (4:21; 5:26) than that Jews *persecuted* Christians under Paul's leadership.

Third, although Paul is alleged to have arrested many Christians in Jerusalem (Acts 9:13, 21), Paul himself claims that no one in the Jerusalem church recognized this enemy of Christianity when he came to Jerusalem for fifteen days to see them (including Peter and James) three years after his conversion. That is, three years after his apparently massive, systematic, and deadly attack on the Church (Gal 1:18), Paul was, he says, unrecognizable throughout the region: "I was still not known by sight to the churches of Christ in Judea." The members of these churches had heard of him as an opponent who had become an ally (Gal 1: 22–23), but how they failed to recognize the scourge of Judea, as Luke portrays Paul, is a little difficult to understand.

In Acts, Luke treats Paul's reception in Jerusalem quite differently. Here, Luke records the only negative reaction to Paul in that city: "And when he had come to Jerusalem he attempted to join the disciples; and they were all afraid of him, for they did not believe that he was a disciple" (Acts 9:26). The problem with this account is that the author of Acts does not explain *why* the disciples did not accept Paul as one of them. It could be because they recognized him as a persecutor, which is contradicted by Galatians 1:22, but it could also be that they rejected him merely because he lacked the credentials of apostleship—that is, because he had not been a part of the Jesus movement until this point.[60] After all, he was so different from all of the original

59. Weiss, *Earliest Christianity*, I, 7–8. Weiss challenges Paul's claim that there was "a great persecution against the church" by noting not only that the church remained in Jerusalem, but also that the leaders, who would have been the first to have been arrested, clearly survived and flourished. Furthermore, given "the horrors of persecution" that Luke describes, "one can hardly understand how anyone could ever have been left alive" (I, 169–70).

60. Brown comments, "The statement in Gal 1:22 that three years after his adherence to Jesus the churches in Judea still did not know his face need not contradict his role in such a persecution" (*Introduction*, 426). But Brown's saying it does not make it so. For an opposing view, see Conzelmann and Lindemann, *Interpreting the New Testament*, 359. To put it simply, Acts 8:1 seems to be contradicted by Gal 1:22.

disciples—an urbanite, a non-Palestinian, a product of Greco-Roman culture. And he was a late-comer to the movement—that is, "one untimely born" (1 Cor 15:8).

How did Paul get accepted by people who, while they might not have known his victims, knew perfectly well that their fellow Christians had been arrested, beaten, flogged, and executed? There is no report that he repented, showed remorse, or even apologized. Barnabas simply told the disciples that Paul had seen and heard Jesus "on the road" and "had preached boldly" in Jesus' name (Acts 9:27). That is, with Barnabas' help, Paul was welcomed into the Jerusalem church not because he at least attempted to explain his past actions, but because he established his "Christian" credentials. Yet, it must be asked, how could the perpetrator of serious attacks on Christians in Judea not only go unrecognized by *anyone* in Judea, *but also not be held accountable for his crimes*? Would Judas, who is the only disciple who actually repented for his betrayal of Jesus (Matt 27:3), ever, under any circumstances, have been accepted by the Jerusalem church?

Fourth, although Paul claims to have participated in the execution of *many* Christians, no one—including Luke, Hegesippus, and Josephus—has reported their names, their number, or anything else about them. In Acts, Luke is (as far as we can tell) unusually scrupulous about reporting every detail of the suffering of Jesus' followers *except* for those who were martyred in Paul's persecution. Luke describes a total of two deaths (Stephen's and James the son of Zebedee's), several arrests of Peter, and many attacks on Paul by Jews, as well as his arrests by Roman authorities (some at the urging of Jews). The execution of James the son of Zebedee—like the later murder of James the brother of Jesus—was independently recorded by the Christian historian Hegesippus and the Jewish historian Josephus, the latter of whom refers to no other examples of Jewish executions of Christians.

The question is, why did the Church itself (as well as Josephus) fail to record not only any other victims' names, but also any other specific acts of violence? That is, considering that Acts provides details on arrests of and assaults on Paul and other Christians in the forties and fifties, why does it fail to provide any information on the arrests, imprisonments, *and* executions of Christians in the early thirties? Unlike Paul's other reports—i.e., his accounts of Jesus' communications with him, especially his description of his conversion experience, which are organized in narrative units, with a beginning, middle, and end—his allusions to his anti-Christian persecutions are mere lists. He arrested Christians in their homes or in synagogues, he bound them and turned them over to the High Priest, he gave witness against them at their trials, and he watched them die, as he watched Stephen, who is the only named victim of this apparently incessant and systematic violence—though, in this instance, at the hands of a mob, instead of an officially appointed deputy of the High Priest.

Fifth, one might also ask, assuming (again) that Paul aided in the arrest and punishment of many Christians without too much difficulty, why the Jews had so much trouble killing *him*. The pattern of arrest and escape in Acts was first established by

Peter and others, who were placed "in hold" three times and then released (Acts 4:3, 21 and 5:18, 40). Earlier, the Christians whom Paul persecuted must have committed the same offenses—i.e., preaching repentance, forgiveness, resurrection, and the messiahship of Jesus (Acts 3:19–21)—but they were supposedly severely punished, if not executed. After their first arrest, Peter and the other Christians were *excused* by the Jewish authorities because they could find "nothing how they might punish them" (Acts 4:21). After the second arrest, "an angel of the Lord opened the prison doors and brought them out" (5:19). And after the third arrest, the Pharisee Gamaliel argued successfully for their release (5:34–40).

In this context, the logical question is unanswerable: How could Christians be arrested and executed just for being professing Christians, while aggressively proselytizing Christians like Peter and Paul could be arrested (and sometimes punished), but neither held for long nor executed? One scholar comments, "[T]he very fact that Paul was able to persist in his controversial ministry for so many years is our best evidence that Jewish opponents employed considerable restraint in dealing with the Apostle to the Gentiles."[61] Furthermore, if Paul was indeed a pupil of Rabbi Gamaliel, who later singlehandedly managed the release of Peter against the rest of the council's strong desire to kill him, where was this esteemed member of the Sanhedrin and former teacher of Paul when his exceptional pupil brought his victims before the same council by which Peter was released for a more serious crime (i.e., proselytizing) than at least some of Paul's arrestees had committed (i.e., merely professing a belief in Jesus)?[62]

The only difference between Paul's experience and Peter's was that Paul was more often pursued than captured. In Damascus, "the Jews plotted to kill him," but he escaped by night in a basket (Acts 9:23–25). Later, Paul was chased out of both Antioch (13:50) and Iconium (14:5–6), in the latter case because the residents tried to stone him. In Lystra, Paul was stoned and left for dead by crowds stirred up by Jews from the two cities he had recently abandoned (Acts 14:19). Paul then escaped from Thessalonica and Beroea (Acts 17:5–7, 13–15). He was apprehended and released in Corinth (Acts 18:12–16) and plotted against upon his return to Greece (Acts 20:3). Finally, in Jerusalem, he was captured by "the people" but saved from execution by Roman soldiers (21:30–31), although some Jews took an oath not to eat or drink until he was killed (22:14). Appearing before the council, Paul eluded any kind of punishment by the Jews for the last time (Acts 23).

This saga of failure and frustration on the part of Jews who could neither kill Paul nor have him executed by the Romans might be interpreted as a consequence of Jesus' loyalty to Paul, but the same inability to kill *any* Christians at this time, except Stephen

61. Hare, *Jewish Persecution of Christians*, 60.

62. Indeed, if the Pharisees, represented by Gamaliel, were less inclined to persecute Christians than the Sadducees were, why would Paul, a self-proclaimed Pharisee, be moved to work for the High Priest and his minions, all of whom were Sadducees? Conzelmann and Lindemann make this point in *Interpreting the New Testament*, 352–53.

and James the son of Zebedee, characterizes the twenty-five or so years of Paul's missionary activity. If nearly all of the Christians were saved from execution during this stretch of time, why were so many so easily executed *before* Paul's conversion? As one historian explains, the same law that prevented Jews from executing Jesus applied to Paul and other Christians as well. Thus, although Luke says that the Jews were Paul's enemies, they failed to execute Paul (assuming that they intended to) because *they could not make the decision without the approval of the Romans*: "[T]hey [could] only bring slanders and no well-founded charges against him."[63] In this context, Paul's claim simply makes no sense. That is, if Jewish officials were unable to execute either Jesus or Paul, then why were they able to execute other Christians?

It is also worth noting that, of the three executions of Christians recorded, only one of them was unquestionably an official act of the state *and* (allegedly) supported by the people. The murder of James the son of Zebedee was carried out by Herod Agrippa in the early forties and "pleased the Jews," according to Acts 12:1–2. However, as one scholar explains, "there is no suggestion in the text that the action was suggested to the king by the Sanhedrin or by the high priest." It was, therefore, not a "religious persecution."[64] Nevertheless, says another scholar, the only people Agrippa "cared about pleasing" were not the peasants, but "the ruling class."[65] The stoning of Stephen is, as I said earlier, usually understood to have been a mob action rather than an official act of the Sanhedrin or any other Jewish authority. Some Jews tried to bite Stephen immediately after his speech (Acts 7:54—in the KJV, but not the RSV), in which he expressed an attitude toward the Temple that, according to at least one Bible scholar, even Christian Jews like Peter could not have accepted.[66]

63. Weiss, *Earliest Christianity*, I, 147. Weiss says, "The Sanhedrin which could not carry out executions at all had to be very cautious in conducting heresy trials." Furthermore, he continues, "It was no breach of the [Jewish] law if ["the Nazarenes"] chose to consider a dead teacher as the Messiah" (170).

64. Hare, *Jewish Persecution of Christians*, 30. Hare accepts the possibility that the Jews were pleased, but he finds it "improbable . . . that the king would have arbitrarily executed a Christian leader simply to please public opinion" (31). Hengel contends, on the other hand, that Agrippa I presumably wanted to make himself popular among the leading groups in Jerusalem, i.e. in Sadduccean circles." For Hengel, this was the group responsible for "a harsh policy towards the new messianic sect in Jerusalem" (*Acts*, 112). Summarizing his review of Jewish executions of Christians, Hare finds no clear example of even one execution "by Jewish religious authorities for purely religious reasons . . . nor did the evidence indicate any systematic effort to eliminate Christianity by treating it as a capital crime." Thus, "Christian martyrdoms were probably few in number, and probably for the most part due to the unprecedented violence of a mob" (78).

65. Hill, *Hellenists and Hebrews*, 36 n. 67.

66. Bruce, *New Testament History*, 217–26. In the years immediately following the Crucifixion, Brown says, the Jewish authorities were more or less tolerant of Christians, "but that did not mean they would tolerate attacks on the Temple from believers in Jesus any more than they tolerated it from other Jews" (*Introduction*, 295). Weiss comments, however, "From the description of Stephen's death, so much may be discerned with certainty, viz. that he was not condemned and executed by due process of law, for which moreover the Sanhedrin had no authority, but that he fell victim to a violent outbreak of popular passion and was put to death without the observance of the prescribed

James the brother of Jesus was murdered by the Sanhedrin under the High Priest Ananus II in 62, at a time (the interregnum between two procurators) when Ananus thought he could get away with it. This execution was considered to be illegal by the new procurator Albinus, who immediately, with the approval of Herod Agrippa, removed the High Priest from office. It was also lamented by Josephus, as well as by Jews whom Josephus describes as fair-minded and "strict in their observance of the law." Of course, why Jews generally would applaud one execution (of James the brother of John) and condemn the other (of James the brother of Jesus) is hard to understand. There is no reason to assume that Jewish peasants would have approved of either execution.

It should be remembered, too, that the Jews had trouble arresting Christians for the same reason that the High Priest had trouble arresting Jesus, at least during the daytime: The people—i.e., *the Jews*—would have stoned the Jewish authorities! As I said earlier, Luke is reluctant to acknowledge that "the people" in all of these passages were in fact Jews, whom he explicitly identifies as such (except for converts) only when they *attack* Christians. The conclusion is inescapable, however, that ordinary Jews were not hostile to Christianity. The only enemies of both Jesus and his followers were the Jewish elite, agents of the Romans.[67]

Furthermore, as I said earlier, when Peter and other disciples were brought to trial before the Sanhedrin and accused their captors of killing Jesus, Rabbi Gamaliel convinced his fellow councilmen, who "were enraged and wanted to kill" the Christians, that, based on past experiences with the followers of other messianic leaders, the Sanhedrin should let the success or failure of Jesus' followers prove whether they were divinely or humanly inspired: "I tell you, keep away from these men and let them alone; because if this plan or this undertaking is of human origin it will fail; but if it is of God, you will not be able to overthrow them" (Acts 5: 33–39). How Paul's account comports with this one is difficult to tell because it is not exactly clear when this event took place. In the view of at least one Bible scholar, however, "After the Sanhedrin session at which Gamaliel spoke, Acts begins (*ca.* AD 35) an era in which, except for the brief rule of the Jewish King Herod Agrippa I over Palestine (AD 41–44; Acts

---

formalities" (*Earliest Christianity*, I, 168). Ruether makes the same point: "Stephen's death appears to have been due to a popular riot rather than a judicial decision of the religious court" (*Faith and Fratricide*, 269 n. 20). Conzelmann and Lindemann suggest that Luke might have used two sources—one including a formal judicial proceeding; the other interpreting the event as "mob justice" (*Interpreting the New Testament*, 90). Hare says that J. Blinzler, in *Trial of Jesus*, "probably is correct in his estimate that the majority of scholars regard the execution of Stephen as an act of lynch law" (*Jewish Persecution of Christians*, 22 n. 1). Hare discusses the episode on 20–30.

67. In the arrests of Jesus and his followers, the class warfare in Palestine manifested itself in (1) hostility toward the Christians from the Jewish elite and (2) support for (or at least indifference to) the Christians from all other Jews. All of which raises questions about the ease with which Paul allegedly rounded up Christians after the Crucifixion and before Peter's arrests. That is, between these events, it seems as though Paul (as Saul, of course) was not restrained by public opposition to the arrest of Christians. Strange interlude.

12:1–23), the branch of the Jerusalem church closely associated with the Twelve *was not persecuted.*"[68]

Paul claims to have been given written permission by the High Priest and the elders, addressed to the Jews in Damascus, to hunt the escapees down and bring them back to Jerusalem (Acts 22:5). However, this claim raises the question as to whether the authority of the High Priest in the capital city of Judea would extend to the capital city of Syria. According to two historians of the early Church, "it is now regarded as highly unlikely that [Paul] was dispatched from Judea as a special agent with the powers of arrest." The High Priest would have risked "violating the judicial sovereignty of the Roman Governor of Syria, who was not only the supreme authority in Damascus but who exercised general supervision of affairs in Judea as as well."[69] At any rate, Paul never made it to Damascus for the purpose of capturing Christians. His intention was undermined by Jesus' personal appeal to him to stop persecuting Jesus by persecuting his followers (Acts 9:4; 22:7–8; 26:14–15).

On the other hand, there is little reason to doubt that Paul was flogged several times by synagogue leaders, stoned by others (2 Cor 11:24), and almost lynched before Roman soldiers saved him (Acts 21:30–36). It should be remembered, however, that he was a victim, by his own account, of the Jews' attempt to stop his proselytizing, not punish him for his beliefs (1 Thess 2:14–15). Indeed, Paul was not only preaching about Jesus in the synagogues of the Diaspora. If his attitude toward the Jews he addressed was anything like his attitude toward the Jews in his letters, he was also insulting them. No wonder, then, he was regularly expelled and subjected to the thirty-nine lashes that were typical of synagogue punishments for such violations at the time.[70] It is also worth noting that every time Paul was flogged, he voluntarily accepted the

---

68. Brown, *Introduction*, 293; my emphasis. Thus, Brown calls Stephen "the first Christian martyr" (296). It is also notable that Paul traveled to Jerusalem after his conversion experience without secrecy. In other words, he traveled, as a Christian, without fear of arrest by the Jewish police force, of which he had formerly been a prominent (if not the leading) member, and who were, presumably, still trying to round up Christians.

69. Horsley and Silberman, *Message*, 120. See also Stegemann and Stegemann, *Jesus Movement*, 344; Hare, *Jewish Persecution of Christians*, 65 n. 1; Maccoby, *Mythmaker*, 86–87; and Conzelmann and Lindemann, *Interpreting the New Testament*, 353–54. The editors of *Oxford Annotated Bible* state, however, that "the empire granted the Jews the right to extradite offenders" (1329).

70. It should be remembered that all of the disputes between Paul and the Christians (if there were any) or, later, between Paul and the Jerusalem church were not yet Jewish-Christian in nature, but intra-Jewish, all disputants being self-described Jews and, probably, until the second century, as I suggested earlier, Jews to the outside world. Thus, "All early conflict occurs within the multifaceted world of Judaism, not only in the sense that various sects and subgroups still identify themselves as 'Israel,' but also in the sense that the nature of the disputes reflects the long tradition of intra-Jewish tensions, especially between prophetic and priestly strains" (Carroll, *Constantine's Sword*, 144). Says Crossan, "Internally, divergent groups within Judaism opposed one another in those same centuries [i.e., from the third century BC to the end of the first century AD] with everything from armed opposition through rhetorical attack to nasty name calling" (*Who Killed Jesus?* 32).

punishment. His submission means that he acknowledged that he was a Jew. Otherwise, he could have evaded the ordeal completely.[71]

It seems to me that the only way to resolve these contradictions is to interpret them in the context of what some scholars have described as the twin purposes of the Acts of the Apostles: to defend Christianity to the Romans and (not unrelatedly) to minimize its connection to Judaism. First, Acts has been called an *apologia* addressed to the gentiles that was intended to fend off the criticisms of Christianity by putting it in the best possible light.[72] Thus, Acts presents the community itself as peaceful, law-abiding, and cooperative; and its leaders as virtuous men who, though devoted to expanding the Church and solving its internal problems, were neither critical of nor hostile to the Roman empire and its pagan citizens. According to some scholars, Luke might also have exaggerated, by implication, the grandeur of Paul's mission and the number of his converts—both, of course, for apologetic purposes.[73]

Second, the Church had no reason to condemn the Romans because, again, according to Acts, its only enemies were the Jews, who were supposedly resolved to destroy Christianity. Thus, Acts shows not only that the Jews rather than the Romans killed Jesus, but also that the Sanhedrin was committed to arresting and executing all Christians. Yet, despite Acts' claim that the Jewish Council authorized a pervasive attempt to crush the Jesus movement, the effort was strangely, unexplainably unsuccessful. This happened, however, not because the Jewish establishment was inept, but because, with James leading the Church and his fellow Christians following the Jewish Law, the Jews had no such intention and therefore made no such effort. In short, the persecution—at least to the extent that it is described in Acts—did not occur.[74]

71. Setzer says that flogging was a punishment given to Jews for a number of proscribed actions, including stealing and attending Temple services in an impure state. "This discipline imposed by the synagogue," Setzer explains, "sought to keep a recalcitrant Jew in good standing in the community. That Paul submitted to this punishment indicates that both he and the synagogue regarded him as a Jew" ("Jewish Responses to Believers in Jesus," 578). Of course, this implies that *anyone* who was flogged by synagogues in the New Testament accepted the punishment voluntarily and thereby acknowledged his Jewishness.

72. Mack says, "Luke wanted Christianity to be recognized as a religion that was good for the Roman order and thus worthy of Roman support." That is why Paul defends "the author's concept of Christianity as a cultural force for producing good citizens" (*Who Wrote?* 230). In other words, "Luke's point was to position Paul clearly as a Christian, distance him from Jews who made trouble for the Romans, and depict him as a loyal citizen, one whose exemplary life and character were no threat to the peace and order of Roman society." He "is uncommonly courteous before these rulers, and they are extremely respectful of Paul and his views" (237).

73. On these points, see Meeks, *First Urban Christians*, 28; Hengel, *Acts*, 60; MacMullen, *Christianizing the Roman Empire*, 107; and Horsley, *Covenant Economics*, 140. Perrin and Duling comment: "As long as Christians expected the world to pass away shortly, they could revile Rome and its Empire in anticipation of its imminent destruction, as John of Patmos does in Revelation 18, but to live in the Empire they must come to terms with it, as the author of Luke-Acts, and no doubt the churches he represents, try to do" (*New Testament*, 300). Thus, "[t]he Christians' difficulties are not the hostility of Roman authorities but the machinations of the Jews" (300.).

74. According to Langmuir, "Since the overwhelming majority of Jews had not been attracted to

Summing up the attitude of the Jewish elite toward Jesus' followers immediately after the Crucifixion, one historian comments: "The Jewish authorities did not . . . interfere; they judged that this movement, like others before it, would eventually disappear. There was not, apparently, a great deal to fear. The followers of Jesus had no political aspirations; they were scrupulous in their observance of the Law and the temple ritual."[75] In short, there was no Jewish persecution of Christians at this time—at least in Judea: "In the pre-war period"—that is, from the Crucifixion in AD 30 to the Revolt in AD 66—"the Church in Palestine suffered little from Jewish intolerance."[76]

In this context, one way of explaining Paul's claim to have been a persecutor of Christians is to see it as a rhetorical ploy. That is, Paul may have created a kind of authenticating history for himself that allowed him to appear to have been a fully committed Jew, willing to do almost anything to defend his faith, who was now, as a result of his life-changing religious experience, a fully committed Christian. That is, he might have been motivated by his need for acceptance among the original disciples of Jesus to use his stellar "record" to prove that he had been not only circumcised, a member of the tribe of Benjamin, a Pharisee, and a student of Gamaliel, but also "a persecutor of the church" (Phil 3:5; Acts 22:3)—i.e., that he had therefore given up more than anyone else in the process of becoming a disciple of Jesus. In other words, according to one scholar, Paul thought that knowledge of his vigilante background "would make his witness convincing."[77] "Thus he informs his audience not only that he was a Torah-observant Jew, but that his credentials as a Christian-hater are also unimpeachable, since he was active in persecuting the church 'unto death' . . . Luke is emphasizing to his readers Paul's Torah fidelity and his earlier hatred of Christianity. His conversion, then, which Luke recounts next, is all the more dramatic by contrast."[78]

Two other actions on the part of the Jews have been used as evidence of their persecution of first-century Christians. The first is the curse on Christians recited in synagogues from an indeterminate starting date, supposedly, until the modern age. The question is, what did the curse actually say, and when did it first appear? Justin

---

the new Christian religiosity, the Jewish authorities did not feel particularly threatened by the relatively small schismatic movement" (*History, Religion, and Antisemitism*, 281). Langmuir adds that, although Jews later "circulate[d] scurrilous stories about Jesus and his followers, which were known in their medieval form as the *Toledot Jesu*, they were very brief and were the kind of slander that religious authorities frequently tell about those they consider heretics." Otherwise, "the authorities of the new Talmudic Judaic religion ignored Christianity almost completely" (282).

75. Peters, *Harvest of Hellenism*, 487. In the time period covered by Acts of the Apostles, says Brown, "The chief priests and the Sanhedrin had implicitly decided to extend grudging tolerance to those who believed in the risen Christ" (*Introduction*, 295).

76. Hare, *Jewish Persecution of Christians*, 167.

77. Tannehill, *Luke-Acts*, II, 282. That is, he was a "'reluctant witness' who ha[d] been forced to testify against his own inclination" (282).

78. Sanders, *Jews in Luke-Acts*, 287. Sanders says later, "This theme . . . [also] prepares for the miracle of [Paul's] conversion, recounted in the following verses, inasmuch as it serves to show that he did not have some kind of inclination towards Christianity before his conversion" (296).

Martyr says three times in his *Dialogue with Trypho*, a fictional debate between Justin and a Jew named Trypho, that the Jews pronounced a curse on Christians in one of their prayers (16:4; 47:4; and 96:2). In many recent studies of Christian-Jewish relations of this period, as well as in the writings of Eusebius and Jerome, it has been assumed that Justin was talking about a curse that allegedly appeared in the late first century (specifically, in the eighties or nineties, composed by Rabbi Gamaliel II)—the *birkat ha-minim,* a measure by which Christians were excluded from synagogues. One surviving version of the curse reads: "And for the apostates let there be no hope; and may the insolent kingdom be uprooted quickly, in our days. And may the nosrim and the minim perish quickly; and may they be erased from the Book of Life; and may they not be inscribed with the righteous." It is usually assumed that the *nosrim* are the Nazarenes (or Christians) and the *minim* are heretics in general.[79]

On the one hand, some scholars have argued that the curse was directed against Jewish Christians and originated in c. AD 85. These scholars explain the curse in the context of two problems: first, a growing impatience among Rabbinical Jews with Jewish dissidents in general, whose mutual hostility was held responsible for the failure of the rebellion against Rome; and, second, hostility toward Jewish Christians in particular for stealing potential converts. Furthermore, the curse was accompanied by laws that forbade commerce between the two groups and, after 135, outlawed Christian writings. Gradually, when Jews came to see Christians not simply as Christworshiping Jews, but as Christians claiming to be the true Israel, they expressed their resentment in their liturgy.

On the other hand, however, some scholars have argued that the concept of heresy among Jews was unknown in the first century (primarily because there was no established orthodoxy); that the prayer did not appear until the third or fourth century, well after curses on Jews were rampant in Christian texts; and that it was, at any rate, a curse on *all* heretics.[80] From this point of view, it seems unlikely that Jewish hostility to Christians—that is, not as proselytizers, but as merely *professing* Christians—manifested itself as early as Justin Martyr claimed.[81] Indeed, Christians were welcome in at

79. Lieu, *Image and Reality*, 30, 132. Lieu adds, "It is probable that, either on a regular basis or in specific circumstances, there might be liturgical expression of the exclusion of those following particular (deviant) beliefs or practices as a means of maintaining the purity of the community" (134).

80. My discussion of this subject rests on the argument by Boyarin (in *Border Lines*, 67–73), who concludes, "There simply is no patristic witness that counts as evidence for the proposition that a formal liturgical curse against Christians existed before the fourth century" (259 n. 170). Stegemann and Stegemann put the earliest date of any specific mention of Christians (Nozrim, or Nazarenes) at 135 (*Jesus Movement*, 234). Brown says: "The dating of it to AD 85 is dubious, and the idea that it was a universal decree against Christians is almost certainly wrong" (*Introduction*, 82). "The inclusion of Christians among the deviants [cursed in the prayer] may have come considerably later than the composition of John" (374 n. 102). See also Horbury, *Jews and Christians*, 67. Elsewhere, Boyarin says that the earliest "firmly attested" date for the prayer is the fifth century (in a letter from Jerome to Augustine), although "earlier forms of it are known from the third century" (*Jewish Gospels*, 18).

81. Schiffman, *From Text to Tradition*, 153–54. The Mishnah, the Jewish collection of oral traditions and composed during the second century, contains, according to Clemens Thoma, nothing that

least some synagogues well into the fourth century, as John Chrysostom discovered, much to his chagrin. If the experience of the bishop of Antioch is at all typical, it would seem that Christian leaders had more trouble keeping Christians *out* of synagogues than getting them *in*: "Up to the fourth century, church fathers were still complaining that Jews welcomed members of their churches into the synagogues."[82]

The second example of anti-Christian actions on the part of first-century Jews is based, as I suggested earlier, on the Gospel predictions of Christians suffering at the hands of the Jews. Among Jesus' Beatitudes in Luke is his warning to his followers that they will be hated and excluded and reviled "on account of the Son of man" (Luke 6:22). In Matthew, Jesus predicts that they will be "persecuted for righteousness' sake" just as the prophets were persecuted (Matt 5:10–12). John's Jesus says, more pointedly, "They will put you out of the synagogues" and even kill you, in what they assume to be "service to God" (16:2). Indeed, John states that the expulsion of Jesus' followers had already begun: "[T]he Jews had already agreed that if any one should confess [Jesus] to be Christ, he was to be put out of the synagogue" (John 9:22; see also 12:42). And at least one scholar claims that Jesus himself was the first victim of exclusion: He began to preach on hillsides and on the shores of Lake Galilee because "the synagogue authorities of the region [were] increasingly disinclined to let him use the synagogues as a platform for his proclamation of the kingdom."[83]

Since neither this claim nor the one made in John 9:22 is corroborated in the synoptic Gospels, however, most historians assume that any expulsion or exclusion of Christians began after Jesus' death.[84] In fact, by the time the Gospels were written, the "predictions" of violence against Christians had been borne out. We have reliable records of three executions from the post-Crucifixion period, from AD 30 to 66. Stephen, according to most accounts, was probably killed by a mob. James the son of Zebedee was executed by Herod Agrippa. And James the brother of Jesus was illegally murdered by the High Priest Ananus, who (as I said earlier and according

---

"clearly denounc[es] Jesus or Christianity." See Carroll, *Constantine's Sword*, 647 n. 13.

82. This point is made by Levine in *Misunderstood Jew*, 106–7; see 105–10, for Levine's full discussion of the subject. Furthermore, Ruether says that, whenever the curse was introduced, it did not prevent Christians from attending synagogue services. It simply stopped Christians from introducing their non-Jewish and anti-Jewish ideas to the congregation (*Faith and Fratricide*, 87). Hare, who thinks the curse was written into the twelfth of the Eighteen Benedictions in AD 85 by Samuel the Small, says that it was not intended to exclude all Christians, but to prevent "sectarians" from proselytizing in synagogues at the invitation of synagogue leaders. Hare adds that the *birkat ha-minim* "involves self-exclusion only and does not constitute excommunication from the synagogue" (*Jewish Persecution of Christians*, 54–56). Boyarin claims that the word *minim* did not refer to all Christians, but to law-abiding Jewish Christians of the kind that Jerome said were neither Jews nor Christians: they were "nothing" (*Jewish Gospels*, 19).

83. Bruce, *New Testament History*, 181.

84. "These specific warnings of Jewish opposition [especially in John 9:22; 12:42; and 16:2] were probably added by the early church to Jesus' predictions of the general resistance that preachers of the Gospel would meet, and the additions were probably made just when Jewish hostility to Christianity was mounting"—i.e., after the Revolt (Kee et al., *Understanding the New Testament*, 240).

to Josephus) was condemned by many pious Jews in Judea, repudiated by the new procurator Albinus, and deposed by Herod Agrippa. Both Peter and Paul, as well as other Christian missionaries, were arrested by both Jewish and Roman officials, and Paul was regularly flogged by synagogue leaders and often attacked by mobs.

Of course, nothing can excuse the three murders. As I suggested above, however, the same tensions that resulted in Jesus' execution only increased as time passed. The procurators after Pilate continued to arrest and execute revolutionaries, including anyone who even *seemed* to be dangerous. According to two scholars, summarizing Josephus' description of Felix, procurator of Judea during the fifties, it "reads like the ghastly accounts of the reign of terror in the French Revolution. Felix was regularly executing one zealot or another . . . and seems to have made it his personal mission to root out Jewish messianic troublemakers," which "only produced more violence among the Jews." In the late fifties, after Paul was arrested outside the Temple, one of Felix's officers asked him if he was "the Egyptian," one of the more notorious rebels of the period, who (in the words of the Roman tribune) "recently stirred up a revolt and led the four thousand men of the Assassins out into the wilderness" (Acts 21:37–38).[85]

Furthermore, lamentable and inexcusable as those Christians deaths were, the number is ridiculously modest compared to the hundreds of thousands of Jews killed by the Romans, the hundreds (if not thousands) of Christians killed by the Romans, and the thousands of Jews killed by Christians—all from the beginning of the Roman occupation of Palestine in 63 BC to the early Middle Ages.[86] As one scholar puts it, whatever the Christians suffered under the Roman emperors, "all that is a trifle in comparison with what they inflicted on Jews."[87] It could be argued, in fact, that, given the social and political turmoil that prevailed in ancient Palestine, particularly in the fifties and sixties, it is less surprising that Peter and Paul were arrested and three Christian leaders were killed than that many more were not beaten, imprisoned, and murdered.

Consider Paul's experience in Pisidian Antioch. At the synagogue on the Sabbath, Paul and his companions listened to "the reading of the law and the prophets," after which the "the rulers of the synagogue" asked them if they had anything to say—"any word of exhortation for the people." In response to this invitation to speak, Paul—like Stephen, who had accused the Jews in his audience of belonging to a race that had habitually disobeyed divine law and murdered its defenders—told the Jews in the synagogue that they had misread the prophets, asked Pilate to kill Jesus, and failed to understand that the law of Moses is inferior to belief in Jesus. Paul presumably

85. Shanks and Witherington, *Brother of Jesus*, 165–66.

86. In the first Jewish war, "Jerusalem was laid waste and hundreds of thousands of Jews were killed" (Carroll, *Constantine's Sword*, 90). Carroll's numbers are based on estimates by Josephus and Tacitus.

87. Herford, *Pharisees*, 235. Earlier in his book, Herford asks, "How many millions of Jews have been slaughtered by Christian hands, harried and afflicted by Christian rulers, and yet the Jews remain, unconquered and unconquerable!" (224).

delivered the same message from city to city, and, although it was appealing to many gentiles and "converts to Judaism," it was evidently offensive to so many Jews that Paul announced, "Since you thrust it from you, and judge yourselves unworthy of eternal life, we turn to the Gentiles" (Acts 13:14–46). At this point, in many of the cities he visited, he was either driven out of town or punished by synagogue officials.

In the most thorough-going study of Jewish violence against Christians, the author argues that it was *only* this kind of behavior (i.e., haranguing the audience with insults and accusations) that resulted in the expulsion of Christians from synagogues and, in egregiously provocative situations, flogging as well. Exclusion was used "against Christian missionaries who threatened the peace of the Jewish community," but not against others. "Flogging was employed as a punishment against Christian missionaries such as Paul," but not "against rank-and-file Christians." Flogging could occur because of incendiary speeches, such as those delivered by Peter (Acts, 2–3), Stephen, and Paul, or because Christians returned to synagogues from which they had been excluded after such speeches had been delivered. Sometimes the reactions were official; sometimes they were mob-engendered. However, "[t]here was little inclination on the part of Jews to persecute Gentile Christians or to instigate Gentile persecution of the Church." Thus, in Acts, only proselytizers were arrested (chs. 4–6), only Stephen and Paul were stoned, and only Paul seems to have been repeatedly beaten (2 Cor 11:24–25). No doubt other Christians suffered the same fate, but, because neither profession nor propagation of Christianity was a capital crime in either Palestine or the Diaspora, actual violence—aside from verbal abuse and social ostracism—was relatively rare.[88]

In the post-Revolt period, given the Jews' vulnerability to criticism because of the failed Revolt itself, Christians may have felt that they could step up their proselytizing in the synagogues—e.g., more aggressive preaching to Jews; more insulting charges of murder and persecution; more direct appeals to God-fearers; or even prophesying, healing, and speaking in tongues. "In other words, there are numerous very good reasons why Jews might have expelled messianists from their synagogues."[89] God-fearers may have increasingly turned to Christianity both because Judaism had fallen into disrepute with the Romans and because they "could become full members of the New Israel without the burden of all 613 *mitzvot*" –i.e., all the laws of the Torah. The Jews themselves may have become "suspicious of converts" and thus disinclined to

---

88. Hare, *Jewish Persecution of Christians*, 78, 103, 169. "When hostility exceeded the bounds of moderation," Hare explains, "Christians were liable to physical violence at the hands of a mob . . . When outspoken missionaries such as Paul strained the tolerance of the Jewish community, mob action was frequently rendered unnecessary by legal recourse to the synagogue council or, in Palestine, to the local Jewish court." Either way, these reactions were unusual: "It would appear that disciplinary action was ad hoc and applied only in obnoxious cases" (167). Matthew "indicates that the number [of Christians who were physically punished] was relatively small" (129).

89. Levine, *Misunderstood Jew*, 109.

proselytize.[90] In short, the atmosphere in the synagogues was less conducive to cordial relations between Jews and Christians than it had been before the war.

As I suggested above, however, whatever the reasons for the sins of the Jews at this time, it makes little sense (comparatively speaking) to view these acts of violence against Christians as the single most important event of the second half of the first century. In the words of one historian, speaking especially of the decades after the Revolt of 66: "This was a period of perhaps the most catastrophic events in Jewish history until the Nazi era, a time when the very survival of Judaism appeared to be at stake. In addition to the terrible losses suffered in the rebellion, Jews in the Diaspora experienced massacres and persecution. The spread of a sect at this moment announcing that God had rejected the Jewish people appeared to the Rabbis to be as profound a threat internally as their social reverses were externally." Thus, the Jews flogged Christians who announced in their synagogues not only that Jesus was the Messiah, but also that Judaism was doomed, as were all Jews who refused to embrace Christianity.[91]

Although there was no central authority among the Jews and therefore no official body that could enforce any kind of conformity, Rabbinical Jews began to see Jewish sects as dangerously divisive and even subversive, and these leaders could afford to take a strong stand on this issue partly because several of those sects—the Essenes, the Sadducees, the Zealots, and the Sicarii—had been either wiped out in or rendered irrelevant by the war: "In the internal Jewish conflicts after 70 . . . the decisive role was no doubt played by the tendency of majority Judaism [represented by the Pharisees, who overlapped with the Rabbis] toward unification, in the course of which, on the one hand, the previous factionalism of Judaism was overcome and, on the other hand, new groups that did not go along with the consensus were excluded."[92]

However, even though Judaism looked inward at the exact moment that Christianity began to look outward, there is (as we have seen) little reason to assume that Jews regularly went after Jesus' followers either during his life or in the few decades after his death—that is, unless provoked by Christian proselytizing *in the synagogues*.[93] The

90. Armstrong, *History of God*, 90.

91. Ruether, *Faith and Fratricide*, 166. Says Ruether: "It was in this period that the basic estrangement of Judaism and Christianity took place and when it is possible to speak of Judaism as 'persecuting' Christians. Christian preachers were flogged for attempting to proselytize the synagogues" (166).

92. Stegemann and Stegemann, *Jesus Movement*, 243. Brown suggests that John's tendency to condemn the Jews generally "may be an attempt to portray the Jewish opponents in the synagogues of John's time—opponents who are persecuting John's community (16:2) even as Jewish opponents in Jesus' time were remembered as persecuting him" (*Introduction*, 339). In addition, Brown says, the accusation that the Jews not only expelled Jesus' followers from the synagogues but killed them as well is also a retrojection from John's time to Jesus' time. (370). Many Bible scholars today argue that no such expulsions (let alone murders) took place even in John's time except in instances of Christian proselytizing in synagogues.

93. Speaking in general about Jewish violence against Christians, Parkes says that, when Christians verbally assaulted Jews, the Jews responded: "To suppose an initiative on the part of the majority,

Jesus sect was no further out of the mainstream than other dissident groups, including the Essenes, some of whom went so far as to live apart from other Jews. The sect's messianism was hardly unique, and its other views matched those of the Sadducees (opposition to the oral tradition), the Pharisees (belief in a physical resurrection), the followers of John the Baptist (demand for repentance), and the prophets (concern for the poor and disenfranchised).[94]

"Thus," in the words of two social historians, "we may presume that everyday relations between confessors of Christ and Jews were relatively harmonious."[95] To be sure, whatever else was going on, Jews continued to proselytize among pagans (and, presumably, among Christians). For that reason, it is important, say the same authors, to evaluate cautiously Luke's insistence in Acts and Paul's insistence in his letters that the Jews were militantly anti-Christian in the post-Crucifixion era.[96] In the words of two other scholars, as far as we can tell, the "widespread systematic persecution of Christians did not take place."[97] Nor did it occur in the second, third, or fourth centuries. There are few references to Christianity in the Talmud of this period, when Christians complained the most about Jewish violence and hostility. And, although many of the second-century Christian apologists—including Justin Martyr, Tertullian, and Origen—accused the Jews of insulting Christians, they cite no examples.[98]

---

which was preoccupied with other matters, is to suppose an unnatural order of events . . . But, in fact, we know that the Christians gave continual provocation. The whole development of teaching in the sub-apostolic period was inevitably infuriating to the Jew. The fact that the Christians considered it essential to the explanation of their position does not alter this truth" (*Conflict*, 81–82). Hare says, "Conflict between Christians and non-Christians in the Jewish community was inevitable, in view of the disrespect shown by Christians for the cherished symbols of ethnic solidarity" (*Jewish Persecution of Christians*, 167). Hare discusses this subject on 3–18.

94. "Theologically the Zealots differed but little from the Pharisees, and neither a Pharisee, a Zealot, nor an Essene need violate his basic theological tenets in order to recognize in Jesus a teacher sent by God" (Bruce, *New Testament History*, 183).

95. Stegemann and Stegemann, *Jesus Movement*, 340.

96. *Jesus Movement*, 342. Stegemann and Stegemann conclude that, if there were Jewish attacks on Christians, they were likely to be "isolated cases" (352). For an overview of both the *birkat ha-minim* and other evidence of Jewish hostility to Christians, see Sanders, *Jews in Luke-Acts*, 306–13.

97. Perrin and Duling, *New Testament*, 138. Summarizing Hare's position in *Jewish Persecution of Christians*, 20–43, Ruether says: He "concludes that execution was never any part of the disciplinary action of Jewish religious courts against Christian preachers [and, we might add, ordinary Christians]. Flogging of dissident sectarians was a disciplinary measure used by the synagogue. This clearly was used against Christian preachers who were trying to convert the synagogue" (*Faith and Fratricide*, 87). "Hare," Ruether continues, "regards the theme of persecution and especially the motif of 'killing' in the Gospels as a theological a priori"—a polite way of describing a fiction made up in the service of a larger fiction (269 n. 20). Thus, Ruether concludes—agreeing with Weiss, Stegemann and Stegemann, Perrin and Duling, Hare, and Zeitlin (*Who Crucified Jesus?*)—there is no evidence that the death sentence was ever passed by Jewish courts (*Faith and Fratricide*, 166–67).

98. Parkes, *Conflict*, 106. Parkes adds that "the Church complained bitterly of the attitude of the Synagogue to Christianity" (106–7). However, none of the accusations can be substantiated. Furthermore, "it is probable that the Jewish attack on Christianity would be less violent than that of the Christians on Judaism" (114)

At the same time, despite the charges from the same writers, there is little evidence that the Jews had a significant role in the Roman persecution of martyrs.[99]

THE ACTS OF THE APOSTLES

With all of these scholarly claims that the Jews did not persecute the Christians in the early years of Christianity, one comes away from Acts of the Apostles with some degree of confusion. This book, after all, shows that Jews arrested, tried, flogged, and imprisoned several leaders of the movement—even *before* the Revolt of 66. Indeed, Acts in its entirety can be read as the record of an ongoing hostile argument between Jewish Christians and non-Christian Jews. The angry dialogue begins with Peter's speeches, arrests, and prison releases. It is followed by Stephen's speech and murder, and it continues with Paul's speeches, arrests, and prison escapes. It ends, after Paul's near murder in Jerusalem, with a number of inconclusive trials or hearings. That is, a series of Christian verbal accusations and Jewish punitive actions is followed by a series of Jewish accusations and Christian defenses. Oddly, every encounter is unresolved. The speeches are, more often than not, unsuccessful—at least, from the point of view of the speakers. In addition, the escapes are followed by more arrests; the charges do not result in punishment; and the defenses do not result in exoneration. In Acts, words are often disruptive, but ineffectual; actions are often obstructive, but inconclusive.[100]

What is especially interesting about this careful orchestration of events is that it also moves, from the very beginning to the very end, within a larger framework that makes the story as tragic as it is surreal. It starts, after all, with Jesus' miraculous reappearance, his promise that his disciples will be "baptized with the Holy Spirit," and his assurance that the Kingdom of God will come. Since Jesus' return to earthly life fulfills a promise he made before his death and his second promise is fulfilled in chapter 2, his followers have every reason to expect the fulfillment of his third promise in subsequent chapters. In addition, before the end of the second chapter, the disciples have established a community; they have heard Peter's reiteration of the Church's new doctrine (supported by three Old Testament quotations proving, to Peter's satisfaction, that Jesus is the source of Life, the Savior, and the King); and they have proceeded to baptize "thousands of souls" in Jesus' name.

---

99. Lieu, *Image and Reality*, 91–92. Justin Martyr claims that Jews wished to kill Christians and would if they could, "but that in the present circumstances of powerlessness it is in fact the gentiles who actually condemn Christians to death" (135).

100. One of the main recurring themes in Tannehill's commentary on Acts is irresolution. There are fulfillments aplenty scattered throughout the work, but most of them occur near the beginning. Tannehill notes that, at the end of Acts, Paul is still a prisoner; he does not appear before Caesar; and he makes no contact with gentiles (*Luke-Acts*, II, 344). Furthermore, the Kingdom has not arrived, and Jesus has not returned.

In the end, however, despite the focus on Paul's journey to Rome, in which the mood should be celebratory, even Paul's prospect of extending his mission to Italy does not brighten the grim story of literal and figurative trials that end without resolving anything, Paul's two near-death experiences (outside the Temple and on Malta), and his final peroration to the Jews of Rome that expresses the utter hopelessness of saving them: "This salvation of God has been sent to the Gentiles; they will listen" (Acts 28:28). From this larger perspective, Paul's sea voyage appears to be a journey to nowhere, and the promise of the early chapters of Acts appears to undergo a slow, but certain demise. At the end, Paul is on his way, not to victory, but to house arrest and, for a short time, literary oblivion—not even Luke read his letters. Beyond the story, violence triumphed in the murders of James, Paul, and Peter and, more grandly, in the bloody Revolt of AD 66. No wonder Luke left those events out of his narrative.

Since the story moves so clearly from expectation to disappointment, from freedom to imprisonment, from certainty to irresolution, it is also worth noting that Acts is composed of three different plots, all of them contradictory and each of the latter two swallowing up—subsuming—its predecessor. Each plot, or layer, features a different apostle: James the brother of Jesus, Peter, or Paul. And all of the layers together constitute a series of parallel universes in which different realities, especially regarding these apostles and their relationship to both Christians and Jews, are presented. In fact, Luke might have woven the three narratives together because he received three different oral traditions (perhaps more), each one passed on by only one of the apostles or his companions. Luke says that he composed his Gospel only after "many [had] undertaken to compile a narrative of the things which have been accomplished among us." Since these accounts "were delivered to us by those who from the beginning were eyewitnesses and ministers of the word," Luke implies that he wrote his own "orderly" record by reworking and interweaving at least some of these first-hand narratives (Luke 1:1–3). No doubt, he used the same method when he wrote Acts.

The first layer focuses on the relationship between the Jerusalem church on one side and the Jews of Jerusalem on the other, especially the Jewish non-elite, frequently referred to as "the people." Of course, as I have suggested, although he was very likely the leader of the church at this time, James goes unmentioned in this role until halfway through Acts. Under his rule, there were three significant facts. First, Jews joined the Church in abundance, evidently without incident. This included not only Pharisees, but priests as well. In other words, Jews were attracted to Christianity, they were welcomed by the Church, and their fellow Jews raised no objections to their becoming members. After all, many Jews were affiliated with one or another of several Jewish sects—Sadducees, Pharisees, and Essenes, for example—which certainly competed with each other for members but did not block each others' attempts to attract new recruits.

Second, Jews converted to Christianity partly because there appeared to be a strong connection between the two religions. As Acts demonstrates, Christian proselytizers quoted the psalms and the words of the prophets (Acts 2:14–35; 3:23–25; 7:2–50), recycled Jewish themes (repentance, forgiveness, the Kingdom of God), retained Jewish concepts (an omnipotent God, the Covenant, the Holy Spirit, the Davidic Messiah, the Sabbath), and continued to pray in the Temple and synagogues, using the only scripture they had, the Jewish Bible. Indeed, it seems that Christians, who referred to their movement as the Way and to themselves as the Brethren, did not think that they were establishing a new faith since most of the religious practices they engaged in were indistinguishable from those of ordinary Jews. And this certainly made it easier for them to live side by side with their non-Christian Jewish neighbors.

Third, relations between Christians and Jews were amicable. As I said earlier, the members of the movement had "favor with all the people" (Acts 2:47), who "held them in high honor" (5:13). And the authorities—the Jewish aristocracy—could neither punish the Christians (4:21) nor treat them violently (5:26) because "the people" were prepared to stone them, if necessary. James the brother of Jesus was revered as a pious Jew, who on two occasions demonstrated his deep devotion to Judaism. At the Jerusalem Conference (Acts 15), he decided that the conversion of gentiles without circumcision was acceptable, but only because the prophets had included gentiles in the future Kingdom of God and because he found a precedent in the Torah for allowing gentiles to convert by following certain minimal requirements. On the occasion of Paul's last visit to Jerusalem (Acts 21), as I explained earlier, James (and the elders) insisted that Paul prove his loyalty to Judaism by sponsoring four Christians who were engaging in an ancient Jewish ritual at the Temple.

As a result of the Jerusalem church's ongoing connection to Judaism, "the church throughout all Judea and Galilee had peace and was built up; and walking in the fear of the Lord and in the comfort of the Holy Spirit it was multiplied" (Acts 9:31). Furthermore, this connection was sustained through the years, so much so that James and the elders of the Jerusalem church could say to Paul, thirty years after the Crucifixion, as a justification for his support of the Nazirite ritual, "You see, brother, how many thousands there are among the Jews who have believed; they are zealous for the law" (21:20). It is useful to recall, in this regard, that when Paul "laid his hands upon" Apollos' disciples in Ephesus, "[t]here were about twelve of them in all" (19:7). It is possible, at least, that some of Paul's other "churches," perhaps a few of them having grown from mere "households," were hardly larger than that. So James' "thousands" of Jews may actually have been a huge number compared to even the sum total of Paul's converts.[101] Yet this story of incredible success is not the final story, the real story, the important story.[102]

The second layer of Acts of the Apostles might be called the Peter narrative. It focuses on the arrests of Peter and other apostles by the Jewish authorities because the Christians were not only preaching Jesus in the Temple, but also criticizing the Jews for killing him. The theme of this narrative is most eloquently expressed by Gamaliel, who, after Peter's second arrest, warned the Sanhedrin "to keep away from these men and let them alone; for if this plan or this undertaking is of men, it will fail; but if it is of God, you will not be able to overthrow them. You might even be found opposing God!" (Acts 5:38–39). His point was that Peter and the Christians had at least a small chance of being on the side of Yahweh. Not surprisingly, then, Peter and the apostles successfully converted many Jews to the faith (4:4, 5:14); and, although some of Jesus' followers were arrested twice by representatives of the Sadducees and once by Herod Agrippa, they were eventually released.

Peter reappears later as a missionary of the Jerusalem church, curing Aeneas in Lydda and Tabitha in Joppa and converting Cornelius in Caesarea. The last of these recipients of Peter's attention was neither a Jew nor a pagan, but a God-fearing gentile, who turned out to be either the first or second non-Jewish convert on record. Peter's path to this conversion involved not a repudiation of Judaism, but a visitation by some divine power, who spoke to Peter when he was in a trance and thereby provided clear evidence that God Himself approved of Cornelius' conversion. First, Peter had a vision in which a celestial "voice" told him that no foods are unclean (Acts 10:15). Second, he saw that Cornelius and his household were inspired by the Holy Spirit when they spoke in tongues and extolled God (10:45).

What makes Peter different from Paul is that he questioned the need for change and subsequently wavered somewhat in his willingness to modify any aspect of

101. Horsley and Silberman estimate that Paul's churches had no "more than a few hundred people" (*Message*, 187). Meeks reminds his readers that "the Pauline churches" as well as "most other early Christian groups" met in "private houses" because, often enough, the so-called churches consisted of individual households—that is, individual families and their slaves or servants (*First Urban Christians*, 75–76). Apparently, in Paul's lifetime there were no buildings in most of the Diaspora that could be called churches in the modern sense of the word.

102. Tannehill points out that success, unity, growth, and fulfillment are the constituents of "a minor theme" in Acts: "This material, although sometimes presented in summary form, is more than filler and bridge between scenes" (*Luke-Acts*, II, 43). Tannehill discusses each constituent on pages 31 (fulfillment); 43 (unity and sharing); and 44–45, 77, and 81 (growth). Ironically, these terms refer only to the Jerusalem church, which actually dominated (and even deliberately guided) Christendom at the time. However, because this church gradually lost its authority, its achievements tended, in retrospect, to be ignored rather than celebrated. They are associated with the church under the rule of James, who appears late and otherwise seldom in Acts and whose successful reign is trumped by the missionary efforts of Paul. Sanders argues that the theme of compatibility between Christians and Jews, which he refers to as the "Jerusalem springtime," is minor because it is short-lived. That is, in Luke's conceptual scheme, the Jews initially support the Christians, only to turn on them after the murder of Stephen, at which point "the role of 'the Jews' in Acts changes markedly" (*Jews in Luke-Acts*, 71).

Judaism. Thus, in the first of the two incidents referred to in the preceding paragraph, he resisted the voice of God twice. As a good Jew, he told God, he had "never eaten anything that is common or unclean" (Acts 10:14). And, as he said to Cornelius, it is "unlawful . . . for a Jew to associate with or visit any one of another nation" (10:28). In these instances, Peter, like James, was willing to make adjustments in his Judaism, but—again, like James—he did so only by citing Jewish sources (albeit, quite indirectly and without identifying them). When he said that "in every nation any one who fears [God] and does what is right is acceptable to him" (10:35), he was echoing Ezekiel 18:5–9, Psalm 15:1–5, and Isaiah 26:2—passages in which all who worship God are welcome and in which worship does not mean performing Jewish rituals but following the fundamental moral precepts of mercy and justice. The door is open, said the prophets, and all are welcome, as long as they love God.

In the third narrative layer, the story of Paul, the reader enters a realm of human experience that is completely different from the world of James and the Jerusalem church and a very large step beyond the world occupied by Peter. Here, the hostility between Christians like Paul and the Jews was unmitigated by uncertainty, reluctance, or compromise. Paul despised the leaders of the Jerusalem church every bit as much as he hated some aspects of Judaism. As a result, whereas Peter was arrested and twice expediently as well as once miraculously released from incarceration, Paul was not only arrested, but beaten and stoned—not once, but repeatedly, as Paul points out to his followers (Acts 20:19; 2 Cor 11:24–25). As I said earlier, the only thing Peter and Paul had in common in this regard is that they always escaped execution. Of course, it helps to remember that most of Paul's worst encounters took place outside of Palestine, where he built up such a bad reputation that Jews sometimes followed him from town to town to prevent him from proselytizing. And when he returned to Jerusalem for the last time, his reputation caught up with him again (Acts 21:20–22).

It is impossible to doubt that Paul was regarded in many cities of the Diaspora—at least by the time he came back to Jerusalem in c. AD 60— as "a pestilent fellow, an agitator among all the Jews throughout the world, and a ringleader of the sect of the Nazarenes," which is how a "spokesman" of the High Priest and Jewish elders described Paul before the procurator Felix after Paul's arrest (Acts 24:5). And it is difficult to imagine that all of this sat well with James and the other leaders of the Jerusalem church, particularly in the context of the quite friendly and peaceful relations they had maintained, for thirty years, between the church and the local Jewish authorities. If Paul had, in fact, persecuted Christians in the thirties as he had certainly raised questions about the missionary goals of the Church in the forties and now drew a crowd so disturbed by the content of his preaching that the Roman police became involved in the ruckus, one can only wonder what James actually thought of him.

Paul was, after all, an iconoclastic, intemperate, and (usually) uncompromising apostle, who compelled many people to say, even after hearing his defense of his actions, "Away with such a fellow from the earth! For he ought not to live" (Acts 22:22).

The crowd he addressed in Jerusalem was so unruly that the Roman tribune who saved Paul from being beaten to death asked him if he was a famous revolutionary who had recently "stirred up a revolt" (21:37–38). That is, the tribune, too, thought of Paul as a Jewish trouble-maker who had created a large disturbance. Of course, James' allegedly strong commitment to both Jewish Law, which Paul had challenged, and civil order, which Paul had disrupted, could not have made the head of the Jerusalem church (and, in some sense, all of Christendom) happy with his fellow Christian. Paul not only offered the world a gospel that James could not have approved of, but also presented it in such a way that crowds traveled long distances to hunt him down (21:27). Perhaps James' silence and inaction after Paul's arrest were a testimony to his dissatisfaction. In any case, within the next few years, all three men—James, Peter, and Paul—were dead, one assassinated in Jerusalem by the High Priest, the others probably executed by Nero in Rome.

Considering these three different layers in Acts of the Apostles—the stories of Peter, James, and Paul—all different in both tone and content, it should come as no surprise that scholars have in fact concluded that the book as a whole was drawn from three different oral traditions or written sources: one section, the equivalent of nine or ten chapters (including most of chapters 1–12), covering the steady expansion of the Jerusalem church; a second, the equivalent of two or three chapters, dealing with the Hellenists and the church in Antioch; and a third, running from chapter 15 to the end, but also including some passages in chapters 9, 13, and 14, and focused on the Pauline mission.[103] It is likely, furthermore, that all of these narrative strands had different purposes and were intended for different audiences, which would explain their differences in content, particularly between the first and the third.

The goal of the author of the Jamesian narrative was evidently to portray the early church in the most favorable light, stressing the good relations between Jews and Christians; the loyalty of the Jerusalem church to both Jesus and the Jewish tradition; its unwillingness to make rash or radical changes in theology, worship, or ethics; and its inoffensiveness as a growing institution. Jews are negatively portrayed as Christ killers, but not as children of the Devil, as they are in the Gospel of John. To be sure, as I said earlier, good deeds (like joining the Church) are usually performed by an anonymous group called *the people*, but bad deeds (like arresting Christians) are usually performed by *Jews*. Otherwise, the hostility between Christians and Jews is minimal.

In this way, the first part of Acts *leans* toward supersessionism, but it stops far short of condemning Jews and Judaism as explicitly or as extensively as Paul does. The audience might have been Jewish Christians living in or near Jerusalem, who continued to see themselves as Jews. However, because of the exclusion of their proselytizers from synagogues and the occasional harassment of their leaders by local Jewish

---

103. Brown, *Introduction*, 317. Brown deals with the problem of sources and historicity in 316–27. Notably, he adds, "Acts has a textual problem more acute than any other N[ew] T[estament] book." It involves the question as to whether the Western or Eastern text is the original one (327).

authorities, measured though it may have been, they were beginning to establish their own separate identity as Christians. Luke might also have hoped to include Romans among his readers, presenting as he does a Church that in no way threatened nonconformity, let alone rebellion.

By contrast, the purpose of the Pauline narrative was clearly to demonstrate the separation between Jews and Christians, as well as the compatibility between Christians and pagans. We see in this picture of the early Church at least a strong verbal commitment to an aggressive gentile mission; a complete rejection of circumcision, at least for gentiles; and a willingness to speak openly, unapologetically, and therefore provocatively about these matters. As a result, Paul is portrayed as a man in constant conflict with Jews all over the Diaspora, and he was subjected to incessant mental and physical harm. He and his companions were plotted against by Jews almost everywhere, and they managed to survive only by a mixture of ingenuity, good fortune, and perhaps divine intervention. Meanwhile, the Romans are represented by the proconsul Gallio, who told the Jews he was uninterested in their intra-Jewish squabbles in chapter 18; the tribune who saved Paul's life in chapters 21 and 23; the procurator Felix, who hoped for a bribe, but did not harm his prisoner in chapter 24; and the centurion Julius, who "treated Paul kindly" and even saved his life in chapter 27.

Although the author of Paul's story does not have the apostle express any of his distinctive theological views, some of which departed significantly not only from orthodox Judaism, but also from orthodox Jewish Christianity (at least of the kind that was practiced in Jerusalem), he nevertheless emphasizes Paul's repudiation of Jews at every opportunity, quite explicitly whenever Paul reacted to their failure to accept his call to conversion (Acts 13:46; 14:27; 18:6; 28:28). What is interesting about this persistent complaint, however, is not only that Paul continued to preach to Jews, as I pointed out in the preceding chapter, but also that he was at least somewhat successful in converting Jews, Jewish proselytes, and God-fearers: "[I]n Acts, all three of the announcements of turning to the Gentiles follow hard on what an impartial observer would surely call descriptions of Paul's considerable success among Diaspora Jews and of reasonably good favour from them."[104]

Speaking first to Jewish and Jewish-leaning audiences in most cities, Paul often received a favorable response. After he preached in the synagogue at Pisidian Antioch—having been invited to do so at the conclusion of the Sabbath service by the synagogue "rulers"—the Jews begged him to continue to explain his views on the following Sabbath. Furthermore, "when the meeting of the synagogue broke up, many Jews and devout converts to Judaism followed Paul and Barnabas, who spoke to them and urged them to continue in the grace of God." The next week, "almost the whole city gathered together to hear the word of God" (13:42–44).

104. Sanders, *Jews of Luke-Acts*, 65. Kee et al. contend that, generally speaking, "the response to Paul's preaching of the Gospel [to the Jews] was mixed" (*Understanding the New Testament*, 224).

This pattern continues in the rest of Acts of the Apostles.[105] As a result of Paul's preaching in the synagogue at Iconium, "a great company believed, both of Jews and of Greeks" (Acts 14:1). In Derbe, presumably in the synagogue of that city, Paul and Silas "made many disciples" (14:21). In Philippi, on his way to "a place of prayer" on the Sabbath, Paul converted a woman named Lydia, "a worshiper of God," and her household (16:13–14). After Paul preached to Jews and proselytes in the synagogue at Thessalonica, "some of them [i.e., the Jews] were persuaded and joined Paul and Silas; as did a great many of the devout Greeks [i.e. Jewish converts or God-fearers]" (17:4). The results were even better in Beroea, where the Jews in the synagogue "received the word with all eagerness . . . Many of them therefore believed" (17:11–12). In Corinth, Paul "argued in the synagogue every Sabbath, and persuaded Jews and Greeks" (18:4). Chased out of the synagogue, Paul continued to preach next door, at the home of "a worshiper of God"—that is, once more, a Jew or Jewish convert. From there, Paul proceeded to convert "Crispus, the ruler of the synagogue, . . . together with all his household; and many of the Corinthians hearing Paul believed and were baptized"— no doubt, more Jews as well as "Greeks" who were Jewish proselytes. One of the latter was Titius Justus, a "worshiper of God" (18:7–8).

Notably, Paul was, in every instance, invited to speak in these synagogues and, more surprisingly, sometimes allowed to preach there for an extended period of time. In Iconium, despite the opposition of "unbelieving Jews," Paul and Barnabas "remained for a long time." They left because eventually "both Gentiles and Jews" tried "to molest them and to stone them" (Acts 14:3–5). Paul spent three weeks in the synagogue at Thessalonica (17:2), "every Sabbath" in the synagogue at Corinth (18:4), and eighteen months at the home of a Jewish convert next door (18:11). Paul argued with the Jews in the synagogue at Ephesus but declined "[w]hen they asked him to stay for a longer period" (18:19–20). Upon his return to Ephesus a short time later, "he entered the synagogue and for three months spoke boldly" (19:8). After he moved his base of operations to the hall of Tyrannus, he stayed for two years, preaching to "Jews and Greeks." During that time, Paul outperformed some "itinerant Jewish exorcists," word of which spread "to all residents of Ephesus, both Jews and Greeks; and fear fell upon them all; and the name of the Lord Jesus was extolled" (19:9–17).

Even in Rome, in his last recorded public address, Paul unpredictably—based on his persistent dismissal of his former co-religionists—"called together the local leaders of the Jews" (Acts 28:17). After he explained to them that he had been arrested in Jerusalem and then sent to Rome, he spoke to them, at their request, about "the kingdom of God" and "Jesus both from the law of Moses and from the prophets" (28:23). As was often the case with the Jews he preached to, "some were convinced by what

---

105. According to Sanders, Paul encountered no Jewish opposition in Salamis, Paphos, Derbe, Philippi, and Athens; and he was more or less successful in Antioch, Iconium, Thessalonica, Beroea, and Corinth (*Jews of Luke-Acts*, 75–76). Later, Sanders refers to "the fixed pattern" of Paul's mission: He "goes first to a synagogue, he either converts or 'persuades' both Jews and Gentiles, and then Jewish persecution breaks out" (272).

he said, while others disbelieved." However—despite the fact that, once again, Paul received a mixed response from his Jewish audience—his final words expressed little more than the major theme of Acts of the Apostles and what appears to be its *raison d'etre*: "The Holy Spirit was right in saying to your fathers through Isaiah the prophet: 'Go to this people and say, You shall indeed hear but never understand, and you shall indeed see but never perceive . . . Let it be known to you then that this salvation of God has been sent to the Gentiles; they will listen'" (28:25–28).[106] Afterward, under house arrest, although he preached "openly and unhindered," he "welcomed all who came to him" (28:30–31)—presumably, the usual crowd of "Jews and Greeks." From Luke's point of view, Paul merely needed another chance to condemn the Jews.

Two more aspects of Paul's mission are worth emphasizing. First, since he was obviously successful in converting some Jews in every city he preached in, it is hard to understand why he and his companions were sooner or later chased out of town. For example, in Pisidian Antioch, despite his warm welcome by Jews in the synagogue, some otherwise unidentified "Jews" argued with him, which led him to condemn *all* Jews, turn to the gentiles, and convert a large number of them. It is hard to believe that the Jews who first reacted positively to Paul's message then drove him away. A change of mind seems unlikely. More probably, there were two different groups, one perhaps made up of ordinary people, the other made up of Jewish leaders. In Jerusalem, after all, it was not the peasants, but the "the chief priests and the principal men of the Jews" who presented the charges against Paul to Festus and persuaded the procurator to join their plot to kill Paul (25:2).[107] That is, the same distinction that must be made between Jesus' enemies (i.e., the Jewish elite) and the Jews who made it difficult for the Jewish authorities to arrest him (i.e., the Jewish peasantry) must also be applied to Paul's Jewish enemies and both his Jewish converts and potential converts. This means that Paul's blanket indictment of *all* Jews is either an exaggeration on his part or a deliberate misrepresentation on the part of Luke.

Second, despite his condemnation of all Jews and his promise to turn his attention to the gentiles, Paul not only continued to preach to Jews, but also never went out of his way to appeal to non-Jews. The complaints in Acts 13, 18, and 28, therefore,

106. Paul restates these sentiments in his Letter to the Romans: "What then? Israel failed to obtain what it sought. The elect obtained it, but the rest were hardened, as it is written, 'God gave them a spirit of stupor, eyes that should not see and ears that should not hear, down to this very day.' And David says, 'Let their feast become a snare and a trap, a pitfall and a retribution for them; let their eyes be darkened so that they cannot see, and bend their backs for ever'" (Rom 11:7–10; see also 2 Cor 3:17–4:4). According to the editors of *Oxford Annotated Bible*, Paul says in this passage, "The resistance to the gospel on the part of the masses of Jews is providential; God has *hardened their hearts* for a loving purpose, namely, that the Gentiles might have an opportunity to hear and receive the gospel" (1371). Paul's quotations are from Isa 29:10 and Ps 69:22–23.

107. Kee et al. similarly identify the angry Jews in Thessalonica and Beroea as "local Jewish authorities" (*Understanding the New Testament*, 177). And who were the gentiles in the same chapter? Tannehill says they were God-fearers who were "in the position of overhearing what Paul is saying to another group" (*Luke-Acts*, II, 165), in which case they were not a new audience.

actually appear to be gratuitous, particularly considering that Paul failed to act on his sentiments. In short, as I said in the preceding chapter (and as far as we can tell from the evidence in Acts of the Apostles), *neither Paul nor any other Christian engaged in a deliberate and systematic gentile mission during the period that Acts covers.*[108] No doubt, some kind of gentile mission occurred; otherwise, the number of gentiles in the Church would not have expanded. But it may well have taken place during Luke's time, rather than Paul's.

Why does Paul *say* he is abandoning the Jews and turning to the gentiles, but never acts on this intention in any serious or sustained way? It is helpful to remember that, in Luke's view (if not in Paul's [e.g., Gal 2:7–9]), Paul's mission was originally directed to both groups. In Luke's Gospel, for example, Simeon announced Jesus' role as "a light for revelation to the Gentiles, and for glory to [God's] people Israel" (Lk 2:32). In Acts, Jesus said to Ananias that Paul was his "chosen instrument . . . to carry [his] name before the Gentiles and kings and the sons of Israel" (Acts 9:15). Summarizing his missionary career to the Ephesians, before his last trip to Jerusalem, Paul said he had testified "both to the Jews and to Greeks of repentance to God and of faith in our Lord Jesus Christ" (20:21). In Jerusalem, he told his audience of Jews that Ananias, under Jesus' direction, told him that he was "appointed" to "be a witness" for Jesus "to all men" (22:15). And, in Caesarea, he said to Agrippa that Jesus had told him in a vision that he was being sent to both "the people" (i.e., the Jews) and "the Gentiles . . . to open their eyes, that they may turn from darkness to light" (26:16–17).

However, despite his clear and unequivocal double commission to Paul, Jesus also seems to prophesy in Acts that the mission to the Jews will be unsuccessful. He says to Paul in a vision that is reported late in this book (22:18–21) but occurs well before Paul's first missionary journey: "Make haste and get quickly out of Jerusalem, because they will not accept your testimony about me . . . Depart; for I will send you away to the Gentiles." This statement reveals two important points. For one thing, the first sentence makes a claim that is inconsistent with Luke's description of the

---

108. For a very different view of the gentile mission of the Church covered in Acts, see Hengel, *Acts,* passim. One of Hengel's main points is that Acts documents Paul's gentile mission clearly and explicitly: Luke's "purpose was to show the course taken by the gospel from the Jewish-Christian community in Jerusalem . . . step by step to Paul's world-wide mission to the Gentiles" (66). Claiming that Luke describes Paul's mission to the gentiles in the second half of Acts (62), Hengel says that, at this point in the narrative, the mission was no longer sporadic, isolated, and limited, but systematic and deliberate (100). Indeed, so focused was Paul on this mission that it "now took the place of a mission to the Jews, which hitherto had been assumed to have priority" (100, 101). This mission did not immediately grow into a world mission, but developed gradually, owing largely to Paul's "super-human programme" in his role as "apostle to the Gentiles," which was accomplished on the "great journeys which took him from one province to another" (110). This sounds impressive, but none of it is documented in Acts of the Apostles. For a critique of Hengel's view of Acts, see Sanders, *Schismatics,* 84–85. Sanders comments, "Acts is tendentious enough to lead the careful scholar to look elsewhere at least for verification of its details." On this point, he quotes Hans-Joachim Schoeps, who says that, in pursuit of "a clear dogmatic goal," Acts "carries out a strenuous legend-building as well as re-stylizing both persons and events according to its own norms and on the basis of its own presuppositions" (261 ns. 9 and 10).

church under James, which was entirely made up of Jews and the growth of which demonstrated that testimony about Jesus was eminently acceptable in Jerusalem. That is, simply as a bearer of the Good News about Jesus, Paul was very likely to do what James did so well: (1) bring in Jewish converts and (2) avoid offending either the Jewish establishment or the Roman government.

In addition, the second sentence suggests that Jesus was sending Paul to the gentiles *because* his message was unacceptable to Jews. This point is important because, in this way, Luke gives Paul a motive for pursuing a gentile mission that Paul himself does not provide in his letters.[109] That is, the failure of Paul's Jewish mission, which is not attested apart from Luke's account of it in Acts, was not a historical fact, but a theological imperative. According to Paul in his letters, he was the self-described "apostle to the uncircumcised," or gentiles (Gal 2:7–8; Rom 11:13; 15:15–16; Eph 3:1, 8). For this reason, Paul had no intention of converting Jews and therefore could not have failed to convert them. This was Peter's assignment (Gal 2:7). As I said in the preceding chapter, however, writing at a time when the gentile mission was beginning to supplant the Jewish mission, Luke provided the Church with a divine rationale for this occurrence. Thus, as Paul and Barnabas said to the Jews in Pisidian Antioch, "It was necessary that the word of God should be spoken first to you" (Acts 13:46). By repeating this idea, Luke turned the failure of the Jewish mission into one of his major themes.[110]

This is the most obvious explanation for the fact that, in Acts, Paul not only overreacted to the Jewish response to his proselytizing, but also failed to initiate a gentile mission that involved a persuasive gospel (unlike the one that only slightly impressed the gentiles of Athens, for example) and convenient venues (like the synagogues, where Paul could at least get an initial welcome and address a large group of people).[111] In Luke's story, Paul was clearly so busy proselytizing to Jews that he had little time left over for gentiles. Writing in the nineties, several decades after the time period of Acts, Luke appears to have retrojected the deteriorating relations between

109. Meeks says that Luke has "Paul trying in every place first to win the Jewish community whole and withdrawing to the gentiles only when forced to by Jewish hostility . . . but Paul says nothing of it" (*First Urban Christians*, 168). Of course, Paul says of the Jews that "through their trespass salvation has come to the Gentiles" (Rom 11:11), but he never claims that he preached to the gentiles only (or even partly) because his own mission to the Jews did not succeed.

110. Tannehill suggests that the announcement was theologically rather than circumstantially driven. That is, in Acts, Paul did not stop preaching to Jews and turned to the gentiles only because the Jews rejected his message. As the quoted passage implies, the mission "must follow a prescribed order. The Jews must be addressed first" because that is the prophetic requirement. In this way, it conforms to "the purpose of God" (*Luke-Acts*, II, 173). Enslin says that "it was but a matter of time until the church should become convinced that [the transition from a Jewish to a Gentile mission] was a part of the unfolding purpose of God . . . Surely this was no accident. God had so ordained it" (*Christian Beginnings*, 181).

111. Brown says that preaching to pagans, in places like Lystra, Paul ran into "the ethos of a different world where the message of the one God (14:15–18) has not really taken root, making it all the more difficult to preach Christ" (*Introduction*, 305).

Christians and Jews that characterized the last quarter of the first century to that earlier period—before the Jewish Revolt.[112] That is, by the time Luke wrote Acts, Jews had become much less hospitable to insulting harangues by visiting Christians.[113] In fact, Luke might have been trying to substantiate two accusations that were becoming increasingly important to the Church because hostilities between the two groups had become more violent and more frequent—first, that the Jews had rejected both Jesus and his disciples and, second, that *many* Jews had had the opportunity to accept them. By this time, strikingly unlike the period in which the Church flourished under James, the separation was slowly, but ineluctably approaching completeness.

Thus, Paul's phrase "to the Jew first and also to the Greek" (Rom 1:16) meant to Luke—assuming that he ever read it or heard it—not only that the Jews received the word of God before the gentiles did, historically, but also that they heard it first from Paul before he turned to the gentiles That is presumably why Paul is shown to go on appealing to these irredeemable people.[114] The facts (as they are given in Acts), however, show that Paul encountered gentiles quite by accident. Furthermore, they appear to have become Christians as reluctantly as the Jews did. Thus, there was no reason to say that the Jews, uniquely, rejected Jesus. For a long time, according to Acts, nearly everybody did. But, again, when Luke wrote Acts, at the end of the first century, the mission to the Jews was floundering, and the mission to the gentiles had found its voice. It was more Hellenized, more accommodating to its audience, and therefore more successful.

If Paul was misunderstood by gentiles in Lystra (14:8–9), attacked by gentiles in Philippi (16:20–24), modestly successful in Athens (17:32–34), and resented by gentiles in Ephesus (19:29), it might fairly be said that, except for the God-fearers in the synagogues, Paul had a hard time finding a successful method of appealing to non-Jewish audiences. After all, since he preached the resurrection of the dead, the Kingdom of God, and the promise of the Messiah—traditionally *Jewish* themes—he could find common ground with Jews, as well as gntiles who were in one way or another affiliated with Judaism. But other gentiles, without that connection, could see little in the faith Paul proffered that could serve as a bridge from paganism to Christianity.[115] According to Acts, Paul thus had little luck with pagans, including Felix

112. Enslin says of the gentile mission that "its whole tone reflects the later practice of the church, already involved on a world mission and is in decided contrast to the attitude of the first Jerusalem followers who apparently shared Jesus' own view of the nature and purpose of his ministry"—i.e., preaching exclusively to the Jews (*Christian Beginnings*, 194).

113. Like many scholars, Fenton argues that Christians were not "excluded from the Jewish synagogues" until "after *c.* A.D. 85" (*Gospel of St. Matthew*, 11).

114. "The *purpose* of Paul's mission, for Luke, is to carry the Gospel to the Gentiles. At the same time, however, an effort must be made to reach Jews, so that the theme of rejection can be carried forward" (Sanders, *Jews in Luke-Acts*, 270).

115. On this point, see Kee et al., *Understanding the New Testament*, 180. The authors mention the concepts of Jesus as judge and the resurrection of the dead as incomprehensible to the pagans of Athens.

and Festus. And, perhaps because he had learned the futility of preaching to gentiles by then, Paul failed to seize the opportunity to preach to the soldiers, sailors, and other passengers on board the ship that took him to Malta. In fact, he even missed the chance to proselytize among the residents of Malta, where he resided for months and, owing to the friendliness of the natives, would have had every reason to expect a positive response to his missionizing.[116]

It is not Paul's failure to initiate a serious and sustained gentile mission in Acts that readers remember, however, but his verbal repudiation of the Jews who rejected Jesus, which is underscored by Paul's frequent attacks on Jewish practices in his letters. Readers also seem to remember only the second and third layers of the story of Acts of the Apostles, the sections that focus on Peter and Paul and the violence that accompanied their missionary efforts. Readers forget the first layer, on James—or, at least, the *church* of James—which preserves an entirely different picture of Jewish-Christian relations and which is generally not characterized by the kind and degree of hostility that pervades the other narratives. Indeed, it is marked by such extraordinary success—at least regarding the conversion of Jews—that one might ask what James did right and Paul did wrong.

That, however, is not Luke's question. Rather, the focus of both his Gospel and Acts of the Apostles is not on the compatibility of Christianity and Judaism, but on the increasing separation of the former from the latter, the increasing persecution of Christians by Jews, and the increasing obviousness of this process, which Luke regarded as inevitable because it was divinely ordained. On the one hand, the Church grew out of Judaism. On the other hand, however, it grew *away* from Judaism, and that paradox (according to Luke) had to be explained. Luke explained it by portraying the Jews as "maliciously opposed to Jesus and the Church," as bearing even greater "culpability in the death of Jesus" than "the received tradition" claimed, and as doing in Acts exactly what they had done in the Gospel of Luke. Of course, the absence of any account of the Roman persecution of Christianity, which by the time Luke wrote Acts was at least notable if not extensive (and which mirrors the absence of any Roman responsibility for the execution of Jesus), strongly suggests that the description of Jewish culpability in both of Luke's books might be a result of Luke's theological interests: "No good reason is ever given for the hostility, and we have ample ground for doubting its complete historicity."[117]

116. "In fact, the whole narrative of the voyage to Rome is remarkable for the absence of any indication that Paul proclaimed Jesus either to his companions on the ship or to the people of Malta" (Tannehill, *Luke-Acts*, II, 337).

117. Sanders, *Jews in Luke-Acts*, 18–19, 22–23. Says Sanders, "Inasmuch as we know that Luke's portrayal of Roman persecution of Christianity (i.e., he gives no such portrayal) is theologically motivated, in order to promote the idea of official Roman friendliness toward Christianity, it would seem likely that his portrayal of Jewish persecution of Christianity is likewise theologically motivated" (23; see also 313). Sanders examines the "symmetry" between Luke's two works on 69–83. And he discusses Luke's main theme—that, although Christianity grew out of Judaism, it eventually became a gentile religion, in accord with God's plan—on 129, 168, 254, 298. Thus, despite the Jewish support of

What disappears at the end of Acts of the Apostles is, thus, not only the great hope embodied in Jesus' reappearance on earth and his promise of salvation, but also the Jerusalem church's slow, but steady development into an institution capable of both celebrating Jesus' return and fulfilling his promises. In place of Jesus' message and its successful promotion by the non-Pauline Church, Paul turns his attention almost entirely to himself. As the story continues, after his oration in Pisidian Antioch, in which he recapitulates Jesus' role in the context of Jewish history (Acts 13:16–41) and his definition of the Christian God in Athens (17:22–31), Paul says less and less about Jesus, but more and more about his own spiritual and physical struggles and sacrifices. In four different orations (20:17–35; 22:1–21; 24:10–21; 26:2–23), he is particularly (and surprisingly) autobiographical.[118] Ironically, the trajectory of hope slowly plummets in Acts' final pages of frustration and bad weather, ending in little more than inconsequence. Christ Redivivus, addressing his adoring disciples and promising them salvation, is supplanted by *San Paulo in vincoli* (26:29), threatening the local Jews with eternal damnation.

The last few chapters of Acts present the strangest combination of events imaginable, especially in relation to the grand first chapter. Paul made a series of speeches to different audiences after his arrest by the Romans, all of which contained the false claims that he was not only Law-obedient,[119] but that he was being attacked by Jews for his belief in the resurrection of the dead. At the end of Paul's speech to Herod Agrippa,

---

the Jerusalem church and the substantial success of Jewish Christianity in the early pages of Acts, Luke reverses his favorable portrait of both Jews and Jewish Christians after chapter 12: "From this point on, 'the Jews' oppose Christianity" (40). And the Diaspora Jews who reject Paul's gospel are as guilty of killing Jesus as are the Jews in Jerusalem (53–55).

118. Tannehill calls two of the four speeches autobiographical, but this word characterizes all of them. In this respect, these speeches "differ markedly from Paul's previous mission speeches" (*Luke-Acts*, II, 274; see also 317). At the same time that Paul's autobiography swells, "references to Jesus' name become less frequent and more scattered," Tannehill says. "The comparative infrequency of references to Jesus' name in Acts 10–28 supports the view that the frequent references in Acts 2–5 and 8–9 are not merely the result of habits of expression but show deliberate emphasis in a section of Acts where this theme contributes to narrative continuity" (49). More important, I think, the early usage supports the theme of "fulfillment," and the later usage suggests the decline of this positive theme in Acts. Notably, Paul replaces Jesus as the focus of the narrative.

119. The editors of *Oxford Annotated Bible* say that the elders of the Jerusalem church were wrong to charge Paul with "teach[ing] all Jews who are among the Gentiles to forsake Moses, telling them not to circumcise their children or observe the customs" (21:21). The editors justify their objection by citing Acts 16:3, in which Paul has Timothy circumcised; 1 Cor 9:20, in which Paul says that he "became as a Jew, in order to win Jews"; and 1 Cor 10:32, in which Paul advises the Corinthians not to offend Jews in order to save them. However, in all of these passages, Paul is not saying that he observes the Jewish Law because he believes in it, but because he is willing to show respect for it in the service of his missionary objectives. That is, he did not encourage Timothy to be circumcised because he (Paul) believed in the efficacy of the act, but "because of the Jews that were in those places" (16:3). In other words, the charge of the elders, as well as the charge by "the Jews from Asia," was certainly correct. On this point, Segal comments, "The charge against Paul is also logical, because Paul comes close to advocating overthrowing Torah in his opinion of its inapplicability to food laws or circumcision" (*Paul the Convert*, 239).

both the king and the procurator Festus made jokes, in a friendly manner, at Paul's expense. Both procurators desired to please the Jews (24:27; 25:9), Felix by keeping Paul in prison, Festus by having Paul sent to Jerusalem so that the Jews could capture and kill him (25:2), but Paul evaded the latter threat by simply demanding to be sent to Rome. The procurator Felix and the missionary Paul discussed theology intermittently during the latter's two-year incarceration (24:26–27).

Paul's sea journey to Rome was cursed by a number of bizarre occurrences, including a violent tempest that made everyone give up all hope (27:20), an abandonment of the ship by sailors (27:30), a shipwreck (27:41), a plot by soldiers to kill the prisoners (including Paul), and a life-saving escape from the ship, in which everyone jumped overboard and swam to shore. On Malta, Paul was unhurt by the bite of a deadly viper (28:3) and helped by the hospitality offered by "the chief man of the island," Publius. It is also notable that, on board the ship, Paul persistently assured everyone that they would be safe, thanks to Jesus' counsel (27:21–23), but his ongoing advice about navigating the vessel was only belatedly heeded by the centurion in charge of the prisoners on board. In these episodes, even though they might bear some resemblance to what actually happened, the details seem irrelevant and insignificant. The lengthy and uneventful stay on Malta seems particularly trivial, following as it does Paul's dramatic appearances before the Sanhedrin, two Roman procurators, and King Herod Agrippa. Indeed, as I have suggested, the entire story ends in an anticlimactic diminuendo.

Yet, as I said earlier, this is not what remains in the memory of the reader. The undramatic story of James comes first, but it is covered up over time, superseded by the later, more theatrical tales. Its rather positive, but unexciting portrayal of Christian life in the mid-first century is easily overshadowed by the pyrotechnics of the Pauline account. Eventually, it is lost in the narrative shuffle. In short, limited in scope as the opposition between Jews and Christians may actually be in the Acts of the Apostles, particularly considering that the book covers a period of thirty years and a territory extending from Jerusalem to Rome, this conflict so dominates the Lucan landscape that it has turned out to be the most memorable aspect of the whole extraordinary story. When we step back from the canvas, if we ever do, what we see is that, at first, Paul is the only named and officially sanctioned perpetrator of violence against Christians and, at the last, except for Stephen (and, of course, Paul's companions), the only named recipient of it. Take this single individual out of the picture, and the brutal struggle between Jews and Christians dissipates into smoke and mirrors.

Chapter Six

Hellenization

"It is not too much to say that the success of the Church in converting the gentile world in the fourth and fifth centuries was due to a process which may be described as a pagan transmutation of Christianity itself." (J. B. Bury)

THE FOURTH CONSEQUENCE OF Paul's mission to the gentiles outside of Palestine was an ongoing transformation of Christianity itself. Here, the agent of change was not merely the gentile-Christian indifference or hostility to Judaism, but the gentile (as well as Diaspora Jewish) understanding of Jesus, worship, and ethics,[1] which had two principal sources: the Platonism of the fourth century BC, which continued to have a powerful influence on Western civilization through the Renaissance; and the mystery religions, which influenced the West, from Italy to Asia Minor to Egypt, from several centuries before Jesus to several centuries after his Crucifixion.

In other words, as I said in the preceding chapter, by merely crossing the line between a thoroughly anti-Hellenistic Jewish Galilee (at least those parts of it that Jesus had visited and the disciples had originally preached in) and a thoroughly Hellenized gentile Diaspora, Christianity was profoundly changed: "The historical presupposition for Paul's theology is not the kerygma of the oldest Church but that of the Hellenistic Church; it was the latter that mediated the former to Paul. His theology presupposes a certain development of primitive Christianity which it had undergone

---

1. Ruether refers to the Hellenization of Christianity as a result of its move into the Diaspora in *Faith and Fratricide*, 33. See also Cullmann, *Early Church*, 161; and Conzelmann and Lindemann, *Interpreting the New Testament*, 355. By the end of the first century after the Crucifixion, says Enslin, Christianity had become "completely acclimated to the wider Mediterranean world" because it "had drunk so deeply at wells which no Jewish hands had delved" (*Christian Beginnings*, vii). Quoting two passages—one from Mark and the other from 2 Peter, Grant says, "Between the two lies a process, whether long or short, in the course of which the Christian gospel was redirected in order to become more fully comprehensible to those who lived and thought in the Graeco-Roman world" (*Historical Introduction*, 89). "I shall be saying in all that follows," comments Lee, "that I believe the distance between Athens and Jerusalem is roughly parallel to the distance between Western Christians and Jews" (*Galilean Jewishness of Jesus*, 8).

after the Christian message had crossed the boundaries of Palestinian Judaism, and congregations of Hellenistic Christians, both Jewish and Gentile, had arisen."[2]

Of course, the most important question we can ask about Christianity, in this context, is the one raised by this quotation: What *was* "the oldest Church"—that is, exactly what message did it inherit from Jesus himself, and what message did it propagate before it was transformed by Hellenism? The scholar quoted in the last paragraph says, *It was not originally Paul's Church.* The evidence weighs heavily in favor of the conclusion that the theology of Paul, as well as that of his Hellenized compatriots, is a secondary development. The *primary* development, as I said earlier, is represented by James the brother of Jesus (especially insofar as the Epistle of James actually expresses his views); the original disciples (including Peter and the two sons of Zebedee, John and James), who either agreed with him or submitted to his authority; and other Jewish-Christian groups that flourished in the first century, particularly the Ebionites, the people who wrote the Q gospel, the *Didache* community, and even the group for which the late second-century *Pseudo-Clementines* was written.[3]

The single most important fact about these groups is their ongoing connection to Judaism, which is manifested in their ethical focus, represented by their common interest in the Sermon on the Mount; their picture of Jesus as a spirit-driven teacher of wisdom; and either their obedience to the Law of Moses or their open embrace of the Jewish Bible as a source of covenantal values, which they implemented by creating model communities based on sharing and mutual aid.[4] In his second-century *Dialogue with Trypho the Jew*, Justin Martyr identifies Jewish Christians by their practice

---

2. Bultmann, *Theology*, I, 63. Based on archeological studies, Reed concludes that "the Galilean world of Jesus was Jewish, and while not completely isolated, relatively sheltered from the overt Pagan aspects of urbanization, the Roman emperor cult, and a Legionary presence, all of which came to Galilee only in the second century after the Second Jewish Revolt against Rome" ("Archeological Contributions to the Study of Jesus and the Gospels," 54).

3. Mack says that Q "provides a documentation for the [original] Jesus movement that the narrative gospels cannot provide" (*Lost Gospel*, 238). In other words, "Q is the best record we have for the first forty years of the Jesus movements." That is why, "[b]y reading Q carefully, it is possible to catch sight of those earliest followers of Jesus" (4). Kloppenborg says that Q "is almost certainly from Jewish Palestine" and "gives us a glimpse of a Gospel formulated by Jesus' Galilean followers, quite different in complexion from the diasporic and Gentile Christianities that we know from other sources" (*Q*, ix). Koester says that "[t]he Q community stood in a demonstrably direct continuity to Jesus' own ministry—indeed the members of this community seem to have emulated Jesus' behavior" (quoted in Crossan, *Birth of Christianity*, 405). Crossan agrees that the tradition from which the Q community derives was created by "the male and female companions of Jesus" in Jerusalem (though they were, like Jesus, originally Galileans), where they "stayed from the very beginning" (573). Crossan refers to two scholars who connect at least parts of the *Pseudo-Clementines* with "earliest Jewish Christianity," or "the primitive church" (512).

4. Distinguishing Q from the Gospels, Kloppenborg says that it contains no controversies over Sabbath regulations or food laws. Indeed, "Q presupposed an exclusively Israelite environment where people naturally circumcised their sons, kept kashrut, and observed the Sabbath." Furthermore, Q shows no interest in a gentile mission because it "presents . . . a rural, Galilean Jewish gospel," which, "along with the letter of James," gives us "one of the very few arguable instances of a document produced by and for the earliest Judean followers of Jesus" (Q, 68–69).

of circumcision and their observance of Sabbath and purity laws. Unlike Irenaeus and Hippolytus, Justin did not believe that these beliefs disqualified Jews from salvation, unless they tried to impose their quasi-heretical views on other Christians. In the eyes of many other Church leaders in the second century, however, Jewish Christianity *was* heretical and therefore expendable.[5]

On the other hand, the logic of identifying the earliest Christians as *Jewish* Christians is simple. If Jesus lived and died a Jew, if his earliest disciples did the same, if the Jerusalem church was a direct creation of those disciples, if their first leader was indeed James the brother of Jesus, if Paul was an outsider whose views were more often than not in the minority,[6] and if the Jewish-Christian communities referred to above were in fact offshoots of the Jewish-Christian community in Jerusalem, then it is apparent that *original* Christianity (or, at least, the original Jesus movement) underwent profound changes on its way to being represented by the letters of Paul, the Gospel of John, and the Passion narratives in the synoptic Gospels. Some scholars have argued that the earliest church was dominated by Stephen and the Hellenists, who yielded control to James only because of Stephen's death.[7] However, only the Hellenists left Jerusalem at this time. The first disciples, e.g., Peter and the sons of Zebedee—those who had actually *known* Jesus—obviously remained in Jerusalem under the leadership of James.

Paul wrote in the fifties; the Passion stories, which have no precedent in "sayings" collections like Q, were written after the destruction of the Temple in AD 70; and John's Gospel was composed in the nineties or later. In other words, the central focus of these works—on the death and resurrection of Jesus—was a later development.[8]

---

5. Speaking of the Q community, Mack argues that "they were not Christians." This is because "[t]hey did not think of Jesus as a messiah or the Christ." Furthermore, they did not believe he had rejected Judaism. They did not consider him to be innately divine or his death as salvific. Rather, "they thought of him as a teacher whose teachings made it possible to live with verve in troubled times" (*Lost Gospel*, 4; see also 8, 42, 48, 246–47). According to this tradition, Jesus did not even intend to reform Judaism (5). Kloppenborg also notes the "lack of an explicit narration of Jesus' death and resurrection" (*Q*, 73). On this point, see also Schillebeeckx, *Jesus*, 284. Later, Schillebeeckx mentions the Q community's renunciation of possessions, embrace of poverty, expectation of transformation, and trust in God (412). Bauckham says that both Jesus and Q have come to be thought of as representative of the wisdom tradition ("James and Jesus," 105). Crossan identifies both Q and *The Didache* as expressions of rural communities that have no Passion-Resurrection stories and therefore concentrate exclusively on Jesus' life and sayings (*Birth of Christianity*, 572–73). Horsley and Silberman say that *The Didache* instructs community members "to observe a rigorous code of nonviolent resistance, communal solidarity, and economic sharing" (*Message*, 229).

6. On the Jerusalem church as normative (rather than conservative) and Paul as radical, see Hill, *Hellenists and Hebrews*, 115, 146–47, 151, 164.

7. On this point, see Ruether, *Faith and Fratricide*, 82. Biblical support for this view comes from Paul, but evidence of the early Church's respect for Sabbath and purity laws, its requirement of circumcision for converts, and early Christians' worship in the Temple—before any suggestion in Acts that James the brother of Jesus was the leader of the Church—is abundant.

8. "By the second century Christianity had grown to that state of maturity where it could no longer be ignored or dismissed. Its Jewish past was fading, and what had occurred almost symbolically

And the idea that the fundamental tenet of Christian faith is not moral, but meta-physical was a product of the influence of Hellenistic religious concepts. For many scholars, these later ideas originated in what they call the Christ cult: "The clue to the logic of the kerygma [i.e., the proclamation of Jesus' divinity and related ideas] lies in the phrase that Christ died 'for us,' namely the congregation of Christians. Such a notion cannot be traced to old Jewish and/or Israelite traditions, for the very idea of a vicarious human sacrifice was anathema in these cultures. But it can easily be traced to a strong Greek tradition of extolling a noble death."[9]

The "cult" of Jesus the Christ has been so labeled because it resembled the mystery cults that were pervasive in the Roman empire, in which worshipers could achieve immortality by participating in the death and rebirth of the mystery god: "A spirited cult formed on the model of the mystery religions, complete with entrance baptisms, rites of recognition (the holy kiss), ritualized meals (the lord's supper), the notion of the spiritual presence of the lord, and the creation of liturgical materials such as acclamations, doxologies, confessions of faith, and Christ hymns."[10] As a result of the growing prominence of this view of Jesus and his message, James was forgotten; the sayings of Q, recounting Jesus' covenantal ethics, were subordinated to the high christology of Paul and John; the Ebionites were transformed into heretics; and *The Didache* simply disappeared completely until a manuscript was discovered in the nineteenth century.[11]

in Paul's own lifetime, the passage from Jerusalem, to the synagogues of Asia, to the Areopagus of Athens, was being reenacted on an ecumenical scale" (Peters, *Harvest of Hellenism*, 614). The main tenet of Paul's teaching, says Vermes, is "the dying and rising Christ" (*Resurrection*, 116, 119), which many scholars contend is absent from the earliest ideas about Jesus. Vermes also argues that Paul's view of Jesus is unprecedented in Judaism. Thus, "whereas the idea of the Resurrection lay at the periphery of the preaching of Jesus, Saint Paul turned it into the centerpiece of his mystical and theological vision, which was soon to become quasi-identical with the essence of the Christian message" (128). Meeks makes a similar point in *Origins of Christian Morality*, 64–65, 87.

9. Mack, *Lost Gospel*, 216–217. For Mack's complete argument on this point, see 207–25. As a result of its move into the Hellenized world of the Jewish Diaspora, Enslin says, Christianity became "a gentile cult" (*Christian Beginnings*, 147). "By the middle of the second century—and probably much earlier," Enslin continues, "it had become one of the Graeco-Oriental cults, and like the others offered salvation to its converts through its divine Lord" (187). Later, Enslin adds, "[I]t is hard to doubt that well before the end of the century a new religion which promised salvation to its converts through union with its crucified and risen Lord and which had its sacred rites of initiation and communion had come to rival the claims of other cults promising precisely the same boon" (200). How thoroughly Christianity became this kind of cult is, of course, open to debate. However, that it "came to be regarded as one of the mystery religions of salvation does not appear to be open to legitimate question" (191).

10. Mack, *Lost Gospel*, 220.

11. "From the fact that there is only a sparse tradition of Jewish Christian witnesses [many scholars] incorrectly conclude that Jewish Christianity was actually insignificant, without taking into consideration that our knowledge is determined by the ecclesiastical tradition" (Strecker, "On the Problem of Jewish Christianity," 242). Strecker identifies the *Kerygmata Petrou* (c. 200) as yet another Jewish-Christian document (257–71). He also rejects the idea that "Jewish Christianity separated itself from the 'great church' and subsequently led a cloistered existence as a sect." Indeed, it was the only church in some areas (271). The search for Q—which is embedded in the Gospels of Matthew

It is important to recognize how far this process went—that is, how thoroughly Christianity changed from the first century to the fourth. It is not simply that it completely lost its identity as a movement within Judaism; it also (and just as importantly) totally abandoned the main theme of Jesus' preaching in the synoptic Gospels: the idea of the Kingdom of God. After a time, the Church turned its back on the Jewish apocalyptic tradition partly because the Kingdom appeared to be unaccountably delayed and because the "eschatological discourses" that announced the coming of a New Age were expressed in what one scholar has called "oriental thought-patterns," which were "incomprehensible" to non-Jews: "So the early Fathers of the Church soon put out of court a type of literature which at one time had been of prime importance for Jesus and the first Christians."[12]

Furthermore, as we shall see, the ethical code embedded in the Jewish Covenant and expressed in the Sermon on the Mount gave way to a more broadly conventional Greco-Roman moral vision. That is, not only did Christianity give up much of its Jewish past, it also replaced what it lost with acquisitions from the Hellenized world: "As Christian doctrine evolved, it managed to incorporate much of the thought and experience of other sects."[13] In the words of another scholar, the Church, responding to the "tremendous influence" of its new environment, "adopted new conceptions, took on a totally different character, borrowed from all with whom it came into contact, and through its extraordinary eclectic character was able to rival the older and more firmly established cults."[14]

Thus, to put it simply, the faith that Jesus founded became, in the long run, a product of both Jewish and Greco-Roman influences: "Christianity began as a Jewish sect with missionary ambitions, but it did not simply arise out of Judaism, nor directly out of the ministry of Jesus." As a result of the spread of Hellenism, "Christianity became deeply enmeshed in the syncretistic process [by which Hellenism affected all of the religions of the Roman empire], and this may very well have been its strength."[15] However, Christianity was transformed not merely because Hellenism was the dominant cultural force in the Roman empire, but also because Christians were increasingly recruited from this world and because the Church realized that its success rested

---

and Luke—was partly inspired by the discovery of another collection of Jesus' sayings, *The Gospel of Thomas*.

12. Koch, "Apocalyptic and Eschatology," 60. Koch says that this literature (including not only the Book of Daniel, but also works attributed to Enoch, Baruch, and Esdras) formed a "bridge" between Old and New Testaments. Specifically, it connected Jesus to the Jewish prophets (61).

13. Grant, "Gnosticism, Marcion, Origen," 318.

14. Enslin, *Christian Beginnings*, 147.

15. Koester, *History, Culture, and Religion*, 166. See also xxix-xxx, 39. According to Latourette, the greatest threat to the survival of Christianity as a unique faith came from Judaism on one end and Hellenism on the other: "As it moved out into the non-Jewish world it was in danger of so far conforming to that environment that it would sacrifice the essential features of the Gospel. The threat was especially acute from Hellenism and the atmosphere of the Hellenistic world" (*History of Christianity*, I, 122).

on its relations with the Romans rather than the Jews. Once the Church both saw itself as gentile and understood its dependence on the Romans for its survival, in the second century, it was compelled to turn its attention from Jews to pagans.[16]

Before we explore these cultural forces and their influence on early Christianity, however, it is important to recognize how powerfully Hellenism affected Judaism—not, of course, in Palestine, except in the Greek cities established there, but in the Diaspora.[17] The Hellenization of Judaism is relevant here because it paved the way for the Hellenization of Christianity. As one scholar puts it, "Christianity, after all, became a Hellenistic movement through and through, largely because Judaism had already marked the path into Hellenistic culture."[18]

PLATONISM AND PAGANISM

Even ordinary Jews outside of Palestine were affected in one way or another by Greek culture. First, they spoke the language. Second, their Bible, the Septuagint, was written in Greek. Third, Jewish worship services were conducted in Greek. And, fourth, all Jews in these areas, especially those who lived in cities, could hardly avoid at least some contact with the material manifestations of Greco-Roman society. The most powerful Jews in the Diaspora—who almost always, after 63 BC, supported the Romans—not only spoke Greek, read the Septuagint, and had Greek temples, gymnasia, and schools in their midst; they also admired Greek culture, welcomed the establishment of all Greek institutions, accepted Greek values, and (at least among the intellectual elite) studied Greek philosophy.[19] Some Jews were so enamored of Greek and Roman

---

16. Lieu, *Image and Reality*, 285; and Parkes, *Conflict*, xii.

17. Armstrong contends that Greek philosophy began to influence Jewish thinking outside of Palestine as early as the fourth century BC (*History of God*, 66). See also Boyarin, *Border Lines*, 92. Schiffman says that the Aegean impact on the Near East goes back to the fourteenth century BC. However, it became an important force in the Diaspora only by the fourth century BC, thanks to the conquests of Alexander, and under the Seleucids in the second century BC (*From Text to Tradition*, 60–65).

18. Koester, *History, Culture, and Religion*, 97–98. Peters explains: "The Jews of the Diaspora were the first great instrument in the Christianization of the oikoumene. The Hellenized synagogue was also the door to the wider world of Hellenism" (*Harvest of Hellenism*, 493). See also Strecker, "On the Problem of Jewish Christianity," 243.

19. Guignebert mentions not only Greek, but also Egyptian, Babylonian, Hittite, Chaldean, and Persian influences (*Jewish World*, 84–88). Furthermore, these influences have been ignored, especially by Christian scholars (83, 84, 159). Even in Jerusalem, Herod the Great constructed a palace, three towers, a fortress, a tomb, a theater, a hippodrome, and the Temple itself—all in the Greco-Roman style (Jeremias, *Jerusalem*, 10, 87). Some scholars argue that all Jews were Hellenized to some extent. As Bauckham says, "It is now usually stressed that the whole of Jewish culture was to some degree Hellenized" ("James and Jesus," 104–5). See also Mack, *Lost Gospel*, 55–59; and Carmichael, *Birth of Christianity*, 19. Crossan contends, however, that Galilee was unaffected by such Hellenistic influences as Platonic dualism (*Birth of Christianity*, xxxiv). Freyne agrees, especially regarding rural areas (*Galilee, Jesus*, 169–70).

culture "and embarrassed to be different" that they paid to have their circumcision reversed by an operation called epispasm.[20]

The most obvious evidence of the Hellenistic influence on Jewish thinking is the appearance, from the second century BC to the time of Jesus, of such Greek-influenced texts as *Ecclesiasticus* (or *The Wisdom of Jesus ben Sirach*); *The Wisdom of Solomon*; *2, 3 and 4 Maccabees*; the *Sybilline Oracles*; and the writings of Philo. One scholar explains: "The Jews, for their part, came into contact with Greek letters and Greek thought, and this placed them in a delicate position with regard to the Torah similar to that occupied by many educated religious persons today with regard to science and dogma. They too managed to convince themselves that there could not be any real contradiction between their knowledge and their faith, and sought to reconcile them."[21]

Thus, Platonism, most obviously the body-soul conflict that was important to both Paul and the author of the Gospel of John, is a prominent theme in *2 Esdras*, for example, a late first-century work, mostly composed in either Hebrew or Aramaic. The writer of *2 Esdras* says, in language that Paul uses in 1 Corinthians 15:52–54, "A man corrupted by the corrupt world can never know the way of the incorruptible" (2 Esd 4:11). In other words, living on earth, we can see nothing beyond it: "[O]nly he who lives above the heavens can understand the things high above heaven" (2 Esd 4:21). At death, after "the spirit leaves the body to return to the One who first gave it," it perceives what it has not perceived before and "join[s] the other souls in their abodes" (2 Esd 7:78, 88, 100–101). Thus, one of the things that forces us to "wander in torment, endless grief, and sorrow" (2 Esd 7:80) is "the contrast between the corruptible world from which [the saved] have joyfully escaped and the future life that is to be their possession" (2 Esd 7:96).

Similarly, the writer of *The Wisdom of Solomon* says it is difficult to know God's will because the soul is not free from the body: "The reasoning of mortals is uncertain, and our plans are fallible, because a perishable body weighs down the soul, and its frame of clay burdens the mind already so full of care." Thus, we struggle to see "things of the earth" and cannot determine "what is in heaven" (Wis 9:13–16). We see through a glass, darkly.

The Septuagint itself shows how much the culture of Greece influenced Jewish religious life in the time of Jesus. First, the order of books in this Bible, following the Greek method of ordering writings by genre rather than by date of canonization, is quite different from the order in the Hebrew Bible. Second, partly because a number of different Hebrew biblical texts existed at the time, parts of the Septuagint were translated from Bibles different from those used in Palestine. Finally, and most important,

---

20. Wylen, *Jews*, 92. Wylen explains: "The Greeks despised circumcision. Because of this, in the Hellenistic era fulfilling the law of circumcision acquired added significance as a sign of adherence to Jewish values" (90–91).

21. Guignebert, *Jewish World*, 223. See also Jeremias, *Jerusalem*, 35, 74; and Cook, *Introduction to the Bible*, 67–68. Cook refers to *The Wisdom of Solomon* as "a stage towards the N.T." (68).

the translation from Hebrew to Greek is not literal. The text was written with the goal of enabling readers of Greek to understand it, which sometimes required using Greek rather than Jewish concepts.[22] Jesus ben Sirach, who purportedly translated his grandfather's *Ecclesiasticus* from Hebrew to Greek, recognized that his translation was flawed because "what was originally expressed in Hebrew does not have exactly the same sense when translated into another language. Not only this work, but even the law itself, the prophecies, and the rest of the books differ not a little as originally expressed."[23]

As a result, Greek culture influenced the Jews in the Diaspora not only insofar as it was embedded in their physical environment, but also to the extent that it was reflected in their religious ideas. Thus, when Paul and other early Christian proselytizers came to them with Greek-influenced ideas of salvation, morality, and divine intermediaries, the Jews in the Diaspora were, as I said earlier, far more prepared to accept them than were the Jews in Palestine.[24] And they were more inclined to accept Paul's interpretation of Jesus than Peter's or James'. As one historian puts it, the Septuagint "provided a basis for a new departure of Jewish theology in a new cultural environment, and made it possible that the ferment for renewal . . . could further develop within the horizons of Hellenistic culture and religion."[25] The translation, which was done exclusively by Christians after the Pentateuch had been translated by Jews, also

---

22. Schiffman discusses this subject in more detail in *From Text to Tradition*, 91–94.

23. Quoted in Bruce, *Canon of Scripture*, 45–46.

24. Furthermore, Jews outside of Palestine were less influenced by Jewish traditions. Guignebert says that the apostles' testimony "found more willing ears among certain Jews of the Dispersion whose religious duties brought them on pilgrimages to the Holy City. Such men, living outside Palestine, in a Gentile environment, no longer clung so firmly as did their brethren to the expectation of a warrior Messiah or the hope of a nationalistic revival of the Davidic Kingdom" (*Jewish World*, 259). Guignebert adds, Christianity's "true antecedents lie on Hellenistic soil, for it was in Hellenistic Judaism that it found its *raison d'être*, there it was born, nurtured and reared, and there it fulfilled its destiny" (261).

25. Koester, *History, Culture, and Religion*, 253. "Thus," Koester adds, "the LXX [Septuagint] became the most significant factor in the process of the Hellenization of Judaism" (253). And, by extension, it became the most important factor in the Hellenization of Christianity: "Greek Judaism with the Septuagint had ploughed the furrows for the gospel seed in the Western world" (A. Deissmann, *New Light*, 95; quoted in Bruce, *Canon of Scripture*, 50). Ruether notes that Diaspora Judaism became spiritualized, universalized, and individualized under the influence of Hellenism (*Faith and Fratricide*, 32, 57). That is, "Judaism in the Greco-Roman period was an evangelical religion that was in the process of breaking its ethnic boundaries to become a universal faith" (26). Conzelmann and Lindemann note the tendency (1) among the Pharisees to conceive of God as transcendent and (2) among Jews in general to think of salvation as spiritual rather than physical and piety as individualized (*Interpreting the New Testament*, 130, 135). On this point, see Wylen, *Jews*, 44–45. On other aspects of the Hellenization of the Pharisees, see Koester, *History, Culture, and Religion*, 241–43. Crossan raises the question of whether—but for the Jewish revolts against Rome and the consequent loss of a Jewish homeland—Judaism would have become more universal and inclusive over time, instead of more parochial (or at least more inward looking) and exclusive, as it did under the Rabbis (*Historical Jesus*, 420). After all, the Greco-Roman philosophical interest in autarky (inner freedom), individualism, and cosmopolitanism (discussed in Conzelmann and Lindemann, *Interpreting the New Testament*, 145) was shared by groups other than the Roman aristocracy in the time of Jesus.

enabled Christian proselytizers to present the Jewish Bible in terms that aided their missionary purposes.[26]

It is also worth noting that aristocratic Jews all over the Roman empire were interested in promoting Judaism as a religious system compatible with Greek philosophy and more cosmopolitan notions of religious practice.[27] They had two main reasons (not necessarily mutually exclusive): (1) a desire to convert pagans to Judaism and (2) a desire to defend Judaism against its detractors. Against such severe critics of the Jewish faith as Cicero and Tacitus, Josephus, for example, portrays the major sects of Judaism as mirror images of different Greek philosophies. Philo, who spent his whole life reconciling Judaism and Platonism, did so not only for his own satisfaction, but also because he wanted Greek-speaking people in general to respect his faith as something grander than a primitive superstition, which it was seen by many pagans to be. And a Jew who called himself Phocylides (after a Greek poet of the sixth century BC) wrote a manual for gentiles in which he tried to demonstrate that the morality of the Jews was not very different from the morality of the pagans. All of these writers described their religion as a monotheistic faith that emphasized ethics rather than ritual because they wished "to present Judaism to the outer world in a form that would not repel it."[28]

As I suggested earlier, however, just as Hellenism affected Christians in different ways in different circumstances—especially their socio-economic status and their location in the empire—Jews were similarly influenced by this dominant cultural force depending on how and where they lived. Most scholars, as we have seen, emphasize the differences between Palestine and the Diaspora, rural versus urban areas, and affiliation with or hostility to Rome as a governing power. Jews who spoke only Aramaic (with perhaps a smattering of Greek used for commercial purposes), lived in villages

26. Cook contends that Greek translations of Jewish texts "prepared the way for the transition from the Hebrew and Jewish O.T. to the Greek and Christian N.T." In these works, he explains, "numerous adjustments were made, and particular usages of Classical Greek words were reshaped theologically" (*Introduction to the Bible*, 38). Bruce says that, on occasion, "the Septuagint translators used a form of words which . . . lent itself to the purposes of New Testament writers better than the Hebrew text would have done" (*Canon of Scripture*, 53).

27. According to Segal, "the most characteristic aspect of Diaspora thinking was its attempt to show that Scripture and Greek philosophy were in complete harmony over the essential issues" (*Rebecca's Children*, 55). See also Ruether, *Faith and Fratricide*, 25.

28. Guignebert, *Jewish World*, 230. On the subject of Jewish propaganda in Jesus' time, see 228–32. See also Ruether, *Faith and Fratricide*, 27, 31–32. Meeks says that Philo walked a thin line between defending what he took to be essential Judaism and demonstrating the similarities between his faith and that of the Romans. Thus, "a large part of what he finds in the biblical narratives and laws [on which he wrote his commentaries] is identical with much that one might hear from the pagan moralists and philosophers who were teaching in the schools of Alexandria." Yet he not only read Moses in terms of Plato, but also read Plato in terms of Moses (*First Urban Christians*, 36–37). Meeks says elsewhere that Philo's work in this regard reveals "the fundamental tension that shaped the ethos of diaspora Israel" (*Origins of Christian Morality*, 45). On the *Sentences of Pseudo-Phocylides*, see Crossan, *Historical Jesus*, 419–20. Brown describes Phocylides as "a very Hellenized Jew" and dates the *Pseudo-Phocylides* to "after 100 BC" (*Introduction*, 740).

or small towns, and regularly attended a synagogue were more inclined to cling to traditional ways, especially in religious matters, and were resistant to Greco-Roman culture generally. Thus, as one scholar says, although "no part of Judaism was untouched by Hellenism," not all Jews "were touched in the same way or to the same extent."[29] Ironically, therefore, as Christianity became more urban, Diasporan, gentile, and Hellenized, it moved away from its Jewish roots and away from the influence of its Jewish leaders—not only James the brother of Jesus, Peter, and the other original disciples, but also the fifteen "Hebrew" bishops of the Jerusalem church listed by Eusebius in his *Ecclesiastical History.*

The least significant influence on the development of Christianity was the official paganism of the empire, which is summarized in a passage from Homer: "It is with sacrifices and humble prayer, / With libation and burnt offering that people implore [the gods] / And turn [their wrath], when any has offended or sinned" (*Iliad*, 9:499–501). In other words, paganism bore this similarity to the Hinduism of the Vedas, the Judaism of Leviticus, and Homeric religion: It emphasized ceremonial and sacrificial acts over ethics.[30] Worshipers were judged much less by their moral actions than by their correct performance of ritual actions, which demonstrated their obedience to the gods and their desire to placate them in any way possible. Thus, "the usual form of prayer was the vow, the prayer accompanied by the promise to pay some tribute named when prayer was answered. It was a transaction with a legal flavor—*Do ut des* ('I give in hope of return from you')."[31]

The Roman gods, particularly the ones derived from the ancient Olympic pantheon, were conceived of anthropomorphically—they were superhuman and immortal, but motivated by humanlike emotions. They were, at least in Homeric times, immanent insofar as they appeared in human form on occasion. And they were thereby, like Yahweh before the termination of Jewish prophecy in the fourth century

29. Lee, *Galilean Jewishness of Jesus*, 59. Lee says, for example, that Greek thought had no influence on Galilee. He cites George Foot Moore's claim (in *Judaism*) that neither the Mishnah nor the two Talmuds show any trace of Greek influence and concludes that "the rabbinic decision to go down a fully Hebraic road is consonant with and disclosive of the deeper impulses that characterized Palestinian Judaism throughout most of its contact with Hellenism" (77–78). It should be emphasized, of course, that many Jews opposed Hellenization of any kind, as the Revolt of 66 demonstrated. On this point, see Koester, *History, Culture, and Religion*, 53, 97.

30. Roman piety, says Koester, had nothing to do with individual religious experience—least of all mysticism. "Rather, piety meant the faithful observation of ritual duties," which were intended "to maintain the favor of the gods and to avert their curse" (*History, Culture, and Religion*, 363). This kind of piety, emphasizing prayer and ritual, was common among all the religions in the Roman empire (Wylen, *Jews*, 84). See also Balsdon, "Rome as a Battleground of Religions," in Balsdon, ed., *Romans*, 198. Unlike the Jews, the Romans, "in the early centuries CE, made no attempt to establish a universal cult or sacred text or priesthood or belief statement" (Clark, *Christianity and Roman Society*, 5).

31. Mattingly, *Roman Imperial Civilisation*, 223. "In time of calamity—invasion, famine or plague—men's thoughts turned naturally" to the possibility that the disaster occurred because the gods had been insufficiently worshiped. "Had something been done to offend the powers?" Then something had to be done to appease them (224).

BC, capable of communicating directly with human beings and influencing their actions. Of course, by the first century AD, the Romans saw these gods far less the way the earlier Greeks had described them and more like the abstract, impersonal gods of Plato and Aristotle. Nevertheless, they had to be appeased—and there were many of them.[32]

The Romans were tolerant of other religions for two reasons. First, they assumed that some of the national gods of other peoples were the same as their own gods, just renamed. Second, in religions in which the gods seemed odd or the manner of worship primitive, the Romans allowed the worshipers to follow their faiths, especially if the religions themselves were ancient, as was the case with Judaism and the religion of Egypt, and as long as the worshipers also honored the Roman gods. (Indeed, Julius Caesar himself had excused the Jews from praying *to* these gods as long as they prayed *for* them.[33]) Worship of the emperor himself, demonstrated in the imperial cult, was a means of achieving some kind of uniformity throughout the empire: "Though each people might be allowed its own indigenous cult, how advantageous it would be for imperial unity if there were at the same time one cult in which all of the peoples could participate!"[34]

Christians were criticized by the Romans only when they appeared to be withdrawn from society, engaging in immoral acts, and (especially) unwilling to worship the official gods. Romans in general seem to have believed that the success of the empire depended on the continuing support of these as well as other gods, who therefore needed to be respected by *all* of the residents of the nation. Failure "to repay divine favor, to avert impending wrath, or to placate the actual rage and fury of the gods"—which Christians seemed to be guilty of—threatened to undermine not only the unity of the empire, but also its very survival.[35]

There was little in this religion, however—except its failure to satisfy people's need for an emotional connection to a god or gods—that would have enhanced its followers' inclination to appreciate Christianity. In the words of one historian of early Christianity: "[I]t may be doubted whether, outside Italy and Greece, . . . these gods gave much spiritual solace to their worshippers." Indeed, "the official pantheon meant

32. Mattingly discusses the polytheism of Roman religions, the general amorality of the gods, and the great number and kinds of deities in ancient Rome on 210–13, 218–22.

33. Under Caesar, says Parkes, "in return for the support of the Jews a certain measure of their political power was returned to them," some of which they lost under Tiberius. Parkes traces the history of Rome's offer of privileges to the Jews from the time of the Maccabees until the Christianization of the empire in the fourth century AD in *Conflict*, 7–11.

34. Bainton, *Early Christianity*, 22.

35. The quotation is from Minucius Felix's *Octavius*, in which Felix, through a fictional Roman character, expresses "the charges commonly made against Christians" (in Ehrman, ed., *After the New Testament*, 54–55). Bainton says: "The cardinal principle throughout antiquity was that the state can prosper only through the favor of the gods. The warfare of peoples was considered to be a warfare between their gods. A state would be wise, therefore, to make an *entente cordiale* with the powers of heaven" (*Early Christianity*, 21).

little to the later pagan world," and the "official worship of the emperors, dead and living, had even less religious content." The imperial cult was "usually a mere form."[36] Besides, by AD 150 paganism was "fading into the background," largely because of the kinds of events ("war and disaster") that would eventually bring down the empire. And it was gradually being replaced, as I suggested earlier, by a monotheism that focused on a single invisible, unknowable, and transcendent god, probably influenced by the still popular concepts of Plato.[37]

At the same time, Platonism itself had a powerful influence on Christianity, which can be seen not only in the writings of Paul and John, but also in the proliferation of Platonic ideas in the post-New Testament period: for example, in Athenagoras' *Plea Regarding the Christians* (4, 10, 15); *Letter to Diognetus* (2, 6); *2 Clement* (6, 12, 14); and Origen's *Homilies on Luke* (3), *Homilies on Genesis* (2), and *On First Principles* (Bk. 1, 1:1, 8:9; Bk. 2, 6:3).[38] One of the most important aspects of Plato's ideas that flourished in the Diaspora in the first century AD (and which we have already seen in *2 Esdras* and *The Wisdom of Solomon*) appeared in the writings of Philo, whose view of Platonic philosophy was probably shared by many educated urban Jews at the time.

For these writers and thinkers, the immortal soul leaves God and enters the world by descending into a mortal body. Ideally, it spends its earthly life trying to return to God by denying the passions that interfere with its perception of and participation in divine (or spiritual) reality. And the final ascent to God, resulting in a union of spirit with Spirit, is prefigured in states of ecstasy, in which spirit perceives Spirit in a moment of transcendence of the body.[39] Peter and Paul's revelations of Jesus' words

36. Jones, *Constantine*, 35. "Official Roman religion," says Chadwick, "was not of a character to evoke religious emotion as distinct from patriotism" (*Early Church*, 152–53).

37. Grant comments, "This attitude made the deities of Olympus acceptable to the more advanced thinking of the day, but it also weakened their hold on the minds of the Roman people as autonomous, individual entities" (*Climax of Rome*, 163). As time passed, says Latourette, "the state religions were no longer believed in as strongly as formerly. However, the continuance of their rites was believed to be necessary for the welfare of society" (*History of Christianity*, I, 23). Chadwick says, "People of high education and rank upheld the old religion . . . [and] participated in the traditional cultic acts on the principle that these rites were received ways of keeping the unseen powers friendly" (*Early Church*, 152).

38. These texts can be found in Ehrman, *After the New Testament*, passim. Koester notes "the wide dissemination beginning in 1 BCE of Platonic thoughts and concepts, which was by no means the success story of a particular philosophical school, namely, of the Academy, but a cultural development." In short, "Platonism determined the general thoughts and world view of the entire subsequent period" (*History, Culture, and Religion*, 143). See also Bainton, *Early Christianity*, 12–13; Cumont, *After Life in Roman Paganism*, 42–43; Young, "A Cloud of Witnesses," 24–25; and Clark, *Christianity and Roman Society*, 36. Latourette says that Neoplatonism, developed by third-century philosophers Ammonias Saccas and Plotinus, "left a permanent impress on Christianity, partly through Augustine of Hippo, partly through its share in shaping Christian thought in general, and especially in its contributions to Christian mysticism" (*History of Christianity*, 95).

39. Koester summarizes the Jewish philosopher Philo's influence on Christianity in *History, Culture, and Religion*, 280. Latourette discusses the Hellenization of Judaism, including the influence of Philo, in *History of Christianity*, I, 14–15. On the expansion of Christianity through the Jewish Diaspora, Latourette says, "Christianity had much of its early spread through the circles of Hellenistic

may reflect the adoption of these ideas in Acts of the Apostles, although they were undoubtedly influenced as well by the Jewish tradition of the Holy Spirit. Needless to say, many of these concepts are entirely foreign to the Jesus of the synoptic Gospels, although they are at the very center of Jesus' ideas in the Gospel of John and in Paul's epistles.

To Philo, soul and body are thus in conflict, as they are in Paul and John, but not in the synoptic Gospels. The words *soul* and *spirit* appear seldom in the Synoptics, where *spirit* most frequently refers to either the Holy Spirit (Matt 4:1, Mark 1:10) or the demonic spirits that Jesus exorcizes (Matt 8:16; 10:1; 12:43; 14:26; Mark 5:2; 9:2). Otherwise (Matt 16:26; 26:41; Luke 1:47; 12:19), *soul* and *spirit* refer to a kind of essential self, equivalent to the word *heart* (Acts 4:32), as they do in the Jewish Bible.[40] Preaching without the concept of an opposition between *body/flesh* and *soul/spirit* in the synoptic Gospels, Jesus warns in the Sermon on the Mount that the "whole body" can be "cast into hell" (Matt 5:29–30), and Matthew describes the "bodies of the saints" arising from their graves—both of which statements suggest the Jewish idea of physical resurrection. Similarly, at his return after his Resurrection, Jesus appears in bodily form. He says, "[A] spirit [i.e., a ghost] hath not flesh and bones, as ye see me have" (Luke 24:39).

By contrast, John adopts whole cloth the Platonic idea that the essential conflict in the moral life of humanity is the enmity between spirit and flesh. As Jesus says to Nicodemus in John's Gospel, "That which is born of the flesh is flesh, and that which is born of the Spirit is spirit" (John 3:6). All of humanity can be "born of the Spirit"— that is, endowed with a spiritual self—because everyone can be inspirited by God, who "is a Spirit." In short, "It is the Spirit [i.e., of God] that quickeneth" (i.e., brings eternal life), as opposed to the "flesh," which "profiteth nothing" (6:63). Thus, "they that worship him must worship him in spirit and in truth" (4:24)—that is, as Plato said in so many words, only a spiritual being can relate to God as a spiritual being.

The other dichotomies in the Gospel of John are similarly little more than extensions of the fundamental contrasts in Plato between the profane and the sacred: mortal and immortal, visible and invisible, and matter and spirit. For John, the Platonic opposites are earth and heaven, death and life, hatred and love, dark and light, the devil and God, blindness and seeing, and damnation and salvation, among others: "Labor not for the meat which perisheth, but for that meat which endureth unto everlasting

---

Judaism, both among those who were Jews by long heredity and those who had either become full proselytes or were on the fringes of the synagogue" (16). Crossan discusses Philo's concept of the present Kingdom of God as a specific example of a Hellenized Christian concept anticipated by a Hellenized Jewish one (*Historical Jesus*, 287–89).

40. Segal says, "There was no strict distinction between body and soul in ancient Hebrew thought" (*Rebecca's Children*, 60). See also Moore, *Judaism*, II-III, 263–64. In fact, there are only two examples of the concept in the entire synoptic Gospels. The first is from Matt 10:28 and Luke 12:4: "And fear not them which kill the body, but are not able to kill the soul." The passage clearly implies that the body is mortal, the soul is immortal, and the latter can exist without the former. The second is from Matthew 26:41 and Mark 14:38: "[T]he spirit indeed is willing, but the flesh is weak."

life" (John 6:27).[41] It was a short road from these dichotomies to the Christian concept of Heaven and Hell, which had its origin in Persian Mazdaism: "The resplendent heights where the gods had their thrones were to be after death the abode of those who had served piously." Those who had not "were to be flung into the murky abysses in which Ahriman [the Spirit of Evil] reigned."[42]

In his epistles, Paul uses many of the same contrasting terms: notably, flesh and spirit (Rom 8:1–14; 1 Cor 5:3–5; 15:44; Gal 5:16–25), death and life (Rom 6:1–14), earth and heaven (1 Cor 15:47–49). Indeed, Paul applies the dichotomous world view of Plato as often and as broadly as John does.[43] He emphasizes the contrast between Spirit and Letter (Rom 2:29; 7:6; 2 Cor 3:6), Adam/Moses/Ishmael and Christ/Isaac (Rom 5:12–17; 1 Cor 15:22, 45; 2 Cor 3:12–15; Gal 4:21–31), Works and Grace (Rom 11:5–6; Gal 2:8–10), Law and Faith (Rom 3:17–31; Gal 2:15–3:29), wisdom and folly (1 Cor 3:18; 4:10), sexuality and chastity (1 Cor 7), and writing and revelation (2 Cor 3:3). Everything important is an expression of this fundamental split, one might say, in the cosmos.

41. Hengel says that John's Gospel was particularly popular in Egypt partly because of the influence of Plato on Alexandrian Judaism "since the second century BC" (*Four Gospels*, 43). On the popularity of dualism in the early centuries, see Grant, *Climax of Rome*, 194–95, 200–203. According to Latourette, the spirit/flesh conflict "seemed to have come into Greek thought through the Orphic movement centuries before Christ." He continues: "It was perpetuated through Platonism and Neoplatonism. By its presence in that cultural tradition, it had so moulded the thinking and the attitude of Christian converts from a Hellenistic background that it often came over with them. Through them and the continued study of Platonism and Neoplatonism it has persisted in the thought, practice, and worship of a large proportion of Christians" (*History of Christianity*, I, 122). Grant says that John's Gospel, though it is more Greek than Jewish, was made canonical because it was assumed to have been written by a real disciple (*Climax of Rome*, 206). Braun also finds the long sermons Jesus is supposed to have recited in the Gospel of John to be less characteristic of Judaism than of Hellenistic-Oriental religion (*Jesus*, 30).

42. Cumont, *After Life*, 88–89. Cumont says that the idea of "an absolute antithesis" between these afterlife abodes was passed on to Alexandrian Jews, Pythagorians, gnostics, Manicheans, and "above all," worshipers of Mithras. Cumont concludes, "This was also the conception which, after some hesitation, became generally accepted by the Church, and which for long centuries was to remain the common faith of all Christendom" (90).

43. Martin says that Paul, unlike earlier Jewish Christians, understood Christianity from a Hellenized perspective: "Although Paul was highly educated in the Jewish tradition (Gal 1:14), he must have been influenced to some extent by the range of religious alternatives present in his native city of Tarsus" (*Hellenistic Religions*, 119). Grant says that 1 Cor 12:12–27, for example, in which Paul refers to the church as the body of Christ, is "derived from Graeco-Roman political thought." Grant continues, "Indeed, everything Paul says in this passage can be paralleled in Greek and Roman writers" (*Historical Introduction*, 398–399). Grant reminds his readers, however, that body/soul language can be found not only in the Hellenized Josephus, but also in the writings of the Essenes (311). Brown briefly discusses Paul's Stoicism in *Introduction*, 90. On Paul's "desire to make his gospel understandable to gentiles," see Mack, *Who Wrote?* 138–43: The alleged Jewish failure to keep the Law was replaced by the idea of universal sin; Mosaic Law was replaced by natural law; the physical resurrection of the dead was replaced by the idea of transformation from materiality to spirituality; and righteousness was replaced by Greek virtue (as self-control). Brandon discusses the differences between the Jewish historical view of Jesus and the Greek mystical view in *Trial of Jesus*, 18–20.

The physical self in Paul's writing is always associated with sin, selfishness, and death: "For I know that nothing good dwells within me, that is, in my flesh" (Rom 7:18). In particular, the flesh is the abode of desire and passion (Gal 5:17, 24; Rom 8:6). It is the "carnal" dimension of the self (Rom 7:14). And although Paul explains the spirit/flesh, mind/body division in different ways at different times, some passages directly echo Plato's mind/body contrast: "I see in my members another law at war with the law in my mind and making me captive to the law of sin which dwells in my members," from which Jesus will deliver him. "So then," he continues, "I of myself serve the law of God with my mind, but with my flesh I serve the law of sin" (7:23–25). In this way, the self is, in the words of one scholar, "inwardly split." And this inner division manifests itself in a kind of psychological warfare, self against self.[44]

One of Paul's strongest themes is the Platonic idea that human beings have direct access to the spiritual world, through revelation, which is no longer reserved only for God's prophets, in Paul's view, but is now available to the saints of the Church: "God hath revealed [things] to us by his Spirit." And we have received these things through "the spirit of man, which is in him"—that is, as John later said and as Plato earlier argued, people experience the spiritual through the spiritual within them (1 Cor 2:6–14; Gal 3:1–6). Thus, "no man can say that Jesus is the Lord, but by the Holy Ghost" (1 Cor 12:3).[45]

Resurrection is, similarly, not a physical, but a spiritual phenomenon: "Now this I say, brethren, that flesh and blood cannot inherit the kingdom of God." And Paul's explanation is Platonic, not Jewish: "[N]either doth corruption inherit incorruption." At the end, "the dead shall be raised incorruptible . . . and this mortal must put on immortality" (1 Cor 15:50–54). Underlying all of these discontinuities, as in John, is the fundamental doctrine of Plato—that human beings live in two worlds, one pure, invisible, and eternal; the other, corrupt, accessible to the senses, and mortal: "[W]e look not at things which are seen, but at things which are not seen: for the things which are seen are temporal; but the things which are not seen are eternal" (2 Cor 4:18).

Palestinian Jews were likely to understand Jesus in the context of the Jewish Bible, in which case John's idea of God would have been, as it was to Nicodemus, a novelty. Jews and gentiles in the Diaspora had a better chance of understanding Jesus' meaning differently because their cultural heritage was different from that of Jews who lived in the small towns and villages of Judea and especially Galilee. In areas outside of

44. Bultmann, *Theology*, I, 244–45. See also 104–6. The subject is also discussed by Crossan (quoting Boyarin) in *Birth of Christianity*, xxii–xxiv; and Kee et al. in *Understanding the New Testament*, 208–9. "For many Christians, as for many pagans," says Markus, "the body became the chief locus of all the frustrating powers of the world. The abuse heaped upon the flesh and the asceticism that flowed from such attitudes were no monopoly of Christianity, even though they continued to infect Christian attitudes" (*Christianity*, 31).

45. Cullmann states that Rabbinism marked the end of prophecy, and the Apostolic movement revived it (*Early Church*, 74).

Palestine, Plato's ideas had a profound effect on the Christian concept of Jesus. John's Jesus, who comes down from heaven and goes up again, may be understood to be presenting an allegory illustrating the pattern that the soul or spirit of his followers would eventually take in their departure from and return to God.[46]

On one hand, John's Jesus says, "No one has ascended into heaven but he who descended from heaven, the Son of man" (John 3:13). On the other hand, however, speaking of anyone "who sees the Son and believes in him," Jesus "will raise him up at the last day" (John 6:40, 44, 54; see also 12:32). In other words, according to John's logic, all of Jesus' followers will ascend to the place they originally came from, which means that they too are Sons of man—that is, immortal souls who come from God, temporarily occupy an earthly body, and finally return to God, as Plato argued.

Furthermore, Philo's description of the *logos* can similarly be understood to have allowed not only Greek-speaking Jews in the Diaspora, but also pagans, to develop a more understandable view of Jesus than the Palestinian Jews could offer. Philo's logos is a means by which God manifests Himself periodically in Jewish history as a divinely inspired prophet who communicates God's will to the Jewish people. Notably, the logos is referred to by Philo as the firstborn son of God, God's likeness, God's messenger, and humanity's intercessor with God. Thus, as one scholar explains: "Philo's writings were preserved and cherished by the church, and provided the inspiration for a sophisticated Christian philosophical theology" based on "a pre-Christian picture of a heavenly intermediary being of the kind Christians were to identify with Jesus." It would have been easy, too, for Hellenized pagans and Jews to connect the logos with the traditional figure of Wisdom, which I discussed in the Introduction (26–27).[47]

The strictly messianic Jesus of the early Gospels, who was understood in the context of Old Testament prophecies, thus gave way to a Platonic Jesus who was understood by Diaspora Jews, God-fearers, and pagans in the context of Greek philosophy.[48] Specifically, the idea of Jesus as the Jewish Messiah who initiates the Golden

---

46. Mack says that the early Christian view of the universe as a "cosmos" derived from the way Greeks thought of the universe. And the Jesus who inhabits this cosmos—the cosmic Jesus—reflects "a variant of the old, standard descent-ascent pattern, whereby a god comes down into the world from the heavenly realm on a mission or with a message and then returns" (*Who Wrote?* 176–82).

47. The quotation is from Young, "Two Roots or a Tangled Mass?" 115. After discussing the similarities between the logos and Wisdom (115–16), Young summarizes what A. D. Nock considered the major pre-Christian influences on the post-Judaic Jesus (118–19). Schiffman, noting that Wisdom is described in *The Wisdom of Solomon* "as an emanation of God, a great light," calls this "concept similar to the logos (divine wisdom) of Philo" (*From Text to Tradition*, 124). According to Peters, Philo himself "makes her an analogue to the creative Logos" (*Harvest of Hellenism*, 658). See also Bainton, *Early Christianity*, 13.

48. Grant argues that the idea of the logos prepared the way for the acceptance of Jesus as a divine mediator: "Plato and the Platonists and others [no doubt, including Philo] had unwittingly played an integral, preparatory part in the Christian achievement . . . The Word [or logos] . . . is what Jesus seemed to be" (*Climax of Rome*, 209). On the circulation of this idea among early Christians, see Mack, *Who Wrote?* 263–66; and Latourette, *History of Christianity*, I, 141–43. Pelikan quotes Clement of Alexandria as saying that Jesus was "the Image of God as the divine and royal Logos" (*Jesus Through*

Age was supplanted by the idea of Jesus as the Greek *logos*, whose eventual return will liberate all human beings from their bodies, judge each individual on his or her merits, and provide everyone with an eternal reward or punishment, in heaven or hell. In other words, the popular understanding of Jesus changed constantly from the first century to the fourth, but eventually Paul's Hellenistic view won out. As one student of this process says: "[T]he Aramaic-speaking Jewish Christians did not interpret Jesus in the same way as the Hellenistic Jews of the Diaspora . . . ; and the non-Jewish Greeks, Syrians, Romans and so forth, who had absolutely no part in Israel's hopes of salvation, naturally enough proceeded to express the salvation they had found in Jesus in quite different categories."[49]

Although it is obvious that Paul's ideas (and John's, as well) had a better chance of succeeding in the Greco-Roman world than in Palestine, they no doubt would have appealed as much to Hellenized Jews in the Diaspora as to Hellenized gentiles. In fact, although Paul may be said to have Hellenized Christianity, it might also be said that, considering the widespread acceptance of Philo's version of Plato among Jews as well as gentiles, at least some Hellenization would have occurred even if the followers of Jesus had remained Jewish. That is, the transformation of Christianity might have had more to do with its movement out of a relatively anti-Hellenistic rural Palestine, especially Galilee, and into a completely Hellenistic Diaspora than its shift in membership from Jews to gentiles.

Specifically, if Philo promoted the ideas of an unchanging and invisible God, the *logos* as an intermediary between God and humanity, an immortal soul, a resurrection for all moral people, ultimate rewards and punishments, and an eternal life in heaven—and if Diaspora Jews agreed—then the ideas of a still-Jewish Jesus could very well have been reinterpreted exactly as they appear in Paul's letters and John's Gospel. Furthermore, many of these concepts were also available to the Jews in the Book of Daniel as well as a number of inter-testamental works, such as *2 Maccabees* and *1 Enoch*.[50] The point is not that all Jews in the Diaspora would have understood Jesus through Philo's eyes, but that many educated Jews would have seen him in the same way that educated gentiles did.

---

the Centuries, 41).

49. Schillebeeckx, *Jesus*, 22. In other words, "The transition from a Jewish Christianity to a 'Gentile' one produces . . . a new 'image' of Jesus inside the Bible itself" (60).

50. Many of the ideas in this paragraph derive from Segal, *Rebecca's Children*, 56–64. Peters says: "What the church had done in the third century was to join itself to the contemporary Hellenic intellectual (and artistic) tradition. Judaism too, though it had earlier apparently declined this step, was more quietly moving in the same direction" (*Harvest of Hellenism*, 634).

THE MYSTERY RELIGIONS

While Platonism affected the more urbanized, more educated Jews and gentiles (like, most notably, Justin Martyr, who "identified Christ with the highest reason"[51]), the early Church appealed more strongly to the poor and unschooled. Among such people, at least among gentiles of the lower classes, Jesus was understood not in the context of Plato's theories or even in the context of either the official, highly ritualistic religion of the Romans or one of the Greco-Roman philosophies that attracted middle-class people (Stoicism, etc.), but in the context of the mystery religions, which the small tradesmen, artisans, and peasants living outside Palestine typically joined.[52] These cults, in which a great variety of gods and goddesses were worshiped (though each cult worshiped a single deity or pair of deities), offered their members an emotional experience that the other religious and philosophical options available to them could not provide. Hence, the attraction.[53]

The ceremonies began with a rite of purification and culminated in a sacred banquet, after which the initiate was delivered from peril, protected against disease, and given immortality—all of which suggests how strongly these movements resembled early Christianity and the extent to which they might have influenced the way pagans who belonged to them understood Jesus.[54] Besides the rituals of baptism and sacred meals, a "high standard of morality," and a "creed of redemption and salvation," these

---

51. Grant, *Antonines*, 119.

52. Koester notes, however, that emperors and intellectuals were drawn to the Eleusinian mysteries. Among Romans, he refers to Cicero, Augustus, Hadrian, Antoninus Pius, Lucius Verus, Marcus Aurelius, and Commodus (*History, Culture, and Religion*, 178). Klingaman notes that the upper classes were turning away from the Roman gods and "adopting more exotic eastern gods instead." In response, Tiberius outlawed all foreign cults in Rome, including Judaism and the cult of Isis, "which apparently had been attracting substantial numbers of converts among freedmen and the nobility" (*First Century*, 113–14). In the first century AD, the cults were popular all over the Roman empire (Grant, *Historical Introduction*, 249).

53. Mattingly comments, "A special vent for personal emotion was provided by the 'mystery' religions. The chief recurring feature in them is the conception of a divine protector and friend who guides and guards men in life and leads them to a happy immortality after death" (*Roman Imperial Civilisation*, 217).

54. On this topic, see White, *From Jesus to Christianity*, 66. Martin offers a lengthy overview of the mystery cults in chapters three and four of *Hellenistic Religions*. For a good general summary, see Bultmann, *Primitive Christianity*, 156–61. Bultmann quotes a prayer to Isis, worshiped as the Queen of Heaven as well as a fertility goddess: "O holy and blessed dame, the perpetual comfort of human kind, who by thy bounty and grace nourishest all the world, and bearest a great affection to the adversities of the miserable as a loving mother" (159). The proliferation of females among the cultic deities suggests how strong was the desire to worship a motherly figure as well as a young male. In fact, says Cook, "The representation of Isis . . . with the young Horus on her knee served to familiarize the Christian world with the figure of the Madonna and the child Jesus" (*Introduction to the Bible*, 23). Mack contends that mystery cults, like shrines and associations, were means by which displaced or transplanted persons could retain their ties to the mother country: "How to keep one's culture alive was the question" (*Who Wrote?* 26–29).

cults also encouraged "strong personal feelings towards the god."[55] Thus, in converting members of the cults (as well as Gnostics), the Church risked being "insidiously corrupted" not merely by newly converted Christians interpreting its doctrines and practices from a different perspective, but also "incorporat[ing] their own ideas into Christian theology."[56]

Many of these religions centered on a divine (or semi-divine) figure who had died and had been reborn or who at least represented the cycle of death and life: Attis, Osiris, Baal, Adonis, Astarte, Cybele, Asclepius, Orpheus, Heracles, and Serapis, among others. The initiate often reenacted the death and rebirth of the deity and thereby earned eternal life. Immortality was acquired when the initiate united with the god or goddess, usually called a savior.[57] The cult of Isis, for example, celebrated the return to life of Osiris with a stately ritual, splendid robes, and riveting drama. This Egyptian cult spread throughout the empire, as did the Greek cults of Dionysus and Demeter. Worship of the former consisted of wine drinking, intoxication, and a vision of the god. Demeter, whose daughter Persephone was lost and found rather than murdered and reborn, was worshiped through a reenactment of her mourning and other aspects of the myth.[58]

Originally fertility rituals, these rites were attractive because, like Christianity, they promised new life to initiates, as well as a sense of brotherhood, in which ethnic, racial, and social distinctions disappeared.[59] The similarity is suggested by the fact that

55. Vermaseren, "Religions in Competition with Christianity," 255.

56. Bainton, *Early Christianity*, 31. Bainton explains: "The Mysteries would find in Christianity some elements unintelligible and uncongenial, such as the creation of the world, the incarnation of god in man, the voluntary dying of Christ, and the doctrine of sin and grace. Other elements would be all too intelligible: the resurrection, the rebirth, and the sacraments." Thus, converts from these religions might "think of the resurrection as the rebirth of a nature god, and Easter would become a fertility rite . . . The Lord's Supper would become [as it did] an actual consuming of the flesh and blood of the god. Jesus would be the only god except for the goddess, the Virgin Mary. Against such misreadings the Church was required to be on guard" (33).

57. On these points, see Conzelmann and Lindemann, *Interpreting the New Testament*, 142–43. Bainton says that the theme of death and resurrection (or "restoration") was common among cults from Babylon, Syria, Asia Minor, Egypt, and Greece (*Early Christianity*, 31–32). Cumont discusses the attainment of immortality in the mystery religions in *After Life*, 116–24. He explains that the acquisition of eternal life was attractive insofar as it promised to save converts from the misery of the physical conditions in which most of them lived and the hopelessness of being victims of Fate. On drinking wine, eating bread, and symbolically consuming the god himself (or herself) at ritual banquets, Cumont says that the practice was universal as well as ancient: "This idea goes back to the most primitive savagery." Its purpose was to allow the participant to acquire the virtues of the deity, including strength, courage, and oracular abilities (120).

58. On the importation of the mystery religions into the Roman empire, see Meeks, *First Urban Christians*, 13, 16–18. On Cybele, Mithras, Isis, and other mystery gods and goddesses, see Mattingly, *Roman Imperial Civilisation*, 213–16.

59. Kee et al., *Understanding the New Testament*, 19–21. Wilken says that Celsus, a Roman critic of Christianity, compared it "to unpopular and arcane religious movements that offended the sensibilities of the Romans"—for example, the worship of Cybele, Mithras, and Sabazius. "In another place [Celsus] compares Christian worship to the superstitious practices of the Egyptians" and the

Paul was mistaken for a cult promoter when he preached about Jesus in Athens: "He seemeth to be a setter forth of strange gods" (Acts 17:18).[60] In Ephesus, Paul enraged the silversmiths, who made their living by selling silver shrines to the worshipers of the cult goddess Diana (Acts 19:28). Clement of Alexandria went so far as to suggest, in the words of one scholar, "that Christianity may be properly understood to be a mystery religion."[61] Justin Martyr found so many similarities between Christianity and Mithraism that he could only attribute them to the work of "wicked demons," whose goal was to deceive potential Christian converts.[62]

worship of Bacchus (*Christians*, 96). See also Koester, *History, Culture, and Religion*, on parallels between Christianity and the worship of Isis (190–91). Parallels between Christianity and Orphism are equally obvious (161–62). In "The Revelation of Isis," a poem in Apuleius' *Metamorphosis* (11), Isis calls herself "the parent of the nature of things," the "initial progeny of the ages," and the "first of heavenly beings," controlling all the forces of the universe by a nod. She is also worshiped everywhere, in the guise of Minerva, Venus, Diana, Proserpina, Ceres, Juno, and others (Henderson, "Apuleius of Madauros," 197–98). See also Carmichael, *Birth of Christianity*, 89–91, 138.

60. On this point, see Bruce, *New Testament History*, 311–12. Perrin and Duling, in *New Testament*, say: "That Christianity could be interpreted as a cult within Hellenism is obvious at first glance. It too had its myth of the hero, the gospel story of Jesus; its initiation rite, baptism; its sacred meal" (82). The idea of individual immortality, special rites by which it could be attained, and common meals celebrating the ensuing sense of community were common features of Hellenism, not limited to, but chiefly represented by, the mystery religions. Thus, once Christianity adopted such beliefs and practices, says Koester, "it immediately came under the suspicion of being a mystery religion." This "was nothing else but an external sign of the fact that Christianity was deeply engaged in a process through which it became one with the Hellenistic world and its religious concepts" (*History, Culture, and Religion*, 200–201). Says Cook, "It would not have been difficult . . . to identify [Jesus] with, or at least to find parallels with Him in, Marduk, or Osiris, or Apollo" (*Introduction to the Bible*, 149). Likewise, according to Clark, "A group called 'Christiani' (Acts 11.26) would initially have seemed like 'Heraklistai' or 'Asklepiasti', worshippers of a god who, like Herakles and Asklepios, had once been mortal" (*Christianity and Roman Society*, 22). Trevor-Roper calls Christianity "[a]nother of these oriental mystery-religions": "But nothing in the third century suggested that this Jewish heresy could rival the more tempting mystery-religions of Persia, Syria or Egypt" (*Rise of Christian Europe*, 58). On parallels between Jesus and Osiris, see Wright, *Evolution of God*, 304–6.

61. Meyer, "The Mithras Liturgy," 182. Meyer notes that Clement wrote in his Exhortation to the Greeks: "O truly sacred mysteries! O pure light! In the blaze of torches I have a vision of heaven and of God. I become holy by imitation. The Lord reveals the mysteries" (182). Perrin and Duling quote six New Testament hymns in which Jesus is described as a descending-redeeming-ascending god: Phil 2:6–11; Col 1:15–20; 1 Pet 3:18–22; Eph 2:14–16; Heb 1:3; 1 Tim 3:16 (*New Testament*, 83–84). On parallels between the mystery cults and Christianity, see 341. As Placher reminds his readers, however, the similarities between Jesus and the mystery gods can be pushed too far. Unlike most of the other "deities," Jesus demanded total loyalty to God, emphasized ethics over ritual, and "called for love and sharing and a transformation of one's life" (*History of Christian Theology*, 41). Yet again, the point is not that there were no differences between Christianity and the mystery religions, but that there were enough similarities to convince members of the latter faiths that Christianity was far from a strange and alien religion.

62. Enslin, *Christian Beginnings*, 198. This was Justin's usual way of explaining unpleasant facts. Maguire comments: "Early Christian dogmas were not very distinctive in their contemporary world. (What was distinctive was the moral vision begun in Judaism and planted in Christianity.) The similarities embarrassed Christian apologetes and sent them scurrying to prove that the multiple 'pagan' prototypes of the Christian dogmas were either mimicries devised by devils to trick the unwary or blessed foreshadowings of the gospel—*praeparatio evangelica*" (*Moral Core*, 95). Maguire discusses

Mithraism also involved an initiation—characterized by harsh ordeals and expiations—and ultimate union with the god Mithras, leading to immortality. Although Mithras was initially merely allied with the sun and was himself known as the god of the Morning Light, he became known as the Sun God in the first century. Constantine, the first Christian emperor, combined a worship of both Jesus and the sun, "or regarded them as interchangeable." The violent (and apparently bizarre) initiations helped worshipers attain imperviousness to pain and suffering; the god was known to be compassionate; and he offered an ethical code emphasizing purity, restraint, and honesty. In other ways as well, Mithraism was very similar to Christianity, with its "baptisms, sacrifices, communal meals, and martyrdoms," which made Christians feel that it was a deliberate imitation of Christianity. The cult worshiped its god all over the Roman empire, from England to North Africa, with fifty shrines in Rome alone.[63]

In fact, it was the popularity of Mithras that influenced Christians to establish December 25 as the date of Jesus' birth—by Donatists, who left the church in AD 311; by the church in Rome in 336; by Christians in Constantinople in 379; and in Antioch, at the urging of John Chrysostom, in 386. Even before Mithras achieved international fame, the Romans had built a temple to *sol invictus*, who was honored by athletic games on December 25. Indeed, so strongly associated with the sun was this particular day of the year that it ultimately won out over birthdays of Jesus celebrated on March 28 (along with other days in the spring) and the rather persistent celebration of Jesus' birth in early January, especially January 6, which was traditionally the birthday of the gods Dionysus and Aeon and, until the early fourth century, the Epiphany, but afterward a celebration of both the baptism and the birth of Jesus.

Though December 25 was resisted by Egyptians until the fifth century and by Palestinians until the sixth century, Emperor Constantine drove the idea across the Roman empire in the fourth century and finally, posthumously, triumphed over supporters of either spring or January. The irony is that no one knows when Jesus was born or when he died. And, before 300, several birth dates competed for special recognition.[64]

some of the similarities (virgin births, healing miracles, deifications, dying and rising gods, young saviors and mortal mothers, divine mediators, and Queens of Heaven) on 95–97.

63. Grant, *Climax of Rome*, 181–86. On the importation of Mithraism, its special features, and its popularity, see Koester, *History, Culture, and Religion*, 372–74. On the sun as the principal pagan symbol, especially in opposition to Christianity, see 158. See also Meyer, "The Mithras Legacy," 179–92. According to Vermaseren, Mithraists thought that "eating the meat or bread and drinking the blood or wine [of the bull sacrificed in the Mithraic ritual] was favoured by the god and was ensuring them a happy after-life" ("Religions in Competition with Christianity," 254). Followers of Mithras were encouraged to imitate the god's "virtue, might, heroism, righteousness, . . . and general morality" as a means of "attaining eternal life" (254).

64. This and the preceding paragrapha are based on Cullmann's discussion of the origins of Christmas in *Early Church*, 21–36. Cullmann notes that Christians were at first far more interested in the death and resurrection of Jesus than in his birth and that Origen objected to the establishment of any birth date for Jesus as a pagan practice. Furthermore, the establishment of December 25 was a case of mythology trumping history: "[T]he first impulse to celebrate Christ's appearance on earth was

The confusion between Jesus and the gods of the mystery cults was enhanced by the fact that the latter were known for their wisdom and their ability to perform miracles. They came to earth for the specific task of redeeming mankind, and they were therefore revered as divine benefactors. Similar characteristics were ascribed to kings, especially in the East. Egyptian pharaohs, for example, were thought of as divine, and even Roman emperors were venerated as gods after their deaths, thus meriting the titles "Lord" and "savior," as well as "Son of God."[65] Indeed, divinity was often attributed to mere mortals, including men who distinguished themselves as brave or wise: "Drawing upon Greek ideas of deification as a reward for merit, the Romans had fostered similar legends relating to Hercules and their own founder Romulus. And just as they had been human beings whose mighty deeds raised them to be gods after their deaths, so Augustus and some of his successors and their wives and relatives were posthumously appointed to this honorific godhead by a grateful state."[66]

Among the most famous of these so-called Divine Men was a first-century Pythagorean philosopher named Apollonius of Tyana, who, like Jesus, "gathered followers, taught, helped the poor, healed the sick, raised the dead, cast out demons, and appeared to his followers after death."[67] Other Divine Men, similarly blessed with a supernatural (virgin) birth and unusual death, but not immortal—like Plato, Empedocles, Pythagoras, and Alexander the Great—were worshiped at shrines all over the empire. As a result of the widespread fame of these figures, early Christians who lived in the Diaspora and who thought of Jesus as both human and divine, earthly yet exalted, could hardly avoid seeing him as a hero of this kind: "Greek-speaking Jews, nurtured on these ideas, were given every occasion, when they heard the message about Jesus of Nazareth and became Christians, to interpret Jesus within the framework of the Hellenistic pattern of the 'divine miracle-man.'"[68]

---

provided, not by a date, but by theological considerations" (23).

65. Borg and Crossan, *Last Week*, 3. These "gods" were thought to have brought "peace on earth." Markus says, "The figure of Jesus could easily be seen in terms of a savior-myth common to many religions" (*Christianity*, 50; see also 29, 38–39).

66. Grant, *Climax of Rome*, 168. See also Grant, *Historical Introduction*, 250. On the concepts of "Savior Gods" and "Divine Men," see Enslin, *Christian Beginnings*, 186–93; Koester, *History, Culture, and Religion*, 11, 15; Crossan, *Historical Jesus*, 354; and Brown, *Making of Late Antiquity*, 59. Brown mentions the Divine Man concept in the context of his larger discussion of the rising popularity of what he calls exceptional men—i.e., those who serve as agents of the supernatural or as mediators between heaven and earth. Thus, Christianity appealed to the masses because its apostles, martyrs, and (later) bishops were seen from this perspective (12–13, 66–68). On the divinization of Augustus, see Crossan, *Birth of Christianity*, 413–14.

67. Perrin and Duling, *New Testament*, 14. On Apollonius, see also Koester, *History, Culture, and Religion*, 375–76.

68. Schillebeeckx, *Jesus*, 425. Schillebeeckx examines this subject in greater detail on 424–28. Grant comments: "The early gentile Christian is called not only to serve God but to await the coming of his Son. Here the gentile would be on familiar ground. There were many stories in antiquity about 'divine men' who had ascended to heaven, even though there does not seem to have been any expectations that they would return. And the resurrection of an individual was not absolutely unheard

Within Christianity, some ideas of the relationship between man and God that developed along the lines of mystery god and Divine Man were eventually rejected by the church as too extreme.[69] The Gnostics—who thought of the world as a fallen place in which no one could be saved—embraced Plato's mind-body dualism, practiced asceticism in order to liberate the mind (ideas that Christians embraced quite strongly at different times and places), and also believed in a Gnostic Redeemer who descends from above, disguises himself as a human being, teaches wisdom, and returns to the world of light.[70] The Carpocracians, similarly influenced by Gnostic notions, nevertheless promoted libertinism, as did some of Paul's followers in Corinth. More important, the Carpocracians combined some features of both mystery cults and Divine Man worship. Their leader, Carpocrates, esteemed Jesus (as well as Plato, Pythagoras, and Aristotle) as a Divine Man and portrayed him as a teacher of "mysteries."[71]

---

of, even though stories of resurrection were usually questioned by the educated" (*Historical Introduction*, 389–90). This is why, MacMullen explains, the pagan world would not have reacted negatively to the Christian worship of Jesus: The idea of a divine-human being was not unusual (*Christianizing the Roman Empire*, 17). Smith discusses examples of Divine Men, including Apollonius, in *Jesus the Magician*, 18–19, 74–75, 89. See also Tabor, *Jesus Dynasty*, 60; Cumont, *After Life*, 111–15; Hengel, *Charismatic Leader*, 25–27; and Horsley and Silberman, *Message*, 155). Koester describes Alexander the Great in the role of Divine Man in *History, Culture, and Religion*, 11. On parallels regarding the virgin birth, see Robertson, *Origins of Christianity*, 75–76. On divine births, see Talbert, "Miraculous Conceptions and Births in Mediterranean Antiquity," 79–85; Nickelsburg, "First and Second Enoch," 92–95, 102–8; and Crossan, *Birth of Christianity*, 28–29.

69. Indeed, the use of this concept would also have alienated the first Christians. Says Maccoby, "Because of his pagan background, Saul [or Paul] would have read into the story of the death and resurrection of Jesus meanings which were in fact absent from the minds of the Nazarenes themselves, for these followers of Jesus were people of Pharisee background on the whole and . . . therefore, as utterly opposed to pagan schemes of salvation based on dying and resurrected deities" (*Mythmaker*, 101). See also 102, 105–6. Nevertheless, although the idea has been frequently challenged, says Young, "the total impact of the evidence has led to widespread acceptance of the view that it was the Greek-speaking Gentile converts who transformed Jesus, the Jewish Messiah of Palestine, into an incarnate divine being" ("Two Roots or a Tangled Mass?" 98). Young goes on to argue that it was particularly the Divine Man concept that influenced this transformation (100–102). She also discusses the Greek influence on Jewish concepts of the Divine Man in the inter-testamental literature (106–10).

70. Latourette says, "When combined with certain elements from Christianity, Gnosticism proved so attractive that, while no accurate figures are obtainable, the suggestion has been made that for a time the majority of those who regarded themselves as Christians adhered to one or another of its many forms" (*History of Christianity*, I, 123). Bultmann discusses the parallels between Christianity and Gnosticism in *Theology*, I, 100–107, 164–82. "One is probably justified in saying that the consciousness of the Gnostics of constituting a community bound together in a mysterious unity and foreign to the world furnishes a certain analogy to Church-consciousness, a part of which is the consciousness of being delimited from the world. And actually the Fourth Gospel's consciousness of Church unity is influenced by Gnosticism" (107).

71. Bruce, *Canon of Scripture*, 312–16. Bruce quotes from a late second-century letter from Clement of Alexandria, first published in Smith's *Clement of Alexandria and a Secret Gospel of Mark*, in which Clement accuses the Carpocracians of "unmentionable doctrines" and even worse practices. Clement refers to a secret Gospel of Mark, which, he says, should be read only by Christians "who were attaining perfection" and were therefore "being initiated into the great mysteries" (302–3).

There is some disagreement as to whether Gnosticism preceded Jesus, but there can be little doubt that the concepts of saviors and redeemers that flourished outside of Palestine in the first century strongly influenced the way Jesus was perceived by people who were exposed to these ideas. It is a commonplace among scholars that Christianity emerged as a compromise between Judaism and Hellenism. That is, it went quite far in the direction of Greco-Roman culture, but it stopped at the point at which Hellenists completely repudiated Judaism, as they did in the Gnostic movement. It is debatable whether Paul similarly repudiated Judaism, but there is no doubt that *his* Jesus, like the mystery gods, both "died and rose," and would sometime in the future "descend from heaven" so that initiates into what Paul frequently called the "mystery" of the faith, a popular word in Gnostic circles, "shall be caught up together" (1 Thess, 4:14–17; see also Eph 4:9–10).[72]

In the view of many historians, at the very time that Christianity moved out of Palestine and into the Diaspora, residents of the Roman empire had arrived at a low point of optimism and personal satisfaction. Beset by economic decline, political oppression, and social disruption, they came to see their lives as dominated by fear and frustration, and they saw the universe as a realm dominated not by opportunity and freedom, but by Fate.[73] While the Jews, especially those who lived in Palestine, clung to their messianic dream, pagans turned to new religions. In a world of transcendent gods unable to provide succor to their worshipers and with traditional religions reduced to mere ritual, the mystery cults fulfilled a need for hope and security.

These were religions in which a particular god or goddess was venerated, as we have seen, because he or she had died and returned to life. By participating in the god's death and rebirth and thereby becoming one with the god and sharing in his or her immortality, the initiate circumvented Fate and transcended the evil powers that control the cosmos. While the early Palestinian church was probably not affected by such ideas, dominated as it was by Jewish messianic concepts, the later Church could hardly avoid this influence: "The churches which arose on Hellenistic soil, even when they were predominantly Jewish Christian in character, came in close contact with the ideas of Hellenistic religion, especially with the mystery cults and the mysticism whose importance for primitive Christianity we are coming to recognize more and more clearly."[74]

72. Strong's *Exhaustive Concordance* lists no uses of the words *mystery* and *mysteries* in the Old Testament, one use in the Gospels (Mark 4:11; Luke 8:10; and Matt 13:11—all referring to "the kingdom of God"), and twenty uses in the Pauline and deutero-Pauline letters.

73. For descriptions of this pervasive sense of alienation, see Sheehan, *First Coming*, 206–8; and Martin, *Hellenistic Religions*, 21–25.

74. Weiss, *Earliest Christianity*, I, 95–97, 177. Weiss continues: "Especially prominent was the conception of a rebirth or of a dying and rising again with the dead and risen Christ. This conception seems to have been still lacking in the primitive church[,] but it emerged suddenly in Hellenistic circles" (177). On this point, Bultmann comments: "Not only do the heathen mysteries [i.e., the mystery cults] know the conception of the dying god of redemption, but the heathen-gnostic mythology above all knows the idea of a pre-existent heavenly being who, in obedience to his father's will, puts on

When Paul recommends to the followers of Jesus that they repeat his baptism, he is suggesting that they undergo something virtually indistinguishable from what millions of participants in the mystery cults experienced: "Therefore," Paul says, "we have been buried with him by baptism into death, so that, just as Christ was raised from the dead by the glory of the Father, so we too might walk in newness of life." And the goal, of course, was union with the god: "For if we have been united with him in a death like his, we will certainly be united with him in a resurrection like his" (Rom 6:4–5; see also 7:4). But it was also, significantly, union with the entire group of worshipers: "For as in one body we have many members, and not all the members have the same function, so we, who are many, have one body in Christ, and individually we are members one of another" (Rom 12:4–5).[75] By such means, members of the mystery cults similarly overcame their sense of helplessness and aloneness. Dying to this world, they were reborn to the next, which was a world of oneness rather than duality, power rather than weakness, and immortality rather than sickness and death.[76]

---

this world's clothing and takes poverty and want, hatred and persecution upon himself in order to lead his people along the path to the heavenly world" (quoted in Augstein, *Jesus Son of Man*, 98). Bultmann notes elsewhere that "the idea of a suffering, dying, rising Messiah or Son of Man was unknown to Judaism" (*Theology*, I, 31). The appeal of the mystery cults, says Latourette, "seems to have been the assurance of immortality which they gave to their members, combined with a fellowship which many craved in a world in which large numbers were uprooted individuals" (*History of Christianity*, I, 25).

75. Maccoby says that "the idea of 'being in Christ', which occurs frequently in Paul's letters, is entirely without parallel in Jewish literature, whether of the Pharisees or of any other sects . . . [H]owever, it can be paralleled without difficulty in the mystery cults" (*Mythmaker*, 63). Maccoby says later, "The basic theme in the Pauline myth can be summed up in one phrase: the descent of the divine saviour. Everything in the so-called theology stems from this": predestination, a world of light and a world of darkness, and Original Sin (184–85; see also 195–96). Chilton and Neusner comment, "Christians' insistence upon their own consciousness of God's spirit made them seem rather like some of the esoteric movements of the Graeco-Roman world, which offered initiation into the secrets of a hidden realm" (*Judaism*, 101).

76. Koester notes, suggestively, that several different concepts of God's intermediary could easily be thought of as interchangeable. That is, Isis bore some resemblance to Wisdom, who, like the logos (and Jesus), "existed before the beginning of creation" and either assisted in the creation or was the means by which the creation occurred. To know Wisdom (or Isis or the logos or Jesus) is to "recognize the true meaning of the course of the world, which will lead [the recipients of knowledge] to final justification and vindication, in spite of the contempt and the persecutions which they may now have to endure" (*History, Culture, and Religion*, 245). Jews associated the logos with Wisdom, according to Wylen, in *Jews*, 84. Cook says that Wisdom was eventually replaced by Philo's logos: "and whereas the Wisdom Literature fell into the background of Jewish thought, the essential conceptions of Wisdom and the Logos took a new form and a new life at the rise of the Jewish sect that became Christianity" (*Introduction*, 68). Cook notes that both Wisdom and the logos became agents of God and intermediaries between God and man (129). Lee says that "the eschatological prophet" of Jewish Christianity gave way before "the Greek interpretations of Jesus in the logos tradition" (*Galilean Jewishness of Jesus*, 144). Brown cites a number of passages in the Old Testament and the Apocrypha in which Wisdom is described in terms similar to those used to describe Jesus: "[B]efore the creation of the world Wisdom is created by or proceeds from God, then comes down to dwell among human beings, and offers them the food and drink of the knowledge of God." Brown continues, "This portrait of Wisdom was a major element in shaping N[ew] T[estament] Christology" (*Introduction*, 491). On Paul as a "bridge" between Jewish apocalypticism and "the normative Hellenistic mystery religion of piety and morality

Thus, it is not surprising that one of the first Hellenized Christian churches—the church in Corinth, whose members Paul addressed rather frantically in his letters to them—embraced Christianity as if it were a mystery cult. As we have seen, Paul criticized them for believing that they had acquired divine wisdom through the apostles by whom they were initiated into Christianity and that these missionaries, as well as Jesus, "became mystagogues, and baptism a mystery rite."[77] The participants displayed all the behaviors characteristic of many mystery cult participants, especially those Christian Corinthians influenced by Gnosticism, including possession of extraordinary abilities (1 Cor 12–14), esoteric wisdom (1 Cor 4:10; 8:1), and total sexual freedom (1 Cor 4:8; 6:12; 10:23). In short, as one historian of Christianity suggests, Paul's Hellenized version of Christianity "spiraled out of control," even in mainstream Christian circles: "It did not take long for those familiar with Greek mythology and Hellenistic mystery cults to catch the spirit of the resurrected Christ. And it did not take long for people with some knowledge of Greek psychology to translate the Christ myth into a symbol of personal transformation via contact with the spirit of Christ."[78]

In other words, Paul's already quasi-Gnostic, quasi-Neoplatonic interpretation of Jesus was carried one step further by the Corinthians, whose concept of deities and their worship was unrestrained by the Jewish influences that kept Paul from embracing these Hellenistic views completely. Paul thus oversold the concept of freedom to people who were ready to accept it outside its original Jewish context and from their own cultural perspective. The important question is whether this misinterpretation occurred elsewhere in the Roman empire, where the ideas that influenced the Corinthians' understanding of Christianity were likely to have influenced thousands, if not millions, of others.[79]

For their part, other Christian leaders, whether or not influenced by Paul, similarly adapted their faith to the new situation and similarly converted Hellenized gentiles who interpreted the Gospels, ineluctably, from their own point of view. This process was strongly influenced by the fact that more and more converts came from the Hellenized pagan world. In the second century, most new Christians were

---

that Christianity was eventually to become," see Segal, *Paul the Convert*, 149. Segal discusses several parallels between Christianity and the mystery religions on 24, 55, 68.

77. Koester, quoted in Crossan, *Historical Jesus*, 228. Schillebeeckx makes the same point regarding Paul's concerns about the Corinthians. He suggests that in much of the apocryphal literature the legends of Jesus and the apostles went too far (*Jesus*, 428, 432).

78. Mack, *Who Wrote?* 123.

79. *Who Wrote?* 124; see also 96, 125–30. "Obviously, the problem Paul faced in Corinth was due to the fact that these Corinthians were thoroughly at home in the Hellenistic environment of Greek life and thought. Their reasons for being interested in the Christ myth were not the same as Paul's . . . Thus the window Paul provides into this Christian congregation is an exceptional treat. The Corinthians are the first example we have of a thoroughly Hellenistic, mainly gentile, urban Christ cult in the heart of Greece. Their experience of the Christ . . . is so far removed from the persuasions of the Jewish movement that the rapid development from one to the other is simply stunning" (126). Mack discusses Paul's struggle to undo the damage on 130–37.

speakers of Greek. Indeed, the "new type of Christian," replacing the Jewish Christian, "had been taught to read . . . by the *grammaticus*, taught the art of public speaking by the *rhetor*, taught to think by the philosopher." The result was "the expression of the Christian faith in a Greek form." In the third century, the Church opened up to an influx of speakers of Latin, which resulted in an interpretation of Christianity far removed—culturally, linguistically, and geographically—from the Galilee of Jesus' life and work.[80]

Under these circumstances, "Christian evangelists rewrote their vision of Jesus and made him into the cosmic redeemer who had conquered the malevolent powers of the world."[81] Christians did not consciously change their message. Rather, later Christian converts—not only Paul, but also the author of the Gospel of John—simply interpreted Jesus from their own strongly Hellenized perspectives. Especially as the expectation of Jesus' imminent return began to fade, Christians found it easier to think of Jesus not as a messiah who would soon redeem the world by transforming it into an earthly paradise, as the Jews believed, but as a savior who would grant them immortality in another world altogether, as many pagans believed.[82] And the latter view they quite readily adopted because it matched their sense of the kind of deity that could save them.[83]

80. Danielou, "Christianity as a Missionary Religion," 293–97.

81. Sheehan, *First Coming*, 209. Sheehan lists a number of works in which scholars have dissented from Bultmann and others' association of the descending/ascending god with Gnosticism (272 n. 17). Toynbee comments: "The Greeks did not . . . adopt this originally Jewish religion without infusing it with some characteristically Greek elements. They diluted Jewish monotheism with a tincture of polytheism; they supplemented the Jewish worship of a transcendent God with the deification of a human being; and they defined the elusive tenets that were implied in this syncretism in terms of Greek logic" ("The Historical Antecedents," 41). Toynbee says in his introduction to this book that the polytheistic element is the Trinity; and the deification of Jesus is modeled on "Graeco-Roman man-worship" (14).

82. Says Wylen, "As objective historians have long realized, the Christian belief that Jesus' messianic action lies in the world of spirit, providing heavenly salvation, evolved as a reaction to Jesus' delay in returning to earth" (*Jews*, 118). Grant adds "that for pious Jews 'heaven' was [not a place, but] often a word substituted for 'God,' and that as the gospel left Jewish soil this use of 'heaven' could easily be misunderstood so that the this-worldly became other-worldly" (*Historical Introduction*, 337). Weiss says that the idea of a "savior" in the sense in which the Church used the term was Hellenistic rather than Jewish (*Earliest Christianity*, I, 113). According to Bultmann, the word "savior" was a title for both "mystery and salvation deities" (*Theology*, I, 79). See also Mack, *Who Wrote?* 146.

83. Enslin emphasizes the inadvertency of this transformation of the Christian message: "When the earliest disciples began to push out and to make proselytes they had no notion of the consequences of their actions. To think that at some specific time they deliberately altered their practice . . . is absurd." Enslin goes on to say that the first Christian proselytes, as "proselytes to Judaism[,] might be fit objects to preach to; they were not fit table companions. The bars were by no means let down overnight" (*Christian Beginnings*, 184). Specifically, the Eucharist and baptism were not "deliberately transformed by the early missionaries . . . into sacramental rites in order to rival the similar rites in the other cults." What happened was that gentiles "saw resemblances where none were originally intended," and that new conceptions of these rites were developed by gentile converts rather than Jewish or gentile preachers (199).

Furthermore, all of the Gospel writers used Greek models in framing their stories. As one scholar says, "The Gospel authors were not simply creating a life of Jesus out of thin air to match a popular literary form," such as *The Life of Aesop* or the Greek "rapture" model; "rather, they placed the teachings and actions of Jesus in narrative form according to an already existing pattern."[84] They used Greek forms for the same reason they used Greek literary techniques: These were the means available to people who spoke and wrote in Greek, studied Greek literature and philosophy, and were immersed in Greek culture.

Thus, Christianity eventually became neither Jewish nor Greek, but a blend of both traditions. However, since Jesus knew nothing about Plato, mind/body dualism, or the *logos* (through either Greek or Jewish texts), it is a legitimate question as to how much of the Hellenization of Christianity he would have approved of.[85] In other words, if, as one scholar says, "[e]very religious movement is *ipso facto* something inextricably involved in a historical and cultural process"[86]—that is, *inevitably* undergoing constant change and development—can the process go too far? In the words of another scholar, "Maybe, Christianity is an inevitable and absolutely necessary 'betrayal' of Jesus, else it might all have died among the hills of Lower Galilee."[87]

84. Wills, "The Aesop Tradition," 225. See also MacDonald, "Imitations of Greek Epic in the Gospels," 374. Schillebeeckx discusses Luke's use of the "rapture" model, which Luke appropriated "in order to get his Christian message across to the Greeks," in *Jesus*, 340–44. "Luke clothes the Christian story in concepts which are open to [the Greeks] and which they can understand"—specifically elements of the Divine Man tradition (342, 346).

85. The work of reconciling these traditions was performed by exceptional men: "Varying blends of Hebrew and Greco-Roman ideas, possessing infinite significance for the spiritual future of millions of Christians who accepted or rejected them, were being moulded by speculative theologians of unprecedented caliber" (Grant, *Climax of Rome*, 249). See also Wilken, *Christians*, 32; and Maguire, *Moral Core*, 92–93. Wright takes issue with this point, suggesting that the pagan world was not, as many scholars contend, "ready for Christianity" (*What St. Paul Really Said*, 85). Wright loses this argument, however, when he says, "My sense is that the pagan world was no more 'ready for the gospel' . . . than the Jewish world was ready to hear the news of a crucified Messiah" (86). The proof to the contrary is in the pudding. The pagan world accepted Jesus; the Jews (ultimately) did not, unless Wright is prepared to contend that the Jews were simply stiff-necked and hardhearted. Although Brown insists that the pagan idea of a Divine Man did not influence the Gospels, he acknowledges that some Greek-speaking converts to Christianity were influenced by Divine Man theology: "The mindset of the audience that received the N[ew] T[estament] message must be taken into account" (*Introduction*, 84). Supporting Wright, Hengel says, "The heart of the Christian message . . . ran counter not only to Roman political thinking, but to the whole ethos of religion in ancient times and in particular to the ideas held by educated people" (*Crucifixion*, 5; see also 10).

86. Schillebeeckx, *Jesus*, 49.

87. Crossan, *Historical Jesus*, 424. Bury makes the same point in *Later Roman Empire*, I, 372. "The power of the state became intertwined with the power of the Church Triumphant, and the original social message of the movement was all too often lost" (Horsley and Silberman, *Message*, 229). Lee contends that Jesus himself would not have understood the logos theory: It "would surely not have been part of [his] assumptive world" (*Galilean Jewishness of Jesus*, 115). Enslin says, "[T]he transfer of [the] essentially Jewish message to the outside world involved startling and tremendous changes undreamt of by the earliest preachers" (*Christian Beginnings*, 184). Of course, Enslin adds, "had there been no change, there would have been no Christianity." Enslin explains: "[T]he challenge of Jesus

ATTACK AND DEFENSE

Christianity grew very slowly at first. There were only 10,000 to 50,000 Christians in the Roman empire in the early second century[88] and 3,000,000 to 6,000,000 by the end of the third century. Supported by Constantine and other Christian emperors in the fourth century, however—and despite the opposition to the faith from Julian the Apostate—Christianity increased five- or tenfold, to 30,000,000 by AD 400.[89] Besides adding modestly to their numbers at first, Christians also slowly acquired a stronger sense of their own identity as they established a canon of distinctly Christian works for liturgical and other uses. As time passed, these writings provided them with a common body of beliefs and practices and helped to distinguish them from both Jews and pagans.

What unified Christians over time, besides the broad agreement over which texts were sacred and therefore authoritative, was the ongoing battle, from the second century on, against heretical groups and ideas; the establishment of bishops as Church leaders with special decision-making powers; and the centralization of the Church, eventually under the Bishop of Rome.[90] At the same time, however, this steady march toward *relative* unity—after all, East and West still remain divided over some theological issues—was delayed and sometimes even temporarily derailed by two things: first,

---

with its insistence on repentance, with its content the impending change, pitched in terms intelligible to Judaism, would have fallen on deaf ears in any portion of the Mediterranean basin except Palestine" (182). The religion that was "willing to adapt its message to the needs of those whom it wished to gain as converts, won" (181). On the unlikelihood that Jesus and his disciples would have accepted or even understood the theology of, say, the fourth-century Church, see references to Hatch and Kung in note 28.

88. For these estimates, see Stark, *Rise of Christianity*, 7, who puts the number of Christians in AD 100 at 7,500; and Wilken, *Christians*, 31, who puts the number in the early second century at less than 50,000. "Between about 40 and 120 CE, literary references to Christians, by pagans and Jews alike, suggest that the church as a whole expanded slowly" (Klinghoffer, *Why the Jews*, 111). Latourette notes that "Christianity had what looked like a most unpromising beginning" (*History of Christianity*, I, 33). And it continued to be relatively unknown throughout much of the first century: "Yet so small were the first Christian groups that most of them escaped the notice of those who were commenting on their times and all but a few of such documents as they themselves left have perished" (66).

89. Ehrman, ed., *After the New Testament*, 7. Ehrman refers to "the conversion mania of the 4th century" (7). Latourette says, "By the close of its first five centuries Christianity had become the professed faith of the overwhelming majority of the population of the Roman Empire" (*History of Christianity*, I, 97). For similar figures, see MacMullen, *Christianizing the Roman Empire*, 86. MacMullen provides a plausible explanation for the remarkable growth of Christianity in 110–11.

90. Says Ehrman: "Early in the second century, there were calls for a rigid church structure that could bring order out of chaos in the early Christian communities and so guarantee the preservation and perpetuation of the true religion. By the middle of the third century, the leaders of the Christian church could exercise considerable power over their congregations" (*After the New Testament*, 5). Church councils, which proliferated in the fourth century, were similarly intended "to introduce uniformity and discipline into the different Christian communities" (Parkes, *Conflict*, 174). Mack says that, as the authority of the bishops increased, the authority of Jesus' sayings declined (*Lost Gospel*, 233). See also, on the influence of both canonization and church organization on the development of Christianity, Markus, *Christianity*, 64–66.

the diversity of early Christianity and, second, Roman hostility toward this (at first) strange, potentially dangerous, and unauthorized "superstition," a word the Romans used to designate belief systems that appeared to be overly emotional, atheistic (particularly insofar as they were espoused by people who did not worship the gods that made Rome great), undistinguished by age (in contrast to Judaism and Mithraism), and therefore inauthentic.[91]

Like Judaism in the first century, "Christianity during the first three centuries of the Common Era was remarkably diverse." Christians argued—often heatedly and sometimes violently—over the relationship between Jesus and God the Father, the relationship between the Church and society at large, the status of the Jews, the efficacy of martyrdom, the status of priests and lay people who had denied their faith under torture, and the role of women in the church.[92] The Christians who eventually established their own views as orthodox were originally called heretics themselves. That is, those who ultimately prevailed in the battle over theology, christology, canonicity, and governance (among many other issues) were themselves dismissed as dissidents by Ebionites, Donatists, Sabellians, Gnostics, Montanists, Docetists, Phibionites, Nazarenes, Carpocracians, and Arians (among many other groups).

Particularly in the fourth and fifth centuries, after Constantine's conversion to Christianity, bishops regularly deposed, anathematized, exiled, and excommunicated other bishops; councils and synods, meeting one right after the other, praised or exonerated bishops, priests, and lay people who had been indicted or condemned by the earlier group; popes and bishops often reversed the decisions of their predecessors. They did these things because, unlike paganism, Christianity was a credal religion in which membership was limited to those who embraced a particular set of beliefs.[93] Thus, the goal of every Christian sect was to establish itself as the representative of the official creed and, if not eliminate all the other competing creeds from the face of the earth, at least limit their power and influence.

Unresolvable as many issues were—that is, insofar as they were based on such abstruse and abstract concepts that they could not be empirically or logically settled one way or another—many Christians (both lay and clerical) resorted to violence. John Chrysostom's supporters set fire to the Sancta Sophia in Constantinople, which was later destroyed by angry Monophysites. Bloody riots broke out between this

91. On Christianity as a superstition, see Wilken, *Christians*, xvii, 32, 50–52, 63.

92. Ehrman, ed., *After the New Testament*, 1. Latourette comments: "Even in the first generation of its existence the Church was torn by dissensions" (*History of Christianity*, I, 114). Elsewhere, Latourette discusses controversies associated with the Persian church, the Gnostics, the Marcionites, the Montanists, the Novatians, and the Donatists (103–4, 123–29, 137–39). Bultmann adds that this diversity also existed among different communities, based on which disciple founded them and the degree to which they were influenced by Judaism, Gnosticism, and Hellenism in general (*Theology*, I, 63; see also Bruce, *Canon of Scripture*, 314; and Brown, *Churches*, 17).

93. "Two of the chief points in which this faith differed from the Roman State religion were its exclusiveness and the vital importance which it assigned to dogma" (Bury, *Later Roman Empire*, I, 365).

group and Nestorians. Circumcellions attacked non-Donatist churches in North Africa. Followers of two men who competed for the papacy in c. 500 murdered priests, burned cloisters, and beat each other up. Supporters of Timothy Aelurus rioted and dismembered the new bishop of Alexandria, Proterius, after which Timothy became the bishop of Alexandria.

In one of the longest theological battles, Arians periodically fought in the streets of Alexandria against Athanasians throughout the fourth century. Like all of the controversies that ignited violence between overcommitted participants, the issue that moved the followers of Athanasius, the bishop of Alexandria, and Arias, a priest who was supported by Eusebius, the bishop of Nicomedia, was the unanswerable question as to the precise relationship between Jesus and God the Father, which was not settled (at least to some people's satisfaction) until half a century *after* the Nicene Creed was first composed in 325.[94] Eusebius of Caesaria, the great historian of the Church and a moderate in the controversy, described Constantine's palace in Nicea as an armed camp at the conclusion of the council that established the Creed. The palace guards, he says, stood at the entrance with drawn swords.[95]

Christianity was also challenged by the negative attitude of the Romans toward a religion that was, ironically, acceptable as a branch of Judaism (which, though peculiar, was nevertheless venerable by virtue of its antiquity), but highly suspect as an independent faith.[96] The Romans saw Christians as "ignorant, lower class, obstinate, superstitious, and antisocial," as well as atheistic.[97] According to one pagan critic, whose remarks were not at all unusual, the Christians were "a gang of outlawed and reckless desperadoes" who hated the gods of the Romans, ate babies and drank their blood, held nocturnal orgies, and lived in poverty—a clear sign of their alienation from the true gods traditionally worshiped by Romans. Minucius Felix, who recorded this attack in *Octavius* (8:3; 9:5; 12:2), defended his religion by failing to mention "the

94. Bruce discusses the fact that every heretical Christian sect thought of itself as orthodox. See, especially, *Canon of Scripture*, 145–48, 168–69, and 312f., on Valentinians, Montanists, and Carpocracians, respectively.

95. Eusebius is quoted in Crossan, *Historical Jesus*, 424.

96. As I said earlier, the Jews had been granted special status by Julius Caesar. That is, among other things, they were exempted from the imperial command to worship the Roman gods. "Christians probably received similar protection," Brown says, "so long as they were thought of as Jews" (*Introduction*, 65–66). Jews and Christians, Jones explains, "had very similar objectionable features, but in the eyes of the Roman government there was one vital difference. The Jews were a race who practised the traditional worship of their ancestors, and had at an early date, while still a political unit, obtained from Rome legal recognition for their peculiar practices. With their great respect for ancestral custom and legal precedent, the Romans therefore tolerated and even privileged Jews. Christians, on the other hand, were innovators, starting a new cult which, on the face of it, being devoted to a criminal duly executed by a Roman governor, was undesirable" (*Constantine*, 44–45).

97. Ehrman, ed., *After the New Testament*, 25. At first, says Wilken, Romans saw Christians as odd, but insignificant (*Christians*, xv): "Most inhabitants of the Roman Empire had never heard of Christianity" (31). However, some pagans knew of Christianity by the second century (92). According to Grant, pagans mocked the Christians for their blind faith (*Climax of Rome*, 209).

most characteristic parts of the faith," including "the stumbling block of the Cross." But this was the path that Christians seem to have most often (or, at least, most effectively) pursued: "There was a large element of compromise."[98]

Although there were no Roman laws against Christians until the reign of Decius in c. 250, they were attacked by Nero in 64 and by Trajan and Marcus Aurelius in the second century. The persecutions continued under Domitian and Diocletian, and—although the number of Christians who were executed might have been greatly exaggerated[99]—certainly hundreds, if not thousands, of Christians were murdered by Romans, and many more were intimidated, beaten, or flogged.[100] All of this ended when Theodosius I made Christianity the official religion of the empire in the late fourth century, almost exactly 350 years after the Crucifixion.

How did this happen? The answer is that, just as pagan ideas were Christianized, so Christianity, as we have seen, was Hellenized.[101] The title "Son of man" disappeared

98. Mattingly, *Roman Imperial Civilisation*, 232–33. Mattingly adds that the radicalism of Christianity "as a religion of poor, simple people," which was "revolutionary in preaching so uncompromisingly the equality of men in the sight of God and the meaninglessness of caste and social orders," had to appeal to "a society which set the highest value on social position." Something had to give (233). Thus, as Mattingly explains later, "The democratic spirit of the early Church began to lose its purity when Christianity came to take a prominent place among the higher as well as the among the lower orders" (236).

99. Ehrman comments: "We do not know how many Christians were martyred in the first three centuries; judging from the details provided in the early Christian historian Eusebius, however, they probably numbered in the hundreds (rather than many thousands)" (*After the New Testament*, 27). Latourette similarly speculates that there might have been "very few" Christian martyrs in the three and a half centuries after the Crucifixion—certainly, he adds, far fewer than there were Jewish martyrs throughout the same period. Rather than being regularly thrown to the lions, Christians suffered confiscation of property, imprisonment, torture, and hard labor in the mines (*History of Christianity*, I, 81, 85–86). MacMullen agrees, citing W. H. C. Frend, *Martyrdom and Persecution in the Early Church* and R. M. Grant, *Early Christianity and Society*, in *Christianizing the Roman Empire*, 33, 134 n. 13. Clark says, "It is not possible to say how many Christians fell victim to such attacks . . . : the numbers may have been in hundreds rather than thousands over three centuries" (*Christianity and Roman Society*, 47). Even the Great Persecution, under Diocletian in 303—which was "a systematic attempt to eliminate" Christianity and resulted in the burning of books and the denunciation of Christian practices—was mostly an attack on Church leaders. Wherever the persecution was severe (depending on the implementation by local administrators), Christians moved away, apostatized, lost their property, went to prison, suffered torture, or faced martyrdom. Manicheans were similarly persecuted (47–51). Priests who ran away, went into hiding, or in any way evaded a direct confession of their faith were later anathematized by Donatists, who regarded all priestly functions, including baptism, by such "apostates" as invalid. Mack calls Nero's persecution "an ad hoc, localized, scape-goating strategy that everyone understood to be the action of a madman." Furthermore, it "was highly exaggerated by Tacitus, who reported it in order to discredit Nero." "Modern scholars," Mack continues, "cannot find any evidence for a Domitian persecution" (*Who Wrote?* 196). Parkes discusses what he calls "a perpetual tendency to exaggerate the persecutions altogether" in *Conflict*, 88–91.

100. Bainton provides a brief, though comprehensive overview of the persecutions through the third century in *Early Christianity*, 23–27.

101. This question should be asked along with a companion question: "Did Christianity transform Roman society, or did Roman society transform Christianity?" Clark answers, as do most historians of this period, "Either case can be argued, and in either case the transformation could be for the better

because it was meaningless to Romans; "Christ" was assumed to be Jesus' last name; and "Son of God" was interpreted in the context of mystery religions, Gnosticism, Stoicism, and the worship of Greek and Roman gods.[102] I do not mean this merely in the sense in which I have described it so far—that is, Christian missionaries in the Diaspora understood Christianity from a Hellenistic perspective; they therefore presented to the pagan world a Hellenized version of their faith; and the recipients of this message interpreted it from their similarly Hellenized point of view.[103] I mean that Christians embarked on a campaign to make Christianity appear to be (1) compatible with the ideas of pagan religion and philosophy; (2) non-threatening, in the sense that it did not challenge the political and economic establishment; (3) tolerant, at least of some aspects of paganism; and (4) superior to both paganism and Judaism.

As the examples in Paul's letters and John's Gospel suggest, the most important bridge between paganism and Christianity was forged, albeit inadvertently, by Plato. Among all the available Greco-Roman philosophies, the "philosophical theism" of Plato proved to be the most attractive to the earliest non-Palestinian Christian thinkers, especially in the second and third centuries and after. Indeed, "it was Platonic theism, as taken over, adapted to the Christian faith, and developed by St. Justin, the Alexandrians Clement and Origen, and the Fathers of the Church of the 4th and 5th centuries, which became the foundation of traditional Christian philosophy and theology in both East and West."[104] These Christian philosophers, among many "philosophically trained gentiles [who] began to flock to Christianity," saw a relationship between Greek philosophical wisdom and Jewish biblical wisdom and concluded that both came from God. Thus, when they attacked Roman polytheism, they claimed that "they were merely following in the footsteps of the best pagan philosophers and that their doctrines, though outlandish, were in agreement with the teachings found in philosophy."[105]

---

or for the worse" (*Christianity and Roman Society*, 115). Clark explains her point on the following two pages.

102. Mack says, "The son of man was not at all a felicitous construction in Greek, nor did it make much sense in Greek" (*Lost Gospel*, 159). Bornkamm says that the early Church spoke "in the language of a particular time and situation"—or, better, in two different times and situations—and therefore in one language for Jews and in another language for pagans (*Jesus of Nazareth*, 189–90).

103. Gonzalez explains (1) that early Christians saw similarities between their ideas on God and immortality and those of Plato and his intellectual heirs; (2) that they used the latter formulations in their criticism of pagan polytheism; and (3) that they began to understand "their own faith" in these terms. In addition, some Christians used the Stoic ideas of natural law and *apatheia*, with the same results. They borrowed concepts that, first, helped demonstrate to potential converts that Christianity was rational and respectable and, second, enabled them to understand Christianity from their own perspective. In the end, the proselytizers themselves saw Christianity from that point of view. In a sense, therefore, they converted themselves (*Story of Christianity*, 16–17). Gonzalez names the early apologists on 52–53.

104. Armstrong, "Greek Philosophy from the Age of Cicero to Plotinus," 212. Armstrong discusses Plotinus' influence on Christianity on 212–14.

105. Wolfson, "Greek Philosophy in Philo and the Church Fathers," 309. On Philo's allegorical

Thus, as one historian explains, "Christianity survived and spread by the classic technique of cells linked by networks, then made itself acceptable by interpreting unfamiliar Jewish scripture through familiar Greek philosophy and by teaching ethics that were already the norm for decent Roman citizens."[106] Justin Martyr, for example, presented Christianity as "the true philosophy" in order to fight off the charge that Christianity was just another cult of the kind that was disdained by the Roman elite and suspected of subversion by the Roman authorities. To this end, Justin compared Christian and Roman beliefs and practices that could be said to be similar, if not the same. For example, he argued that the two groups' views of final punishment were identical: "Plato . . . said that Rhadamanthus and Minos would punish the wicked who came before them. We say that this will happen, but at the hands of Christ."[107]

Before Theodosius established Christianity as the official religion of the Roman empire and, therefore, as the main religion of the Western world, Christians made every effort to convince pagans that Christianity did not significantly contradict paganism and that it in no way threatened the status quo. In short, they tried to persuade the gentiles in the Diaspora that, particularly unlike Judaism, whose adherents rebelled against the Roman empire in AD 66 and 132, Christianity represented cooperation, common sense, and conservatism. Three centuries before Theodosius' world-changing act, Christians began to write *apologias*—defenses—intended to fend off Roman persecution, the first of which, some scholars believe, was Acts of the Apostles, "written to a Roman administrator named Theophilus precisely to show that Christians are socially innocuous and therefore should not be persecuted."[108]

method of interpretation and its influence on Christianity, see 309–10. On Philo's and Christianity's theory of the logos, see 312–15. This discussion is very thorough.

106. Clark, *Christianity and Roman Society*, 14. As Danielou says, even the "Christian code of morals" matched that of the pagans, a point made by a Christian apologist in the *Epistle to Diognetus*. That is, "the way of life within which this moral code was given expression was the way of Hellenistic society" ("Christianity as a Missionary Religion," 296).

107. Meeks makes the first point about Justin in *First Urban Christians*, 81; and the second in *Origins of Christian Morality*, 123. "Justin's was the first serious attempt in the history of Christian thought to find a way of relating Christian belief with the thought of the Greco-Roman world" (Markus, *Christianity in the Roman World*, 43).

108. Ehrman, ed., *After the New Testament*, 51. Parkes says that by the mid-second century Christianity was "a separate religion busily engaged in apologetics to the Greek and Roman world, and anxious to establish its antiquity, respectability and loyalty" (*Conflict*, 77). Part of the goal was to fend off persecution. Another was to establish common ground, for example, by emphasizing the Christian concern for piety, which was important to Romans, who sometimes charged the Church with "disloyalty to the gods of city and state" (Lieu, *Image and Reality*, 163, 187). Wilson notes that Luke's portrait of Paul as a Roman citizen "completely in harmony with the rest of the Christian community, though much at odds with the troublesome synagogues," makes the same point. Wilson includes among the earliest apologias the Gospel of Luke: "It was to safeguard Christians against this sort of bad press [i.e., the kind that came from Romans like Tacitus] that Luke wrote his accounts of Roman soldiers being commended by Christ for their faithfulness [and] of a centurion standing at the foot of the Cross and exclaiming that Jesus was the son of God" (*Jesus*, 26–27). Horsley and Silberman, after making the same point, add this comment on Luke's Gospel: "The story of the omen-rich birth of the world savior, adored by the humble shepherds and praised by the angels who heralded a new era of peace

Even earlier, of course, Paul was concerned about the proper behavior of his followers not only in terms of its effect on group unity, but also in terms of how it was perceived by non-Christians. He told the Thessalonians "to aspire to live quietly, to mind your own affairs, and to work with your hands, as we charged you; so that you may command the respect of outsiders, and be dependent on nobody" (Thess 4:11; see also Col 4:5 [RSV]). He ordered Corinthians to tone down their physical manifestations of spirituality, especially speaking in tongues, lest outsiders think them insane (1 Cor 14:23). In other words, Christians should be guided by both "the will of God" (Thess 4:3, 5:18) *and* the expectations of the pagan world. Paul's purpose was (1) to prevent pagans from developing negative opinions about Christianity and (2) to appeal to pagans as potential converts. Later works, both canonical and otherwise, contended that Christians were not atheistic, promiscuous, cannibalistic, antisocial, or disloyal to the emperor, as had been charged by non-Christians, as well as Christians attacking other Christians.

Indeed, the writers of the deutero-Pauline letters, following Paul's lead in 1 Corinthians 11:3–10, emphasized the need for Christians to maintain a hierarchical order in their homes, which required the strict obedience of wives to husbands, children to parents, and slaves to masters (Col 3:18–22; Eph 5:22–25; 6:1–5). In 1 Timothy, women are told not only to subordinate themselves to their husbands, but to dress modestly, reject adornments, maintain silence, and never assume the role of teacher (2:9–14). This advice was derived from the so-called *haustafeln*—a household code popular in the pagan world and intended as a guide to family and community organization. By the time 1 Peter was written, early in the second century, the rule of submission was extended to all Christians in relation to all existing laws and governments: "Submit yourselves to every ordinance of man for the Lord's sake: whether it be to the king, as supreme; or unto governors . . . For so is the will of God" (2:13–15, Titus 3:1). According to one historian, such rules "serve[d] as a defense against the typical objection which Greco-Roman writers urged against novel cults: that they corrupt households and hence threaten the basis of the whole social fabric."[109]

and prosperity, offered a familiar literary opening that was routinely used in the personality cults of the emperors" (*Message*, 227). On Luke, see also Mack, *Lost Gospel*, 186. Mack adds later, "Reading the New Testament against the background of the institutional and theological history of Christianity from the second to the fourth centuries, one senses a very strong flavor of accommodation" (235). Brown says that the pastoral letters, with their emphasis on the subordination of women, were meant to show that Christianity was not extreme (*Churches*, 44, 46). Brown adds that 1 Peter was intended to show that Christians were both moral and obedient (78 n. 12). Lieu reminds her readers that Jews, like Christians, appealed to Romans for acceptance, as in Philo's *Apology on Behalf of the Jews* and Josephus' *Against Apion*. In fact, she adds, the second-century Christian apologies were unquestionably indebted to these predecessors (*Image and Reality*, 157–59).

109. Meeks, *First Urban Christians*, 106. "The household duty code," says White, from which Paul drew his moral principles, "was a well-known formula drawn from Greek philosophical discussions on household management" (*From Jesus to Christianity*, 274–75). Commenting on the code as it appears in 1 Peter, Mack says that, although Christians were "preparing for the final judgment" as exiles and aliens, they nevertheless took great care to respect the earthly powers (that is, the emperor and

In the *Letter to Diognetus*, an anonymous work of c. 200, the writer argues that Christians "obey the established laws" and even transcend them "in their private lives" (5:10). In his *Apology*, written at about the same time, Tertullian says, "We pray, also, for the emperors, for their ministers and those in power, that their reign may continue, that the state may be at peace, and *that the end of the world may be postponed*" (39:2; my emphasis). In short, "Thy kingdom come—later."[110] Under the same political pressures, "Render to Caesar the things that are Caesar's" came to mean—for example, in Justin's *Apology*—that Christians have been directed by Jesus to be loyal to whichever Caesar happens to be in power.[111] After all, obedience to and respect for (as well as the payment of taxes to) established authority had been urged, not only in 1 Peter and Titus, but by Paul: "Let every person be subject to the governing authorities; for there is no authority except from God, and those authorities that exist have been instituted by God" (Rom 13:7).

As we have seen, some of these apologias, following Justin Martyr's example, were written by pagan converts to Christianity who not only defended their religion against pagan accusations, but also presented themselves as thoughtful and responsible people who embraced a rational faith that was, properly understood, compatible with paganism. Like Philo, who interpreted Judaism in the light of his Platonic ideas, these Hellenized Christians could hardly avoid both understanding and promoting Christianity as reasonable and respectable. For example, the author of *1 Clement*, writing at the end of the first century, embraced many of the values of the Roman aristocracy: "idealization of civic harmony (*homonoia*) and dislike of strife (*stasis, eris, schism*), firm support for the patriarchal household, and approval of the hierarchy of status in the city, with deference due to the patrons."[112]

---

local governor) and live obediently according to the will of God and the law of the land (*Who Wrote?* 208–9). The code was "well loved by Hellenistic moralists and readily adapted by Jewish apologetic self-descriptions in the Hellenistic environment. Here [in the New Testament] it is used to underline the stability and harmony of the Christian household, in contrast to the mystical preoccupations and sexual asceticism of the opponents" (Meeks, *First Urban Christians*, 127). Meeks also touches on the tendency of Christians to adopt the conventional morality in *Origins of Christian Morality*, 15, 66–69. "Perhaps the chief point that emerges from our survey of some of the commonest forms of early Christian moral speech is how ordinary this morality seems to have been, in both form and content" (84).

110. Pelikan connects Tertullian's statement to his (and, to some extent, the Church's) "new understanding of the meaning of history, an understanding according to which Jesus was not simply going to be the end of history by his second coming in the future, but already was the Turning Point of History, a history that even if it were to continue, had been transformed and overturned by his first coming in the past" (*Jesus Through the Centuries*, 25–26).

111. In *Jesus of Nazareth*, Bornkamm rejects this interpretation as a distortion of Jesus' sentiments (123). Borg and Crossan discuss this misreading of Jesus' words in *Last Week*, 61–64. The quotations from the *Letter to Diognetus* and Tertullian can be found in Ehrman, ed., *After the New Testament*, 73, 350.

112. Meeks, *Origins of Christian Morality*, 46. Markus says that, although "[e]ducated Romans" might have continued to disparage Christians as "barbarians," "the distance which separated Christianity from the cultivated paganism of the townsman was very much less than that which separated

For the two centuries preceding Julian's brief reign, Roman Christians thus worked hard to establish connections between Christianity and paganism.[113] Specifically, they argued that the God they worshiped was the God worshiped by Greeks and Romans. They described Him in terms that their audience could appreciate (e.g., "ineffable" and "inexpressible")[114] and battled against the contention of such anti-Christian writers as Celsus and Porphyry that there were no legitimate links between paganism and this upstart religion. Justin Martyr claimed that the most outstanding Greek philosophers—for example, Socrates and Heraclitus—were actually Christians, as were some people who were otherwise known as Jews, including Abraham and Elijah.[115] Melito went as far as to suggest that the success of the empire under Augustus owed something to Christianity, which flowered at the same time.[116]

In the interest of toning down the radical overtones of Luke's seemingly unequivocal opposition to riches in his Gospel, as well as his portrait of the earliest Christian communities as overtly communistic in Acts of the Apostles, Clement of Alexandria suggested that Jesus was more interested in "the use rather than the accident of possession." That is, despite the implications of Luke 18:22 and 24 (Matt 19:21, 24; Mark

---

both from the life and outlook of the backward peoples of the countryside" (*Christianity*, 79; see also 45–46, 85).

113. Justin Martyr, Clement of Alexandria, Origen, and Augustine were equally interested in reconciling these religions. For the first three, the concept of the logos helped them to both comprehend and explain Jesus. On the ideas of these writers, see Grant, *Climax of Rome*, 209–11. It is indicative of their success that, as Grant says, Jesus was portrayed frequently on the sarcophagi of the late third century as a philosopher (211). According to Latourette, St. Ambrose "combined a Stoic background with Christian faith" (*History of Christianity*, I, 98), and St. Augustine was influenced by both Manicheism and Neoplatonism (96). Grant says elsewhere that Justin's *Dialogue with Trypho* is "significant because it recognizes Greek philosophy, and especially Platonism, as a preparation for the truths of the Christian religion" (*Antonines*, 120). Responding to pagan attacks on Christianity and "knowing that Scripture would not convince his opponents," Lactantius (in *Divine Institutes*) "argued from classical sources." Answering the charge that Christians ignored the wisdom of Greco-Roman philosophers, "he replied that Christianity fulfilled their ideals and therefore deserved toleration until its merits were recognized" (Clark, *Christianity and Roman Society*, 51).

114. In *Theology*, Bultmann provides examples of the "Hellenistic manner of describing the nature of God by the via negationis" (the way of negation), which, he says, was "appropriated" by Christians, such as Paul, Ignatius, and Clement (I, 72). Akenson notes that the New Testament writers changed God's name from Yahweh to Theos. "Since this does not occur in the Greek translations of the Hebrew scriptures which predate Christianity, it has to be taken as an intentional management of vocabulary by either the framers or the copyists of the New Testament." The goal, Akenson says, was to present to Greek-speaking readers not "a Semitic deity," but a god "more compatible with Hellenistic and Roman civilizations" (*Saint Saul*, 59).

115. On Justin's connections to "pagan philosophy," see Gonzalez, *Story of Christianity*, 54–56. Justin particularly made use of the logos as a bridge between Christianity and paganism. Hilary made a similar journey from pagan philosophy to Christianity, according to MacMullen, *Christianizing the Roman Empire*, 69–70.

116. On both subjects, see Lieu, *Image and Reality*, 177, 182–83. Like Aristides, Melito argues that all good things happen because of Christianity, and, he adds (in Lieu's words), "if Christianity should cease to flourish, no one will be answerable for the consequences to the Empire but the Emperor himself" (183).

10:21, 25), Christian converts, Clement said, did not really have to sell their possessions and give the proceeds to the poor. Thus, despite his passionate opposition to "any luxury and ostentation," Clement was interested, as Paul was, in making converts and therefore emphasized the Aristotelian middle way.[117] Similarly, the author of *The Shepherd of Hermas* says, "Blessed are they who are wealthy and understand that their riches are from the Lord, for he who understands this will be able to do some service." The statement is closer to the common-sense wisdom of the Book of Proverbs than to the sentiments of the speaker in Luke 6:20 and 6:24: "Blessed are you poor," and "Woe to you who are rich."[118]

Many Church leaders had been pagan intellectuals before they became Christians, and many, like Clement of Alexandria, were comfortable reading Greek literature and philosophy along with the New Testament.[119] Some, like Origen, repudiated their pagan past, but Christian leaders of the second century and after, including Origen, could not entirely renounce their earlier immersion in Hellenism because it was an indispensable part of their mental training.[120] Augustine, who was impressed by Ambrose's ability to express Christian doctrine in the language of Greek philosophy, seems to have become a Neoplatonist at nearly the same time that he became a Christian.[121] And he was slow to reject the classical Greek works that had shaped his thinking and, in fact, enabled him to appreciate Christianity. Classically educated Christians "continued to use the vocabulary and thought-patterns of philosophical debates." And even in the fifth and sixth centuries, philosophers in the cultural centers of the eastern Mediterranean continued to lecture their Christian and non-Christian students on Platonism and argue that the old Roman gods were "authentic symbols of the divine."[122]

It might have been disingenuous of Jews to accuse Christians of falsely interpreting the Jewish Bible by reading it allegorically since the exegetical method of allegorical interpretation was originally developed by Philo. However, when they claimed that

117. In, e.g., *The Educator*, Bk. 2:1, Bk. 3:10. On Clement, see Gonzalez, *Story of Christianity*, 71–73; and Chadwick, *Early Church*, 98. The relevant passages from *The Educator* can be found in Ehrman, ed., *After the New Testament*, 389, 398. Lucian ridiculed Christians for both their flight from reason and their naïve insistence on common ownership (Grant, *Antonines*, 125).

118. These passages are quoted and commented on in Crossan, *Birth of Christianity*, 402.

119. On Clement's theory that Greek philosophy was a necessary preparation for Christianity, see Pelikan, *Jesus Through the Centuries*, 38–45.

120. "[T]hough Origen sold his library of Greek literature and gave up this kind of teaching, the influence of philosophy on his thought is very clear not only from fragments of his lost *Miscellanies* but also from the structure and content of his treatise *On First Principles* and from the ideas and references provided in his late apology *Against Celsus*" (Grant, "Gnosticism, Marcion, Origen," 328). Grant's brief introduction to Origen (328–30) is excellent.

121. Markus says, "It was with the aid of Plotinus' metaphysics that Augustine of Hippo, converted from Manichean dualism, would find a way of reconciling evil with the goodness of the universe created by an all-powerful and perfectly good God" (*Christianity*, 38).

122. Clark, *Christianity and Roman Society*, 113–14. On the treatment of Christianity as a philosophy as well as a religion, see Markus, *Christianity*, 40–43.

Christians radically adjusted "the unalterable religion revealed to Moses to make it more palatable to Gentile prejudices" they were at least half right.[123] After all, Tertullian, one of the great Christian apologists of the second century, citing Paul's rejection of philosophy, derided his Christian contemporaries for dressing up their religion in Greek philosophical terms: "For worldly wisdom culminates in philosophy with its rash interpretation of God's nature and purpose. It is philosophy that supplies the heresies with their equipment." What disturbed Tertullian in particular was Greek philosophy, from Stoicism to Heraclitus to Aristotle. "What," he asked, "has Jerusalem to do with Athens?" (*Prescription of the Heretics*, chap. 7).[124]

Like Tertullian, many gentile Christians accused other gentile Christians of over-paganizing or over-Hellenizing the Church. Tatian, author of a synthesis of the Gospels and a student of Justin's, questioned his mentor's interest in philosophy and defended Christianity as a "barbarism." Other Church leaders, like Hippolytus (a second-century Roman priest) and Cyprian (the second-century Roman bishop) applied Tertullian's anti-Hellenist attitude to the Church itself, insisting on a strict separation between the "true Church of the Spirit" and the corrupting secularism of the outside world. By the fourth century, Jerome and Augustine were prepared to abandon the classical heritage, which they once thought had nurtured their minds and enriched their spirits. The latter wrote *On Christian Teaching*, an attempt to supplant the classical curriculum with a biblical one.[125] Epiphanius, bishop of Salamis in the fourth century, charged Origen with "adulterating the purity of true faith with the poison of pagan culture." In fact, Epiphanius criticized Origen for using the exegetical method that the Jews accused Christians of abusing. Vigilantius regarded vigils and the worship of the saints to be "pagan infiltrations into the church."[126]

Before Christianity became the official religion of the empire, Christians generally pursued a policy of conciliation with potential converts. Thus, Christian congregants in Spain were permitted to hold official positions in the cult of the emperor. In the third century, Gregory, bishop of Pontus (in Asia Minor), aided the conversion of almost the entire populace of his native city by "substituting festivals in honour of the Christian martyrs for the feasts of the old gods." Also, the king of Armenia sustained

123. Chadwick, *Early Church*, 66.

124. The quoted passage is from Ehrman, ed., *After the New Testament*, 213. Julian the Apostate similarly charged that Christians had compromised their principles and thereby corrupted Christianity itself by embracing the ideas of paganism. "The process, he claimed, had begun with the New Testament writing for it was John's Gospel which made Jesus a God as the other three did not. In the succeeding centuries, Christians, he said, had departed from the primitive pattern in their veneration of the relics of martyrs and in the exaltation of Mary as the Mother of God" (Bainton, *Early Christianity*, 71).

125. Markus, *Christianity*, 44–45, 104, 131, 138. Markus explains Tertullian's position on 49–51, and the difference between Ambrose, as a supporter of the "imperial" Church, and both Jerome and Augustine, who lost confidence in the Church's ability to influence Roman culture without suffering some degree of corruption and contamination, on 120–22.

126. Chadwick, *Early Church*, 184, 214. See also Clark, *Christianity and Roman Society*, 58.

the mass conversion of his subjects by transforming pagan shrines into Christian ones and encouraging pagan priests to retain the same title when they became Christians.[127] In this way, says one historian, "[t]he church baptised—invested with new Christian meaning—as much of the old paganism as it could."[128]

Even as representatives of the dominant faith in the empire, Christians were willing to proceed slowly. On the one hand, the state made every effort to close down temples and otherwise stop pagans from participating in religious ceremonies. For example, although many Christians, like Constantine, worshiped the Sun God as well as the Christian God (and also, in Constantine's case, Cybele), Pope Leo I chastised worshipers at St. Peter's for praying to the Sun God on the steps of the basilica before they went inside to pray to Jesus. On the other hand, however, the Church was often willing to compromise. Faced with the problem of imposing Christianity on *all* the residents of the empire, especially when the local population strongly resisted the change, some priests and bishops repackaged pagan temples, relics, and ritual practices as Christian. Local gods were replaced by saints and martyrs. The relics and bodies of the latter replaced the relics and bodies of the former.[129] Pagan symbols were Christianized.

The Parthenon in Athens, for example, was fitted out as a church and renamed St. Mary, allowing formerly pagan patrons of the temple to return with less pain and uncertainty to their place of worship. The Virgin Mary herself substituted for fertility goddesses. The good shepherd, a boy or young man carrying a sheep, which had been a pagan symbol of *philanthropia*, was recycled as a symbol of Jesus. Such pagan symbols as peacocks, doves, and (of course) fish were appropriated by Christians and given new meanings. At Caesarea Philippi, a pair of bronze statues of a woman bending on one knee and appealing to a standing man for help, originally a pagan work, was taken over by Christians as a symbol of Jesus healing a petitioner. Finally, it was destroyed by anti-Christian pagan vandals. Clearly, at some point—or, better, at different points in different places—it was difficult to tell what was Christian and what was pagan.

Among the more difficult of pagan practices for the newly empowered Church to suppress were dancing and drinking. Several bishops, including Ambrose and Augustine, were appalled when their congregants danced before, during, and after worship services. Former pagans were also accustomed to playing pipes, clapping hands, and beating drums to accompany their own (pagan) religious ceremonies. The Church compromised by simply Christianizing the music—i.e., allowing these activities (at least, drumming and piping) to accompany hymns: "The church, considering how the

127. Latourette, *History of Christianity*, I, 76, 79.

128. Mattingly, *Roman Imperial Civilisation*, 242.

129. Clark, *Christianity and Roman Society*, 57–58. On the continuation of these transformations of pagan into Christian practices in the Middle Ages, see Heer, *Medieval World*, 56. According to Trevor-Roper, "[P]agan ceremonies . . . quickly crystallized round the teaching of Christ" (*Rise of Christian Europe*, 62).

boundaries around itself were defined, and to set it off from rival cults without too much reducing the rewards of life for those who were converted, had to take account of such practical considerations" as defiance or resentment. As for drinking, which was customary at pagan festivals, the Church made the same accommodation. Since resistance to the prohibition of drinking on religious occasions was widespread and unshakable, the official policy was to allow "the cheerful gathering of Our subjects and communal general happy mood," induced by the consumption of wine.[130]

In many instances, manifestations of paganism persisted because they were clandestine or grudgingly tolerated or willingly incorporated into Christianity. Rites were practiced secretly. Peasants continued to honor the old gods. Pagan shrines endured, especially in remote places. Some priests passed out amulets with biblical inscriptions. Pagan festivals had to be continually suppressed, even in Rome. Incense, lights, and flowers—formerly used in pagan ceremonies—showed up in Christian church services. In Julian's reign, two men named Apollinaris (father and son), in an attempt to get Christian ideas back into the official curriculum from which Julian had banned them, rewrote the scriptures in Greek form, including epic poems, odes, and plays. As a result of all of these efforts, in the late fourth century, after the triumph of Christianity, the Roman elite read Greek classics *and* Christian scriptures with the assumption that both referred to the same spiritual reality and outlined the same moral program.[131]

CHRISTIAN SUPERSESSIONISM

Eventually, Christians began to think of their religion as the successor of Judaism and of themselves as "the true Israel." The idea started with Paul and is attributed to Jesus in the Gospel of John.[132] The reasons for this development are complex. It could have

130. MacMullen provides this overview in *Christianizing the Roman Empire*, 74–76. He also refers to his longer examinations of these topics in *Paganism in the Roman Empire*, 20–25, 39f., 47, 57. MacMullen discusses other pagan activities that were slow to die out (including the practice of magic, burial ceremonies, and slaveholding) and the areas of the empire that remained non-Christian (including most of Sardinia, most rural areas, and half of Rome). On the last point, see also Mattingly, *Roman Imperial Civilisation*, 236.

131. For a discussion of these matters, see Wilken, *Christians*, 166–76. "Christian preaching shows that it was only too easy . . . for Christians to accommodate their Christianity to Roman society. Some of Augustine's congregation showed a devotion to saints and martyrs that looked to non-Christians very much like worship of lesser gods; some of John Chrysostom's congregation used amulets, rather than prayer, against illness. Paulinus of Nola adapted the tradition of animal sacrifice so that farmers could continue to make an offering, but in honour of St. Felix and for distribution to the poor" (Clark, *Christianity and Roman Society*, 114–15).

132. "Christianity has traditionally regarded itself as the universal messianic fulfillment of all the promises of election in the Old Testament, proclaiming that the Israel of the spirit (Christianity) has completely replaced the old, particularist Israel of the flesh (Judaism)" (Segal, *Rebecca's Children*, 172). On Paul's radical supersessionism, which is not merely historical, but also ontological and moral, see Ruether, *Faith and Fratricide*, 102–4, 164. Brown says that Christian supersessionism arose in the Johannine community in response to the "withdrawal or expulsion" of its members from the synagogues. These Christians claimed "that Jesus had replaced all the essentials of Judaism (Temple

happened, for example, that Christians declared themselves to be simply followers of a new religion founded by Jesus. However, in the first century, the Romans were unfriendly toward new sects that had no claim to longevity. As I said earlier, guardedly respectful of Judaism because of its pedigree, the Romans were highly suspicious of similarly "irrational" faiths that were not national religions representing a particular people living in a particular territory. Rejecting an identity defined by ethnicity or land—deliberately so as a universal faith open to everyone, regardless of gender, status, and nationality—Christianity was more susceptible to criticism than Judaism and more vulnerable to occasional expressions of hostility.

Partly for that reason, Christians maintained their tie to the older religion by claiming that the Jewish scripture predicted the appearance of Jesus, that Jesus was the natural heir of the Jewish prophets, and that Jesus was the son of the Jewish God. In short, "The early Christian apologists tried to argue that the Christians were not a new religious sect but the legitimate heirs of the venerable ancient religion of Israel."[133] Clearly, James the brother of Jesus—and the first leader of the movement after the Crucifixion—presented himself and his religion this way. As Jews, Christians were not compelled to offer incense to the Roman emperor and were exempt from military service.[134] Furthermore, as Jews, Christians could claim to be "radically renewing the institutions of Israel," including both the Temple and the Torah.[135] Thus, for an entire generation after Jesus' death, Christians continued to direct their missionary efforts mainly to the Jews, as Paul did, even in the face of rejection.

What transformed this relationship, however, was the Revolt of 66, which had two consequences for Jews. First, as a rebellious people, although they retained their religious rights, they lost some of their prestige. Educated Romans who formerly scoffed at Judaism as barbaric could now condemn it as also hostile and dangerous. Second,

---

worship, feasts, natural birth from Jewish parents)" (*Introduction*, 405). That is, Parkes explains, "[i]f Jesus was the Messiah promised to Israel, then [Christians] were the true Israel" (*Conflict*, 100). Lieu says that Justin Martyr was the first to call Christians Israelites. He also uses the terms "high priestly race" and "holy people" to indicate that the Jews had lost their once-privileged position with God (*Image and Reality*, 136). Lieu explains that the "rhetoric of reversal"—appropriating another group's identifying labels and characteristics— is typical of breakaway sects as a "recognised means of differentiation and self-justification" (119).

133. Koester, *History, Culture, and Religion*, 366. Hence, the powerful incentive for Christians to claim a connection to Judaism while at the same time repudiating it. Fredriksen adds: "So firmly were Jewish 'religious rights' established, so definitely was conversion to Judaism (especially for men, with the dramatic and consequential decision to be circumcised) a known social fact, that, according to the fourth-century Christian writer Eusebius, during Rome's anti-Christian persecutions a gentile Christian could consider converting to Judaism to avoid harassment" (*Jesus of Nazareth*, 287).

134. "As long as they were thought to be just another Jewish synagogue, [Christians] were exempt from having to demonstrate their loyalty." However, "as a distinctly new religion, Christians could no longer count on that protection" (Mack, *Who Wrote?* 195).

135. Brown, *Introduction*, 696. According to Horsley and Silberman, the *Didache* community saw itself as "a Renewed Israel," which preserved some of the moral traditions of Palestinian villages and prayed to "the God of David" (*Message*, 230). That is, the Christians in this group were not entirely turning their backs on the faith of their fathers.

not only had the Jews been defeated, but the Temple had been destroyed, which meant that, like the Romans, God Himself no longer favored these people. Thus, "after 70 and the destruction of the Temple," as one scholar explains, "the perception [of the Jewish-Christian relationship] changed, as can be witnessed in John . . . Christ was now seen to have *replaced* what went before."[136]

Signs of this change appear even in the synoptic Gospels, where Jesus is sometimes provided with this post-Revolt consciousness.[137] In Matthew, for example, Jesus says, after he heals the servant of the Roman centurion, "Truly, I say to you, not even in Israel have I found such faith," after which he concludes, "I tell you, many will come from the east and west [i.e., gentiles] and sit at the table with Abraham, Isaac, and Jacob in the kingdom of heaven, while the sons of the kingdom [i.e., the Jews] will be thrown into the outer darkness" (Matt 8:11–12). Later, at the end of the Parable of the Vineyard, he concludes that the owner of the vineyard will kill the tenants who have murdered his servants as well as his son. And then Jesus says directly to his listeners, the chief priests and elders, "Therefore I tell you, the kingdom of God will be taken away from you and given to a nation producing the fruits of it" (Matt 21:43).

This kind of anti-Judaic preaching must have been characteristic of the post-war period, when the Gospels were written. However, while the Hellenists, who left Jerusalem after the murder of Stephen, may well have spoken to their Jewish audiences the way Stephen and Paul evidently did (and elicited the kind of hostility and violence we see throughout Acts), it is difficult to believe that James and the Jerusalem church indulged in the same kind of polemic.[138] How else could they have converted thousands of Jews, including priests and Pharisees? Yet, again, there is no doubt that after the war the rhetoric changed, Christian proselytizers were expelled from synagogues, and the divide between Judaism and Christianity widened. Eventually, Christianity was seen not only to have superseded Judaism, but to have rendered it null and void. Just as Jesus had fulfilled the messianic prophecies, Christianity had fulfilled the promise of Judaism, *and the latter was no longer necessary.*[139]

136. Brown, *Introduction*, 696; my emphasis. See also Parkes, *Conflict*, 84.

137. As Klingaman explains, "[I]n the aftermath of the Jewish revolt, the Gospels (particularly John, the last one written) took great pains to distinguish Jesus from the Jewish elite of his day, to criticize Jews at every opportunity for their obstinacy and blindness, and to charge the Jewish authorities in Jerusalem—and not the Roman government, in the person of Pontius Pilate—with responsibility for the crucifixion of Jesus" (*First Century*, 369). Of course, in Matthew, all of the Jews blame themselves; and in John Jesus himself blames all of the Jews, not just the aristocracy.

138. Enslin, however, argues that Christians in Jerusalem "became stigmatized as a nuisance and menace to law and order." Since Enslin assumes that the speeches in Acts actually represent Christian proselytizing, he finds the lack of conflict far more surprising than the eventual conflict itself (*Christian Beginnings*, 196). Still, James could not have retained the support of the Jewish community for thirty years if the preachers in his church spoke to Jews the way Paul, Peter, and Stephen are said to have spoken. The angry, accusatory, and insulting rhetoric of Christian leaders is more likely to have occurred after the Revolt of 66 than before it.

139. Ehrman notes that this is the view of the author of the Epistle to the Hebrews and of Melito of Sardis (*After the New Testament*, 96). "Jesus Christ," Cook says, "gathered up into one all that had gone

One problem with this new picture of the relationship between Judaism and Christianity is that Judaism was not simply ignored, which might have occurred if Christians had not developed an ambivalent attitude toward their mother church, which later became their enemy. First, as an "apostate" religion, from the perspective of Christianity, Judaism was denuded of its identity and deprived of its most sacred possessions. Not only was it no longer the true Israel, it was no longer the "elect" of God (1 Peter 2:9).[140] As one scholar explains, "Calling itself the new Israel and the true Israel, the church appropriated the schema of historical meaning that had arisen in the interpretation of the redemption of Israel accomplished by the exodus from Egypt, and adapted this schema to the redemption of humanity accomplished by the resurrection of Jesus Christ from the dead."[141]

Indeed, Christianity conceived of itself as Abraham's "free" wife, Sarah, and of Judaism as Abraham's "slave" wife, Hagar.[142] Christians also appropriated Jewish heroes like Abraham, Moses, David, Jonah, and Joshua; the Hebrew prophets; the Holy Spirit; and Jerusalem, which became the center of the Jesus movement and from which the Jews were exiled after the Revolt of 132.[143] Christians claimed to possess

---

before . . . He is the climax of the O.T. functions of prophet and priest, the second Adam superseding the old era which began with the first Adam" (*Introduction to the Bible*, 127). According to Wylen, Emil Schurer is one of the chief modern architects of the supersessionist theory (*Jews*, 118). By the mid-second century, some Church leaders, like Justin Martyr, were no longer interested in Jewish conversions. When the Jews had begun to be described as "prophet killers," as well as "idolaters, law breakers, and sinners of every kind," they had ceased to be a worthy audience (Ruether, *Faith and Fratricide*, 123–25, 148).

140. Meeks says of this passage, "The experience of Israel as a self-conscious and organized community of resident aliens in the diaspora cities is here simply commandeered by the new offshoot cult and used to explain their own social and moral situation in those same cities" (*Origins of Christian Morality*, 48). Flusser discusses the transition from the shared "election" of Jews and gentiles (in, for example, John 11:52) to the elimination of the Jews (in Paul's letter to the Thessalonians and later works). In the latter, including 5 *Esdras* and the writings of Justin Martyr, "[i]t is not the Jews, but Gentile Christians who will inherit the Holy Land and Jerusalem" (*Sage from Galilee*, 130).

141. Pelikan, *Jesus Through the Centuries*, 22. Pelikan explains: "The new interpretation of the historical process began with the history of Israel, whose principal goal was now taken to be the life, death, and resurrection of Jesus" (26). Mack says: "The remarkable thing about this Christian view of the world is that its complex system of thought was created to support a single claim. The claim was that Christians were the legitimate heirs of the epic of Israel, that the Jews had never understood the intentions of their God, and that the story of Israel, if one read it rightly, was 'really' about the coming of Christ" (*Who Wrote?* 252).

142. See Weiss, *Early Christianity*, II, 662–63; and Ruether, *Faith and Fratricide*, 137–43.

143. Bultmann says that "the idea of tradition and succession [that is, the Christian supersessionist treatment of Jews and Judaism] finds characteristic expression in the fact that Jerusalem is regarded as the center of the whole church"—by Paul as well as the Jerusalem church itself (*Theology*, I, 60–61). Paul "asserted that all the main prophets of the Hebrew Bible were proto-Christians" (Maccoby, *Mythmaker*, 190). Parkes says that "all the heroes and religious leaders of the Old Testament" were assimilated into the Church: "The mother and her seven sons who braved the wrath of Antiochus [i.e., Jews who suffered from the anti-Judaism of the Seleucid king in the second century BC] were already celebrated by a feast in the fourth century . . . Later on at different periods the others were added, until the memory of every reputable character in the Old Testament was associated with the past of

the true Temple, the true priesthood, and the true saints. They took over Pentecost, which became their day of foundation, and Passover, which was now superseded and subsumed by Easter. They borrowed the Paschal Lamb and the story of the Exodus, as well as the Sabbath, baptism, and fasting.[144] They even claimed that the Jews were not really Jews, but members of "the synagogue of Satan" (Rev. 2:9, 3:9).

Ironically, as we have seen, the Christians used Philo's allegorical method of interpretation to demonstrate that the Jewish Bible had nothing to do with Judaism, but everything to do with Christianity, since it prophesied the coming of Christ.[145] Eventually, they included the sacred scriptures of the Jews in their own Bible and called it, subordinately, the Old Testament.[146] The greatest theft, of course, was accomplished by the transformation of Jesus, if not from a Jewish prophet into a Hellenized mystery god, then at least from the leader of an exclusively Jewish sect into a gentile deity who seemed to authorize the humiliation and destruction of the people who first acknowledged his greatness. By the time the Christians finished with this massive and comprehensive dismantling of Judaism, there was little left, from the point of view of the heirs of Jesus, but an outdated religion that should have perished because of its

---

the Church rather than the ancestors of contemporary Jews." Parkes mentions Abraham, Moses (and his siblings), Job, Elijah and Elisha, as well as all the prophets (*Conflict*, 104–06). Ignatius claims that the prophets were Christians (Lieu, *Image and Reality*, 30, 36–37).

144. Brown, *Churches*, 26, 77. "Early Christian documents show how Christians appropriated the spiritual message of the festivals and reinterpreted them using Christian symbols . . . Christians made Passover into Easter, the Christian celebration of Christ as redeemer. Christians adopted Pentecost, the [Jewish] celebration of divine revelation, as the day of the descent of the Holy Spirit into the congregation of Christian believers" (Wylen, *Jews*, 100–101). See, for additional examples of Christian thefts from Judaism: Latourette, *History of Christianity*, I, 12; Lieu, *Image and Reality*, 77; Brown, *Introduction*, 701, 708, 710, 722; Chilton, "James in Relation to Peter, Paul, and the Remembrance of Jesus," 153; and Bultmann, *Theology*, I, 38, 41, 95–99.

145. Sterling discusses the Christian adoption of Philo in "Philo of Alexandria," 297–98. The Christian historian Eusebius "stopped short of calling Philo a Christian, [but] later Christians did not" (298). On the Christian appropriation of Jewish methods of exegesis, see Koester, *History, Culture, and Religion*, 253–54.

146. Meeks says that, like 1 Peter and the Epistle of James, the Letter to the Hebrews "invites a Christian audience . . . to hear great parts of the Jewish scripture as a message addressed now to themselves" (*Origins of Christian Morality*, 81). Bultmann comments on the paradox that the Christians accepted the Old Testament as scripture, "but at the same time denied the validity of the Old Testament Law for Christians" in *Theology*, I, 108–9. On this point, see also Bainton, *Early Christianity*, 37–38. Bruce adds: "The Old Testament, as Christians in due course came to call these writings, was a book about Jesus. Here was the church's Bible" (*Canon of Scripture*, 28). Thus, by the fourth century, this book had become "almost exclusively the property of the church" (275–76). See also Mack, *Lost Gospel*, 242. Today, as in the fourth century, Christians assume that the Jewish Bible cannot be understood without the assumption that it is about Christ and that it "is a heritage with which the Christian church was endowed at its inception" (Bruce, *Canon of Scripture*, 275–76). According to Bruce, Christians considered the Septuagint, but not the Hebrew Bible, to be divinely inspired. They, rather than the Jews, translated the rest of the Bible into Greek (only the Torah itself had been translated by Jews). And all of the complete Septuagint manuscripts now in existence were written by Christians (44–45). Bruce also mentions the Christian thefts of the Exodus, the paschal lamb, manna, and water from a rock (61).

irrelevancy or should have been destroyed because of its apostasy and incorrigibility. Fortunately, the Grand Theft was finished by the end of the first century because there was nothing more to take.[147]

Second, Judaism in this guise became an object of such unremitting scorn that it is hard to imagine how it survived. The letters of Paul and the Gospel of John make it very clear that only believers in the divinity of Jesus are the children of God.[148] As I suggested before, all others, according to John, are the children of the Devil. And John is generally so hostile to Jews as to mark a clear moment in history when at least one group of Christians—the Johannines, i.e., those who adopted John's Gospel—seems to have rejected not only all Jews, but Judaism in its entirety. In time, from the second to the sixth century, the Jews were subjected to the *Adversos Judaeos,* a series of writings by Church leaders that at first merely accused the Jews of blindness, disobedience, carnality, hypocrisy, stubbornness, reprobation, and perversity, but later added the charges of child murder and deicide.

All of these deficiencies prevented the Jews from correctly reading their Bible, which justified taking it away from them, and also made it impossible for them to acknowledge Jesus' divinity, which justified reducing them to less than second-class citizens throughout the Roman empire and subjecting them to every conceivable in- dignation. Justin Martyr went so far as to accuse the Jews of corrupting their Bible (i.e., rewriting it) "so as to obscure the scriptures' plain prophetic testimony to Jesus as the Christ."[149] And just as he claimed that evil demons had made Mithraism look like Christianity, so he argued that these very demons had also made Judaism look like his faith.[150] Jews were vilified in sermons, commentaries, tracts, testimonials,

147. Parkes comments: "The main transference took place in the first century. What Christianity required from its parent religion it had taken at that time." However, Church fathers continued to dig into Jewish lore, examining "Jewish legend and story which are not included in the Old Testament" and consulting with Jewish scholars for help in interpreting Jewish texts (*Conflict*, 117).

148. Brown, *Churches*, 83, 118–19.

149. Bruce, *Canon of Scripture*, 70. Bruce earlier notes that Justin found Jesus everywhere in the Old Testament, often in the guise of an angel of God. Thus, it was Jesus who spoke to Moses from a burning bush, announced the birth of Isaac to Abraham, spoke to Joseph in his dreams, and fought beside Joshua. Bruce concludes that Justin, "going beyond the limits of the rational use of language," went too far (64–66). Similarly, Moule argues that the *Letter of Barnabas* "is an extreme example of one of the ways in which Christians treated the Jewish scriptures." Here, as in other Christian texts, Jesus is the "coping-stone" of Judaism, and the Old Testament foreshadows his coming. "To treat scrip- ture as 'Barnabas' does [however] is merely to force upon it what is really derived from elsewhere and already believed on other independent grounds. The *Letter of Barnabas* served as a stick with which to beat those non-Christian Jews who used the same methods in interpreting scripture for their own purposes." In Christian hands, this method became "a way of bending Jewish scripture to Christian belief, a way which cannot commend itself to an honest mind" ("How the New Testament Came into Being," 107–8).

150. Enslin, *Christian Beginnings*, vii. Justin Martyr also said that "The government will be upon his shoulder" (Isa 9:6) meant "Christ will be hung on the cross." The passage from which the verse was taken (and which was read by Jews to refer to the accession of a king of Judea, such as Hezekiah) was understood by Christians to refer to Jesus as the Messiah. No Jew would have read it as meaning

imaginary dialogues, liturgical dramas, and Old Testament exegeses. They were not only the Hagar to Sarah, but also the Esau to Jacob, the Cain to Abel, and the Judah to Joseph. Dead Christians were martyrs, but dead Jews were simply being punished for their sins.[151]

Thus, while Christians incessantly fought among themselves, both before and after the conversion of Constantine, they also tried hard to minimize the influence of Judaism, as well as paganism, on the Church. There were still many Jewish Christians—that is, Christians who still followed the Jewish Law—around in the second century.[152] And many gentile as well as Jewish Christians continued to believe that Judaism and Christianity were compatible. By the fourth century, however, when the Christian population rose into the millions and Constantine showed a lively interest in Jesus as a talisman, things took a turn for the worse.[153] The Church Fathers agreed that Christians could not simultaneously be Jews. As we have seen, John Chrysostom, bishop of Antioch and the most famous preacher of the day, hunted down Judaizers and insisted that the members of his diocese stop all Jewish practices.[154] In short, when Christianity became a dominant force in the empire, the Church went after Jews and their synagogues, just as it attacked pagans and their temples. In doing so, of course, it "chose violence as a major means of extending and defending the gospel."[155]

By the early fourth century, as one scholar explains, the Church had become "an international Gentile community hostile to diversity both within and without: Christians outside the officially sanctioned Church were persecuted as heretics; pagan non-participants increasingly became the object of legal harassment; Jews, though permitted their peculiar worship, were universally condemned as enemies of the prophets and murderers of Christ."[156] The only thing that saved the Jews from *con-*

---

anything except that the new king (whether Hezekiah or the Messiah) would govern since "his government" is referred to in Isaiah 9:7 (90).

151. "[I]f Christian suffering was to have its testificatory value, Jewish suffering had to be disqualified. Indeed, it even becomes the 'negative' of Christian experience, a testimony to disobedience, to rejection by God, and to exclusion from the promises" (Lieu, *Image and Reality*, 282). On the Christian charge that the Jews had misread their own Bible, see Herford, *Pharisees*, 222.

152. Klinghoffer, *Why the Jews*, 123.

153. On Constantine's anti-Semitism, see Jones, *Constantine*, 140.

154. On John Chrysostom, see Ruether, *Faith and Fratricide*, 170–71. On Augustine and Jerome's discussion of this issue, see 171–72: "[B]oth agree that the continued observance of the [Jewish] Law by Christians now is inadmissible." The alternative would suggest that salvation does not come "through Christ alone." Bury claims that when Constantine turned toward Christianity, without actually declaring it to be the official religion of the state, there were only a few million Christians in the Roman empire: "It must never be forgotten that Constantine's revolution was perhaps the most audacious act ever committed by an autocrat in disregard and defiance of the vast majority of his subjects. For at least four-fifths of the population of the Empire were still outside the Christian Church" (*Later Roman Empire*, I, 366). Bury says that estimates of the number of Christians in the empire at that time "vary from one-twentieth to one-sixth of the total population" (366 n. 1).

155. Manschreck, *History of Christianity*, 106.

156. Fredriksen, "The Birth of Christianity and the Origins of Christian Anti-Judaism," 8.

stant harassment, torture, and exile (or simply complete annihilation) was the power of the imperial government to prevent attacks that were encouraged by the Church, which, vigorous though its encouragement was, failed "to persuade the State to introduce measures to suppress their worship or banish them from the Empire."[157]

Short of losing their right to attend their synagogues and of being completely exiled, however, the Jews had their problems. St. Ambrose thought that "the Church and the secular authorities should consider the ruin of Judaism their common cause." He called the synagogue "a haunt of infidels, a home of the impious, a hiding place of madmen, under the damnation of God himself." St. John Chrysostom called it "not only a whorehouse and a theater; it [was] also a den of thieves and a haunt of wild animals," characterized by debauchery and gluttony, which made the Jews "ready for slaughter."[158]

Pagans, too, who, unlike the Jews, had enjoyed majority status in the Roman empire before the late fourth century, had to deal with attacks on their places of worship and persistent, often violent attempts to convert them to Christianity. Christian mobs, which had played a large role in the intra-Christian conflicts of the third and fourth centuries, were at the forefront of Church-engendered attacks on paganism when the Church had the power to support such actions without much fear of retaliation, after 380. Community leaders were encouraged to use whatever means were necessary to eliminate paganism. Laws were passed to make pagan places of worship inaccessible. And the militant hordes from monasteries and churches—"the zealots for conversion"—"took to the streets or crisscrossed the countryside, destroying no doubt," says one historian, "more of the architectural and artistic treasure of their world than any passing barbarians thereafter."[159]

Despite the efforts of anti-Semites like many of the Church leaders in the fourth and fifth centuries, the Jews survived. However, although the claim was somewhat premature, Emperor Theodosius II announced in the fifth century that there were no pagans left in the empire: "In a hundred years," says one historian, "the Empire had been transformed from a state in which the immense majority of inhabitants

157. Bury, *Later Roman Empire*, I, 382. "Under the Christian Empire," says Bury, "the Jews remained for the most part in possession of the privileges which they had before enjoyed" (382). But this situation did not last very long. On one hand, it would seem, despite the efforts "by churchmen not to afford proper protection to the Jews against Christian fanatics," the Jews only had to put up with occasional (but increasing) attacks and the slow erosion of their freedom as the Middle Ages dawned (382 n. 3). On the other hand, as Carroll says, "Rampant violence, sanctioned by the Church and the State, was ubiquitous," and "the Jews were increasingly targeted" (*Constantine's Sword*, 212–13). Perhaps Jones has it right: "The day on which a Roman emperor was converted to Christianity proved an unfortunate one for the Jewish people. From henceforth the contemptuous toleration which the Roman government had hitherto shown towards Judaism changed slowly but steadily into hostility, culminating in the drastic penal laws of the most orthodox emperor, Justinian" (*Constantine*, 140). See also Chadwick, *Early Church*, 170–71.

158. Quoted in Carroll, *Constantine's Sword*, 201, 207, 213. Chrysostom made such remarks as part of eight homilies, called *Against the Jews*, in Antioch in the middle of the fourth century.

159. MacMullen, *Christianizing the Roman Empire*, 119.

were devoted to pagan religions, into one in which an Emperor could say, with gross exaggeration, but without manifest absurdity, that not a pagan survived."[160] The Delphic oracle spoke, the Olympic games were played, and the Eleusinian mysteries were celebrated for the last time at the end of the fourth century. In the sixth century, the Platonic Academy in Athens, the last outpost of pagan philosophy, was closed, signaling that the Church had completely turned its back on the Hellenism that had helped to shape the form and content of Christianity.

Ironically, when Christians were a vulnerable minority in the Roman empire, they pleaded fervently for religious tolerance. Writing to Marcus Aurelius and his son in AD 177, Athenagoras praised them for maintaining freedom of religion in the empire, where "different peoples observe different laws and customs; and no one is hindered by law or fear of punishment from devotion to his ancestral ways, even if they are ridiculous." The Romans were tolerant, he said, because atheism was the only attitude toward the gods which they disliked and because all religions kept their followers from "wrongdoing by fear of the divine." For that reason, Athenagoras wondered why the Romans treated Christians so badly, allowing them "to be harassed, plundered, and persecuted"—not because of what they had done, being believers in a God whose punishment they feared, but just because of their name (*Plea Regarding the Christians*, chap. 1). Roughly twenty years later, Tertullian made the same request to the Roman authorities, asking them not "to take away one's freedom of religion and put a ban on one's free choice of a god." He reminded his readers that only Christians were being discriminated against: "We are the only ones kept from having our own religion." And Tertullian knew why: "We offend the Romans and are not considered Romans because we do not worship the gods of the Romans" (*Apology*, 24:6, 9).[161]

These two Christians were right about the Roman empire. The state offered no explanation of how the universe worked; it had no creed that could be argued about or disputed; and its gods were not offended by the worship of other gods. However, by the time the Christians assumed power in AD 381, they had been battling each other for three centuries over theological, christological, and ecclesiological issues because these matters were the heart and soul of their faith: "Doctrine had to be defined, and heretics suppressed. [Thus], the Church, which had once claimed freedom for itself, denied freedom to others when it was victorious, and would not suffer rival cults.

---

160. Bury, *Later Roman Empire*, I, 372.

161. The quoted passages are from Ehrman, ed., *After the New Testament*, 65–66, 79. Nearly a century after Tertullian, Lactantius said: "Sacrificing to the gods, when it is done against a man's will, is a curse . . . We, on the contrary, although our God is the God of all men, whether they like it or not, do not require that anyone should be compelled to worship him, nor are we angry if a man does not do so . . . We leave vengeance to God" (quoted in de Ste. Croix, "Christianity's Encounter with the Roman Imperial Government," 350). In the Edict of Milan, issued in AD 313, Constantine and Licinius state again and again that "liberty of religion ought to be complete and unrestricted" (350).

Hence a systematic policy of religious intolerance, such as the Greek and Roman world had never known, was introduced."[162]

In the late fourth century, their shrines destroyed, their temples pillaged, and their gods defamed, pagans pleaded for the same tolerance that Christians had pleaded for in the past. The secular power might have been willing to show some sympathy for the Roman aristocrats who clung to the old-time religion, but Church leaders, like Ambrose, intervened on behalf of intolerance and arrogance. This was the fate of the pagan Symmachus, whose address to the emperor in 384, "requesting the restoration of religious privileges to the pagan world he represented," was denied.[163] Symmachus simply asked, "What does it matter by what system of knowledge each one of us seeks the truth?" He explained, "It is not by one single path that we arrive at so great a secret." But the point was made in vain because "Christians of all kinds, orthodox as well as heretics, were quick to denounce persecution only when they themselves were at the receiving end."[164]

In this regard, it was not merely anti-Semitism that drove the Church. Its leaders hated *everyone* else as much as its members often hated each other: Contempt for non-Christians could be found not only in Constantine's edicts, but also in the demands of ordinary Christian converts to overthrow "the baneful contamination of a dead idolatry." Augustine called upon Christians to destroy all manifestation of paganism because that is what "God wants, God commands, God proclaims!"[165] The violence that ensued was simply the consequence of Christianity's absolute commitment to dogmatism and its absolute intolerance of dissent. It was a life-and-death issue whether a person believed that people are saved by Grace or Works; whether Jesus was equal or subordinate to God the Father; and whether the bishop of Rome was *primus inter pares* among all the bishops in Christendom.

162. Bury, *Later Roman Empire*, I, 348. Parkes says, simply, "The claim for equal toleration with others which was advanced by the apologists in the days of their suffering, the Church did not grant to others in the days of her triumph" (*Conflict*, 157). Thus, Lieu adds, although "Christians opened their message to all, as they were at such great pains to emphasize, . . . they developed new patterns of exclusiveness which often must have seemed far more threatening to the stability of society than the Jewish form" (*Image and Reality*, 161–62).

163. MacMullen, *Christianizing the Roman Empire*, 117, 79.

164. De Ste. Croix, "Christianity's Encounter with the Roman Imperial Government," 351. De Ste. Croix supports this point by quoting A. H. M. Jones on the shifting attitudes of the Athanasians. When they were powerless, they pleaded for tolerance, but denied it when they had the support of the Roman emperor. The same writer argues that the Christians were much more hostile to heretics than to pagans. He quotes Ammianus Marcellinus: "[W]ild beasts are not such enemies to mankind as are most Christians in their deadly hatred of one another." In the section on heretics, the *Theodosian Code* "contains no less than sixty-six laws issued between 326 and 435" (351).

165. MacMullen, *Christianizing the Roman Empire*, 91, 95. MacMullen adds: "Abuse . . . barely sufficed to express the feelings of a considerable sampling of church champions when they spoke of people whose religious beliefs differed from their own. Small wonder that their behavior should match their words in explosive animus!" (91).

Of course, since the Jews appeared to take an extreme position on each of these questions, they were regarded as even worse enemies of Christendom than the heretics. They would certainly have rejected the idea of Grace as predestination, as Paul, Augustine, and Calvin saw it. They would have understood Jesus as a prophet, if anything. And they had had a bad experience with bishops—i.e., their own High Priests, who betrayed them at almost every turn. Indeed, after the failed revolts of 66 and 132, some Jews, at least, were inclined to treat every dogma as debatable and every promise as questionable.

By the fourth century, the great divide between Jews and Christians had, in the words of one historian, "hardened into hostility." The so-called New Israel concluded that the so-called Old Israel "was to have no rights." And "[t]he long sad story of Christian anti-semitism" commenced with repressive imperial legislation and culminated, eventually, in unrestrained mob violence.[166] By the fifth and sixth centuries, Jews in many places were physically attacked, they were expelled from Antioch and Alexandria, their synagogues were destroyed, and their Torahs were burned. Jews were not allowed to own slaves or hold land; they were forbidden to even socialize with Christians, to become lawyers or judges, and to join the military; they were forced to become tax collectors and money lenders; they were prevented from repairing synagogues or building new ones; they were compelled to listen to Christian sermons and, in some instances, to convert to Christianity.

These things did not happen to all Jews at all times. But, sooner or later, the Jews all over the empire lost most, if not all of their freedoms. Constantine denied them the right to convert either Christians or pagans in 315. His son Constantius forbade marriages between Jewish men and Christian women and disallowed the Jewish ownership of slaves in 339. Theodosius II prohibited Jews from holding honorable offices in the Roman state in the fifth century. And Justinian made it unlawful for Jews to testify against Christians in the sixth century. Expulsions, compulsory conversions, and massacres continued throughout the Middle Ages. Eventually, Jews were moved into ghettoes and required to wear special clothing. That way, they could be not only blamed, but also punished for starting all the plagues; initiating all the anti-religious ideas, including (in the twentieth century) both socialism and capitalism; and promoting the disease of the modern age, secularism.[167]

166. Markus, *Christianity*, 23. On the replacement of the Old Israel by the New in Paul's letters, see Meeks, *First Urban Christians*, 165–68. To put it simply, "Christianity took over the Jewish position [of exclusivity] completely" (165). Richardson says that, although the Church eventually took on the identity of the New Israel ("inevitably"!), "[t]here is no instance in the New Testament in which 'Israel' applies to Jesus himself. Moreover, there is no place in the New Testament where 'Israel' must refer to the Church and the Church alone. Always 'Israel' retains an intimate connection with the Old Testament people of God, the nation Israel" ("The Israel-Idea in the Passion Narratives," 1).

167. According to Langmuir, "Many [Christians] who felt threatened by industrialism, urbanism, capitalism, socialism, rationalism, and all other activities that were destroying their sense of security associated them in contradictory ways with Jews and accused the Jews of instigating them" (*History, Religion, and Antisemitism*, 321). See, for example, Werner Sombart, *The Jews and Modern Capitalism*

For many historians, theologians, and Bible scholars, this nearly 2,000-year assault on the Jews derived directly from the New Testament writings, especially of Paul and John, but also the Passion stories of the other evangelists. Thanks to the Gospel of John, in which the Jews are portrayed as completely rejecting Jesus, the Church was able to explain "to a beleaguered community of Jews expelled from their synagogues the meaning of their own alienation"—as exiles from the Kingdom of God. Indeed, the Church's exclusivity and its "way of stigmatizing [its] enemies" eventually, especially in the Church Triumphant, bore "the bitter fruit of Christian anti-Semitism."[168] And it was perpetuated by the anti-Semitic crusade of the Church Fathers, especially Sts. Jerome, Augustine, Ambrose, and Hilary, but also, more recently, Martin Luther.[169] "Among others," says one scholar, "Christians share the blame for a Western anti-Semitism that made possible the Nazi *Endlosung*."[170]

The only question that remains is whether it will ever really end. For many scholars, anti-Semitism is inextricably tied to the Holy Scriptures of Christianity, which means that it will endure as long as the rationale for it remains enshrined in these sacred texts: "Already we have seen the deeply problematic legacy of Jew hatred in foundational Christian texts, in the implicitly anti-Jewish idea of revelation as prophecy fulfillment, and most damaging of all, in the dominant Christian theology of Jesus, not only as the enemy of the Jewish people but as the Son of God who obliterates the integrity of all other ways to God."[171] Luke's nobleman in the Parable of the Pounds,

---

(1911).

168. Meeks, *Origins of Christian Morality*, 206. Meeks mentions in the ensuing pages the supersessionism of the *Epistle of Barnabas*, Justin Martyr, Marcion, and Irenaeus. The point is, their portrayal of Judaism as not only out of date, but supplanted by Christianity, led inevitably to the idea that it was unworthy of survival.

169. Late in his life, Luther wrote what Kung has called a "passionately anti-Jewish work," *On the Jews and Their Lies*. After accusing Jews of poisoning wells, infanticide, avarice, blood lust, blindness, and hardness of heart, Kung continues, Luther then recommends "the burning of synagogues, the destruction of houses, the confiscation of the holy scriptures; indeed, he calls for a ban on teaching and worshipping on pain of death, an abolition of safe-conducts, confiscation of cash and jewellery, hard physical labour, and finally, if even all this is of no use, banishment from Christian lands and a return to Palestine" (*Judaism*, 182–83).

170. Schillebeeckx, *Jesus*, 32.

171. Carroll, *Constantine's Sword*, 232. In *History, Religion, and Antisemitism*, Langmuir argues that the Christian "hostility toward Jews" is intrinsic to Christianity (18–20). That is, Christians "hated Jews . . . because they were Christians" (303). Langmuir notes that the case has been made over the past century by, among other scholars, James Parkes (25–26), Marcel Simon (32–33), and Rosemary Ruether (38–39). These writers "make it more impossible now to argue cogently that anti-Judaism has not been inherent in Christianity from the beginning" (40). Obviously, Langmuir adds later, the "fantasies" about Jews that were perpetrated in the Middle Ages—that they murdered Christian children, consumed Christian blood and flesh, contaminated the Eucharist, and started the Black Death—"became deeply embedded in the mentality of millions of normally rational Christians" and led to "the killing of thousands of Jews for actions that no Jew had ever been observed to commit" (304). Less obviously, however, these accusations were made possible by "the New Testament account of Jesus' life and death," the latter of which was unequivocally attributed to the Jews (320). Sanders comments, "Thus all those apologists for the 'no antisemitism-in-the-New-Testament' position, who

obviously representing Jesus, goes "to a far country to receive kingly power." Because the citizens of his realm hate him and reject his authority, he returns after his acquisition of authority and says, "[A]s for these enemies of mine, who did not want me to reign over them, bring them here and slay them before me" (Luke 19:11–27). The lesson of this parable has not been lost on Luke's readers in the two millennia that have passed since it was written.[172] John Chrysostom read it and used it as an excuse for his own virulent anti-Jewish crusades.

---

seek to deny that Luke and John really meant what they wrote . . . , are mistaken" (*Schismatics*, 233). See also, by the same scholar, *Jews in Luke-Acts*, xv-xvi. On this point, see also Segal, *Paul the Convert*, xvi. Because Jews were perceived to be hostile to Jesus and therefore hostile to all Christians in all times and places, they were thought to be worthy of subordination (almost always), persecution (quite often), and death (on occasion).

172. Brown says, "This prepares for the rejection of Jesus in Jerusalem, his crucifixion as King of the Jews, his return in resurrection, and the ultimate destruction of Jerusalem" (*Introduction*, 253). The same message, as Schillebeeckx suggests, is offered by the Parable of the Vineyard (Luke 20:9–18, Matt 21:33–46), in which the tenants are threatened with destruction and the vineyard is given "to others" because the tenants killed the owner's "beloved son" (*Jesus*, 168–69). Hare, commenting on the parable in Matthew, says that it represents a "radical discontinuity between Israel and her successor" (*Jewish Persecution of Christians*, 153). This paragraph is based on the discussion of Christian anti-Semitism in Ruether, *Faith and Fratricide*, 117–21, 171–98, 208–13.

Bibliography

Primary Texts

The Revised English Bible. New York: Oxford and Cambridge University Press, 1989.

The Oxford Annotated Bible. Translated by Herbert G. May and Bruce M. Metzger. New York: Oxford University Press, 1962.

The New Oxford Annotated Bible. Translated by Bruce M. Metzger and Roland E. Murphy. New York: Oxford University Press, 1991.

The Holy Bible (KJV). New York: American Bible Society, n.d.

Secondary Texts

Akenson, Donald Harmon. *Saint Saul: A Skeleton Key to the Historical Jesus.* New York: Oxford University Press, 2000.

Allen, J. R. "Why Pilate?" In *The Trial of Jesus,* edited by E. Bammel, 78–83. London: SCM, 1970.

Applebaum, Shimon. "Economic Life in Palestine." In *The Jewish People in the First Century,* edited by S. Safrai and M. Stern, 631-700. Vol. II. Assen: Netherlands: Van Gorcum, 1976.

Armstrong, A. Hilary. "Greek Philosophy from the Age of Cicero to Plotinus." In *The Crucible of Christianity,* edited by A. Toynbee, 203–214. New York: World, 1975.

Armstrong, Karen. *The Great Transformation: The Beginning of Our Religious Traditions.* New York: Anchor, 2006.

———. *A History of God: The 4,000-Year Quest of Judaism, Christianity and Islam.* New York: Ballantine, 1993.

Aslan, Reza. *Zealot: The Life and Times of Jesus of Nazareth.* New York: Random House, 2013.

Augstein, Rudolf. *Jesus Son of Man.* Translated by Hugh Young. New York: Urizen, 1977.

Bainton, Roland H. *Early Christianity.* Princeton, NJ: D. Van Nostrand, 1960.

Balsdon, J. P. V. D., ed. *The Romans.* New York: Basic Books, 1965.

———. "Rome as a Battleground of Religions." In *The Romans,* edited by J. P. V. D. Balsdon, 192-210. New York: Basic Books, 1965.

Barclay, William. *Introduction to the First Three Gospels.* Philadelphia: Westminster, 1975.

Barton, John. *Ethics and the Old Testament.* London: SCM, 1998.

Bammel, Ernst, ed. "*Ex illa itaque die consilium fecerunt . . ..*" In *The Trial of Jesus,* edited by E. Bammel, 11–40. London: SCM, 1970.

———. *The Trial of Jesus.* London: SCM, 1970.

Basser, Herbert W. "Gospel and Talmud." In *The Historical Jesus in Context*, edited by Amy-Jill Levine et al., 285–295. Princeton: Princeton University Press, 2006.

Bauckham, Richard J. ed. *The Book of Acts in Its First Century Setting*. Vol. IV (*Palestinian Setting*). Grand Rapids, MI: Wm. B. Eerdmans, 1995.

———. *James*. London: Routledge, 1999.

———. "James and Jesus." In *The Brother of Jesus*, edited by B. Chilton and J. Neusner, 100–137. Louisville: Westminster John Knox, 2001.

Bauer, Walter. *Orthodoxy and Heresy in Earliest Christianity*, edited by R. A. Kraft and Gerhard Krodel. Philadelphia: Fortress, 1979.

Birdsall, J. N. "How the New Testament Came to Us." In *Understanding the New Testament*, edited by O. J. Lace, 121–144. London: Cambridge University Press, 1965.

Blinzler, Ernst. "The Jewish Punishment of Stoning in the New Testament Period." In *The Trial of Jesus*, edited by E. Bammel, 147–161. London: SCM, 1970.

Borg, Marcus J. *Jesus: Uncovering the Life, Teachings, and Relevance of a Religious Revolutionary*. HarperSanFrancisco, 2006.

———. *Meeting Jesus Again for the First Time: The Historical Jesus & the Heart of Contemporary Faith*. HarperSanFrancisco, 1995.

Borg, Marcus, and John Dominic Crossan. *The Last Week: What the Gospels Really Teach About Jesus's Final Days in Jerusalem*. HarperSanFrancisco, 2006.

Bornkamm, Gunther. *Jesus of Nazareth*. Translated by I. and F. McLuskey, with J. M. Robinson. Minneapolis: Fortress, 1995.

Boyarin, Daniel. *Border Lines: The Partition of Judaeo-Christianity*. Philadelphia: University of Pennsylvania Press, 2004.

———. *The Jewish Gospel: The Story of the Jewish Christ*. New York: New, 2012.

Brandon, S. G. F. *The Trial of Jesus of Nazareth*. London: Batsford, 1968.

Braun, Herbert. *Jesus: The Man from Nazareth and His Time*. Philadelphia: Fortress, 1979.

———. "The Qumran Community." In *Jesus in His Time*, edited by H. J. Schultz, 66–74. Philadelphia: Fortress, 1971.

Brown, Peter. *The Making of Late Antiquity*. Cambridge: Harvard University Press, 1976.

Brown, Raymond E. *The Churches the Apostles Left Behind*. New York: Paulist, 1994.

———. *An Introduction to the New Testament*. New York: Doubleday, 1997.

Brown, Raymond E., Joseph A. Fitzmyer, and Roland E. Murphy, eds. *The Jerome Bibilical Commentary*. Englewood Cliffs, NJ: Prentice-Hall, 1968.

Bruce, F. F. *The Canon of Scripture*. Downers Grove, IL: IVP Academic, 1998.

———. *New Testament History*. Garden City: Doubleday, 1980.

Bultmann, Rudolf. *Jesus and the Word*. Translated by L. P. Smith and E. H. Lantero. New York: Scribner's, 1958.

———. *Primitive Christianity in Its Contemporary Setting*. Translated by R. H. Fuller. New York: Meridian, 1956.

———. *Theology of the New Testament*. Vol. I. Translated by Kendrick Grobel. New York: Scribner's, 1951.

Burrows, Millar. *The Dead Sea Scrolls*. New York: Viking, 1955.

Bury, J. B. *History of the Later Roman Empire: From the Death of Theodosius I to the Death of Justinian*. Vol. I. New York: Dover, 1965.

Caird, G. B. *The Gospel of St. Luke*. The Pelican Gospel Commentaries. Baltimore: Penguin, 1968.

Cameron, Ronald D. *The Other Gospels: Non-Canonical Gospel Texts.* Philadelphia: Westminster, 1982.

Capper, Brian. "The Palestinian Cultural Context of Earliest Christian Community of Goods." In vol. IV of *The Book of Acts in Its First Century Setting*, edited by R. Bauckham, 323–356. Grand Rapids, MI: Wm. B. Eerdmans, 1995.

Catchpole, D. R. "The Problem of the Historicity of the Sanhedrin Trial." In *The Trial of Jesus*, edited by E. Bammel, 47–65. London: SCM, 1970.

Carroll, James. *Constantine's Sword: The Church and the Jews.* Boston: Houghton Mifflin, 2002.

Chadwick, Henry. *The Early Church.* Harmondsworth, England: Penguin, 1967.

Chilton, Bruce. "James in Relation to Peter, Paul, and the Remembrance of Jesus." In *The Brother of Jesus*, edited by B. Chilton and J. Neusner, 138–160. Louisville: Westminster John Knox, 2001.

———. *Rabbi Jesus: An Intimate Biography.* New York: Doubleday, 2000.

———. "Targum, Jesus, and the Gospels." In *The Historical Jesus in Context*, edited by A. Levine et al., 238–255. Princeton: Princeton University Press, 2006.

Chilton, Bruce, and Jacob Neusner, eds. *The Brother of Jesus: James the Just and His Mission.* Louisville: Westminster John Knox, 2001.

———. *Judaism in the New Testament: Practices and Beliefs.* London: Routledge, 1995.

Clark, Gillian. *Christianity and Roman Society.* London: Cambridge University Press, 2006.

Collins, John J., and Robert A. Kugler, eds. *Religion in the Dead Sea Scrolls.* Grand Rapids, MI: Wm. B. Eerdmans, 2000.

Conzelmann, Hans, and Andreas Lindemann. *Interpreting the New Testament: An Introduction to the Principles and Methods of N. T. Exegesis.* Translated by J. C. B. Mohr. Peabody, MA: Hendrickson, 1999.

Cook, Stanley. *An Introduction to the Bible.* Harmondsworth, England: Penguin, 1950.

Cornfeld, Gaalyah. *Archeology of the Bible: Book by Book.* New York: Harper & Row, 1976.

Crossan, John Dominic. *The Birth of Christianity: Discovering What Happened in the Years Immediately After the Execution of Jesus.* HarperSanFrancisco, 1998.

———. *The Historical Jesus: The Life of a Mediterranean Jewish Peasant.* HarperSanFrancisco, 1992.

———. *Jesus: A Revolutionary Biography.* HarperSanFrancisco, 1994.

———. *Who Killed Jesus?* HarperSanFrancisco, 1996.

Cullman, Oscar. *The Early Church: Studies in Early Christian History and Theology.* Abridged edition. Translated by A. J. B. Higgins and Stanley Goodman. Philadelphia: Westminster, 1966.

Cumont, Franz. *After Life in Roman Paganism.* New Haven: Yale University Press, 1922.

Cuppitt, Don. "The Christ of Christendom." In *The Myth of God Incarnate*, edited by J. Hick, 133–147. London: SCM, 1977.

Cwiekowski, Frederick J. *The Beginnings of the Church.* New York: Paulist, 1988.

D'Angelo, Mary Rose. "Abba and Father: Imperial Theology in the Contexts of Jesus and the Gospels." In *The Historical Jesus in Context*, edited by A. Levine et al., 64–78. Princeton: Princeton University Press, 2006.

Danielou, Cardinal Jean. "Christianity as a Jewish Sect." In *The Crucible of Christianity*, edited by A. Toynbee, 261–282. New York: World, 1975.

———. "Christianity as a Missionary Religion." In *The Crucible of Christianity*, edited by A. Toynbee, 283–298. New York: World, 1975.

Davids, Peter H. "James's Message: The Literary Record." In *The Brother of Jesus*, edited by B. Chilton and J. Neusner, 66–87. Louisville: Westminster John Knox, 2001.

Davies, W. D. *Invitation to the New Testament: A Guide to Its Main Witnesses*. New York: Doubleday, 1969.

Deason, Gary B. "Reformation Theology and the Mechanistic Conception of Nature." In *God and Nature*, edited by D. C. Lindberg and R. L. Numbers, 167–191. Berkeley: University of California Press, 1986.

Deissmann, Adolph. *New Light on the New Testament*. Translated by Lionel R.M. Strachan. Edinburgh: T.& T. Clark, 1907.

De Ste. Croix, G. E. M. "Christianity's Encounter with the Roman Imperial Government." In *The Crucible of Christianity*, edited by A. Toynbee, 331–351. New York: World, 1975.

De Vaux, Roland. *Ancient Israel*. Vol. I. Translated by Darton, Longman & Todd Ltd. New York: McGraw-Hill, 1965.

Dihle, Albrecht. "The Graeco-Roman Background." In *Jesus in His Time*, edited by H. J. Schultz, 10–18. Philadelphia: Fortress, 1971.

Ehrman, Bart D., ed. *After the New Testament: A Reader in Early Christianity*. New York: Oxford University Press, 1999.

———. *Lost Christianities: The Battles for Scripture and the Faiths We Never Knew*. New York: Oxford University Press, 2003.

———, ed. *Lost Scriptures: Books That Did Not Make It into the New Testament*. New York: Oxford University Press, 2005.

———. *Misquoting Jesus: The Story Behind Who Changed the Bible and Why*. HarperSanFrancisco, 2007.

Enslin, Martin Scott. *Christian Beginnings*. New York: Harper, 1938.

Evans, Craig A. "Comparing Judaisms: Qumranic, Rabbinic, and Jacobean Judaisms Compared." In *The Brother of Jesus*, edited by B. Chilton and J. Neusner, 161–183. Louisville: Westminster John Knox, 2001.

———. "Josephus on John the Baptist." in *The Historical Jesus in Context*, edited by A. Levine et al., 55–63. Princeton: Princeton University Press, 2006.

Fenton, J. C. *The Gospel According to St Matthew*. The Pelican Gospel Commentaries. Harmondsworth, England: Penguin, 1963.

Finkelstein, R. L. *The Pharisees: The Sociological Background of Their Faith*. 2nd ed. Philadelphia: Jewish Publication Society of America, 1938.

Fitzmyer, Joseph A. *Essays on the Semitic Background of the New Testament*. Missoula: Scholars', 1974.

———. *Luke the Theologian*. New York: Paulist, 1989.

Flint, Peter. "Jesus and the Dead Sea Scrolls." In *The Historical Jesus in Context*, edited by A. Levine et al., 110–131. Princeton: Princeton University Press, 2006.

Flusser, David. "Jesus in the Context of History." In *The Crucible of Christianity*, edited by A. Toynbee, 215–234. New York: World, 1975.

———. *The Sage from Galilee: Rediscovering Jesus's Genius*. Grand Rapids, MI: Eerdmans, 1997.

Foster, Donald. "John Come Lately: The Belated Evangelist." In *The Bible and the Narrative Tradition*, edited by F. McConnell, 113–131. New York: Oxford University Press, 1986.

Fox, Robin Lane. *The Unauthorized Version: Truth and Fiction in the Bible*. New York: Knopf, 1992.

Fredriksen, Paula. *From Jesus to Christ: The Origins of the New Testament Images of Jesus*. 2nd ed. New Haven: Yale University Press, 2000.

———. *Jesus of Nazareth: King of the Jews*. New York: Vintage, 2000.

Fredriksen, Paula, and Adele Reinhartz, eds. *Jesus, Judaism, and Christian Anti-Semitism: Reading the New Testament after the Holocaust*. Louisville: Westminster John Knox, 2002.

Freyne, Sean. *Galilee from Alexander to Hadrian*. South Bend: Notre Dame University Press, 1980.

———. *Galilee, Jesus and the Gospels*. Philadelphia: Fortress, 1988.

Friedman, Richard Elliott. *Who Wrote the Bible?* New York: Harper & Row, 1989.

Gager, John G. *The Origins of Anti-Semitism: Attitudes Toward Judaism in Pagan and Christian Antiquity*. New York: Oxford University Press, 1985.

———. "Paul the Apostle of Judaism." In *Jesus, Judaism, and Christian Anti-Semitism*, edited by P. Fredriksen and A. Reinhartz, 56–76. Louisville: Westminster John Knox, 2002.

Gonzalez, Justo L. *The Story of Christianity: The Early Church to the Dawn of the Reformation*. Vol. I. HarperSanFrancisco, 1984.

Goulder, Michael. "Jesus, the Man of Universal Destiny." In *The Myth of God Incarnate*, edited by J. Hick, 48–63. London: SCM, 1977.

———. "The Two Roots of the Christian Myth." In *The Myth of God Incarnate*, edited by J. Hick, 64–86. London: SCM, 1977.

Grant, F. C. "Foreword." In E. Hatch, *The Influence of Greek Ideas on Christianity*, vii–xvii. New York: Harper, 1957.

Grant, Michael. *The Antonines: The Roman Empire in Transition*. London: Routledge, 1994.

———. *The Climax of Rome: The Final Achievement of the Ancient World AD* 161–337. London: Weidenfeld, 1993.

———. *Jesus: An Historian's Review of the Gospels*. New York: Scribner's, 1977.

———. *Saint Peter*. New York: Scribner's, 1995.

Grant, Robert M. "Gnosticism, Marcion, Origen." In *The Crucible of Christianity*, edited by A. Toynbee, 317–330. New York: World, 1975.

———. *A Historical Introduction to the New Testament*. New York: Harper & Row, 1963.

Guignebert, Charles. *The Jewish World in the Time of Jesus*. New York: University Books, 1959.

Hare, Douglas R. A. *The Theme of Jewish Persecution of Christians in the Gospel According to St. Matthew*. London: Cambridge University Press, 1967.

Hatch, Edwin. *The Influence of Greek Ideas on Christianity*. New York: Harper, 1957.

Heer, Friedrich. *The Medieval World: Europe* 1100–1350. Translated by Janet Sondheimer. New York: New American Library, 1962.

Helms, Randel. *Gospel Fictions*. New York: Prometheus, 1988.

Henderson, Ian H. "Apuleis of Madauros." In *The Historical Jesus in Context*, edited by A. Levine et al., 193–205. Princeton: Princeton University Press, 2006.

Hengel, Martin. *Acts and the History of Earliest Christianity*. Translated by John Bowden. Eugene: Wipf and Stock, 2003.

———. *The Charismatic Leader and His Followers*. Translated by James Greig. New York: Crossroad, 1981.

———. *Crucifixion in the Ancient World and the Folly of the Message of the Cross*. Translated by John Bowden. Philadelphia: Fortress, 1977.

———. *The Four Gospels and the One Gospel of Jesus Christ.* Translated by John Bowden. Harrisburg, PA: Trinity, 2000.

Herford, R. Travers. *The Pharisees.* Boston: Beacon, 1962.

Herzog II, William R. *Jesus, Justice, and the Reign of God: A Ministry of Liberation.* Louisville: Westminster John Knox, 2000.

Heschel, Abraham J. *The Prophets: An Introduction.* Vol. I. New York: Harper, 1962.

Hick, John, ed. *The Myth of God Incarnate.* London: SCM, 1977.

Hill, Craig C. *Hellenists and Hebrews: Reappraising Divison within the Earliest Church.* Minneapolis: Fortress, 1992.

Hoehner, Harold W. "Why Did Pilate Hand Jesus over to Antipas?" In *The Trial of Jesus,* edited by E. Bammel, 84–90. London: SCM, 1970.

Horbury, William. *Jews and Christians in Contact and Controversy.* London: T&T Clark, 1998.

Horsley, Richard A. (with John S. Hanson). *Bandits, Prophets & Messiahs: Popular Movements in the Time of Jesus.* Harrisburg, PA: Trinity, 1999.

———. *Covenant Economics: A Biblical Vision of Justice for All.* Louisville: Westminster John Knox, 2009.

Horsley, Richard A., and Neil Asher Silberman. *The Message and the Kingdom: How Jesus and Paul Ignited a Revolution and Transformed the Ancient World.* Philadelphia: Fortress, 2002.

Hunter, A. M. *The Gospel According to John.* London: Cambridge University Press, 1965.

Jaher, Frederic Cople. *A Scapegoat in the New Wilderness: The Origins and Rise of Anti-Semitism in America.* Cambridge: Harvard University Press, 1994.

Jeremias, Joachim. *Jerusalem in the Time of Jesus: An Investigation into Economic and Social Conditions during the New Testament Period.* Translated by F. H. and C. H. Cave. Philadelphia: Fortress, 1987.

———. *The Parables of Jesus.* Translated by S. H. Hooke. New York: Scribner's, 1963.

Johnson, Luke Timothy. *The Living Jesus: Learning the Heart of the Gospels.* HarperSanFrancisco, 1999.

———. *The Real Jesus: The Misguided Quest for the Historical Jesus and the Truth of the Traditional Gospels.* HarperSanFrancisco, 1996.

Jones, A. H. M. *Constantine and the Conversion of Europe.* New York: Collier, 1962.

Kaufmann, Yehezkel. *The Religion of Israel: From Its Beginnings to the Babylonian Exile.* Abridged and translated by Moshe Greenberg. New York: Schocken, 1972.

Kaylor, R. David. *Jesus the Prophet: His Vision of the Kingdom of Earth.* Louisville: Westminster John Knox, 1994.

Kee, Howard Clark, Franklin W. Young, and Karlfried Froelich. *The New Testament.* 2nd ed. Englewood Cliffs, NJ: Prentice-Hall, 1965.

Klausner, Joseph. *Jesus of Nazareth: His Life, Times, and Teaching.* New York: Macmillan, 1929.

Klawans, Jonathan. "Moral and Ritual Purity." In *The Historical Jesus in Context,* edited by A. Levine et al., 266–284. Princeton: Princeton University Press, 2006.

Klein, Charlotte. *Anti-Judaism in Christian Theology.* Translated by Edward Quinn. Philadelphia: Fortress, 1978.

Klingaman, William K. *The First Century: Emperors, Gods, and Everyman.* San Francisco: Harper Perennial, 1991.

Klinghoffer, David. *Why the Jews Rejected Jesus: The Turning Point in Western History.* New York: Three Leaves, 2005.

Kloppenborg, John S. *Q, the Earliest Gospel: An Introduction to the Original Stories and Sayings of Jesus.* Louisville: Westminster John Knox, 2008.

Koch, Klaus. "Apocalyptic and Eschatology." In *Jesus in His Time,* edited by H. J. Schultz, 57–65. Philadelphia: Fortress, 1971.

Koester, Helmut. *History, Culture, and Religion in the Hellenistic Age.* Vol. I. New York: Walter de Gruyter, 1987.

Kung, Hans. *Judaism: Between Yesterday and Tomorrow.* Translated by John Bowden. New York: Crossroad, 1992.

Lace, O. Jessie, ed. "The Historical Background of New Testament Times." In *Understanding the New Testament,* edited by O. J. Lace, 11–63. London: Cambridge University Press, 1965.

———. *Understanding the New Testament.* London: Cambridge University Press, 1965.

———. "What the New Testament Is About." In *Understanding the New Testament,* edited by O. J. Lace, 145–163. London: Cambridge University Press, 1965.

Lang, Bernhard. "Segregation and Intolerance." In *What the Bible Really Says,* edited by M. Smith and R. J. Hoffman, 115–136. HarperSanFrancisco, 1989.

Langmuir, Gavin I. *History, Religion, and Anti-Semitism.* Berkeley: University of California Press, 1990.

Latourette, Kenneth Scott. *A History of Christianity.* Vol. I. HarperSanFrancisco, 1975.

Lee, Bernard J. *The Galilean Jewishness of Jesus.* New York: Paulist, 1988.

Levenson, David B. "Messianic Movements." In *The Jewish Annotated New Testament,* edited by A. Levine and M. Z. Brettler, 530–535. New York: Oxford University Press, 2011.

Levine, Amy-Jill. "Introduction." In *The Historical Jesus in Context,* edited by A. Levine et al., 1–39. Princeton: Princeton University Press, 2006.

———. *The Misunderstood Jew: The Church and the Scandal of the Jewish Jesus.* HarperSanFrancisco, 2006.

Levine, Amy-Jill, Dale C. Allison Jr., and John Dominic Crossan, eds. *The Historical Jesus in Context.* Princeton: Princeton University Press, 2006.

Levine, Amy-Jill, and Marc Zvi Brettler, eds. *The Jewish Annotated New Testament.* New York: Oxford University Press, 2011.

Lieu, Judith. *Image and Reality: The Jews in the World of the Christians in the Second Century.* London: T&T Clark, 2003.

Lindberg, David C., and Roland L. Numbers, eds. *God and Nature: Historical Essays on the Encounter between Christianity and Science.* Berkeley: University of California Press, 1986.

Lohse, Eduard. "Temple and Synagogue." In *Jesus in His Time,* edited by H. J. Schultz, 75–83. Philadelphia: Fortress, 1971.

Lovejoy, Arthur O. *Essays in the History of Ideas.* New York: Capricorn, 1960.

Maccoby, Hyam. *The Mythmaker: Paul and the Invention of Christianity.* New York: Barnes and Noble, 1986.

———. *Paul and Hellenism.* Valley Forge, PA: Trinity Press International, 1991.

MacDonald, Dennis R. "Imitations of Greek Epic in the Gospels." In *The Historical Jesus in Context,* edited by A. Levine et al., 372–384. Princeton: Princeton University Press, 2006.

Mack, Burton L. *The Lost Gospel: The Book of Q and Christian Origins.* HarperSanFrancisco, 1993.

————. *Who Wrote the New Testament? The Making of the Christian Myth.* Harper-SanFrancisco, 1995.

MacMullen, Ramsay. *Christianizing the Roman Empire (A.D. 100–400).* New Haven: Yale University Press, 1984.

Maguire, Daniel C. *The Moral Core of Judaism and Christianity: Reclaiming the Revolution.* Minneapolis: Augsburg Fortress, 1993.

Manschreck, Clyde. *The History of Christianity in the World.* Englewood Cliffs, NJ: Prentice-Hall, 1974.

Markus, R. A. *Christianity in the Roman World.* New York: Scribner's, 1974.

Martin, Luther. *Hellenistic Religions: An Introduction.* New York: Oxford University Press, 1987.

Mattingly, Harold. *Roman Imperial Civilisation.* New York: Norton, 1971.

McConnell, Frank, ed. *The Bible and the Narrative Tradition.* New York: Oxford University Press, 1986.

————. "Introduction." In *The Bible and the Narrative Tradition*, edited by F. McConnell, 3–18. New York: Oxford University Press, 1986.

McKenzie, John L. *The New Testament Without Illusion.* New York: Crossroad, 1980.

————. *The Old Testament Without Illusion.* Chicago: Thomas Moore, 1999.

Meeks, Wayne A. *The First Urban Christians: The Social World of the Apostle Paul.* New Haven: Yale University Press, 1983.

————. *The Origins of Christian Morality: The First Two Centuries.* New Haven: Yale University Press, 1993.

Meier, John P. *A Marginal Jew: Rethinking the Historical Jesus.* Vols. I, II, and III. New York: Doubleday, 1991, 1994, 2001.

Metzger, Bruce M. *The Bible in Translation: Ancient and English Versions.* Grand Rapids, MI: Baker Academics, 2001.

Metzger, Bruce M., and Bart D. Ehrman. *The Text of the New Testament: Its Transmission, Corruption, and Restoration.* New York: Oxford University Press, 2005.

Meyer, Marvin. "The Mithras Legacy." In *The Historical Jesus in Context*, edited by A. Levine et al., 179–192. Princeton: Princeton University Press, 2006.

Moltmann, Jürgen. *The Church in the Power of the Spirit: A Contribution to Messianic Ecclesiology.* Translated by Margaret Kohl. Minneapolis: Fortress, 1993.

Moore, George F. *Judaism in the First Centuries of the Christian Era.* Vol. I. Cambridge: Harvard University Press, 1958.

————. *Judaism in the First Centuries of the Christian Era.* Vols. II–III. Peabody, MA: Hendrickson, 1960.

Moule, C. D. F. "How the New Testament Came into Being." In *Understanding the New Testament*, edited by O. J. Lace, 64–120. London: Cambridge University Press, 1965.

Neusner, Jacob. *Judaism in the Beginning of Christianity.* Philadelphia: Fortress, 1984.

————. *Judaism in the Matrix of Christianity.* Philadelphia: Fortress, 1986.

Newsome Jr., James D. *The Hebrew Prophets.* Atlanta: John Knox, 1984.

Nickelsburg, George W. E. "*First* and *Second Enoch*: A Cry Against Oppression and the Promise of Deliverance." In *The Historical Jesus in Context*, edited by Amy-Jill Levine et al., 87–109. Princeton: Princeton University Press, 2006.

Nineham, D. E. "Epilogue." *The Gospel of St. Mark.* The Pelican New Testament Commentaries. Baltimore: Penguin, 1964.

————. In *The Myth of God Incarnate*, edited by J. Hick, 186–204. London: SCM, 1977.

Oesterly, W. O. E. *The Jewish Background of the Christian Liturgy*. Oxford: Clarendon, 1925.

O'Neill, J. C. "The Charge of Blasphemy at Jesus' Trial before the Sanhedrin." In *The Trial of Jesus*, edited by E. Bammel, 72–77. London: SCM, 1970.

Pagels, Elaine. *The Gnostic Gospels*. New York: Random House, 1979.

Painter, John. *Just James: The Brother of Jesus in History and Tradition*. Minneapolis: Fortress, 1999.

———. "Who Was James?" In *The Brother of Jesus*, edited by B. Chilton and J. Neusner, 10–65. Louisville: Westminster John Knox, 2001.

Parkes, James. *The Conflict of the Church and the Synagogue: A Study in the Origins of Anti-Semitism*. New York: Hermon, 1974.

Payne, Robert. *Ancient Rome*. American Heritage Series. New York: McGraw-Hill, 1970.

Pelikan, Jaroslav. *Jesus Through the Centuries: His Place in the History of Culture*. New Haven: Yale University Press, 1985.

Peper, Bradley M., and Mark DelCogliano. "The Pliny and Trajan Correspondence." In *The Historical Jesus in Context*, edited by A. Levine et al., 366–371. Princeton: Princeton University Press, 2006.

Perrin, Norman, and Dennis C. Duling. *The New Testament: An Introduction*. 2nd ed. San Diego: HBJ, 1982.

Peters, E. F. *The Harvest of Hellenism: A History of the Near East from Alexander the Great to the Triumph of Christianity*. New York: Simon and Schuster, 1970.

Placher, William C. *A History of Christian Theology: An Introduction*. Philadelphia: Westminster, 1983.

Pobee, John. "The Cry of the Centurion—A Cry of Defeat." In *The Trial of Jesus*, edited by E. Bammel, 91–102. London: SCM, 1970.

Popkes, Wiard. "The Mission of James in His Time." In *The Brother of Jesus*, edited by B. Chilton and J. Neusner, 88–99. Louisville: Westminster John Knox, 2001.

Porton, Gary G. "The Parable in the Hebrew Bible and Rabbinic Literature." In *The Historical Jesus in Context*, edited by A. Levine et al., 206–221. Princeton: Princeton University Press, 2006.

Reed, Jonathan. "Archeological Contributions to the Study of Jesus and the Gospels." In *The Historical Jesus in Context*, edited by A. Levine et al., 40–54. Princeton: Princeton University Press, 2006.

Reicke, Bo. "Galilee and Judea." In *Jesus in His Time*, edited by H. J. Schultz, 28–35. Philadelphia: Fortress, 1971.

Reinhartz, Adele. "The Gospel of John: How the 'Jews' Became Part of the Plot." In *Jesus, Judaism, and Christian Anti-Judaism*, edited by P. Fredriksen and A. Reinhartz, 99–116. Louisville: Westminster John Knox, 2002.

Reumann, John H. P. *Jesus in the Church's Gospels*. Philadelphia: Fortress, 1968.

Richardson, Alan. *The Gospel According to St. John: A Commentary*. New York: Collier, 1962.

Richardson, Peter. "The Israel-Idea in the Passion Narratives." In *The Trial of Jesus*, edited by E. Bammel, 1–10. London: SCM, 1970.

Robertson, Archibald. *The Origins of Christianity*. New York: International, 1954.

Robinson, James M. "The Gospels as Narrative." In *The Bible in the Narrative Tradition*, edited by F. McConnell, 97–112. New York: Oxford University Press, 1986.

———. *The Gospel of Jesus: A Historical Search for the Original Good News*. HarperSanFrancisco, 2006.

Rostovtzeff, M. *The Social and Economic History of the Roman Empire*. New York: Oxford University Press, 1957.

Rubenstein, Richard E. *When Jesus Became God: The Struggle to Define Christianity During the Last Days of Rome*. New York: Harcourt, 1999.

Ruether, Rosemary Radford. *Faith and Fratricide: The Theological Roots of Anti-Semitism*. Eugene: Wipf and Stock, 1997.

Russell, Jeffrey Burton. *A History of Heaven: The Singing Silence*. Princeton: Princeton University Press, 1997.

Safrai, S. and M. Stern, eds. *The Jewish People in the First Century*. Vol. II. Assen, Netherlands: Van Gorcum, 1976.

Sanders, E. P. *The Historical Figure of Jesus*. London: Penguin, 1993.

———. "Jesus, Ancient Judaism, and Modern Christians: The Quest Continues." In *Jesus, Judaism, and Christian Anti-Semitism*, edited by P. Fredriksen and A. Reinhartz, 31–55. Louisville: Westminster John Knox, 2002.

———. *Jesus and Judaism*. Philadelphia: Fortress, 1985.

———. *Paul and Palestinian Judaism*. London: SCM, 1977.

Sanders, Jack T. *The Jews in Luke-Acts*. London: SCM, 1987.

———. *Schismatics, Sectarians, Dissidents, Deviants: The First One Hundred Years of Jewish-Christian Relations*. Valley Forge, PA: Trinity Press International, 1993.

Sandmel, Samuel. *A Jewish Understanding of the New Testament*. New York: Ktav, 1974.

Schalit, Abraham. "Herod and His Successors." In *Jesus in His Time*, edited by H. J. Schultz, 36–46. Philadelphia: Fortress, 1971.

———. "Palestine under the Seleucids and Romans." In *The Crucible of Christianity*, edited by A. Toynbee, 47–76. New York: World, 1975.

Schiffman, Lawrence H. *From Text to Tradition: A History of Second Temple & Rabbinic Judaism*. Hoboken, NJ: Ktav, 1991.

Schillebeeckx, Edward. *Jesus: An Experiment in Christology*. New York: Crossword, 1989.

Schubert, Kurt. "Jewish Religious Parties and Sects." In *The Crucible of Christianity*, edited by A. Toynbee, 77–98. New York: World, 1975.

Schultz, Hans Jurgen, ed. *Jesus in His Time*. Translated by Brian Watchorn. Philadelphia: Fortress, 1971.

Segal, Alan F. *Paul the Convert: The Apostolate and Apostasy of Saul the Pharisee*. New Haven: Yale University Press, 1990.

———. *Rebecca's Children: Judaism and Christianity in the Roman World*. Cambridge: Harvard University Press, 1986.

Senior, Donald. *Jesus: A Gospel Portrait*. New York: Paulist, 1992.

Setzer, Claudia. "Jewish Responses to Believers in Jesus." In *The Jewish Annotated New Testament*, edited by A. Levine and M. Z. Brettler, 577–579. New York: Oxford University Press, 2011.

Shanks, Hershel, and Ben Witherington III. *The Brother of Jesus: The Dramatic Story & Meaning of the First Archeological Link to Jesus & His Family*. HarperSanFrancisco, 2003.

Sheehan, Thomas. *The First Coming: How the Kingdom of God Became Christianity*. New York: Dorset, 1990.

Sider, Ronald J. "Sharing the Wealth: The Church as Biblical Model for Public Policy." *Christian Century*, June 8–15, 1977, 570f. Sider's pages are unnumbered in the online version of his essay.

Smith, Morton. *Jesus the Magician*. New York: Barnes & Noble, 1993.

Smith, Morton, and R. Joseph Hoffmann, eds. *What the Bible Really Says*. HarperSanFrancisco, 1993.

Spong, John Shelby. *Liberating the Gospels: Reading the Bible with Jewish Eyes*. HarperSanFrancisco, 1996.

Stark, Rodney. *The Rise of Christianity*. Princeton: Princeton University Press, 1996.

Stegemann, Ekkehard W., and Wolfgang Stegemann. *The Jesus Movement: A Social History of the First Century*. Translated by O. C. Dean Jr. Minneapolis: Fortress, 1999.

Stein, Robert H. *The Synoptic Problem: An Introduction*. Grand Rapids, MI: Baker Books, 1987.

Sterling, Gregory E. "Philo of Alexandria." In *The Historical Jesus in Context*, edited by A. Levine et al., 296–308. Princeton: Princeton University Press, 2006.

Stern, M. "Aspects of Jewish Society: The Priesthood and Other Classes." In *The Jewish People of the First Century*, edited by S. Safrai and M. Stern, 561–630. Vol. II. Assen, Netherlands: Van Gorcum, 1976.

Strecker, Georg. "On the Problem of Jewish Christianity." In Bauer, *Orthodoxy and Heresy in Earliest Christianity*, 241–285. Philadelphia: Fortress, 1979.

Strong, James. *Exhaustive Concordance of the Bible*. Peabody, MA: Hendrickson, n.d.

Tabor, James D. *The Jesus Dynasty: The Hidden History of Jesus, His Royal Family, and the Birth of Christianity*. New York: Simon and Schuster, 2006.

Talbert, Charles H. "Miraculous Conceptions and Births in Mediterranean Antiquity." In *The Historical Jesus in Context*, edited by A. Levine et al., 79–86. Princeton: Princeton University Press, 2006.

Tannehill, Robert C. *The Narrative Unity of Luke-Acts: A Literary Interpretation*. Vol. II. Minneapolis: Fortress, 1990.

Theissen, Gerd. *Sociology of Early Palestinian Christianity*. Translated by John Bowden. Philadelphia: Fortress, 1978.

Townsend, John. "Wisdom." In *What the Bible Really Says*, edited by M. Smith and R. J. Hoffmann, 187–196. HarperSanFrancisco, 1993.

Toynbee, Arnold, ed. *The Crucible of Christianity: Judaism, Hellenism, and the Historical Background to the Christian Faith*. New York: World, 1975.

———. "The Historical Antecedents." In *The Crucible of Christianity*, edited by A. Toynbee, 19–46. New York: World, 1975.

Trafton, Joseph L. "The *Psalms of Solomon*." In *The Historical Jesus in Context*, edited by Amy-Jill Levine et al., 256–265. Princeton: Princeton University Press, 2006.

Trevor-Roper, Hugh. *The Rise of Christian Europe*. New York: Harcourt, Brace and World, 1965.

Turner, Victor. *The Ritual Process: Structure and Anti-Structure*. New York: Aldine, 1969.

Van Leeuwen, Arend Theodoor. *Christianity in World History: The Meeting of the Faiths of East and West*. Translated by H. H. Hoskins. New York: Scribner's, 1965.

Vermaseren, M. J. "Religion in Competition with Christianity." In *The Crucible of Christianity*, edited by A. Toynbee, 235–260. New York: World, 1975.

Vermes, Geza. *The Changing Faces of Jesus*. New York: Penguin, 2002.

———. *The Dead Sea Scrolls in English*. Harmondsworth, England: Penguin, 1973.

———. *Jesus the Jew*. Philadelphia: Fortress, 1981.

———. *The Resurrection: History and Myth*. New York: Doubleday, 2008.

Vogt, Joseph. "Augustus and Tiberius." In *Jesus in His Time*, edited by H. J. Schultz, 1–9. Philadelphia: Fortress, 1971.

Weiss, Johannes. *Earliest Christianity: A History of the Period A.D. 30–150.* Vols. I and II. Translated by F. C. Grant. New York: Harper, 1959. Vol. II was completed by Rudolf Knopf.

White, L. Michael. *From Jesus to Christianity: How Four Generations of Visionaries & Storytellers Created the New Testament and Christian Faith.* HarperSanFrancisco, 2004.

Wilken, Robert L. *The Christians as the Romans Saw Them.* New Haven: Yale University Press, 1984.

Wills, Lawrence M. "The Aesop Tradition." In *The Historical Jesus in Context*, edited by A. Levine et al., 222–237. Princeton: Princeton University Press, 2006.

Wilson, A. N. *Jesus: A Life.* New York: Fawcett Columbine, 1992.

Winter, Paul. *On the Trial of Jesus.* Berlin: Walter de Gruyer, 1974.

———. "Sadducees and Pharisees." In *Jesus in His Time*, edited by H. J. Schultz, 47–56. Philadelphia: Fortress, 1971.

Witherington III, Ben. *The Jesus Quest: The Third Search for Jesus of Nazareth.* 2nd ed. Downers Grove, IL: InterVarsity, 1997.

———. *What Have They Done with Jesus?* HarperSanFrancisco, 2006.

Wolfson, Harry. "Greek Philosophy in Philo and the Church Fathers." In *The Crucible of Christianity*, edited by A. Toynbee, 299–316. New York: World, 1975.

Wright, N. T. *Simply Jesus: A New Vision of Who He Was, What He Did, and Why He Matters.* New York: HarperOne, 2011.

———. *What Saint Paul Really Said: Was Paul of Tarsus the Real Founder of Christianity?* Grand Rapids, MI: Wm. B. Eerdmans, 1997.

Wright, Robert. *The Evolution of God.* New York: Little, Brown, 2009.

Wylen, Stephen M. *The Jews in the Time of Jesus.* New York: Paulist, 1996.

Yoder, John Howard. *The Politics of Jesus.* Grand Rapids, MI: Wm. B. Eerdmans, 1972.

Young, Frances. "A Cloud of Witnesses." In *The Myh of God Incarnate*, edited by J. Hick, 13–47. London: SCM, 1977.

———. "Two Roots or a Tangled Mass?" In *The Myth of God Incarnate*, edited by J. Hick, 87–124. London: SCM, 1977.

Zeitlin, Solomon. *Who Crucified Jesus?* New York: Bloch, 1964.

CPSIA information can be obtained
at www.ICGtesting.com
Printed in the USA
LVHW101347160920
666180LV00009B/1080